BLACK PANTHER BY CHRISTOPHER PRIEST: THE COMPLETE COLLECTION VOL. 4. Contains material originally published in magazine form as BLACK PANTHER #50-56 and #59-62, and THE CREW #1-7. First printing 2016. ISBN# 978-1-302-90058-8. Published by MARVEL WORLDWIDE, INC., a subsidiary of MARVEL ENTERTAINMENT, LLC. OFFICE OF PUBLICATION: 135 West 50th Street, New York, NY 10020. Copyright © 2016 MARVEL No similarity between any of the names, characters, persons, and/or institutions in this magazine with those of any living or dead person or institution is intended, and any such similarity which may exist is purely coincidental. **Printed in the U.S.A.** ALAN FINE, President, Marvel Entertainment; DAN BUCKLEY, President, TV, Publishing & Brand Management; JOE QUESADA, Chief Creative Officer; TOM BREVOORT, SVP of Publishing; DAVID BOGART, SVP of Business Affairs & Operations, Publishing & Partnership; C.B. CEBULSKI, VP of Brand Management & Development, Asia; DAVID GABRIEL, SVP of Sales & Marketing, Publishing; JEFF YOUNGQUIST, VP of Production & Special Projects; DAN CARR, Executive Director of Publishing Technology; ALEX MORALES, Director of Publishing Operations; SUSAN CRESPI, Production Manager; STAN LEE, Chairman Emeritus. For information regarding advertising in Marvel Comics or on Marvel.com, please contact Vit DeBellis, Integrated Sales Manager, at vdebellis@marvel.com. For Marvel subscription inquiries, please call 888-511-5480. Manufactured between 6/17/2016 and 7/25/2016 by R.R. DONNELLEY, INC., SALEM, VA, USA.

9 8 7 6 5 4 3 2 1

WRITER **CHRISTOPHER PRIEST**

BLACK AND WHITE

PENCILERS **DAN FRAGA** (#50),
JORGE LUCAS (#51-54)
& **JIM CALAFIORE** (#55-56)

INKERS **LARY STUCKER** (#50),
JORGE LUCAS (#51-54)
& **MARK McKENNA** (#55-56)

COLORIST **JENNIFER SCHELLINGER**

LETTERER **PAUL TUTRONE**

ASSISTANT EDITOR **NOVA REN SUMA**

ASSOCIATE EDITOR **MIKE RAICHT**

EDITOR **MIKE MARTS**

ASCENSION

PENCILERS **PATRICK ZIRCHER** (#59-60)
& **JIM CALAFIORE** (#61-62)

INKER **NORM RAPMUND**

COLORIST **JENNIFER SCHELLINGER**

LETTERER **DAVE SHARPE**

ASSISTANT EDITORS **JENNY HUANG**
& **NICK LOWE**

EDITOR **MIKE MARTS**

THE CREW

PENCILER **JOE BENNETT**

INKERS **CRIME LAB STUDIOS' DANNY MIKI** WITH **RICH PERROTTA** (#7)

COLORIST **AVALON STUDIOS**

LETTERERS **KEN LOPEZ** (#1-2) AND
VIRTUAL CALLIGRAPHY'S RUS WOOTON (#3-5)
& **DAVE SHARPE** (#6-7)

ASSISTANT EDITORS **MARC SUMERAK** & **ANDY SCHMIDT**

EDITOR **TOM BREVOORT**

BLACK PANTHER CREATED BY STAN LEE & JACK KIRBY

FRONT COVER ARTISTS **PATRICK ZIRCHER, NORM RAPMUND** & **JOSE VILLARRUBIA**
BACK COVER ARTISTS **JIM CALAFIORE, NORM RAPMUND** & **JENNIFER SCHELLINGER**

COLLECTION EDITOR MARK D. BEAZLEY
ASSOCIATE EDITOR SARAH BRUNSTAD   ASSOCIATE MANAGER, DIGITAL ASSETS JOE HOCHSTEIN
ASSOCIATE MANAGING EDITOR ALEX STARBUCK   SENIOR EDITOR, SPECIAL PROJECTS JENNIFER GRÜNWALD
VP, PRODUCTION & SPECIAL PROJECTS JEFF YOUNGQUIST
RESEARCH & LAYOUT JEPH YORK   BOOK DESIGNER JAY BOWEN
SVP PRINT, SALES & MARKETING DAVID GABRIEL

EDITOR IN CHIEF AXEL ALONSO   CHIEF CREATIVE OFFICER JOE QUESADA
PUBLISHER DAN BUCKLEY   EXECUTIVE PRODUCER ALAN FINE

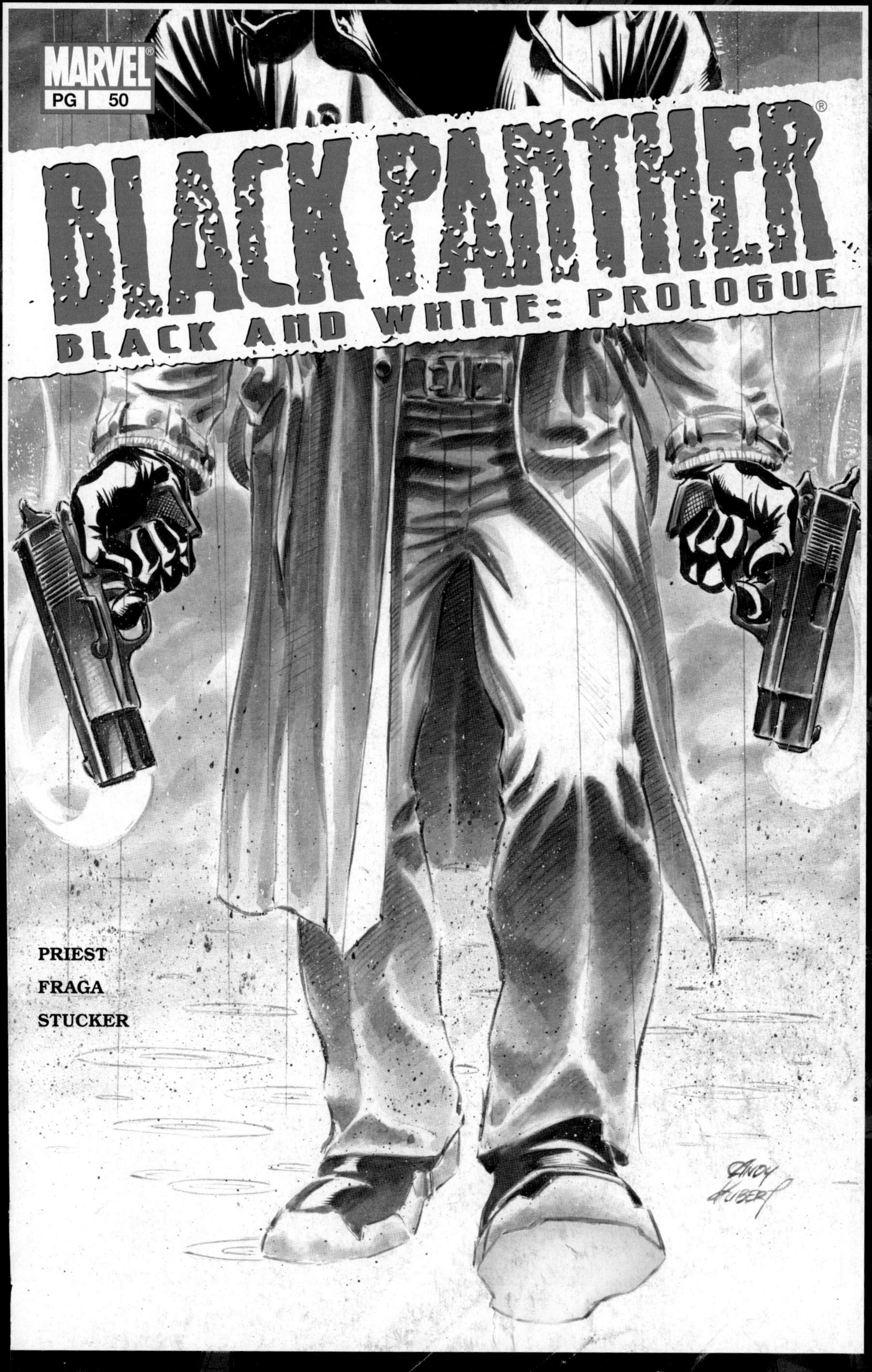
MARVEL
PG 50
BLACK PANTHER
BLACK AND WHITE: PROLOGUE
PRIEST
FRAGA
STUCKER

NEW YORK CITY

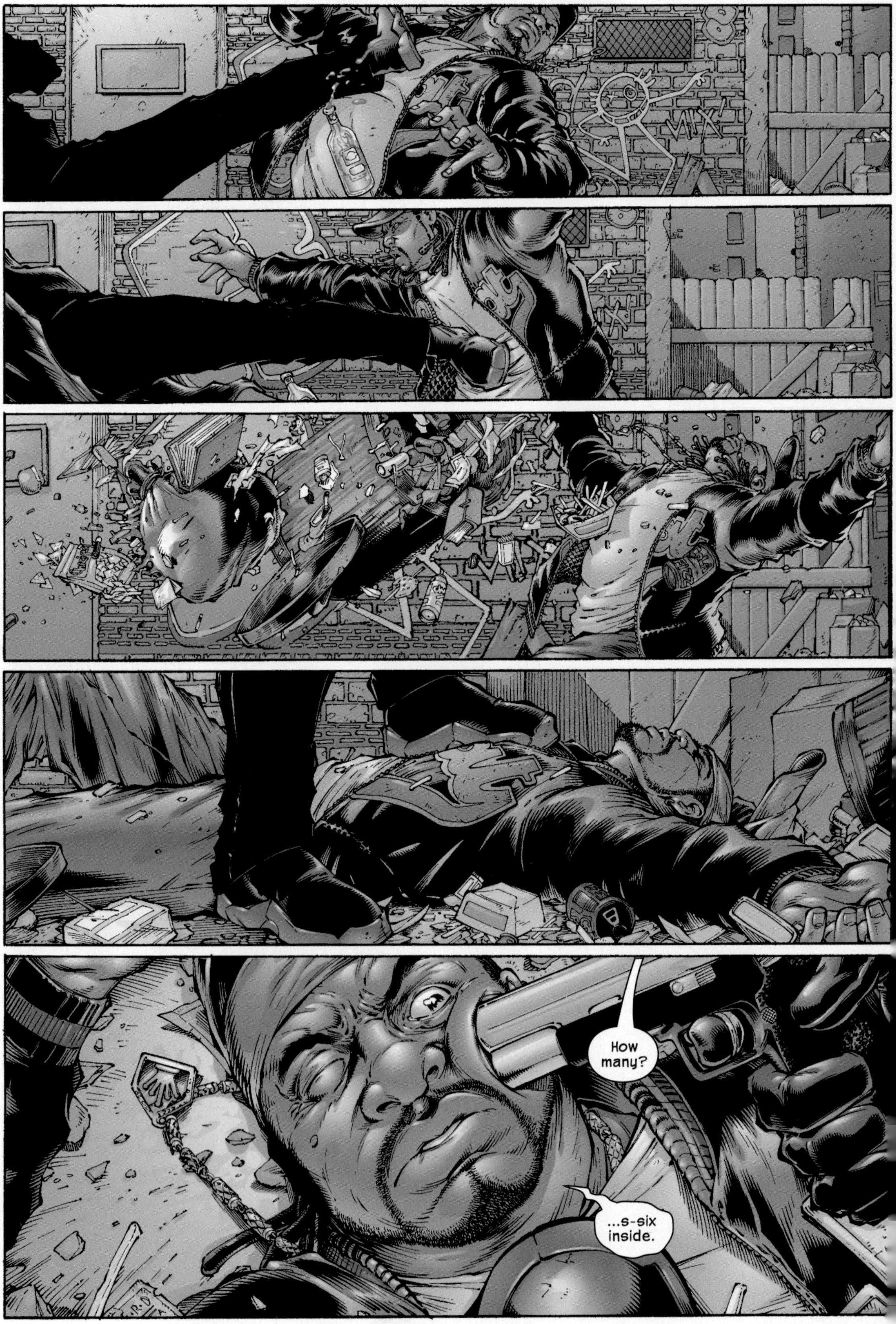
How many?
...s-six inside.

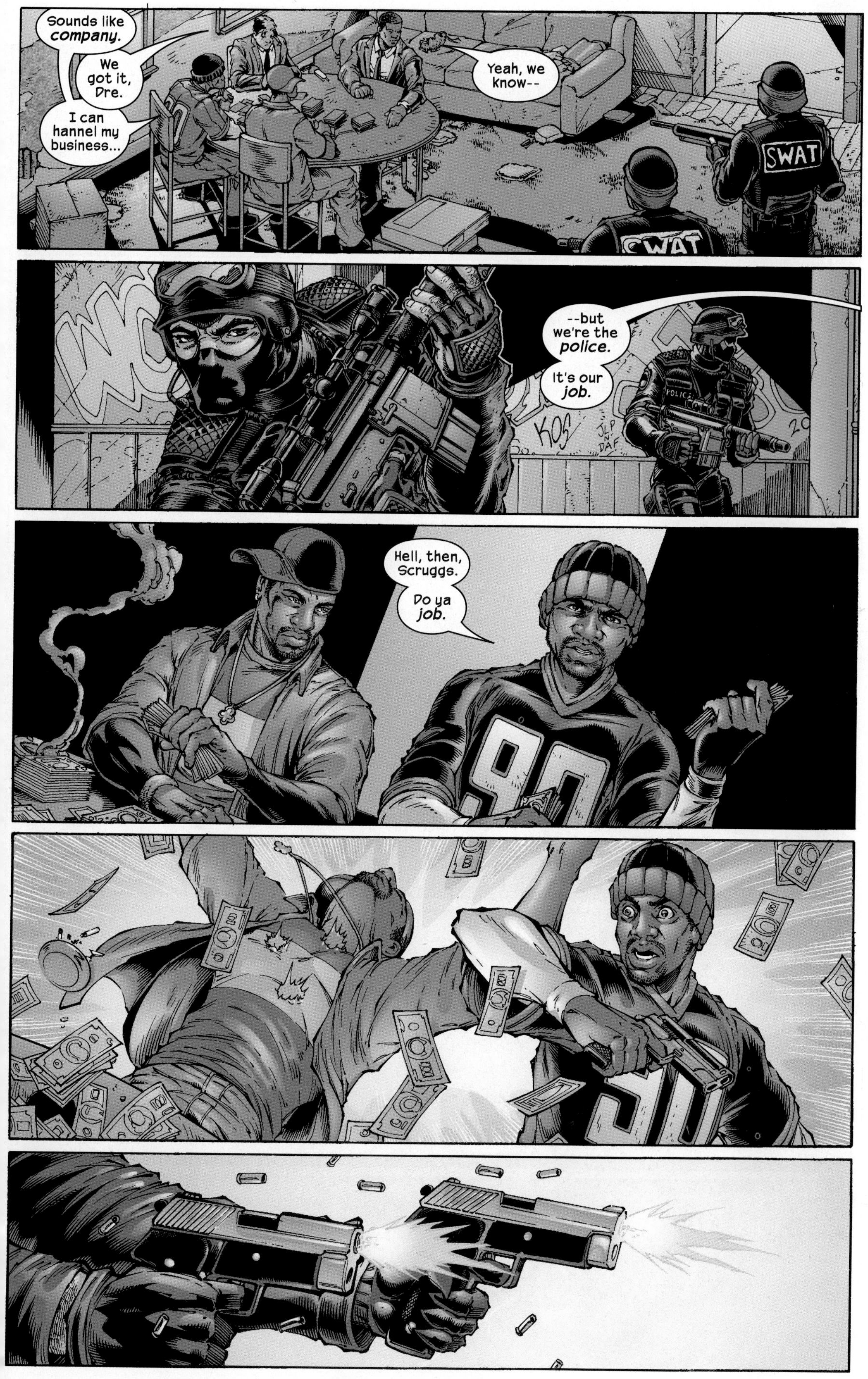
Sounds like company.
We got it, Dre.
I can hannel my business...
Yeah, we know--
--but we're the police.
It's our job.
Hell, then, Scruggs.
Do ya job.
SWAT
POLICE
KOS

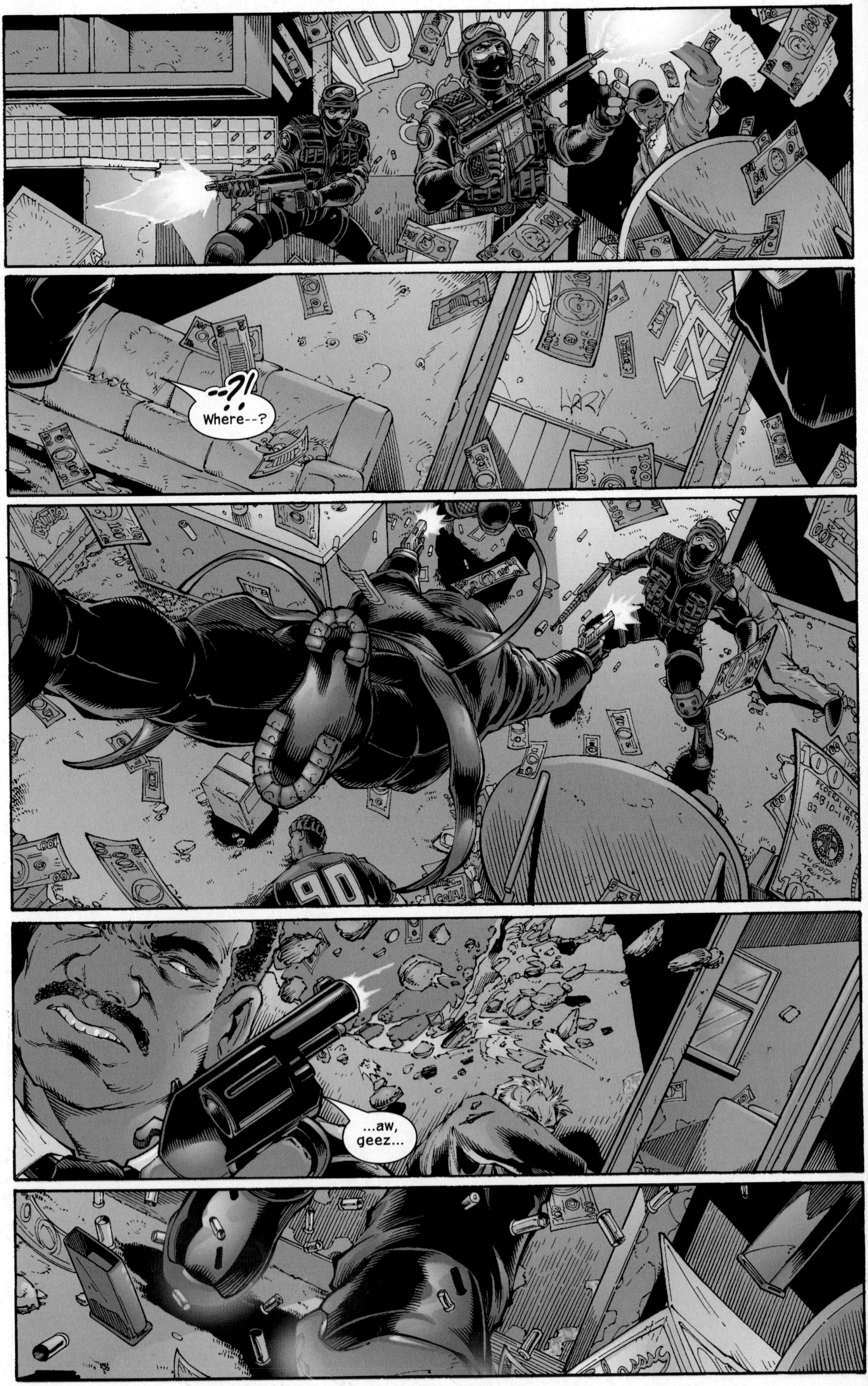
--?! Where--?
...aw, geez...

BLACK AND WHITE: A CRIME NOVEL

PROLOGUE: TIN MEN IN THE GARDEN OF GOOD & EVIL

PRIEST & DAN FRAGA STORYTELLERS
LARY STUCKER INKER PAUL TUTRONE LETTERING JENNIFER SCHELLINGER COLORIST
MIKE RAICHT AND NOVA REN SUMA ASSISTANT EDITORS MIKE MARTS EDITOR
JOE QUESADA EDITOR IN CHIEF BILL JEMAS PRESIDENT

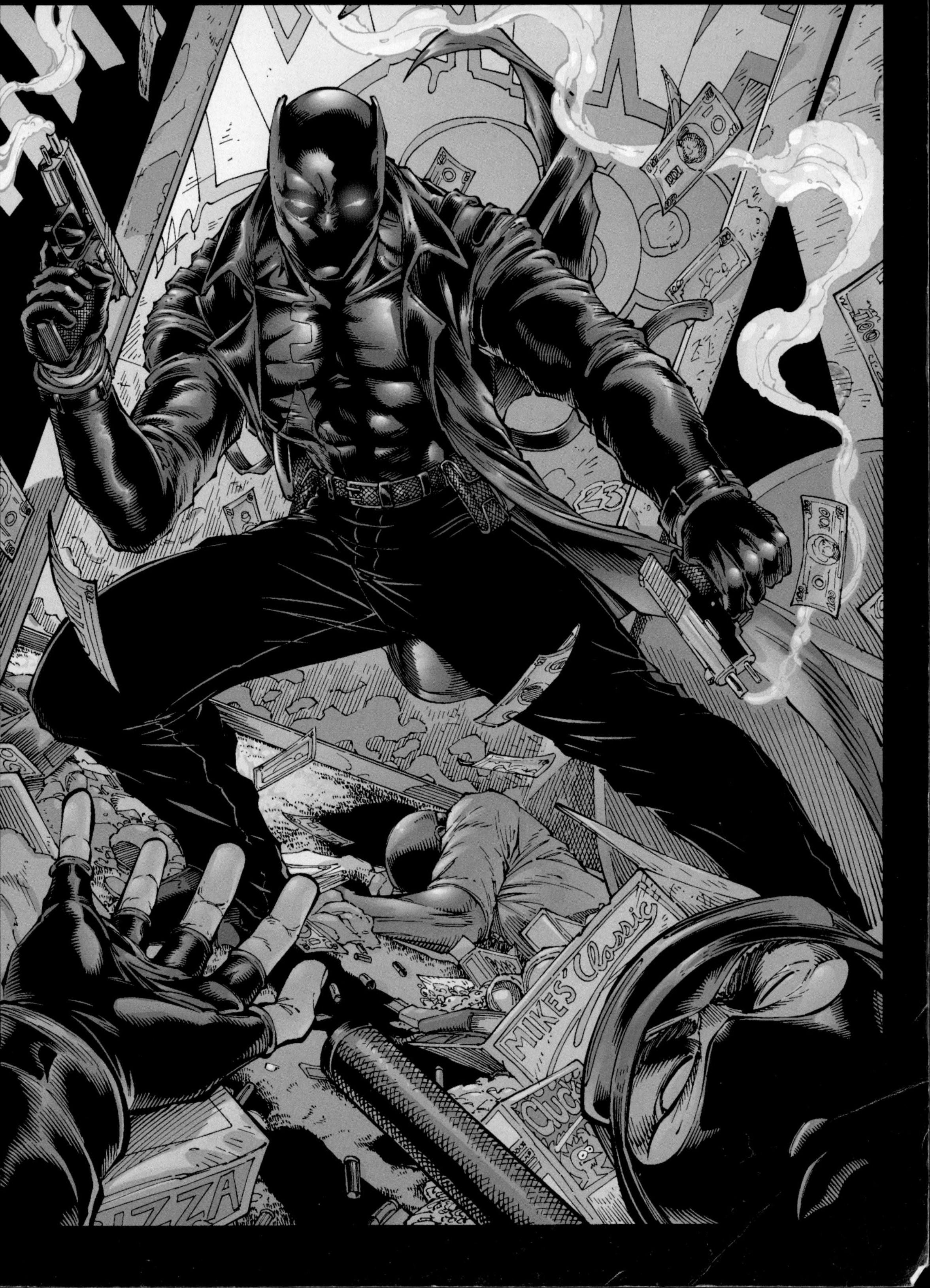
MIKE'S Classic

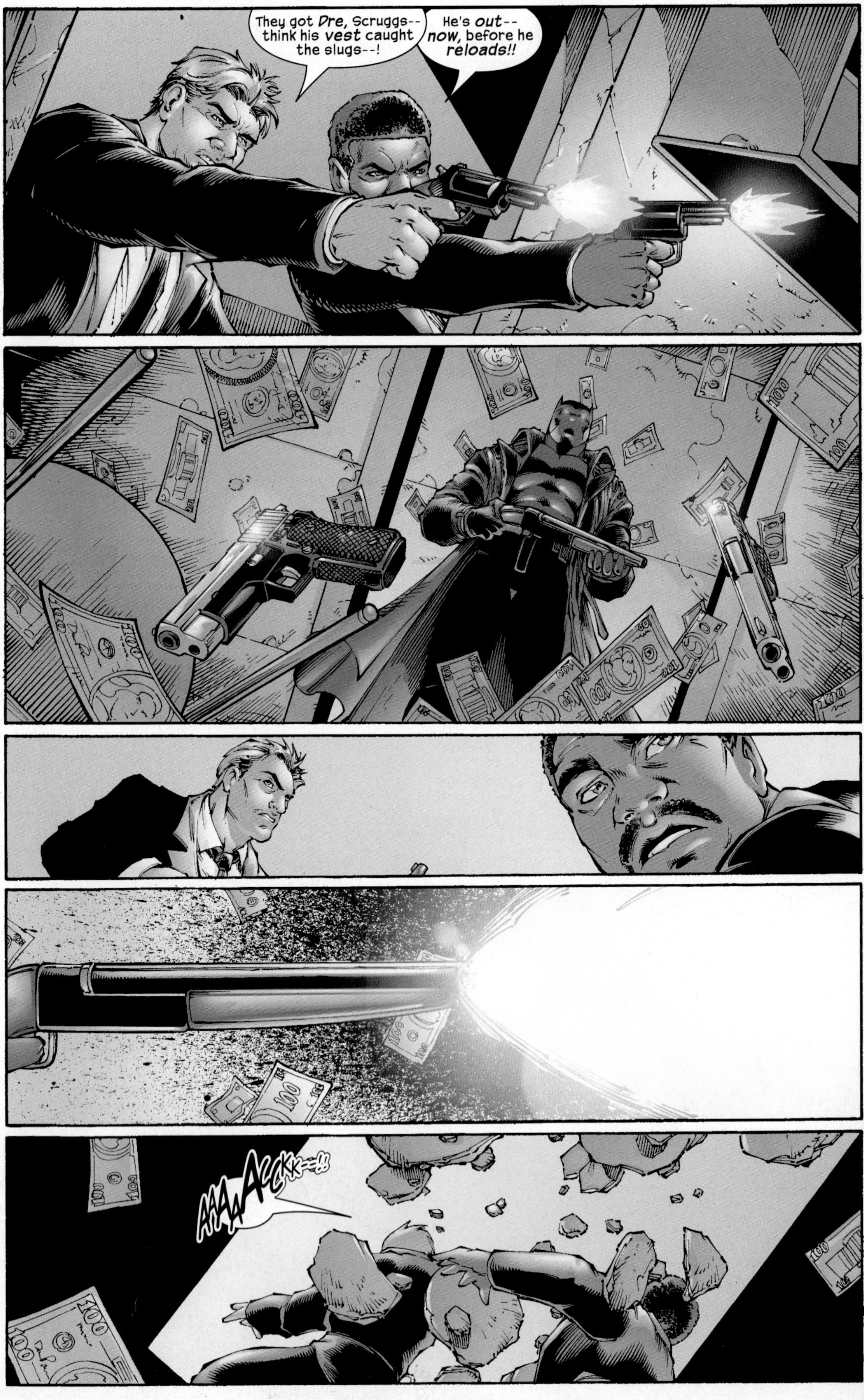
They got Dre, Scruggs-- think his vest caught the slugs--!
He's out-- now, before he reloads!!
AAAAACKK--!!

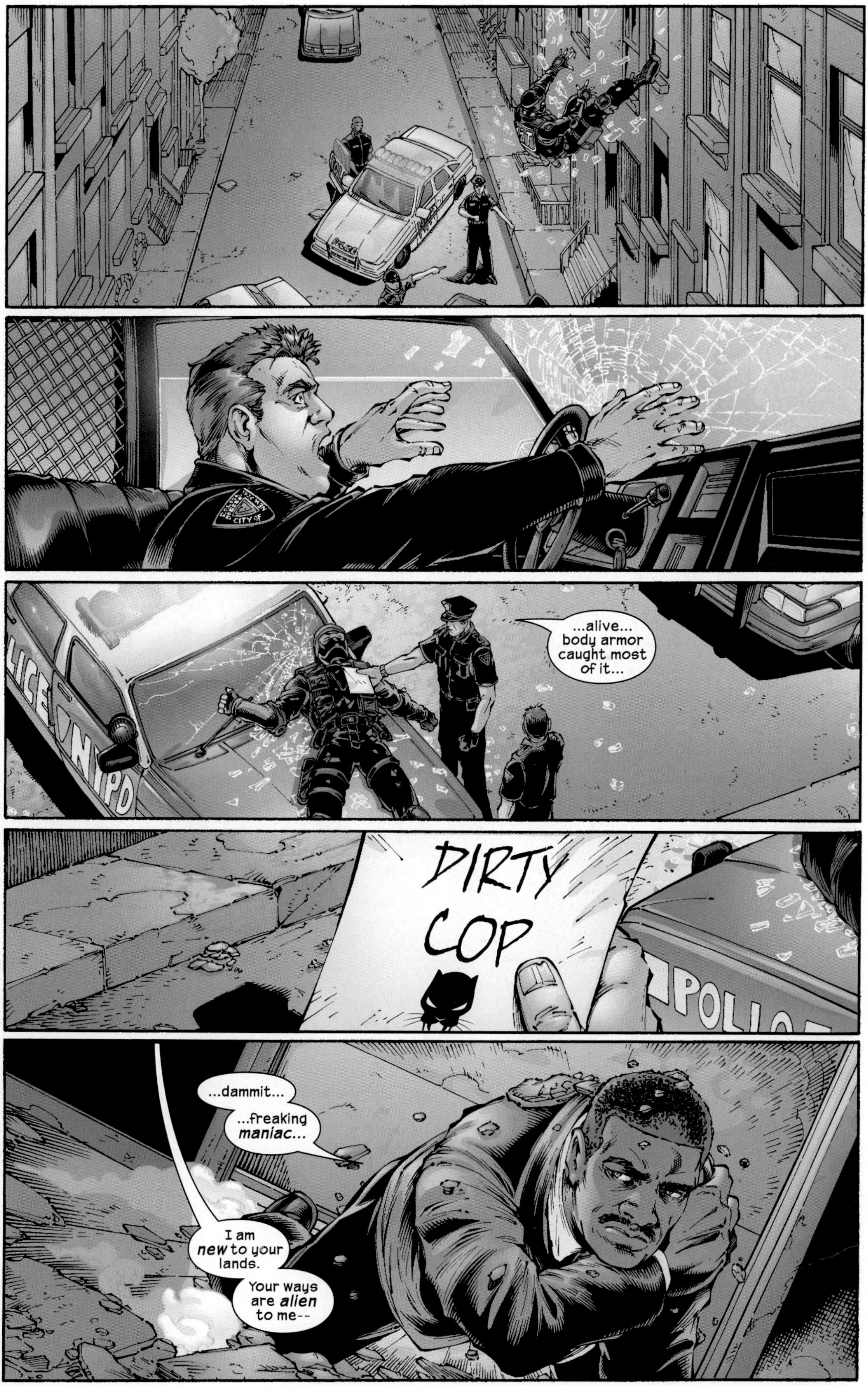

...alive... body armor caught most of it...
DIRTY COP
...dammit...
...freaking *maniac*...
I am *new* to your lands.
Your ways are *alien* to me--

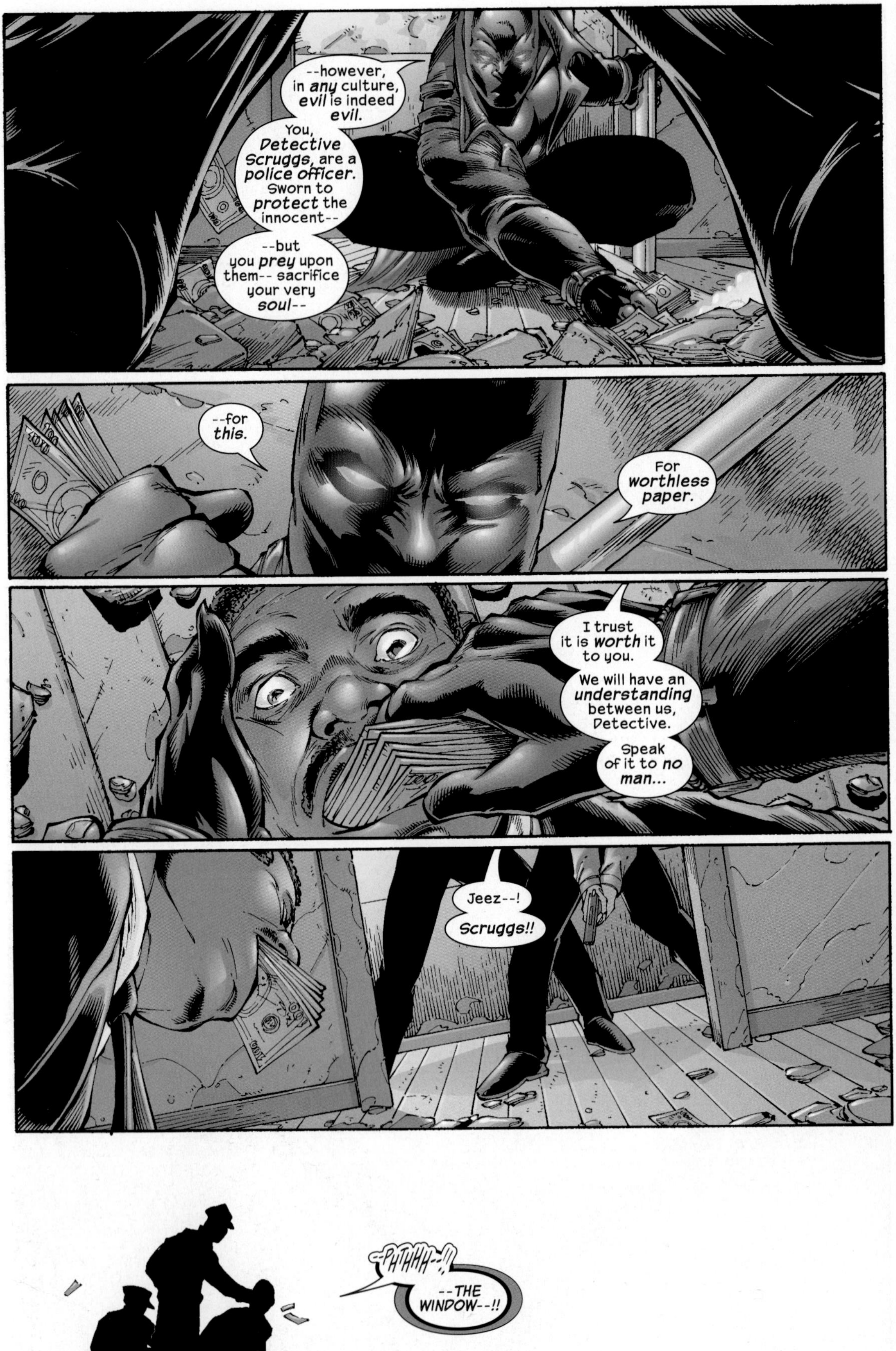
--however, in any culture, evil is indeed evil.
You, Detective Scruggs, are a police officer. Sworn to protect the innocent--
--but you prey upon them-- sacrifice your very soul--
--for this.
For worthless paper.
I trust it is worth it to you.
We will have an understanding between us, Detective.
Speak of it to no man...
Jeez--! Scruggs!!
--PHTHHH--!!
--THE WINDOW--!!

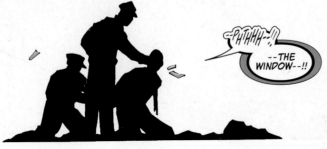

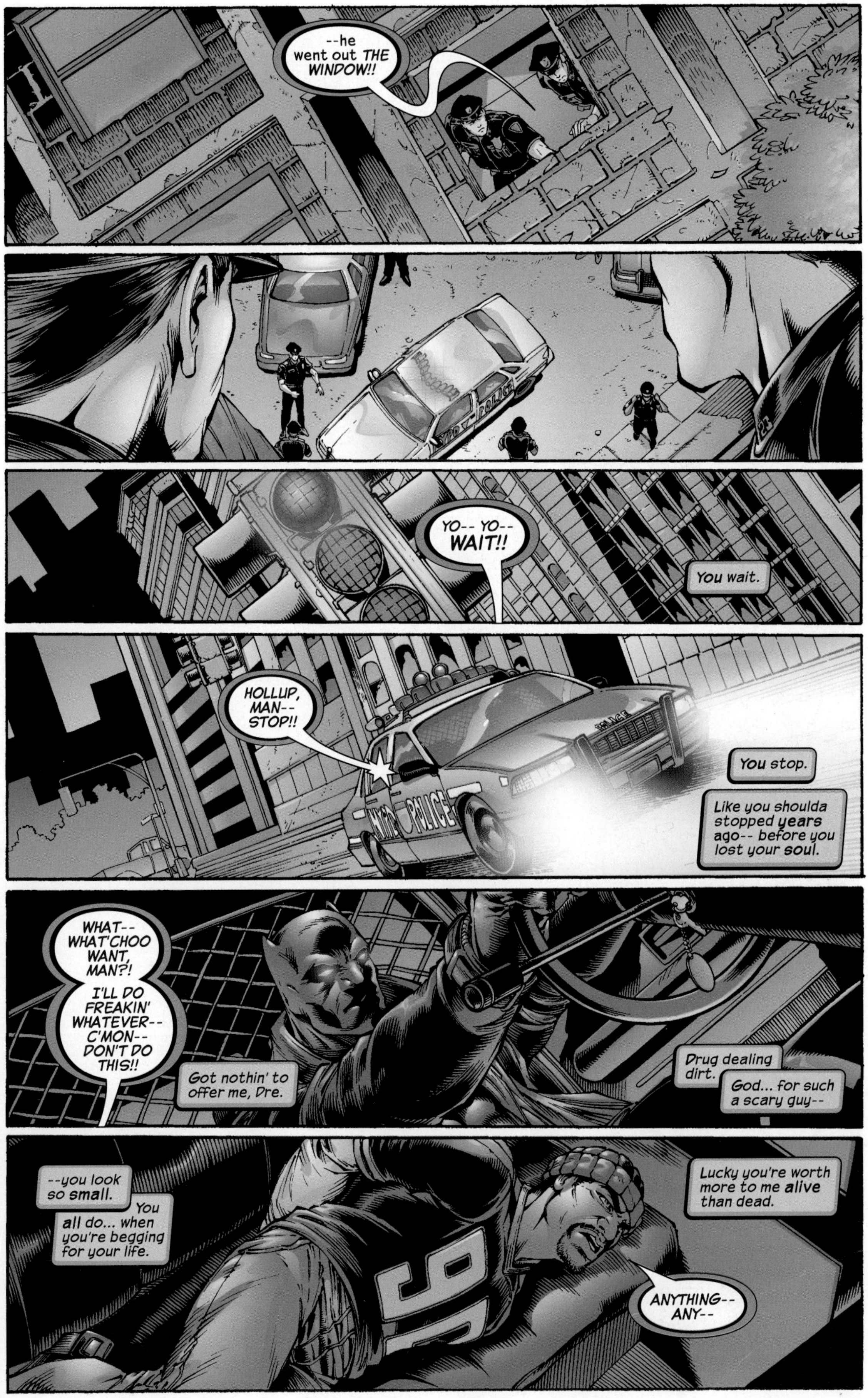
--he went out THE WINDOW!!
YO-- YO-- WAIT!!
You wait.
HOLLUP, MAN-- STOP!!
POLICE
NYPD POLICE
You stop.
Like you shoulda stopped years ago-- before you lost your soul.
WHAT-- WHAT'CHOO WANT, MAN?!
I'LL DO FREAKIN' WHATEVER-- C'MON-- DON'T DO THIS!!
Got nothin' to offer me, Dre.
Drug dealing dirt.
God... for such a scary guy--
--you look so small.
You all do... when you're begging for your life.
Lucky you're worth more to me alive than dead.
ANYTHING-- ANY--

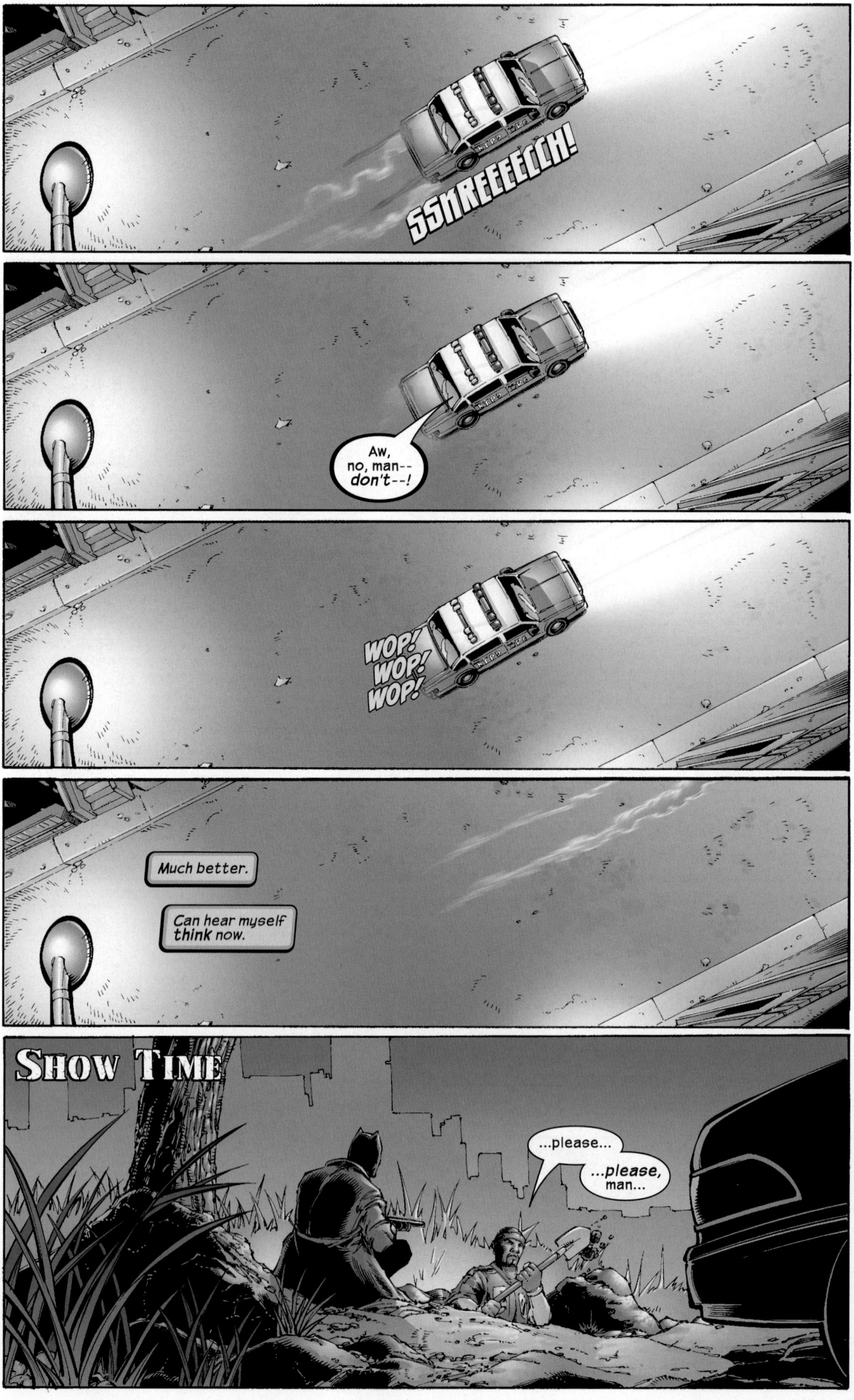
SSKREEEECCH!
Aw, no, man-- don't--!
WOP! WOP! WOP!
Much better.
Can hear myself think now.
SHOW TIME
...please...
...please, man...

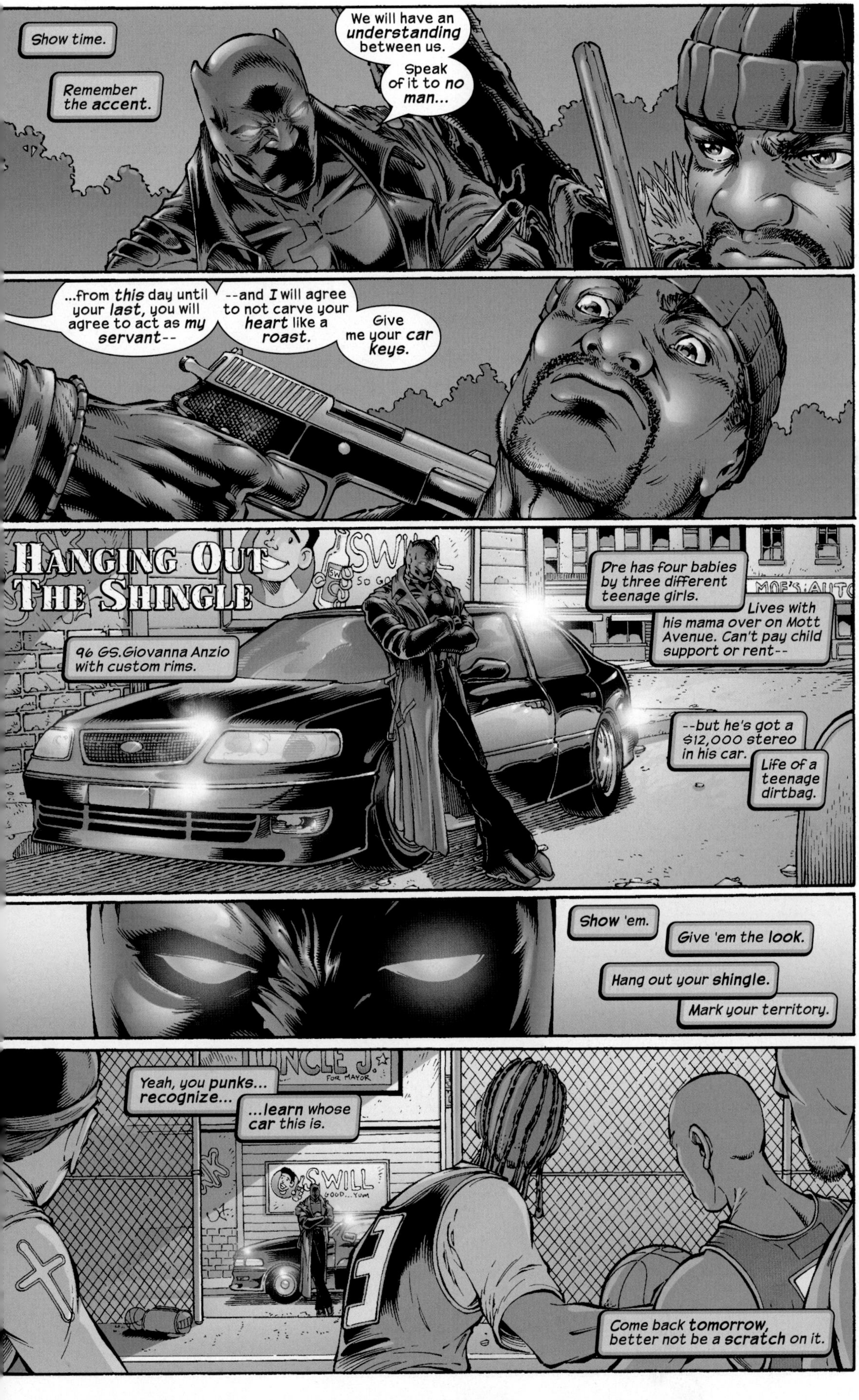
Show time.
Remember the accent.
We will have an understanding between us.
Speak of it to no man...
...from this day until your last, you will agree to act as my servant--
--and I will agree to not carve your heart like a roast.
Give me your car keys.
HANGING OUT THE SHINGLE
Dre has four babies by three different teenage girls.
Lives with his mama over on Mott Avenue. Can't pay child support or rent--
96 GS.Giovanna Anzio with custom rims.
--but he's got a $12,000 stereo in his car.
Life of a teenage dirtbag.
Show 'em.
Give 'em the look.
Hang out your shingle.
Mark your territory.
Yeah, you punks... recognize...
...learn whose car this is.
Come back tomorrow, better not be a scratch on it.

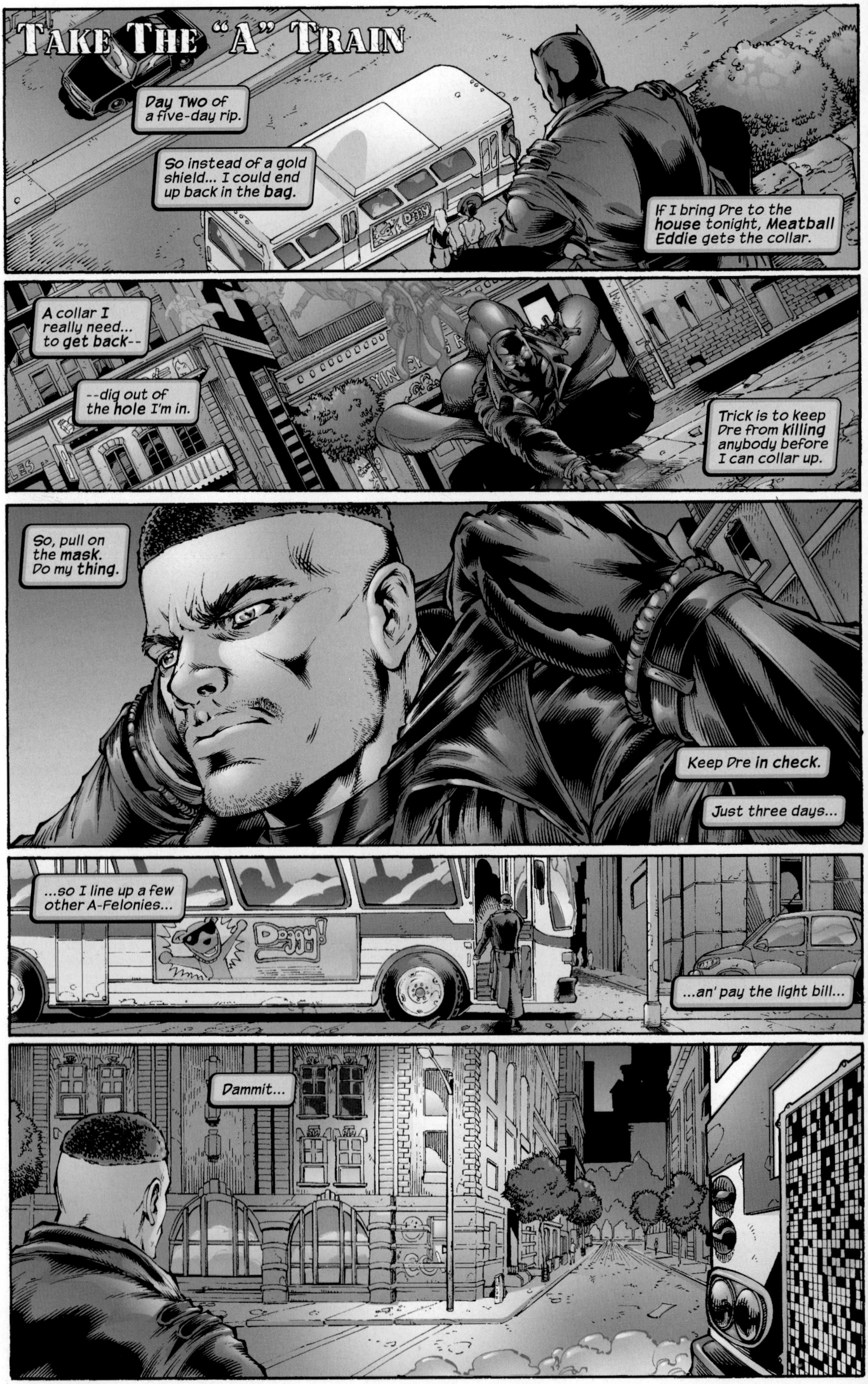
TAKE THE "A" TRAIN
Day Two of a five-day rip.
So instead of a gold shield... I could end up back in the bag.
If I bring Dre to the house tonight, Meatball Eddie gets the collar.
A collar I really need... to get back--
--dig out of the hole I'm in.
Trick is to keep Dre from killing anybody before I can collar up.
So, pull on the mask. Do my thing.
Keep Dre in check.
Just three days...
...so I line up a few other A-Felonies...
...an' pay the light bill...
Dammit...

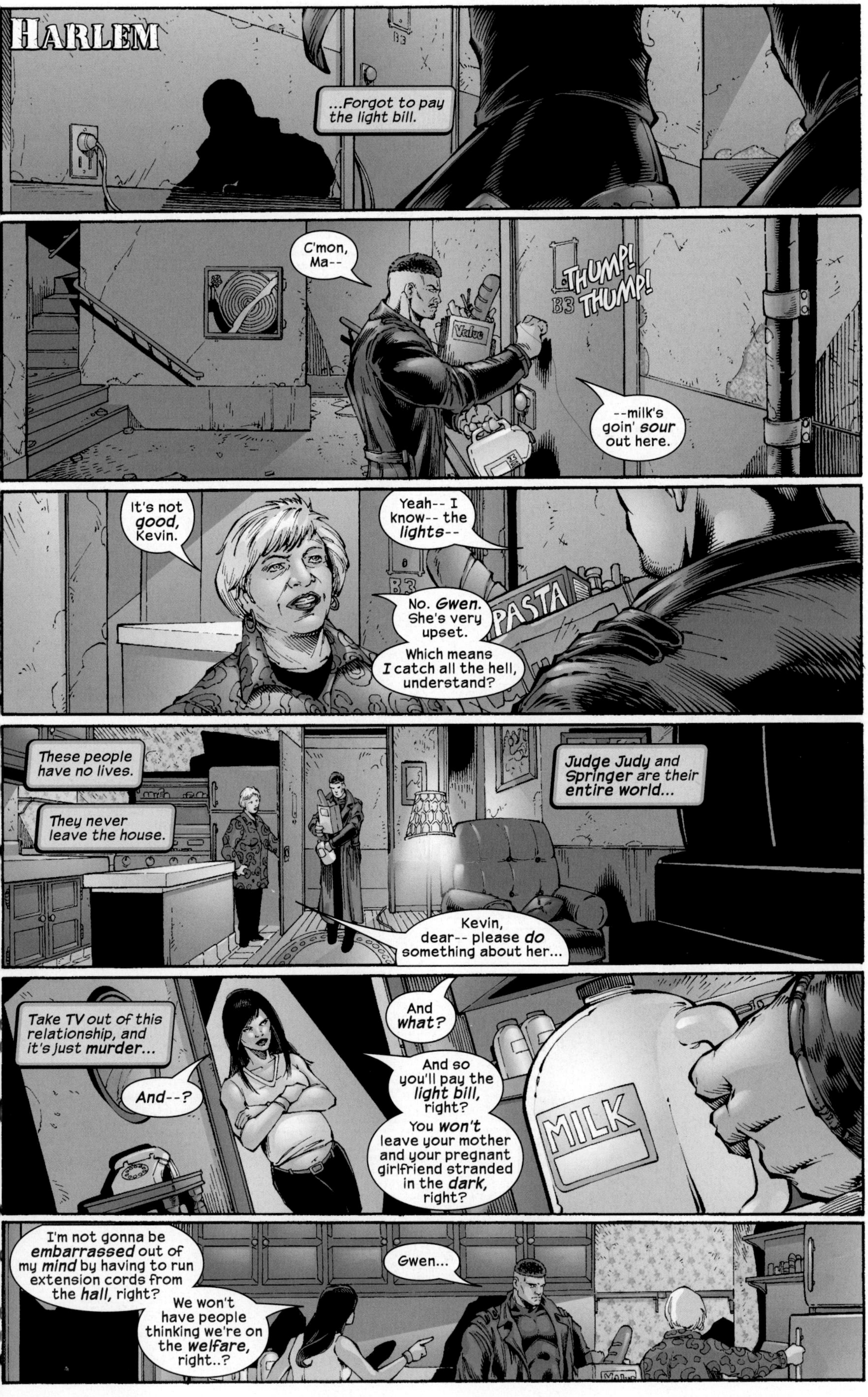
HARLEM
...Forgot to pay the light bill.
C'mon, Ma--
THUMP! THUMP!
B3
--milk's goin' sour out here.
It's not good, Kevin.
Yeah-- I know-- the lights--
No. Gwen. She's very upset.
Which means I catch all the hell, understand?
PASTA
These people have no lives.
They never leave the house.
Judge Judy and Springer are their entire world...
Kevin, dear-- please do something about her...
Take TV out of this relationship, and it's just murder...
And--?
And what?
And so you'll pay the light bill, right?
You won't leave your mother and your pregnant girlfriend stranded in the dark, right?
MILK
I'm not gonna be embarrassed out of my mind by having to run extension cords from the hall, right?
We won't have people thinking we're on the welfare, right..?
Gwen...

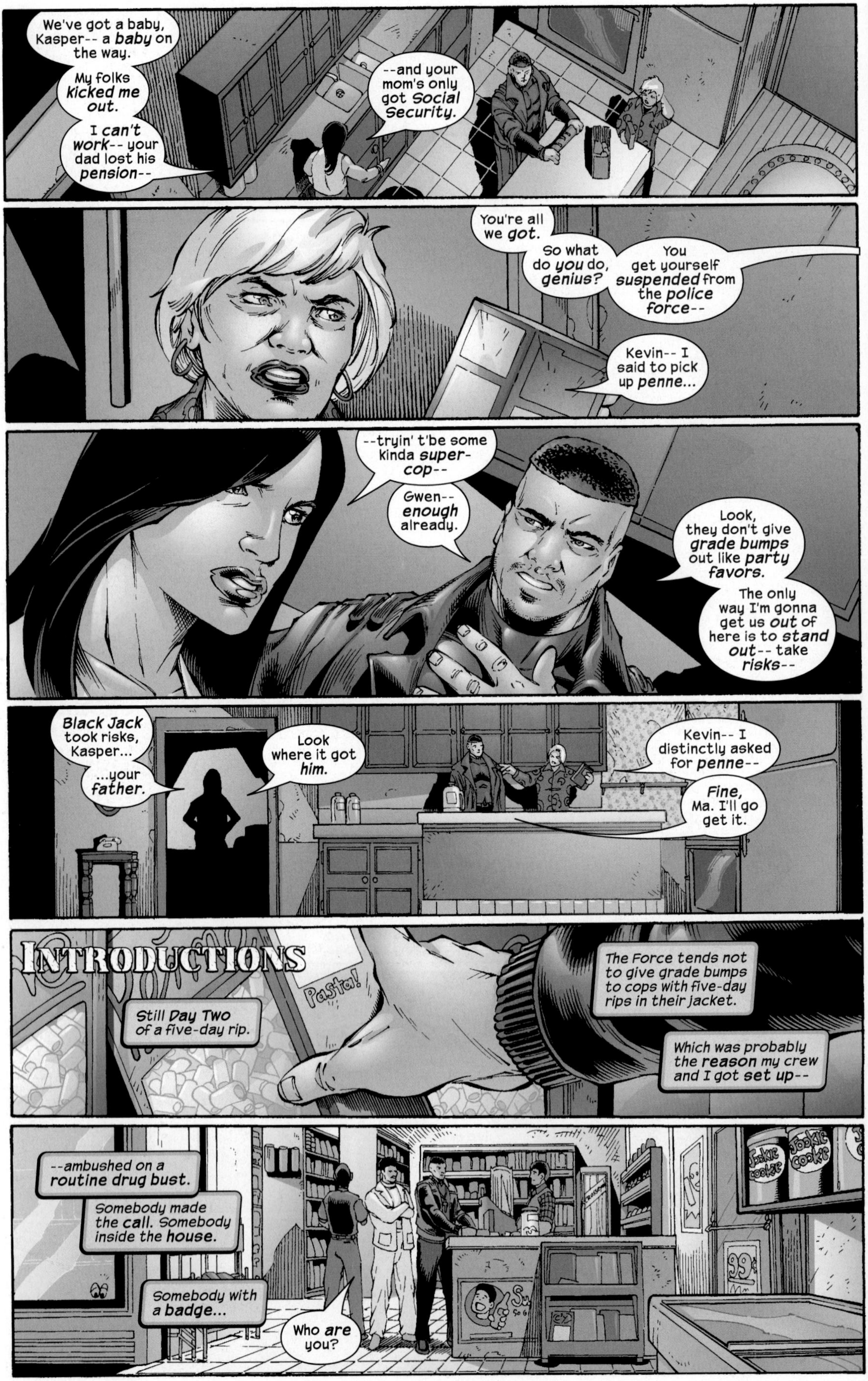
We've got a baby, Kasper-- a baby on the way.
My folks kicked me out.
I can't work-- your dad lost his pension--
--and your mom's only got Social Security.
You're all we got.
So what do you do, genius?
You get yourself suspended from the police force--
Kevin-- I said to pick up penne...
--tryin' t'be some kinda super-cop--
Gwen-- enough already.
Look, they don't give grade bumps out like party favors.
The only way I'm gonna get us out of here is to stand out-- take risks--
Black Jack took risks, Kasper...
...your father.
Look where it got him.
Kevin-- I distinctly asked for penne--
Fine, Ma. I'll go get it.
INTRODUCTIONS
Pasta!
Still Day Two of a five-day rip.
The Force tends not to give grade bumps to cops with five-day rips in their jacket.
Which was probably the reason my crew and I got set up--
--ambushed on a routine drug bust.
Somebody made the call. Somebody inside the house.
Somebody with a badge...
Who are you?
Jookie Cookie
99¢

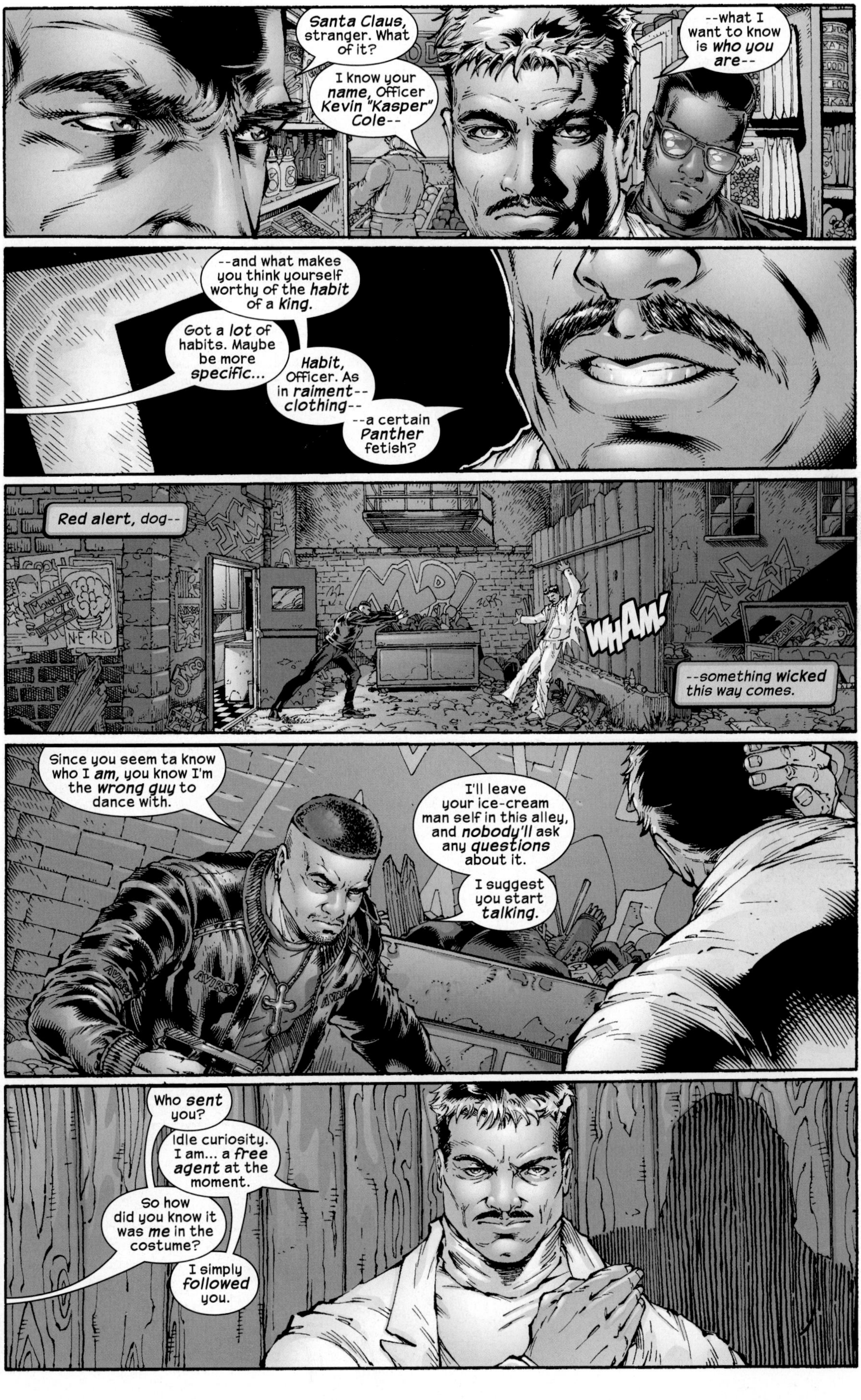

Santa Claus, stranger. What of it?
I know your name, Officer Kevin "Kasper" Cole--
--what I want to know is who you are--
--and what makes you think yourself worthy of the habit of a king.
Got a lot of habits. Maybe be more specific...
Habit, Officer. As in raiment--clothing--
--a certain Panther fetish?
Red alert, dog--
WHAM!
--something wicked this way comes.
Since you seem ta know who I am, you know I'm the wrong guy to dance with.
I'll leave your ice-cream man self in this alley, and nobody'll ask any questions about it.
I suggest you start talking.
Who sent you?
Idle curiosity. I am... a free agent at the moment.
So how did you know it was me in the costume?
I simply followed you.

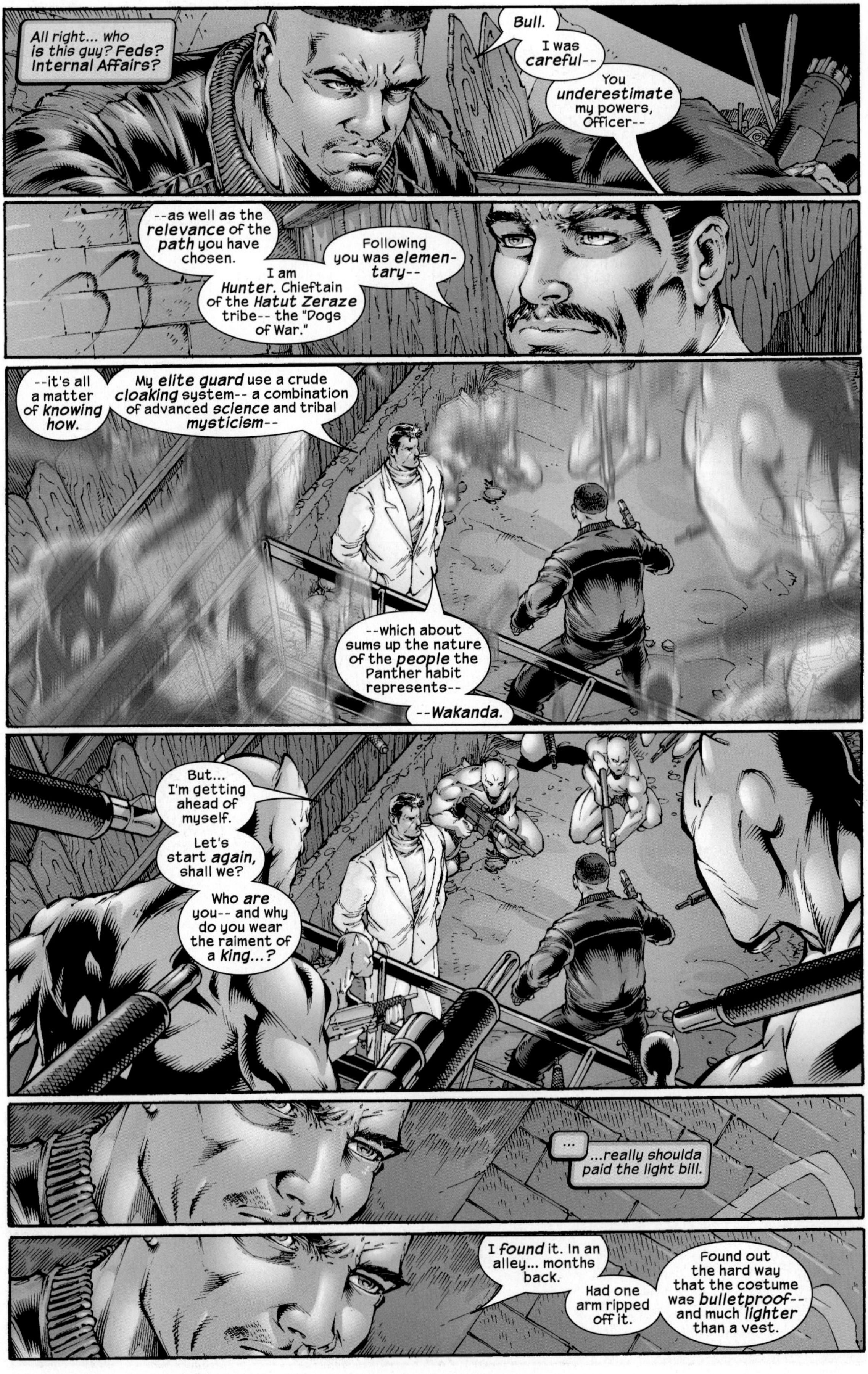

All right... who is this guy? Feds? Internal Affairs?
Bull.
I was careful--
You underestimate my powers, Officer--
--as well as the relevance of the path you have chosen.
Following you was elementary--
I am Hunter. Chieftain of the Hatut Zeraze tribe-- the "Dogs of War."
--it's all a matter of knowing how.
My elite guard use a crude cloaking system-- a combination of advanced science and tribal mysticism--
--which about sums up the nature of the people the Panther habit represents--
--Wakanda.
But... I'm getting ahead of myself.
Let's start again, shall we?
Who are you-- and why do you wear the raiment of a king...?
...
...really shoulda paid the light bill.
I found it. In an alley... months back.
Had one arm ripped off it.
Found out the hard way that the costume was bulletproof-- and much lighter than a vest.

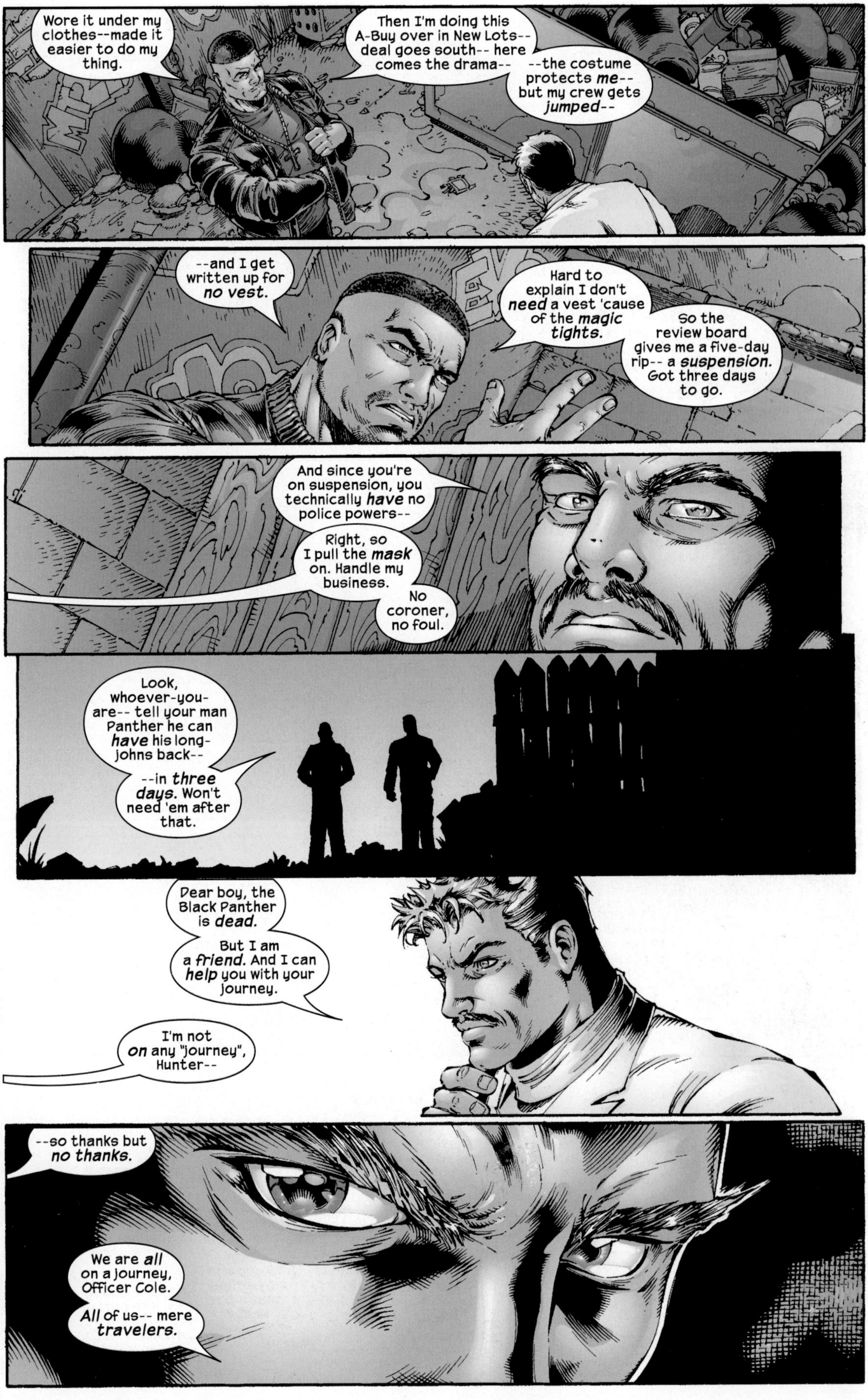
Wore it under my clothes--made it easier to do my thing.
Then I'm doing this A-Buy over in New Lots-- deal goes south-- here comes the drama--
--the costume protects me-- but my crew gets jumped--
--and I get written up for no vest.
Hard to explain I don't need a vest 'cause of the magic tights.
So the review board gives me a five-day rip-- a suspension. Got three days to go.
And since you're on suspension, you technically have no police powers--
Right, so I pull the mask on. Handle my business.
No coroner, no foul.
Look, whoever-you-are-- tell your man Panther he can have his long-johns back--
--in three days. Won't need 'em after that.
Dear boy, the Black Panther is dead.
But I am a friend. And I can help you with your journey.
I'm not on any "journey", Hunter--
--so thanks but no thanks.
We are all on a journey, Officer Cole.
All of us-- mere travelers.

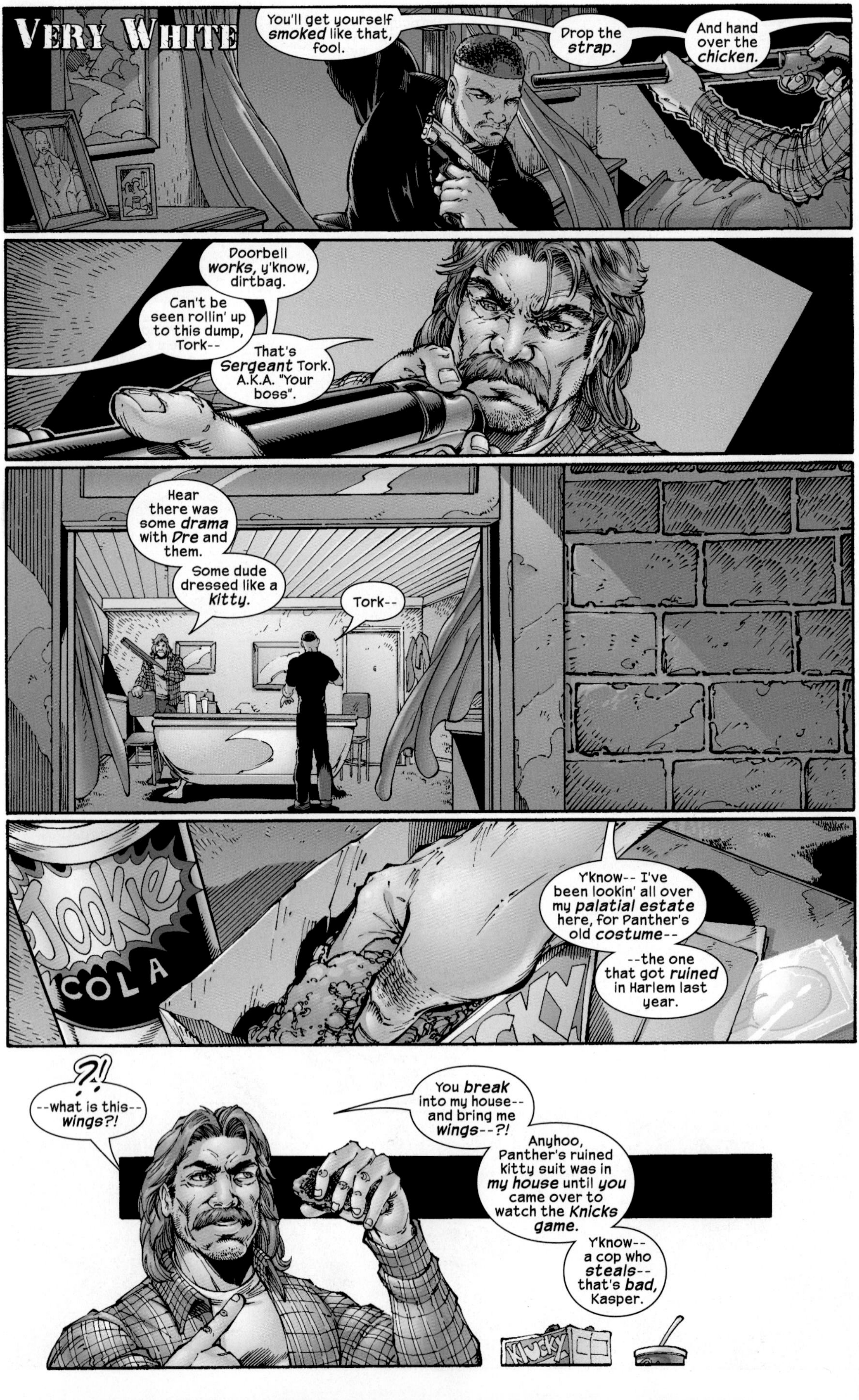
VERY WHITE
You'll get yourself *smoked* like that, fool.
Drop the *strap*.
And hand over the *chicken*.
Doorbell *works*, y'know, dirtbag.
Can't be seen rollin' up to this dump, Tork--
That's *Sergeant* Tork. A.K.A. "Your boss".
Hear there was some *drama* with *Dre* and them.
Some dude dressed like a *kitty*.
Tork--
Y'know-- I've been lookin' all over my *palatial estate* here, for Panther's old *costume*--
--the one that got *ruined* in Harlem last year.
Jookie COLA
?!
--what is this-- *wings?!*
You *break* into my house-- and bring me *wings*--?!
Anyhoo, Panther's ruined kitty suit was in *my house* until *you* came over to watch the *Knicks game*.
Y'know-- a cop who *steals*-- that's *bad,* Kasper.

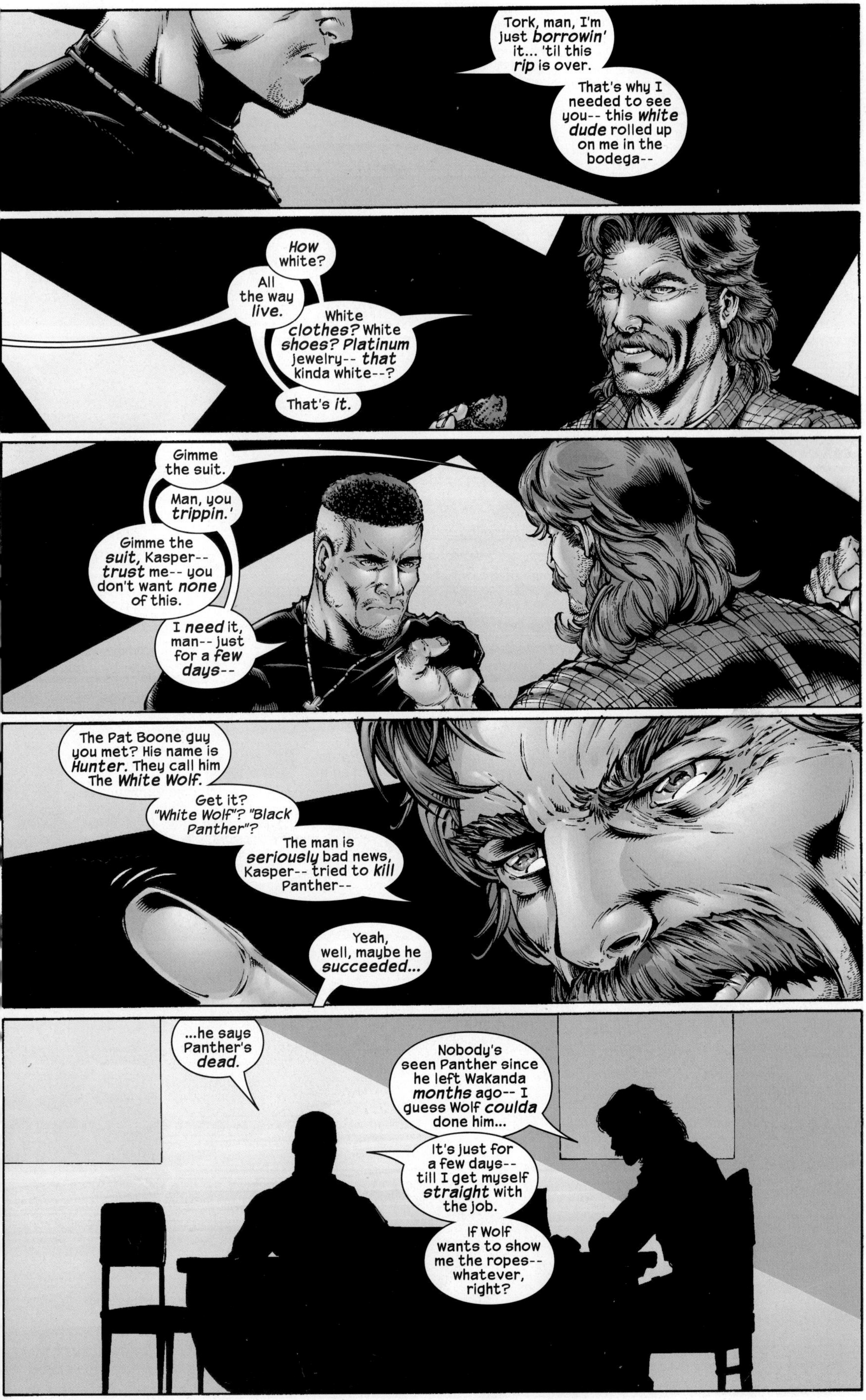
Tork, man, I'm just borrowin' it... 'til this rip is over.
That's why I needed to see you-- this white dude rolled up on me in the bodega--
How white?
All the way live.
White clothes? White shoes? Platinum jewelry-- that kinda white--?
That's it.
Gimme the suit.
Man, you trippin.'
Gimme the suit, Kasper-- trust me-- you don't want none of this.
I need it, man-- just for a few days--
The Pat Boone guy you met? His name is Hunter. They call him The White Wolf.
Get it? "White Wolf"? "Black Panther"?
The man is seriously bad news, Kasper-- tried to kill Panther--
Yeah, well, maybe he succeeded...
...he says Panther's dead.
Nobody's seen Panther since he left Wakanda months ago-- I guess Wolf coulda done him...
It's just for a few days-- till I get myself straight with the job.
If Wolf wants to show me the ropes-- whatever, right?

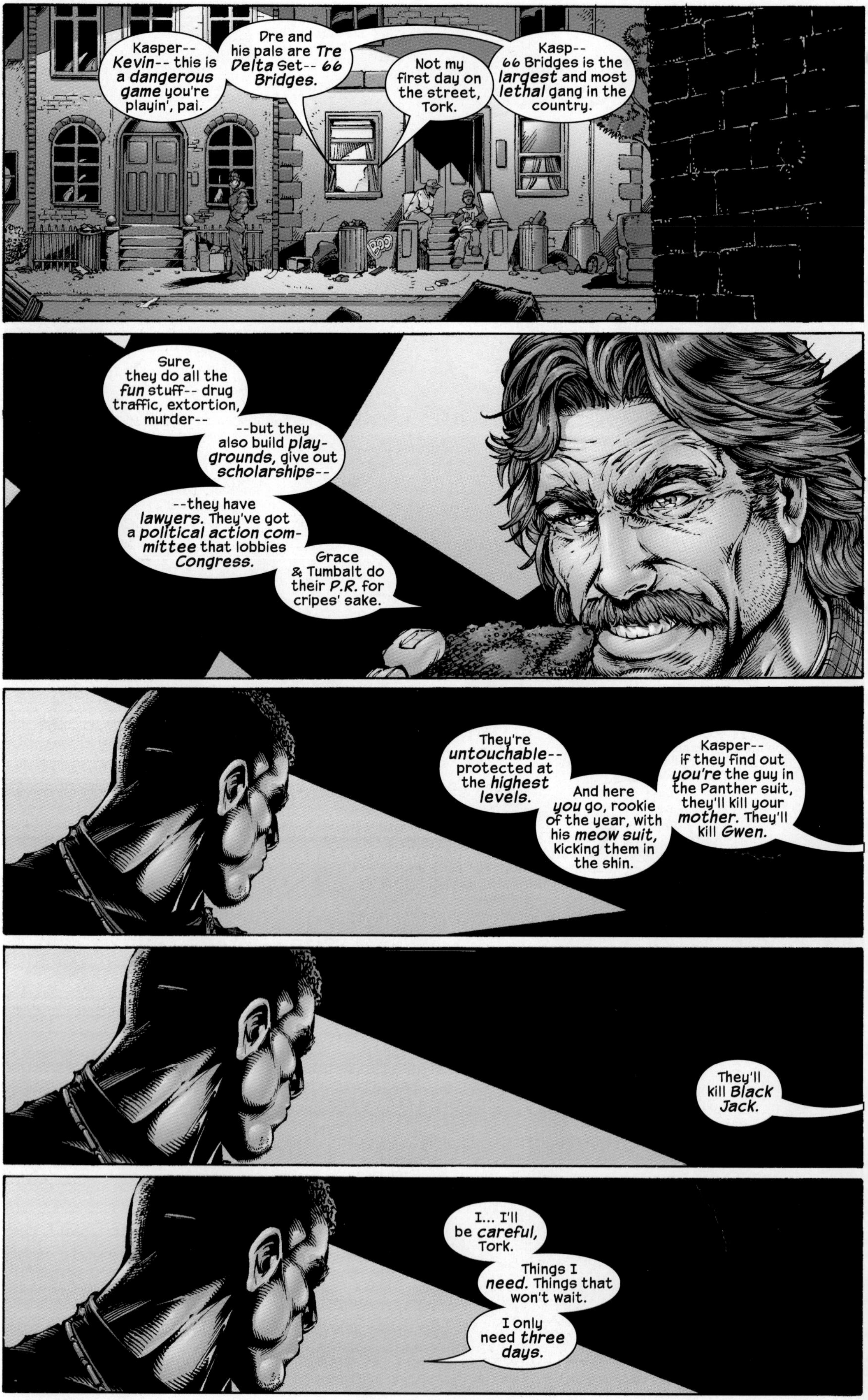
Kasper-- Kevin-- this is a dangerous game you're playin', pal.
Dre and his pals are Tre Delta Set-- 66 Bridges.
Not my first day on the street, Tork.
Kasp-- 66 Bridges is the largest and most lethal gang in the country.
Sure, they do all the fun stuff-- drug traffic, extortion, murder--
--but they also build play-grounds, give out scholarships--
--they have lawyers. They've got a political action com-mittee that lobbies Congress.
Grace & Tumbalt do their P.R. for cripes' sake.
They're untouchable-- protected at the highest levels.
And here you go, rookie of the year, with his meow suit, kicking them in the shin.
Kasper-- if they find out you're the guy in the Panther suit, they'll kill your mother. They'll kill Gwen.
They'll kill Black Jack.
I... I'll be careful, Tork.
Things I need. Things that won't wait.
I only need three days.

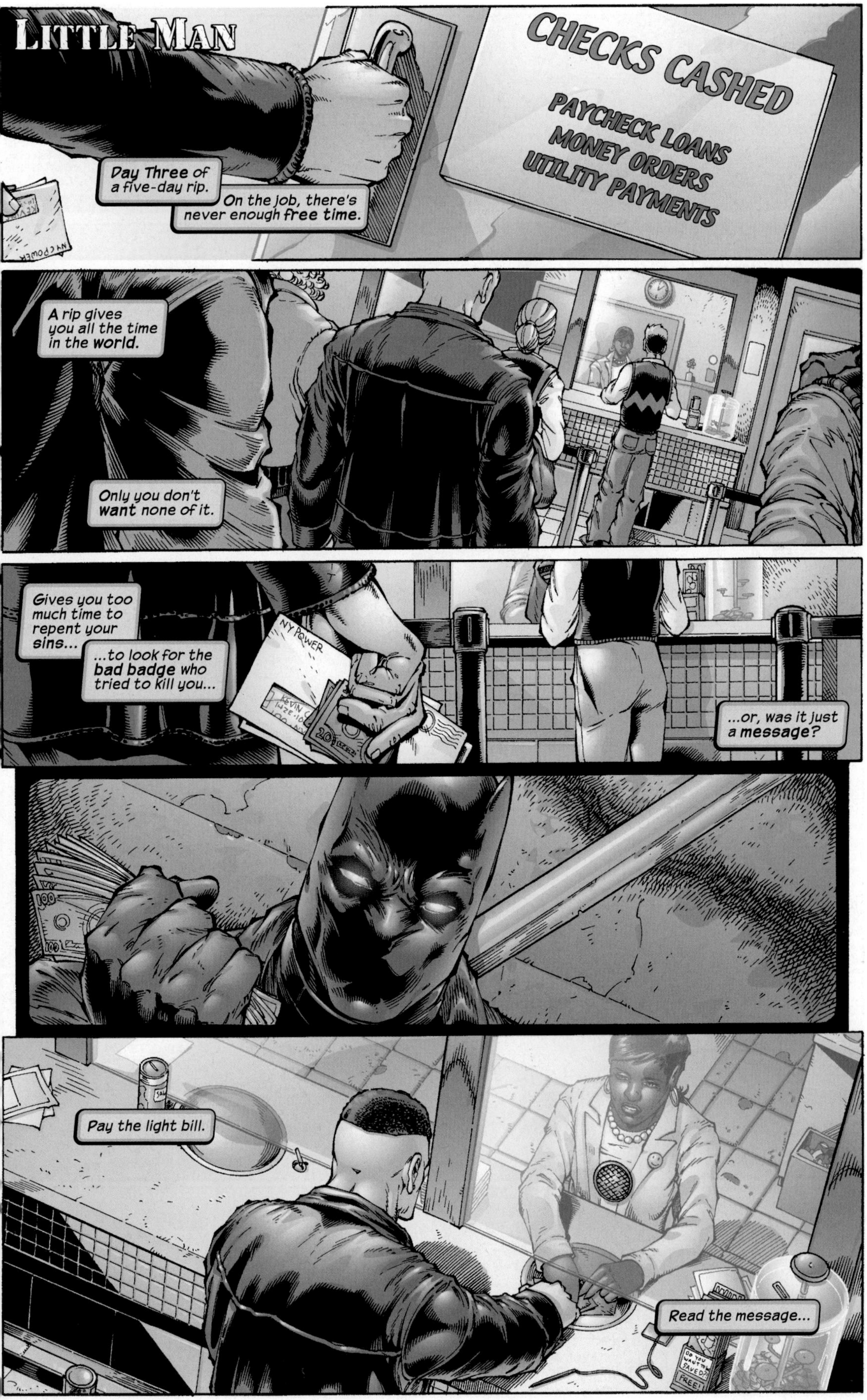
LITTLE MAN
CHECKS CASHED
PAYCHECK LOANS
MONEY ORDERS
UTILITY PAYMENTS
Day Three of a five-day rip.
On the job, there's never enough free time.
NY POWER
A rip gives you all the time in the world.
Only you don't want none of it.
Gives you too much time to repent your sins...
...to look for the bad badge who tried to kill you...
NY POWER
...or, was it just a message?
Pay the light bill.
Read the message...
DO YOU WANT TO BE SAVED? FREE!

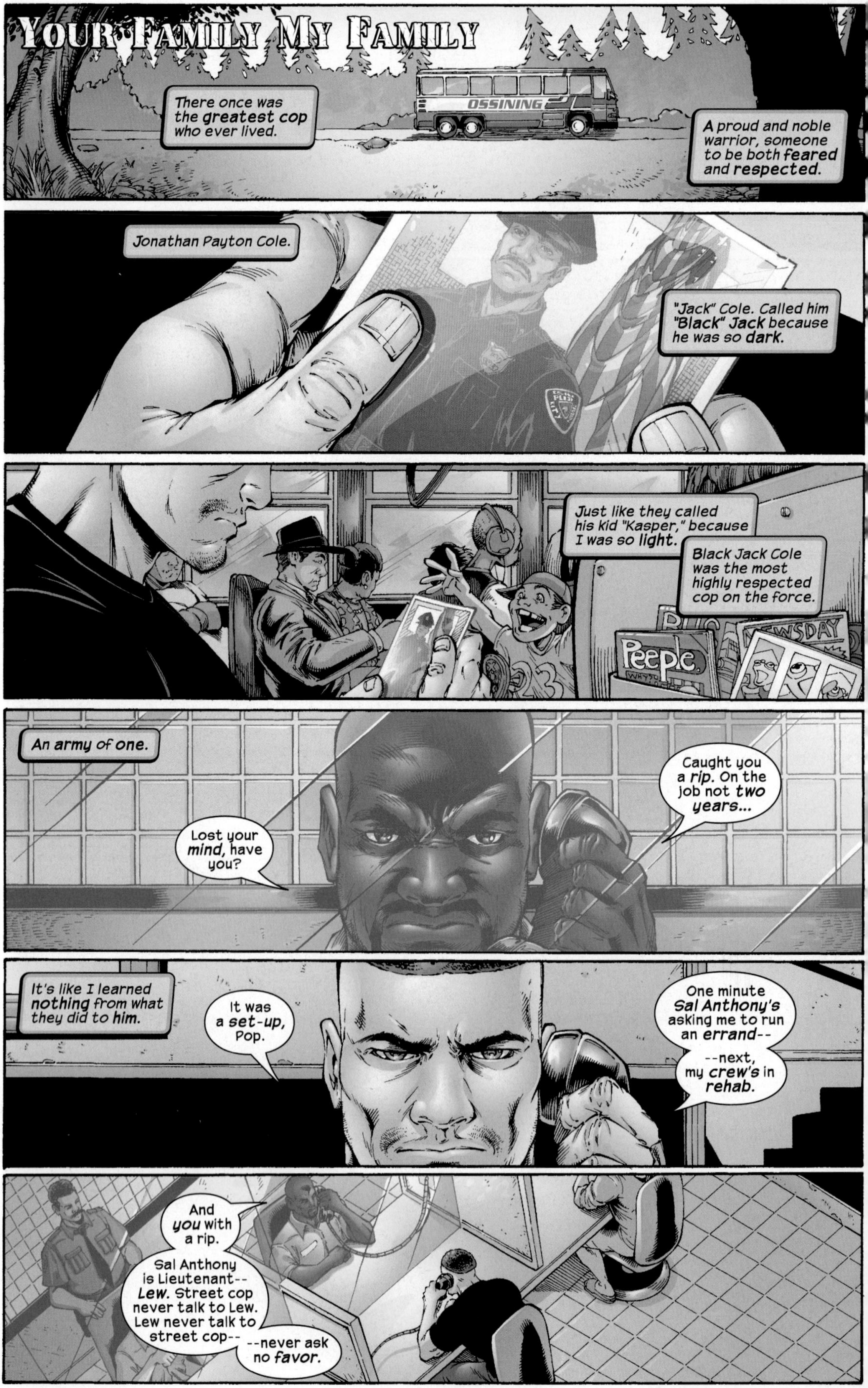

YOUR FAMILY MY FAMILY
There once was the greatest cop who ever lived.
OSSINING
A proud and noble warrior, someone to be both feared and respected.
Jonathan Payton Cole.
"Jack" Cole. Called him "Black" Jack because he was so dark.
Just like they called his kid "Kasper," because I was so light.
Black Jack Cole was the most highly respected cop on the force.
Peeple
NEWSDAY
An army of one.
Caught you a rip. On the job not two years...
Lost your mind, have you?
It's like I learned nothing from what they did to him.
It was a set-up, Pop.
One minute Sal Anthony's asking me to run an errand--
--next, my crew's in rehab.
And you with a rip.
Sal Anthony is Lieutenant--Lew. Street cop never talk to Lew. Lew never talk to street cop--
--never ask no favor.

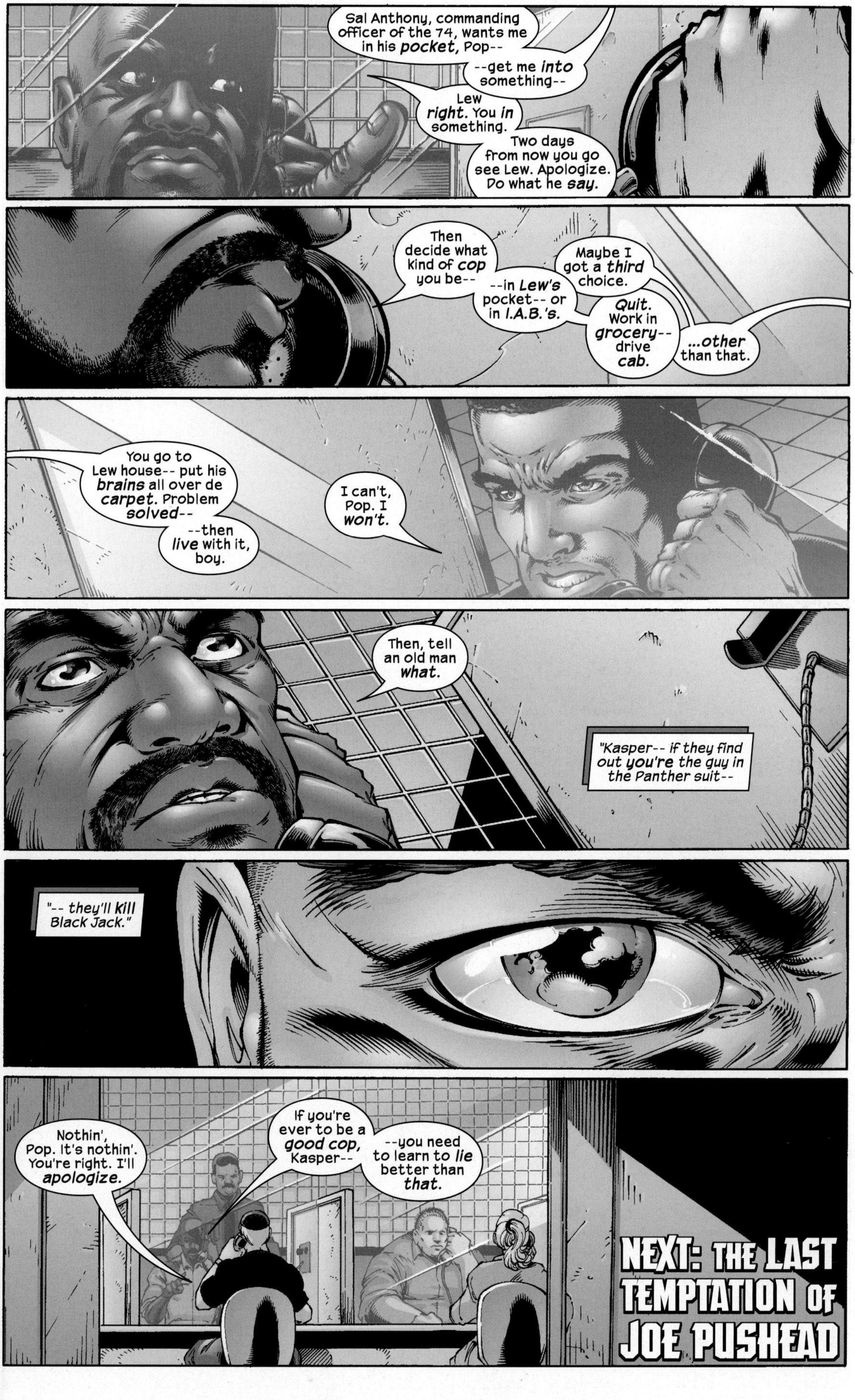

Sal Anthony, commanding officer of the 74, wants me in his pocket, Pop--
--get me into something--
Lew right. You in something.
Two days from now you go see Lew. Apologize. Do what he say.
Then decide what kind of cop you be--
--in Lew's pocket-- or in I.A.B.'s.
Maybe I got a third choice.
Quit. Work in grocery-- drive cab.
...other than that.
You go to Lew house-- put his brains all over de carpet. Problem solved--
--then live with it, boy.
I can't, Pop. I won't.
Then, tell an old man what.
"Kasper-- if they find out you're the guy in the Panther suit--
"-- they'll kill Black Jack."
Nothin', Pop. It's nothin'. You're right. I'll apologize.
If you're ever to be a good cop, Kasper--
--you need to learn to lie better than that.
NEXT: THE LAST TEMPTATION OF JOE PUSHEAD

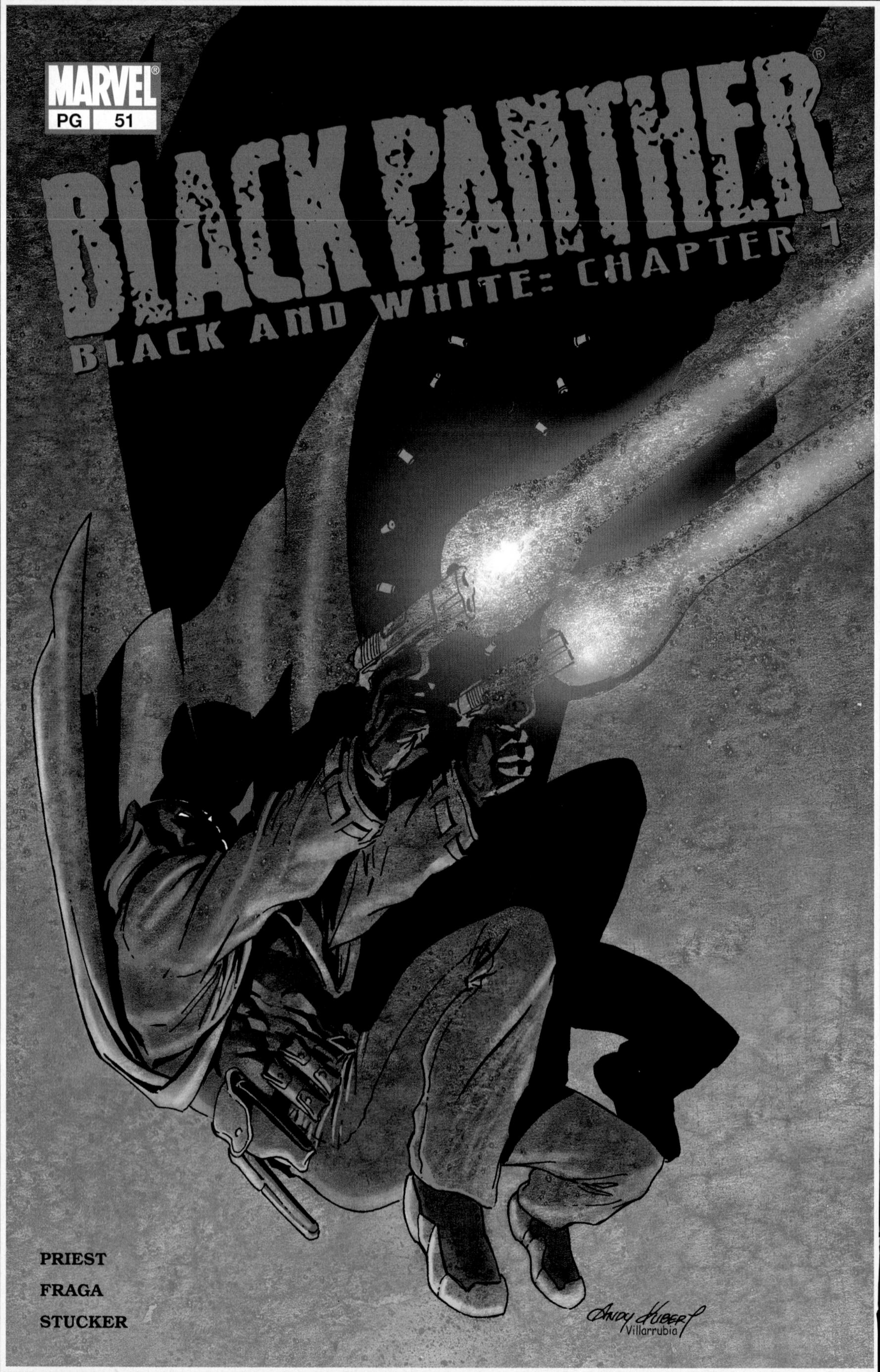
MARVEL
PG 51
BLACK PANTHER
BLACK AND WHITE: CHAPTER 1
PRIEST
FRAGA
STUCKER
Andy Kubert
Villarrubia

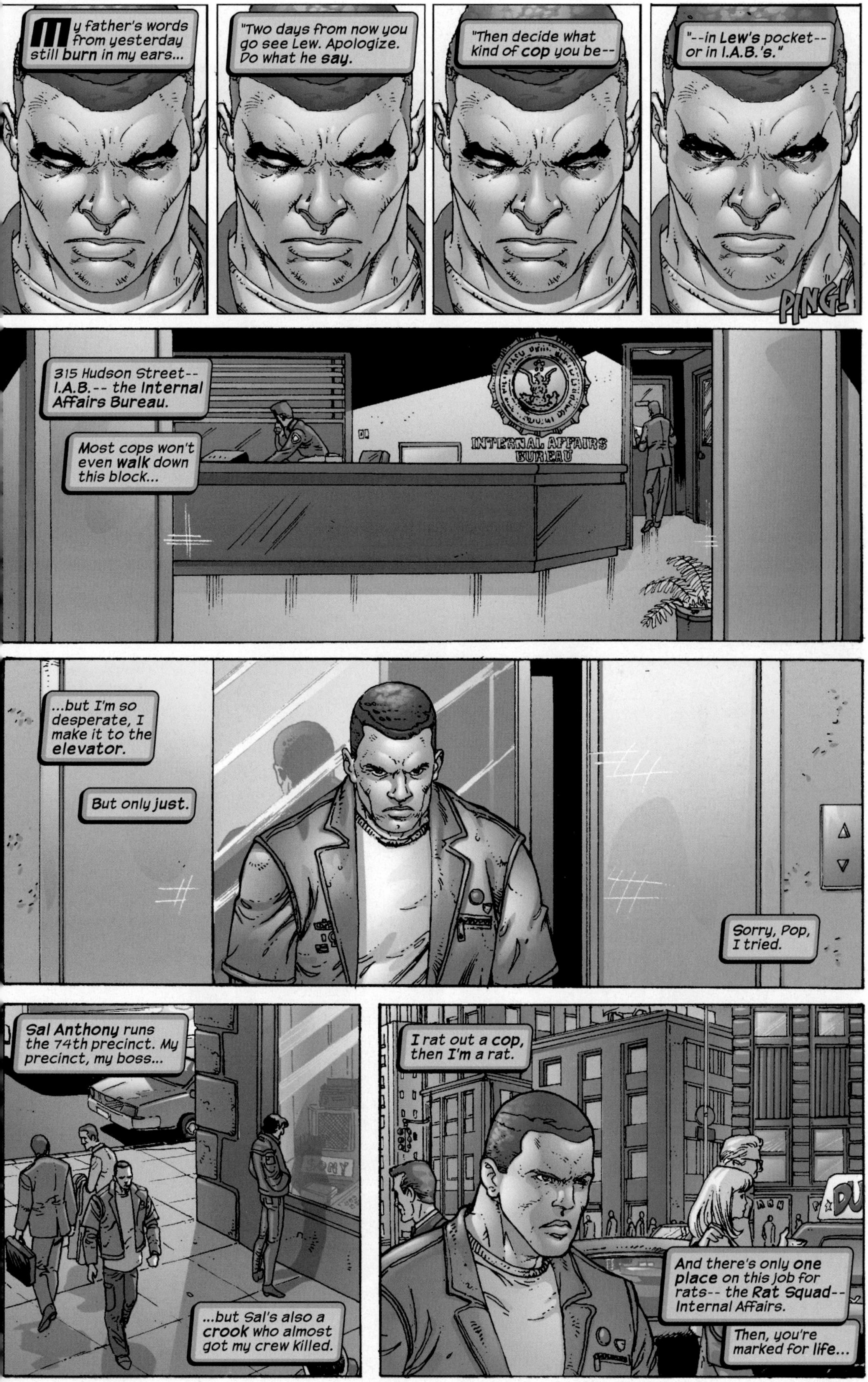
My father's words from yesterday still burn in my ears...
"Two days from now you go see Lew. Apologize. Do what he say.
"Then decide what kind of cop you be--
"--in Lew's pocket--or in I.A.B.'s."
PING!
315 Hudson Street--I.A.B.-- the Internal Affairs Bureau.
Most cops won't even walk down this block...
INTERNAL AFFAIRS BUREAU
...but I'm so desperate, I make it to the elevator.
But only just.
Sorry, Pop, I tried.
Sal Anthony runs the 74th precinct. My precinct, my boss...
...but Sal's also a crook who almost got my crew killed.
I rat out a cop, then I'm a rat.
And there's only one place on this job for rats-- the Rat Squad--Internal Affairs.
Then, you're marked for life...

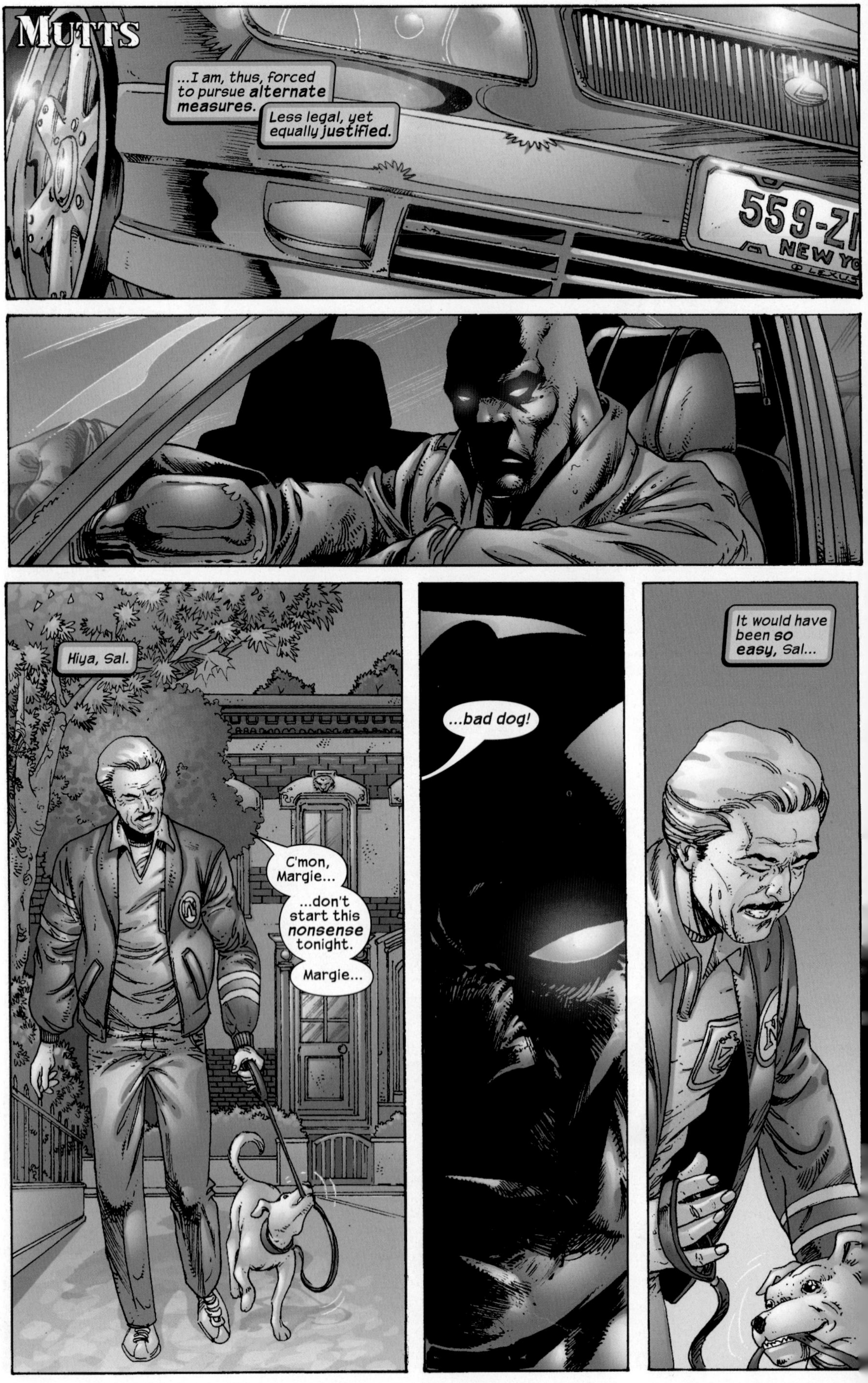
MUTTS
...I am, thus, forced to pursue alternate measures.
Less legal, yet equally justified.
559-ZI
NEW YO
LEXUS
Hiya, Sal.
C'mon, Margie...
...don't start this nonsense tonight.
Margie...
...bad dog!
It would have been so easy, Sal...

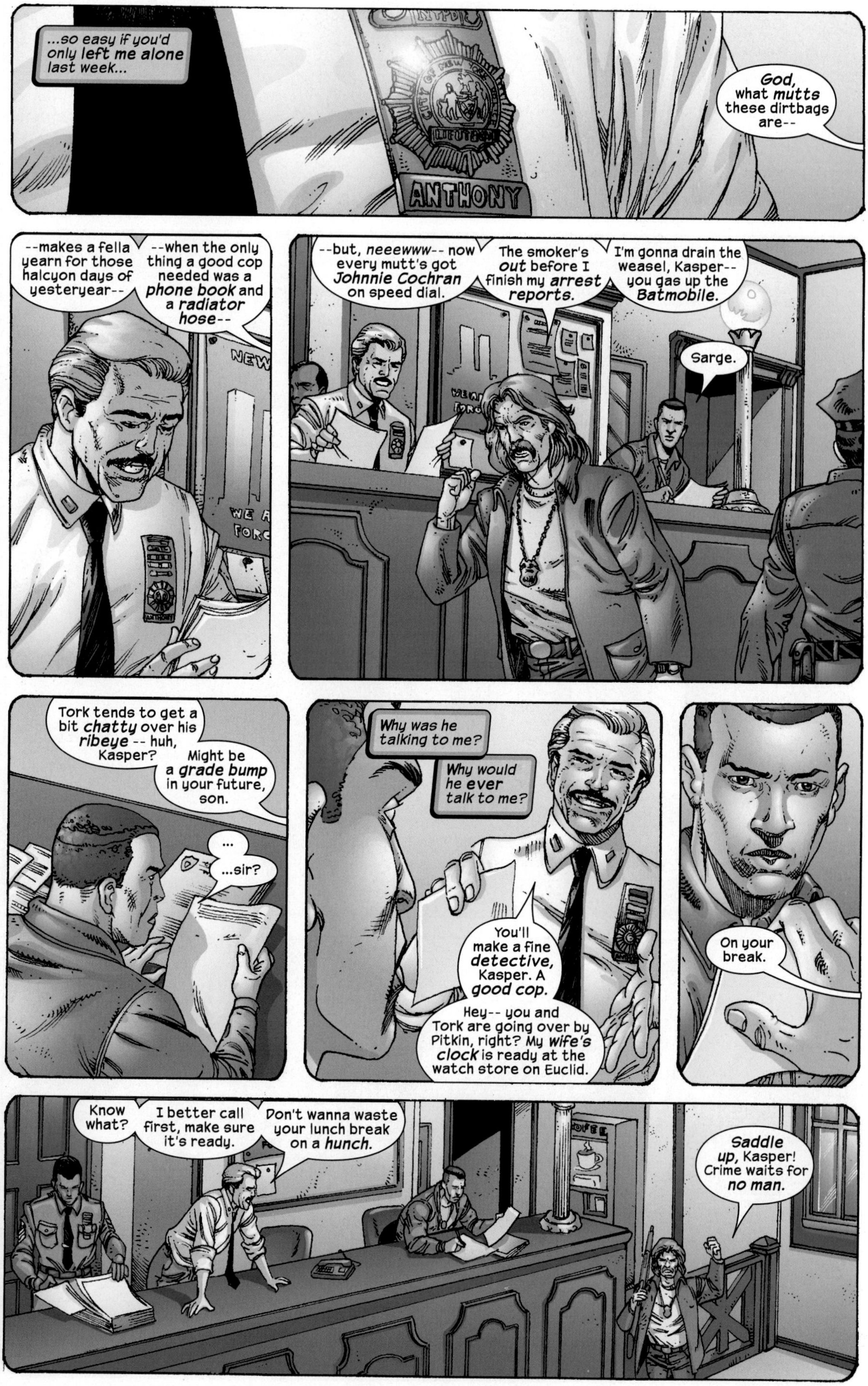
...so easy if you'd only left me alone last week...
ANTHONY
God, what mutts these dirtbags are--
--makes a fella yearn for those halcyon days of yesteryear--
--when the only thing a good cop needed was a phone book and a radiator hose--
--but, neeewww-- now every mutt's got Johnnie Cochran on speed dial.
The smoker's out before I finish my arrest reports.
I'm gonna drain the weasel, Kasper-- you gas up the Batmobile.
Sarge.
Tork tends to get a bit chatty over his ribeye -- huh, Kasper?
Might be a grade bump in your future, son.
...
...sir?
Why was he talking to me?
Why would he ever talk to me?
You'll make a fine detective, Kasper. A good cop.
Hey-- you and Tork are going over by Pitkin, right? My wife's clock is ready at the watch store on Euclid.
On your break.
Know what?
I better call first, make sure it's ready.
Don't wanna waste your lunch break on a hunch.
Saddle up, Kasper! Crime waits for no man.

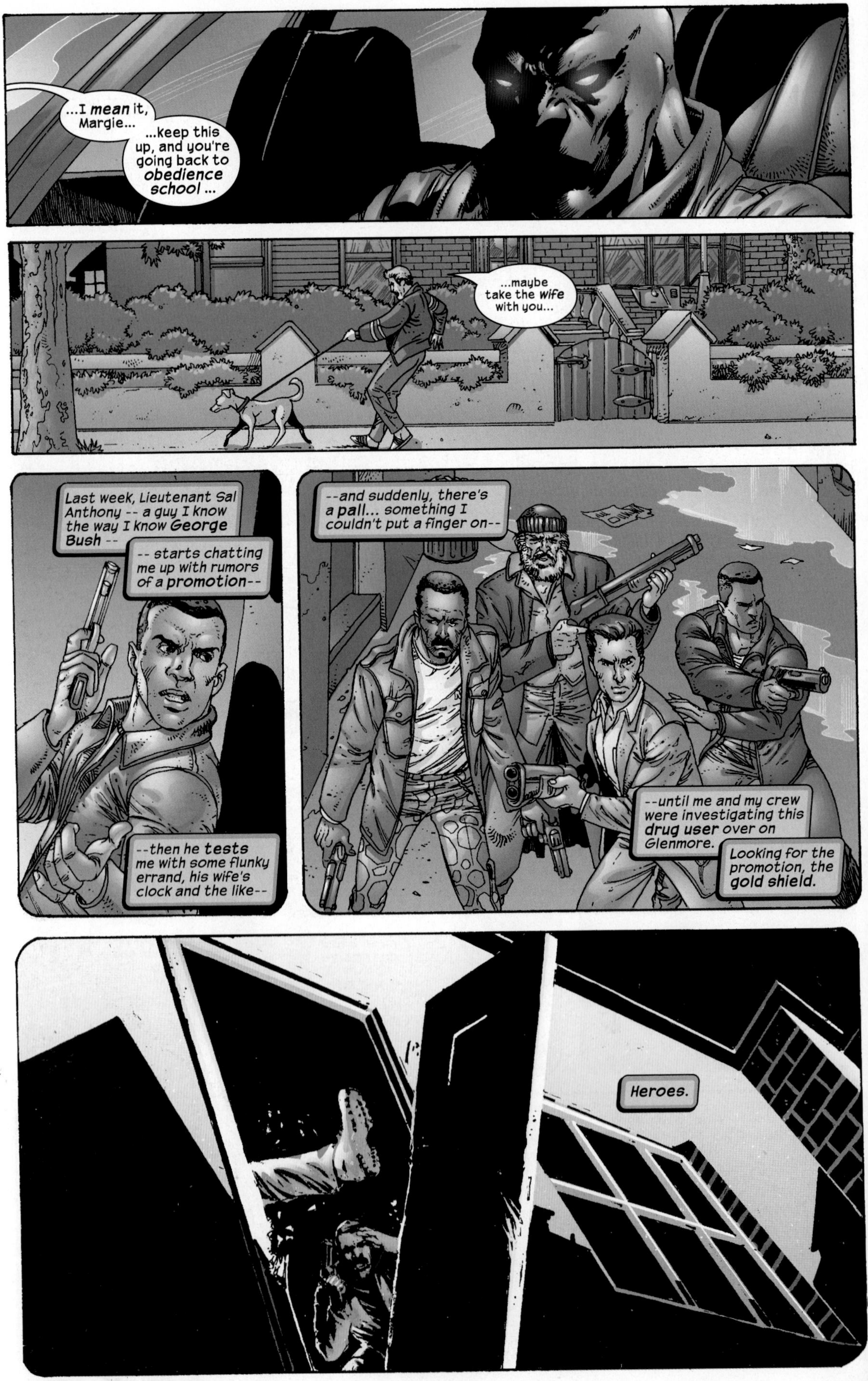
...I mean it, Margie...
...keep this up, and you're going back to obedience school ...
...maybe take the wife with you...
Last week, Lieutenant Sal Anthony -- a guy I know the way I know George Bush --
-- starts chatting me up with rumors of a promotion--
--then he tests me with some flunky errand, his wife's clock and the like--
--and suddenly, there's a pall... something I couldn't put a finger on--
--until me and my crew were investigating this drug user over on Glenmore.
Looking for the promotion, the gold shield.
Heroes.

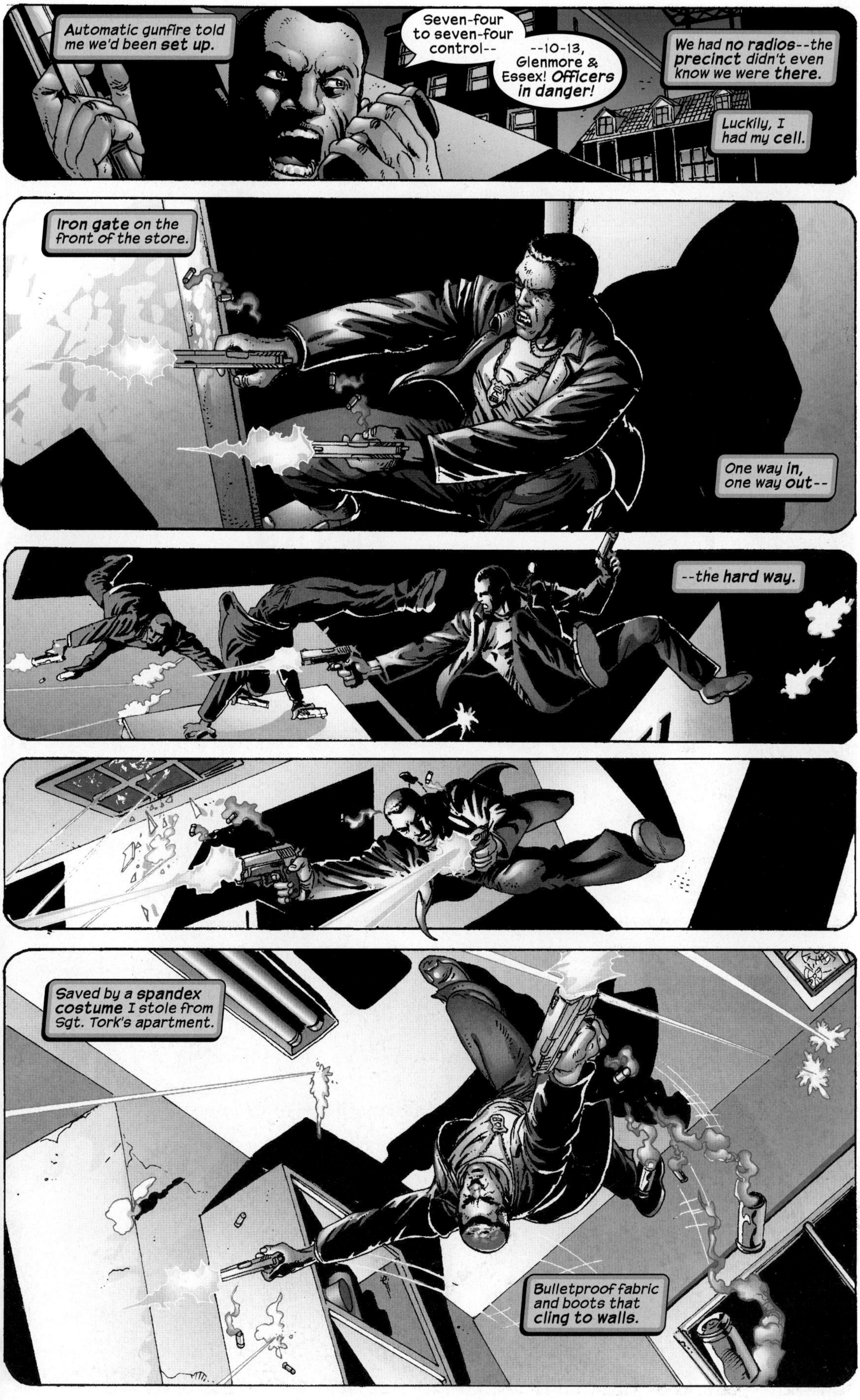
Automatic gunfire told me we'd been set up.
Seven-four to seven-four control--
--10-13, Glenmore & Essex! Officers in danger!
We had no radios--the precinct didn't even know we were there.
Luckily, I had my cell.
Iron gate on the front of the store.
One way in, one way out--
--the hard way.
Saved by a spandex costume I stole from Sgt. Tork's apartment.
Bulletproof fabric and boots that cling to walls.

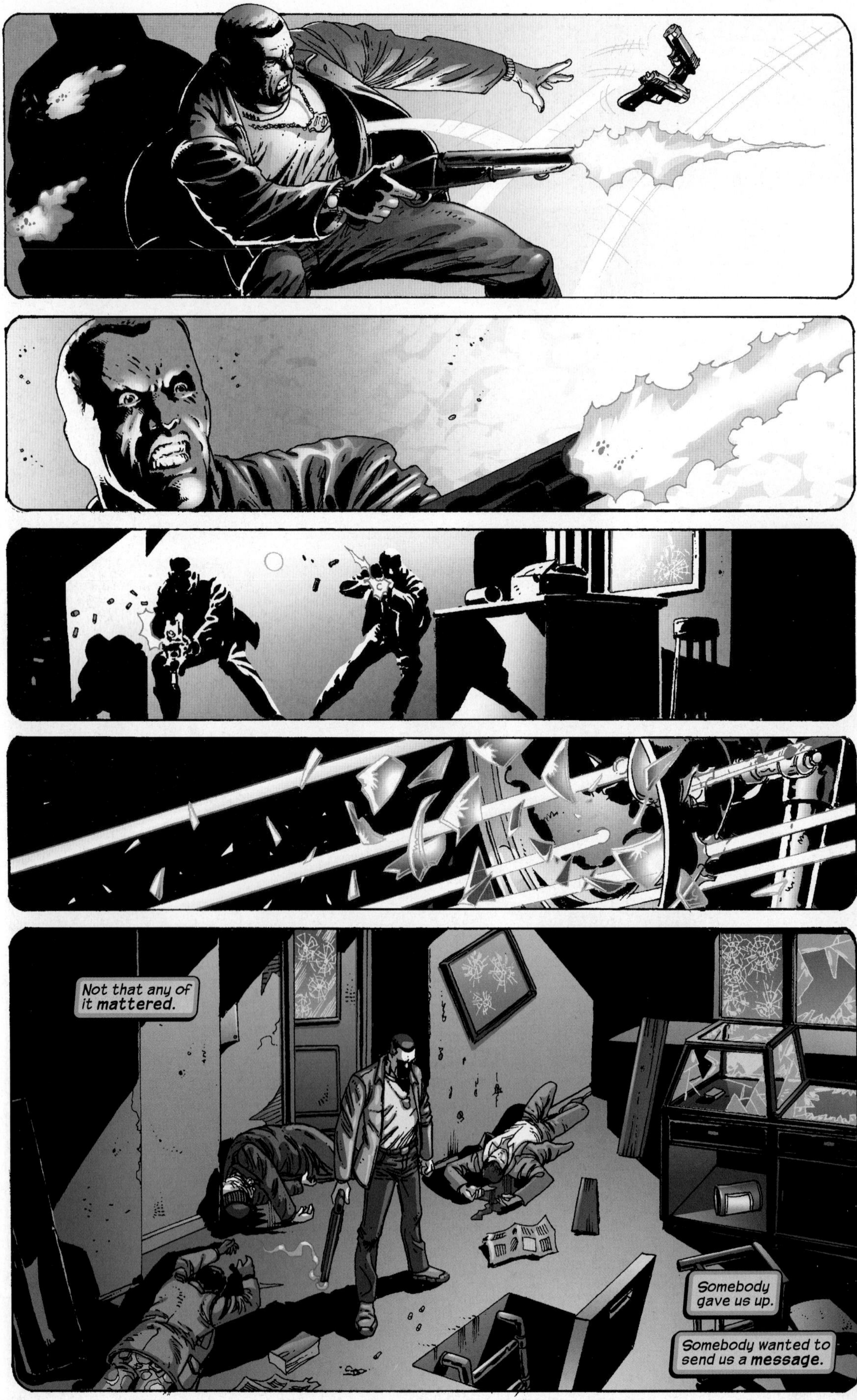
Not that any of it mattered.
Somebody gave us up.
Somebody wanted to send us a message.

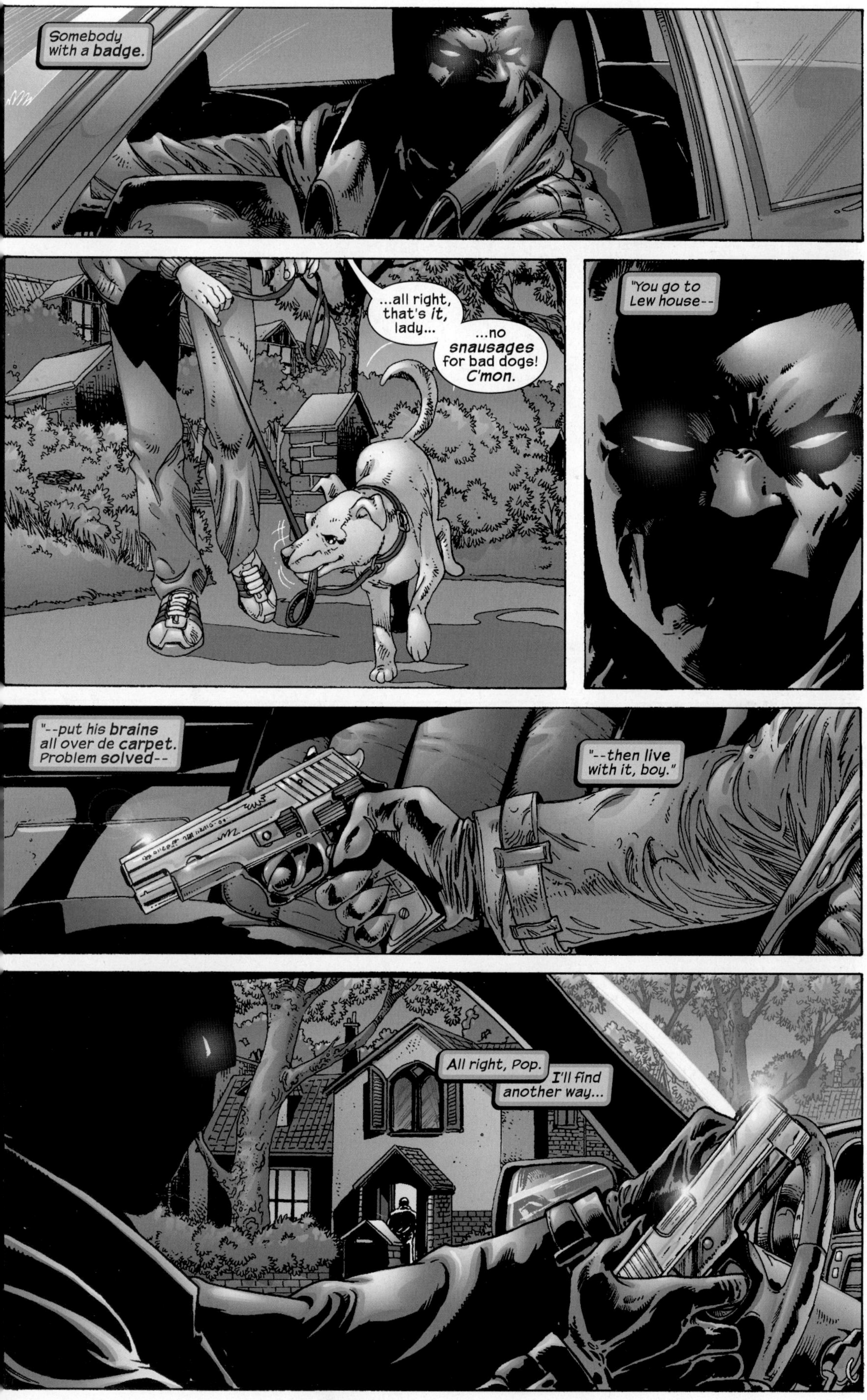
Somebody with a badge.
...all right, that's it, lady...
...no snausages for bad dogs! C'mon.
"You go to Lew house--
"--put his brains all over de carpet. Problem solved--
"--then live with it, boy."
All right, Pop. I'll find another way...

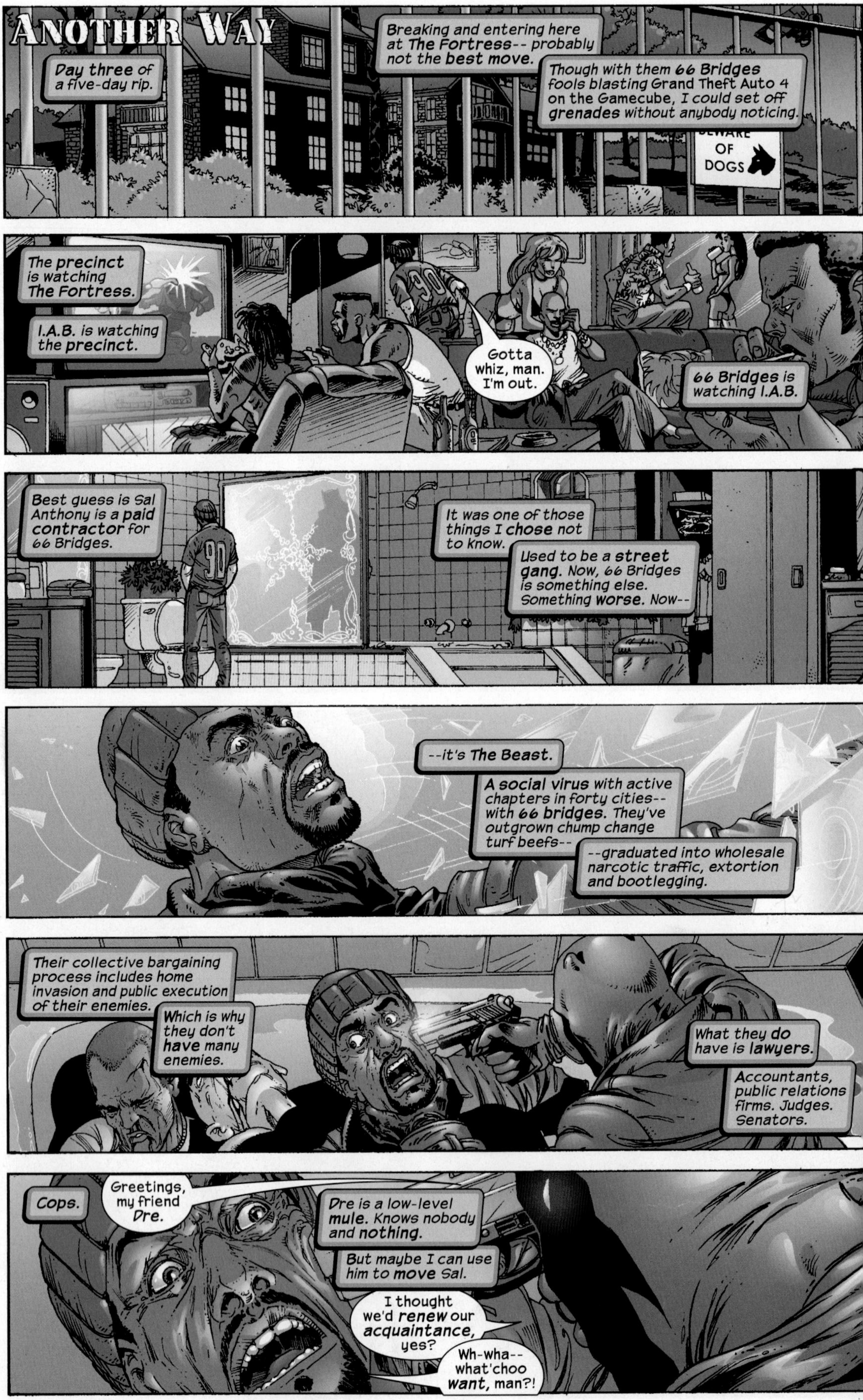
ANOTHER WAY
Day three of a five-day rip.
Breaking and entering here at The Fortress-- probably not the best move.
Though with them 66 Bridges fools blasting Grand Theft Auto 4 on the Gamecube, I could set off grenades without anybody noticing.
OF
DOGS
The precinct is watching The Fortress.
I.A.B. is watching the precinct.
Gotta whiz, man. I'm out.
66 Bridges is watching I.A.B.
Best guess is Sal Anthony is a paid contractor for 66 Bridges.
It was one of those things I chose not to know.
Used to be a street gang. Now, 66 Bridges is something else. Something worse. Now--
--it's The Beast.
A social virus with active chapters in forty cities-- with 66 bridges. They've outgrown chump change turf beefs--
--graduated into wholesale narcotic traffic, extortion and bootlegging.
Their collective bargaining process includes home invasion and public execution of their enemies.
Which is why they don't have many enemies.
What they do have is lawyers.
Accountants, public relations firms. Judges. Senators.
Cops.
Greetings, my friend Dre.
Dre is a low-level mule. Knows nobody and nothing.
But maybe I can use him to move Sal.
I thought we'd renew our acquaintance, yes?
Wh-wha-- what'choo want, man?!

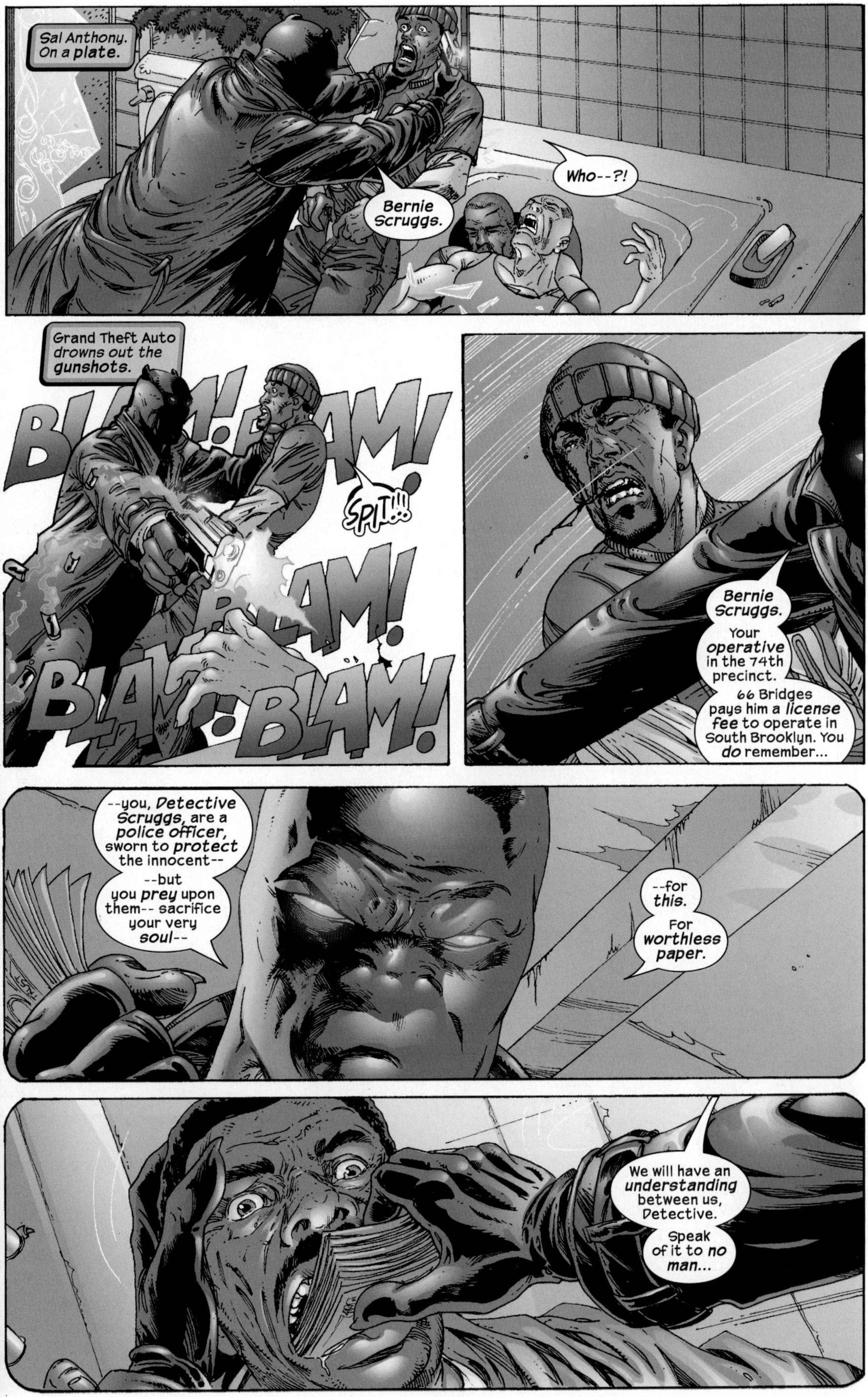
Sal Anthony. On a plate.
Bernie Scruggs.
Who--?!
Grand Theft Auto drowns out the gunshots.
BLAM! BLAM!
SPIT!!!
BLAM!
BLAM! BLAM!
Bernie Scruggs. Your operative in the 74th precinct. 66 Bridges pays him a license fee to operate in South Brooklyn. You do remember...
--you, Detective Scruggs, are a police officer, sworn to protect the innocent-- --but you prey upon them-- sacrifice your very soul--
--for this. For worthless paper.
We will have an understanding between us, Detective. Speak of it to no man...

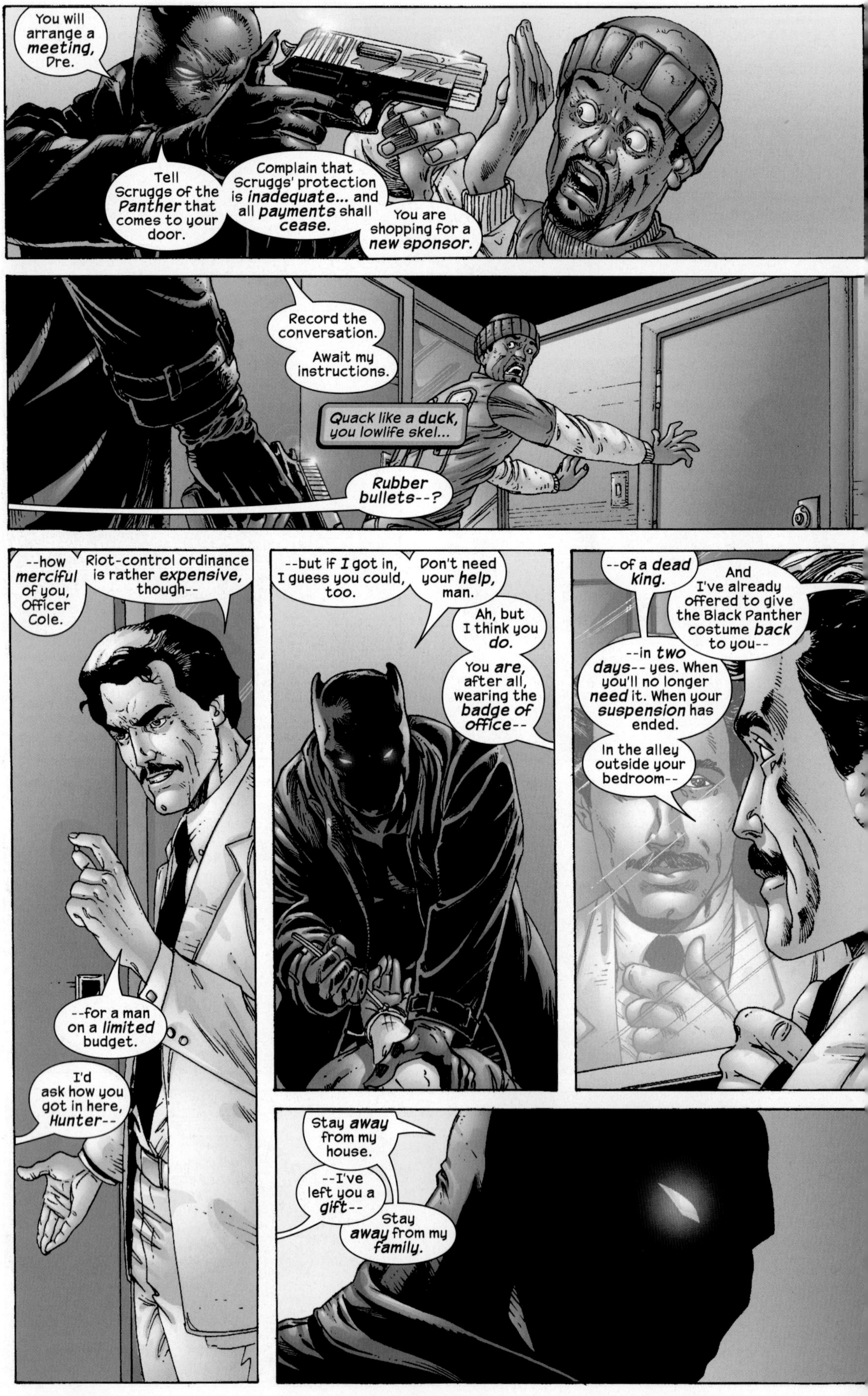

You will arrange a meeting, Dre.
Tell Scruggs of the Panther that comes to your door.
Complain that Scruggs' protection is inadequate... and all payments shall cease.
You are shopping for a new sponsor.
Record the conversation.
Await my instructions.
Quack like a duck, you lowlife skel...
Rubber bullets--?
--how merciful of you, Officer Cole.
Riot-control ordinance is rather expensive, though--
--for a man on a limited budget.
I'd ask how you got in here, Hunter--
--but if I got in, I guess you could, too.
Don't need your help, man.
Ah, but I think you do.
You are, after all, wearing the badge of office--
--of a dead king.
And I've already offered to give the Black Panther costume back to you--
--in two days-- yes. When you'll no longer need it. When your suspension has ended.
In the alley outside your bedroom--
Stay away from my house.
--I've left you a gift--
Stay away from my family.

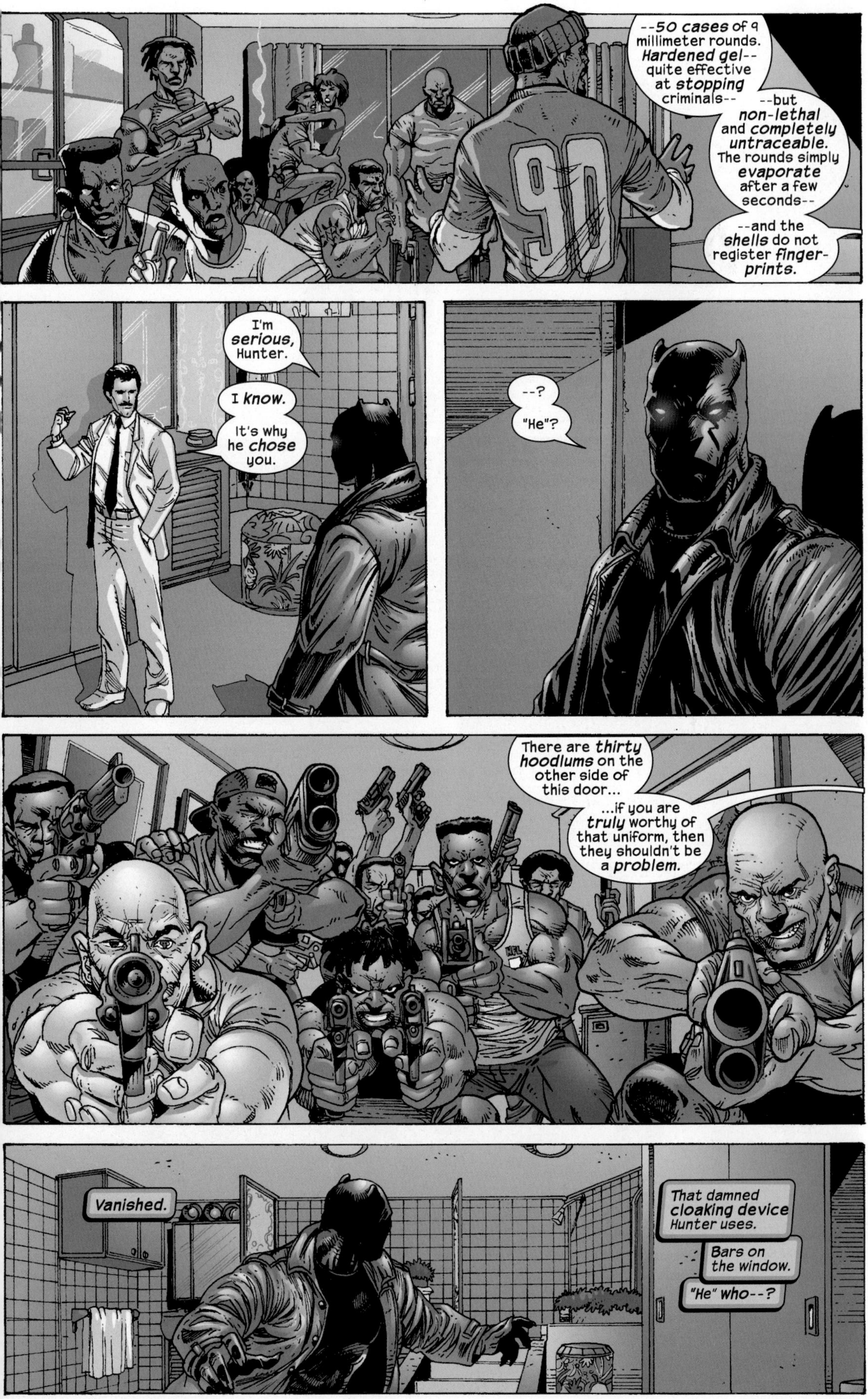
--50 cases of 9 millimeter rounds. Hardened gel-- quite effective at stopping criminals--
--but non-lethal and completely untraceable. The rounds simply evaporate after a few seconds--
--and the shells do not register finger-prints.
I'm serious, Hunter.
I know.
It's why he chose you.
--?
"He"?
There are thirty hoodlums on the other side of this door...
...if you are truly worthy of that uniform, then they shouldn't be a problem.
Vanished.
That damned cloaking device Hunter uses.
Bars on the window.
"He" who--?

Hunter-- a white man-- is chieftain of an African tribe called the *Hatut Zeraze.*

"The Dogs of War."

The Zeraze use a personal *cloaking* device that lets them *vanish* into thin air.

Wish I had it that easy.

The closet--!

All I've got is a bulletproof costume I *stole* from my sergeant's apartment...

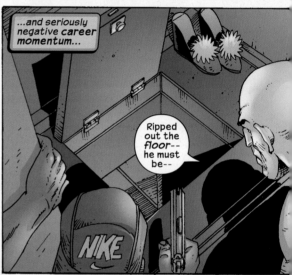

...and seriously negative *career* momentum...

Ripped out the *floor--* he must be--

NIKE

BLAM! BLAM! BLAM!

BLAM! BLAM! BLAM!

Yeah. Yeah, you mothers.

Let's go.

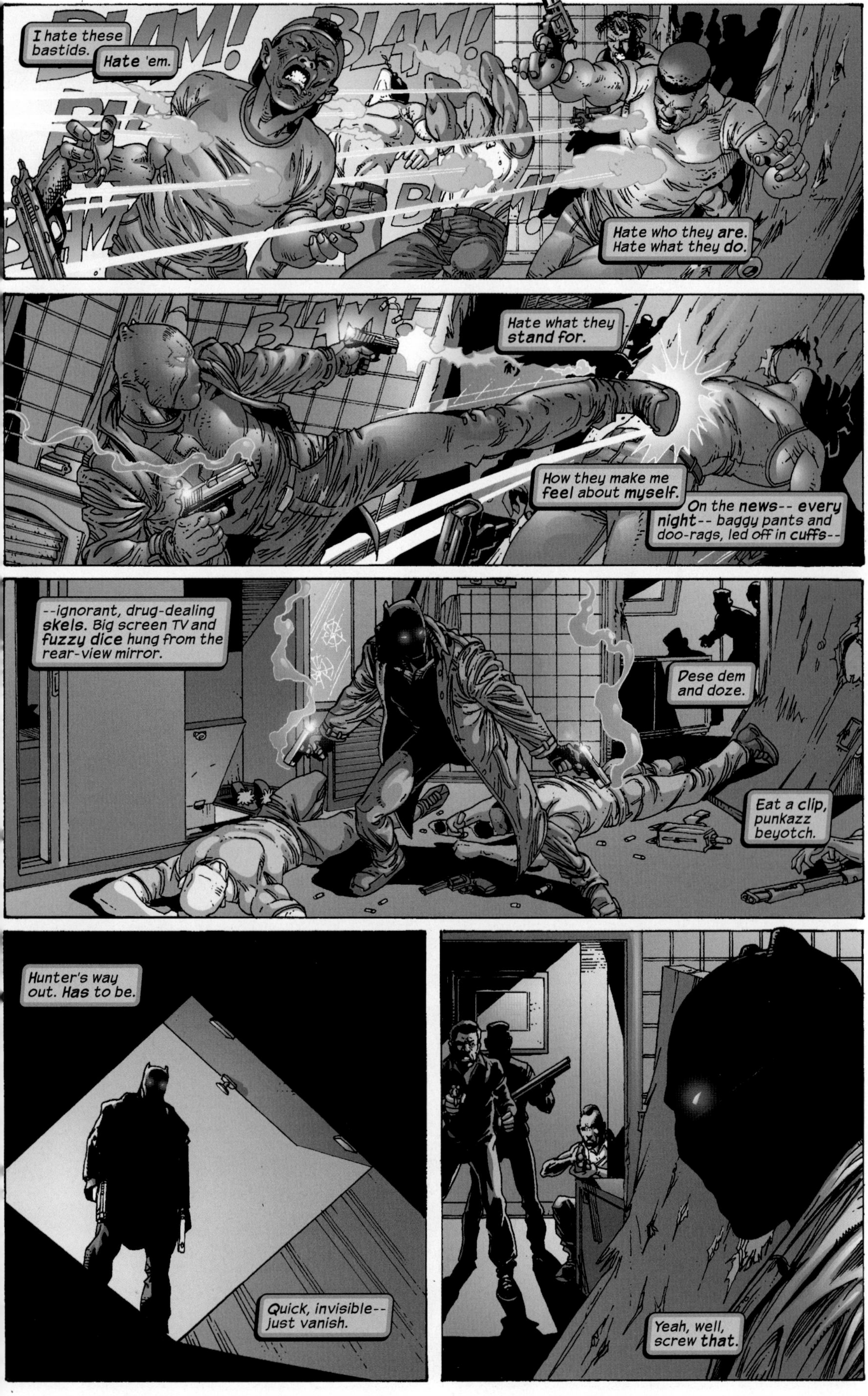
BLAM!
BLAM!
I hate these bastids.
Hate 'em.
Hate who they are. Hate what they do.
BLAM!
Hate what they stand for.
How they make me feel about myself.
On the news-- every night-- baggy pants and doo-rags, led off in cuffs--
--ignorant, drug-dealing skels. Big screen TV and fuzzy dice hung from the rear-view mirror.
Dese dem and doze.
Eat a clip, punkazz beyotch.
Hunter's way out. Has to be.
Quick, invisible-- just vanish.
Yeah, well, screw that.

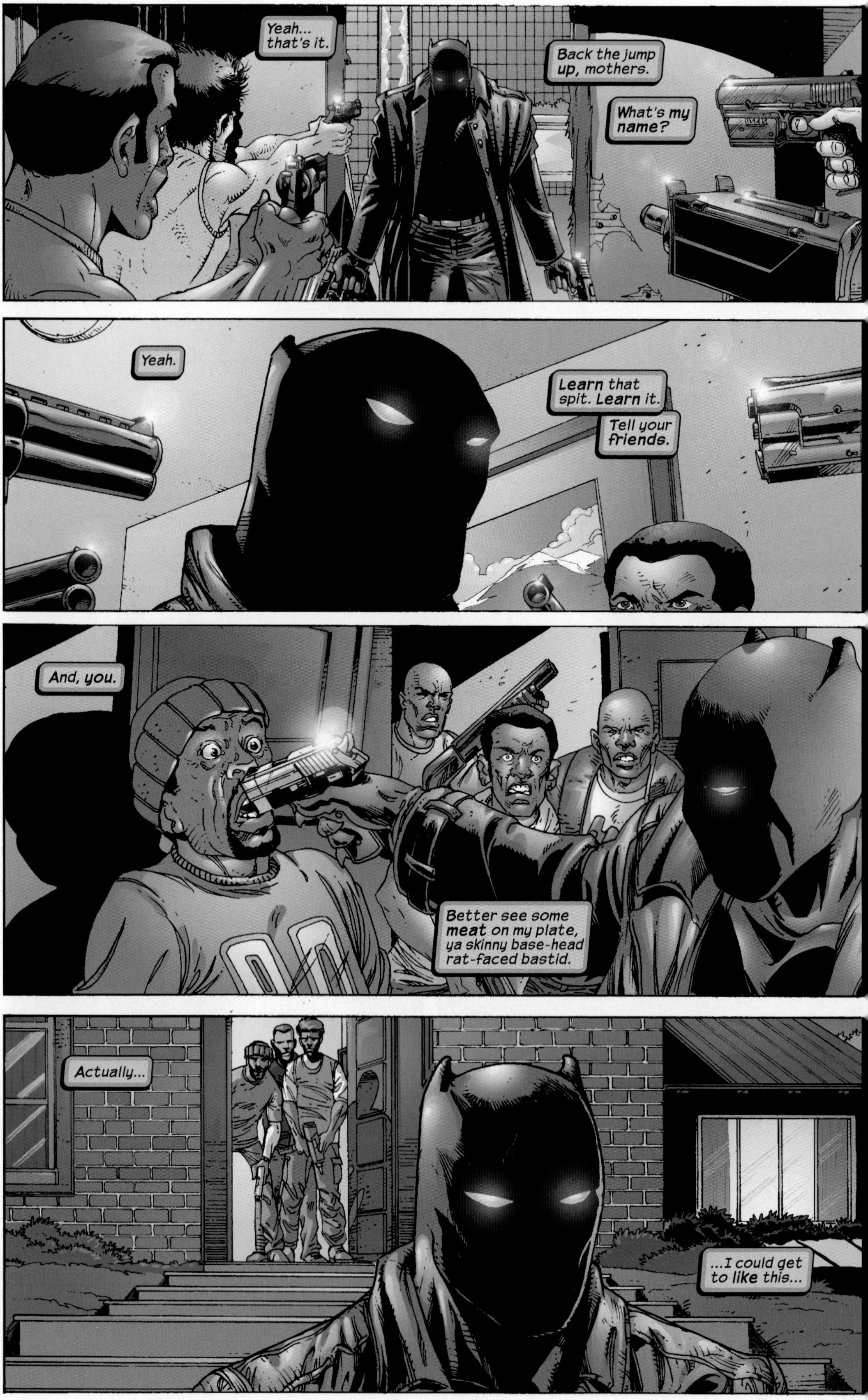
Yeah... that's it.
Back the jump up, mothers.
What's my name?
Yeah.
Learn that spit. Learn it.
Tell your friends.
And, you.
Better see some meat on my plate, ya skinny base-head rat-faced bastid.
Actually...
...I could get to like this...

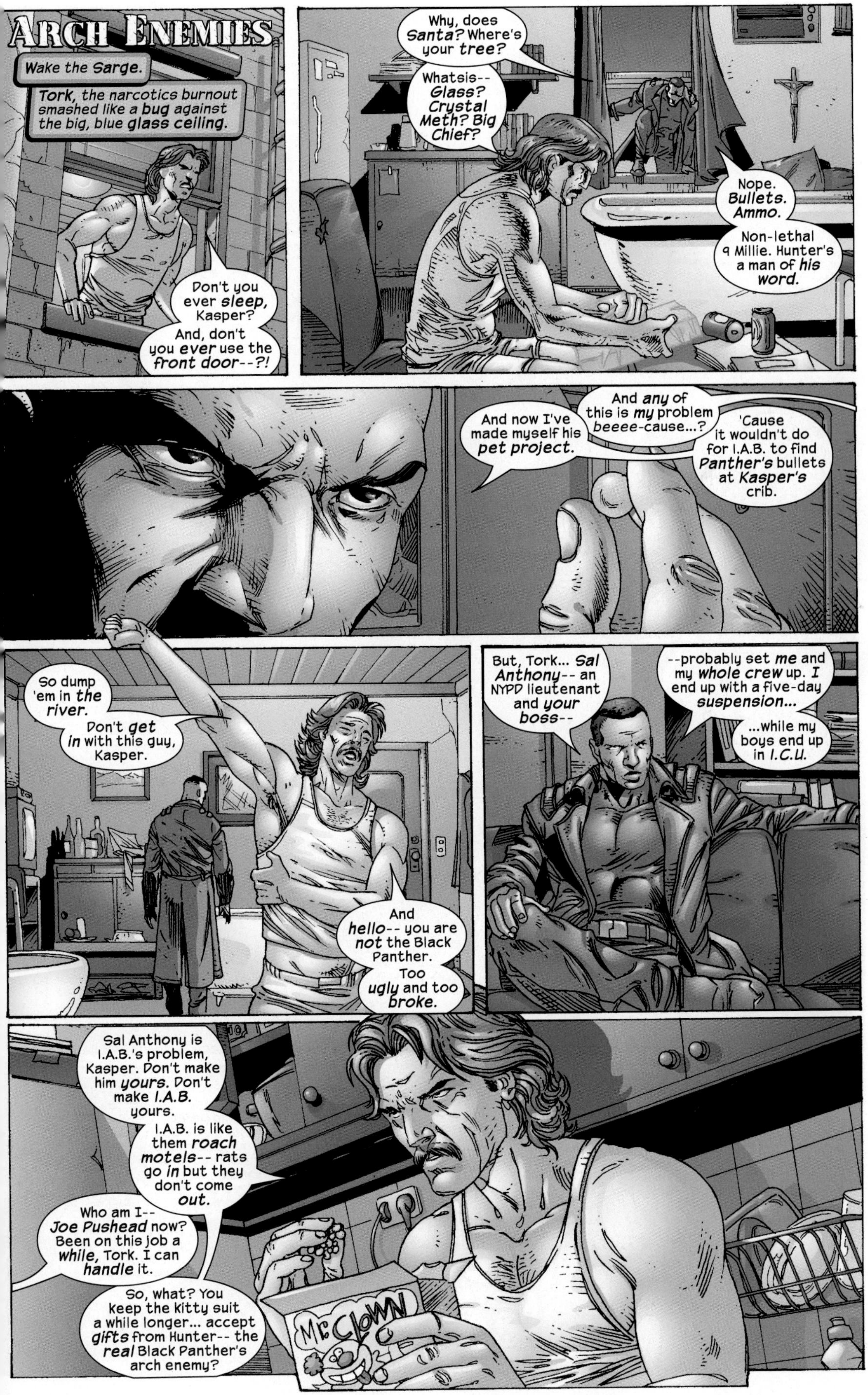

Arch Enemies
Wake the Sarge.
Tork, the narcotics burnout smashed like a bug against the big, blue glass ceiling.
Don't you ever sleep, Kasper?
And, don't you ever use the front door--?!
Why, does Santa? Where's your tree?
Whatsis-- Glass? Crystal Meth? Big Chief?
Nope. Bullets. Ammo.
Non-lethal 9 Millie. Hunter's a man of his word.
And now I've made myself his pet project.
And any of this is my problem beeee-cause...?
'Cause it wouldn't do for I.A.B. to find Panther's bullets at Kasper's crib.
So dump 'em in the river.
Don't get in with this guy, Kasper.
And hello-- you are not the Black Panther.
Too ugly and too broke.
But, Tork... Sal Anthony-- an NYPD lieutenant and your boss--
--probably set me and my whole crew up. I end up with a five-day suspension...
...while my boys end up in I.C.U.
Sal Anthony is I.A.B.'s problem, Kasper. Don't make him yours. Don't make I.A.B. yours.
I.A.B. is like them roach motels-- rats go in but they don't come out.
Who am I-- Joe Pushead now? Been on this job a while, Tork. I can handle it.
So, what? You keep the kitty suit a while longer... accept gifts from Hunter-- the real Black Panther's arch enemy?
Mr. Clown

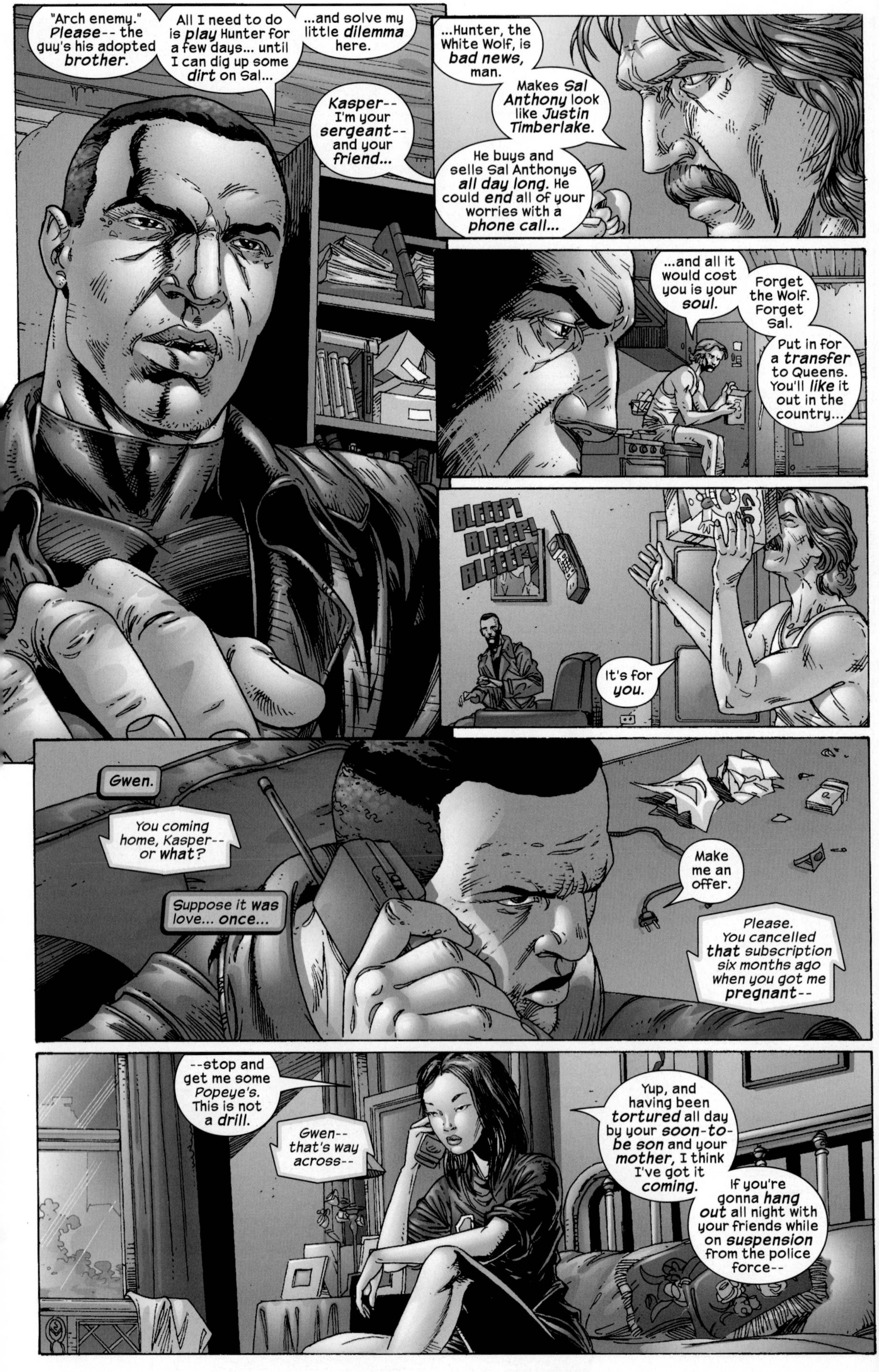
"Arch enemy." Please-- the guy's his adopted brother.
All I need to do is play Hunter for a few days... until I can dig up some dirt on Sal...
...and solve my little dilemma here.
Kasper-- I'm your sergeant-- and your friend...
...Hunter, the White Wolf, is bad news, man.
Makes Sal Anthony look like Justin Timberlake.
He buys and sells Sal Anthonys all day long. He could end all of your worries with a phone call...
...and all it would cost you is your soul.
Forget the Wolf. Forget Sal.
Put in for a transfer to Queens. You'll like it out in the country...
BLEEEP! BLEEEP! BLEEEP!
It's for you.
Gwen.
You coming home, Kasper-- or what?
Suppose it was love... once...
Make me an offer.
Please. You cancelled that subscription six months ago when you got me pregnant--
--stop and get me some Popeye's. This is not a drill.
Gwen-- that's way across--
Yup, and having been tortured all day by your soon-to-be son and your mother, I think I've got it coming.
If you're gonna hang out all night with your friends while on suspension from the police force--

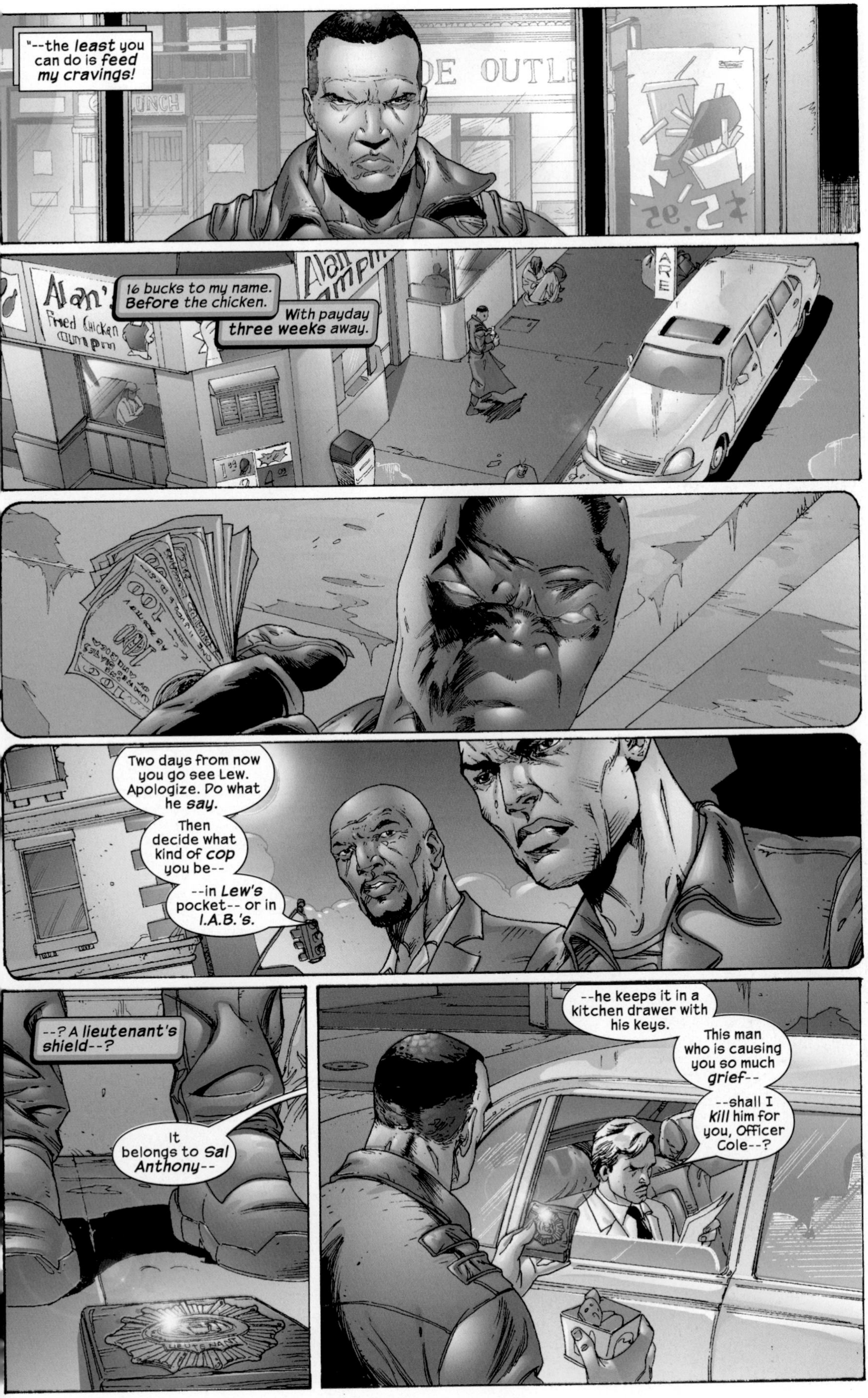
"--the least you can do is feed my cravings!
DE OUTLE
LUNCH
$2.95
Alan's Fried Chicken
16 bucks to my name. Before the chicken.
With payday three weeks away.
ARE
100
Two days from now you go see Lew. Apologize. Do what he say.
Then decide what kind of cop you be--
--in Lew's pocket-- or in I.A.B.'s.
--? A lieutenant's shield--?
It belongs to Sal Anthony--
LIEUTENANT
--he keeps it in a kitchen drawer with his keys.
This man who is causing you so much grief--
--shall I kill him for you, Officer Cole--?

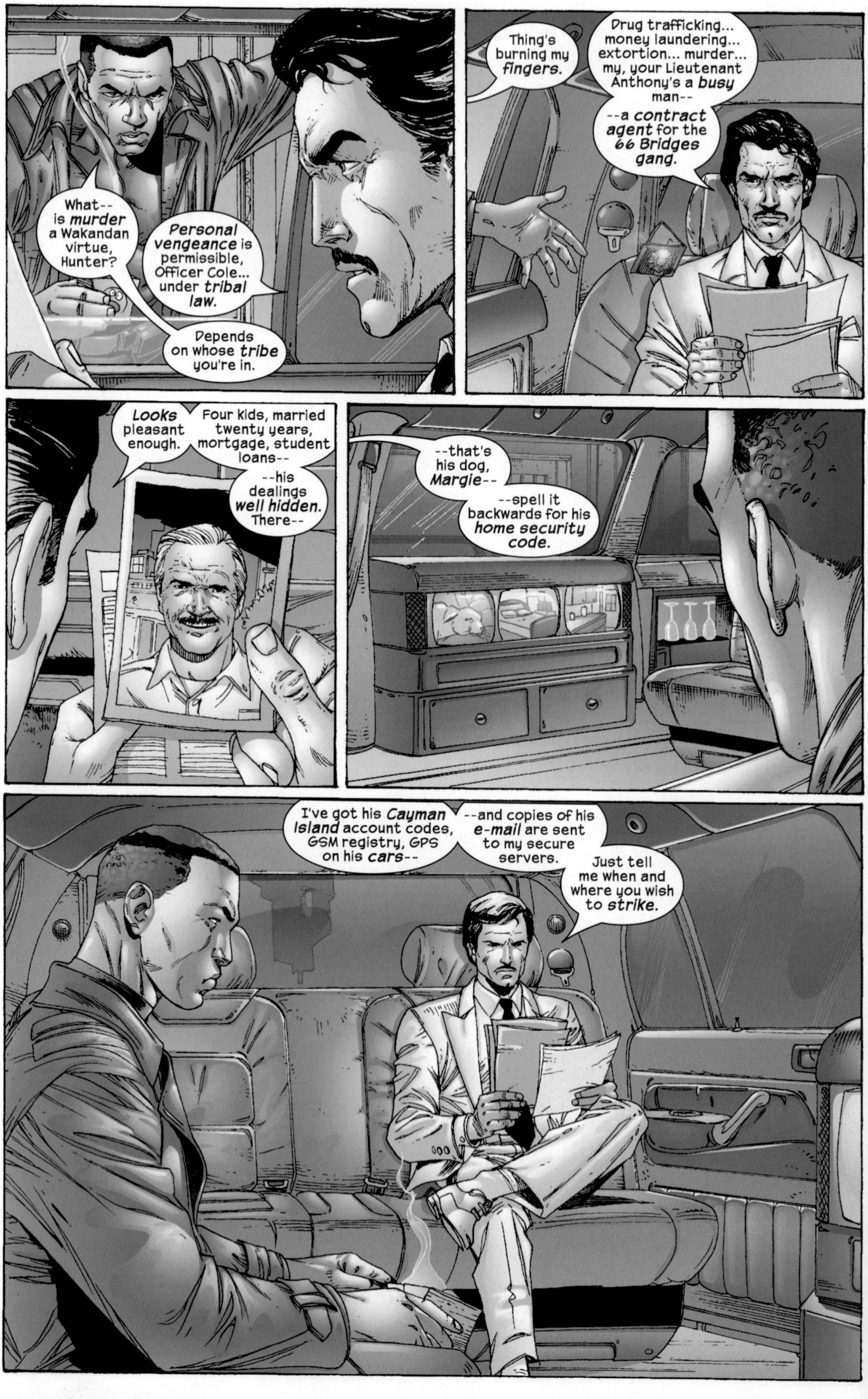

What-- is murder a Wakandan virtue, Hunter?
Personal vengeance is permissible, Officer Cole... under tribal law.
Depends on whose tribe you're in.
Thing's burning my fingers.
Drug trafficking... money laundering... extortion... murder... my, your Lieutenant Anthony's a busy man--
--a contract agent for the 66 Bridges gang.
Looks pleasant enough.
Four kids, married twenty years, mortgage, student loans--
--his dealings well hidden. There--
--that's his dog, Margie--
--spell it backwards for his home security code.
I've got his Cayman Island account codes, GSM registry, GPS on his cars--
--and copies of his e-mail are sent to my secure servers.
Just tell me when and where you wish to strike.

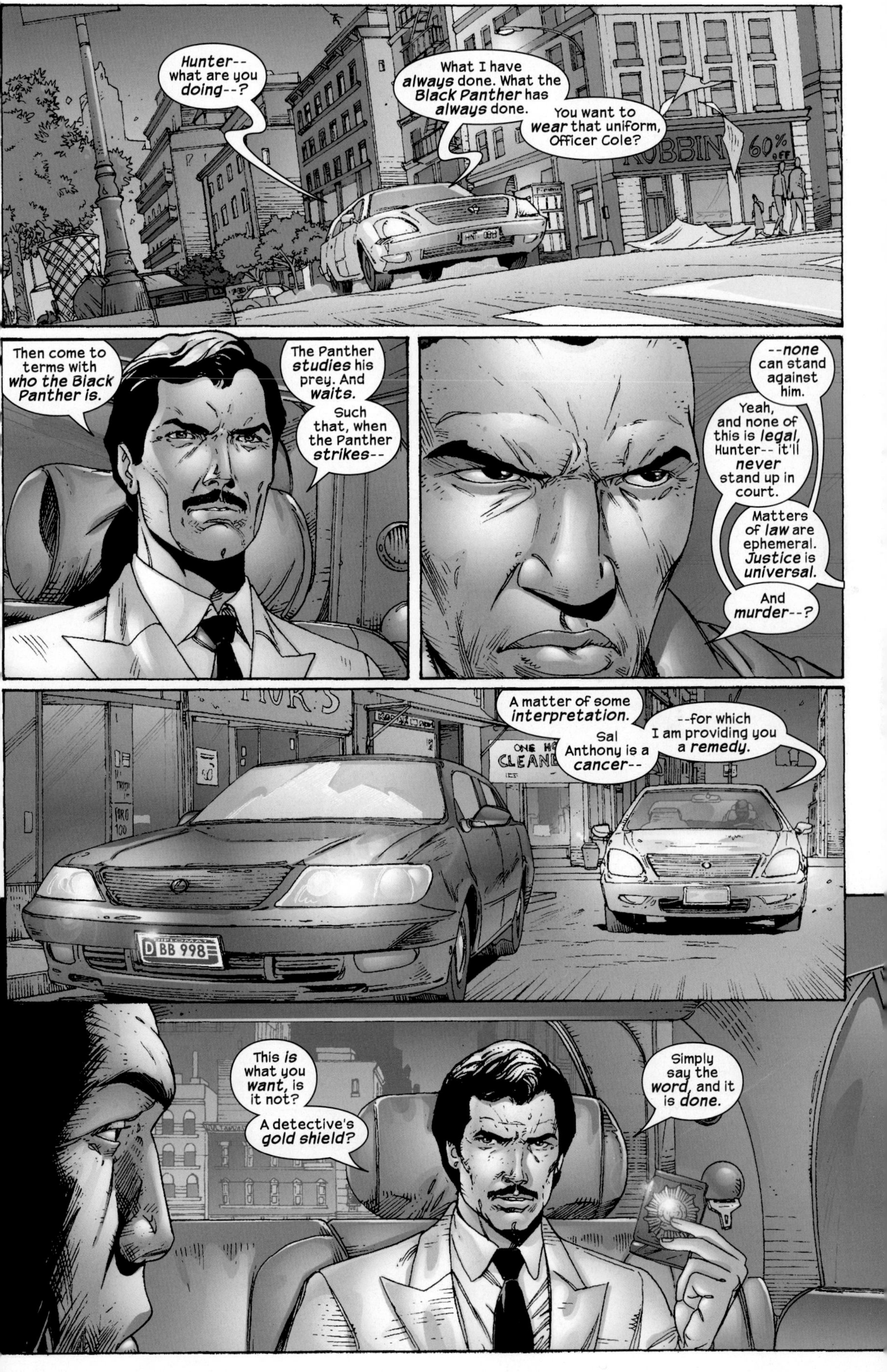
Hunter--
what are you
doing--?
What I have
always done. What the
Black Panther has
always done.
You want to
wear that uniform,
Officer Cole?
ROBBIN
60% OFF
Then come to
terms with
who the Black
Panther is.
The Panther
studies his
prey. And
waits.
Such
that, when
the Panther
strikes--
--none
can stand
against
him.
Yeah,
and none of
this is legal,
Hunter-- it'll
never
stand up in
court.
Matters
of law are
ephemeral.
Justice is
universal.
And
murder--?
A matter of some
interpretation.
Sal
Anthony is a
cancer--
--for which
I am providing you
a remedy.
D BB 998
This is
what you
want, is
it not?
A detective's
gold shield?
Simply
say the
word, and it
is done.

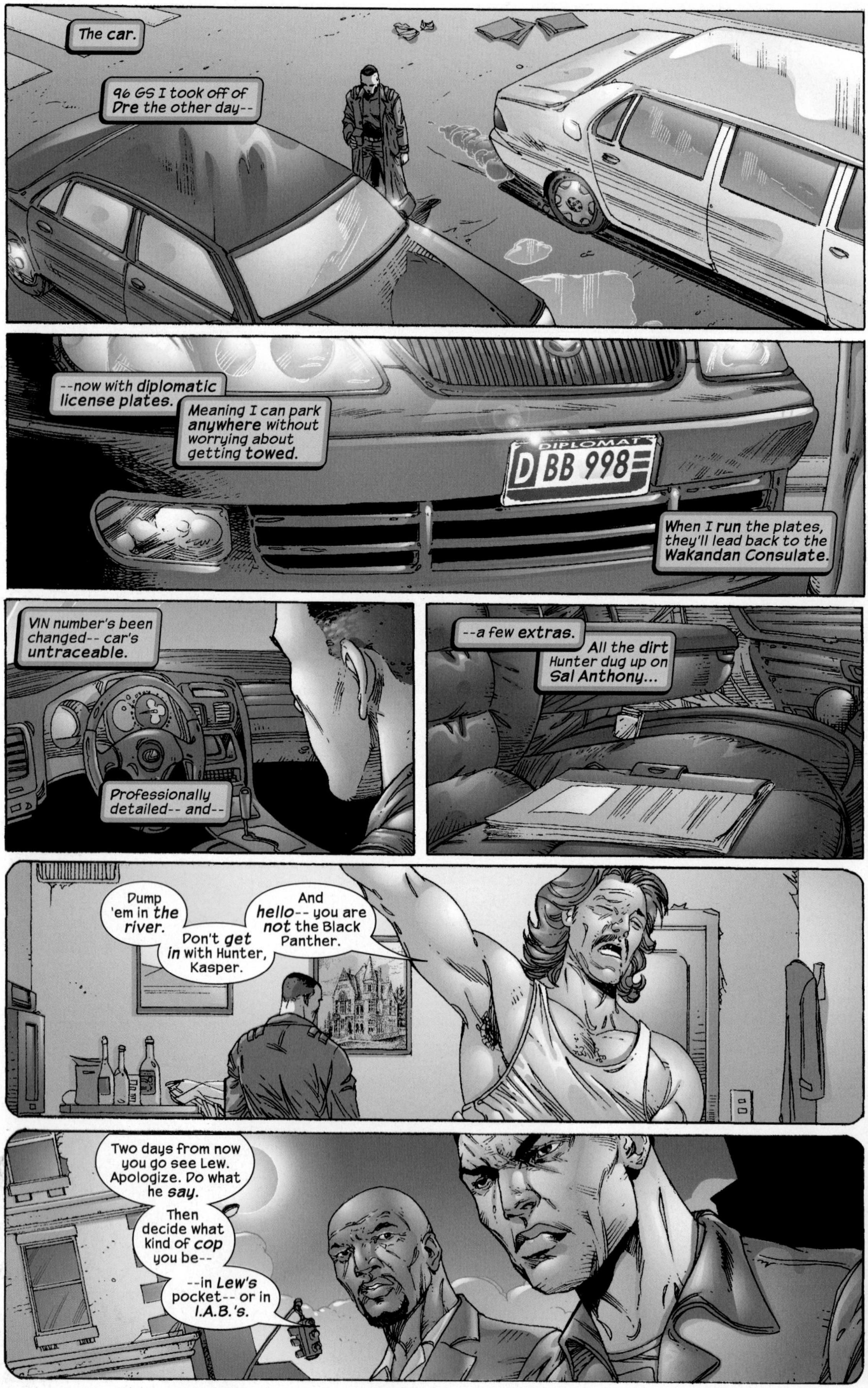

The car.
96 GS I took off of Dre the other day--
--now with diplomatic license plates.
Meaning I can park anywhere without worrying about getting towed.
DIPLOMAT
D BB 998
When I run the plates, they'll lead back to the Wakandan Consulate.
VIN number's been changed-- car's untraceable.
Professionally detailed-- and--
--a few extras.
All the dirt Hunter dug up on Sal Anthony...
Dump 'em in the river.
Don't get in with Hunter, Kasper.
And hello-- you are not the Black Panther.
Two days from now you go see Lew. Apologize. Do what he say.
Then decide what kind of cop you be--
--in Lew's pocket-- or in I.A.B.'s.

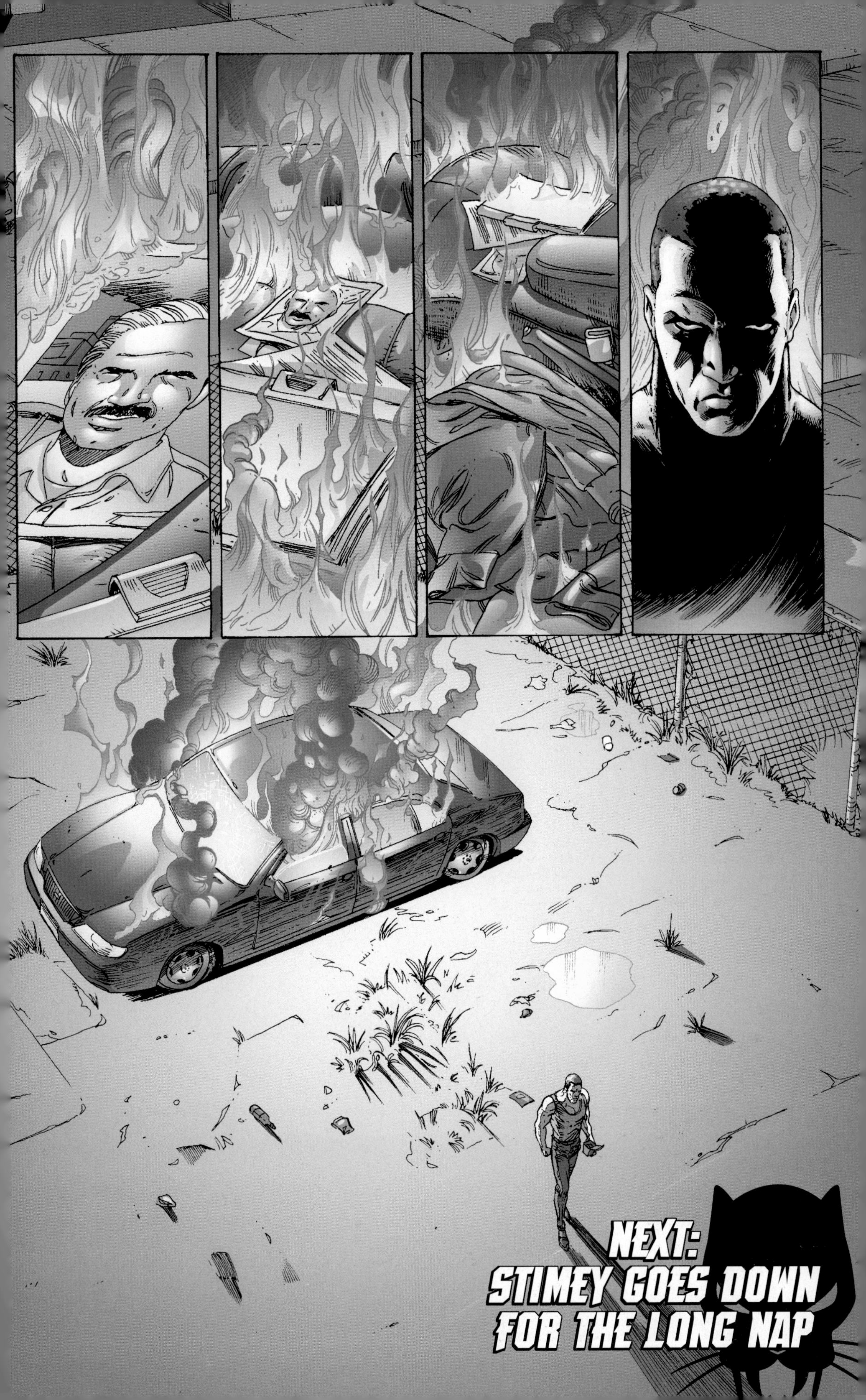
NEXT:
STIMEY GOES DOWN
FOR THE LONG NAP

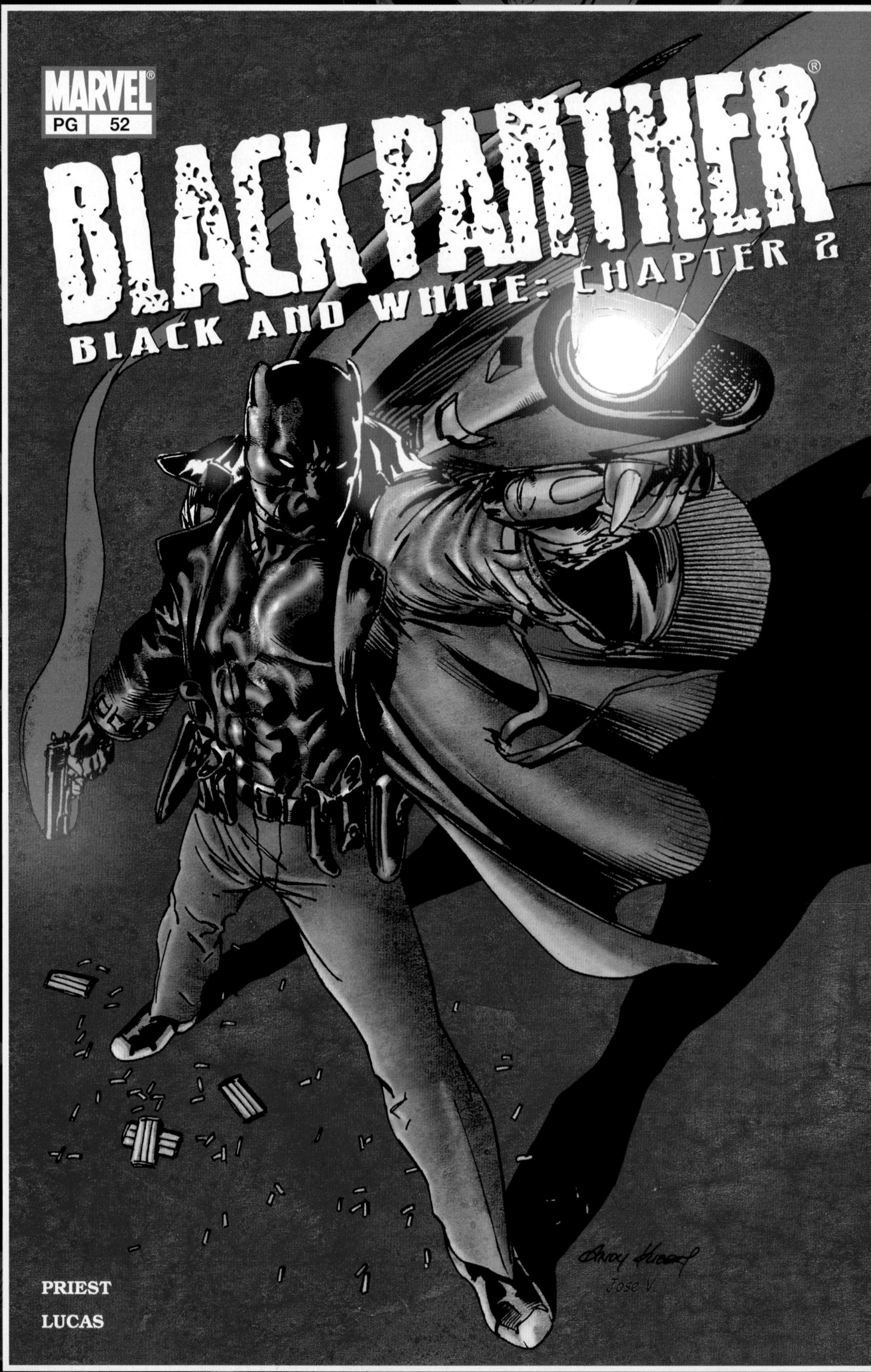
MARVEL
PG 52
BLACK PANTHER
BLACK AND WHITE: CHAPTER 2
PRIEST
LUCAS

...42-foot, three decks, 390hp... named her *"Jess"*, after my wife.

They're *both* a lotta work...

Still showing off the old *rust bucket*, Skip--?

Yeah, *Sal*-- and my *boat*, too.

Long way from *Shangri-La*, aren't we?

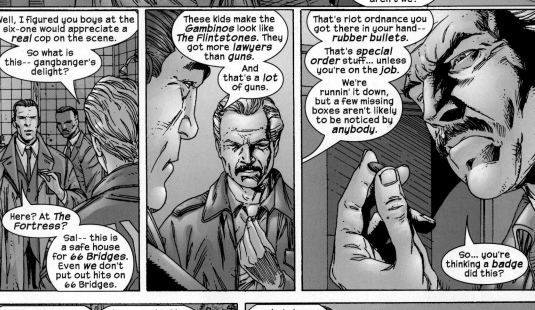

Well, I figured you boys at the six-one would appreciate a *real* cop on the scene.

So what is this-- gangbanger's delight?

Here? At *The Fortress?*

Sal-- this is a safe house for *66 Bridges*. Even *we* don't put out hits on 66 Bridges.

These kids make the *Gambinos* look like *The Flintstones*. They got more *lawyers* than *guns*.

And that's a *lot* of guns.

That's riot ordnance you got there in your hand-- *rubber bullets*.

That's *special order* stuff... unless you're on the *job*.

We're runnin' it down, but a few missing boxes aren't likely to be noticed by *anybody*.

So... you're thinking a *badge* did this?

Nope-- the skels are screaming *Black Panther.*

They say the *king guy* broke in here and started shooting up the place.

Yay *him*, so far as that goes.

Skip, that *boat* of yours--

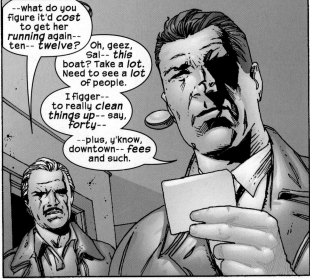

--what do you figure it'd *cost* to get her *running* again-- ten-- *twelve?*

Oh, geez, Sal-- *this* boat? Take a *lot*. Need to see a *lot* of people.

I figger-- to really *clean things up*-- say, *forty*--

--plus, y'know, downtown-- *fees* and such.

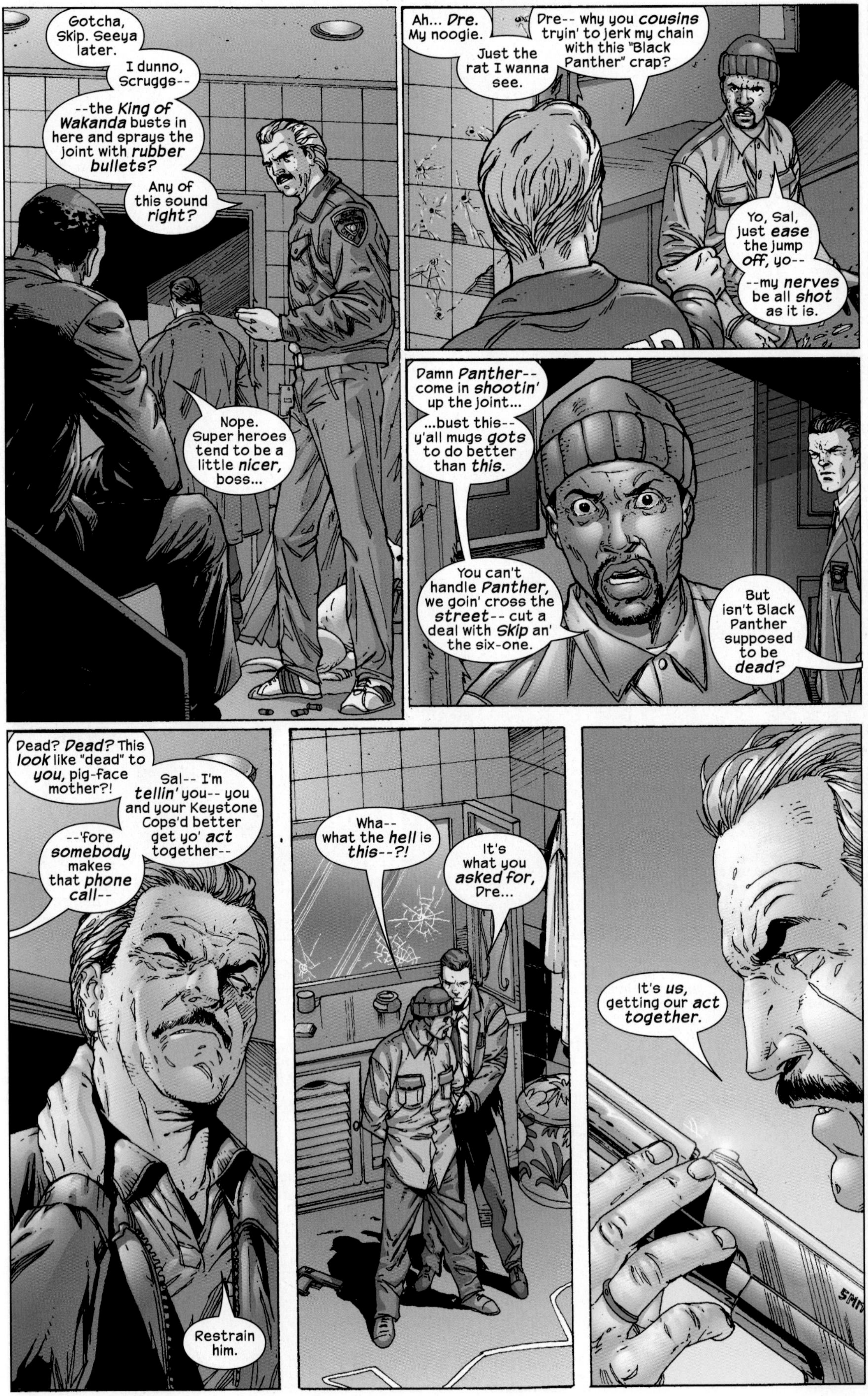
Gotcha, Skip. Seeya later.
I dunno, Scruggs--
--the King of Wakanda busts in here and sprays the joint with rubber bullets?
Any of this sound right?
Nope. Super heroes tend to be a little nicer, boss...
Ah... Dre. My noogie.
Just the rat I wanna see.
Dre-- why you cousins tryin' to jerk my chain with this "Black Panther" crap?
Yo, Sal, just ease the jump off, yo--
--my nerves be all shot as it is.
Damn Panther-- come in shootin' up the joint...
...bust this-- y'all mugs gots to do better than this.
You can't handle Panther, we goin' cross the street-- cut a deal with Skip an' the six-one.
But isn't Black Panther supposed to be dead?
Dead? Dead? This look like "dead" to you, pig-face mother?!
Sal-- I'm tellin' you-- you and your Keystone Cops'd better get yo' act together--
--'fore somebody makes that phone call--
Restrain him.
Wha-- what the hell is this--?!
It's what you asked for, Dre...
It's us, getting our act together.

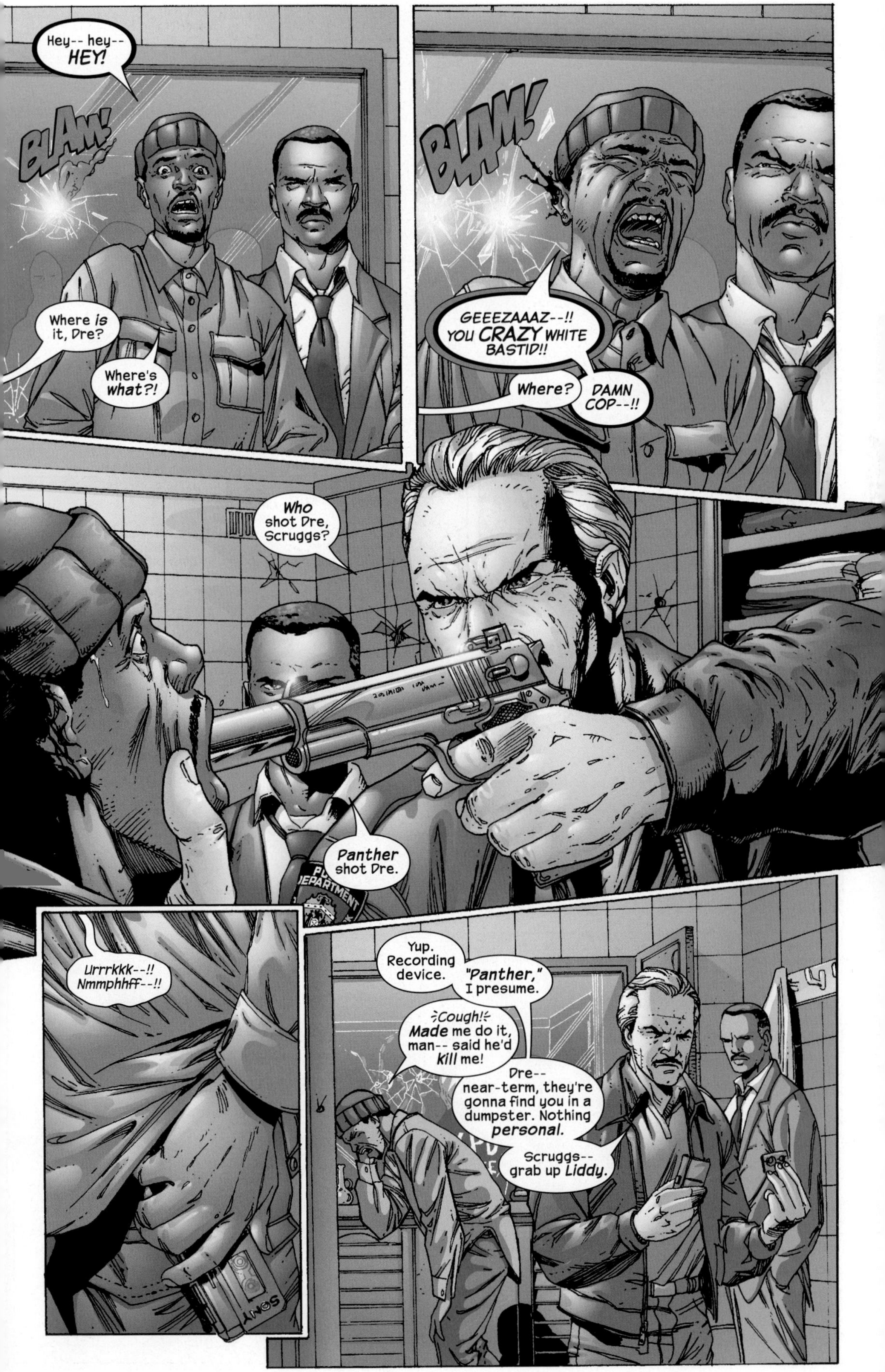
Hey-- hey-- HEY!
BLAM!
Where is it, Dre?
Where's what?!
BLAM!
GEEEZAAAZ--!! YOU CRAZY WHITE BASTID!!
Where?
DAMN COP--!!
Who shot Dre, Scruggs?
Panther shot Dre.
Urrrkkk--!! Nmmphhff--!!
Yup. Recording device.
"Panther," I presume.
Cough! Made me do it, man-- said he'd kill me!
Dre-- near-term, they're gonna find you in a dumpster. Nothing personal.
Scruggs-- grab up Liddy.

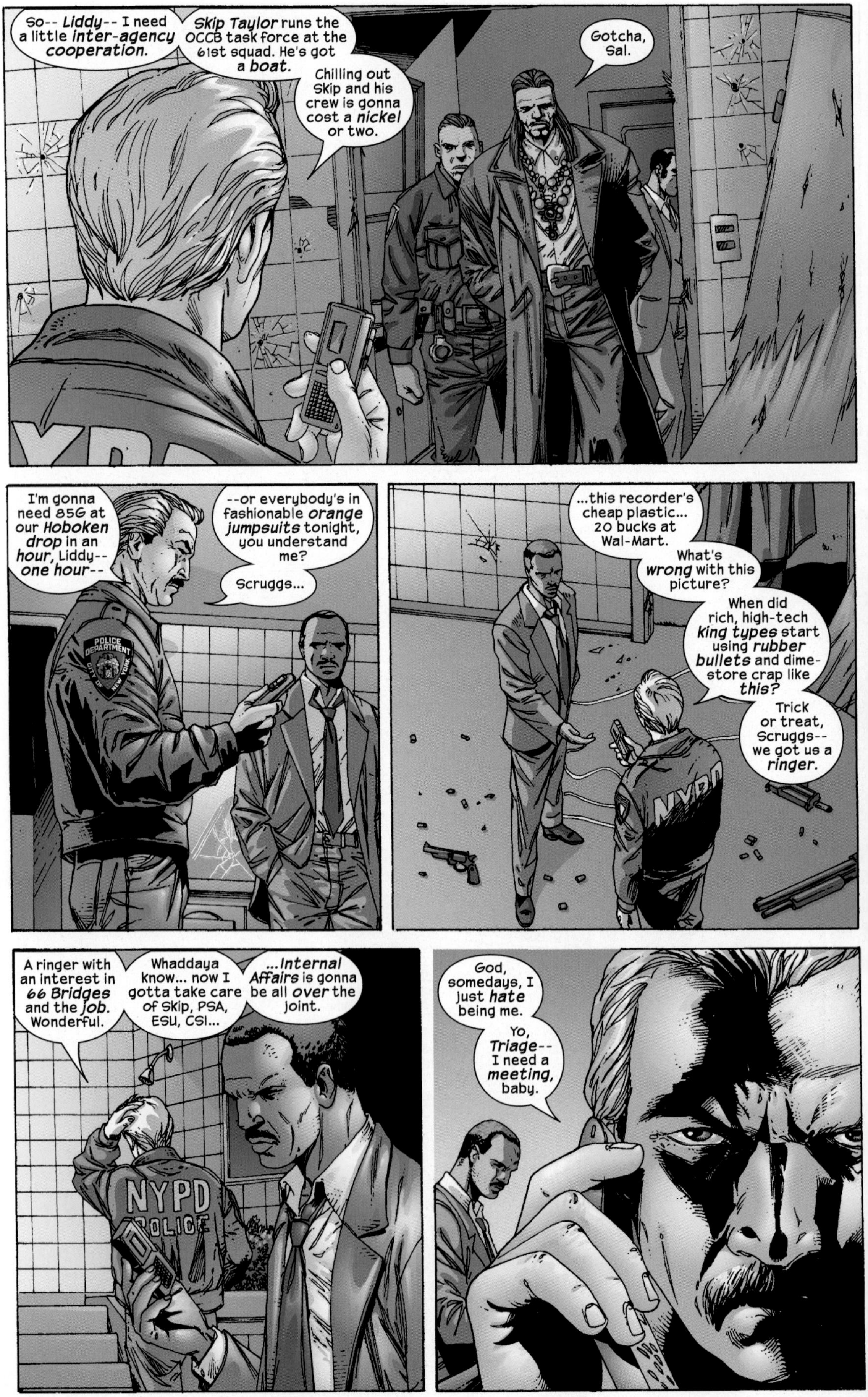
So-- Liddy-- I need a little inter-agency cooperation.
Skip Taylor runs the OCCB task force at the 61st squad. He's got a boat.
Chilling out Skip and his crew is gonna cost a nickel or two.
Gotcha, Sal.
I'm gonna need 85G at our Hoboken drop in an hour, Liddy-- one hour--
--or everybody's in fashionable orange jumpsuits tonight, you understand me?
Scruggs...
POLICE DEPARTMENT CITY OF NEW YORK
...this recorder's cheap plastic... 20 bucks at Wal-Mart.
What's wrong with this picture?
When did rich, high-tech king types start using rubber bullets and dime-store crap like this?
Trick or treat, Scruggs-- we got us a ringer.
NYPD
A ringer with an interest in 66 Bridges and the job. Wonderful.
Whaddaya know... now I gotta take care of Skip, PSA, ESU, CSI...
...Internal Affairs is gonna be all over the joint.
NYPD
God, somedays, I just hate being me.
Yo, Triage-- I need a meeting, baby.

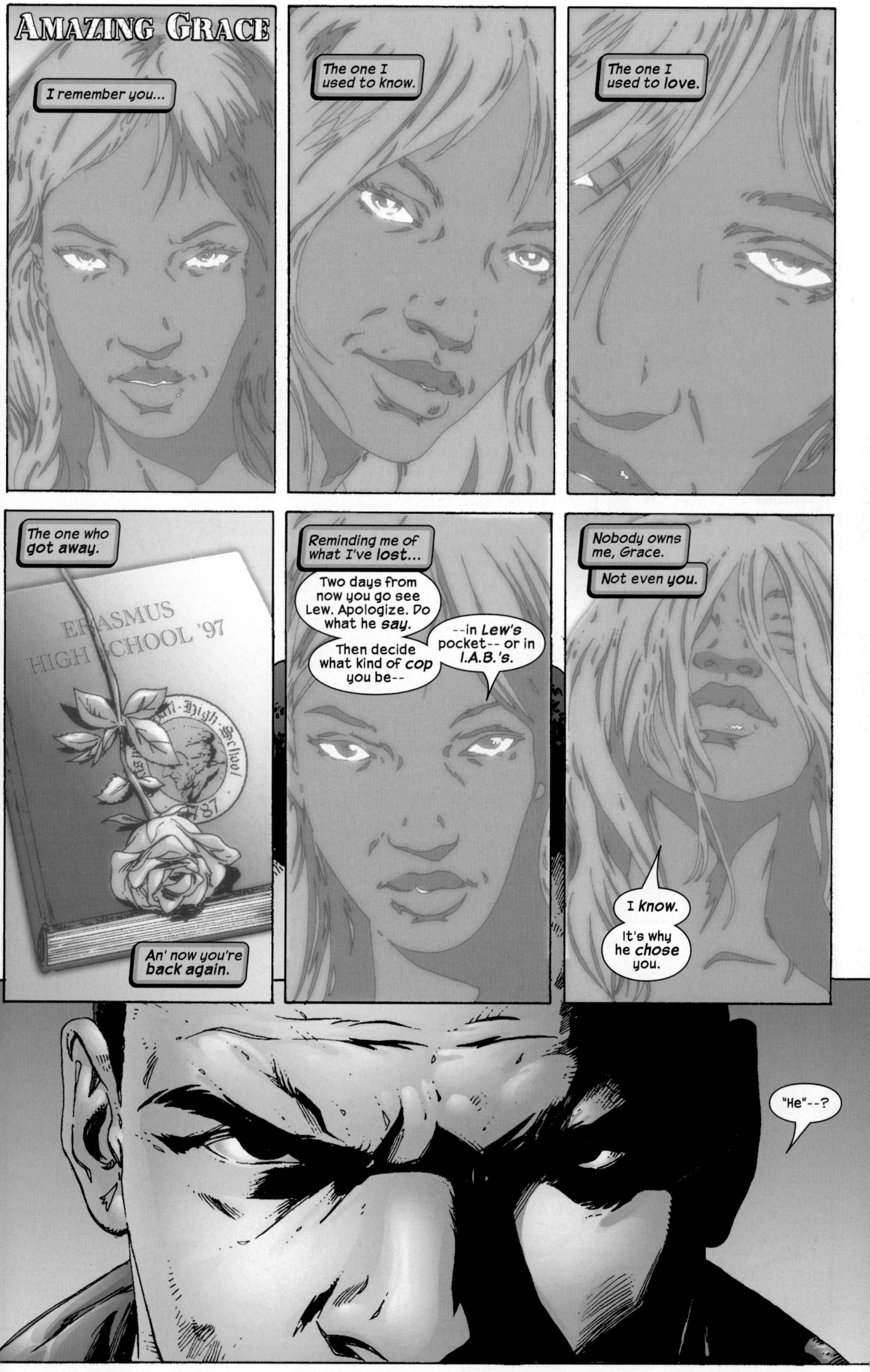
AMAZING GRACE
I remember you...
The one I used to know.
The one I used to love.
The one who got away.
An' now you're back again.
ERASMUS HIGH SCHOOL '97
Reminding me of what I've lost...
Two days from now you go see Lew. Apologize. Do what he say.
Then decide what kind of cop you be--
--in Lew's pocket-- or in I.A.B.'s.
Nobody owns me, Grace.
Not even you.
I know.
It's why he chose you.
"He"--?

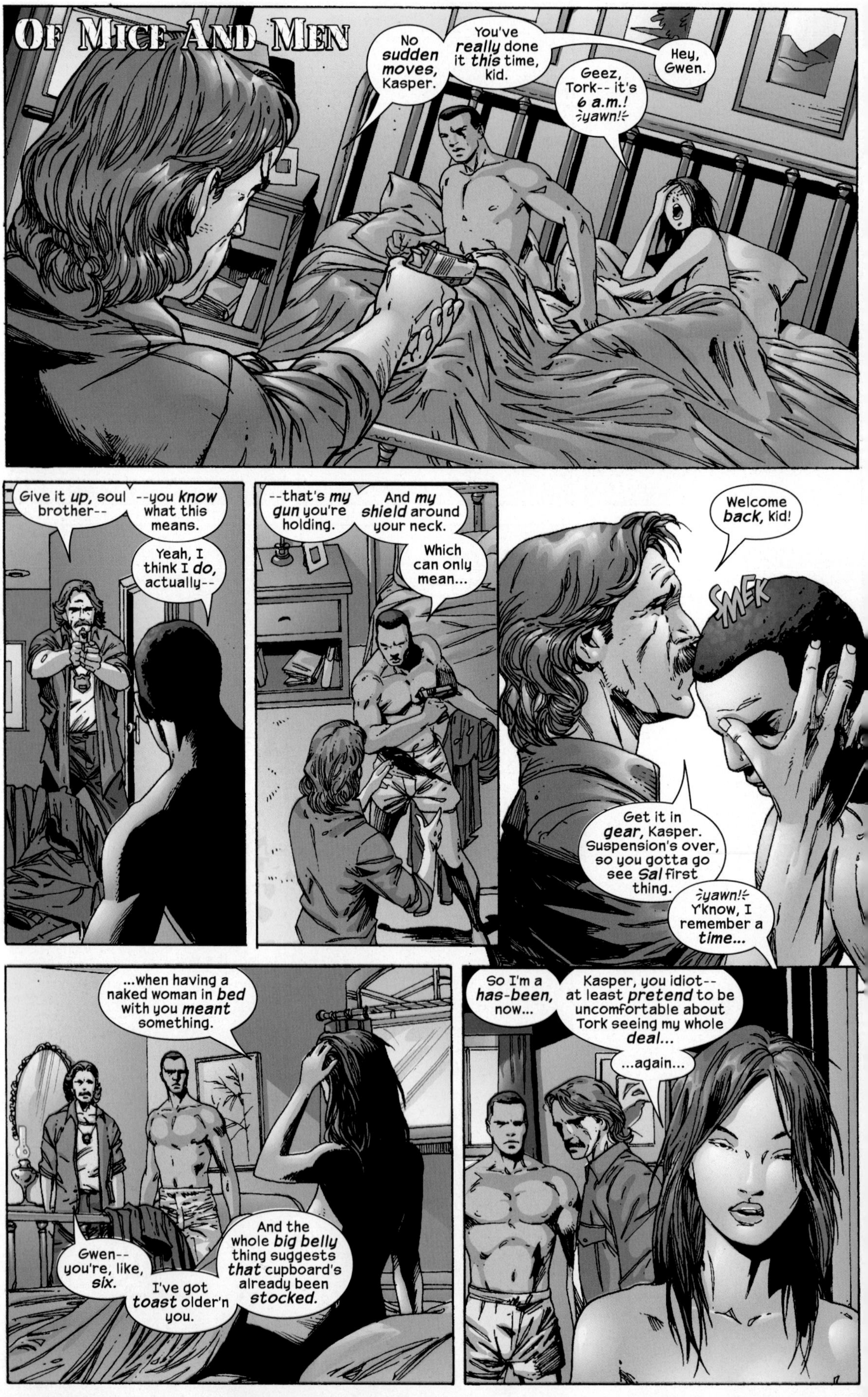

OF MICE AND MEN
No sudden moves, Kasper.
You've really done it this time, kid.
Hey, Gwen.
Geez, Tork-- it's 6 a.m.! ⁓yawn!⁓
Give it up, soul brother--
--you know what this means.
Yeah, I think I do, actually--
--that's my gun you're holding.
And my shield around your neck.
Which can only mean...
Welcome back, kid!
SMEK
Get it in gear, Kasper. Suspension's over, so you gotta go see Sal first thing.
⁓yawn!⁓ Y'know, I remember a time...
...when having a naked woman in bed with you meant something.
Gwen-- you're, like, six.
I've got toast older'n you.
And the whole big belly thing suggests that cupboard's already been stocked.
So I'm a has-been, now...
Kasper, you idiot-- at least pretend to be uncomfortable about Tork seeing my whole deal...
...again...

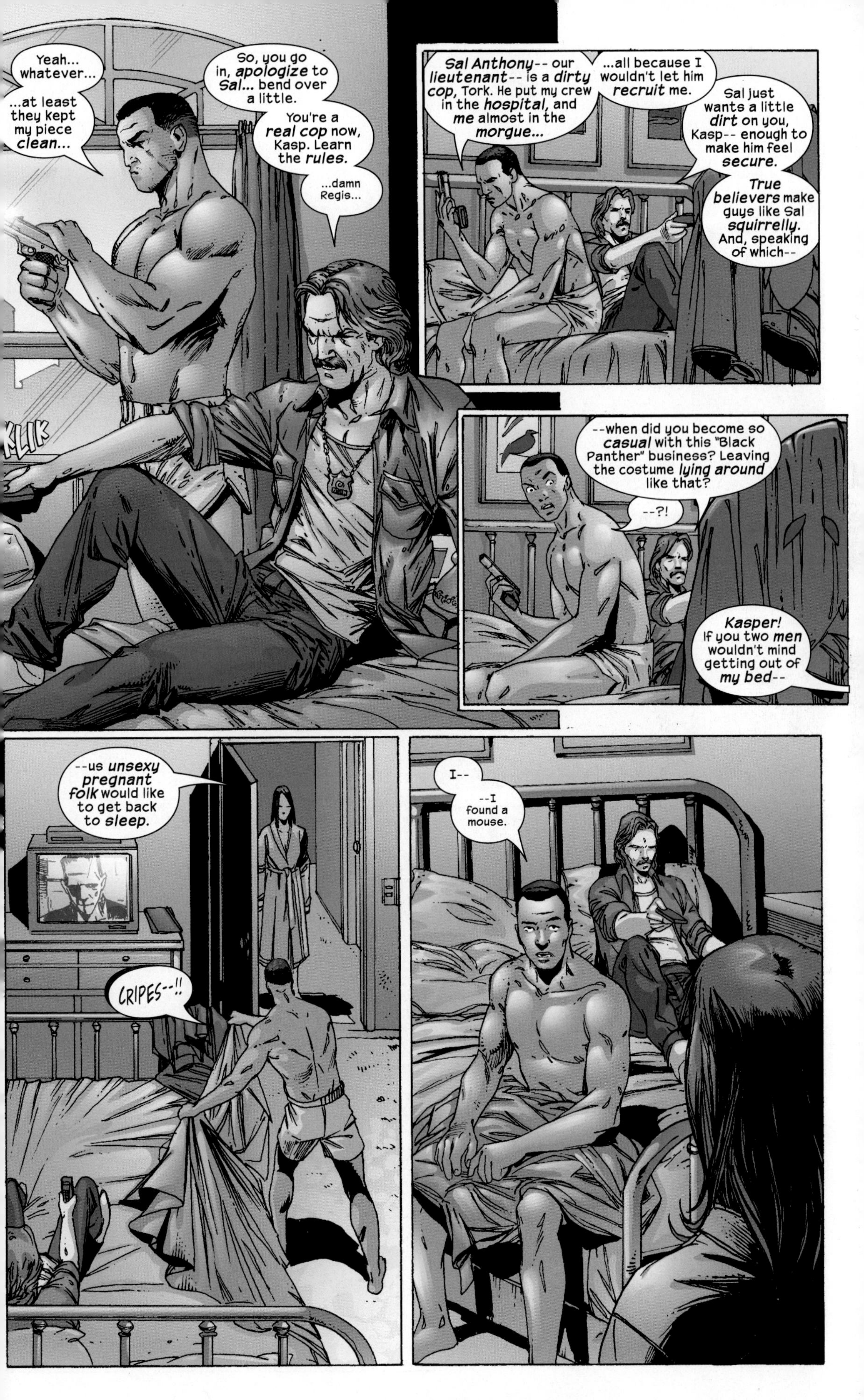

Yeah... whatever...
...at least they kept my piece clean...
So, you go in, apologize to Sal... bend over a little.
You're a real cop now, Kasp. Learn the rules.
...damn Regis...
KLIK
Sal Anthony-- our lieutenant-- is a dirty cop, Tork. He put my crew in the hospital, and me almost in the morgue...
...all because I wouldn't let him recruit me.
Sal just wants a little dirt on you, Kasp-- enough to make him feel secure.
True believers make guys like Sal squirrelly. And, speaking of which--
--when did you become so casual with this "Black Panther" business? Leaving the costume lying around like that?
--?!
Kasper! If you two men wouldn't mind getting out of my bed--
--us unsexy pregnant folk would like to get back to sleep.
CRIPES--!!
I--
--I found a mouse.

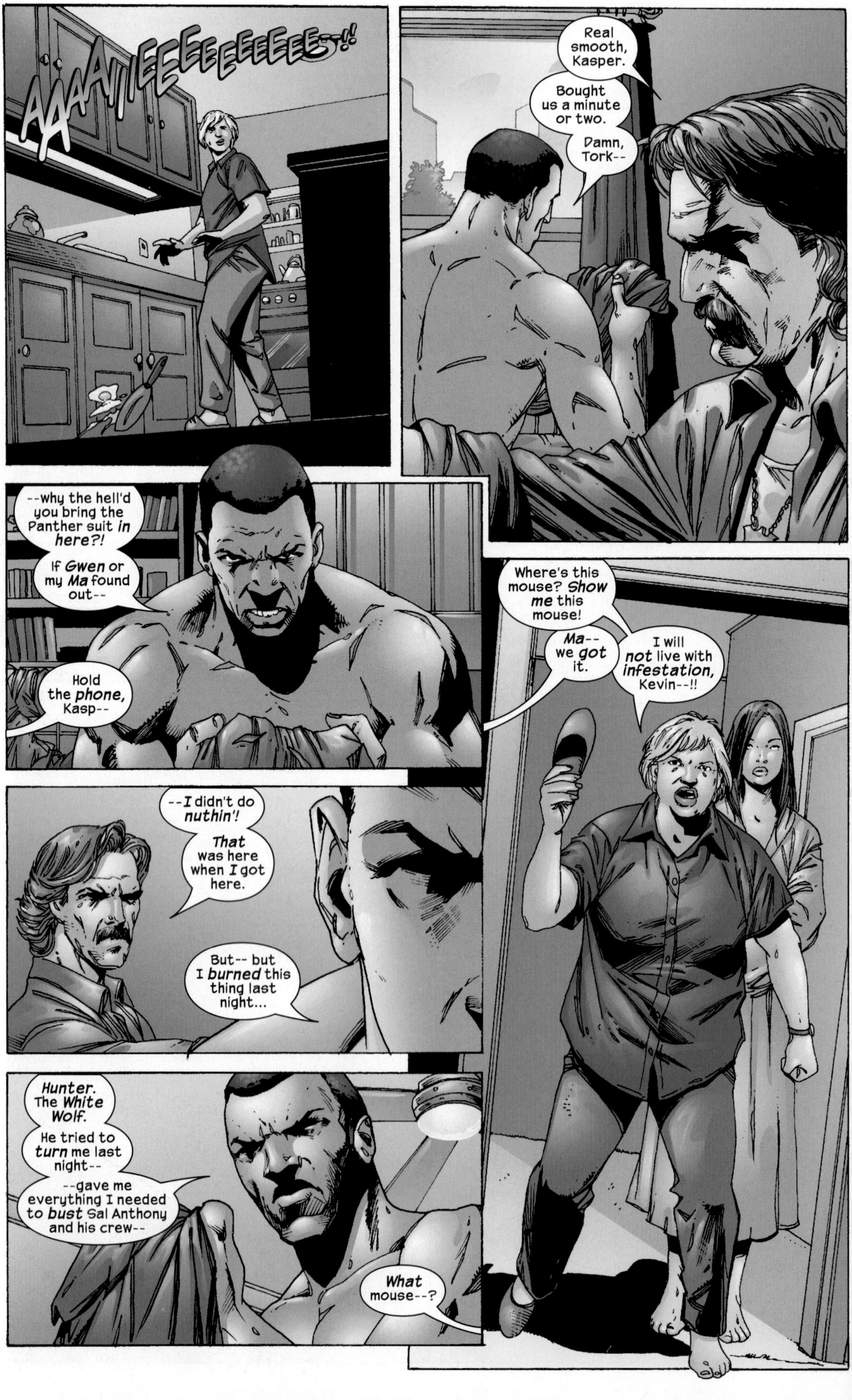
AAAAIIIEEEEEEEEEEE--!!
Real smooth, Kasper.
Bought us a minute or two.
Damn, Tork--
--why the hell'd you bring the Panther suit in here?!
If Gwen or my Ma found out--
Hold the phone, Kasp--
Where's this mouse? Show me this mouse!
Ma-- we got it.
I will not live with infestation, Kevin--!!
--I didn't do nuthin'!
That was here when I got here.
But-- but I burned this thing last night...
Hunter. The White Wolf.
He tried to turn me last night--
--gave me everything I needed to bust Sal Anthony and his crew--
What mouse--?

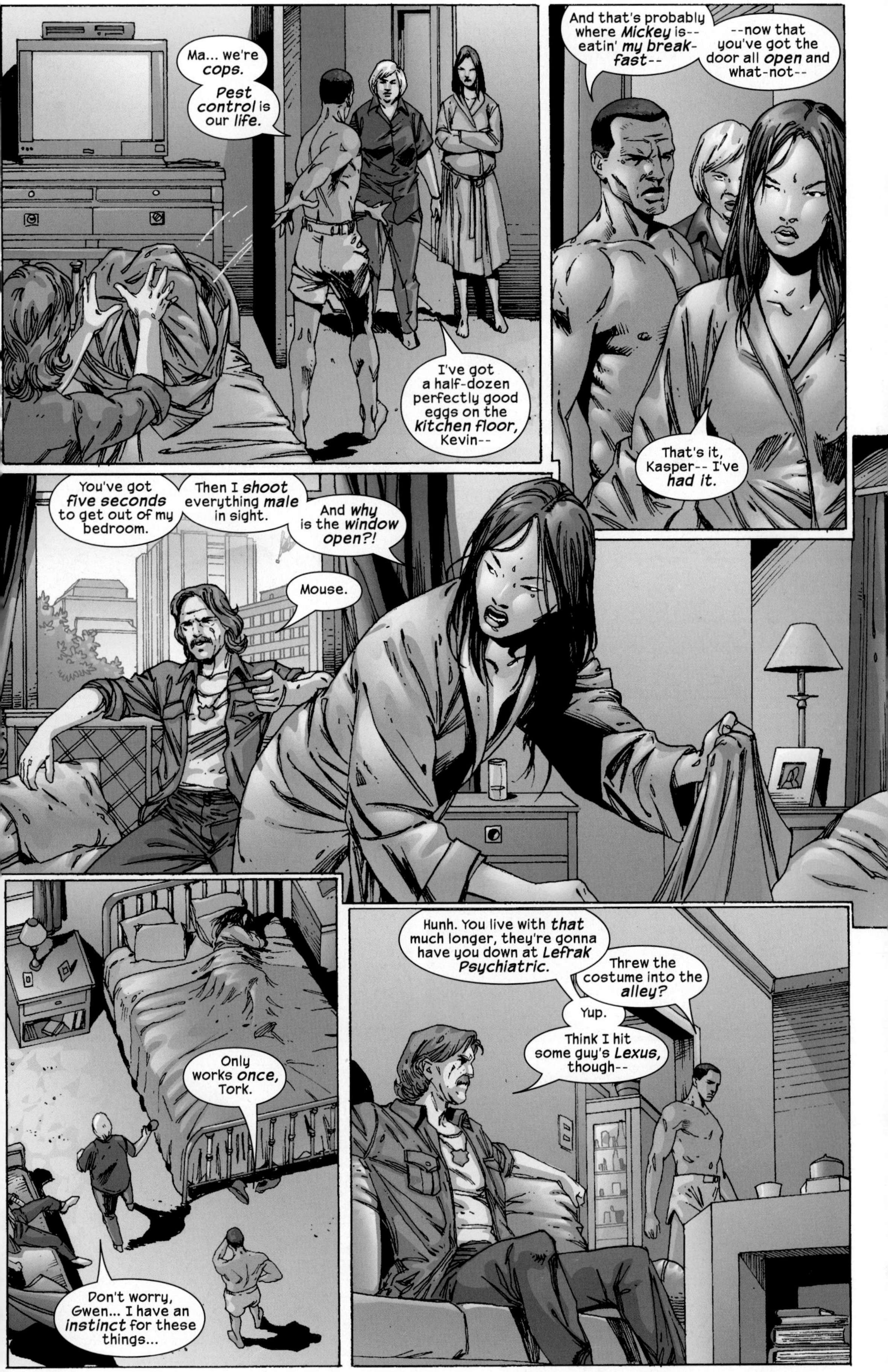
Ma... we're cops.
Pest control is our life.
I've got a half-dozen perfectly good eggs on the kitchen floor, Kevin--
And that's probably where Mickey is-- eatin' my breakfast--
--now that you've got the door all open and what-not--
That's it, Kasper-- I've had it.
You've got five seconds to get out of my bedroom.
Then I shoot everything male in sight.
And why is the window open?!
Mouse.
Only works once, Tork.
Don't worry, Gwen... I have an instinct for these things...
Hunh. You live with that much longer, they're gonna have you down at Lefrak Psychiatric.
Threw the costume into the alley?
Yup.
Think I hit some guy's Lexus, though--

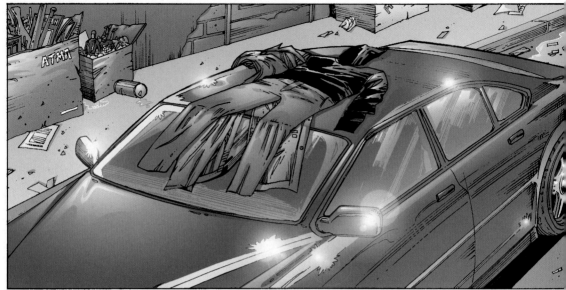

This is a *nightmare.*

I *torched* this Lex last night--

--less than *six* hours ago-- *and* I left the *costume* in it.

There's *no way* Wolf could have had this car rebuilt that fast...

Kasp-- the White Wolf is the adopted brother of *King T'Challa* of Wakanda--

--the Avenger they call the *Black Panther.*

The guy *you've* been *impersonating* the last few days, during your suspension from the police force.

Wakanda is one of the most technologically advanced countries in the *world--* and one of the *richest.*

Hunter was the head of the *Hatut Zeraze--* the Wakandan *Secret Police.* Very scary fellows, they.

You piecin' this *together,* Sherlock--?

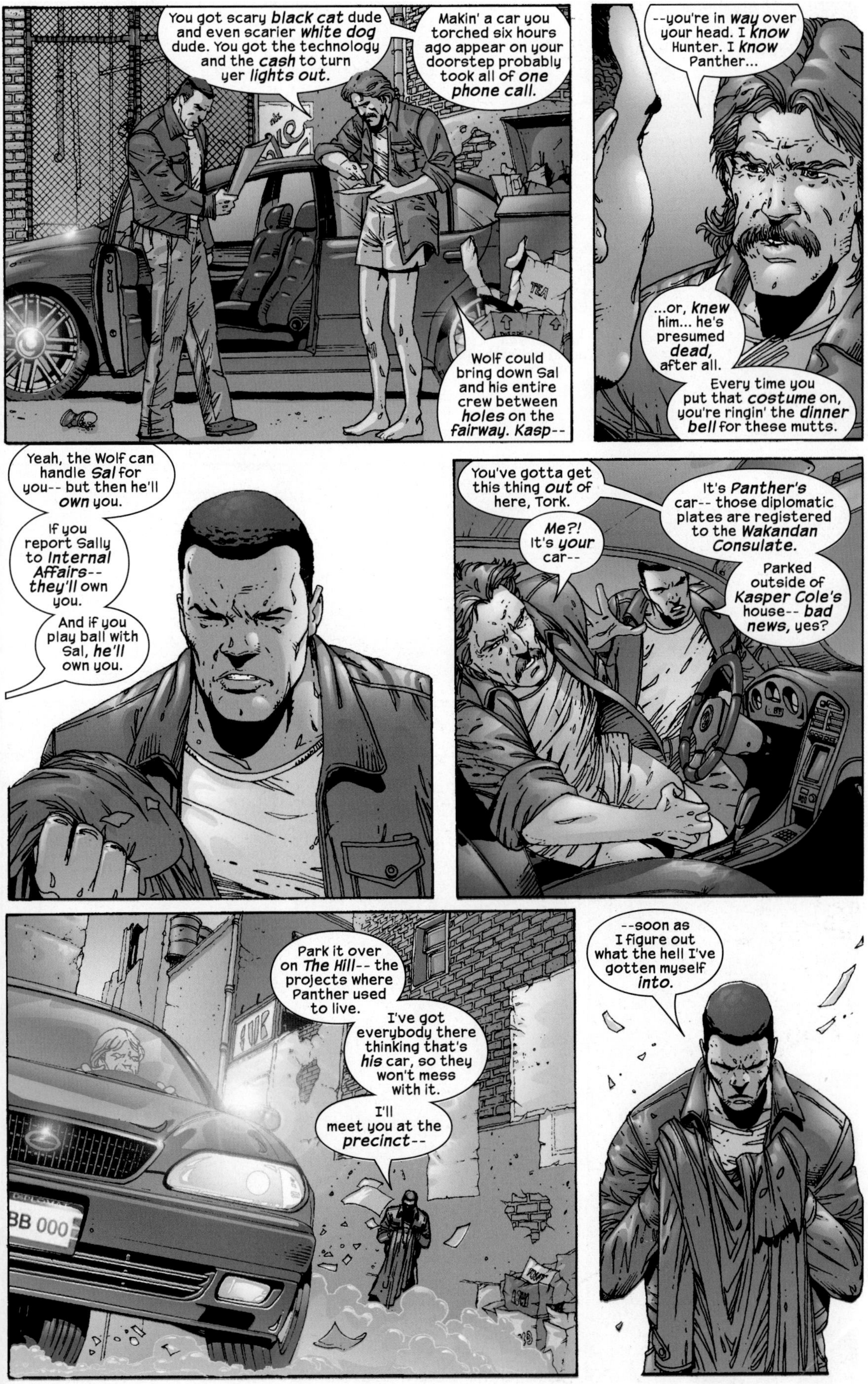
You got scary *black cat* dude and even scarier *white dog* dude. You got the technology and the *cash* to turn yer *lights out.*
Makin' a car you torched six hours ago appear on your doorstep probably took all of *one phone call.*
Wolf could bring down Sal and his entire crew between *holes* on the *fairway.* Kasp--
--you're in *way* over your head. I *know* Hunter. I *know* Panther...
...or, *knew* him... he's presumed *dead,* after all.
Every time you put that *costume* on, you're ringin' the *dinner bell* for these mutts.
Yeah, the Wolf can handle *Sal* for you-- but then he'll *own* you.
If you report Sally to *Internal Affairs-- they'll* own you.
And if you play ball with Sal, *he'll* own you.
You've gotta get this thing *out* of here, Tork.
Me?! It's *your* car--
It's *Panther's* car-- those diplomatic plates are registered to the *Wakandan Consulate.*
Parked outside of *Kasper Cole's* house-- *bad news,* yes?
Park it over on *The Hill*-- the projects where Panther used to live.
I've got everybody there thinking that's *his* car, so they won't mess with it.
I'll meet you at the *precinct*--
--soon as I figure out what the hell I've gotten myself *into.*

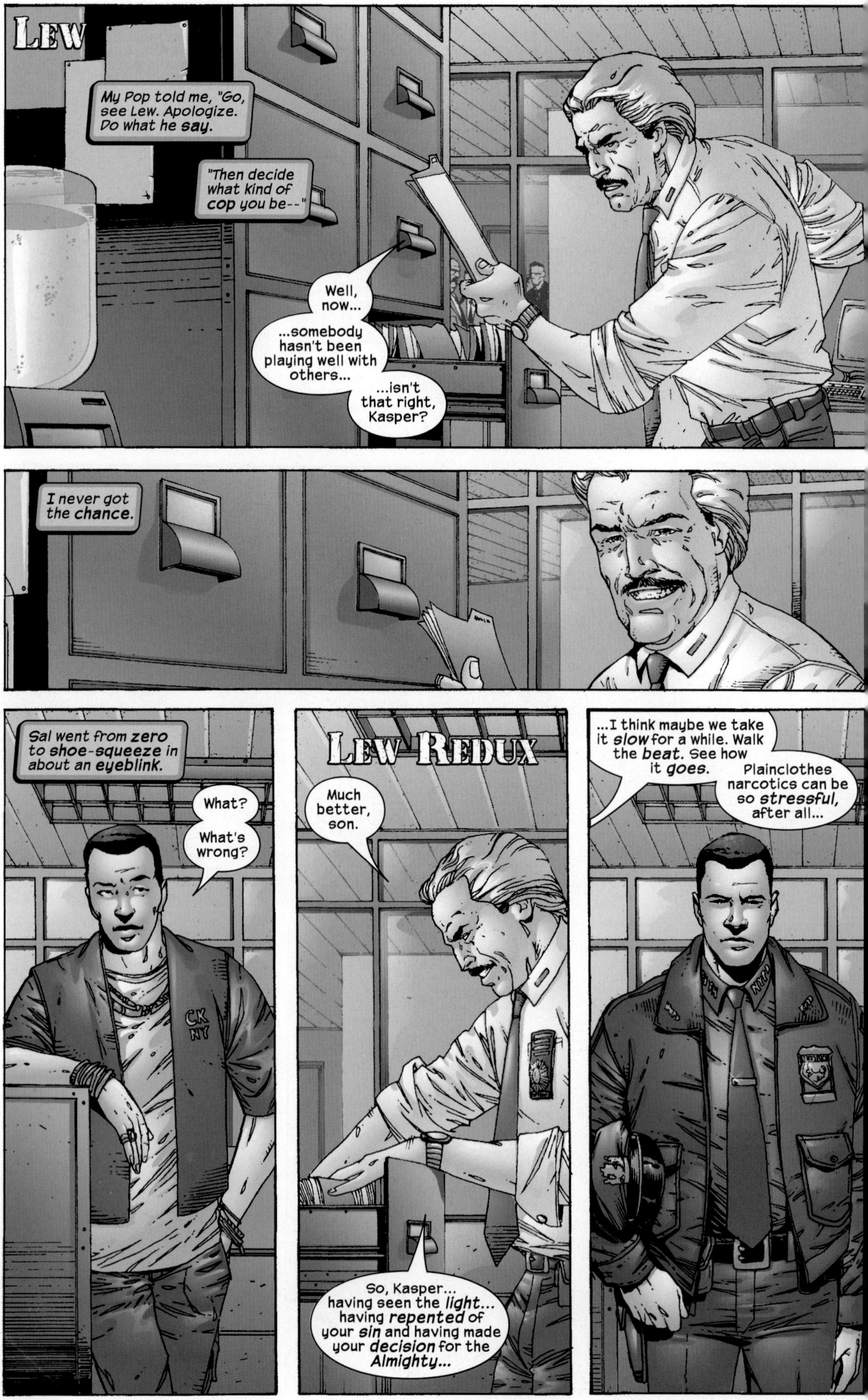
LEW
My Pop told me, "Go, see Lew. Apologize. Do what he say.
"Then decide what kind of cop you be--"
Well, now...
...somebody hasn't been playing well with others...
...isn't that right, Kasper?
I never got the chance.
Sal went from zero to shoe-squeeze in about an eyeblink.
What?
What's wrong?
LEW REDUX
Much better, son.
So, Kasper... having seen the light... having repented of your sin and having made your decision for the Almighty...
...I think maybe we take it slow for a while. Walk the beat. See how it goes.
Plainclothes narcotics can be so stressful, after all...

How It Goes

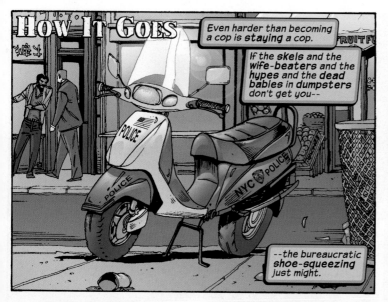

Even harder than becoming a cop is *staying* a cop.

If the skels and the wife-beaters and the hypes and the *dead babies in dumpsters* don't get you--

--the bureaucratic shoe-squeezing just might.

This is Sal asking a question: Is Kasper Cole an I.A.B. *rat*?

Two choices: punch Sal out, leave my shield on his desk--

--or find a way to *squeeze* into this thing.

--? Now what--?

Damn heroes.

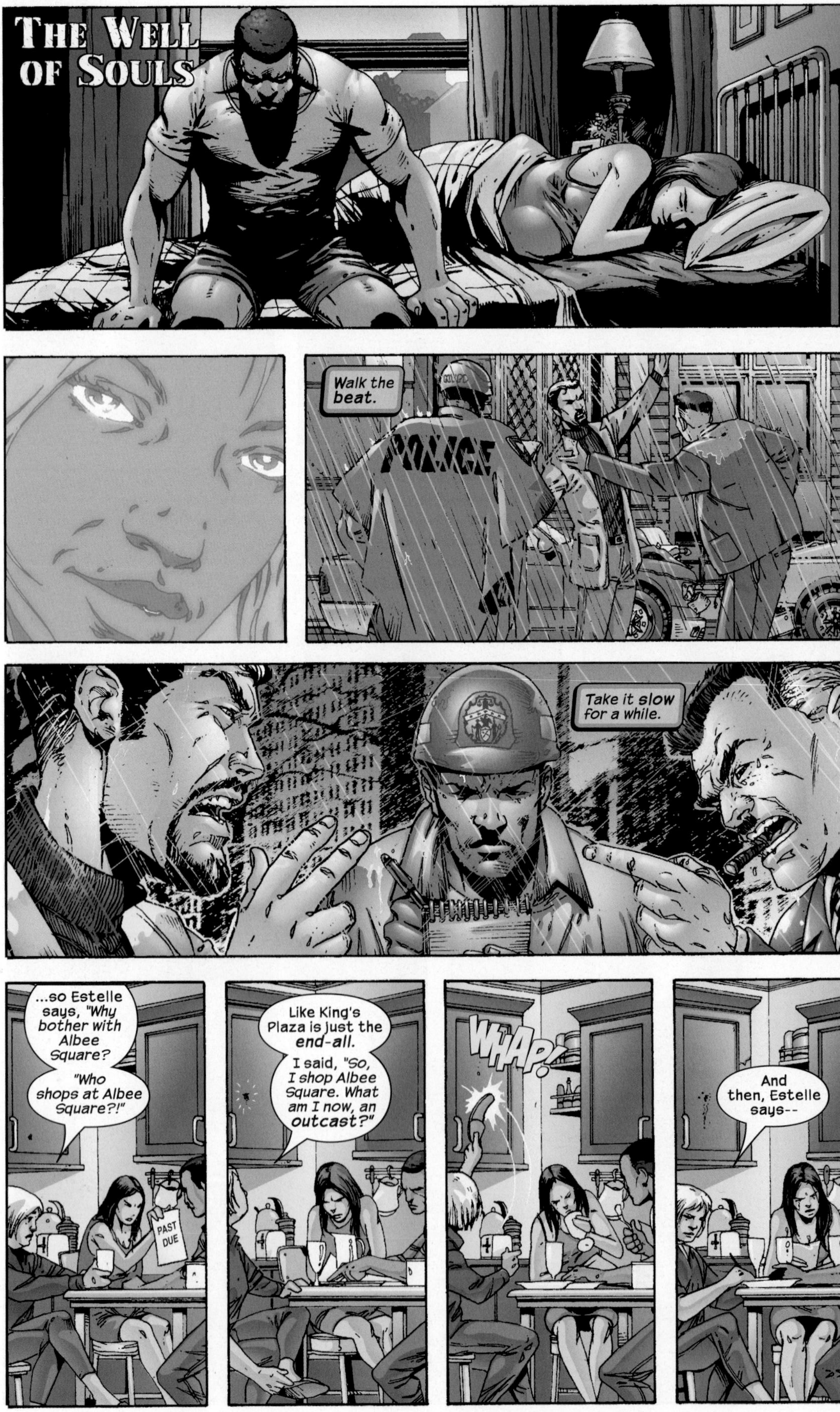
THE WELL OF SOULS
Walk the beat.
POLICE
Take it slow for a while.
...so Estelle says, "Why bother with Albee Square?
"Who shops at Albee Square?!"
PAST DUE
Like King's Plaza is just the end-all.
I said, "So, I shop Albee Square. What am I now, an outcast?"
WHAP!
And then, Estelle says--

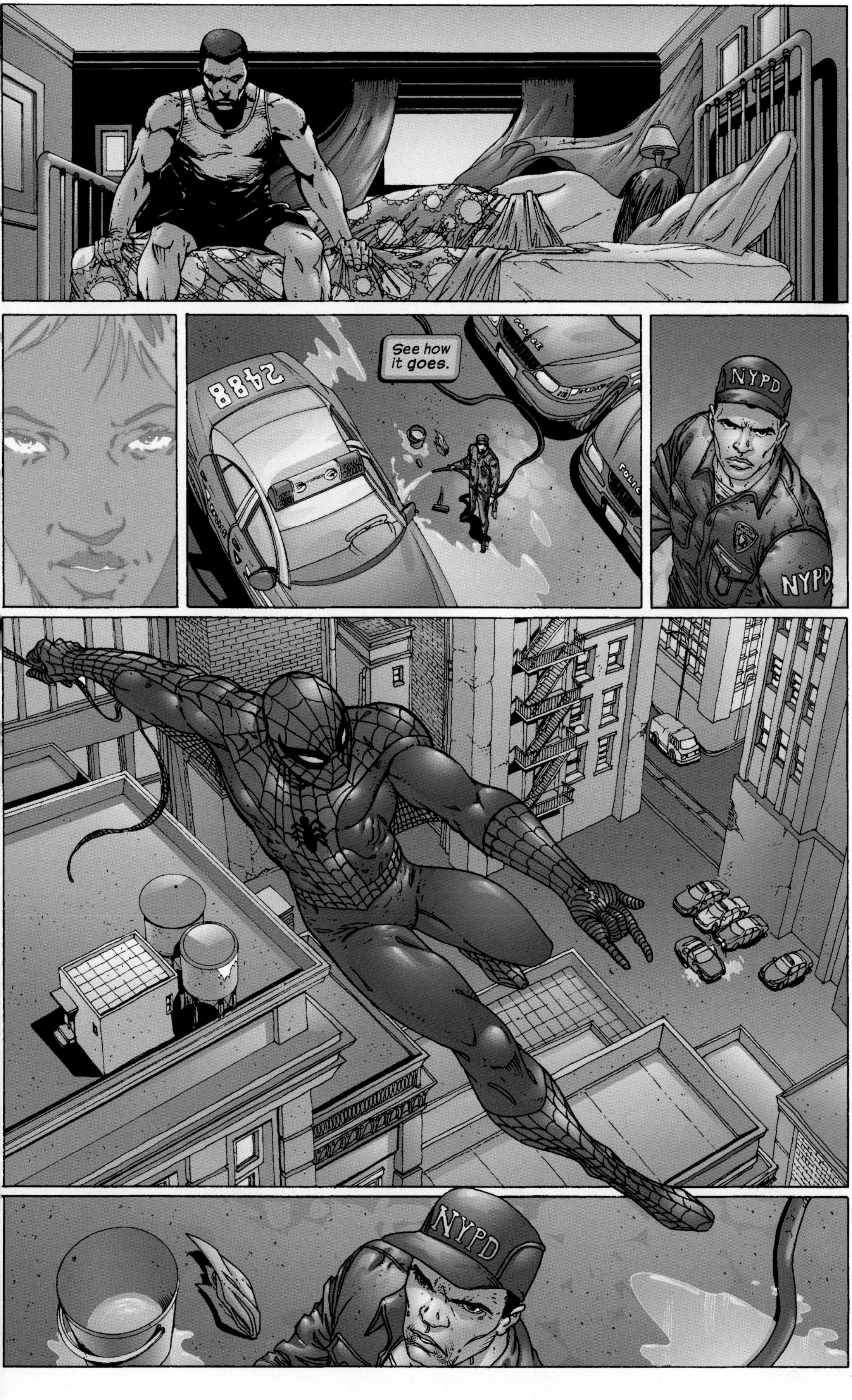
See how it goes.
2488
POLICE
NYPD
NYPD
NYPD

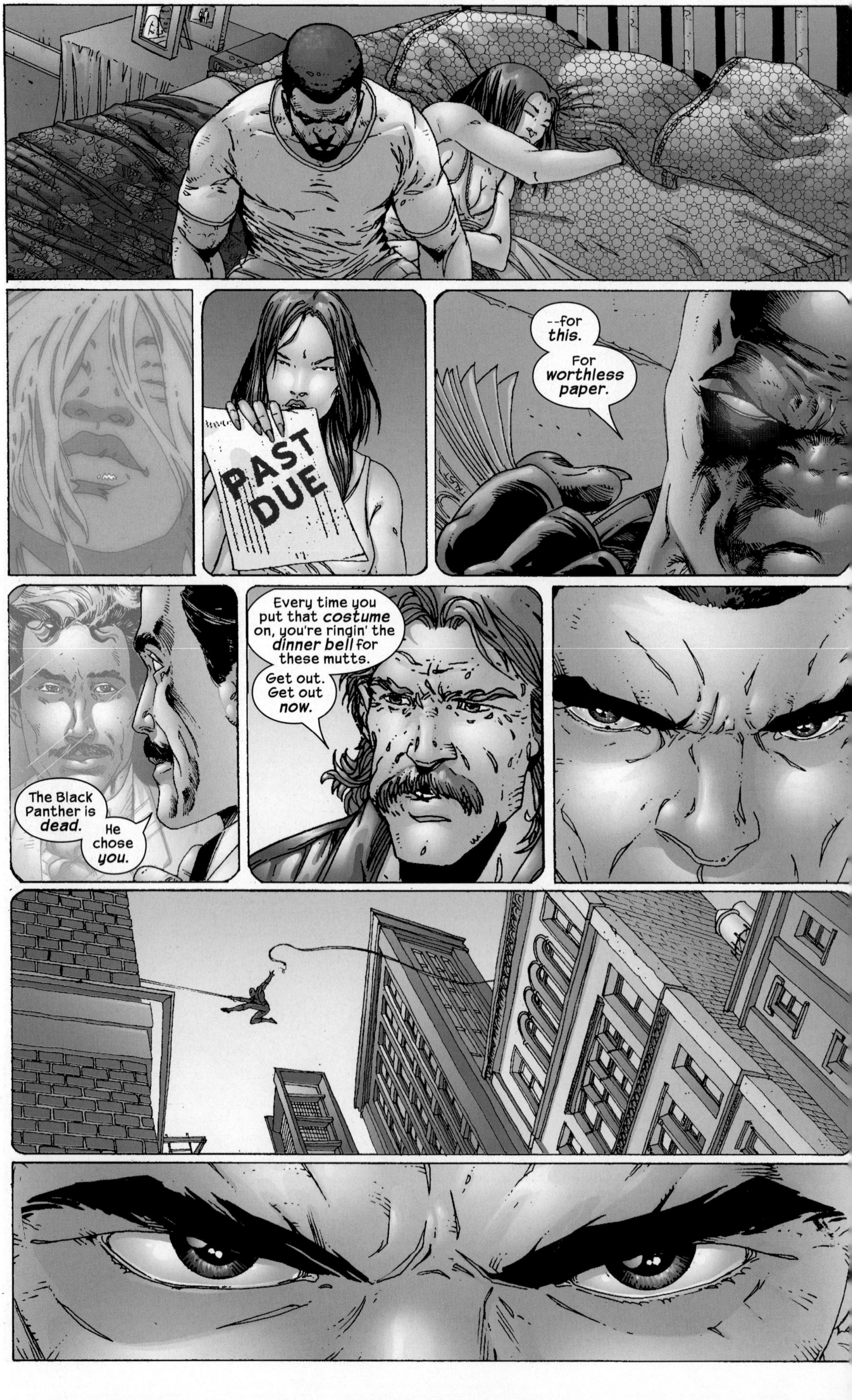
PAST DUE
--for this.
For worthless paper.
The Black Panther is dead.
He chose you.
Every time you put that costume on, you're ringin' the dinner bell for these mutts.
Get out. Get out now.

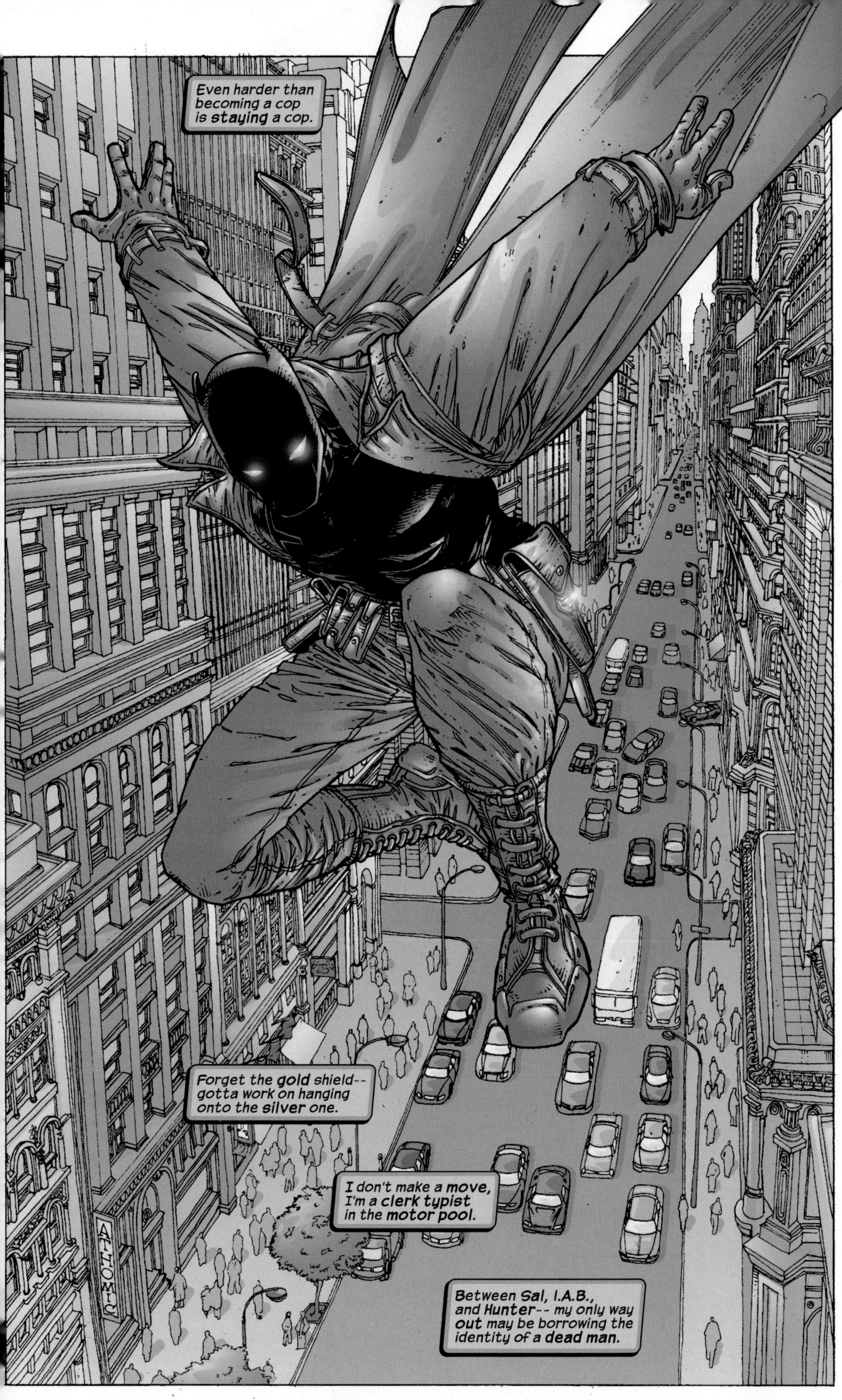
Even harder than becoming a cop is staying a cop.
Forget the gold shield-- gotta work on hanging onto the silver one.
I don't make a move, I'm a clerk typist in the motor pool.
Between Sal, I.A.B., and Hunter-- my only way out may be borrowing the identity of a dead man.

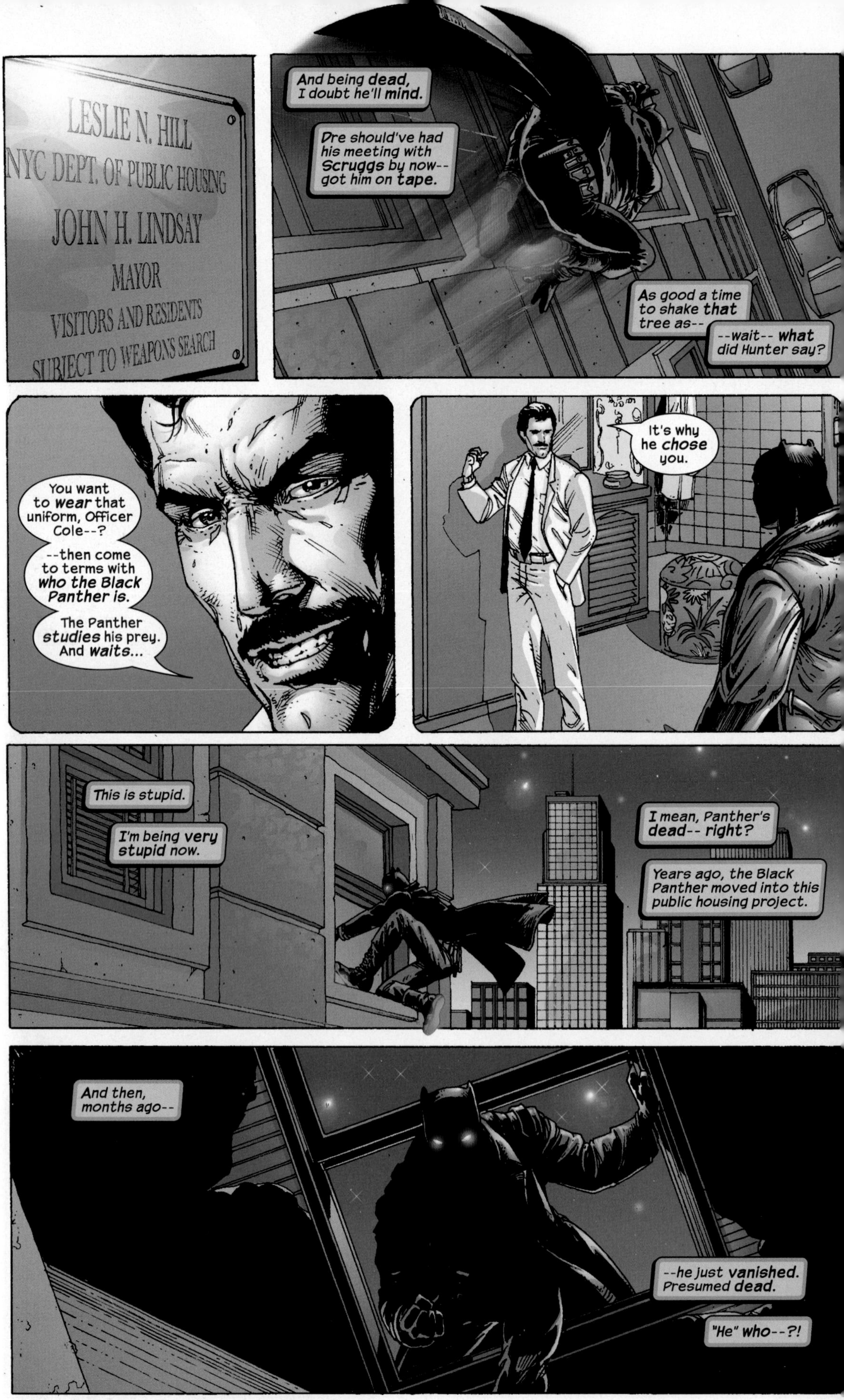
LESLIE N. HILL
NYC DEPT. OF PUBLIC HOUSING
JOHN H. LINDSAY
MAYOR
VISITORS AND RESIDENTS
SUBJECT TO WEAPONS SEARCH
And being dead, I doubt he'll mind.
Dre should've had his meeting with Scruggs by now--got him on tape.
As good a time to shake that tree as--
--wait-- what did Hunter say?
You want to wear that uniform, Officer Cole--?
--then come to terms with who the Black Panther is.
The Panther studies his prey. And waits...
It's why he chose you.
This is stupid.
I'm being very stupid now.
I mean, Panther's dead-- right?
Years ago, the Black Panther moved into this public housing project.
And then, months ago--
--he just vanished. Presumed dead.
"He" who--?!

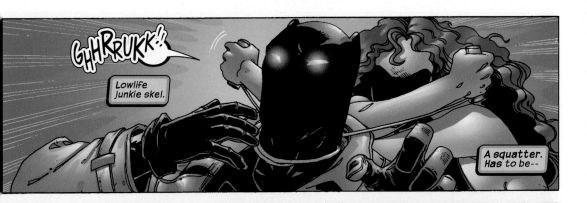

GHHRRUKK!!

Lowlife junkie skel.

A squatter. Has to be--

GHHRRUKK!! GRRRR!!

G-Grace--?

Grace.
Grace.

Grace...
...I remember you...

Okay.

Probably not Grace.

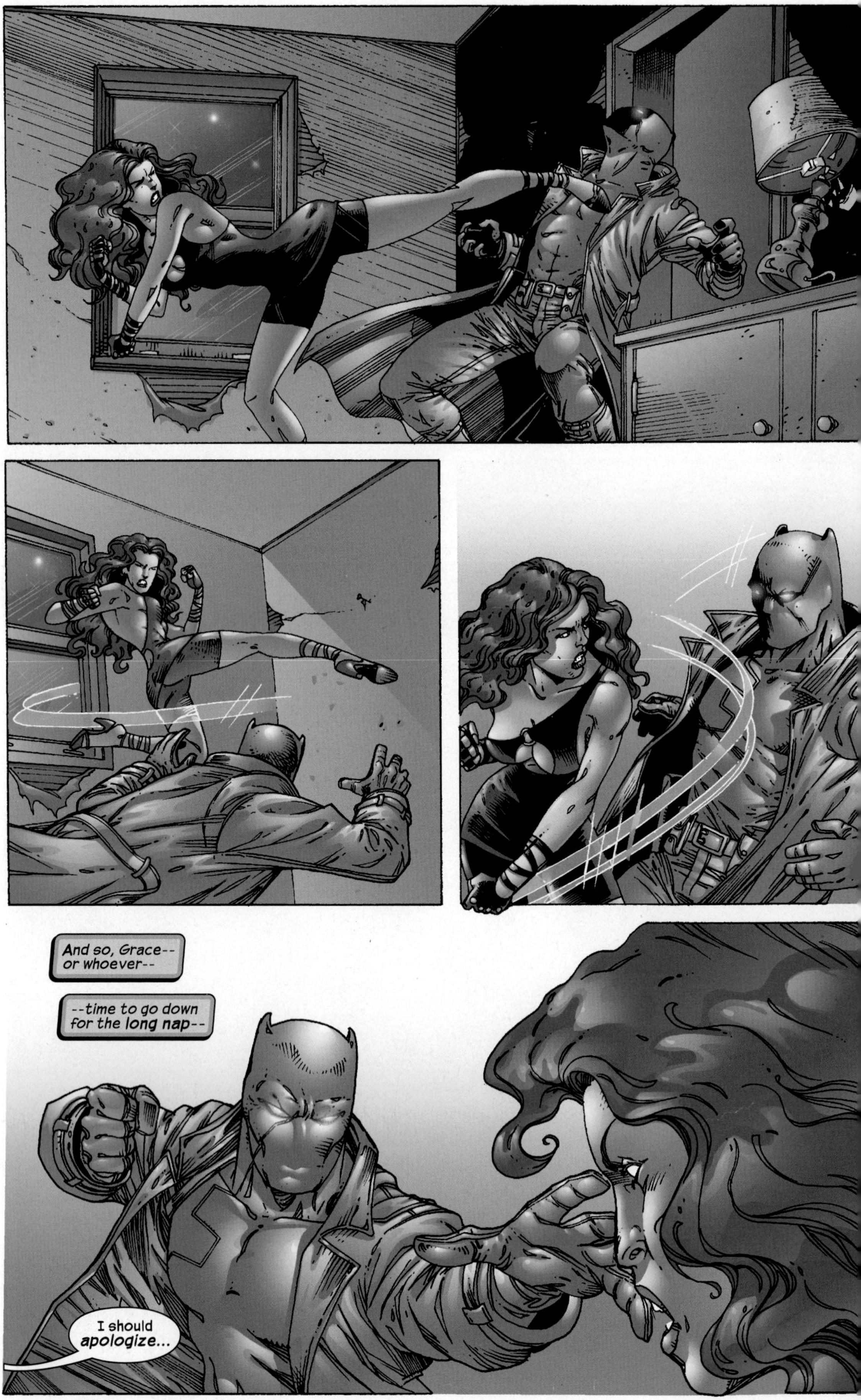

And so, Grace--
or whoever--
--time to go down
for the long nap--
I should
apologize...

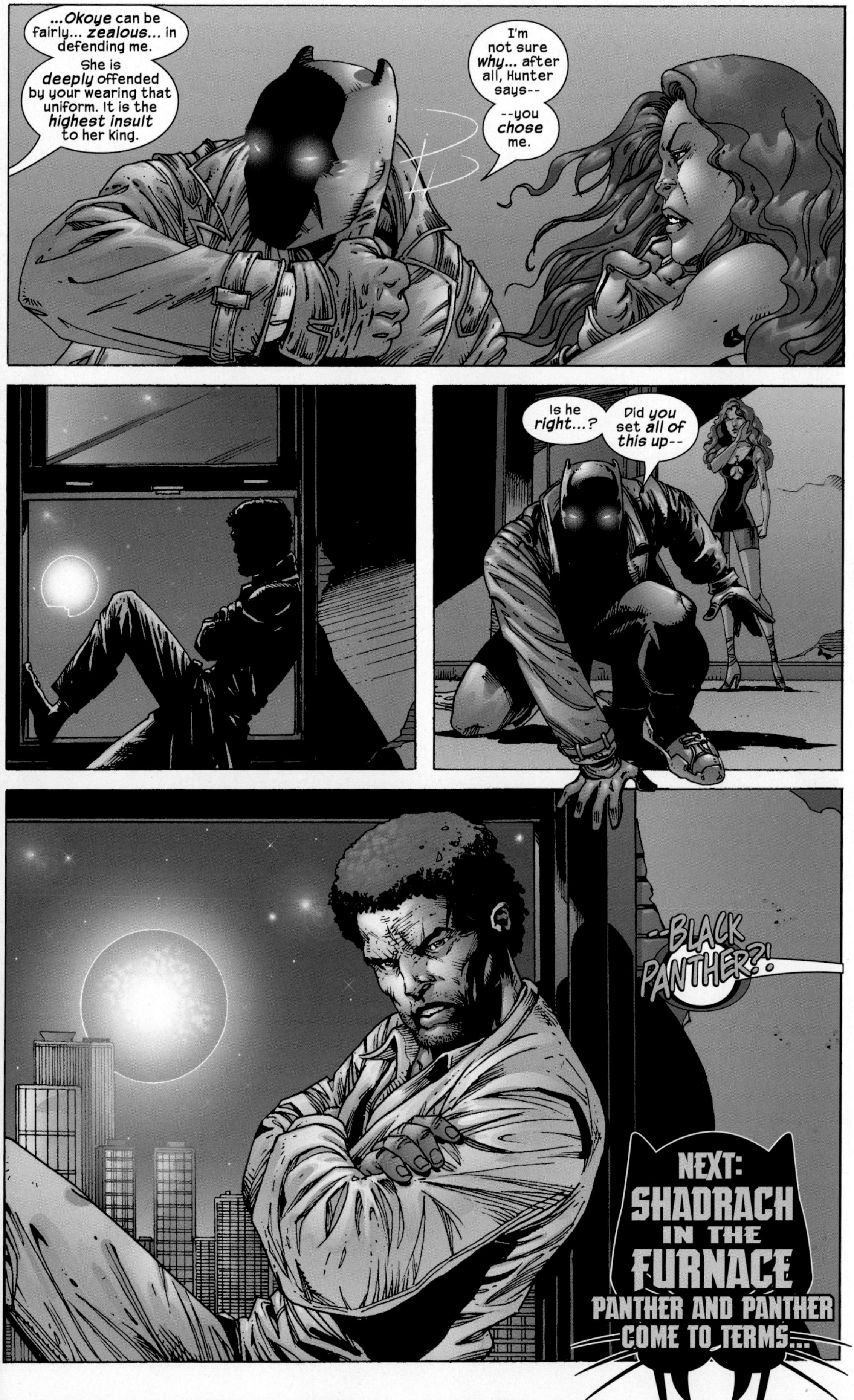
...Okoye can be fairly... zealous... in defending me.
She is deeply offended by your wearing that uniform. It is the highest insult to her king.
I'm not sure why... after all, Hunter says--
--you chose me.
Is he right...?
Did you set all of this up--
--BLACK PANTHER?!
NEXT:
SHADRACH IN THE FURNACE
PANTHER AND PANTHER COME TO TERMS...

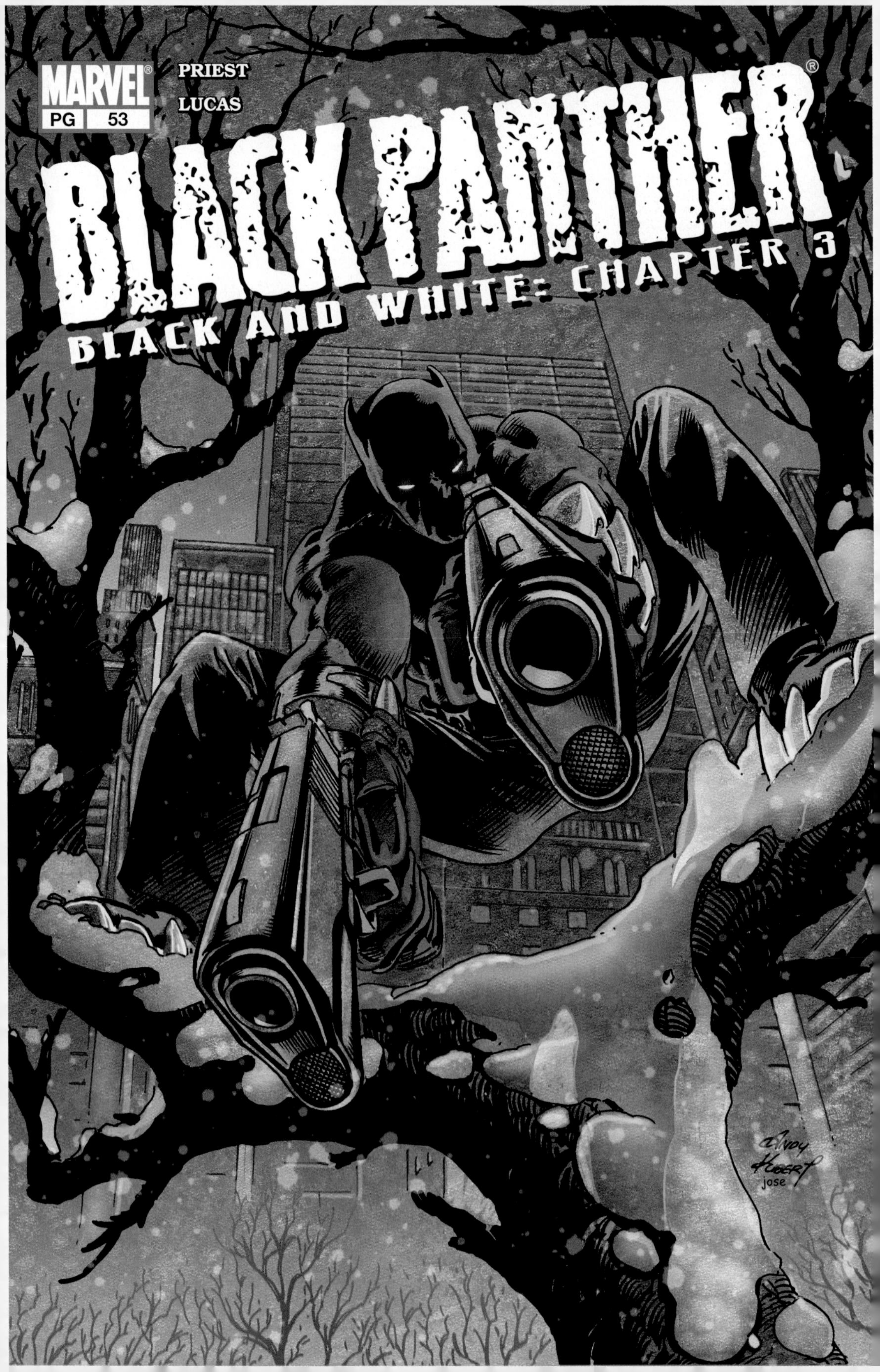
MARVEL®
PG 53
PRIEST
LUCAS
BLACK PANTHER®
BLACK AND WHITE: CHAPTER 3
jose

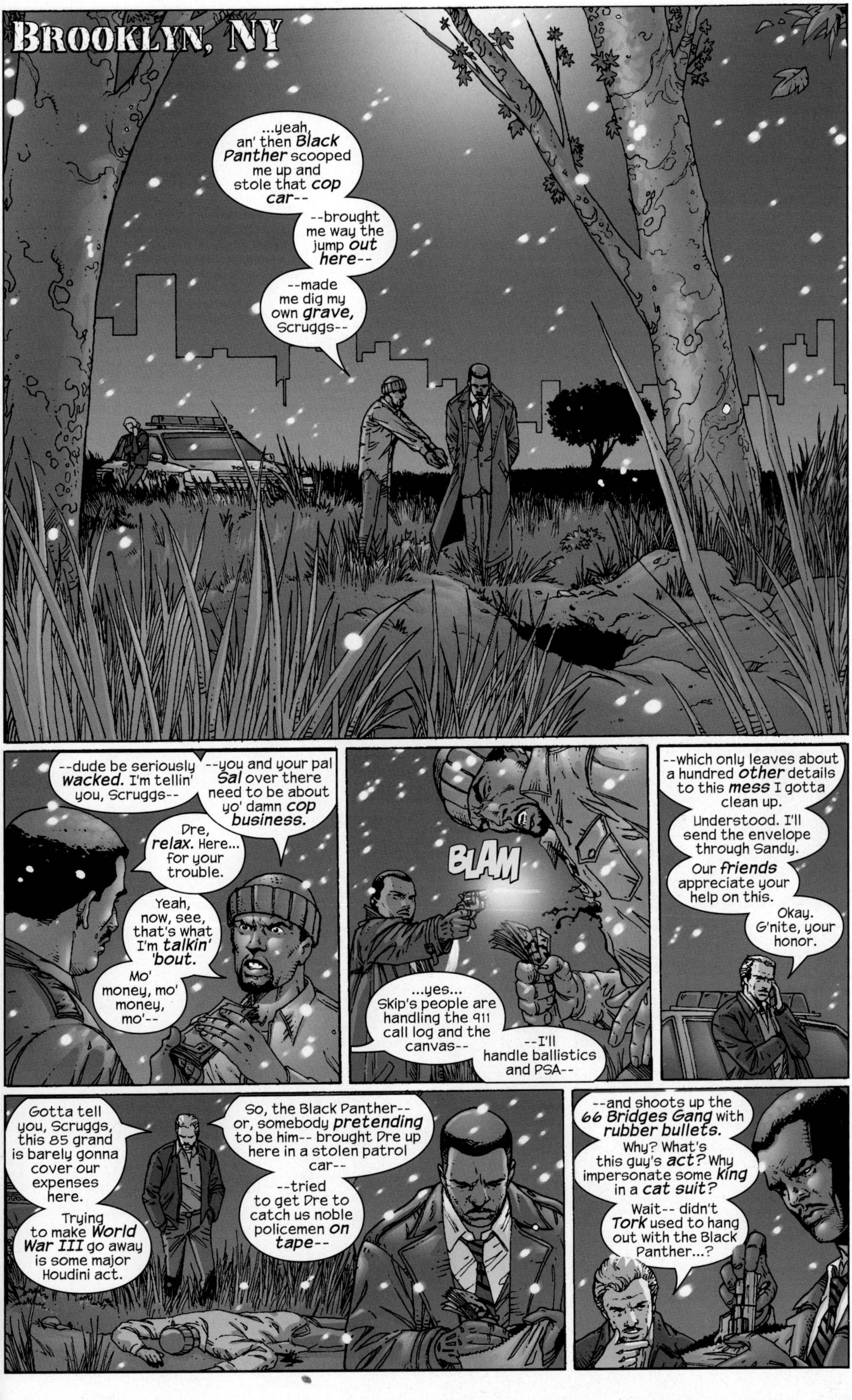

BROOKLYN, NY
...yeah, an' then Black Panther scooped me up and stole that cop car--
--brought me way the jump out here--
--made me dig my own grave, Scruggs--
--dude be seriously wacked. I'm tellin' you, Scruggs--
--you and your pal Sal over there need to be about yo' damn cop business.
Dre, relax. Here... for your trouble.
Yeah, now, see, that's what I'm talkin' 'bout.
Mo' money, mo' money, mo'--
BLAM
...yes... Skip's people are handling the 911 call log and the canvas--
--I'll handle ballistics and PSA--
--which only leaves about a hundred other details to this mess I gotta clean up.
Understood. I'll send the envelope through Sandy.
Our friends appreciate your help on this.
Okay. G'nite, your honor.
Gotta tell you, Scruggs, this 85 grand is barely gonna cover our expenses here.
Trying to make World War III go away is some major Houdini act.
So, the Black Panther-- or, somebody pretending to be him-- brought Dre up here in a stolen patrol car--
--tried to get Dre to catch us noble policemen on tape--
--and shoots up the 66 Bridges Gang with rubber bullets.
Why? What's this guy's act? Why impersonate some king in a cat suit?
Wait-- didn't Tork used to hang out with the Black Panther...?

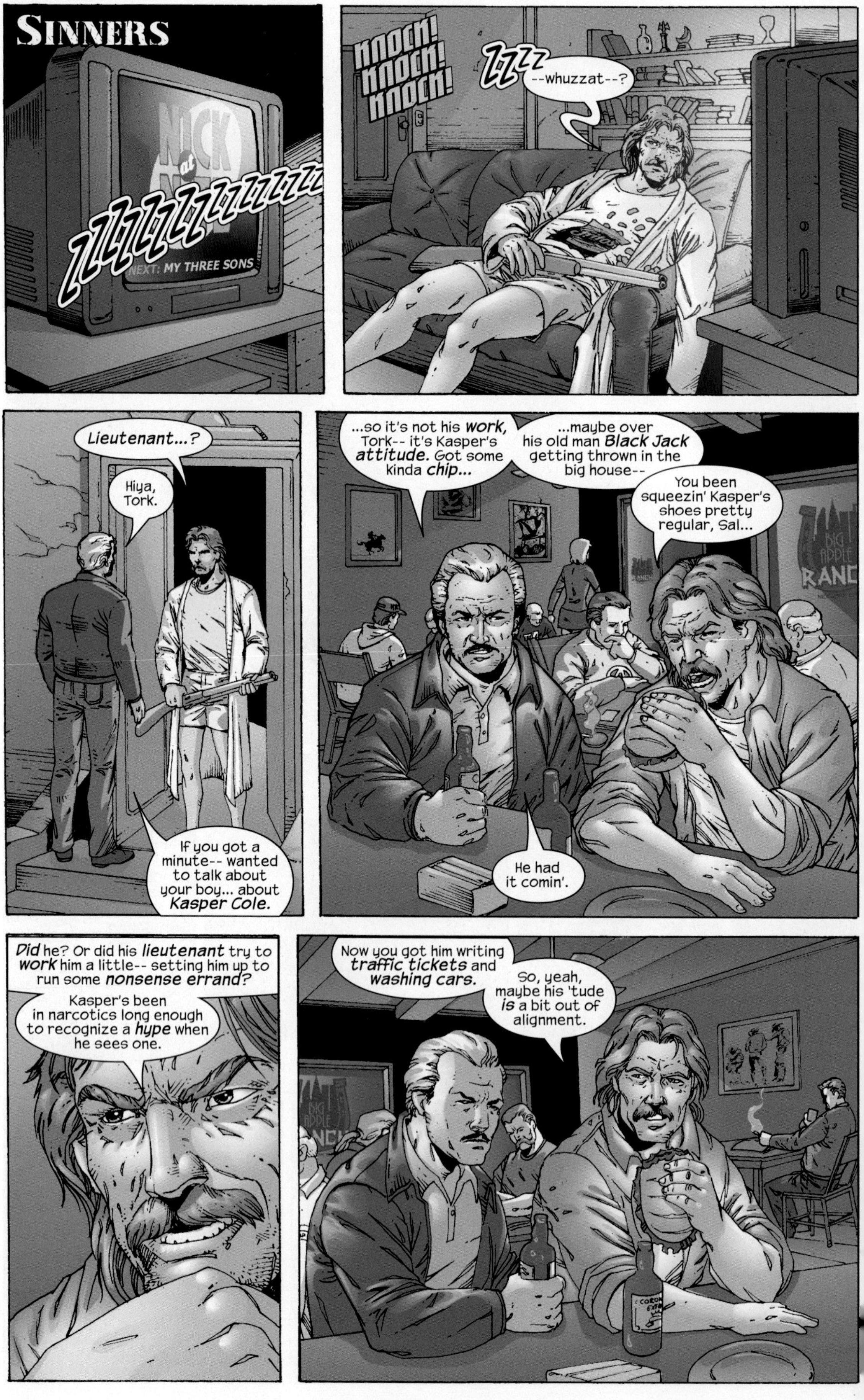
SINNERS
NICK at NITE
ZZZZZZZZZZZZZZZZZZ
NEXT: MY THREE SONS
KNOCK! KNOCK! KNOCK!
ZZZZ
--whuzzat--?
Lieutenant...?
Hiya, Tork.
If you got a minute-- wanted to talk about your boy... about Kasper Cole.
...so it's not his work, Tork-- it's Kasper's attitude. Got some kinda chip...
...maybe over his old man Black Jack getting thrown in the big house--
You been squeezin' Kasper's shoes pretty regular, Sal...
He had it comin'.
Did he? Or did his lieutenant try to work him a little-- setting him up to run some nonsense errand?
Kasper's been in narcotics long enough to recognize a hype when he sees one.
Now you got him writing traffic tickets and washing cars.
So, yeah, maybe his 'tude is a bit out of alignment.

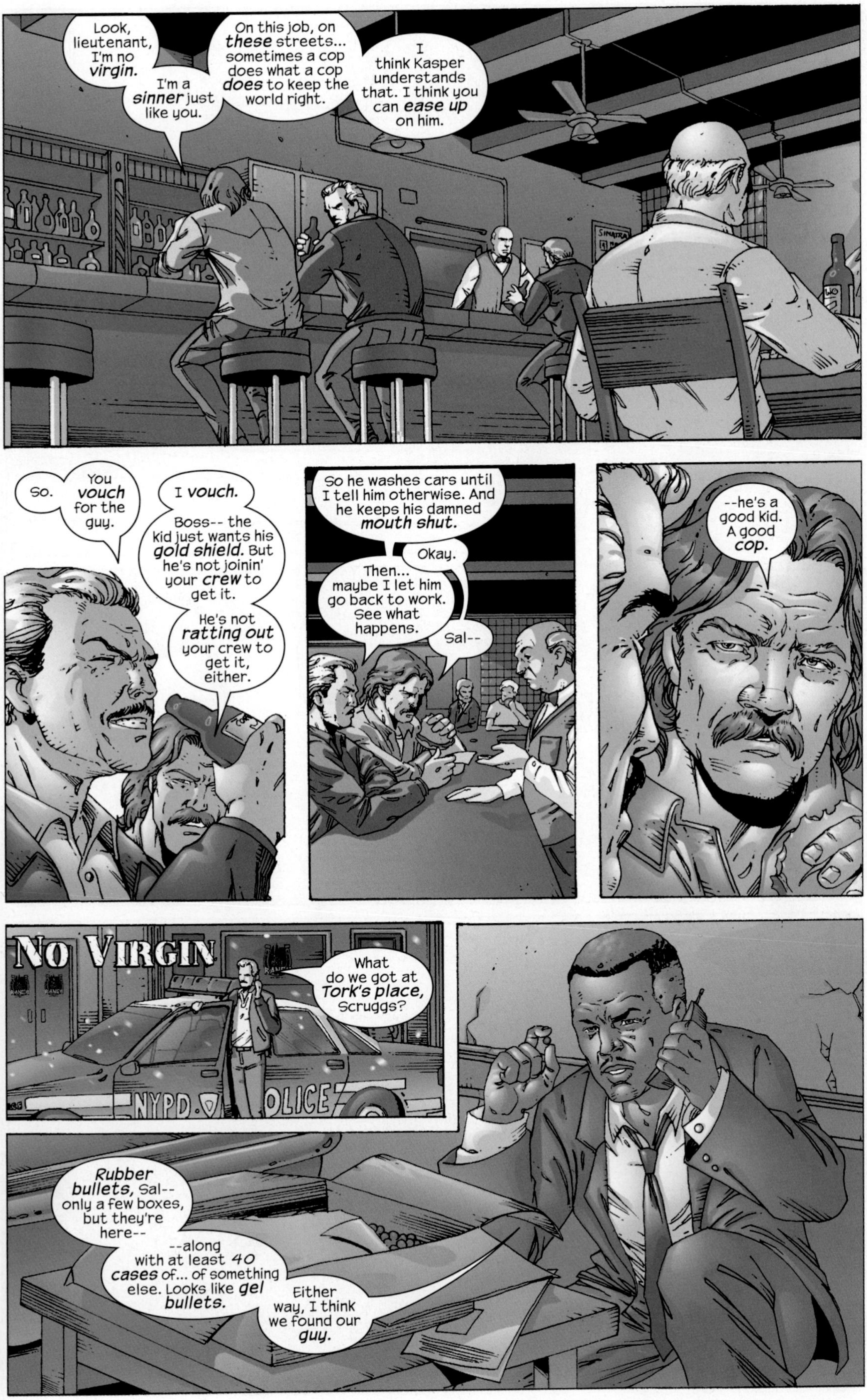
Look, lieutenant, I'm no virgin.
I'm a sinner just like you.
On this job, on these streets... sometimes a cop does what a cop does to keep the world right.
I think Kasper understands that. I think you can ease up on him.
SINATRA
So.
You vouch for the guy.
I vouch.
Boss-- the kid just wants his gold shield. But he's not joinin' your crew to get it.
He's not ratting out your crew to get it, either.
So he washes cars until I tell him otherwise. And he keeps his damned mouth shut.
Okay.
Then... maybe I let him go back to work. See what happens.
Sal--
--he's a good kid. A good cop.
No Virgin
What do we got at Tork's place, Scruggs?
NYPD
OLICE
Rubber bullets, Sal-- only a few boxes, but they're here--
--along with at least 40 cases of... of something else. Looks like gel bullets.
Either way, I think we found our guy.

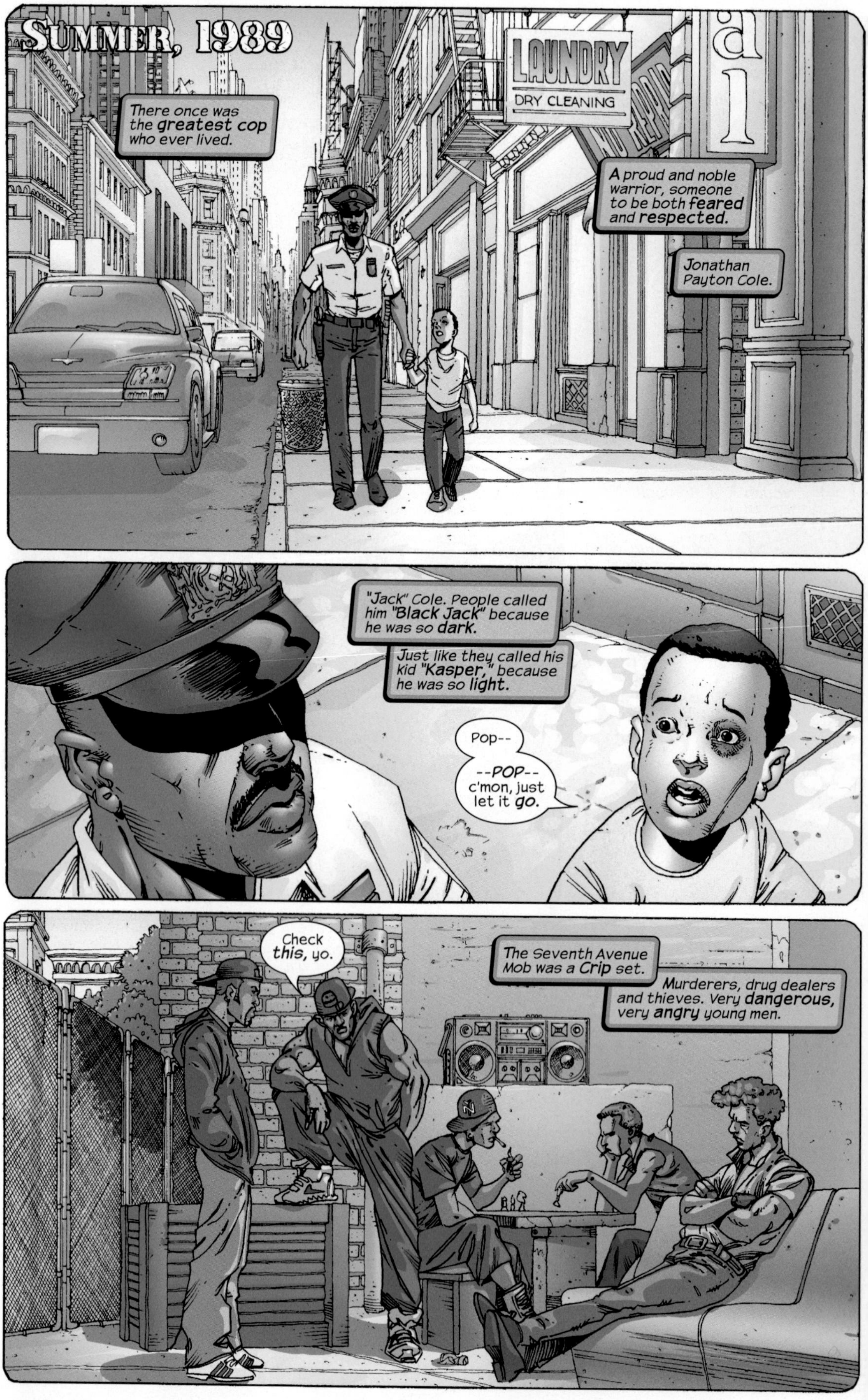
Summer, 1989
There once was the greatest cop who ever lived.
LAUNDRY
DRY CLEANING
A proud and noble warrior, someone to be both feared and respected.
Jonathan Payton Cole.
"Jack" Cole. People called him "Black Jack" because he was so dark.
Just like they called his kid "Kasper," because he was so light.
Pop--
--POP-- c'mon, just let it go.
Check this, yo.
The Seventh Avenue Mob was a Crip set.
Murderers, drug dealers and thieves. Very dangerous, very angry young men.

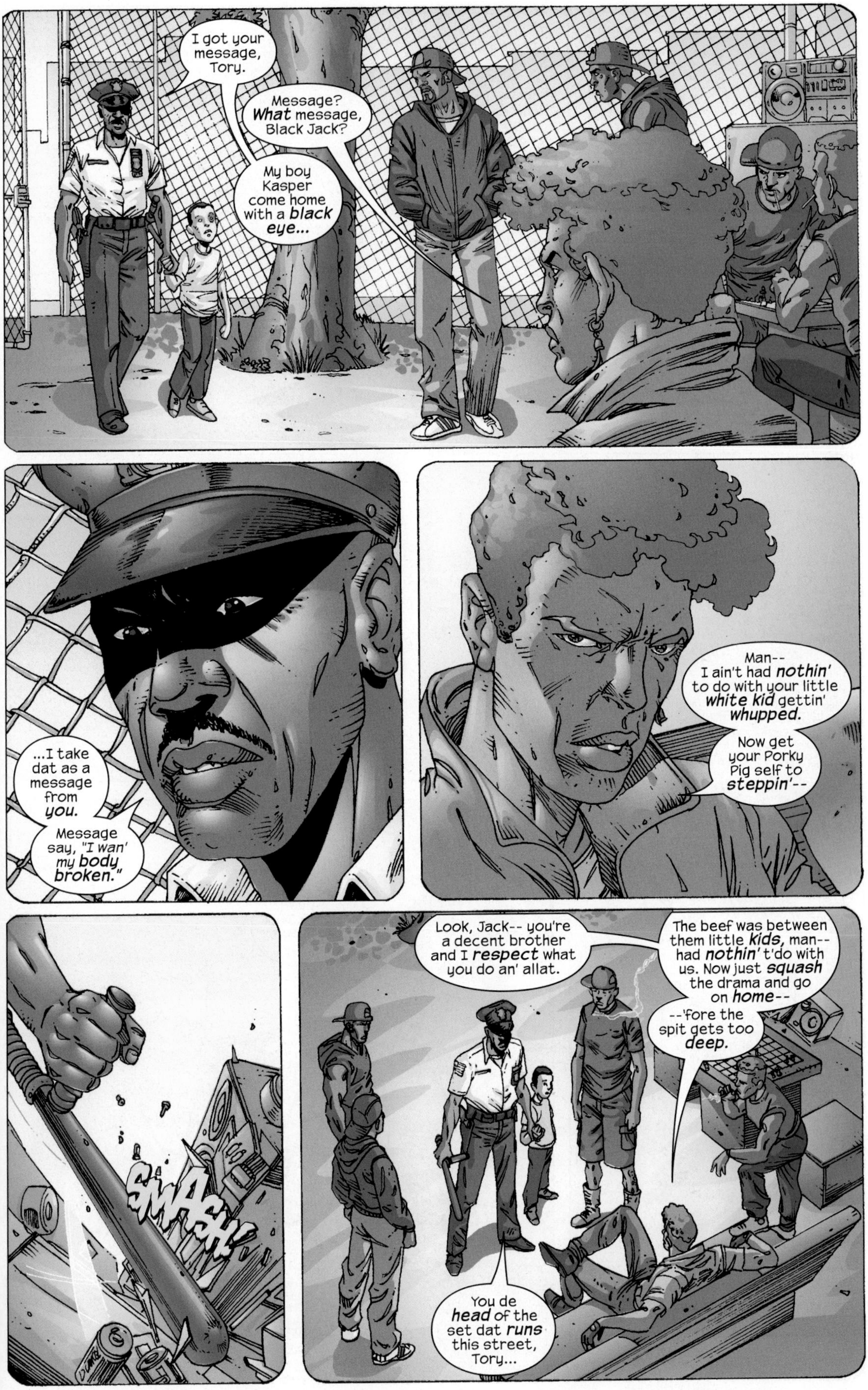

I got your message, Tory.
Message? What message, Black Jack?
My boy Kasper come home with a black eye...
...I take dat as a message from you.
Message say, "I wan' my body broken."
Man-- I ain't had nothin' to do with your little white kid gettin' whupped.
Now get your Porky Pig self to steppin'--
SMASH!
Look, Jack-- you're a decent brother and I respect what you do an' allat.
The beef was between them little kids, man-- had nothin' t'do with us. Now just squash the drama and go on home--
--'fore the spit gets too deep.
You de head of the set dat runs this street, Tory...

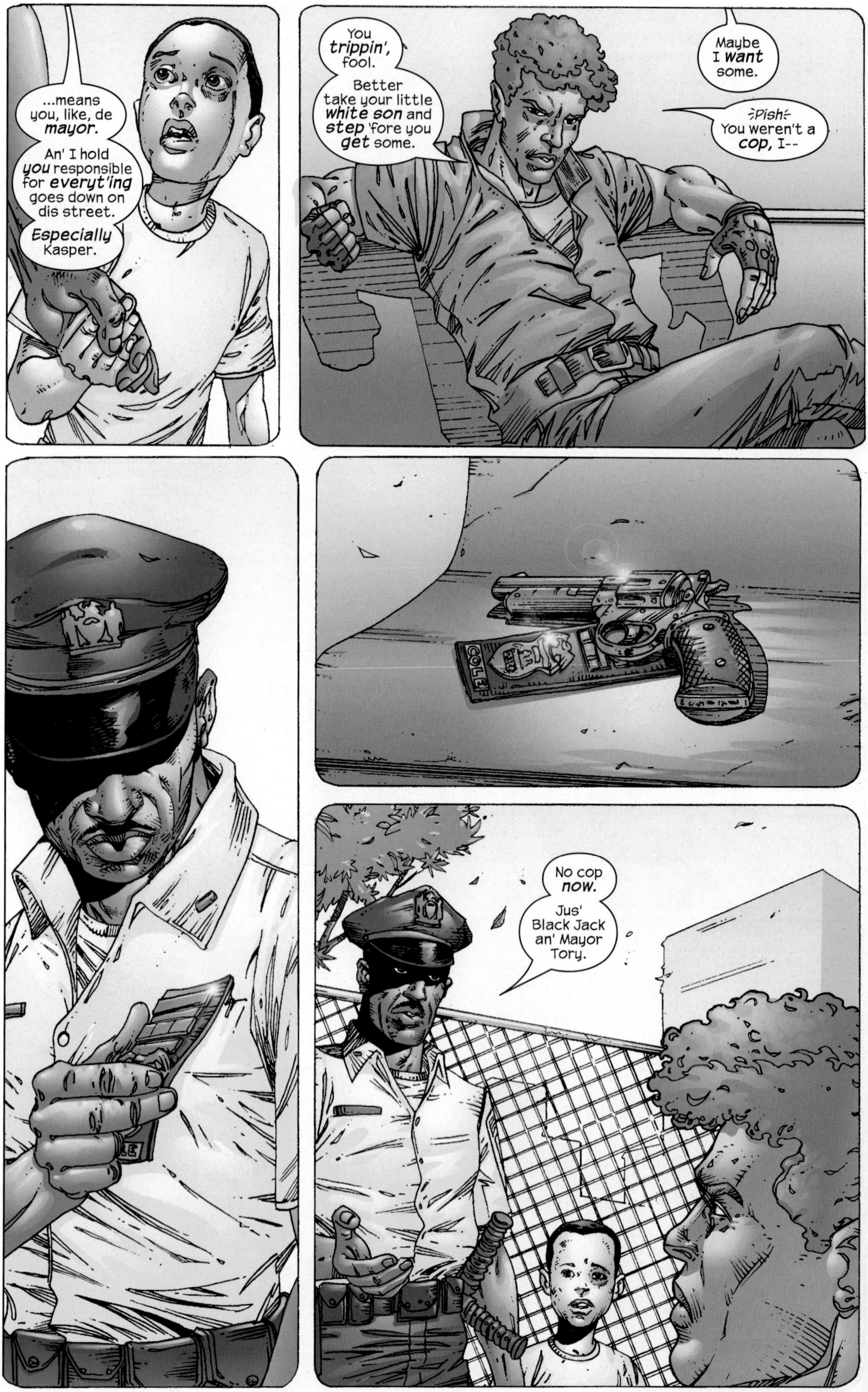
...means you, like, de mayor.
An' I hold you responsible for everyt'ing goes down on dis street.
Especially Kasper.
You trippin', fool.
Better take your little white son and step 'fore you get some.
Maybe I want some.
Pish
You weren't a cop, I--
COLE
No cop now.
Jus' Black Jack an' Mayor Tory.

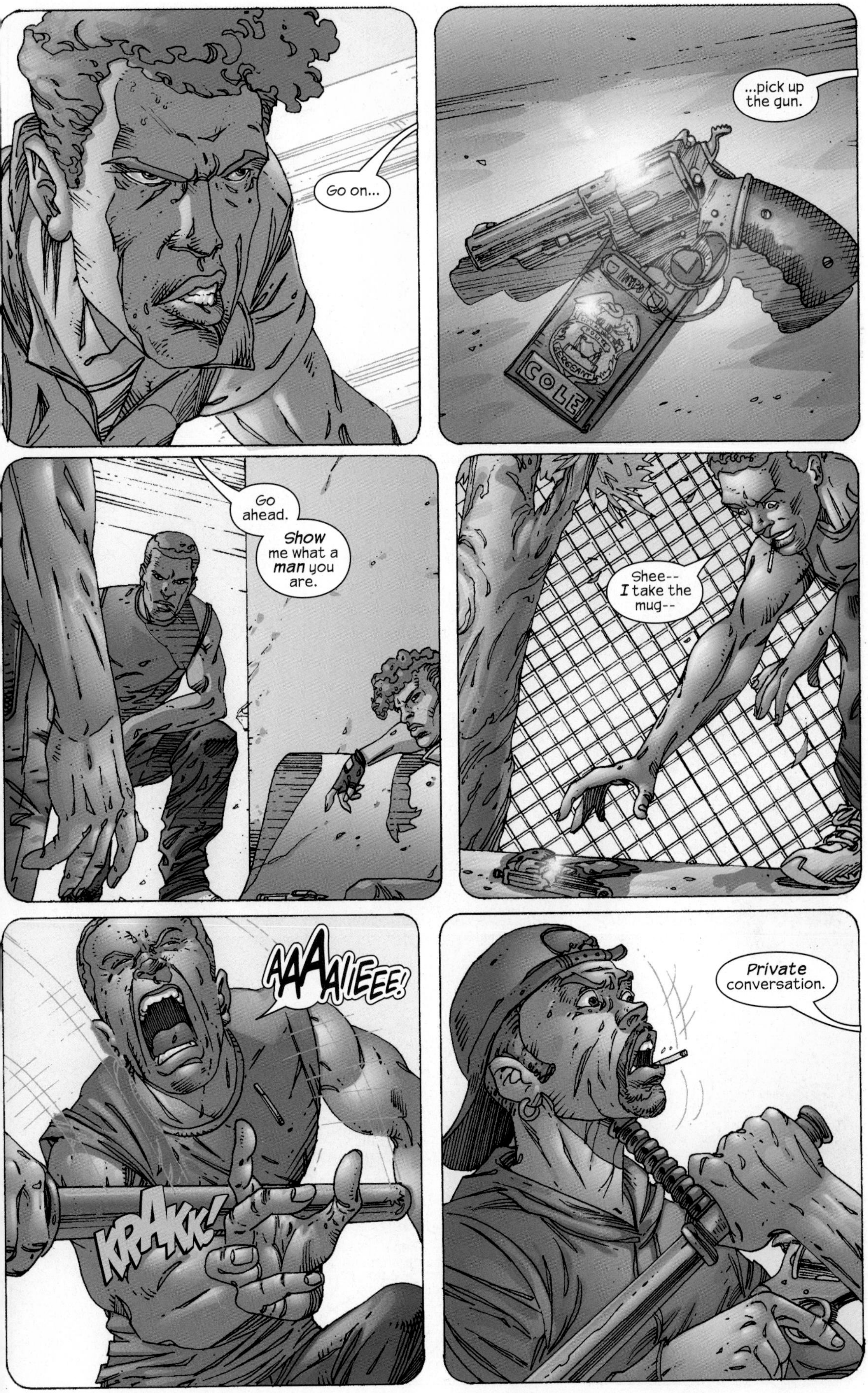

Go on...
...pick up the gun.
COLE
Go ahead.
Show me what a man you are.
Shee-- I take the mug--
AAAAAIIEEE!
KRAKK!
Private conversation.

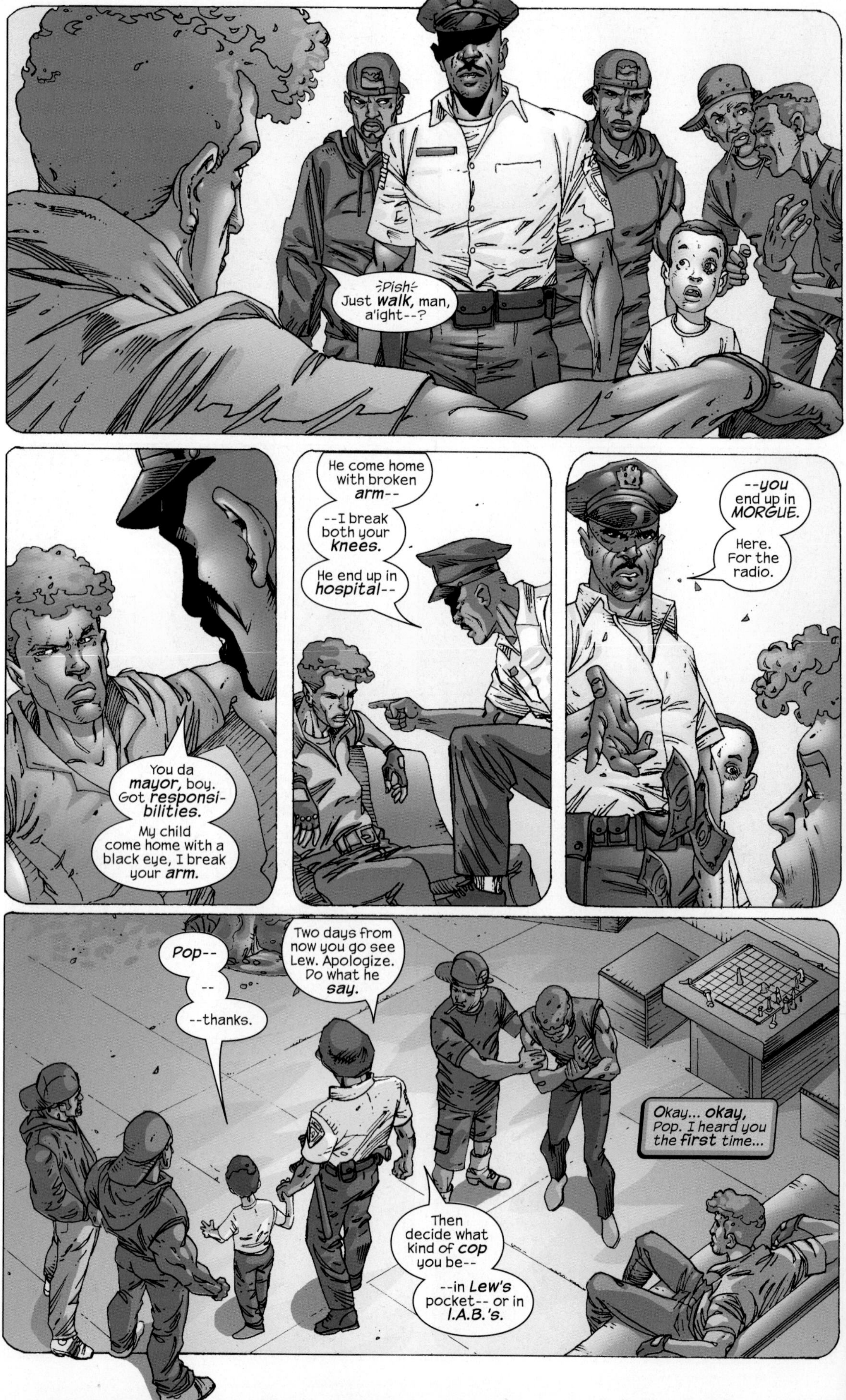

Pish
Just walk, man, a'ight--?
You da mayor, boy. Got responsi-bilities.
My child come home with a black eye, I break your arm.
He come home with broken arm--
--I break both your knees.
He end up in hospital--
--you end up in MORGUE.
Here. For the radio.
Pop--
--
--thanks.
Two days from now you go see Lew. Apologize. Do what he say.
Then decide what kind of cop you be--
--in Lew's pocket-- or in I.A.B.'s.
Okay... okay, Pop. I heard you the first time...

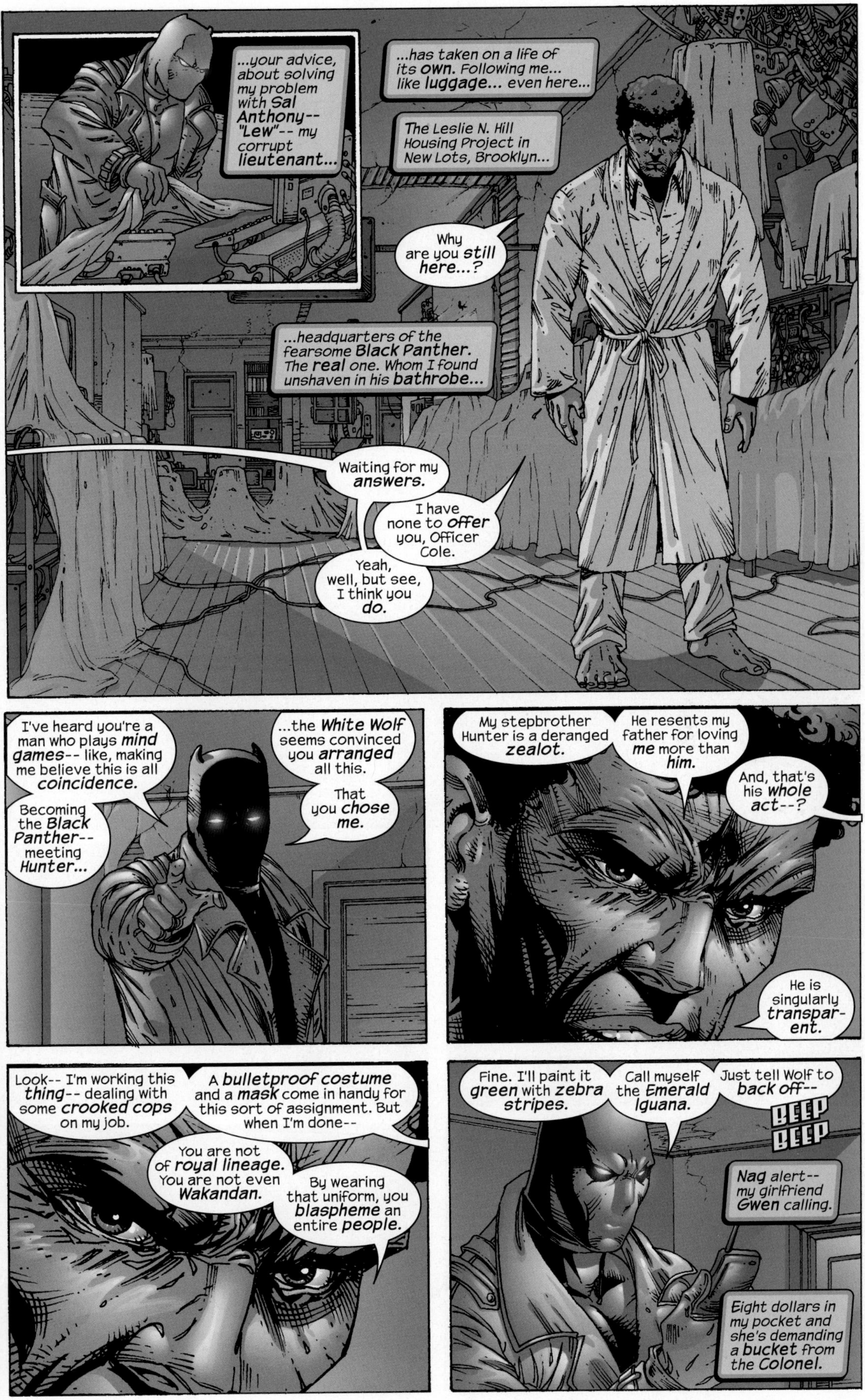
...your advice, about solving my problem with Sal Anthony-- "Lew"-- my corrupt lieutenant...
...has taken on a life of its own. Following me... like luggage... even here...
The Leslie N. Hill Housing Project in New Lots, Brooklyn...
Why are you still here...?
...headquarters of the fearsome Black Panther. The real one. Whom I found unshaven in his bathrobe...
Waiting for my answers.
I have none to offer you, Officer Cole.
Yeah, well, but see, I think you do.
I've heard you're a man who plays mind games-- like, making me believe this is all coincidence.
Becoming the Black Panther-- meeting Hunter...
...the White Wolf seems convinced you arranged all this.
That you chose me.
My stepbrother Hunter is a deranged zealot.
He resents my father for loving me more than him.
And, that's his whole act--?
He is singularly transpar-ent.
Look-- I'm working this thing-- dealing with some crooked cops on my job.
A bulletproof costume and a mask come in handy for this sort of assignment. But when I'm done--
You are not of royal lineage. You are not even Wakandan.
By wearing that uniform, you blaspheme an entire people.
Fine. I'll paint it green with zebra stripes.
Call myself the Emerald Iguana.
Just tell Wolf to back off--
BEEP BEEP
Nag alert-- my girlfriend Gwen calling.
Eight dollars in my pocket and she's demanding a bucket from the Colonel.

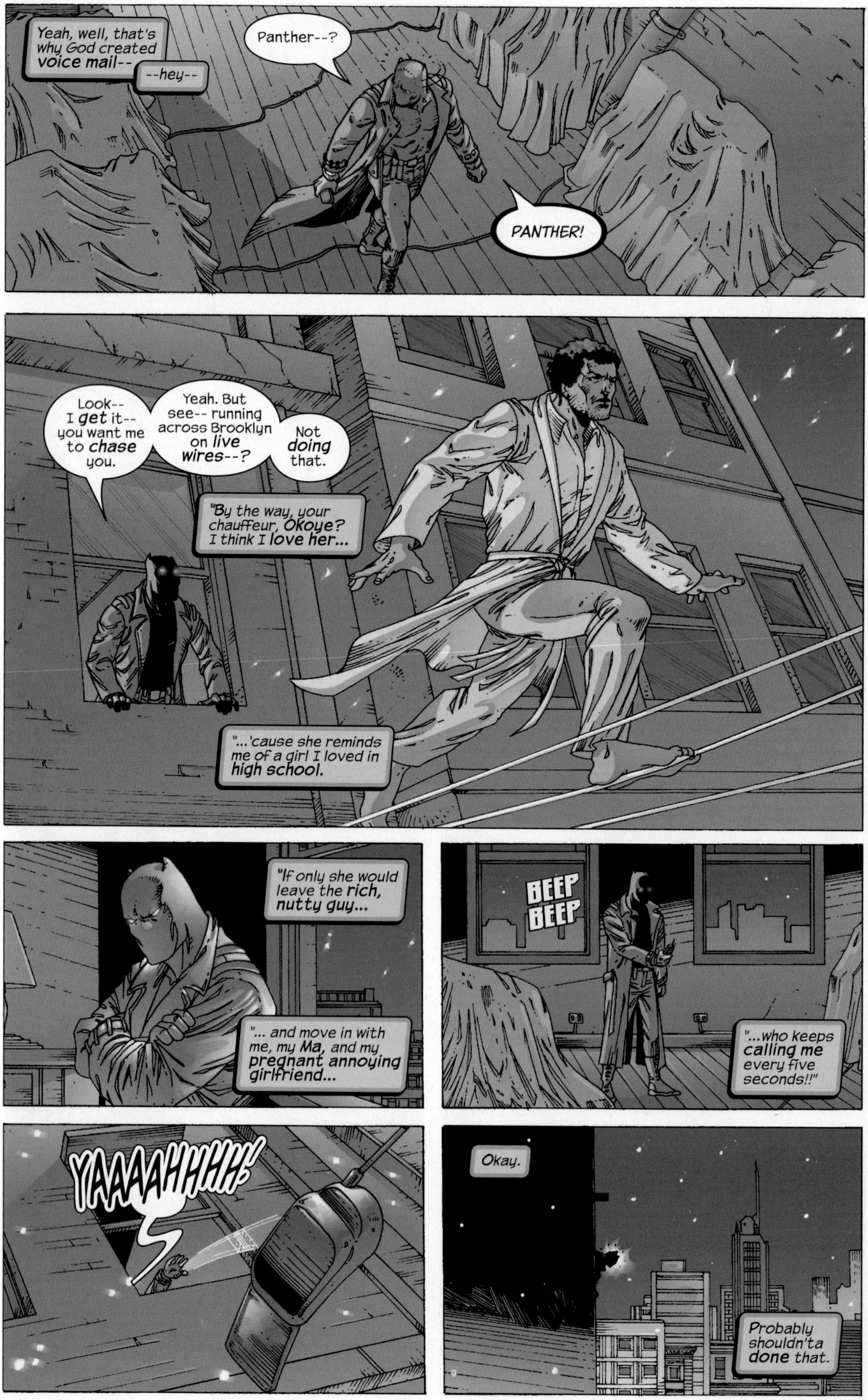

Yeah, well, that's why God created voice mail--
--hey--
Panther--?
PANTHER!
Look-- I get it-- you want me to chase you.
Yeah. But see-- running across Brooklyn on live wires--?
Not doing that.
"By the way, your chauffeur, Okoye? I think I love her...
"...'cause she reminds me of a girl I loved in high school.
"If only she would leave the rich, nutty guy...
"... and move in with me, my Ma, and my pregnant annoying girlfriend...
BEEP BEEP
"...who keeps calling me every five seconds!!"
YAAAAHHHH!
Okay.
Probably shouldn'ta done that.

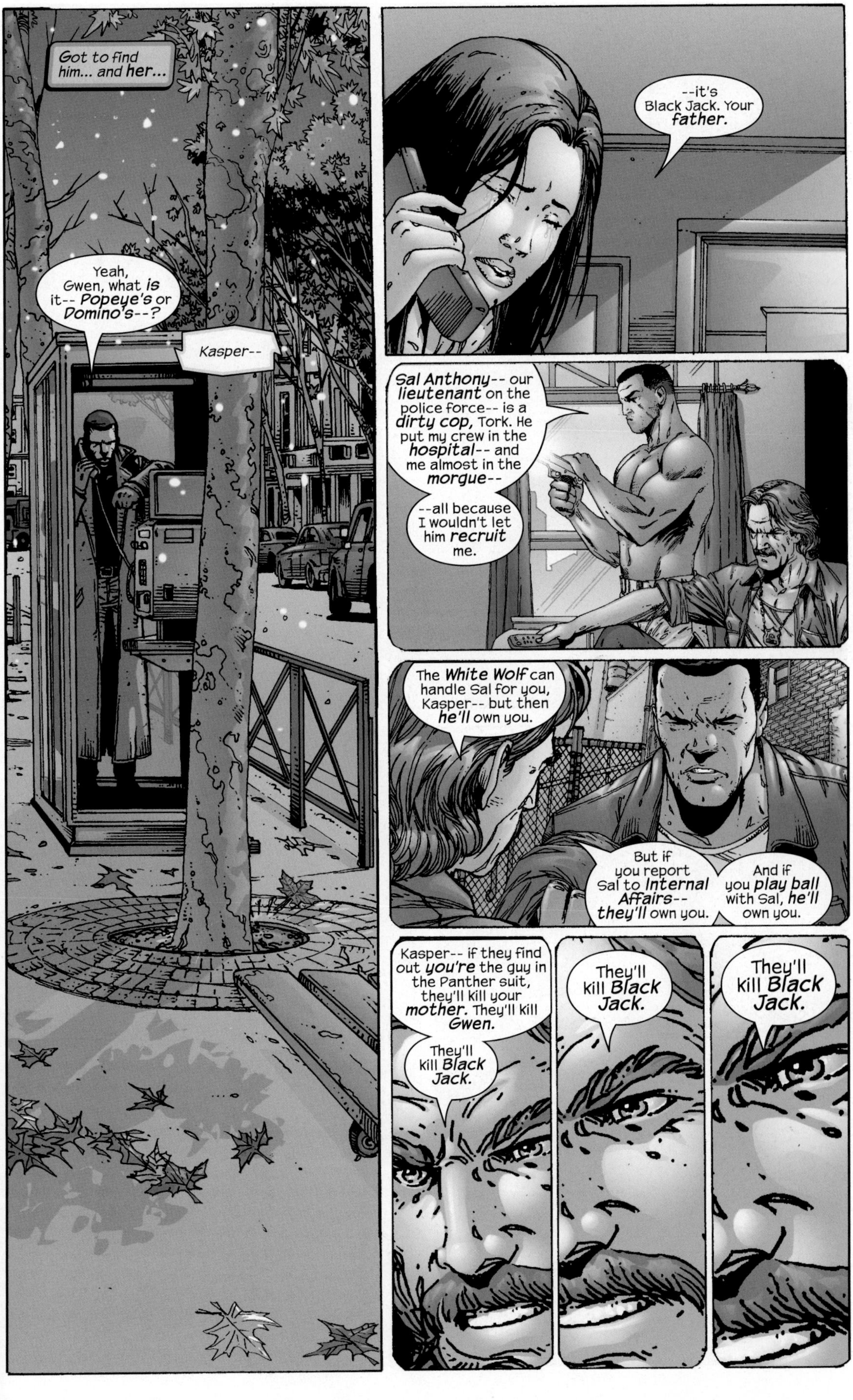
Got to find him... and her...
Yeah, Gwen, what is it-- Popeye's or Domino's--?
Kasper--
--it's Black Jack. Your father.
Sal Anthony-- our lieutenant on the police force-- is a dirty cop, Tork. He put my crew in the hospital-- and me almost in the morgue--
--all because I wouldn't let him recruit me.
The White Wolf can handle Sal for you, Kasper-- but then he'll own you.
But if you report Sal to Internal Affairs-- they'll own you.
And if you play ball with Sal, he'll own you.
Kasper-- if they find out you're the guy in the Panther suit, they'll kill your mother. They'll kill Gwen.
They'll kill Black Jack.
They'll kill Black Jack.
They'll kill Black Jack.

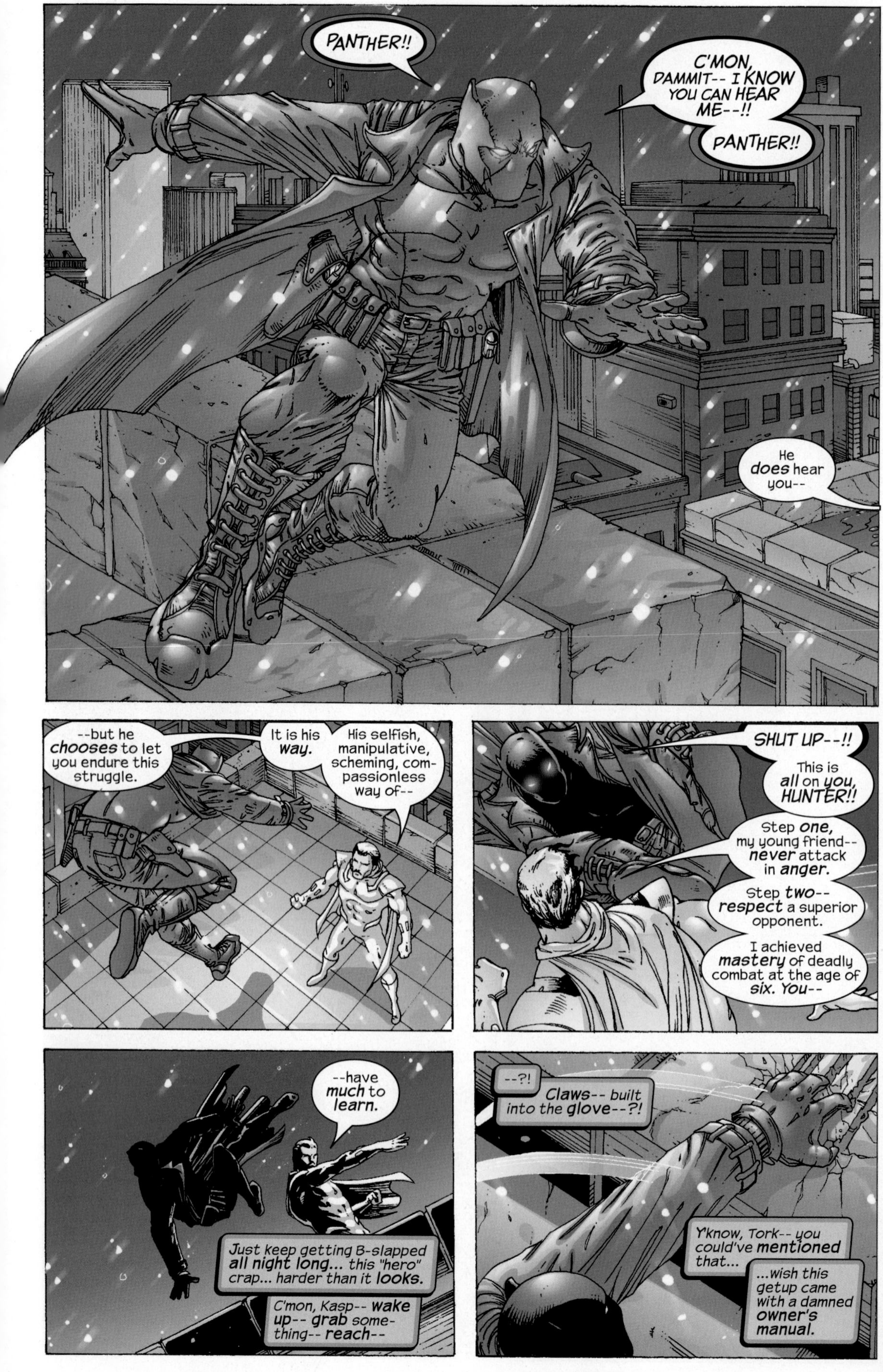
PANTHER!!
C'MON, DAMMIT-- I KNOW YOU CAN HEAR ME--!!
PANTHER!!
He does hear you--
--but he chooses to let you endure this struggle.
It is his way.
His selfish, manipulative, scheming, compassionless way of--
SHUT UP--!!
This is all on you, HUNTER!!
Step one, my young friend-- never attack in anger.
Step two-- respect a superior opponent.
I achieved mastery of deadly combat at the age of six. You--
--have much to learn.
Just keep getting B-slapped all night long... this "hero" crap... harder than it looks.
C'mon, Kasp-- wake up-- grab some-thing-- reach--
--?!
Claws-- built into the glove--?!
Y'know, Tork-- you could've mentioned that...
...wish this getup came with a damned owner's manual.

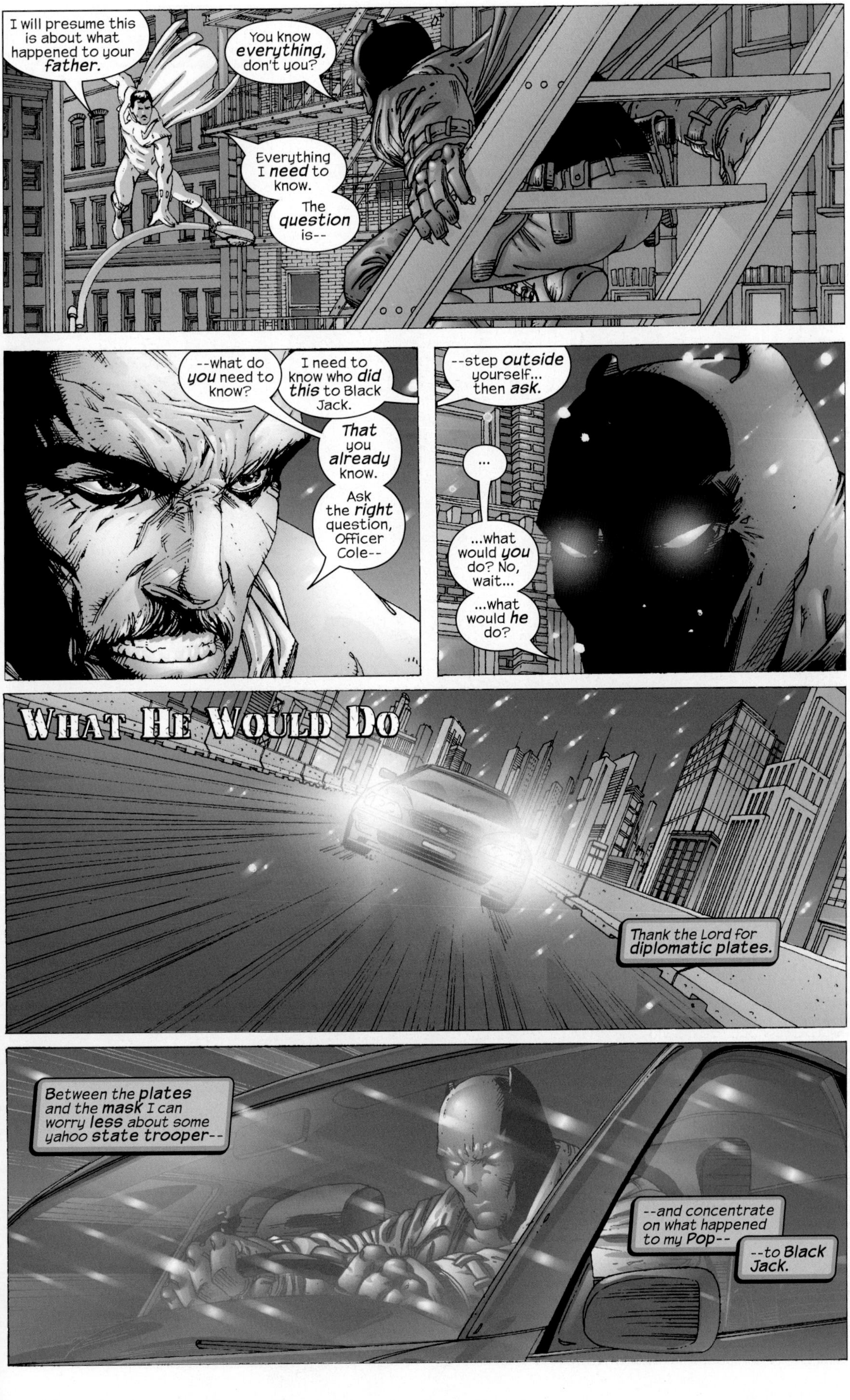
I will presume this is about what happened to your father.
You know everything, don't you?
Everything I need to know.
The question is--
--what do you need to know?
I need to know who did this to Black Jack.
That you already know.
Ask the right question, Officer Cole--
--step outside yourself... then ask.
...
...what would you do? No, wait...
...what would he do?
WHAT HE WOULD DO
Thank the Lord for diplomatic plates.
Between the plates and the mask I can worry less about some yahoo state trooper--
--and concentrate on what happened to my Pop--
--to Black Jack.

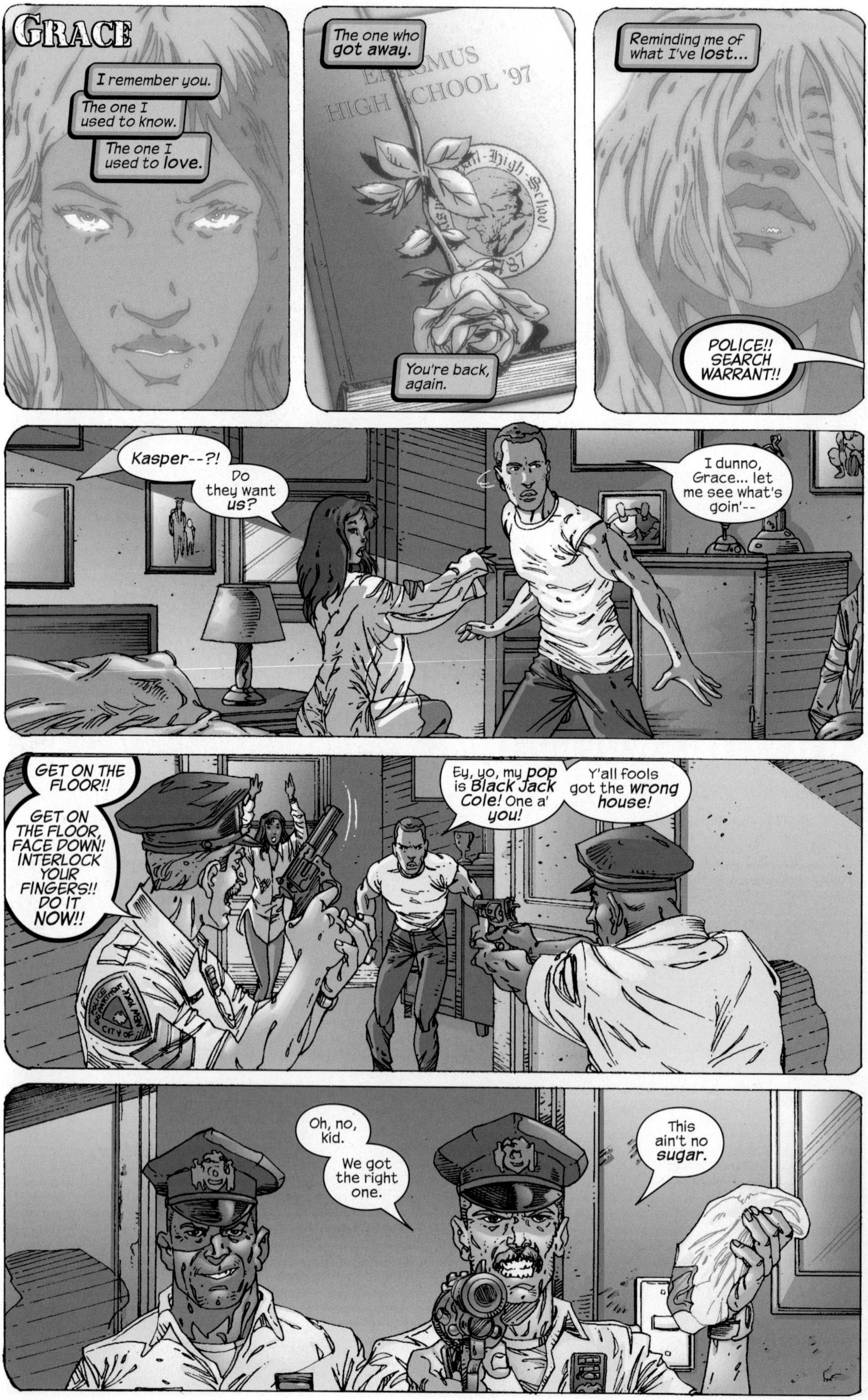
GRACE
I remember you.
The one I used to know.
The one I used to love.
The one who got away.
ERASMUS HIGH SCHOOL '97
You're back, again.
Reminding me of what I've lost...
POLICE!! SEARCH WARRANT!!
Kasper--?!
Do they want us?
I dunno, Grace... let me see what's goin'--
GET ON THE FLOOR!!
GET ON THE FLOOR, FACE DOWN! INTERLOCK YOUR FINGERS!! DO IT NOW!!
Ey, yo, my pop is Black Jack Cole! One a' you!
Y'all fools got the wrong house!
Oh, no, kid.
We got the right one.
This ain't no sugar.

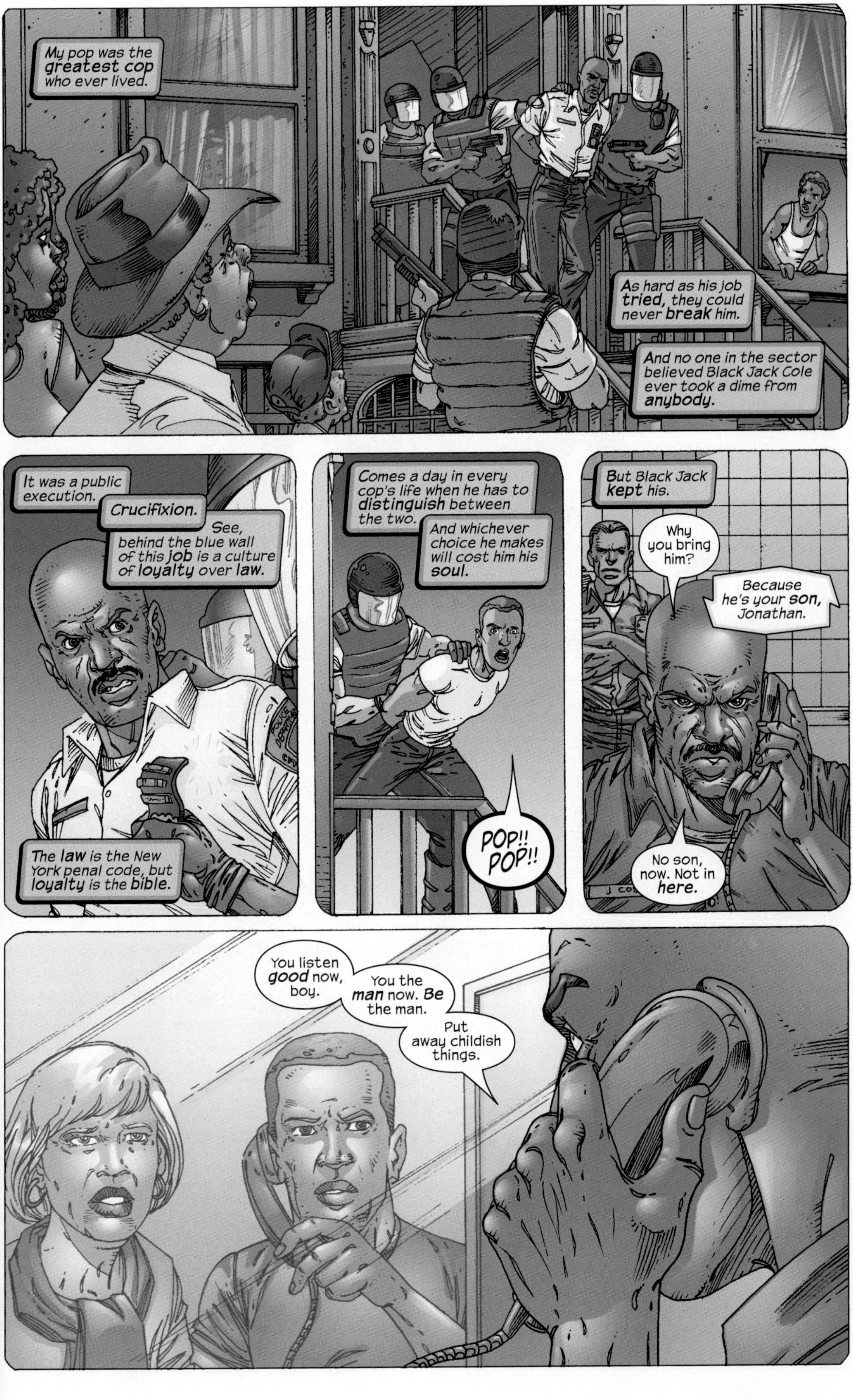
My pop was the greatest cop who ever lived.
As hard as his job tried, they could never break him.
And no one in the sector believed Black Jack Cole ever took a dime from anybody.
It was a public execution.
Crucifixion.
See, behind the blue wall of this job is a culture of loyalty over law.
The law is the New York penal code, but loyalty is the bible.
Comes a day in every cop's life when he has to distinguish between the two.
And whichever choice he makes will cost him his soul.
POP!! POP!!
But Black Jack kept his.
Why you bring him?
Because he's your son, Jonathan.
No son, now. Not in here.
You listen good now, boy.
You the man now. Be the man.
Put away childish things.

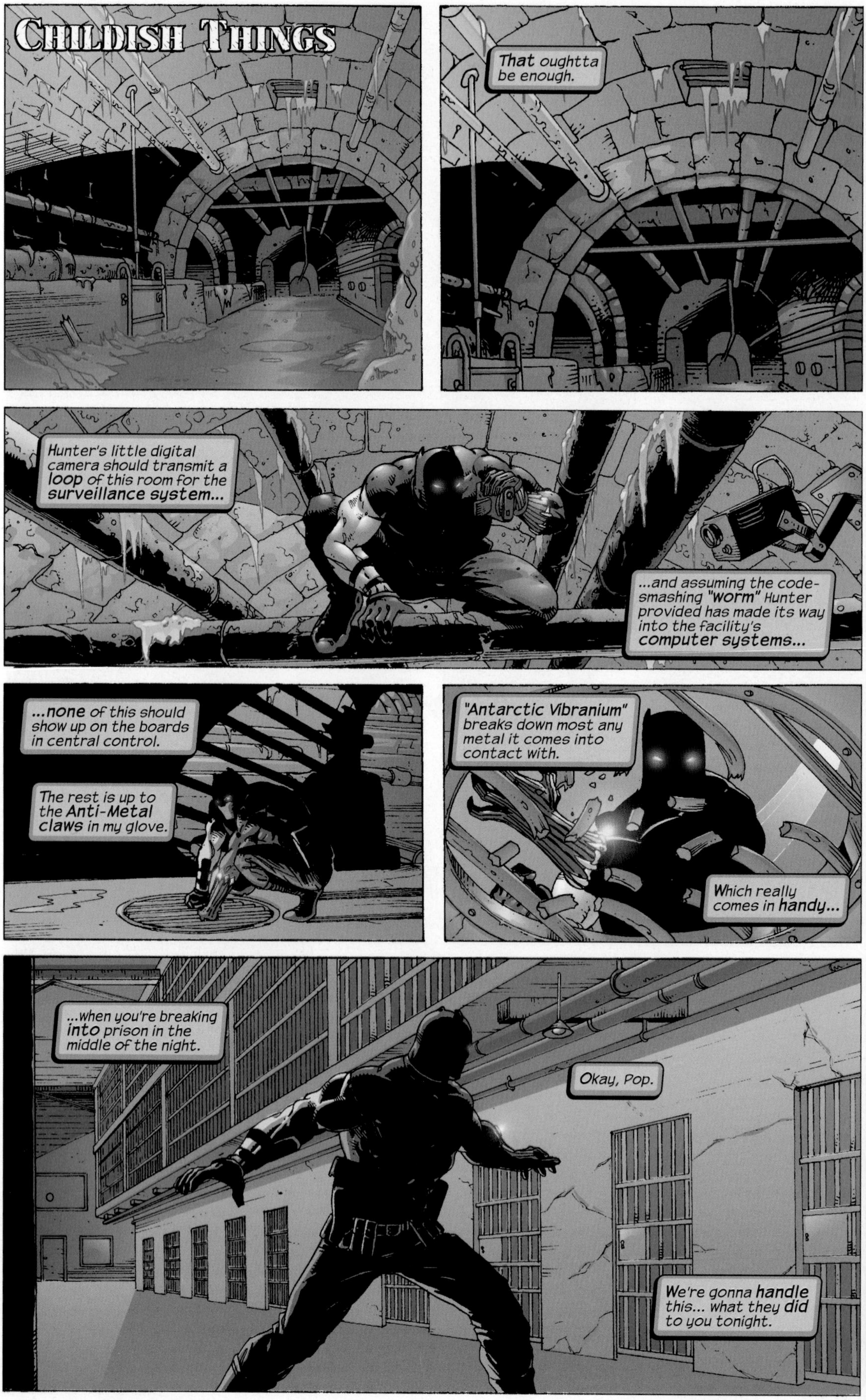
CHILDISH THINGS
That oughtta be enough.
Hunter's little digital camera should transmit a loop of this room for the surveillance system...
...and assuming the code-smashing "worm" Hunter provided has made its way into the facility's computer systems...
...none of this should show up on the boards in central control.
The rest is up to the Anti-Metal claws in my glove.
"Antarctic Vibranium" breaks down most any metal it comes into contact with.
Which really comes in handy...
...when you're breaking into prison in the middle of the night.
Okay, Pop.
We're gonna handle this... what they did to you tonight.

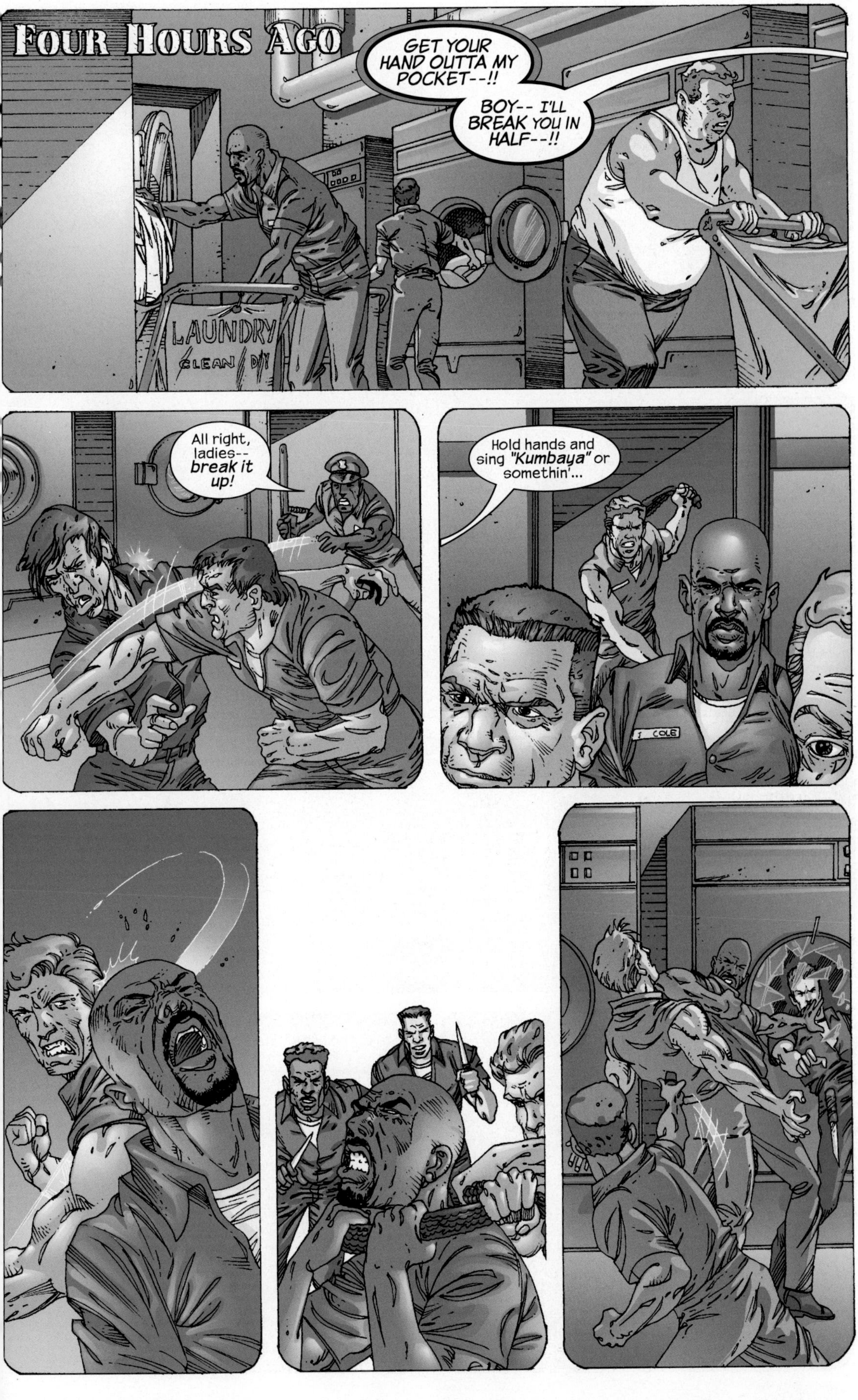
FOUR HOURS AGO
GET YOUR HAND OUTTA MY POCKET--!!
BOY-- I'LL BREAK YOU IN HALF--!!
LAUNDRY
CLEAN / DIY
All right, ladies-- break it up!
Hold hands and sing "Kumbaya" or somethin'...
J. COLE

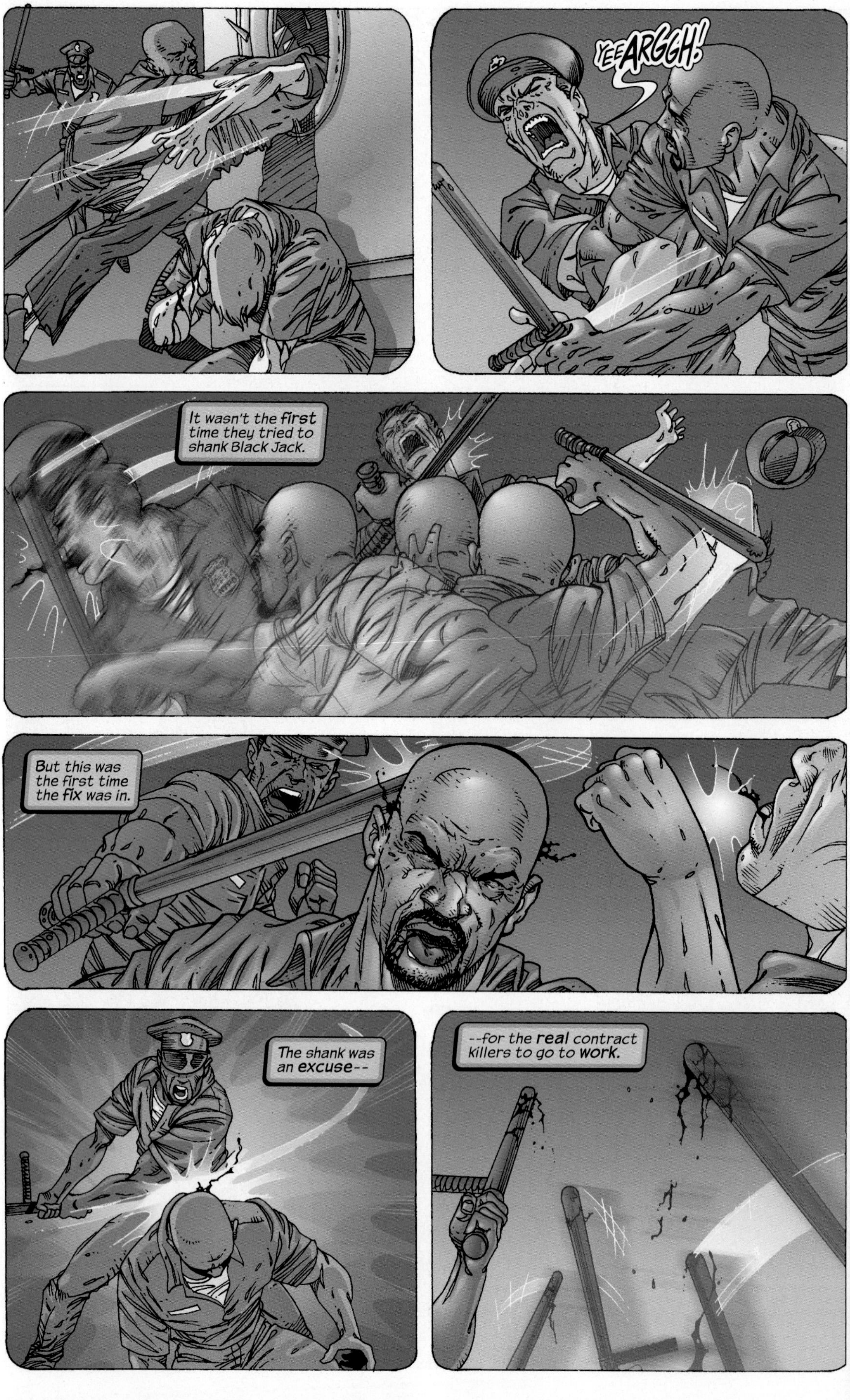
YEEARGGH!
It wasn't the first time they tried to shank Black Jack.
But this was the first time the fix was in.
The shank was an excuse--
--for the real contract killers to go to work.

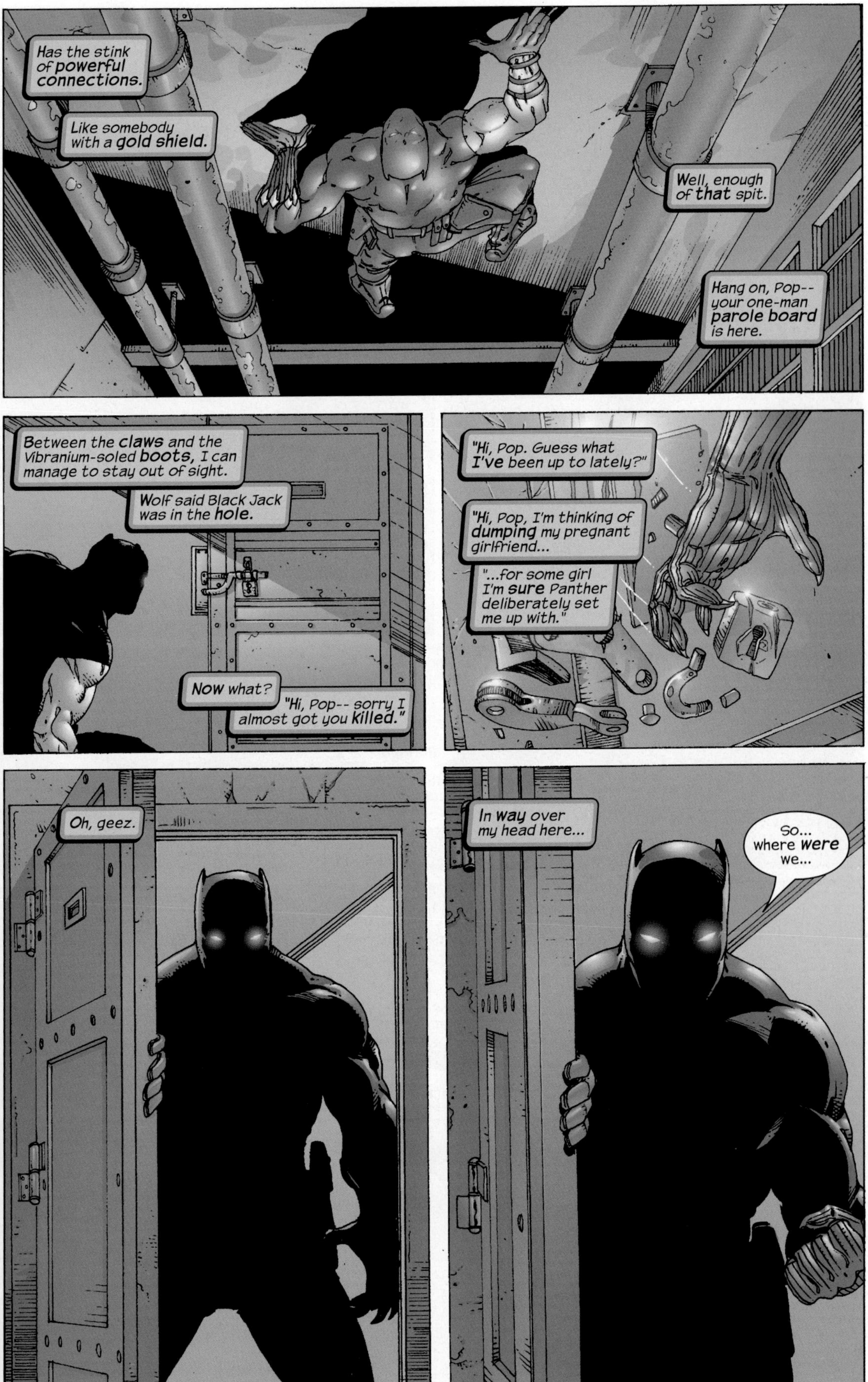
Has the stink of powerful connections.
Like somebody with a gold shield.
Well, enough of that spit.
Hang on, Pop-- your one-man parole board is here.
Between the claws and the Vibranium-soled boots, I can manage to stay out of sight.
Wolf said Black Jack was in the hole.
Now what?
"Hi, Pop-- sorry I almost got you killed."
"Hi, Pop. Guess what I've been up to lately?"
"Hi, Pop, I'm thinking of dumping my pregnant girlfriend...
"...for some girl I'm sure Panther deliberately set me up with."
Oh, geez.
In way over my head here...
So... where were we...

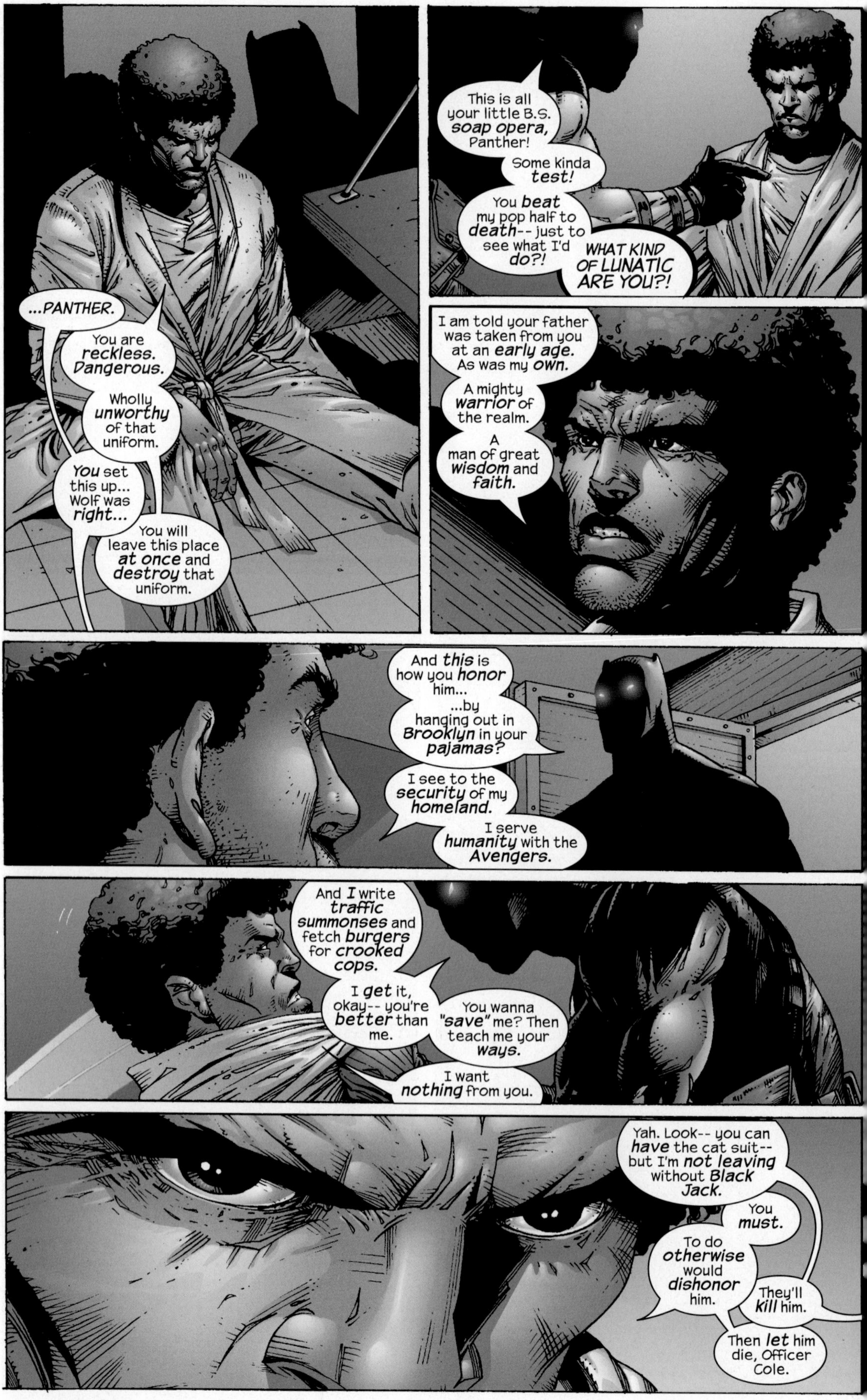

...PANTHER.
You are reckless. Dangerous.
Wholly unworthy of that uniform.
You set this up... Wolf was right...
You will leave this place at once and destroy that uniform.
This is all your little B.S. soap opera, Panther!
Some kinda test!
You beat my pop half to death-- just to see what I'd do?!
WHAT KIND OF LUNATIC ARE YOU?!
I am told your father was taken from you at an early age. As was my own.
A mighty warrior of the realm.
A man of great wisdom and faith.
And this is how you honor him...
...by hanging out in Brooklyn in your pajamas?
I see to the security of my homeland.
I serve humanity with the Avengers.
And I write traffic summonses and fetch burgers for crooked cops.
I get it, okay-- you're better than me.
You wanna "save" me? Then teach me your ways.
I want nothing from you.
Yah. Look-- you can have the cat suit-- but I'm not leaving without Black Jack.
You must.
To do otherwise would dishonor him.
They'll kill him.
Then let him die, Officer Cole.

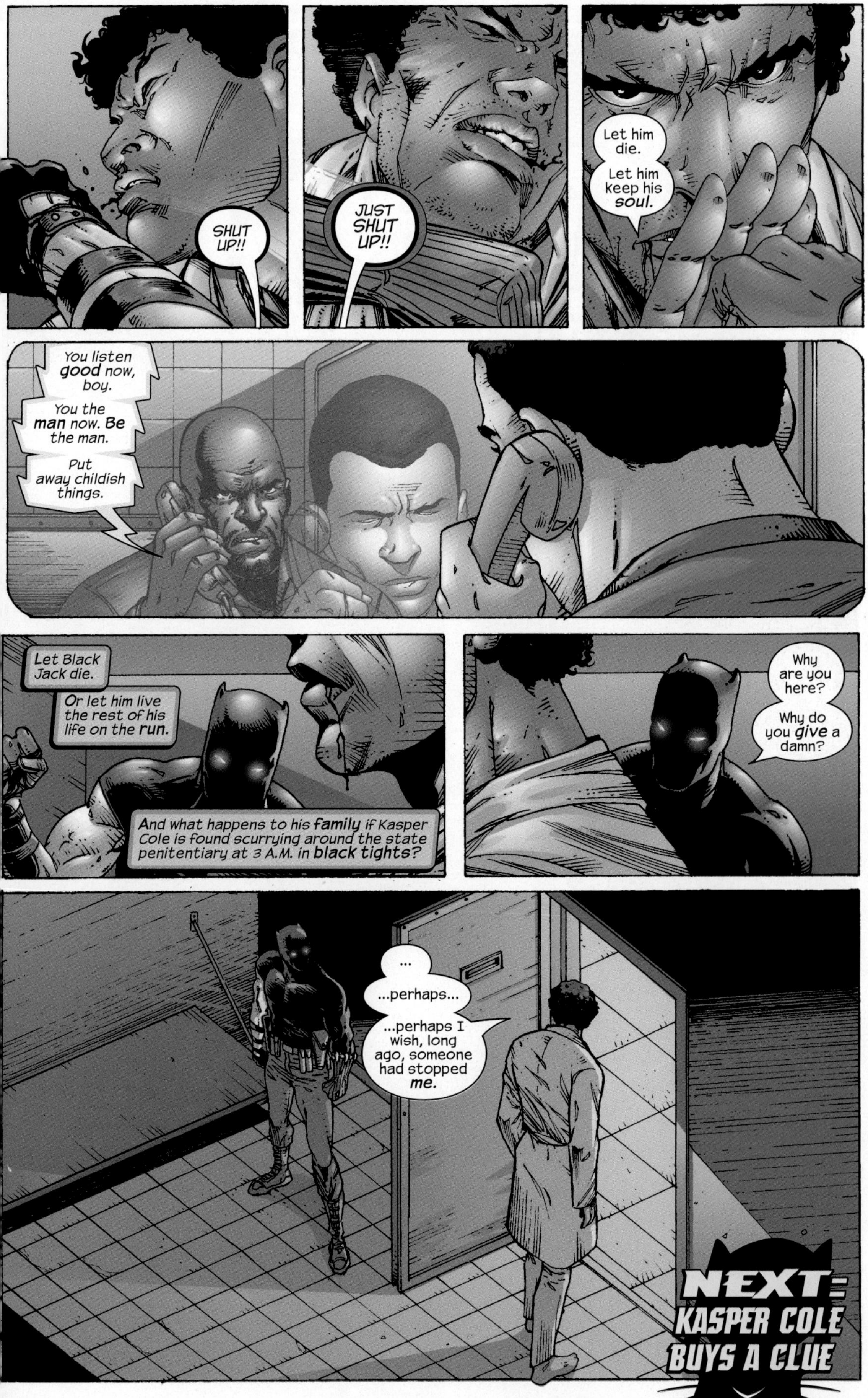
SHUT UP!!
JUST SHUT UP!!
Let him die.
Let him keep his soul.
You listen good now, boy.
You the man now. Be the man.
Put away childish things.
Let Black Jack die.
Or let him live the rest of his life on the run.
And what happens to his family if Kasper Cole is found scurrying around the state penitentiary at 3 A.M. in black tights?
Why are you here?
Why do you give a damn?
...
...perhaps...
...perhaps I wish, long ago, someone had stopped me.
NEXT: KASPER COLE BUYS A CLUE

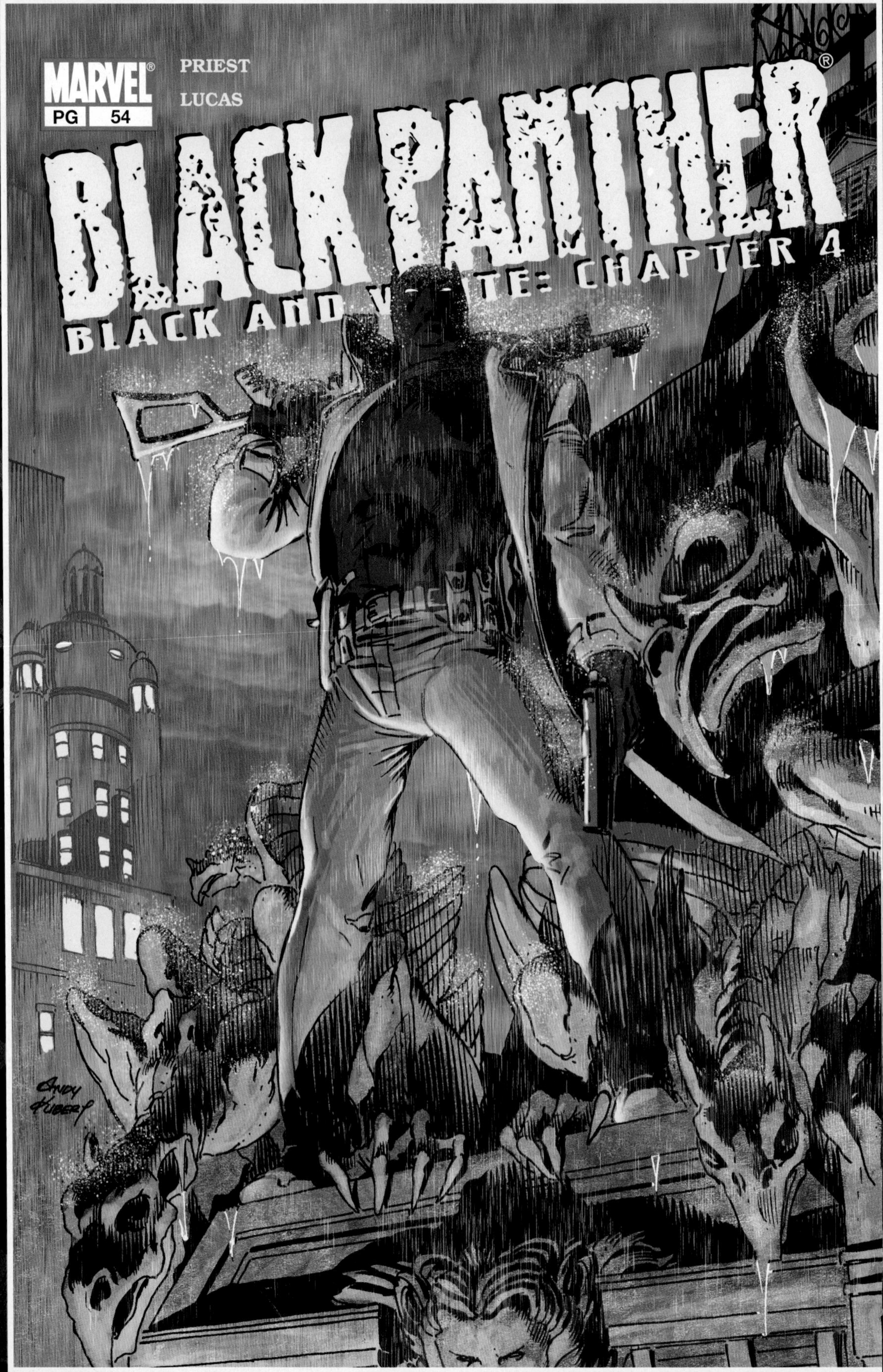

MARVEL
PG 54
PRIEST
LUCAS
BLACK PANTHER
BLACK AND W TE: CHAPTER 4
ANDY KUBERT

FACES

There once was the **greatest cop** who ever lived.

A proud and noble warrior, someone to be both **feared** and **respected**.

Jonathan Payton Cole.

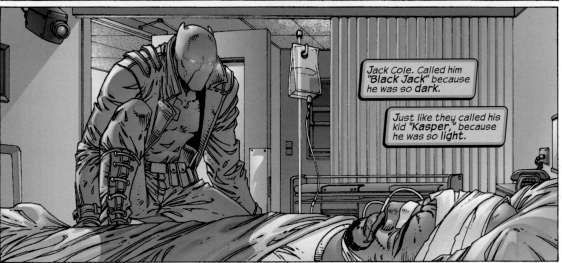

Jack Cole. Called him **"Black Jack"** because he was so **dark**.

Just like they called his kid **"Kasper,"** because he was so **light**.

Pop--

--what have they **done**... what have **I** done?

This was a **warning**... a **message**...

...from a **bad badge**.

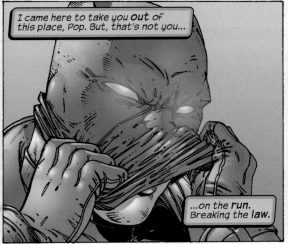

I came here to take you **out** of this place, Pop. But, that's not you...

...on the **run.** Breaking the **law.**

King T'Challa-- the **real** Black Panther-- made me see that.

Damn. I've **gotta** do better than this.

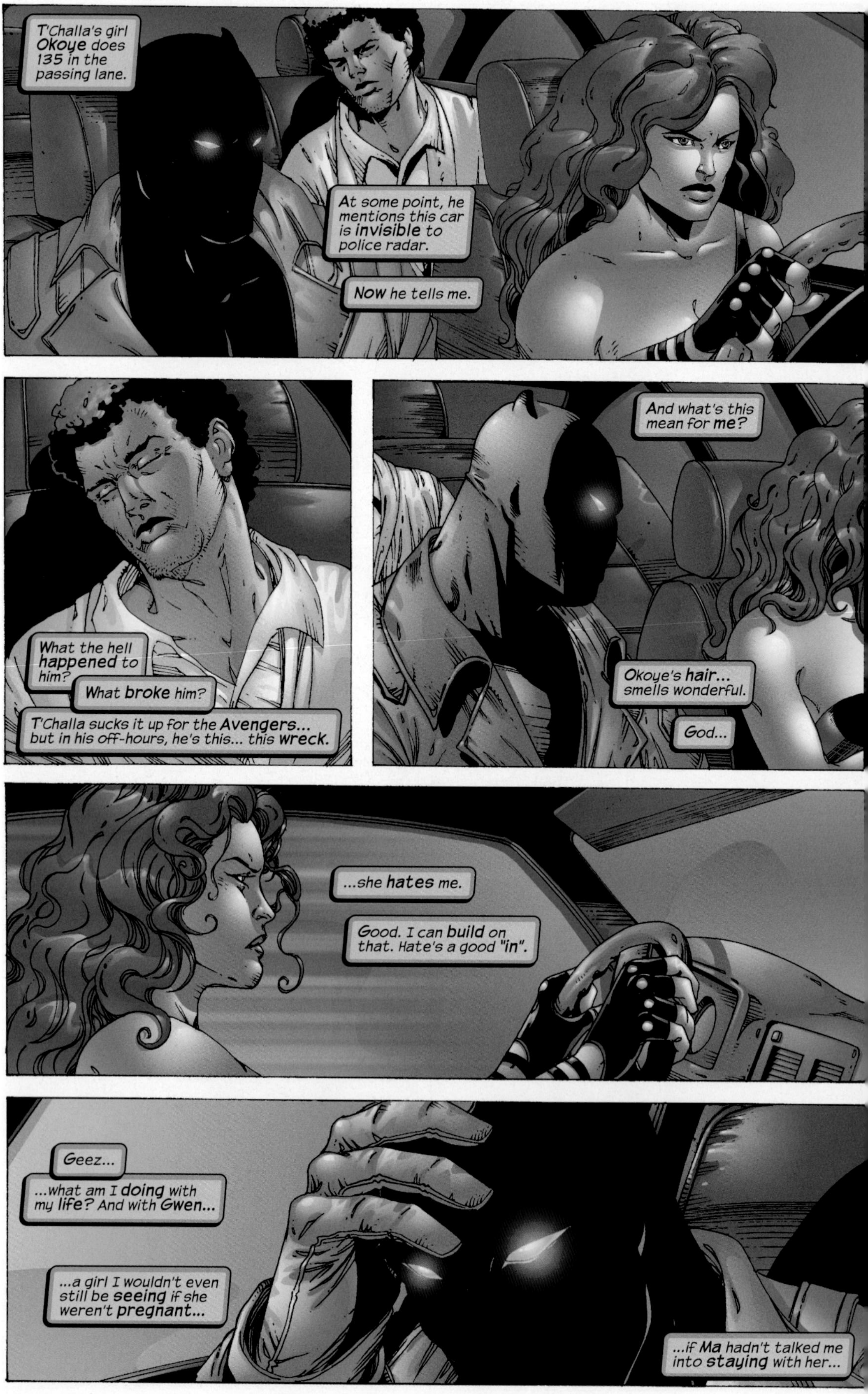
T'Challa's girl Okoye does 135 in the passing lane.
At some point, he mentions this car is invisible to police radar.
Now he tells me.
What the hell happened to him?
What broke him?
T'Challa sucks it up for the Avengers... but in his off-hours, he's this... this wreck.
And what's this mean for me?
Okoye's hair... smells wonderful.
God...
...she hates me.
Good. I can build on that. Hate's a good "in".
Geez...
...what am I doing with my life? And with Gwen...
...a girl I wouldn't even still be seeing if she weren't pregnant...
...if Ma hadn't talked me into staying with her...

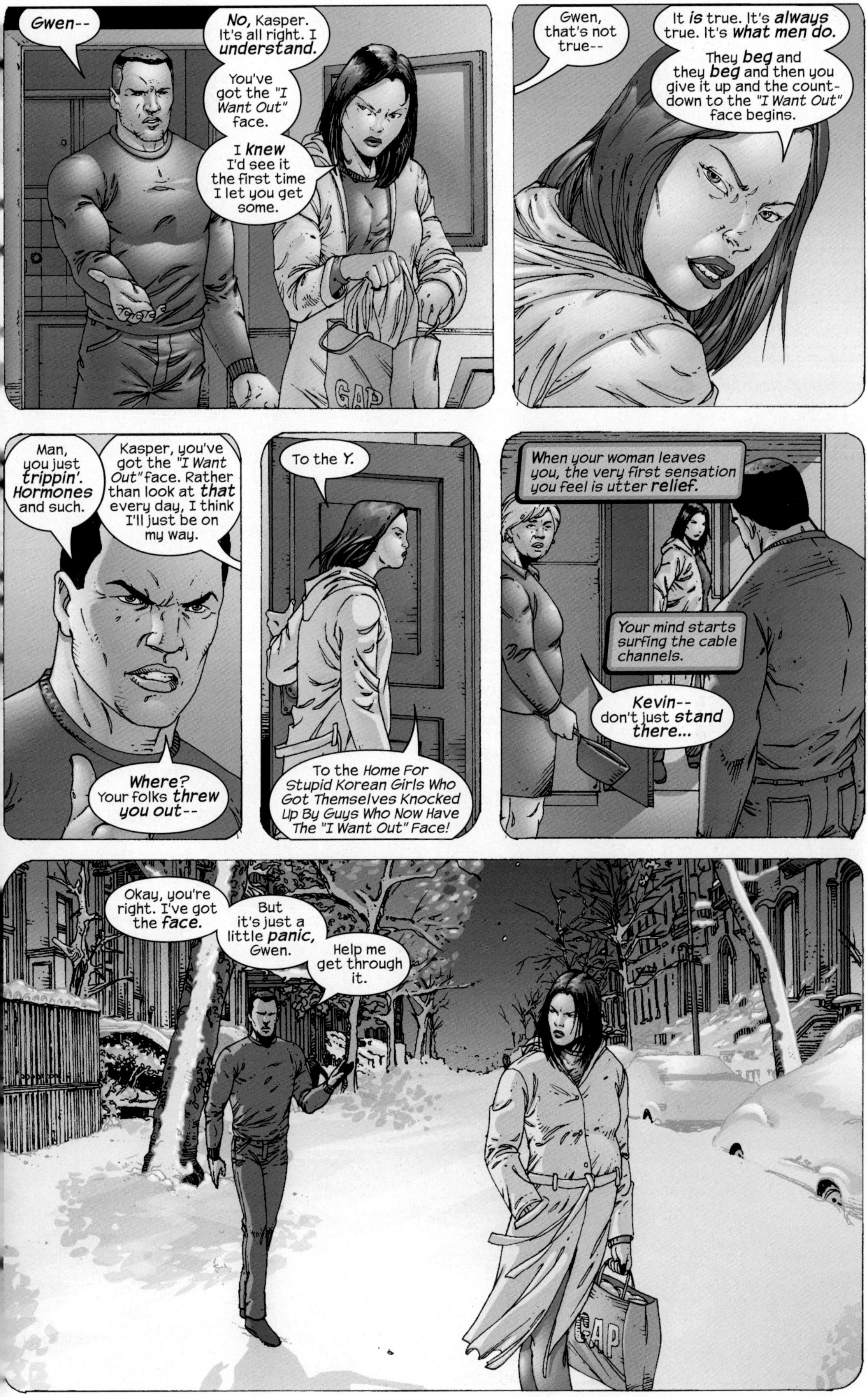
Gwen--
No, Kasper. It's all right. I understand.
You've got the "I Want Out" face.
I knew I'd see it the first time I let you get some.
Gwen, that's not true--
It is true. It's always true. It's what men do.
They beg and they beg and then you give it up and the count-down to the "I Want Out" face begins.
Man, you just trippin'. Hormones and such.
Kasper, you've got the "I Want Out" face. Rather than look at that every day, I think I'll just be on my way.
Where? Your folks threw you out--
To the Y.
To the Home For Stupid Korean Girls Who Got Themselves Knocked Up By Guys Who Now Have The "I Want Out" Face!
When your woman leaves you, the very first sensation you feel is utter relief.
Your mind starts surfing the cable channels.
Kevin-- don't just stand there...
Okay, you're right. I've got the face.
But it's just a little panic, Gwen.
Help me get through it.

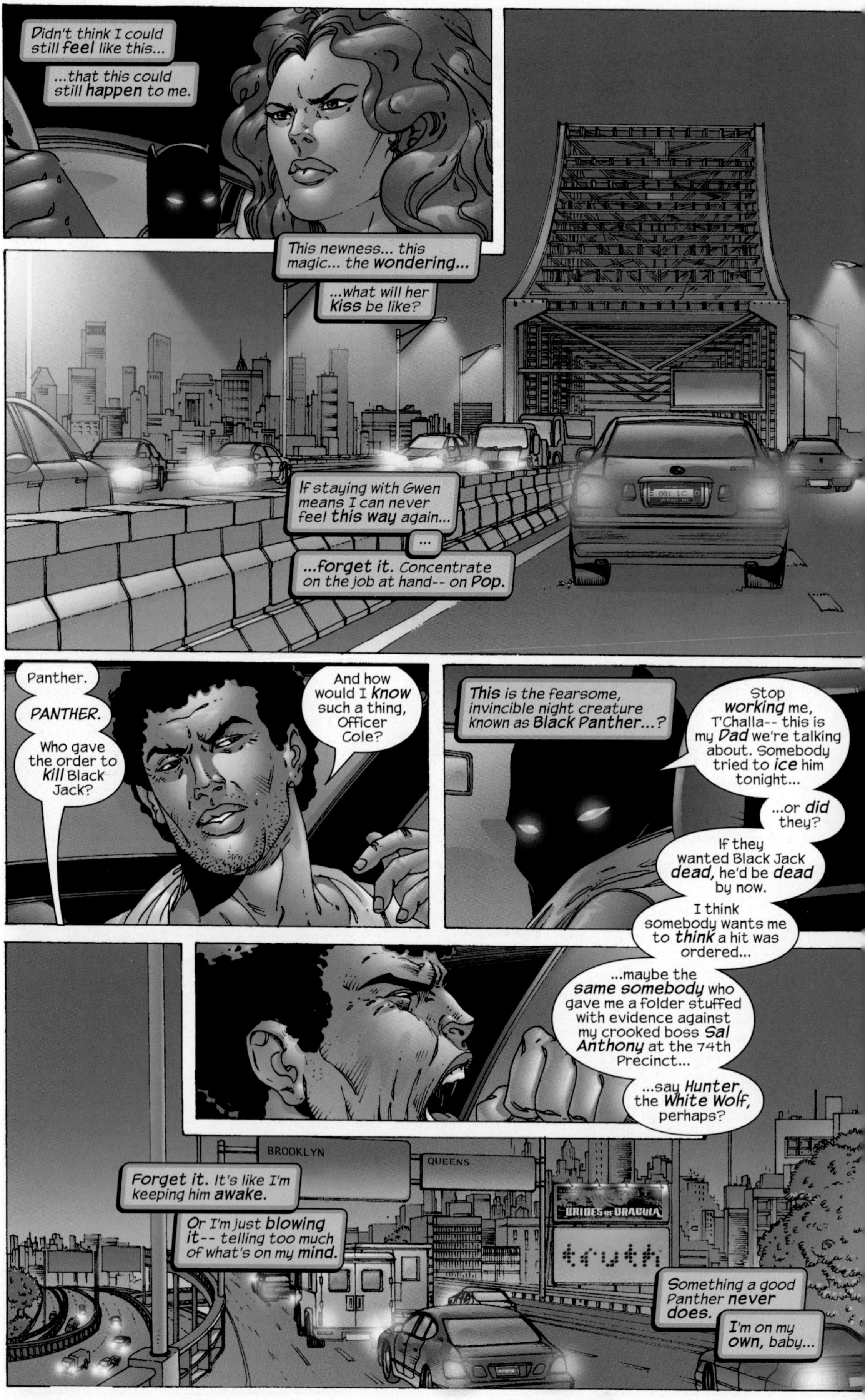

Didn't think I could still feel like this...
...that this could still happen to me.
This newness... this magic... the wondering...
...what will her kiss be like?
If staying with Gwen means I can never feel this way again...
...
...forget it. Concentrate on the job at hand-- on Pop.
Panther.
PANTHER.
Who gave the order to kill Black Jack?
And how would I know such a thing, Officer Cole?
This is the fearsome, invincible night creature known as Black Panther...?
Stop working me, T'Challa-- this is my Dad we're talking about. Somebody tried to ice him tonight...
...or did they?
If they wanted Black Jack dead, he'd be dead by now.
I think somebody wants me to think a hit was ordered...
...maybe the same somebody who gave me a folder stuffed with evidence against my crooked boss Sal Anthony at the 74th Precinct...
...say Hunter, the White Wolf, perhaps?
BROOKLYN
QUEENS
BRIDES OF DRACULA
truth
Forget it. It's like I'm keeping him awake.
Or I'm just blowing it-- telling too much of what's on my mind.
Something a good Panther never does.
I'm on my own, baby...

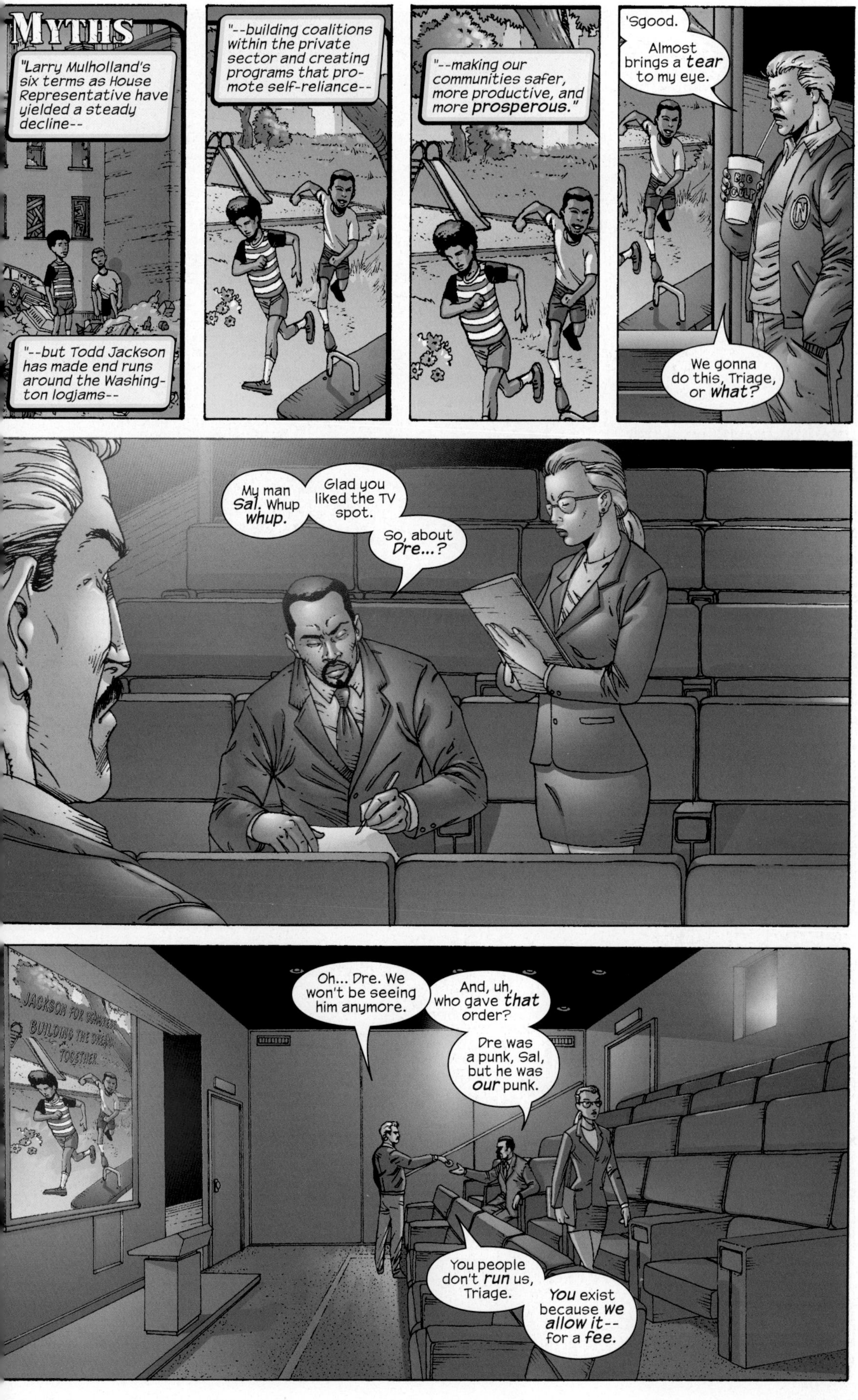
MYTHS
"Larry Mulholland's six terms as House Representative have yielded a steady decline--
"--but Todd Jackson has made end runs around the Washington logjams--
"--building coalitions within the private sector and creating programs that promote self-reliance--
"--making our communities safer, more productive, and more prosperous."
'Sgood.
Almost brings a tear to my eye.
We gonna do this, Triage, or what?
My man Sal. Whup whup.
Glad you liked the TV spot.
So, about Dre...?
JACKSON FOR CONGRESS
BUILDING THE DREAM TOGETHER
Oh... Dre. We won't be seeing him anymore.
And, uh, who gave that order?
Dre was a punk, Sal, but he was our punk.
You people don't run us, Triage.
You exist because we allow it-- for a fee.

You know, Sal, I think you actually *believe* that-- that you still *matter* in the scheme of things.

That we don't have people in your own ring of *crooked cops* who'd sell out your pasta-ass for Knicks tickets and a ham sandwich.

I believe in a *lot* of things, Triage-- Santa Claus, the Easter Bunny--

GRACE & TUMBALT

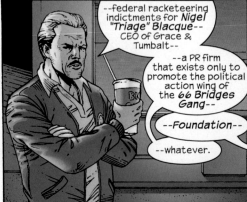

--federal racketeering indictments for *Nigel* "*Triage*" *Blacque*-- CEO of Grace & Tumbalt--

--a PR firm that exists only to promote the political action wing of the *66 Bridges Gang*--

--Foundation--

--whatever.

Okay, so I'm not your *prom date,* Sal.

Still... you shouldn't have moved on Dre without getting that spit *cleared.*

Upsets all them uh, *checks* and *balances* you in law enforcement have worked so diligently to propagate here in the *private sector.*

Can't have *anarchy,* Sal.

News footage-- just a *glimpse* of something we all missed from that *debacle* a couple weeks back--

--when *Dre* and *Scruggs* were making the *count split*--

--and the *Black Panther* dropped in. Only--

--I don't think that's the *real Panther.*

Since *when* does Panther bust up *drug deals?* Carry *guns?* Wear a *coat?*

He stole a *squad car* to escape-- why would Panther even *need* to escape?

Then he sets up *Dre* to get Scruggs *on tape?*

Sal-- giving me a *headache,* man.

Why the jump do *I* give a damn about any of this Panther crap?

Cuz the guy's too *amateur night* to be Agency or FBI...

...I think he might be a *badge.*

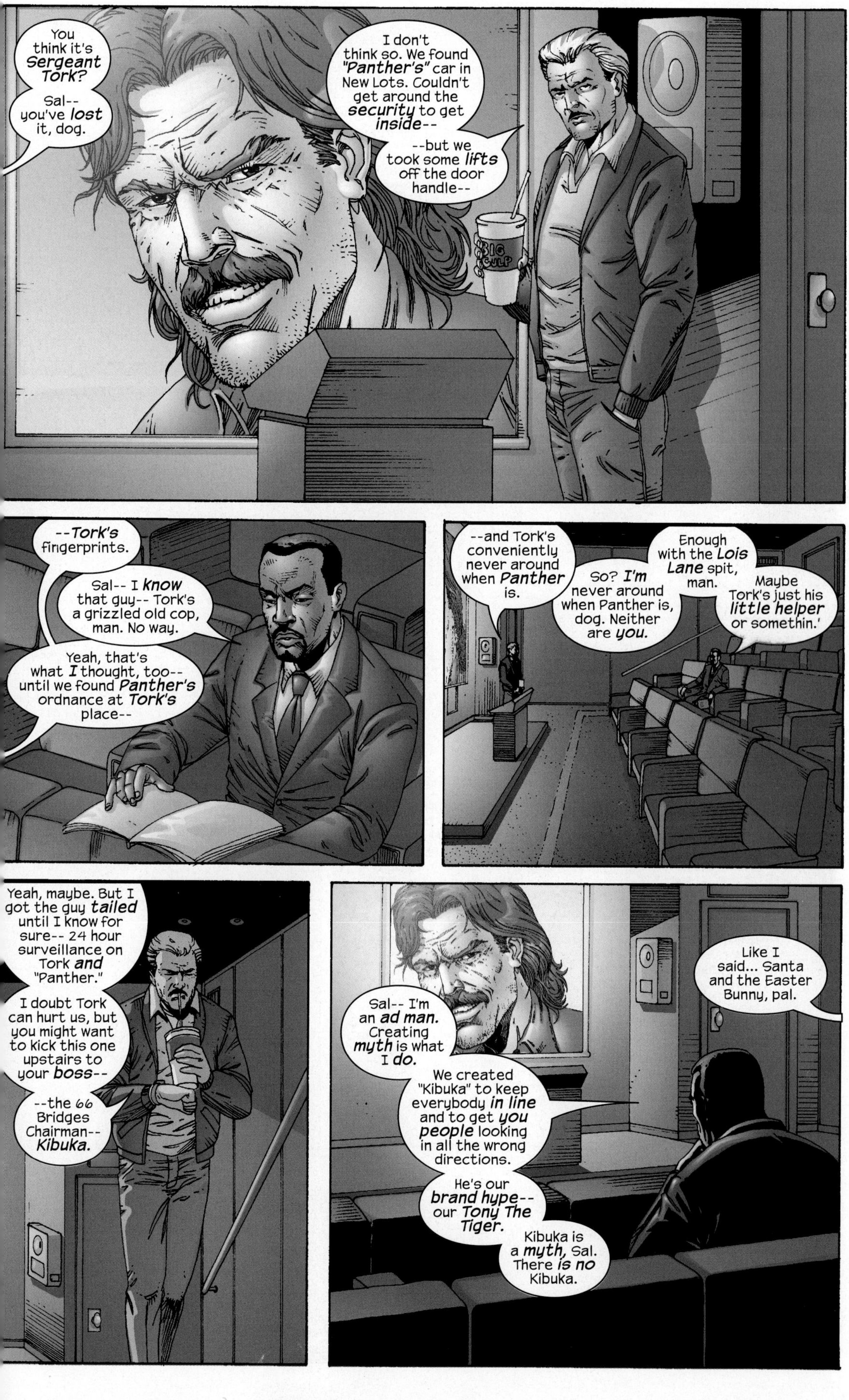
You think it's *Sergeant Tork?*
Sal-- you've *lost* it, dog.
I don't think so. We found *"Panther's"* car in New Lots. Couldn't get around the *security* to get *inside*--
--but we took some *lifts* off the door handle--
BIG GULP
--*Tork's* fingerprints.
Sal-- I *know* that guy-- Tork's a grizzled old cop, man. No way.
Yeah, that's what *I* thought, too-- until we found *Panther's* ordnance at *Tork's* place--
--and Tork's conveniently never around when *Panther* is.
So? *I'm* never around when Panther is, dog. Neither are *you.*
Enough with the *Lois Lane* spit, man.
Maybe Tork's just his *little helper* or somethin.'
Yeah, maybe. But I got the guy *tailed* until I know for sure-- 24 hour surveillance on Tork *and* "Panther."
I doubt Tork can hurt us, but you might want to kick this one upstairs to your *boss*--
--the 66 Bridges Chairman-- *Kibuka.*
Sal-- I'm an *ad man.* Creating *myth* is what I *do.*
We created "Kibuka" to keep everybody *in line* and to get *you people* looking in all the wrong directions.
He's our *brand hype*-- our *Tony The Tiger.*
Kibuka is a *myth,* Sal. There *is no* Kibuka.
Like I said... Santa and the Easter Bunny, pal.

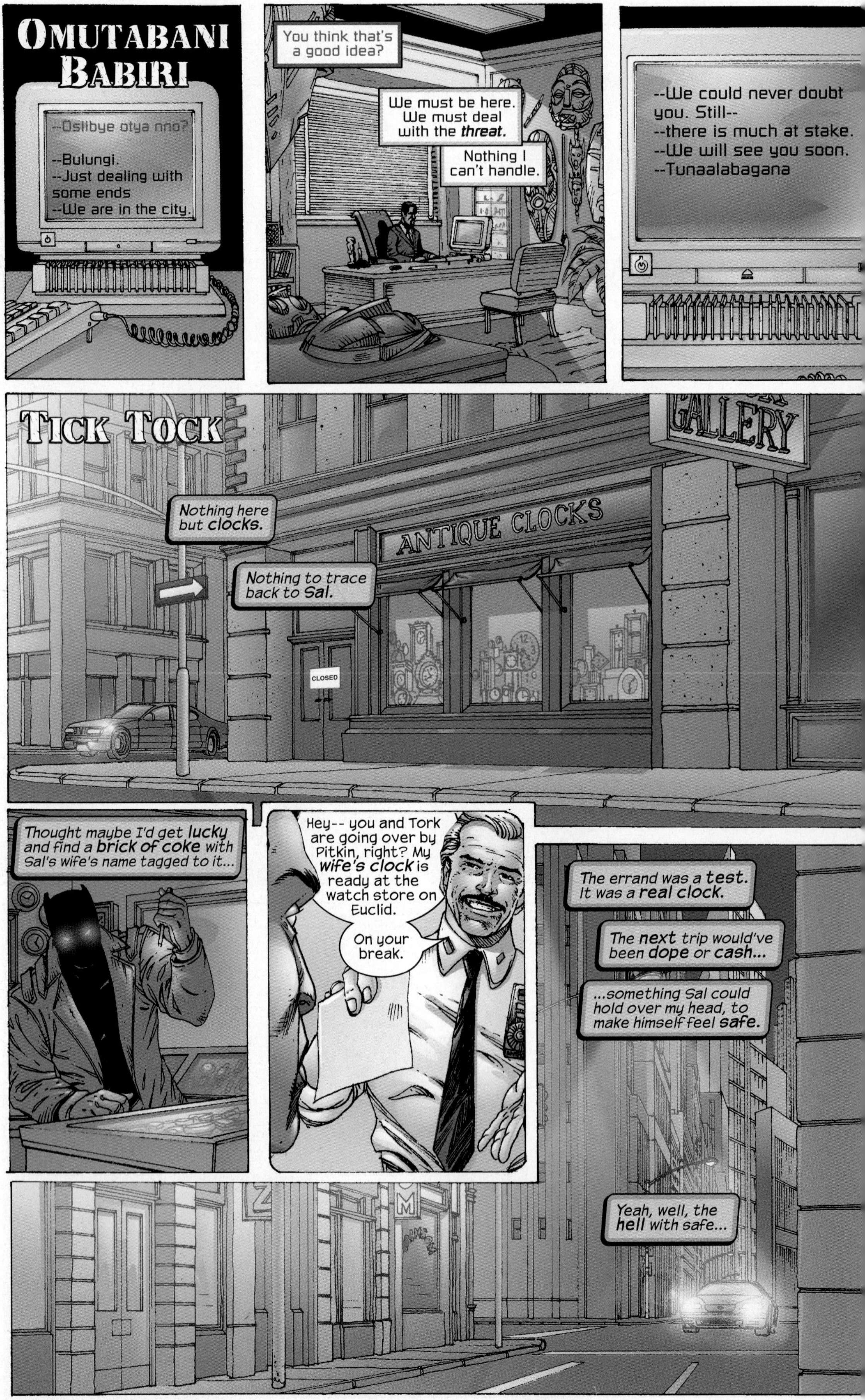

OMUTABANI BABIRI
--Osiibye otya nno?
--Bulungi.
--Just dealing with some ends
--We are in the city.
You think that's a good idea?
We must be here. We must deal with the threat.
Nothing I can't handle.
--We could never doubt you. Still--
--there is much at stake.
--We will see you soon.
--Tunaalabagana
TICK TOCK
GALLERY
Nothing here but clocks.
ANTIQUE CLOCKS
Nothing to trace back to Sal.
CLOSED
Thought maybe I'd get lucky and find a brick of coke with Sal's wife's name tagged to it...
Hey-- you and Tork are going over by Pitkin, right? My wife's clock is ready at the watch store on Euclid.
On your break.
The errand was a test. It was a real clock.
The next trip would've been dope or cash...
...something Sal could hold over my head, to make himself feel safe.
Yeah, well, the hell with safe...

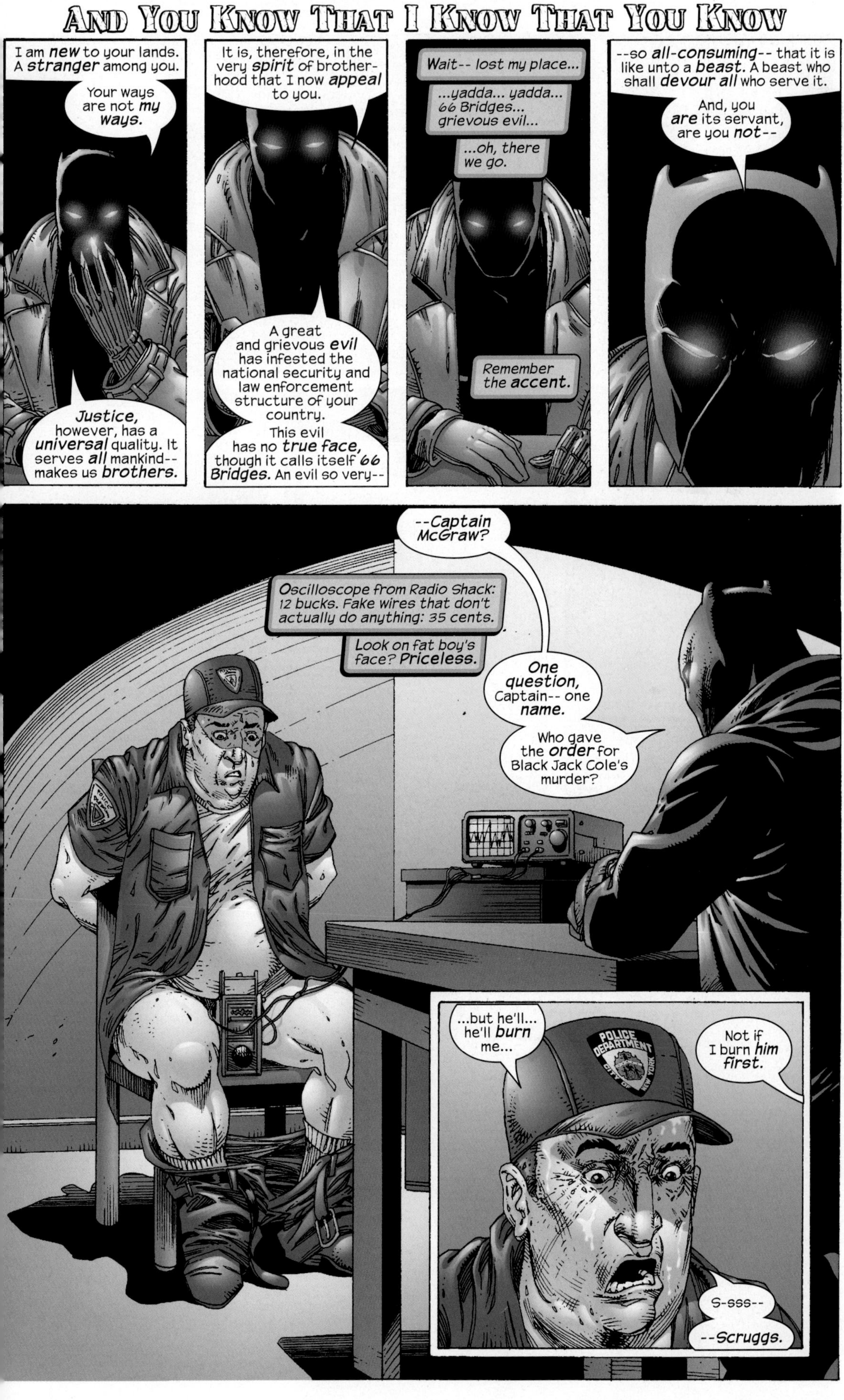
And You Know That I Know That You Know
I am new to your lands. A stranger among you.
Your ways are not my ways.
Justice, however, has a universal quality. It serves all mankind-- makes us brothers.
It is, therefore, in the very spirit of brotherhood that I now appeal to you.
A great and grievous evil has infested the national security and law enforcement structure of your country.
This evil has no true face, though it calls itself 66 Bridges. An evil so very--
Wait-- lost my place...
...yadda... yadda... 66 Bridges... grievous evil...
...oh, there we go.
Remember the accent.
--so all-consuming-- that it is like unto a beast. A beast who shall devour all who serve it.
And, you are its servant, are you not--
--Captain McGraw?
Oscilloscope from Radio Shack: 12 bucks. Fake wires that don't actually do anything: 35 cents.
Look on fat boy's face? Priceless.
One question, Captain-- one name.
Who gave the order for Black Jack Cole's murder?
...but he'll... he'll burn me...
Not if I burn him first.
POLICE DEPARTMENT CITY OF NEW YORK
S-sss--
--Scruggs.

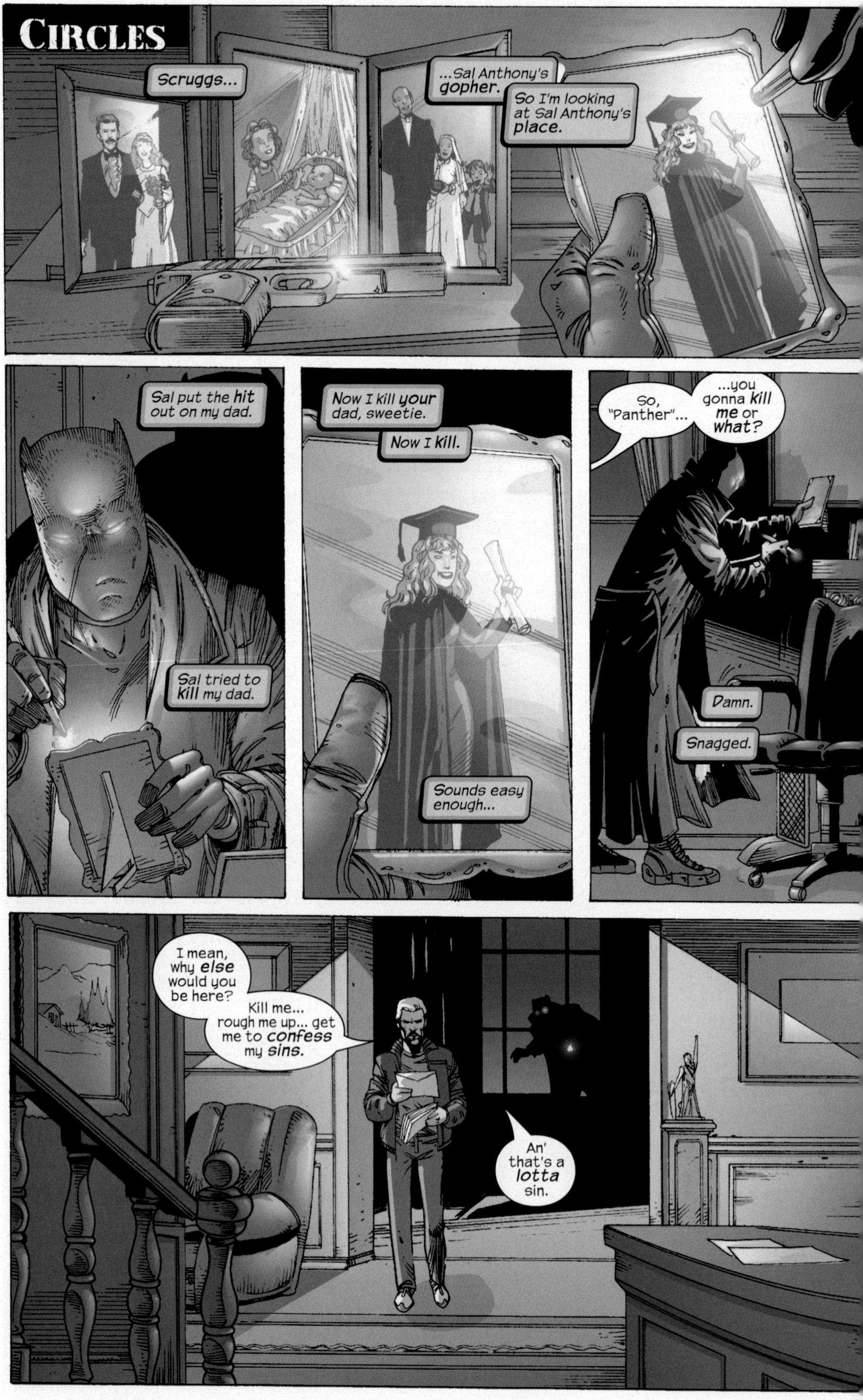
CIRCLES
Scruggs...
...Sal Anthony's gopher.
So I'm looking at Sal Anthony's place.
Sal put the hit out on my dad.
Sal tried to kill my dad.
Now I kill your dad, sweetie.
Now I kill.
Sounds easy enough...
So, "Panther"...
...you gonna kill me or what?
Damn.
Snagged.
I mean, why else would you be here?
Kill me... rough me up... get me to confess my sins.
An' that's a lotta sin.

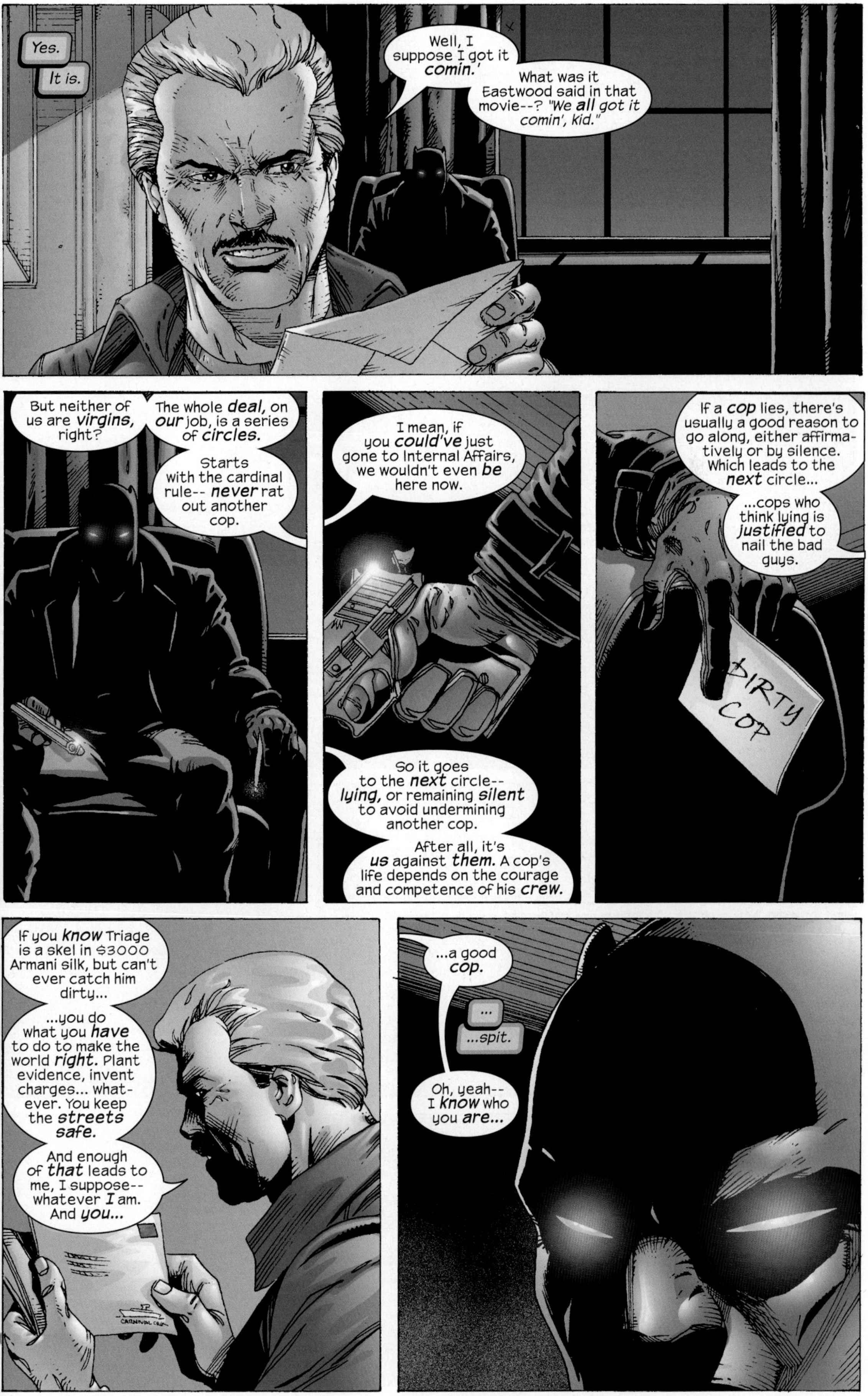
Yes.
It is.
Well, I suppose I got it comin.'
What was it Eastwood said in that movie--? "We all got it comin', kid."
But neither of us are virgins, right?
The whole deal, on our job, is a series of circles.
Starts with the cardinal rule-- never rat out another cop.
I mean, if you could've just gone to Internal Affairs, we wouldn't even be here now.
So it goes to the next circle-- lying, or remaining silent to avoid undermining another cop.
After all, it's us against them. A cop's life depends on the courage and competence of his crew.
If a cop lies, there's usually a good reason to go along, either affirmatively or by silence. Which leads to the next circle...
...cops who think lying is justified to nail the bad guys.
DIRTY COP
If you know Triage is a skel in $3000 Armani silk, but can't ever catch him dirty...
...you do what you have to do to make the world right. Plant evidence, invent charges... whatever. You keep the streets safe.
And enough of that leads to me, I suppose-- whatever I am. And you...
...a good cop.
...
...spit.
Oh, yeah-- I know who you are...

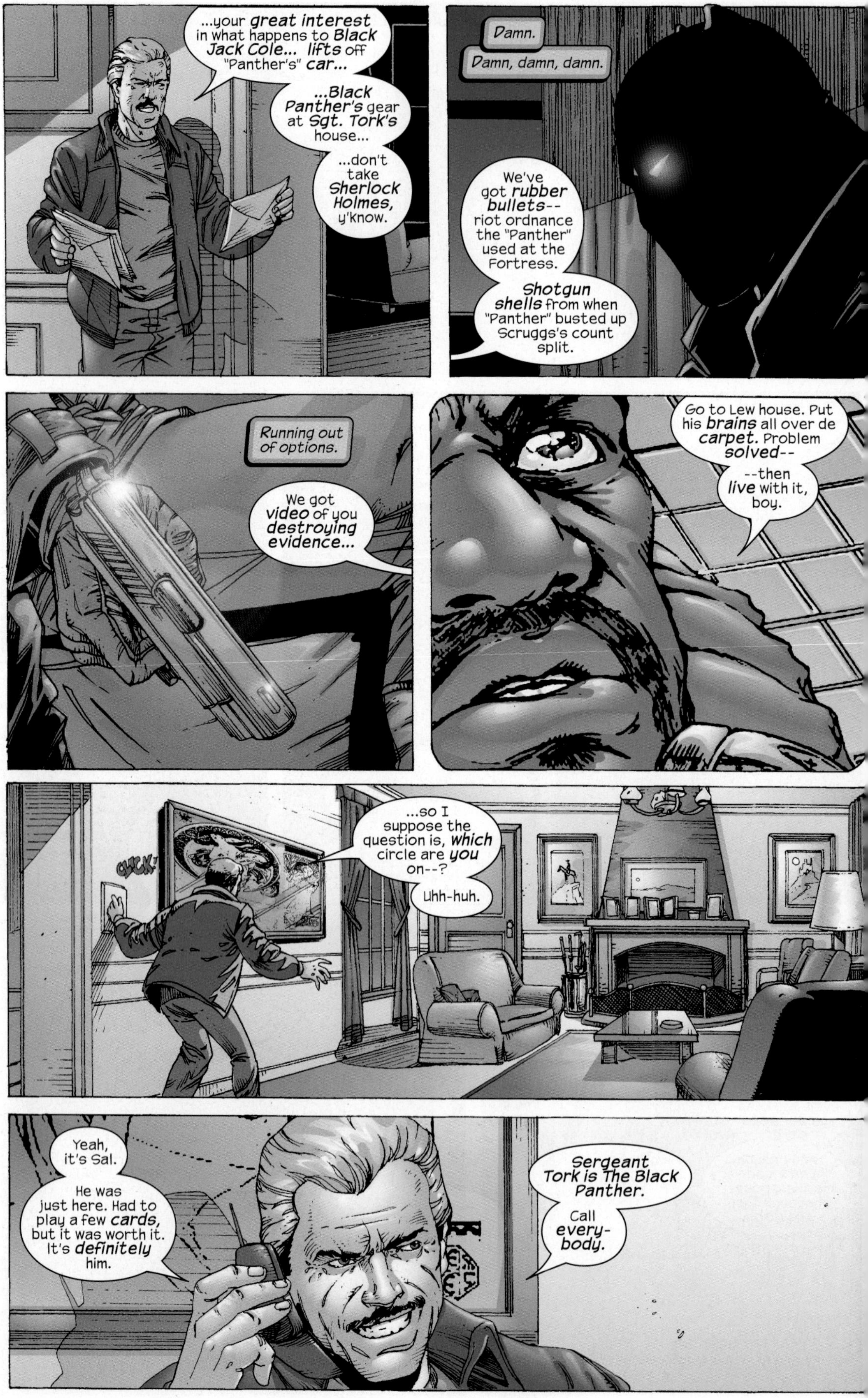

...your great interest in what happens to Black Jack Cole... lifts off "Panther's" car...
...Black Panther's gear at Sgt. Tork's house...
...don't take Sherlock Holmes, y'know.
Damn.
Damn, damn, damn.
We've got rubber bullets-- riot ordnance the "Panther" used at the Fortress.
Shotgun shells from when "Panther" busted up Scruggs's count split.
Running out of options.
We got video of you destroying evidence...
Go to Lew house. Put his brains all over de carpet. Problem solved--
--then live with it, boy.
CLICK!
...so I suppose the question is, which circle are you on--?
Uhh-huh.
Yeah, it's Sal.
He was just here. Had to play a few cards, but it was worth it. It's definitely him.
Sergeant Tork is The Black Panther.
Call every-body.

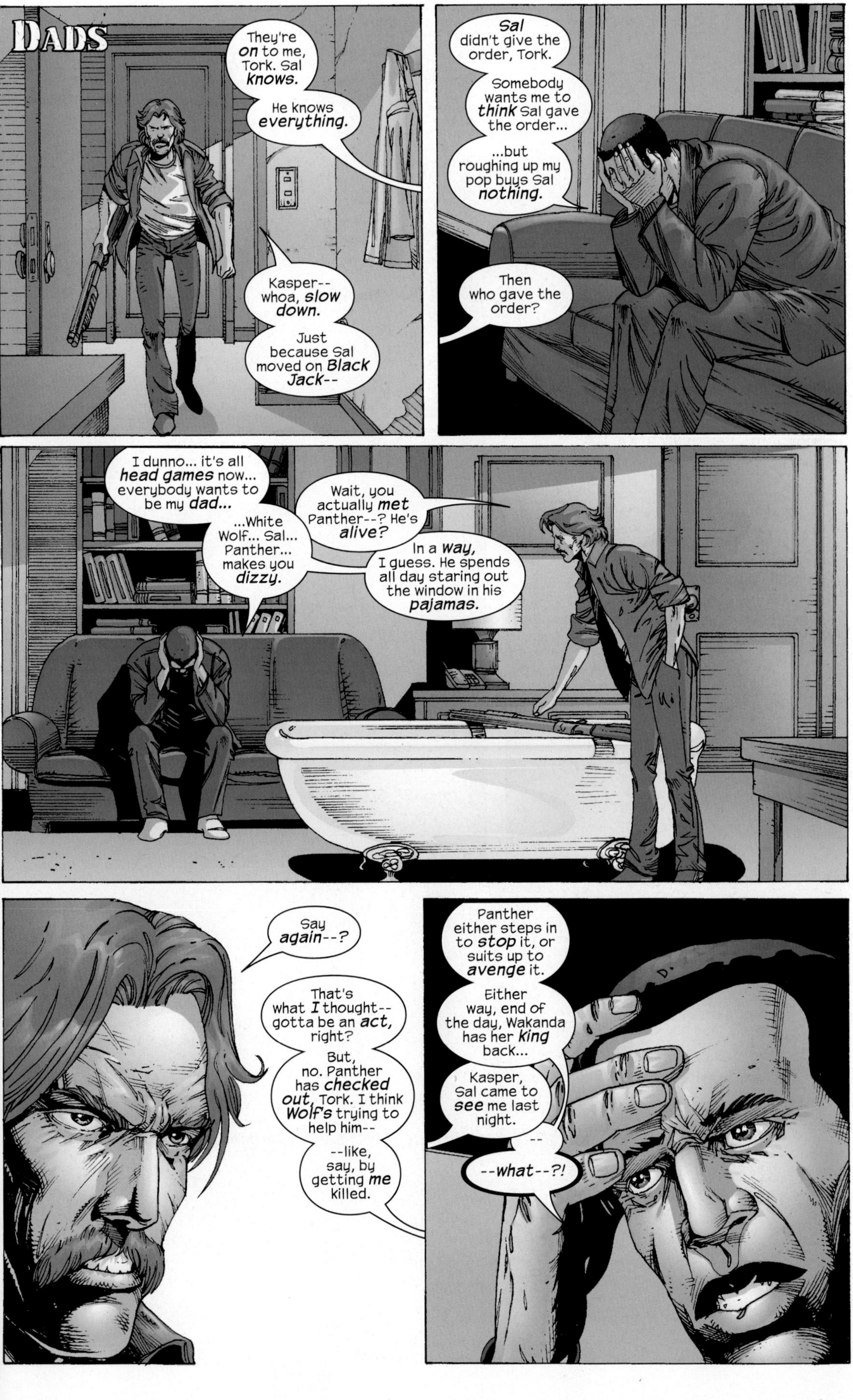

DADS
They're on to me, Tork. Sal knows.
He knows everything.
Kasper-- whoa, slow down.
Just because Sal moved on Black Jack--
Sal didn't give the order, Tork.
Somebody wants me to think Sal gave the order...
...but roughing up my pop buys Sal nothing.
Then who gave the order?
I dunno... it's all head games now... everybody wants to be my dad...
...White Wolf... Sal... Panther... makes you dizzy.
Wait, you actually met Panther--? He's alive?
In a way, I guess. He spends all day staring out the window in his pajamas.
Say again--?
That's what I thought-- gotta be an act, right?
But, no. Panther has checked out, Tork. I think Wolf's trying to help him--
--like, say, by getting me killed.
Panther either steps in to stop it, or suits up to avenge it.
Either way, end of the day, Wakanda has her king back...
Kasper, Sal came to see me last night.
--
--what--?!

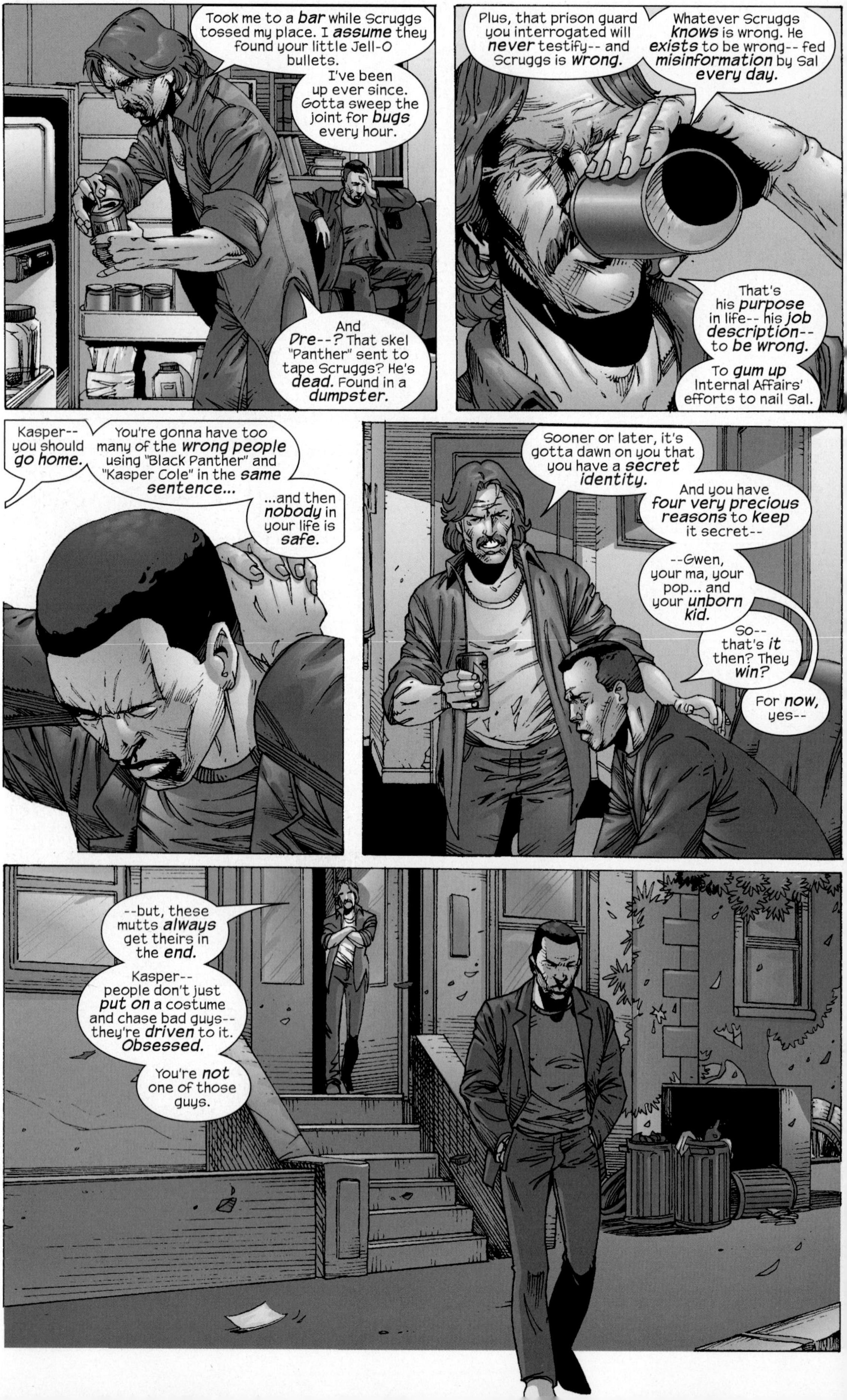
Took me to a bar while Scruggs tossed my place. I assume they found your little Jell-O bullets.
I've been up ever since. Gotta sweep the joint for bugs every hour.
And Dre--? That skel "Panther" sent to tape Scruggs? He's dead. Found in a dumpster.
Plus, that prison guard you interrogated will never testify-- and Scruggs is wrong.
Whatever Scruggs knows is wrong. He exists to be wrong-- fed misinformation by Sal every day.
That's his purpose in life-- his job description-- to be wrong.
To gum up Internal Affairs' efforts to nail Sal.
Kasper-- you should go home.
You're gonna have too many of the wrong people using "Black Panther" and "Kasper Cole" in the same sentence...
...and then nobody in your life is safe.
Sooner or later, it's gotta dawn on you that you have a secret identity.
And you have four very precious reasons to keep it secret--
--Gwen, your ma, your pop... and your unborn kid.
So-- that's it then? They win?
For now, yes--
--but, these mutts always get theirs in the end.
Kasper-- people don't just put on a costume and chase bad guys-- they're driven to it. Obsessed.
You're not one of those guys.

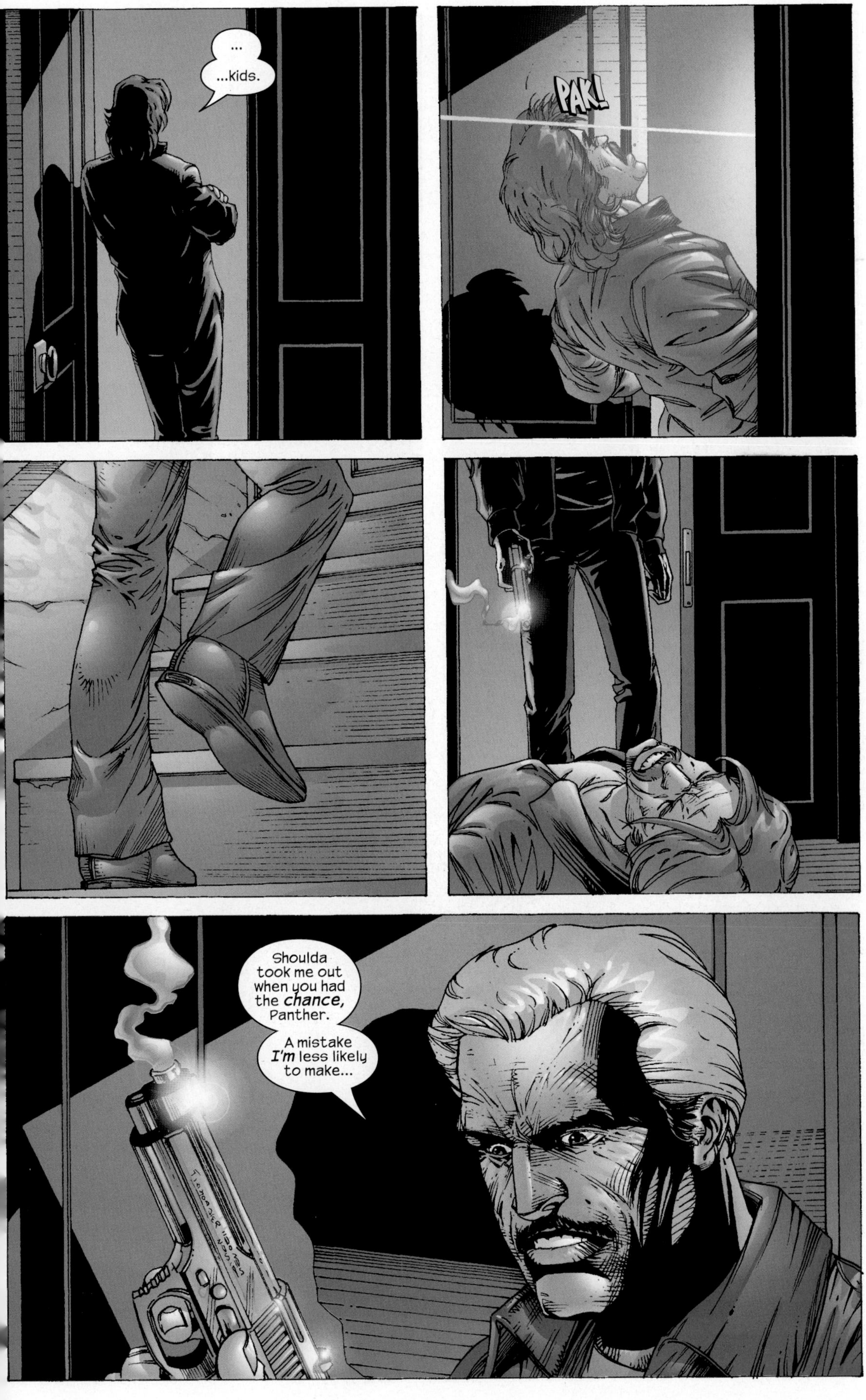
...
...kids.
PAK!
Shoulda took me out when you had the *chance,* Panther.
A mistake *I'm* less likely to make...

PRECIOUS REASONS

NOTICE:
LATE FEE $50
LEGAL ACTION
IF RENT AND
FEE ARE NOT
PAID WITHIN
10 DAYS

My Ma and Gwen have been home **all day.** TV so *hot* you could fry an *egg.*

Which leaves **two** possibilities...

NOTICE:
LATE FEE $50
LEGAL ACTION
IF RENT AND
FEE ARE NOT
PAID WITHIN
10 DAYS

(A) They didn't **see** the notice.

(B) They deliberately **left** it here so I'd see it.

NOTICE:
LATE FEE $50
LEGAL ACTION
IF RENT AND
FEE ARE NOT
PAID WITHIN
10 DAYS

Twelve minutes.

Still can't get the **key** in the door.

Can't lose the "I Want Out" face.

Gwen sees that, it's gonna be an **all night** kind of deal...

KRASH!

Eureka.

I can use the shouting match as **cover.**

Make it to the bathroom demilitarized zone...

Kevin-- Kevin, dear-- **tell** her--!

I-am-not-listening-to-maniacs-I-am-not!

Kasper--

--hurry or we'll be *late!*

"Late?"

What'd I forget...?

Late... for...?

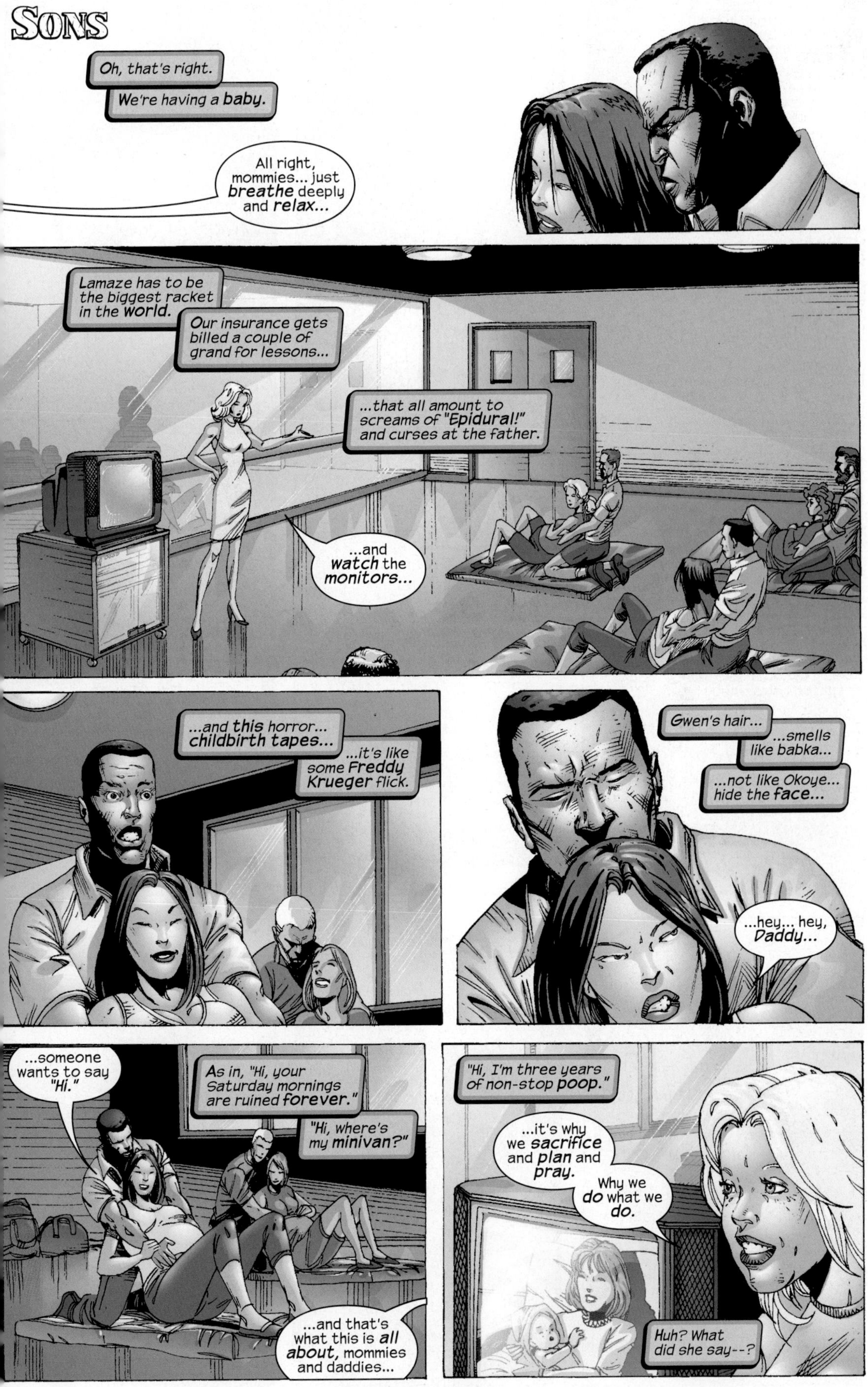
SONS
Oh, that's right.
We're having a baby.
All right, mommies... just breathe deeply and relax...
Lamaze has to be the biggest racket in the world.
Our insurance gets billed a couple of grand for lessons...
...that all amount to screams of "Epidural!" and curses at the father.
...and watch the monitors...
...and this horror... childbirth tapes...
...it's like some Freddy Krueger flick.
Gwen's hair...
...smells like babka...
...not like Okoye... hide the face...
...hey... hey, Daddy...
...someone wants to say "Hi."
As in, "Hi, your Saturday mornings are ruined forever."
"Hi, where's my minivan?"
...and that's what this is all about, mommies and daddies...
"Hi, I'm three years of non-stop poop."
...it's why we sacrifice and plan and pray.
Why we do what we do.
Huh? What did she say--?

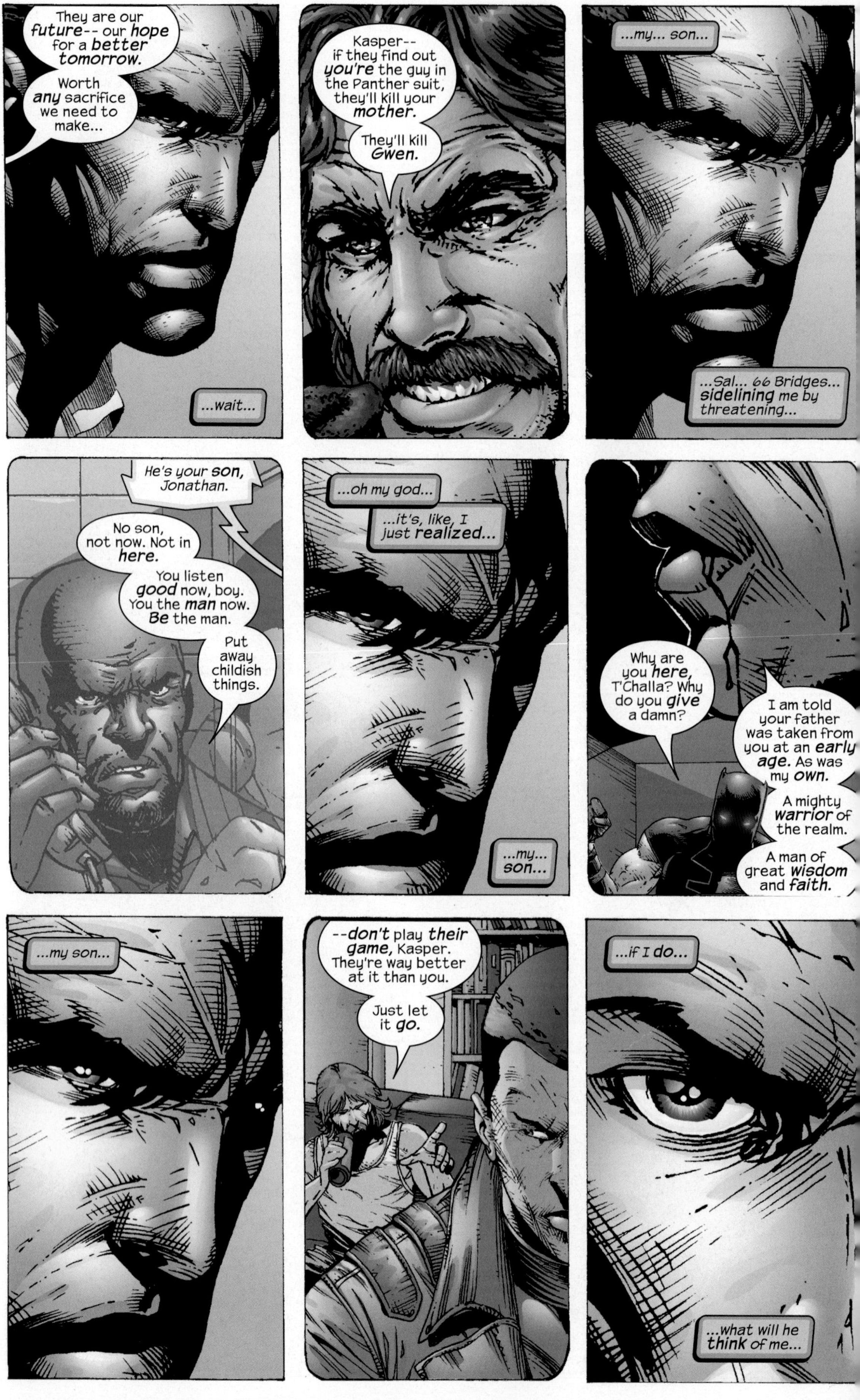

They are our future-- our hope for a better tomorrow.
Worth any sacrifice we need to make...
...wait...
Kasper-- if they find out you're the guy in the Panther suit, they'll kill your mother.
They'll kill Gwen.
...my... son...
...Sal... 66 Bridges... sidelining me by threatening...
He's your son, Jonathan.
No son, not now. Not in here.
You listen good now, boy. You the man now. Be the man.
Put away childish things.
...oh my god...
...it's, like, I just realized...
...my... son...
Why are you here, T'Challa? Why do you give a damn?
I am told your father was taken from you at an early age. As was my own.
A mighty warrior of the realm.
A man of great wisdom and faith.
...my son...
--don't play their game, Kasper. They're way better at it than you.
Just let it go.
...if I do...
...what will he think of me...

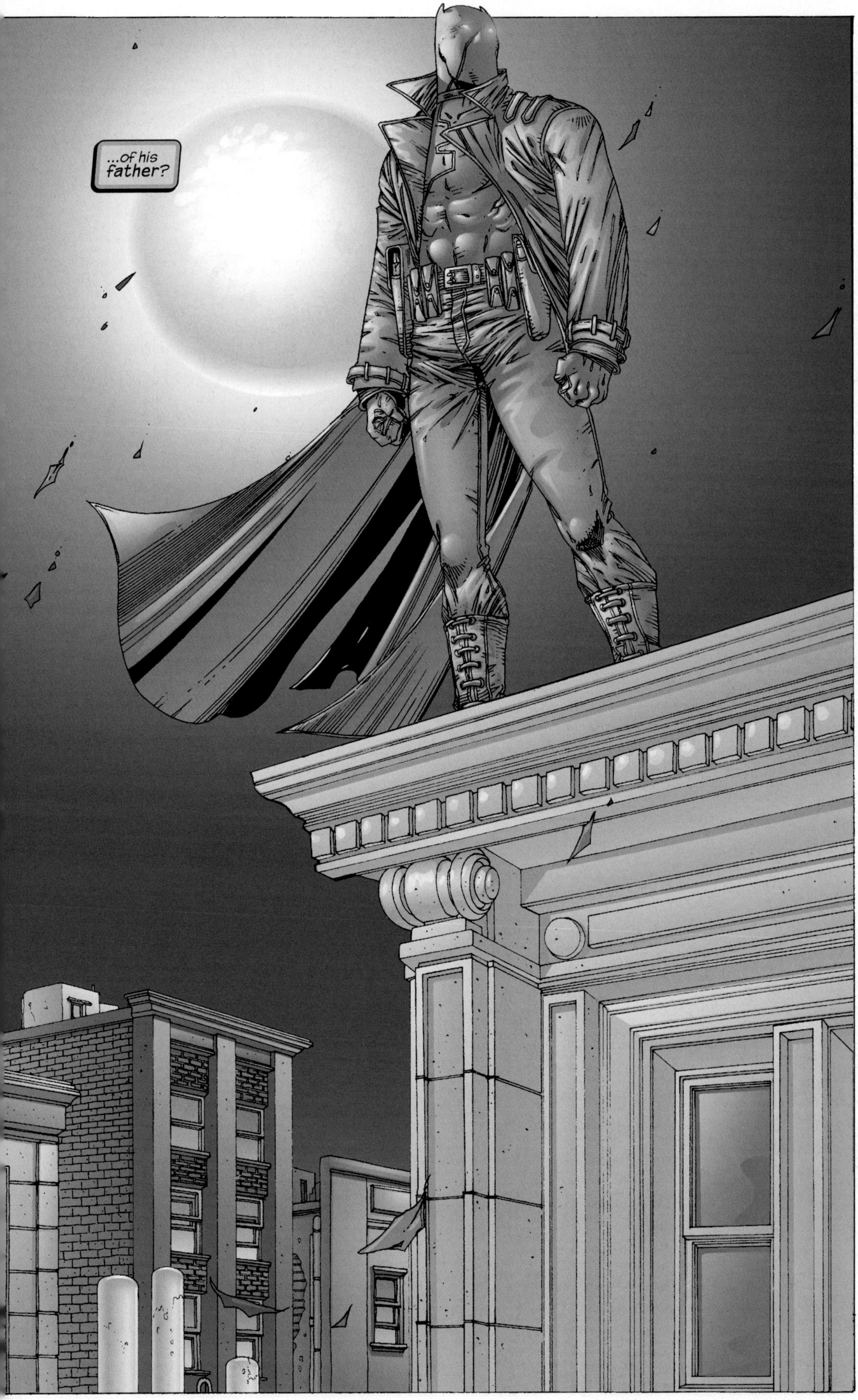
...of his father?

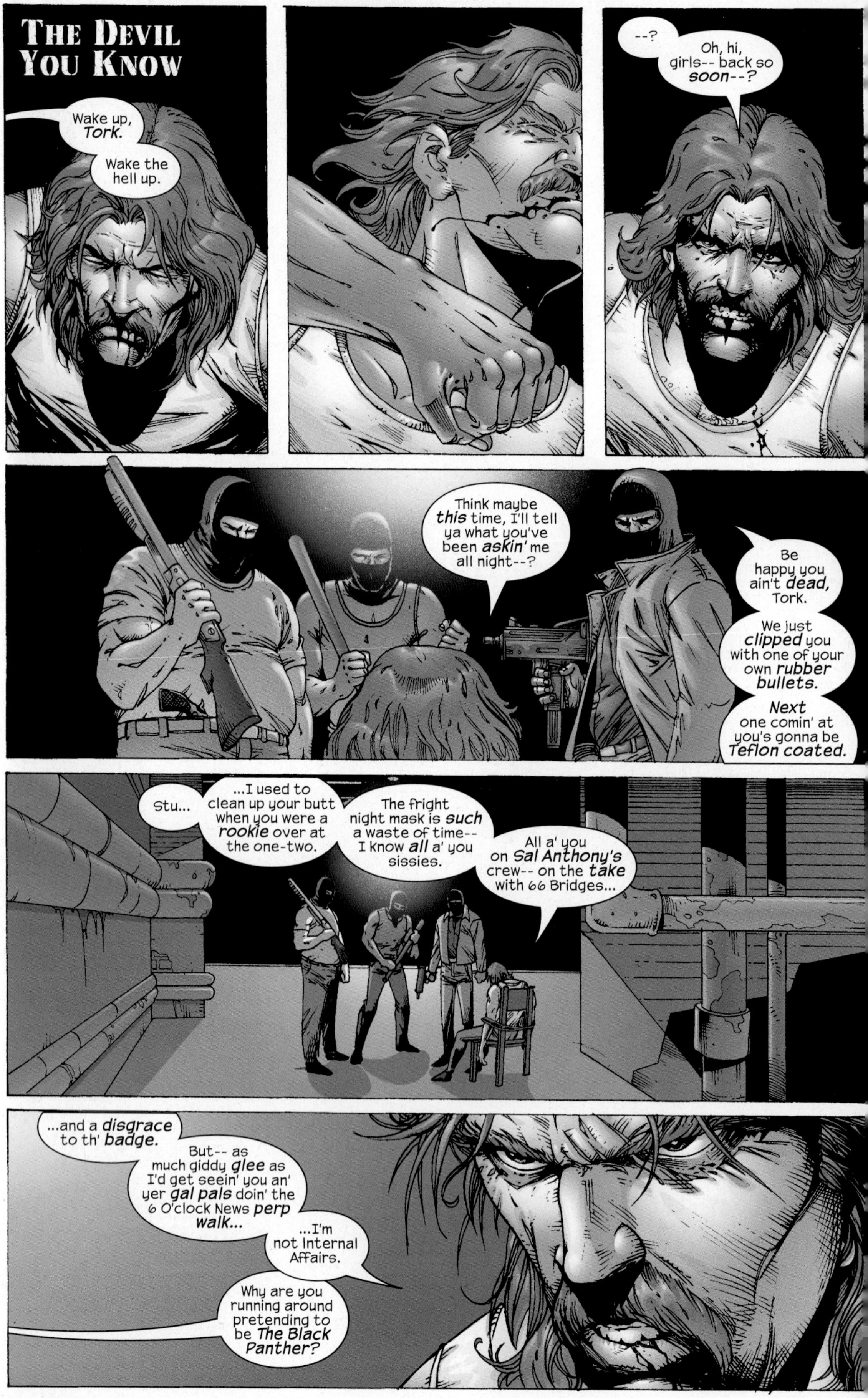
THE DEVIL YOU KNOW
Wake up, Tork.
Wake the hell up.
--?
Oh, hi, girls-- back so soon--?
Think maybe this time, I'll tell ya what you've been askin' me all night--?
Be happy you ain't dead, Tork.
We just clipped you with one of your own rubber bullets.
Next one comin' at you's gonna be Teflon coated.
Stu...
...I used to clean up your butt when you were a rookie over at the one-two.
The fright night mask is such a waste of time-- I know all a' you sissies.
All a' you on Sal Anthony's crew-- on the take with 66 Bridges...
...and a disgrace to th' badge.
But-- as much giddy glee as I'd get seein' you an' yer gal pals doin' the 6 O'clock News perp walk...
...I'm not Internal Affairs.
Why are you running around pretending to be The Black Panther?

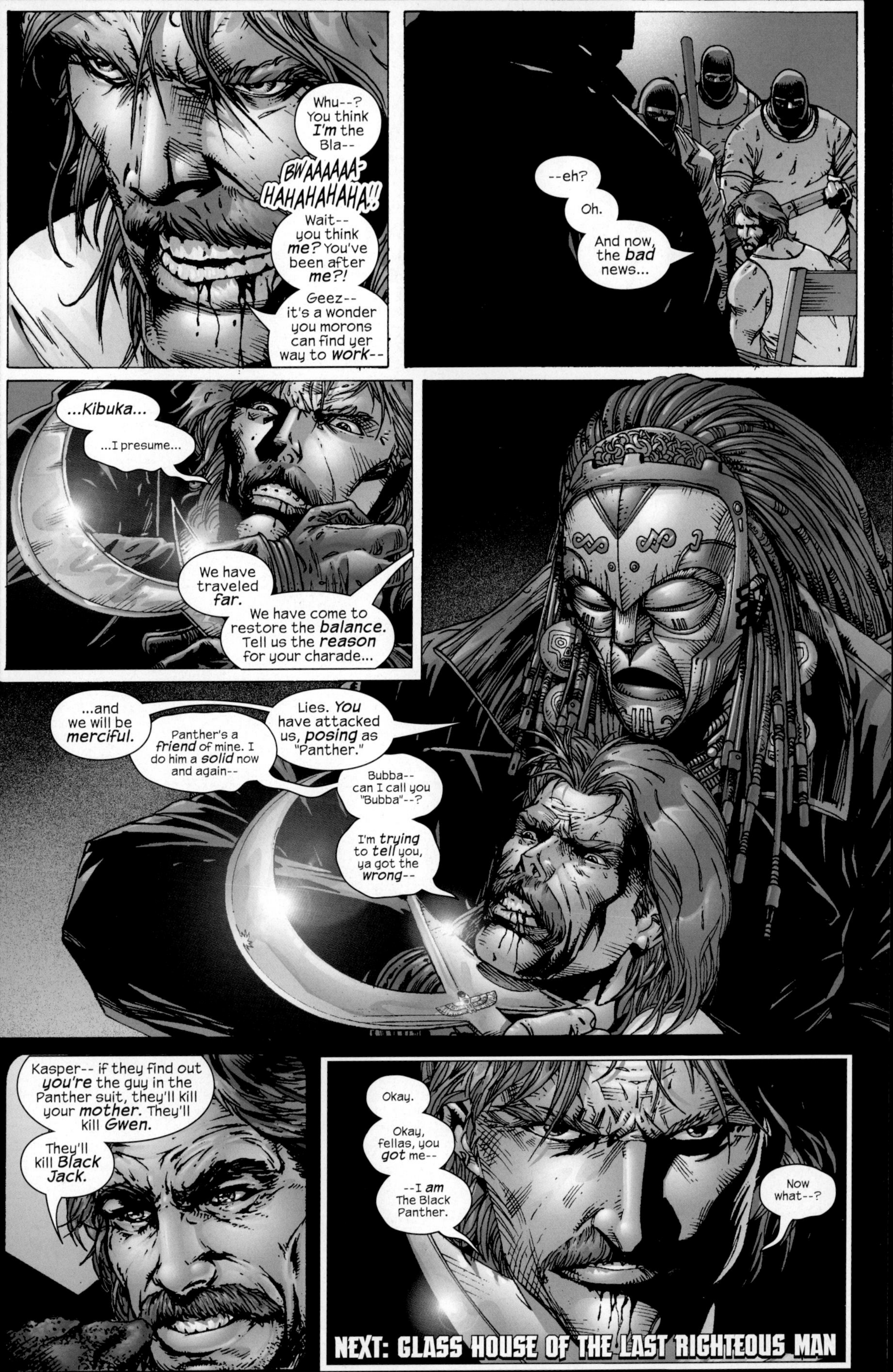
Whu--? You think I'm the Bla--
BWAAAAAA-HAHAHAHAHA!!
Wait-- you think me? You've been after me?!
Geez-- it's a wonder you morons can find yer way to work--
--eh?
Oh.
And now, the bad news...
...Kibuka...
...I presume...
We have traveled far.
We have come to restore the balance. Tell us the reason for your charade...
...and we will be merciful.
Panther's a friend of mine. I do him a solid now and again--
Lies. You have attacked us, posing as "Panther."
Bubba-- can I call you "Bubba"--?
I'm trying to tell you, ya got the wrong--
Kasper-- if they find out you're the guy in the Panther suit, they'll kill your mother. They'll kill Gwen.
They'll kill Black Jack.
Okay.
Okay, fellas, you got me--
--I am The Black Panther.
Now what--?
NEXT: GLASS HOUSE OF THE LAST RIGHTEOUS MAN

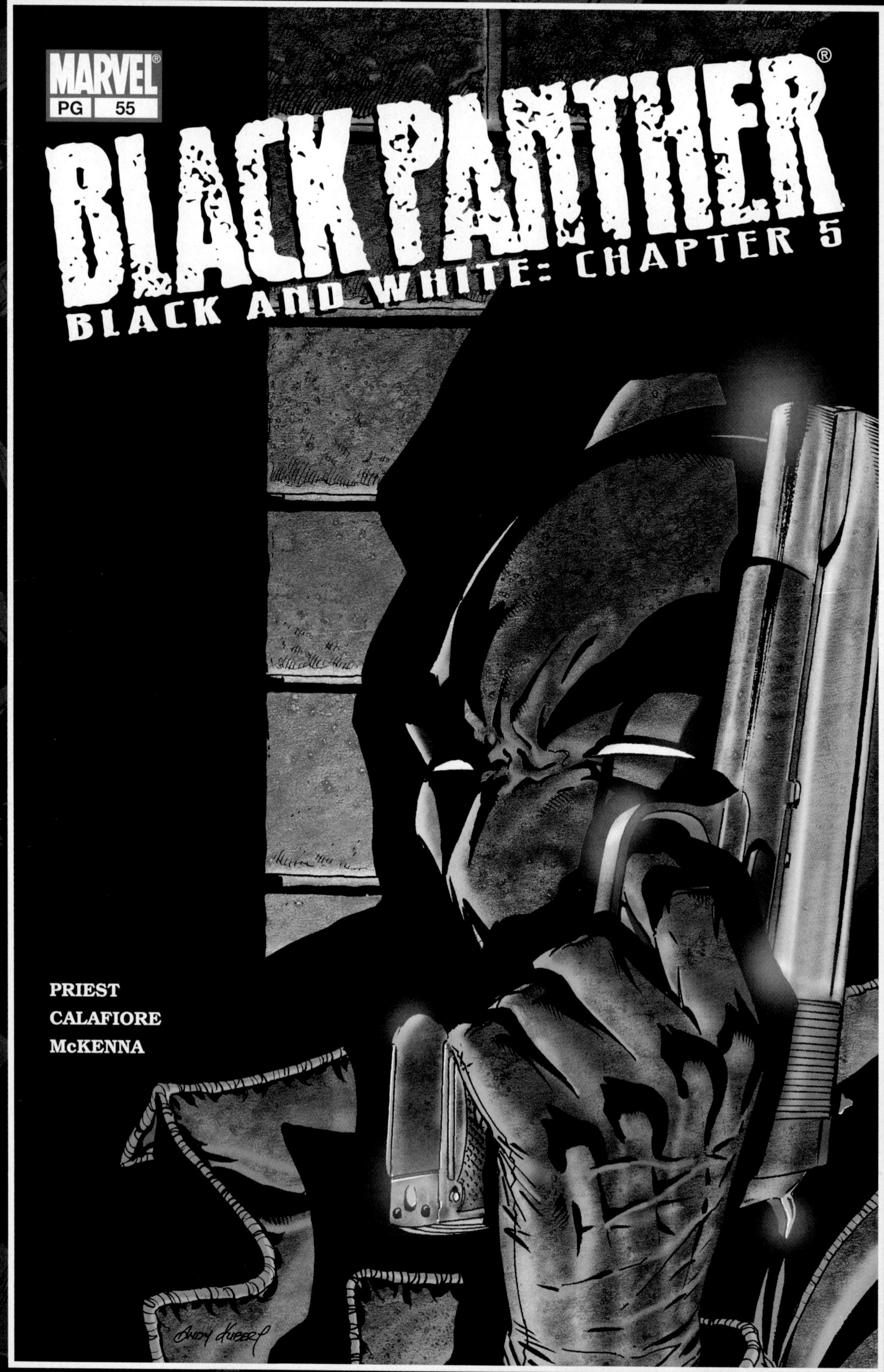
MARVEL®
PG 55
BLACK PANTHER®
BLACK AND WHITE: CHAPTER 5
PRIEST
CALAFIORE
McKENNA
ANDY KUBERT

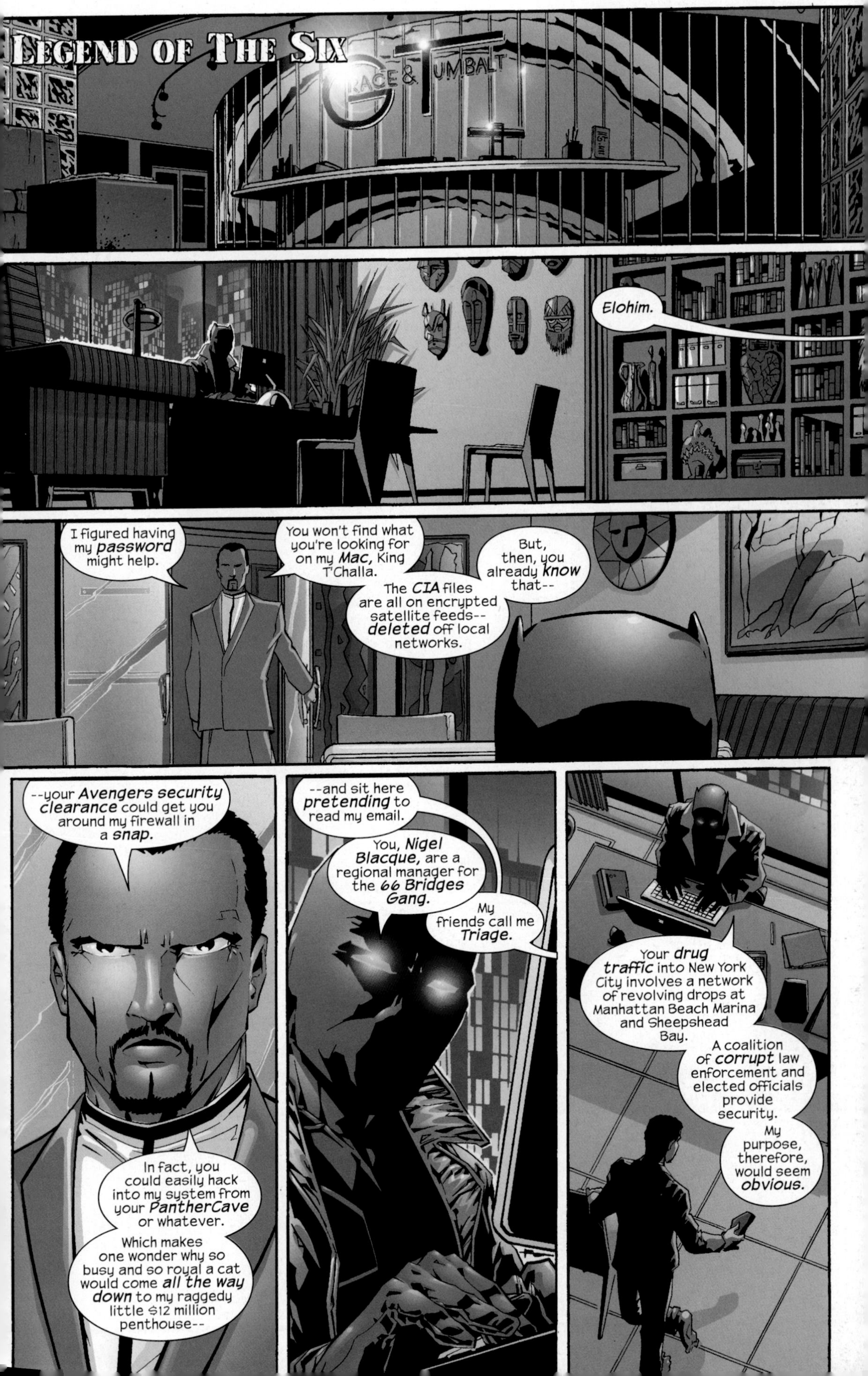
LEGEND OF THE SIX
GRACE & TUMBALT
Elohim.
I figured having my password might help.
You won't find what you're looking for on my Mac, King T'Challa.
The CIA files are all on encrypted satellite feeds-- deleted off local networks.
But, then, you already know that--
--your Avengers security clearance could get you around my firewall in a snap.
In fact, you could easily hack into my system from your PantherCave or whatever.
Which makes one wonder why so busy and so royal a cat would come all the way down to my raggedy little $12 million penthouse--
--and sit here pretending to read my email.
You, Nigel Blacque, are a regional manager for the 66 Bridges Gang.
My friends call me Triage.
Your drug traffic into New York City involves a network of revolving drops at Manhattan Beach Marina and Sheepshead Bay.
A coalition of corrupt law enforcement and elected officials provide security.
My purpose, therefore, would seem obvious.

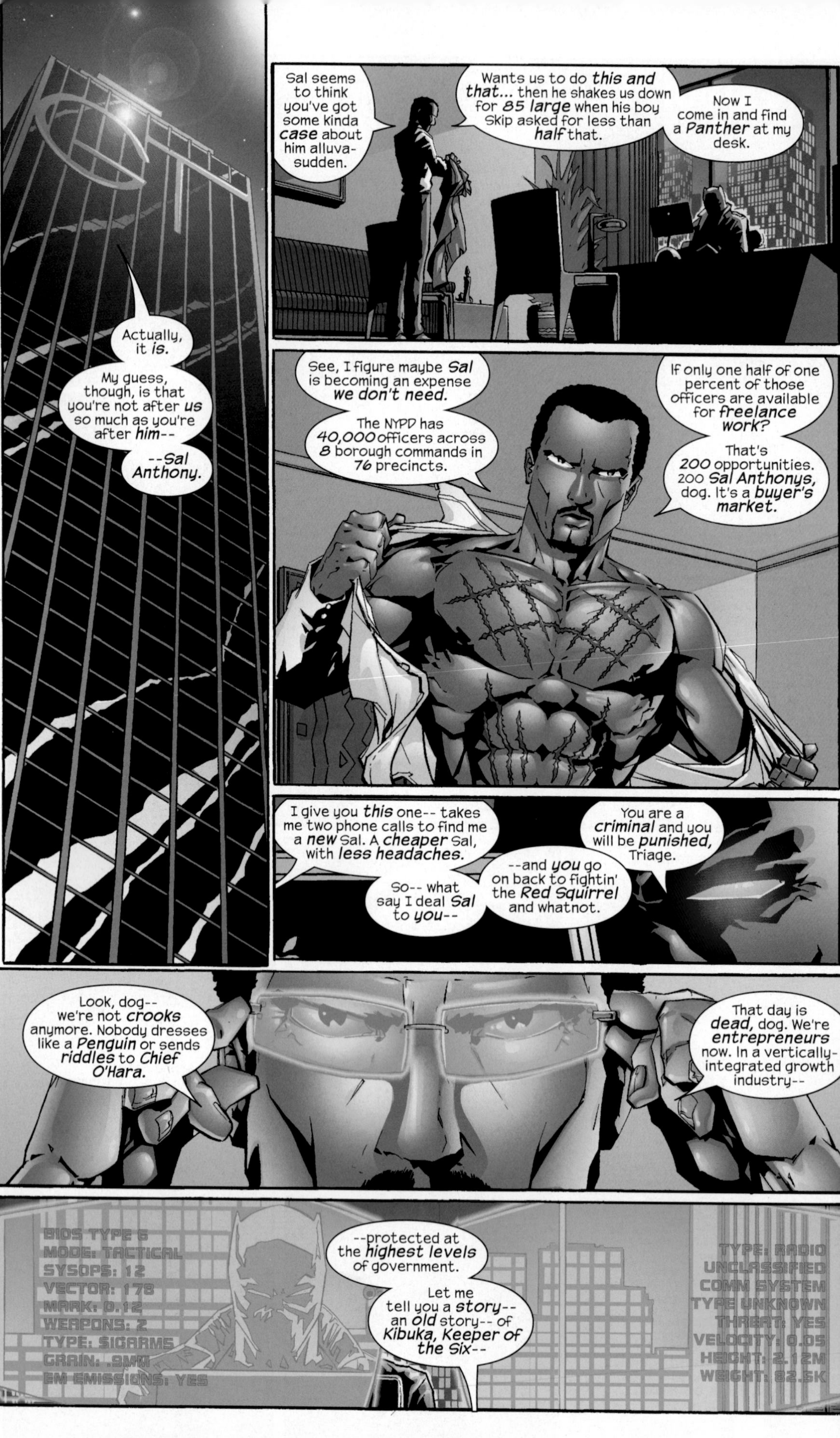
Actually, it is.
My guess, though, is that you're not after us so much as you're after him--
--Sal Anthony.
Sal seems to think you've got some kinda case about him alluva-sudden.
Wants us to do this and that... then he shakes us down for 85 large when his boy Skip asked for less than half that.
Now I come in and find a Panther at my desk.
See, I figure maybe Sal is becoming an expense we don't need.
The NYPD has 40,000 officers across 8 borough commands in 76 precincts.
If only one half of one percent of those officers are available for freelance work?
That's 200 opportunities. 200 Sal Anthonys, dog. It's a buyer's market.
I give you this one-- takes me two phone calls to find me a new Sal. A cheaper Sal, with less headaches.
So-- what say I deal Sal to you--
--and you go on back to fightin' the Red Squirrel and whatnot.
You are a criminal and you will be punished, Triage.
Look, dog-- we're not crooks anymore. Nobody dresses like a Penguin or sends riddles to Chief O'Hara.
That day is dead, dog. We're entrepreneurs now. In a vertically-integrated growth industry--
BIOS TYPE 6
MODE: TACTICAL
SYSOPS: 12
VECTOR: 178
MARK: 0.12
WEAPONS: 2
TYPE: SIGARMS
GRAIN: .9MM
EM EMISSIONS: YES
--protected at the highest levels of government.
Let me tell you a story-- an old story-- of Kibuka, Keeper of the Six--
TYPE: RADIO
UNCLASSIFIED
COMM SYSTEM
TYPE UNKNOWN
THREAT: YES
VELOCITY: 0.05
HEIGHT: 2.12M
WEIGHT: 82.5K

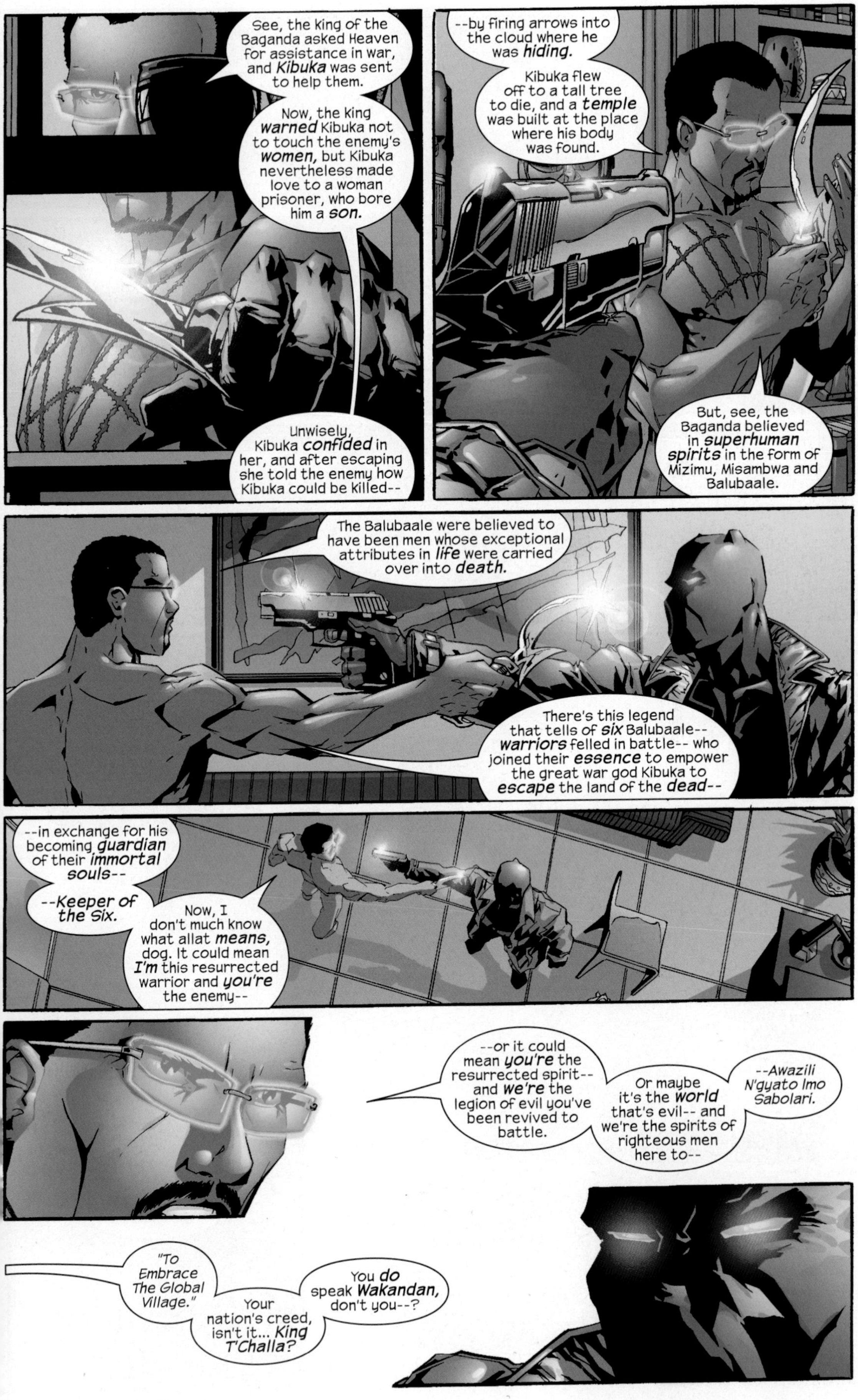

See, the king of the Baganda asked Heaven for assistance in war, and Kibuka was sent to help them.
Now, the king warned Kibuka not to touch the enemy's women, but Kibuka nevertheless made love to a woman prisoner, who bore him a son.
Unwisely, Kibuka confided in her, and after escaping she told the enemy how Kibuka could be killed--
--by firing arrows into the cloud where he was hiding.
Kibuka flew off to a tall tree to die, and a temple was built at the place where his body was found.
But, see, the Baganda believed in superhuman spirits in the form of Mizimu, Misambwa and Balubaale.
The Balubaale were believed to have been men whose exceptional attributes in life were carried over into death.
There's this legend that tells of six Balubaale-- warriors felled in battle-- who joined their essence to empower the great war god Kibuka to escape the land of the dead--
--in exchange for his becoming guardian of their immortal souls--
--Keeper of the Six.
Now, I don't much know what allat means, dog. It could mean I'm this resurrected warrior and you're the enemy--
--or it could mean you're the resurrected spirit-- and we're the legion of evil you've been revived to battle.
Or maybe it's the world that's evil-- and we're the spirits of righteous men here to--
--Awazili N'gyato Imo Sabolari.
"To Embrace The Global Village."
Your nation's creed, isn't it... King T'Challa?
You do speak Wakandan, don't you--?

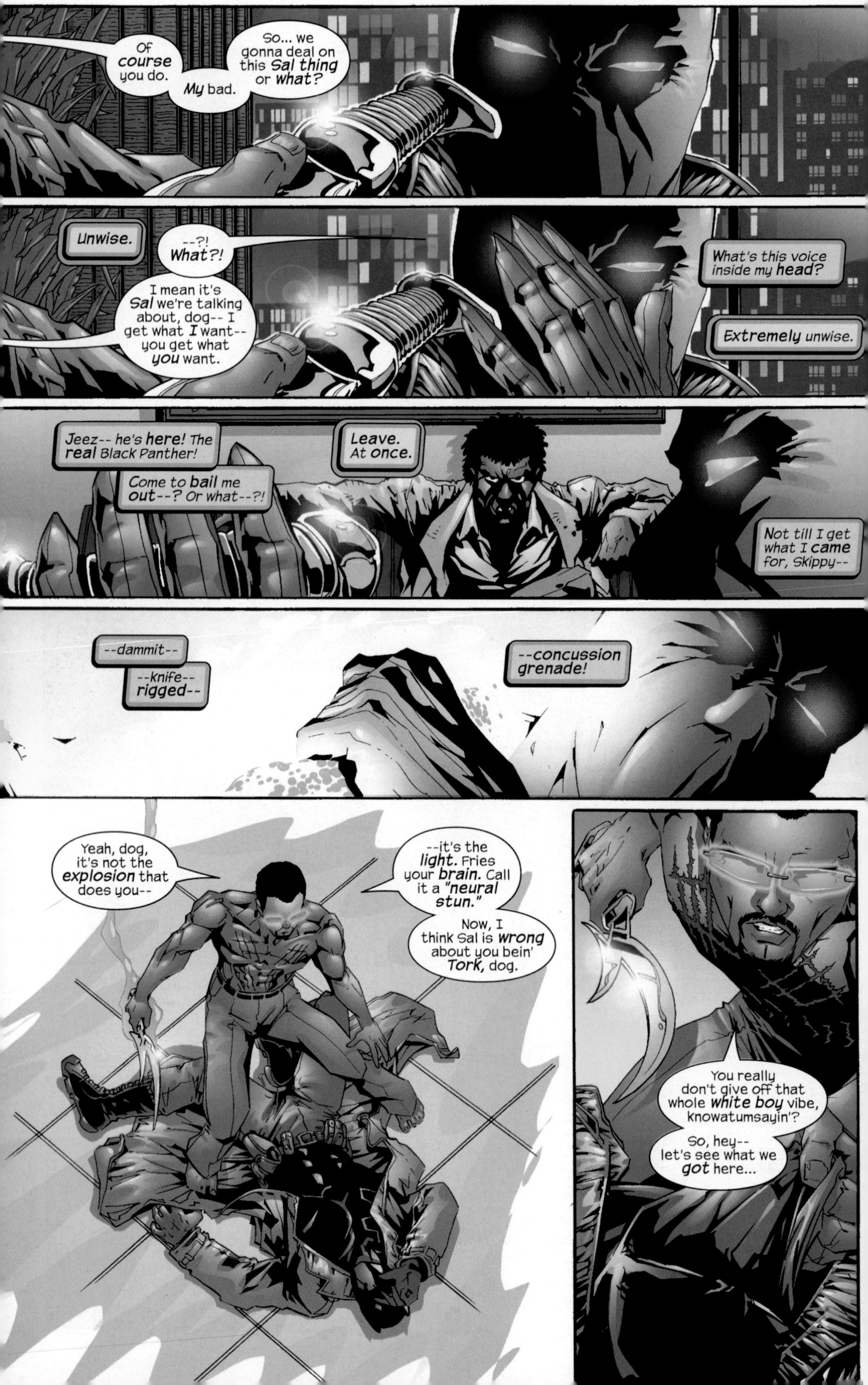
Of course you do.
My bad.
So... we gonna deal on this Sal thing or what?
Unwise.
--?! What?!
I mean it's Sal we're talking about, dog-- I get what I want-- you get what you want.
What's this voice inside my head?
Extremely unwise.
Jeez-- he's here! The real Black Panther!
Come to bail me out--? Or what--?!
Leave. At once.
Not till I get what I came for, Skippy--
--dammit--
--knife-- rigged--
--concussion grenade!
Yeah, dog, it's not the explosion that does you--
--it's the light. Fries your brain. Call it a "neural stun."
Now, I think Sal is wrong about you bein' Tork, dog.
You really don't give off that whole white boy vibe, knowatumsayin'?
So, hey-- let's see what we got here...

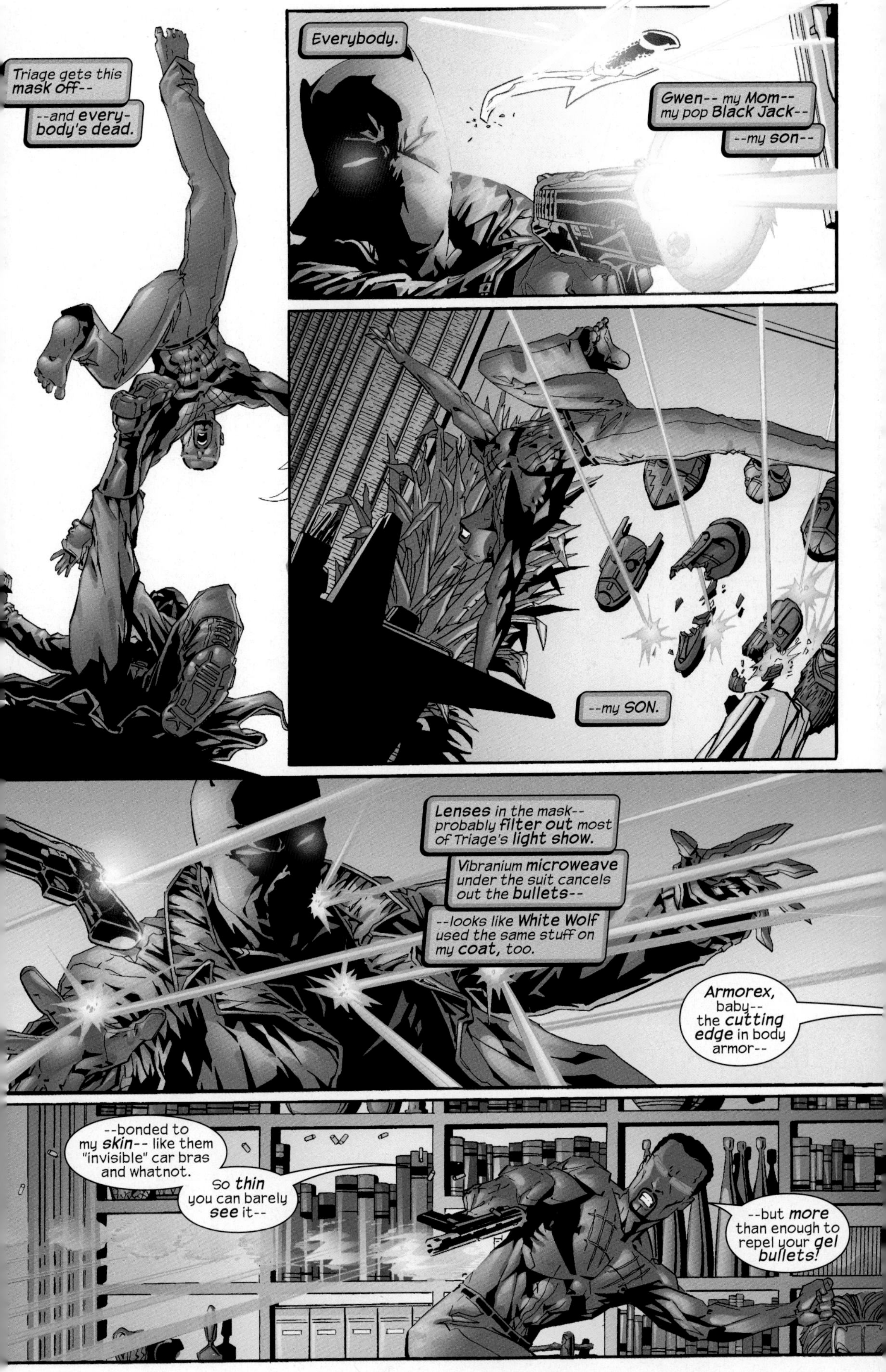

Triage gets this mask off--
--and everybody's dead.
Everybody.
Gwen-- my Mom-- my pop Black Jack--
--my son--
--my SON.
Lenses in the mask-- probably filter out most of Triage's light show.
Vibranium microweave under the suit cancels out the bullets--
--looks like White Wolf used the same stuff on my coat, too.
Armorex, baby-- the cutting edge in body armor--
--bonded to my skin-- like them "invisible" car bras and whatnot.
So thin you can barely see it--
--but more than enough to repel your gel bullets!

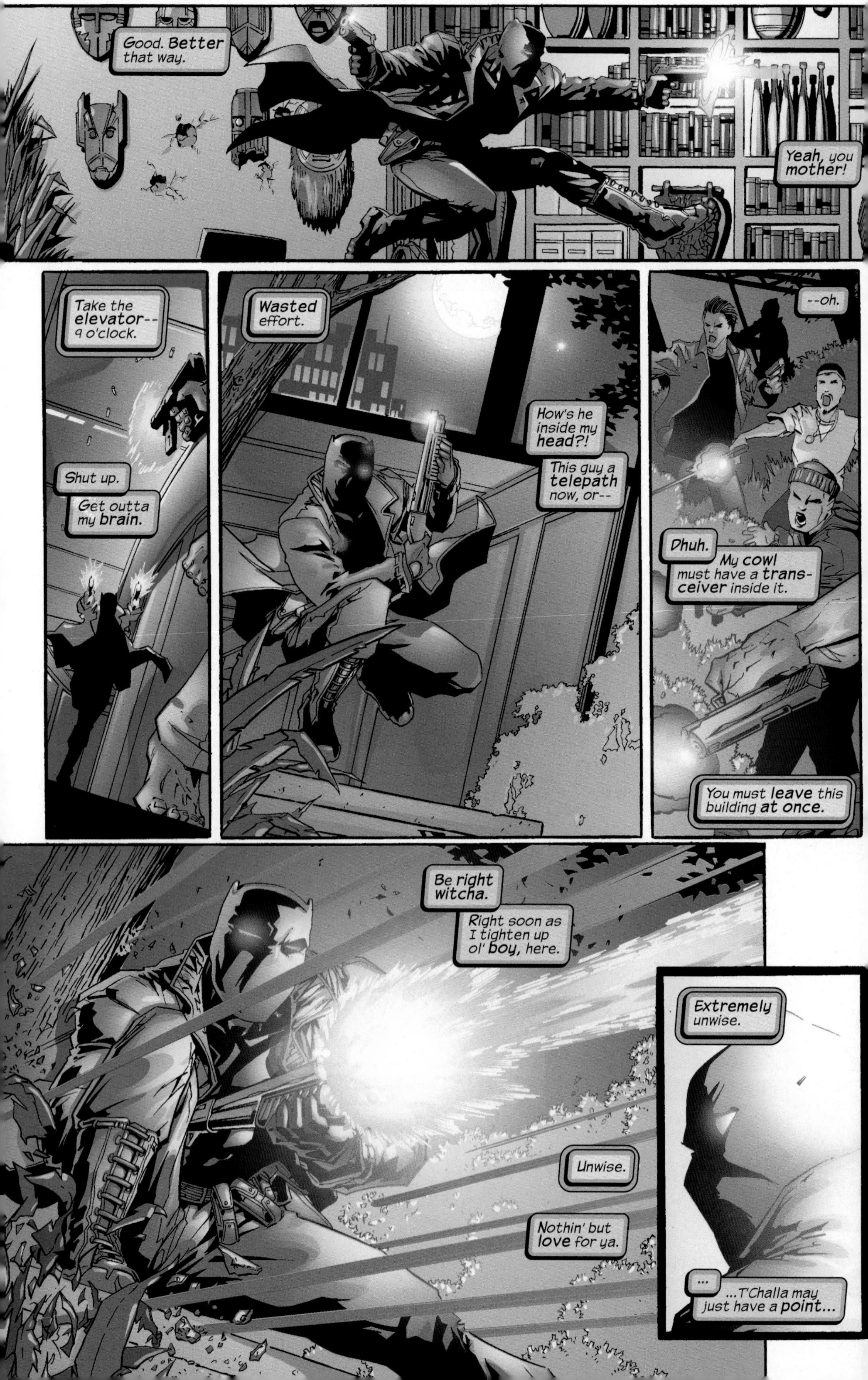

Good. Better that way.
Yeah, you mother!
Take the elevator-- 9 o'clock.
Shut up.
Get outta my brain.
Wasted effort.
How's he inside my head?!
This guy a telepath now, or--
--oh.
Dhuh.
My cowl must have a trans-ceiver inside it.
You must leave this building at once.
Be right witcha.
Right soon as I tighten up ol' boy, here.
Unwise.
Nothin' but love for ya.
Extremely unwise.
...
...T'Challa may just have a point...

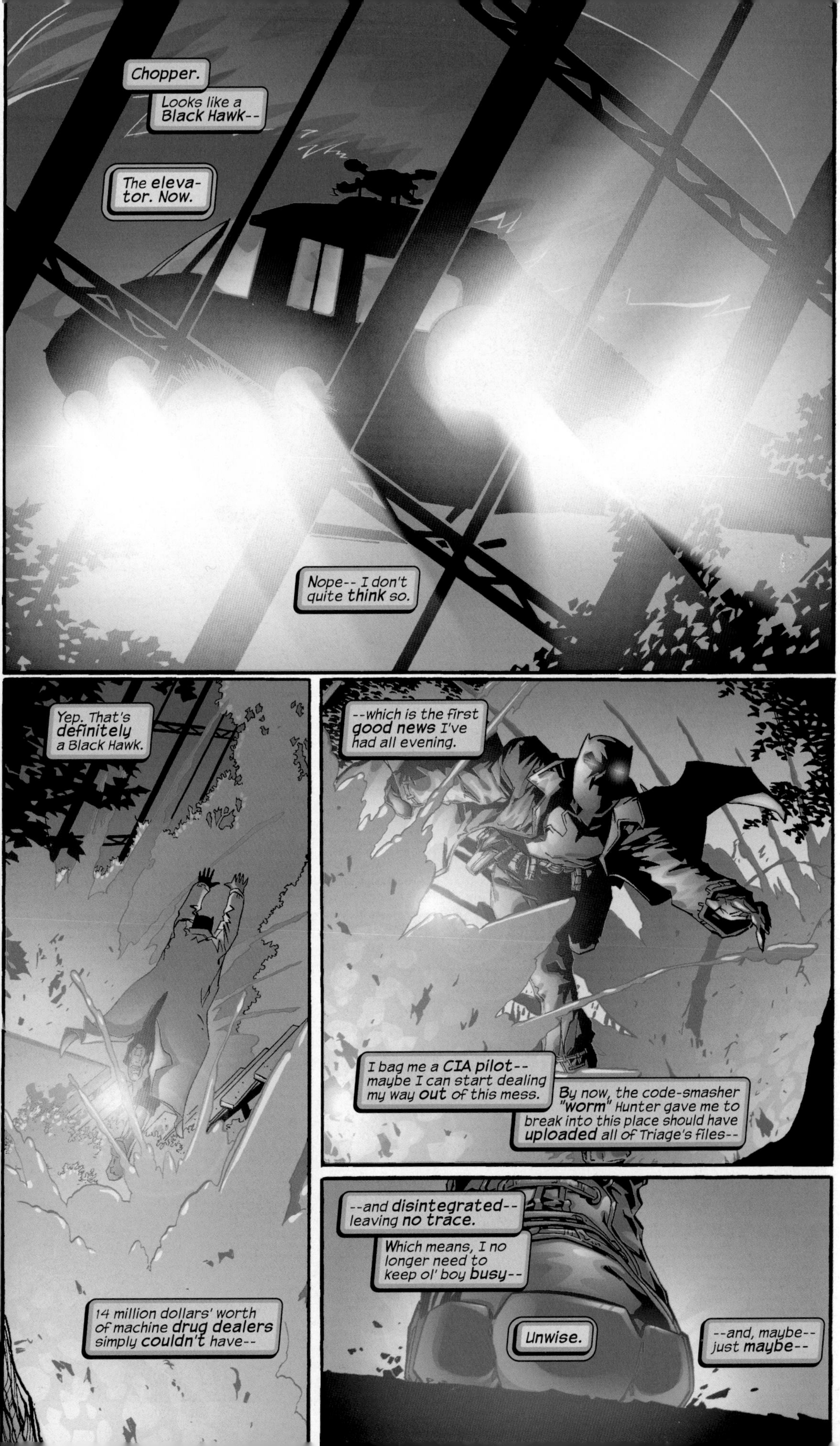
Chopper.
Looks like a Black Hawk--
The elevator. Now.
Nope-- I don't quite think so.
Yep. That's definitely a Black Hawk.
14 million dollars' worth of machine drug dealers simply couldn't have--
--which is the first good news I've had all evening.
I bag me a CIA pilot-- maybe I can start dealing my way out of this mess.
By now, the code-smasher "worm" Hunter gave me to break into this place should have uploaded all of Triage's files--
--and disintegrated-- leaving no trace.
Which means, I no longer need to keep ol' boy busy--
Unwise.
--and, maybe-- just maybe--

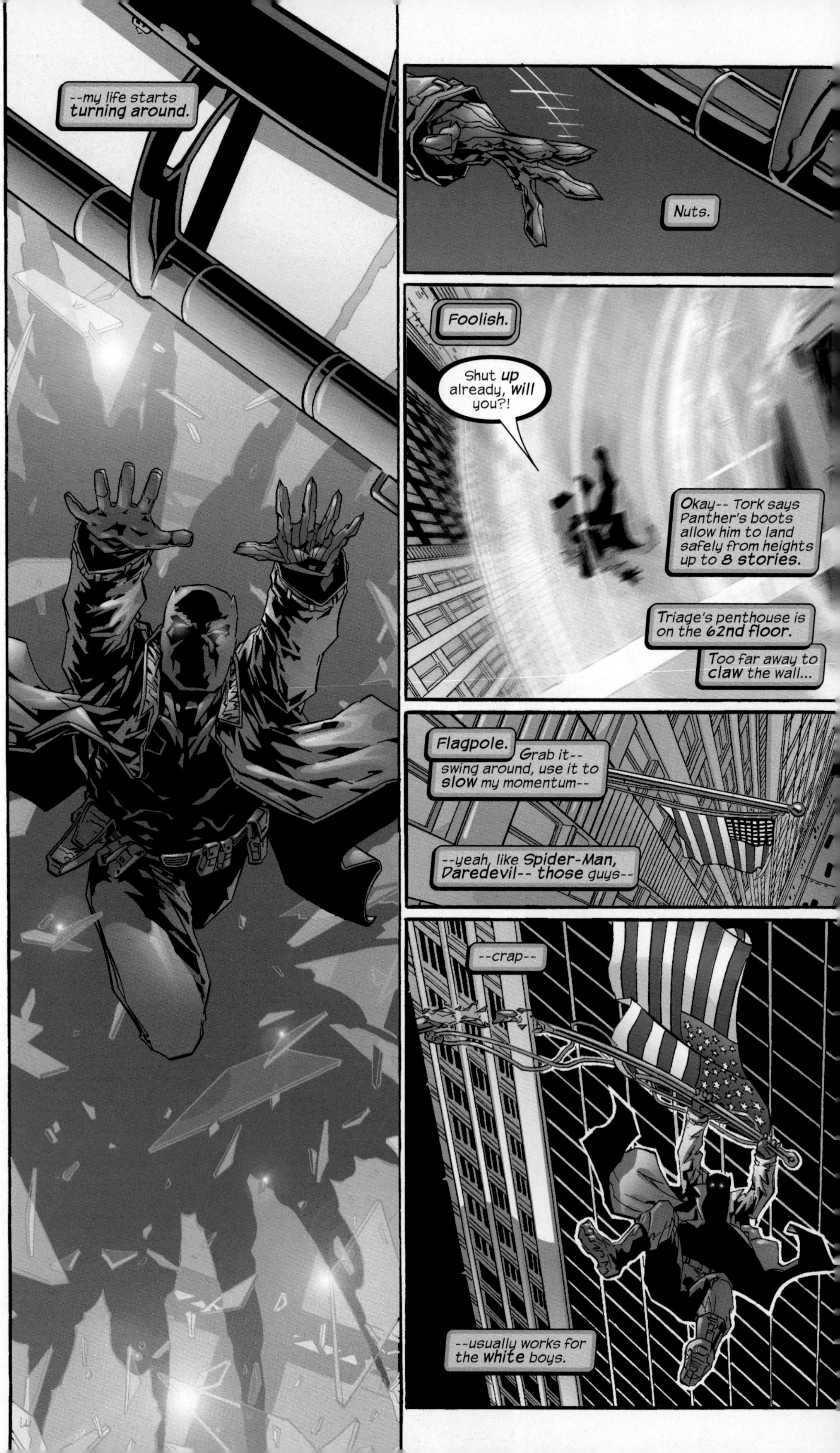
--my life starts turning around.
Nuts.
Foolish.
Shut up already, will you?!
Okay-- Tork says Panther's boots allow him to land safely from heights up to 8 stories.
Triage's penthouse is on the 62nd floor.
Too far away to claw the wall...
Flagpole. Grab it-- swing around, use it to slow my momentum--
--yeah, like Spider-Man, Daredevil-- those guys--
--crap--
--usually works for the white boys.

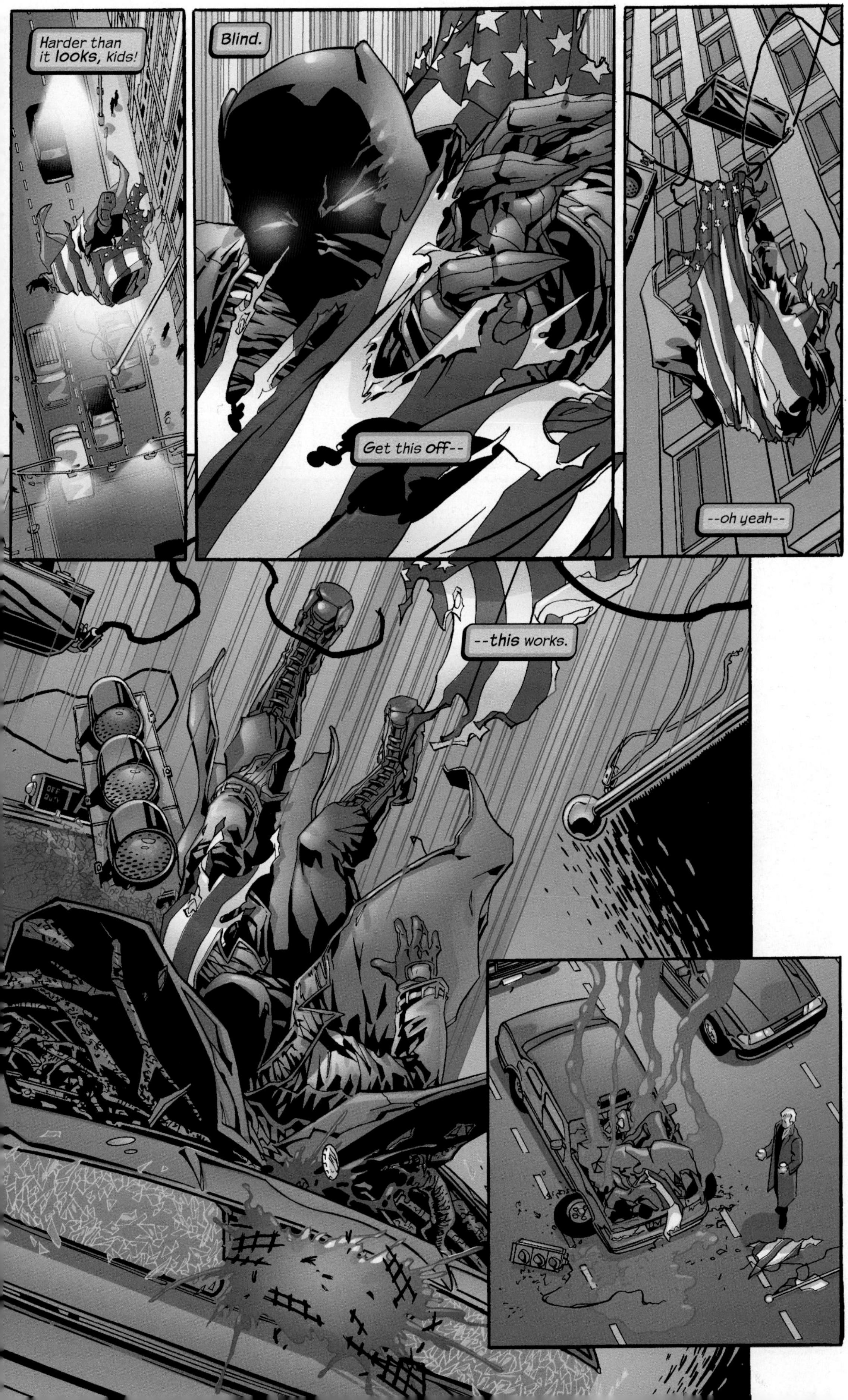

Harder than it looks, kids!
Blind.
Get this off--
--oh yeah--
--this works.

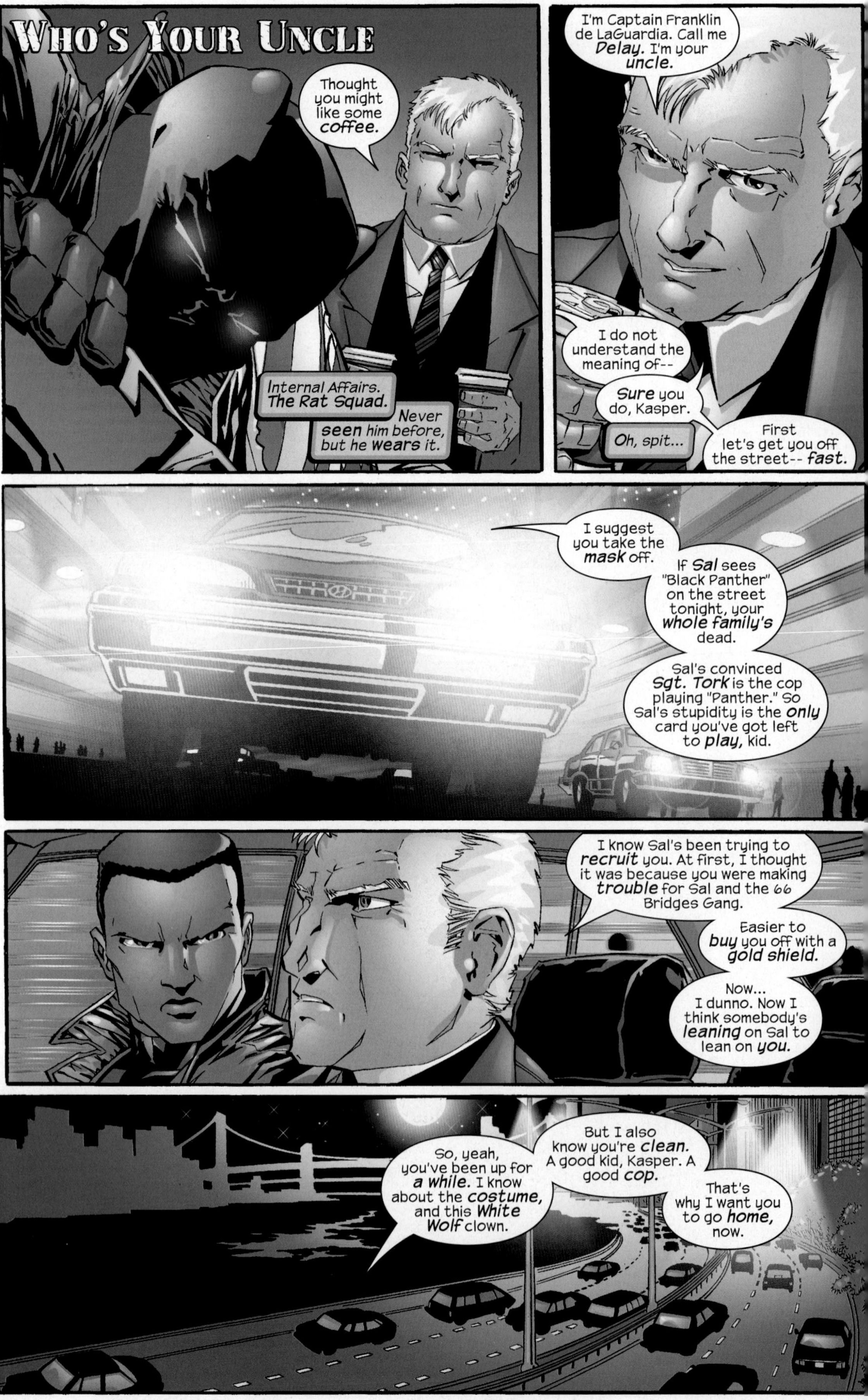

WHO'S YOUR UNCLE
Thought you might like some coffee.
Internal Affairs. The Rat Squad.
Never seen him before, but he wears it.
I'm Captain Franklin de LaGuardia. Call me Delay. I'm your uncle.
I do not understand the meaning of--
Sure you do, Kasper.
Oh, spit...
First let's get you off the street-- fast.
I suggest you take the mask off.
If Sal sees "Black Panther" on the street tonight, your whole family's dead.
Sal's convinced Sgt. Tork is the cop playing "Panther." So Sal's stupidity is the only card you've got left to play, kid.
I know Sal's been trying to recruit you. At first, I thought it was because you were making trouble for Sal and the 66 Bridges Gang.
Easier to buy you off with a gold shield.
Now... I dunno. Now I think somebody's leaning on Sal to lean on you.
So, yeah, you've been up for a while. I know about the costume, and this White Wolf clown.
But I also know you're clean. A good kid, Kasper. A good cop.
That's why I want you to go home, now.

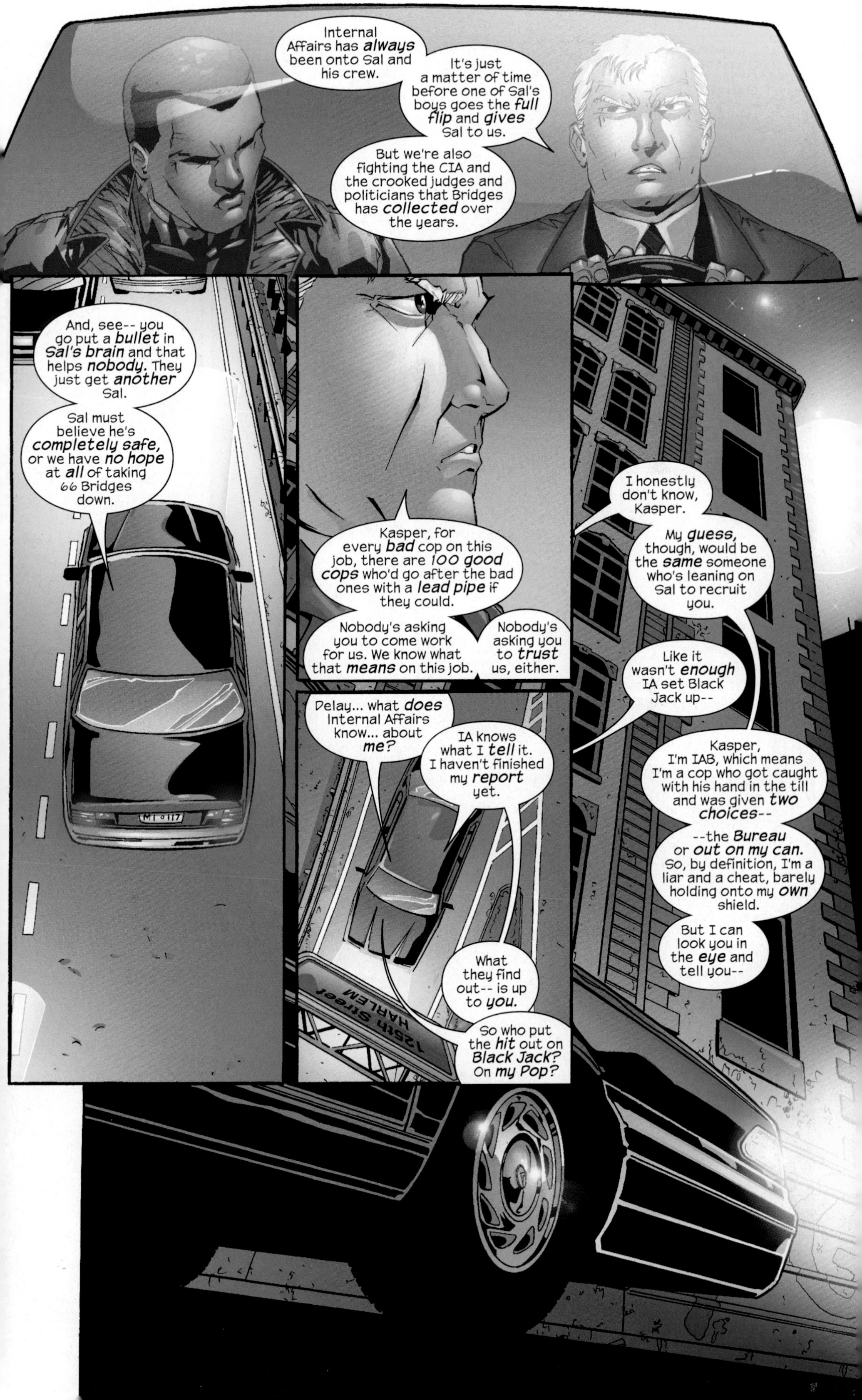

Internal Affairs has always been onto Sal and his crew.
It's just a matter of time before one of Sal's boys goes the full flip and gives Sal to us.
But we're also fighting the CIA and the crooked judges and politicians that Bridges has collected over the years.
And, see-- you go put a bullet in Sal's brain and that helps nobody. They just get another Sal.
Sal must believe he's completely safe, or we have no hope at all of taking 66 Bridges down.
Kasper, for every bad cop on this job, there are 100 good cops who'd go after the bad ones with a lead pipe if they could.
Nobody's asking you to come work for us. We know what that means on this job.
Nobody's asking you to trust us, either.
Delay... what does Internal Affairs know... about me?
IA knows what I tell it. I haven't finished my report yet.
What they find out-- is up to you.
So who put the hit out on Black Jack? On my Pop?
I honestly don't know, Kasper.
My guess, though, would be the same someone who's leaning on Sal to recruit you.
Like it wasn't enough IA set Black Jack up--
Kasper, I'm IAB, which means I'm a cop who got caught with his hand in the till and was given two choices--
--the Bureau or out on my can. So, by definition, I'm a liar and a cheat, barely holding onto my own shield.
But I can look you in the eye and tell you--
125th Street
HARLEM

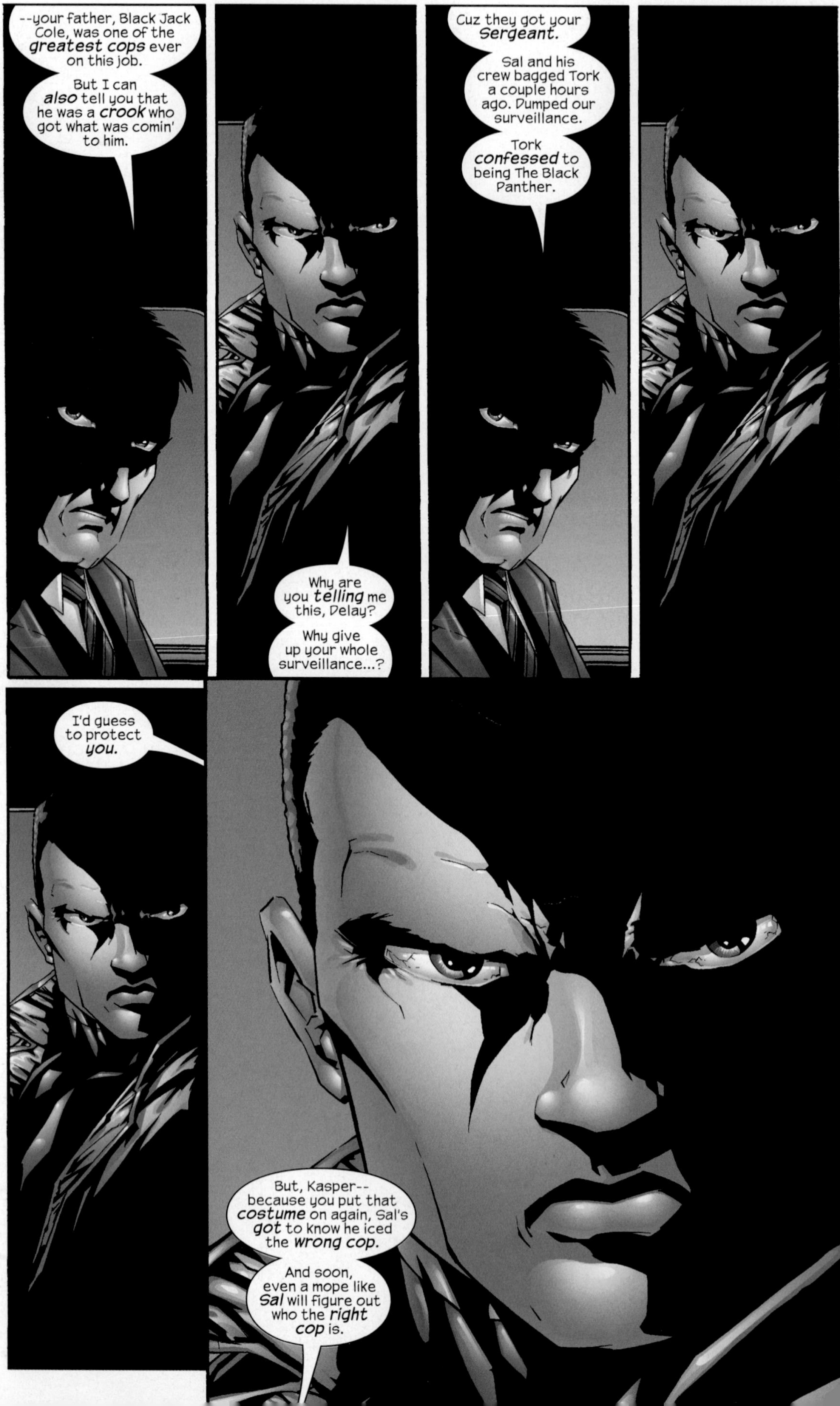
--your father, Black Jack Cole, was one of the greatest cops ever on this job.
But I can also tell you that he was a crook who got what was comin' to him.
Why are you telling me this, Delay?
Why give up your whole surveillance...?
Cuz they got your Sergeant.
Sal and his crew bagged Tork a couple hours ago. Dumped our surveillance.
Tork confessed to being The Black Panther.
I'd guess to protect you.
But, Kasper--because you put that costume on again, Sal's got to know he iced the wrong cop.
And soon, even a mope like Sal will figure out who the right cop is.

GOD AND MAN

God.
Please, God.

Father... I'm *begging* you...

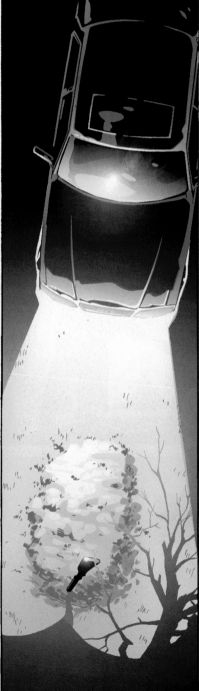

...please...

...don't make me carry this...

You've gotta get this car *out* of here for me, Tork.

Park it over on *The Hill*-- the *projects* where Panther used to live.

Tork's *prints* on that *car*...

...got him *killed*.

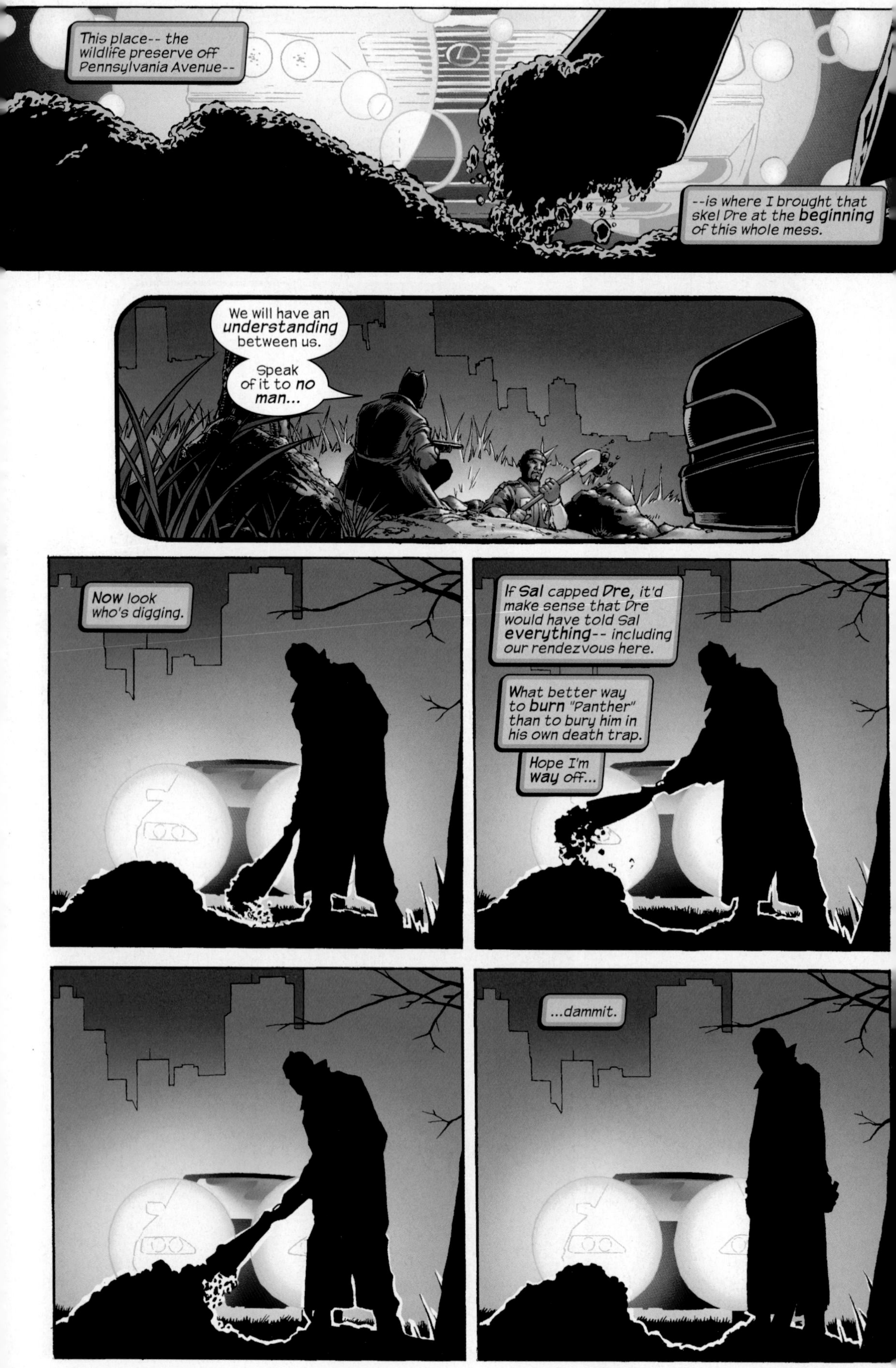
This place-- the wildlife preserve off Pennsylvania Avenue--
--is where I brought that skel Dre at the beginning of this whole mess.
We will have an understanding between us.
Speak of it to no man...
Now look who's digging.
If Sal capped Dre, it'd make sense that Dre would have told Sal everything-- including our rendezvous here.
What better way to burn "Panther" than to bury him in his own death trap.
Hope I'm way off...
...dammit.

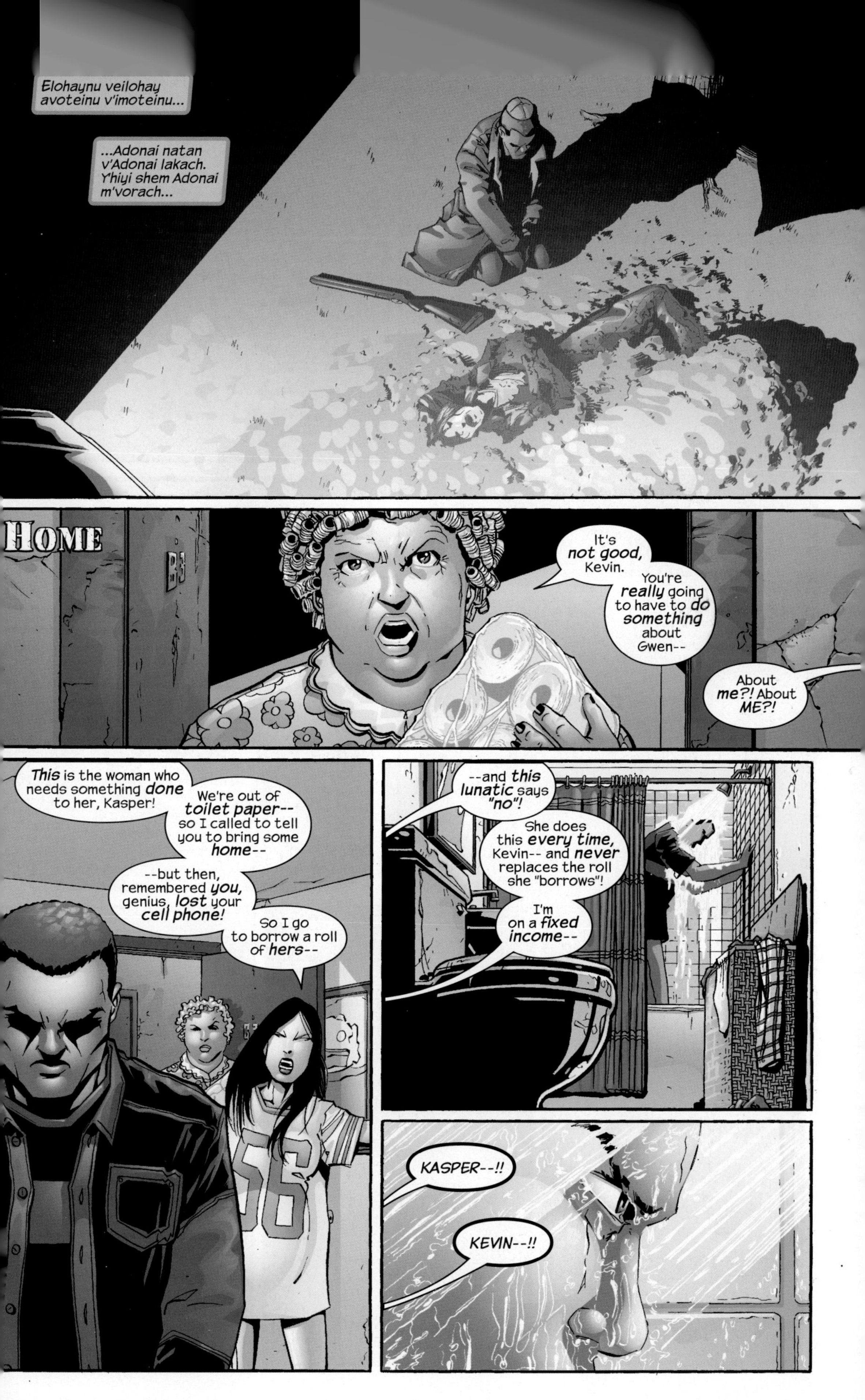
Elohaynu veilohay avoteinu v'imoteinu...
...Adonai natan v'Adonai lakach. Y'hiyi shem Adonai m'vorach...
HOME
It's not good, Kevin.
You're really going to have to do something about Gwen--
About me?! About ME?!
This is the woman who needs something done to her, Kasper!
We're out of toilet paper-- so I called to tell you to bring some home--
--but then, remembered you, genius, lost your cell phone!
So I go to borrow a roll of hers--
--and this lunatic says "no"!
She does this every time, Kevin-- and never replaces the roll she "borrows"!
I'm on a fixed income--
KASPER--!!
KEVIN--!!

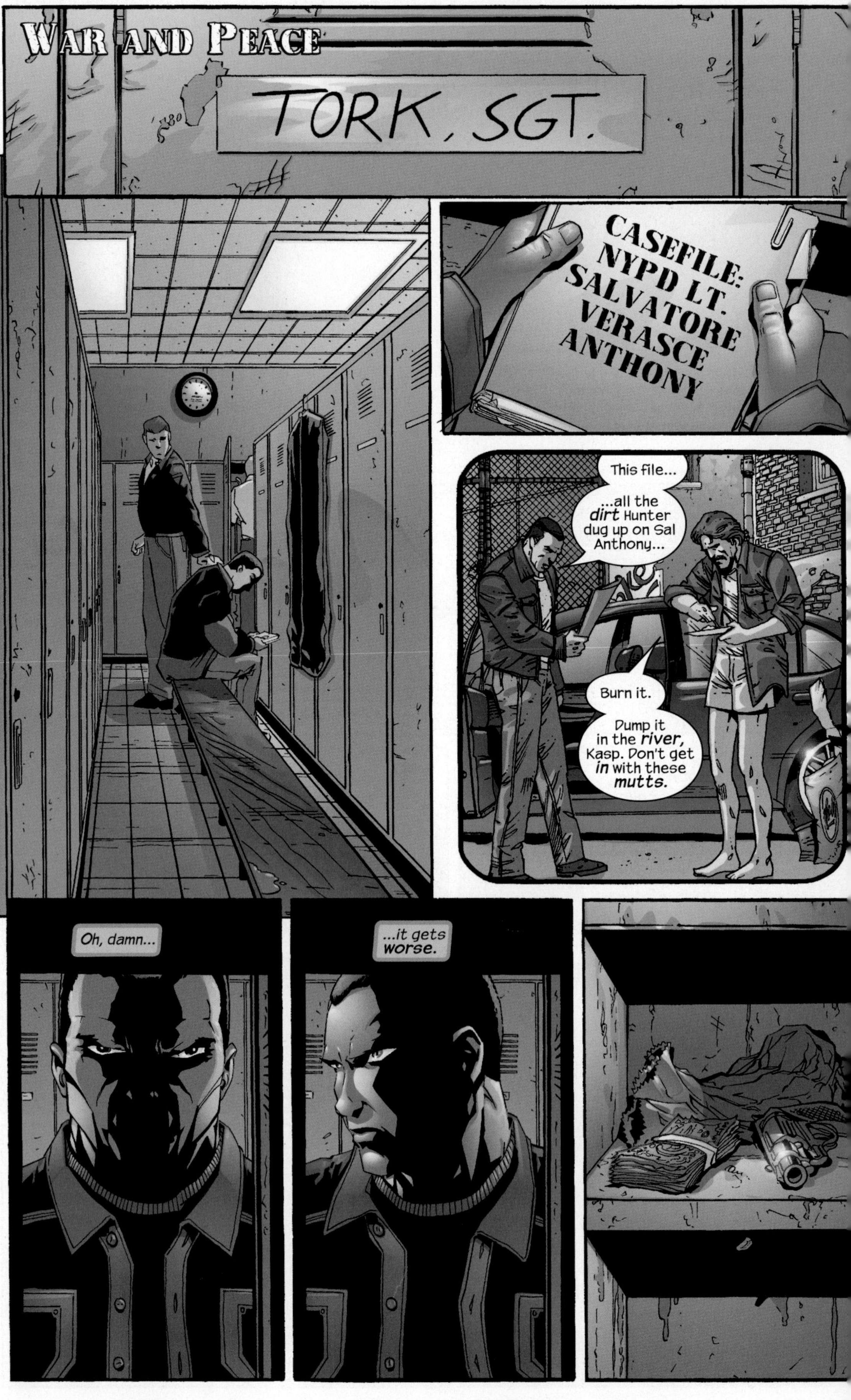
WAR AND PEACE
TORK, SGT.
CASEFILE: NYPD LT. SALVATORE VERASCE ANTHONY
This file...
...all the dirt Hunter dug up on Sal Anthony...
Burn it.
Dump it in the river, Kasp. Don't get in with these mutts.
Oh, damn...
...it gets worse.

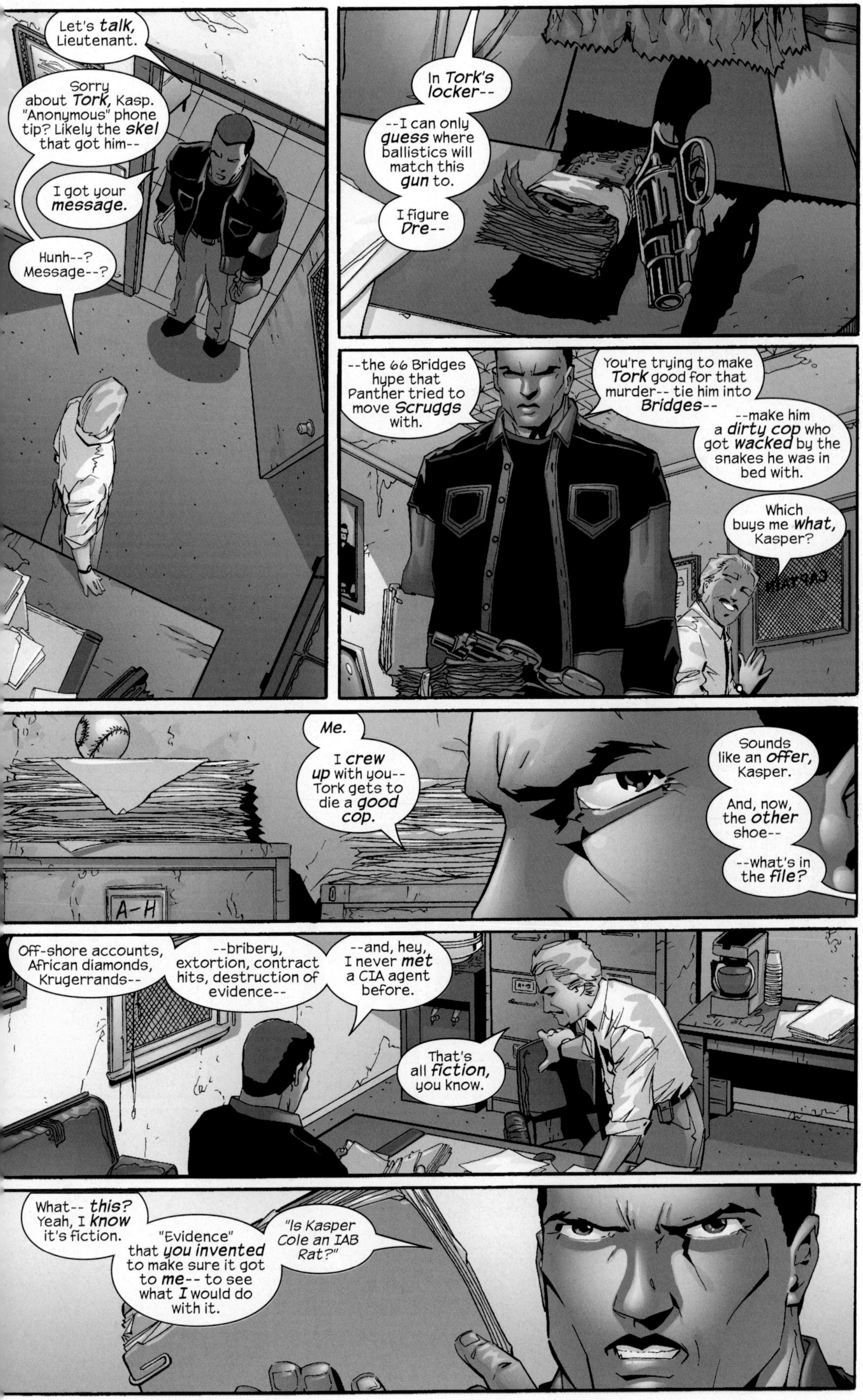

Let's talk, Lieutenant.
Sorry about Tork, Kasp. "Anonymous" phone tip? Likely the skel that got him--
I got your message.
Hunh--? Message--?
In Tork's locker--
--I can only guess where ballistics will match this gun to.
I figure Dre--
--the 66 Bridges hype that Panther tried to move Scruggs with.
You're trying to make Tork good for that murder-- tie him into Bridges--
--make him a dirty cop who got wacked by the snakes he was in bed with.
Which buys me what, Kasper?
Me.
I crew up with you-- Tork gets to die a good cop.
Sounds like an offer, Kasper.
And, now, the other shoe--
--what's in the file?
A-H
Off-shore accounts, African diamonds, Krugerrands--
--bribery, extortion, contract hits, destruction of evidence--
--and, hey, I never met a CIA agent before.
That's all fiction, you know.
What-- this? Yeah, I know it's fiction.
"Evidence" that you invented to make sure it got to me-- to see what I would do with it.
"Is Kasper Cole an IAB Rat?"

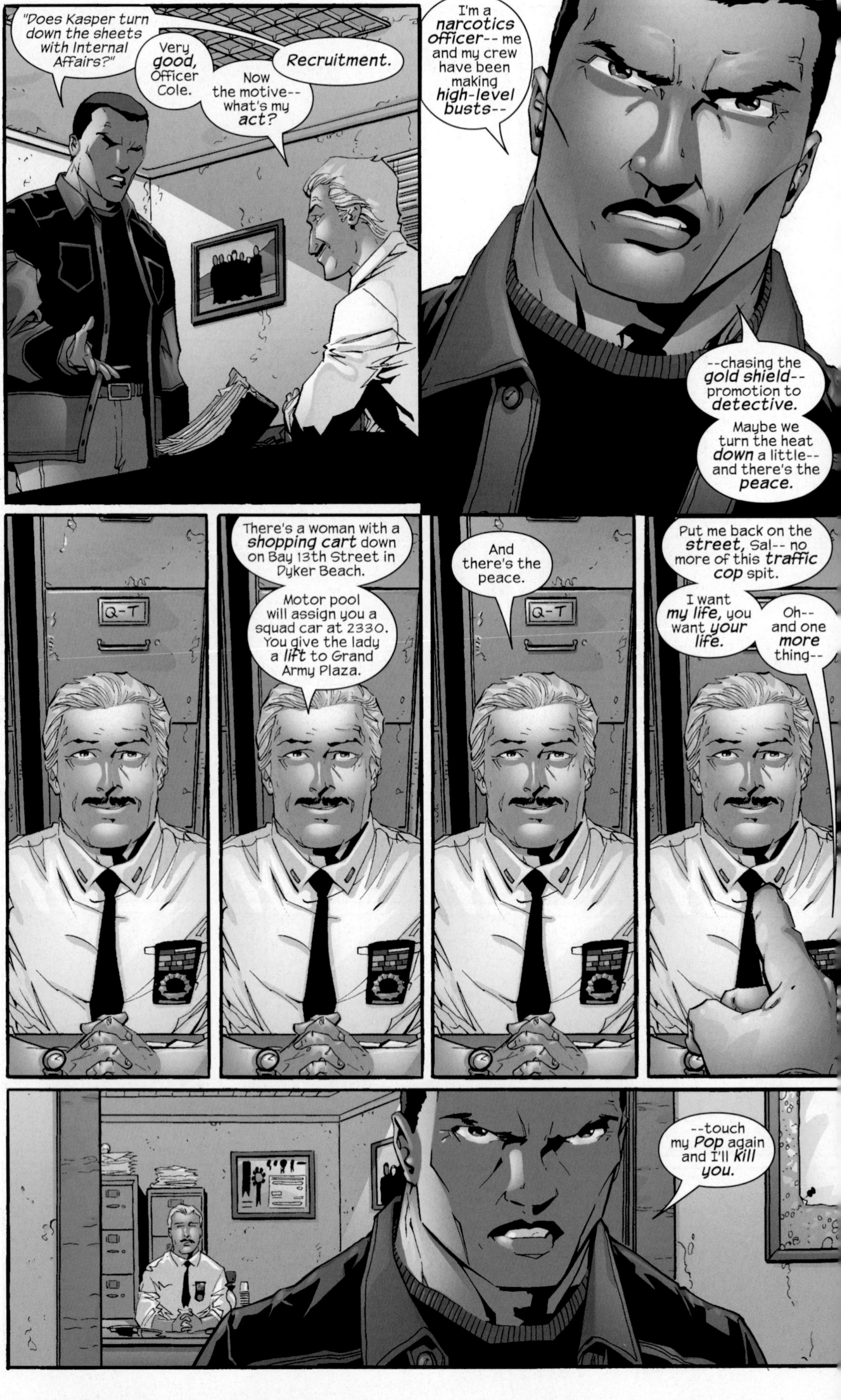
"Does Kasper turn down the sheets with Internal Affairs?"
Very good, Officer Cole.
Recruitment.
Now the motive-- what's my act?
I'm a narcotics officer-- me and my crew have been making high-level busts--
--chasing the gold shield-- promotion to detective.
Maybe we turn the heat down a little-- and there's the peace.
There's a woman with a shopping cart down on Bay 13th Street in Dyker Beach.
Motor pool will assign you a squad car at 2330. You give the lady a lift to Grand Army Plaza.
Q-T
And there's the peace.
Q-T
Put me back on the street, Sal-- no more of this traffic cop spit.
I want my life, you want your life.
Oh-- and one more thing--
--touch my Pop again and I'll kill you.

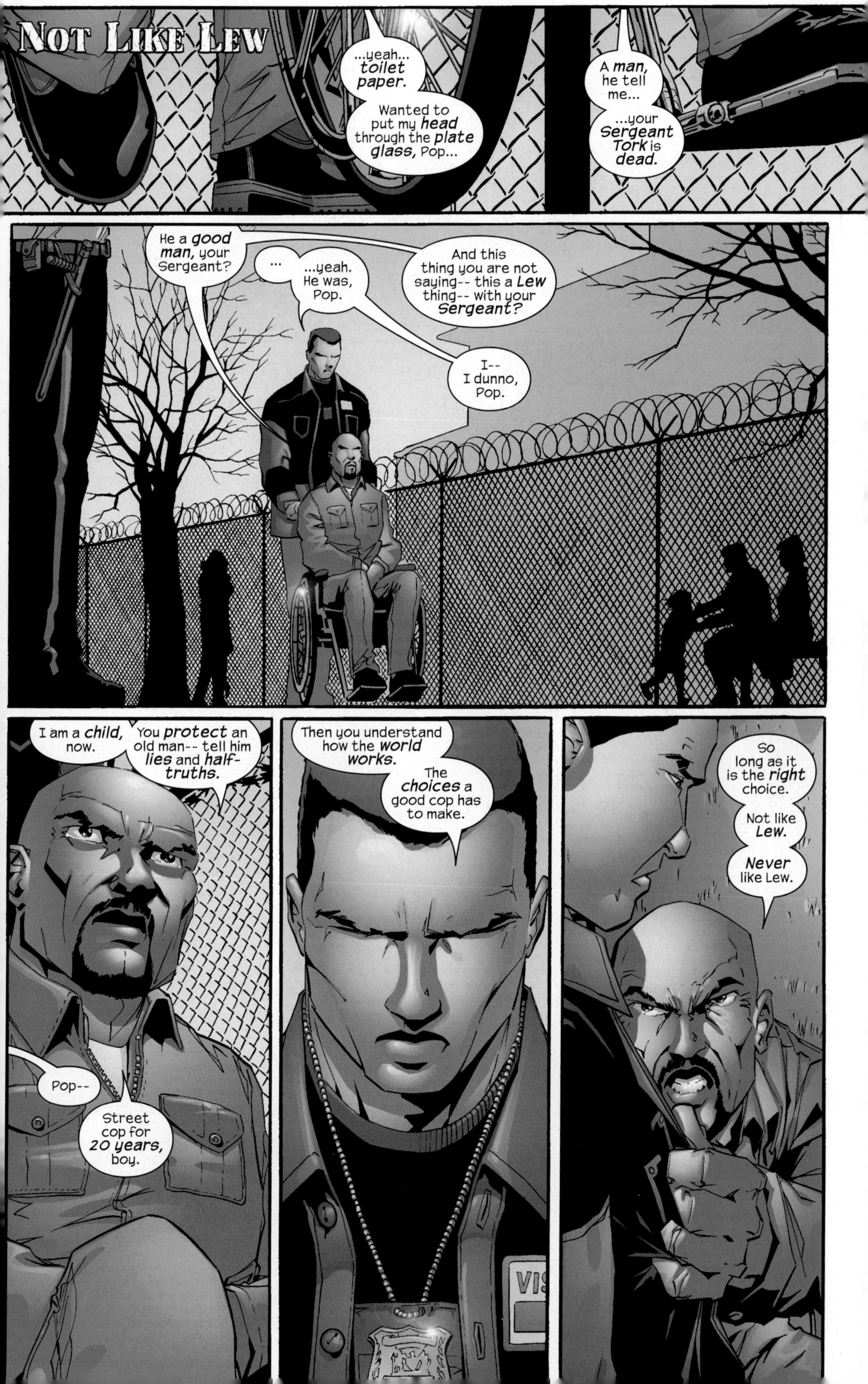
Not Like Lew
...yeah... toilet paper.
Wanted to put my head through the plate glass, Pop...
A man, he tell me...
...your Sergeant Tork is dead.
He a good man, your Sergeant?
...
...yeah. He was, Pop.
And this thing you are not saying-- this a Lew thing-- with your Sergeant?
I-- I dunno, Pop.
I am a child, now.
You protect an old man-- tell him lies and half-truths.
Pop--
Street cop for 20 years, boy.
Then you understand how the world works.
The choices a good cop has to make.
So long as it is the right choice.
Not like Lew.
Never like Lew.

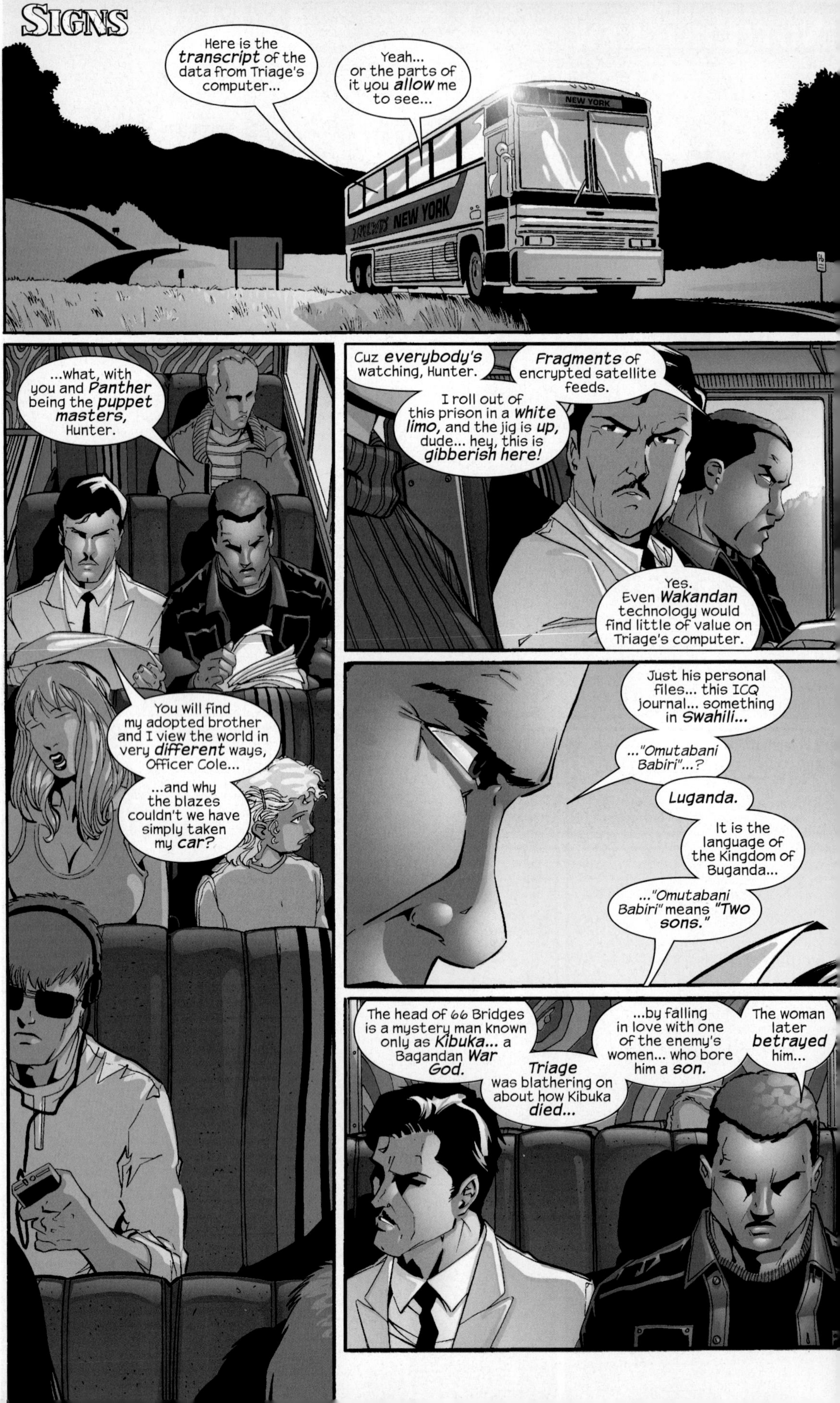
SIGNS
Here is the *transcript* of the data from Triage's computer...
Yeah... or the parts of it you *allow* me to see...
NEW YORK
NEW YORK
...what, with you and *Panther* being the *puppet masters,* Hunter.
You will find my adopted brother and I view the world in very *different* ways, Officer Cole...
...and why the blazes couldn't we have simply taken my *car?*
Cuz *everybody's* watching, Hunter.
I roll out of this prison in a *white limo,* and the jig is *up,* dude... hey, this is *gibberish here!*
Fragments of encrypted satellite feeds.
Yes. Even **Wakandan** technology would find little of value on Triage's computer.
Just his personal files... this ICQ journal... something in *Swahili...*
..."*Omutabani Babiri*"...?
Luganda.
It is the language of the Kingdom of Buganda...
..."*Omutabani Babiri*" means *"Two sons."*
The head of 66 Bridges is a mystery man known only as *Kibuka...* a Bagandan *War God.*
Triage was blathering on about how Kibuka *died...*
...by falling in love with one of the enemy's women... who bore him a *son.*
The woman later *betrayed* him...

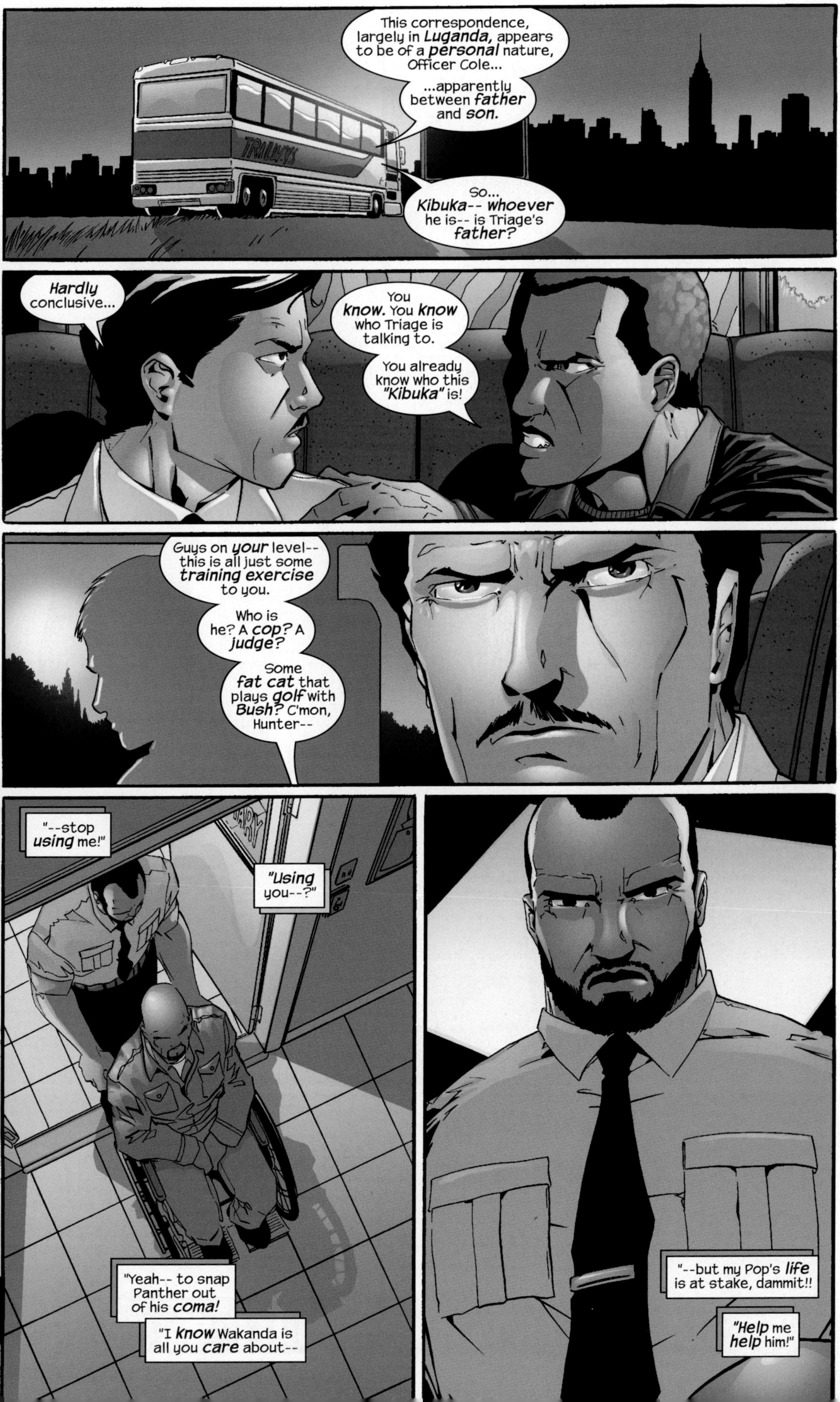

This correspondence, largely in Luganda, appears to be of a personal nature, Officer Cole...
...apparently between father and son.
So... Kibuka-- whoever he is-- is Triage's father?
Hardly conclusive...
You know. You know who Triage is talking to.
You already know who this "Kibuka" is!
Guys on your level-- this is all just some training exercise to you.
Who is he? A cop? A judge?
Some fat cat that plays golf with Bush? C'mon, Hunter--
"--stop using me!"
"Using you--?"
"Yeah-- to snap Panther out of his coma!
"I know Wakanda is all you care about--
"--but my Pop's life is at stake, dammit!!
"Help me help him!"

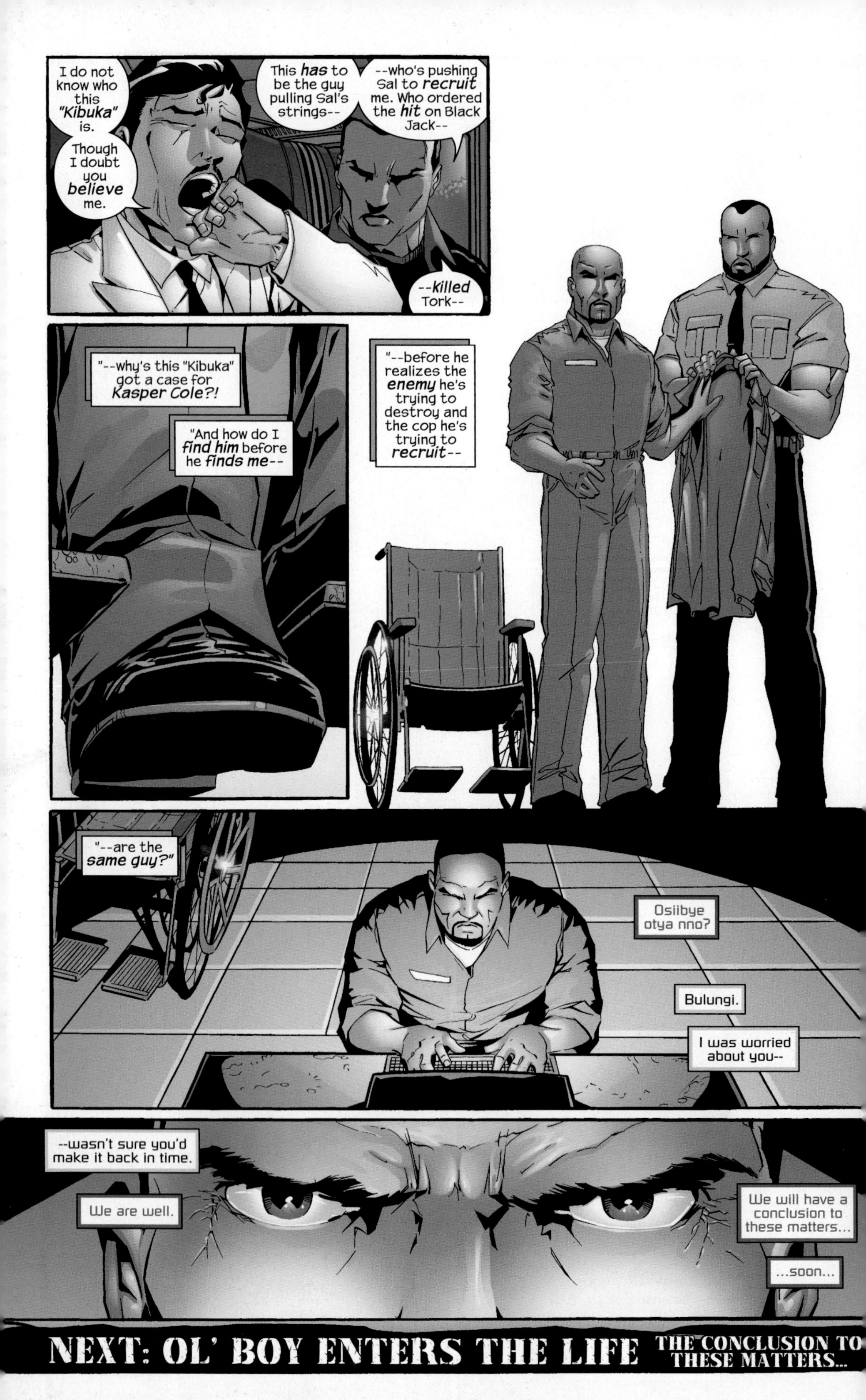
I do not know who this "Kibuka" is.
Though I doubt you believe me.
This has to be the guy pulling Sal's strings--
--who's pushing Sal to recruit me. Who ordered the hit on Black Jack--
--killed Tork--
"--why's this "Kibuka" got a case for Kasper Cole?!
"And how do I find him before he finds me--
"--before he realizes the enemy he's trying to destroy and the cop he's trying to recruit--
"--are the same guy?"
Osiibye otya nno?
Bulungi.
I was worried about you--
--wasn't sure you'd make it back in time.
We are well.
We will have a conclusion to these matters...
...soon...
NEXT: OL' BOY ENTERS THE LIFE
THE CONCLUSION TO THESE MATTERS...

MARVEL
PG 56
BLACK PANTHER
BLACK AND V
CHAPTER 6
PRIEST
CALAFIORE
McKENNA

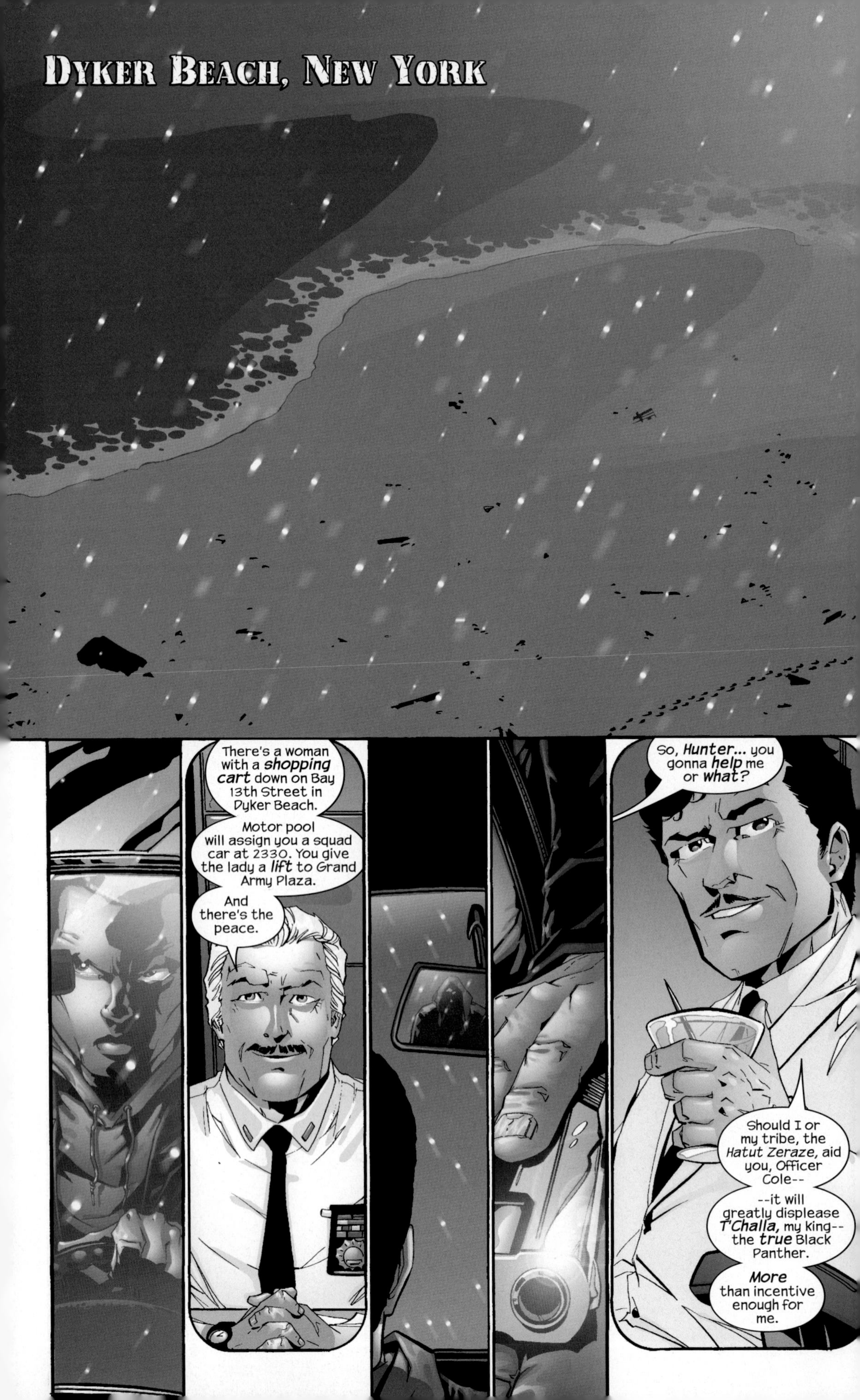
DYKER BEACH, NEW YORK
There's a woman with a shopping cart down on Bay 13th Street in Dyker Beach.
Motor pool will assign you a squad car at 2330. You give the lady a lift to Grand Army Plaza.
And there's the peace.
So, Hunter... you gonna help me or what?
Should I or my tribe, the Hatut Zeraze, aid you, Officer Cole--
--it will greatly displease T'Challa, my king-- the true Black Panther.
More than incentive enough for me.

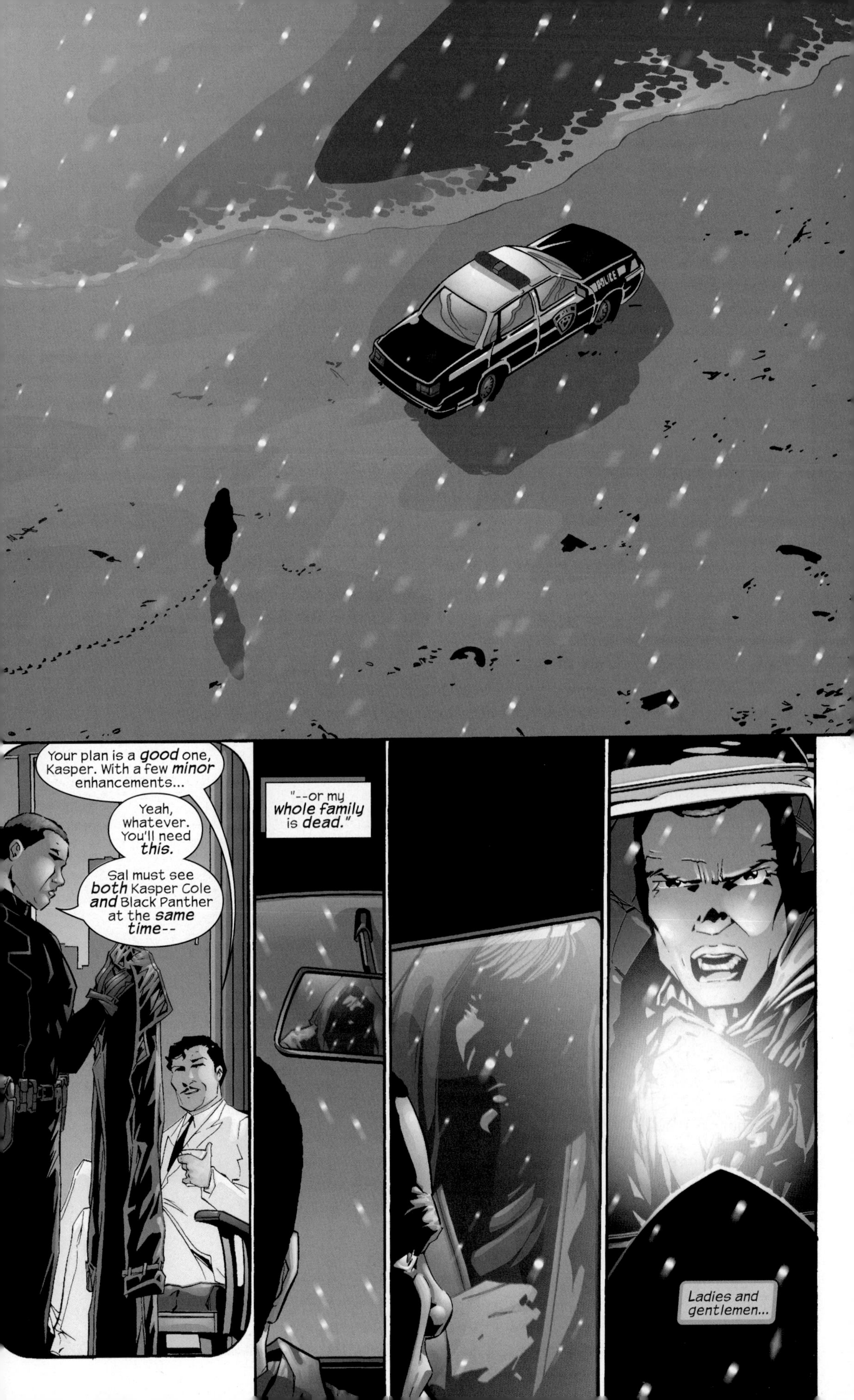

Your plan is a good one, Kasper. With a few minor enhancements...
Yeah, whatever. You'll need this.
Sal must see both Kasper Cole and Black Panther at the same time--
"--or my whole family is dead."
Ladies and gentlemen...

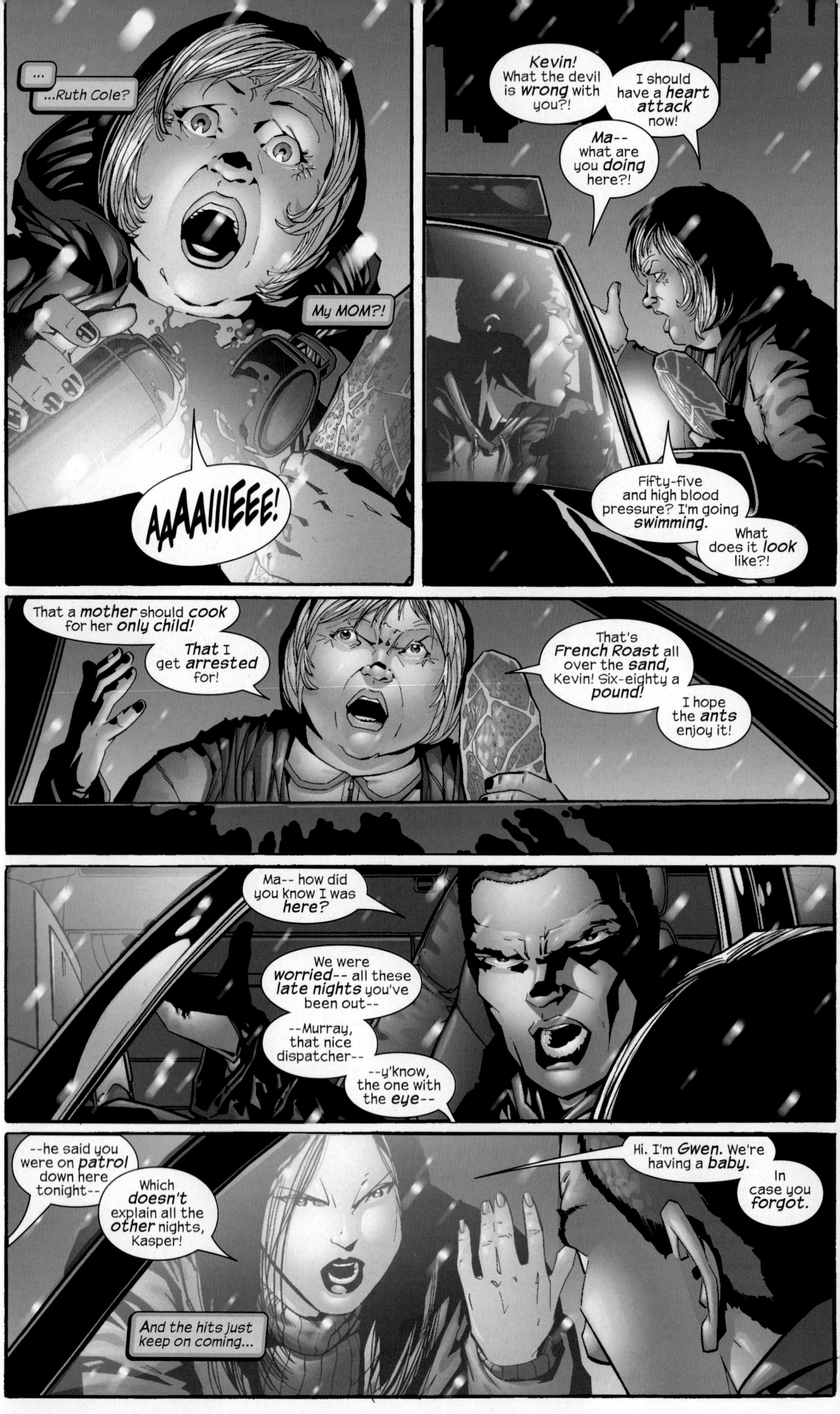
...
...Ruth Cole?
My MOM?!
AAAAIIIIEEE!
Kevin! What the devil is wrong with you?!
I should have a heart attack now!
Ma-- what are you doing here?!
Fifty-five and high blood pressure? I'm going swimming.
What does it look like?!
That a mother should cook for her only child!
That I get arrested for!
That's French Roast all over the sand, Kevin! Six-eighty a pound!
I hope the ants enjoy it!
Ma-- how did you know I was here?
We were worried-- all these late nights you've been out--
--Murray, that nice dispatcher--
--y'know, the one with the eye--
--he said you were on patrol down here tonight--
Which doesn't explain all the other nights, Kasper!
Hi. I'm Gwen. We're having a baby.
In case you forgot.
And the hits just keep on coming...

And where's your **uniform?**

Oy, you look like a **thug...**

...you should be in the **back** seat... in **handcuffs...**

Where ya **been,** Kasper? Don't you **like** your family anymore?

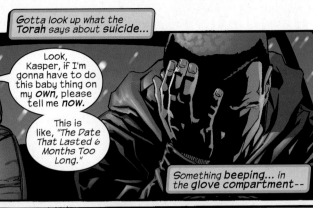

Gotta look up what the **Torah** says about **suicide...**

Look, Kasper, if I'm gonna have to do this baby thing on my **own,** please tell me **now.**

This is like, "The Date That Lasted 6 Months Too Long."

Something **beeping...** in the **glove compartment**--

--somebody left a **cell phone** in here?

--at least run the **motor** and turn some **lights** on-- you'll catch your **death**--

My parents threw me **out,** Kasper-- so if you're not gonna hold up **your end**--

Internal Affairs. Captain de LaGuardia...

Kasper, it's **Delay.**

Internal Affairs **knows** about Sal's little initiation tonight, Kasper--

--you pick up a **mule**-- deliver her and her **package** to Grand Army Plaza.

Then Sal's **comfortable** that he has something **on** you-- he leaves you be.

But we **both** know that's **not** gonna happen.

You do this, and Sal will **own** you forever.

Look, Kasper-- if you don't report this, I gotta write it up. But if you **do** report it, well... then you're working for **us.**

Either choice means you're not a **cop** anymore.

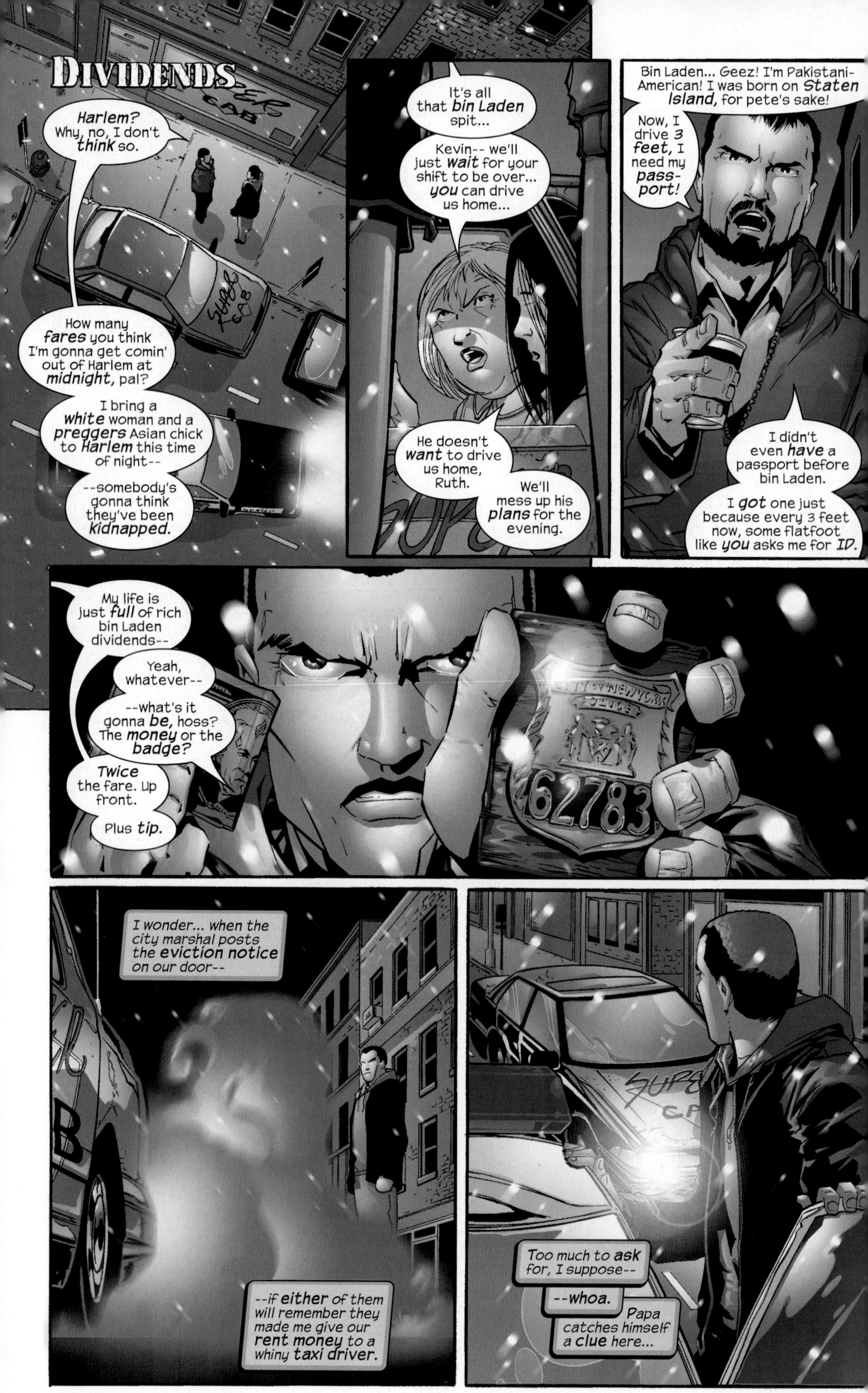
DIVIDENDS
Harlem? Why, no, I don't think so.
How many fares you think I'm gonna get comin' out of Harlem at midnight, pal?
I bring a white woman and a preggers Asian chick to Harlem this time of night--
--somebody's gonna think they've been kidnapped.
It's all that bin Laden spit...
Kevin-- we'll just wait for your shift to be over... you can drive us home...
He doesn't want to drive us home, Ruth.
We'll mess up his plans for the evening.
Bin Laden... Geez! I'm Pakistani-American! I was born on Staten Island, for pete's sake!
Now, I drive 3 feet, I need my pass-port!
I didn't even have a passport before bin Laden.
I got one just because every 3 feet now, some flatfoot like you asks me for ID.
My life is just full of rich bin Laden dividends--
Yeah, whatever--
--what's it gonna be, hoss? The money or the badge?
Twice the fare. Up front.
Plus tip.
CITY OF NEW YORK POLICE
62783
I wonder... when the city marshal posts the eviction notice on our door--
--if either of them will remember they made me give our rent money to a whiny taxi driver.
Too much to ask for, I suppose--
--whoa.
Papa catches himself a clue here...

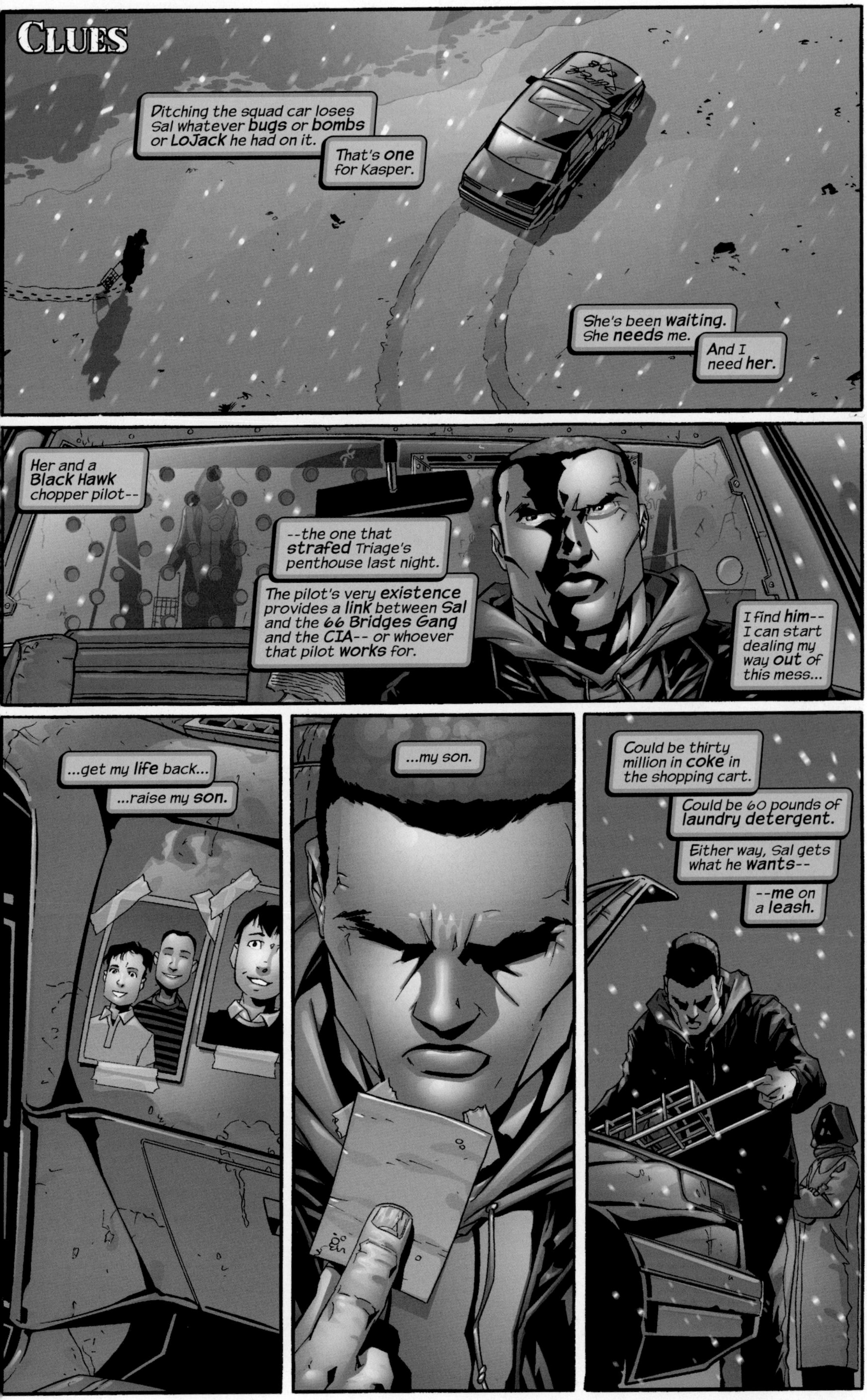
CLUES
Ditching the squad car loses Sal whatever bugs or bombs or LoJack he had on it.
That's one for Kasper.
She's been waiting. She needs me.
And I need her.
Her and a Black Hawk chopper pilot--
--the one that strafed Triage's penthouse last night.
The pilot's very existence provides a link between Sal and the 66 Bridges Gang and the CIA-- or whoever that pilot works for.
I find him-- I can start dealing my way out of this mess...
...get my life back...
...raise my son.
...my son.
Could be thirty million in coke in the shopping cart.
Could be 60 pounds of laundry detergent.
Either way, Sal gets what he wants--
--me on a leash.

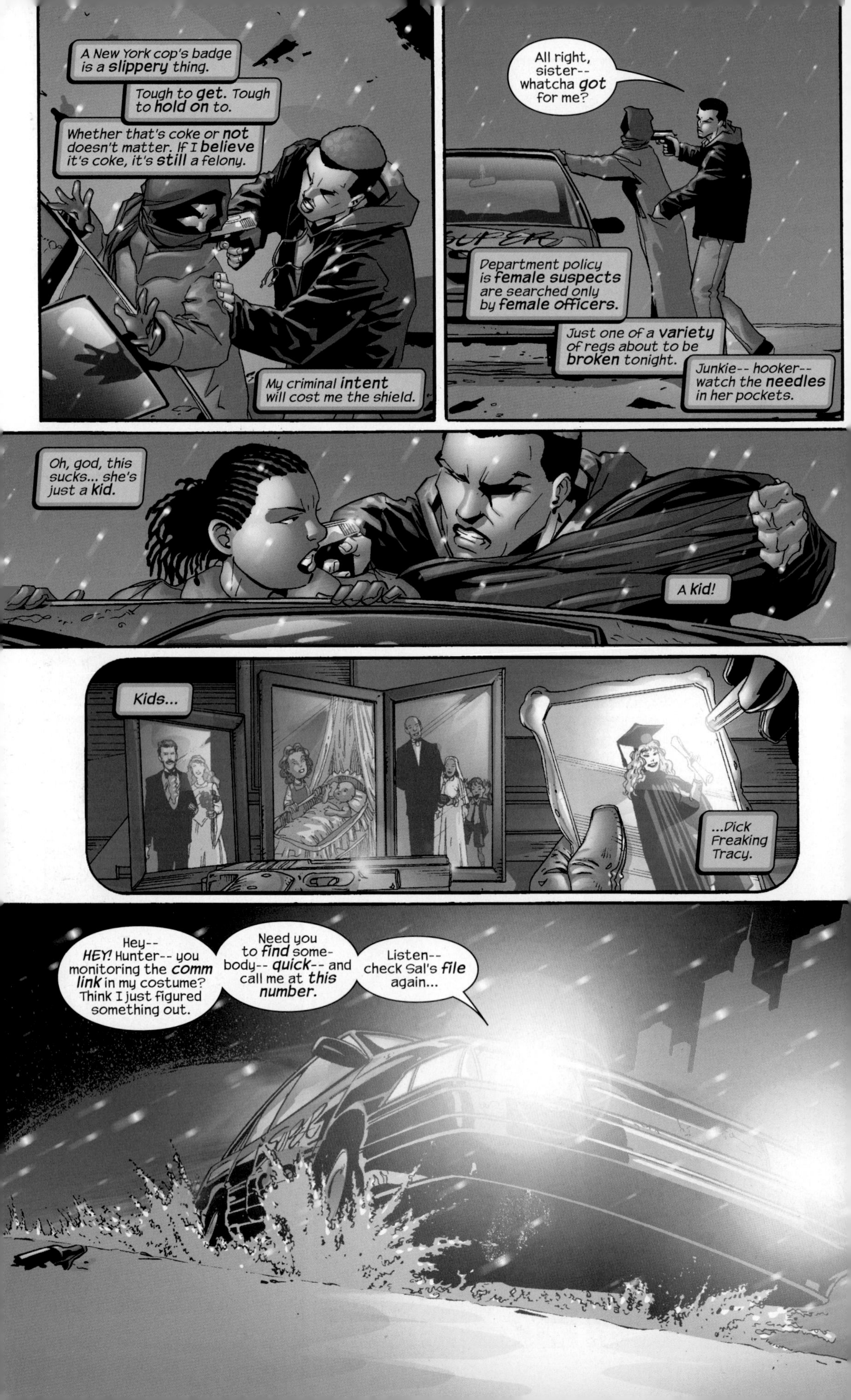
A New York cop's badge is a slippery thing.
Tough to get. Tough to hold on to.
Whether that's coke or not doesn't matter. If I believe it's coke, it's still a felony.
My criminal intent will cost me the shield.
All right, sister-- whatcha got for me?
Department policy is female suspects are searched only by female officers.
Just one of a variety of regs about to be broken tonight.
Junkie-- hooker-- watch the needles in her pockets.
Oh, god, this sucks... she's just a kid.
A kid!
Kids...
...Dick Freaking Tracy.
Hey-- HEY! Hunter-- you monitoring the comm link in my costume? Think I just figured something out.
Need you to find some-body-- quick-- and call me at this number.
Listen-- check Sal's file again...

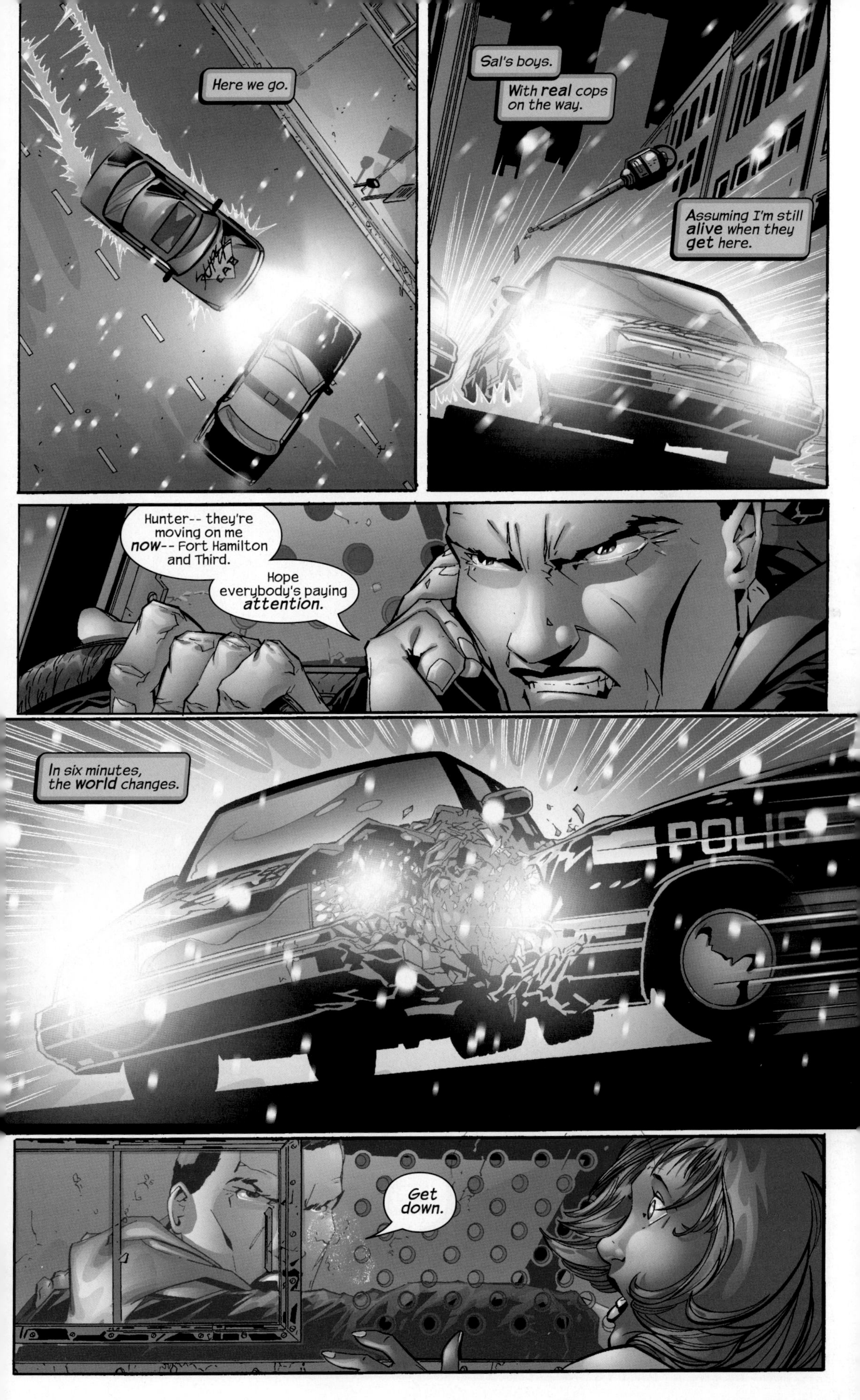
Here we go.
Sal's boys.
With real cops on the way.
Assuming I'm still alive when they get here.
Hunter-- they're moving on me now-- Fort Hamilton and Third.
Hope everybody's paying attention.
In six minutes, the world changes.
POLIC
Get down.

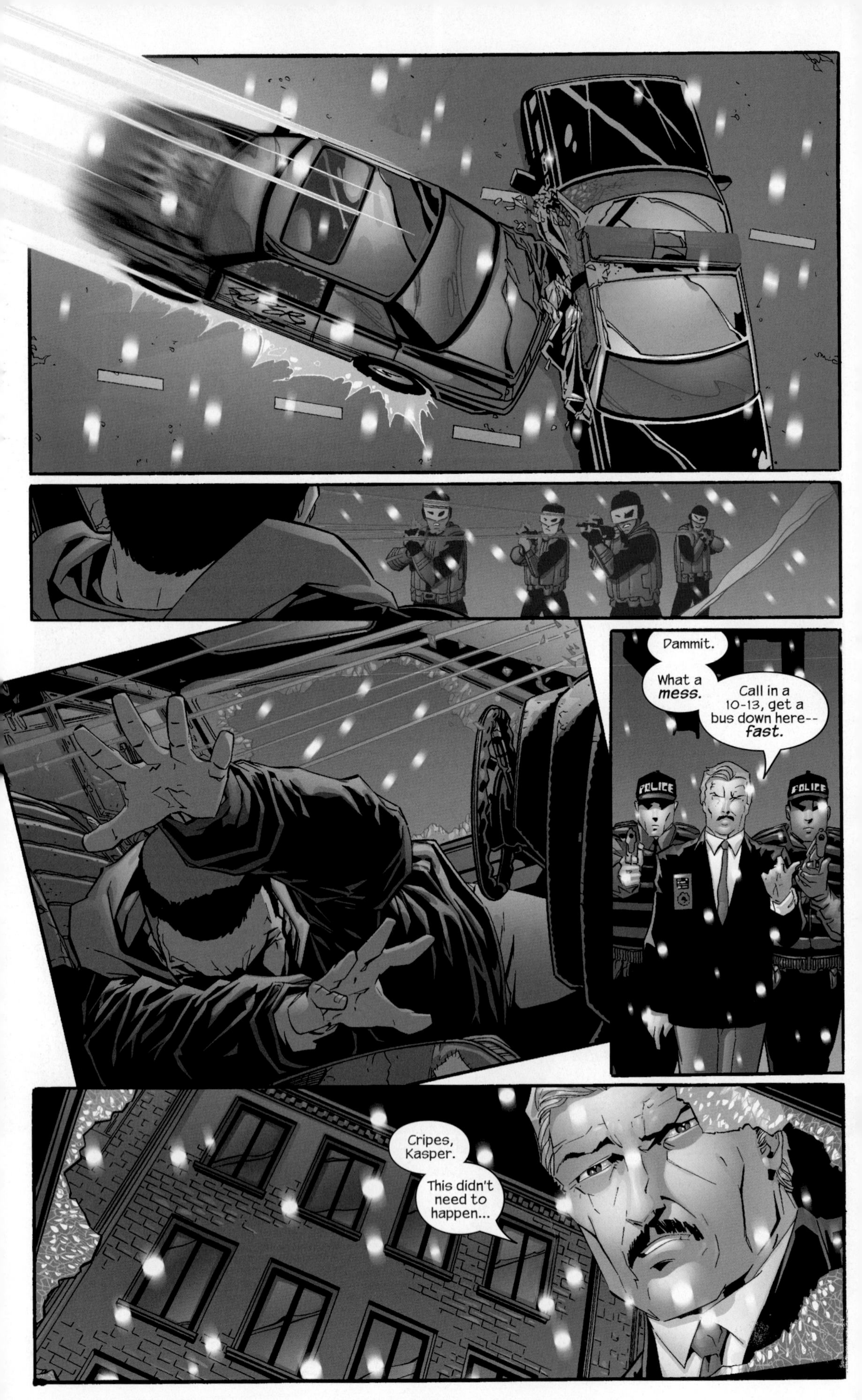
Dammit.
What a mess.
Call in a 10-13, get a bus down here--fast.
POLICE
POLICE
Cripes, Kasper.
This didn't need to happen...

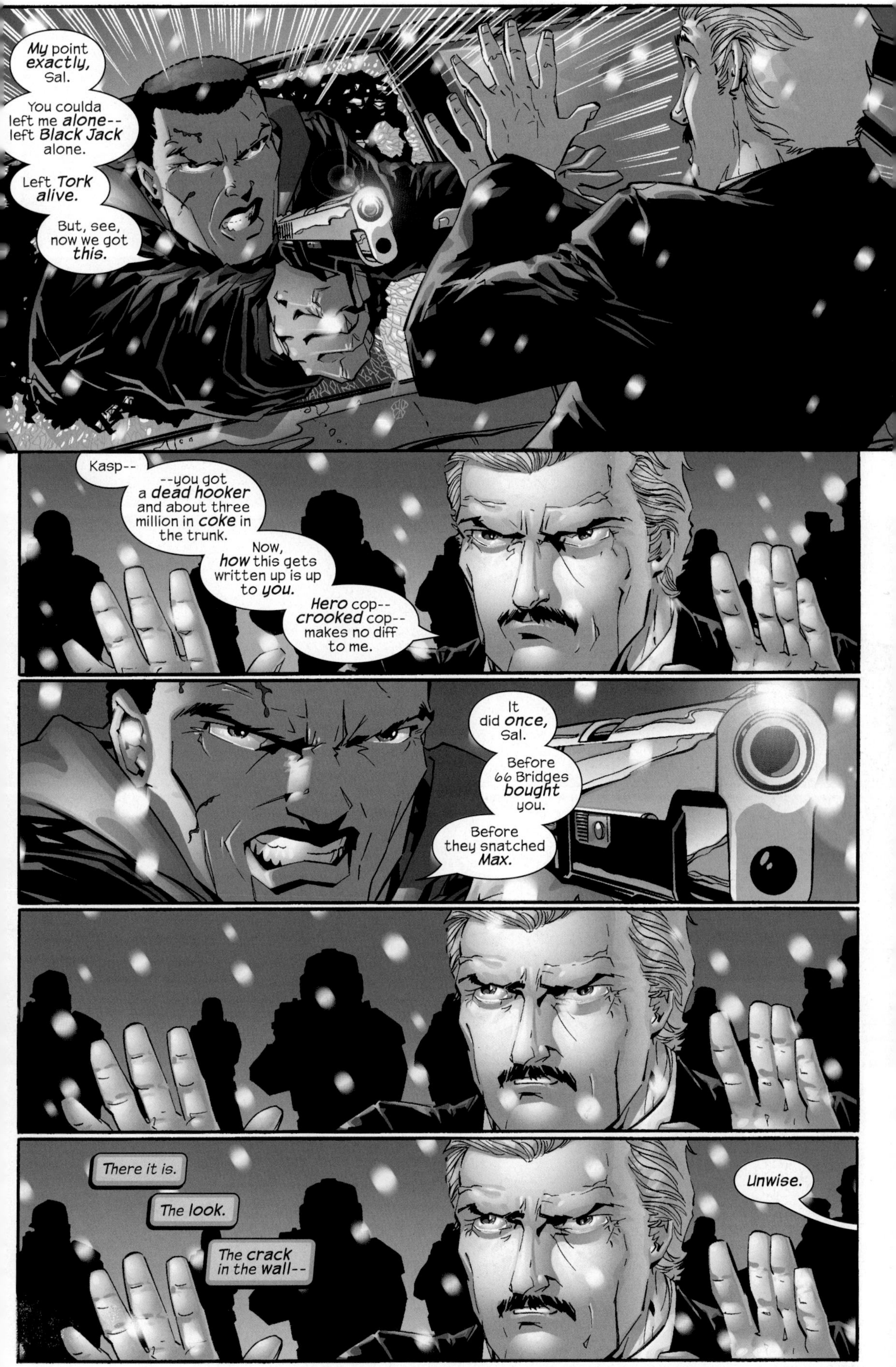
My point exactly, Sal.
You coulda left me alone-- left Black Jack alone.
Left Tork alive.
But, see, now we got this.
Kasp--
--you got a dead hooker and about three million in coke in the trunk.
Now, how this gets written up is up to you.
Hero cop-- crooked cop-- makes no diff to me.
It did once, Sal.
Before 66 Bridges bought you.
Before they snatched Max.
There it is.
The look.
The crack in the wall--
Unwise.

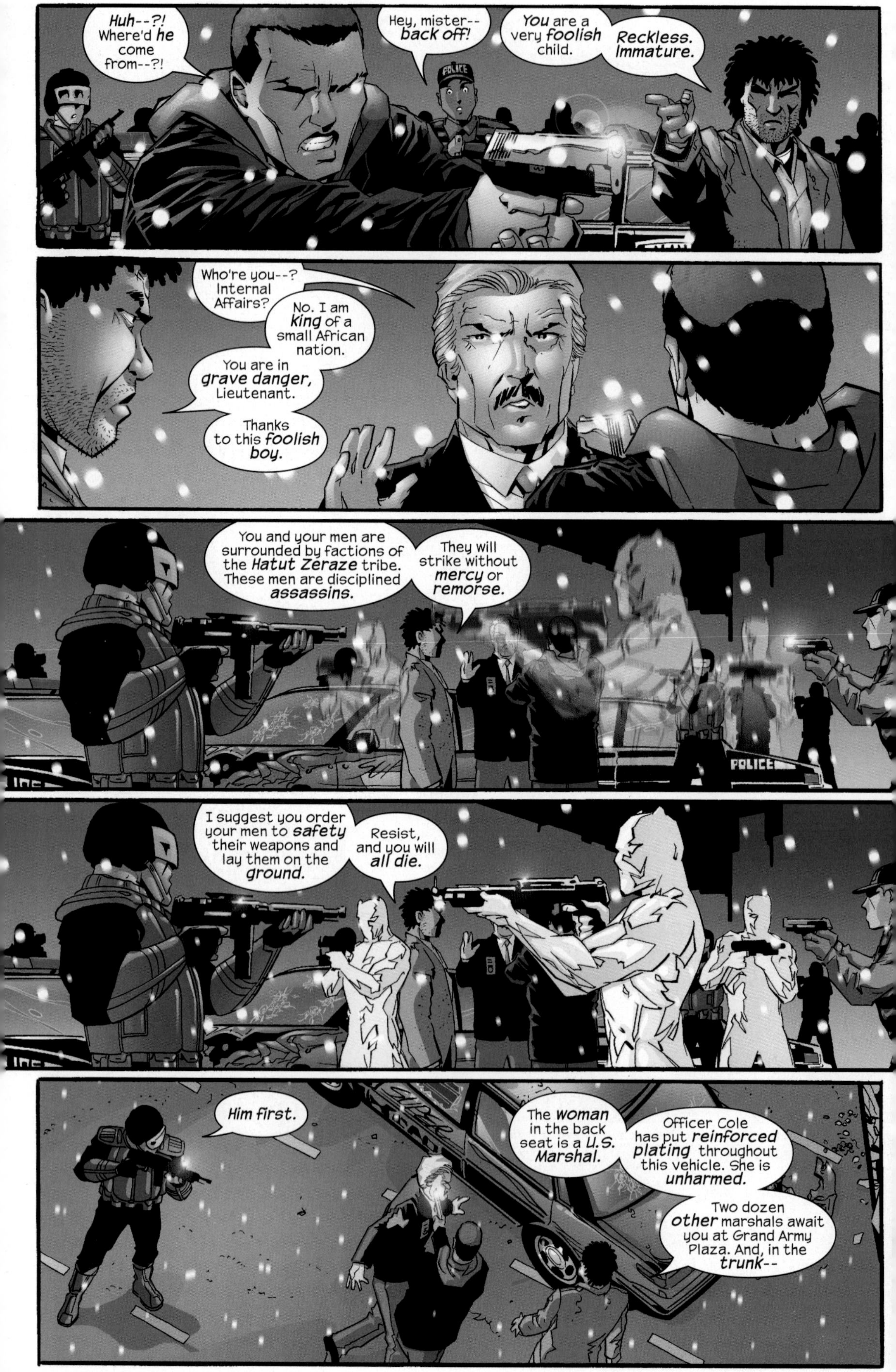
Huh--?! Where'd he come from--?!
Hey, mister-- back off!
You are a very foolish child.
Reckless. Immature.
POLICE
Who're you--? Internal Affairs?
No. I am king of a small African nation.
You are in grave danger, Lieutenant.
Thanks to this foolish boy.
You and your men are surrounded by factions of the Hatut Zeraze tribe. These men are disciplined assassins.
They will strike without mercy or remorse.
POLICE
I suggest you order your men to safety their weapons and lay them on the ground.
Resist, and you will all die.
Him first.
The woman in the back seat is a U.S. Marshal.
Officer Cole has put reinforced plating throughout this vehicle. She is unharmed.
Two dozen other marshals await you at Grand Army Plaza. And, in the trunk--

--the *pilot* of the Black Hawk helicopter Triage used to try and *kill me.*

Kill you-- *you?!*

Wait-- are you saying you-- you're--?

--*very* annoyed.

I leave you all to your *foolishness.*

You ain't goin' *nowhere,* you son of--

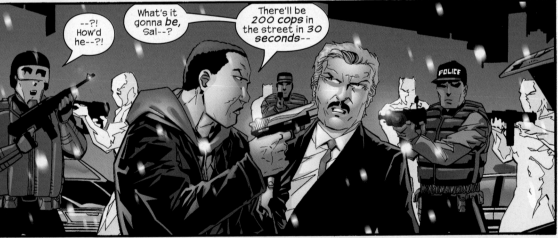

--?! How'd he--?!

What's it gonna *be,* Sal--?

There'll be *200 cops* in the street in *30 seconds*--

--what say we take a *ride?*

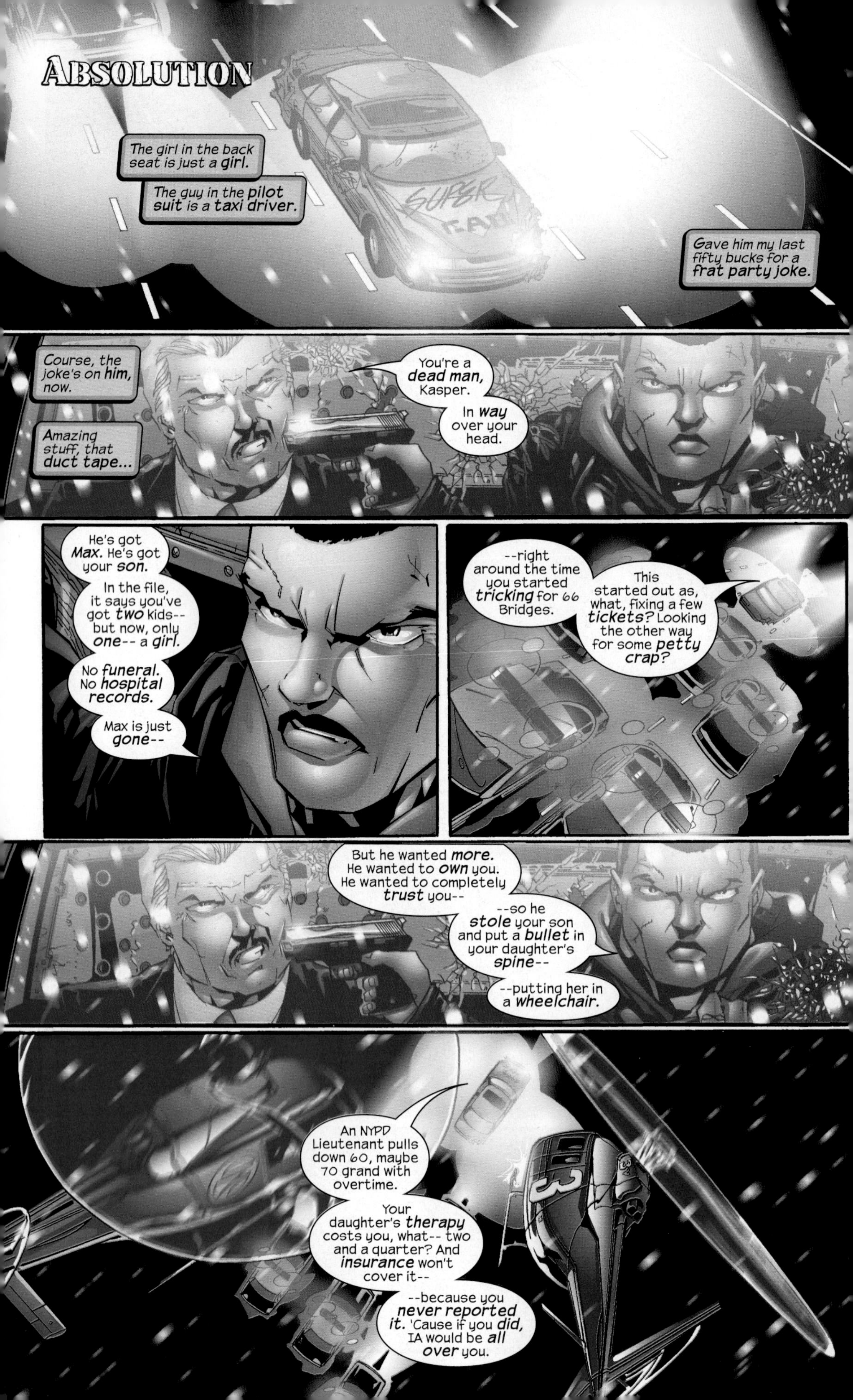
ABSOLUTION
The girl in the back seat is just a girl.
The guy in the pilot suit is a taxi driver.
SUPER
Gave him my last fifty bucks for a frat party joke.
Course, the joke's on him, now.
Amazing stuff, that duct tape...
You're a dead man, Kasper.
In way over your head.
He's got Max. He's got your son.
In the file, it says you've got two kids-- but now, only one-- a girl.
No funeral. No hospital records.
Max is just gone--
This started out as, what, fixing a few tickets? Looking the other way for some petty crap?
--right around the time you started tricking for 66 Bridges.
But he wanted more. He wanted to own you. He wanted to completely trust you--
--so he stole your son and put a bullet in your daughter's spine--
--putting her in a wheelchair.
An NYPD Lieutenant pulls down 60, maybe 70 grand with overtime.
Your daughter's therapy costs you, what-- two and a quarter? And insurance won't cover it--
--because you never reported it. 'Cause if you did, IA would be all over you.

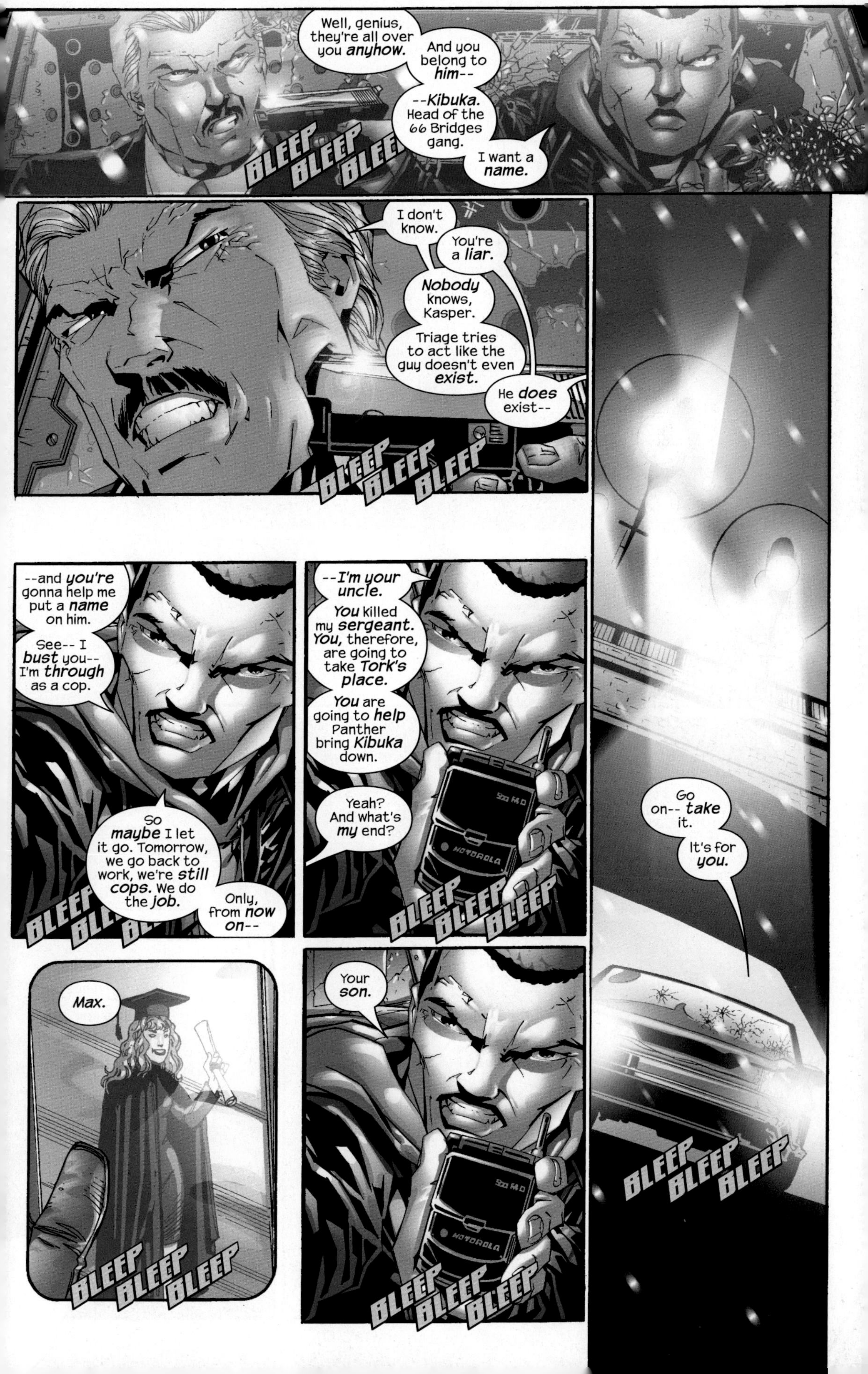
Well, genius, they're all over you anyhow.
And you belong to him--
--Kibuka. Head of the 66 Bridges gang.
I want a name.
BLEEP BLEEP BLEEP
I don't know.
You're a liar.
Nobody knows, Kasper.
Triage tries to act like the guy doesn't even exist.
He does exist--
BLEEP BLEEP BLEEP
--and you're gonna help me put a name on him.
See-- I bust you-- I'm through as a cop.
So maybe I let it go. Tomorrow, we go back to work, we're still cops. We do the job.
Only, from now on--
--I'm your uncle.
You killed my sergeant. You, therefore, are going to take Tork's place.
You are going to help Panther bring Kibuka down.
Yeah? And what's my end?
BLEEP BLEEP BLEEP
Max.
BLEEP BLEEP BLEEP
Your son.
BLEEP BLEEP BLEEP
Go on-- take it.
It's for you.
BLEEP BLEEP BLEEP

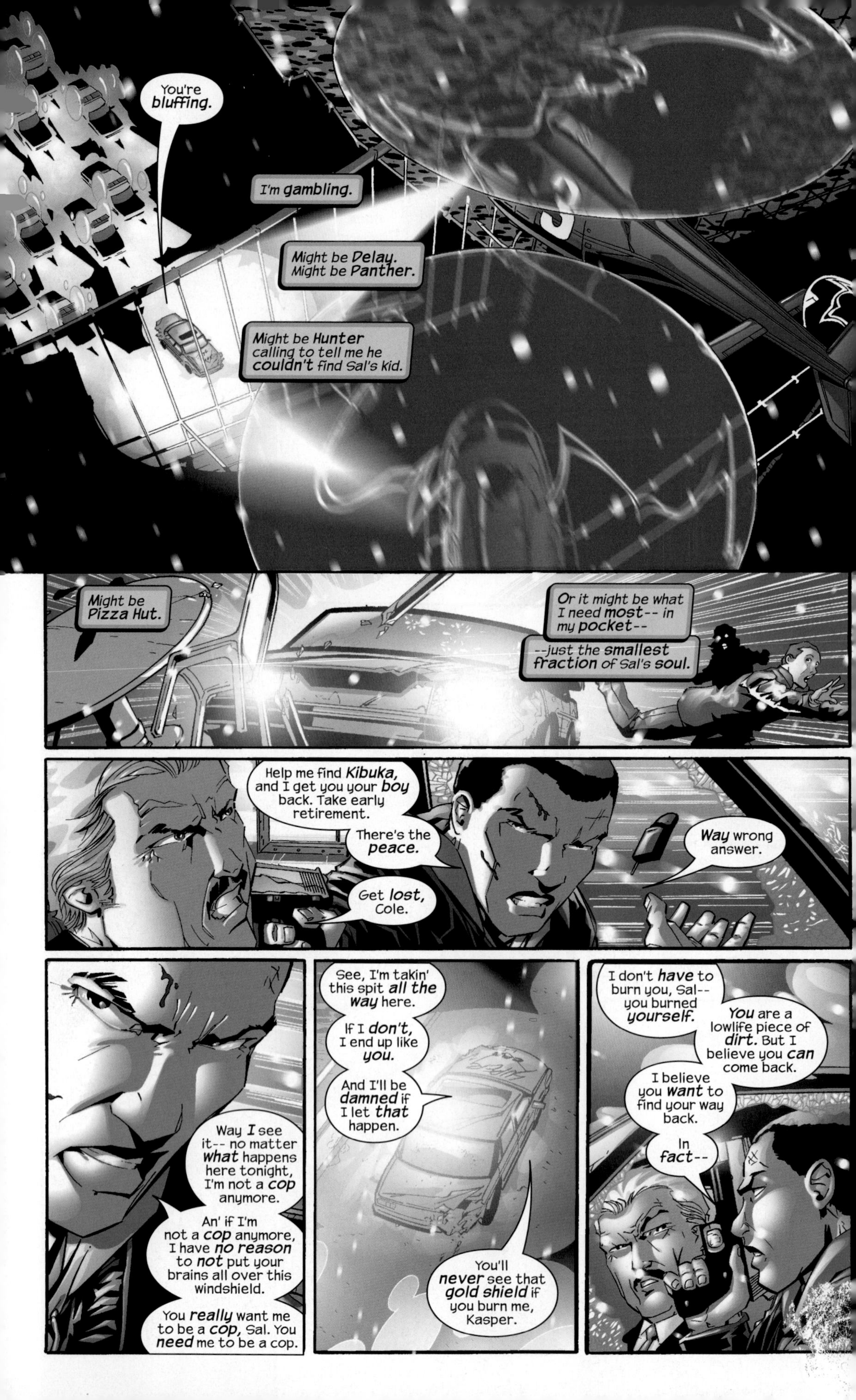
You're bluffing.
I'm gambling.
Might be Delay. Might be Panther.
Might be Hunter calling to tell me he couldn't find Sal's kid.
Might be Pizza Hut.
Or it might be what I need most-- in my pocket--
--just the smallest fraction of Sal's soul.
Help me find Kibuka, and I get you your boy back. Take early retirement.
There's the peace.
Get lost, Cole.
Way wrong answer.
Way I see it-- no matter what happens here tonight, I'm not a cop anymore.
An' if I'm not a cop anymore, I have no reason to not put your brains all over this windshield.
You really want me to be a cop, Sal. You need me to be a cop.
See, I'm takin' this spit all the way here.
If I don't, I end up like you.
And I'll be damned if I let that happen.
You'll never see that gold shield if you burn me, Kasper.
I don't have to burn you, Sal-- you burned yourself.
You are a lowlife piece of dirt. But I believe you can come back.
I believe you want to find your way back.
In fact--

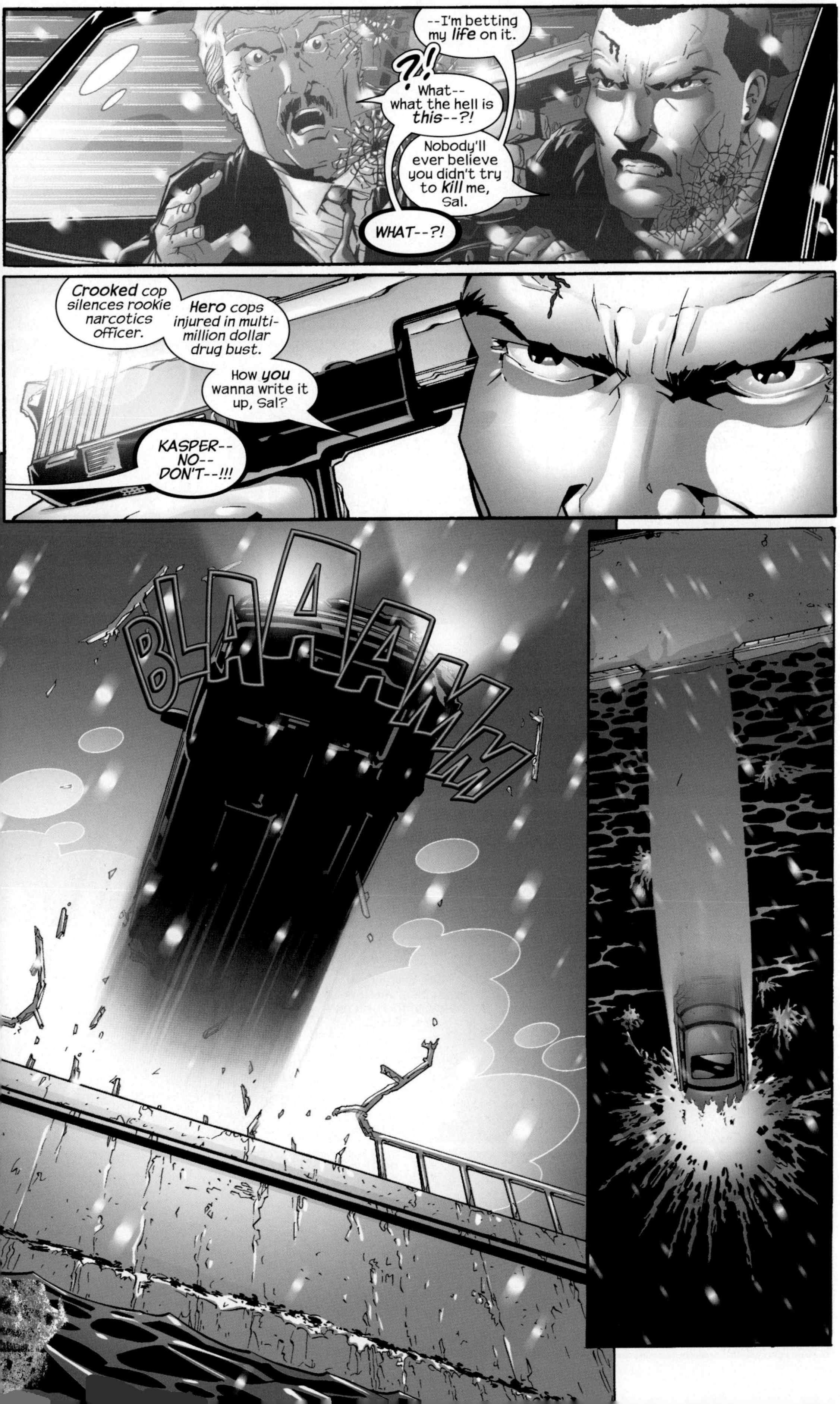

--I'm betting my life on it.
?!
What-- what the hell is this--?!
Nobody'll ever believe you didn't try to kill me, Sal.
WHAT--?!
Crooked cop silences rookie narcotics officer.
Hero cops injured in multi-million dollar drug bust.
How you wanna write it up, Sal?
KASPER-- NO-- DON'T--!!!
BLAAAMM

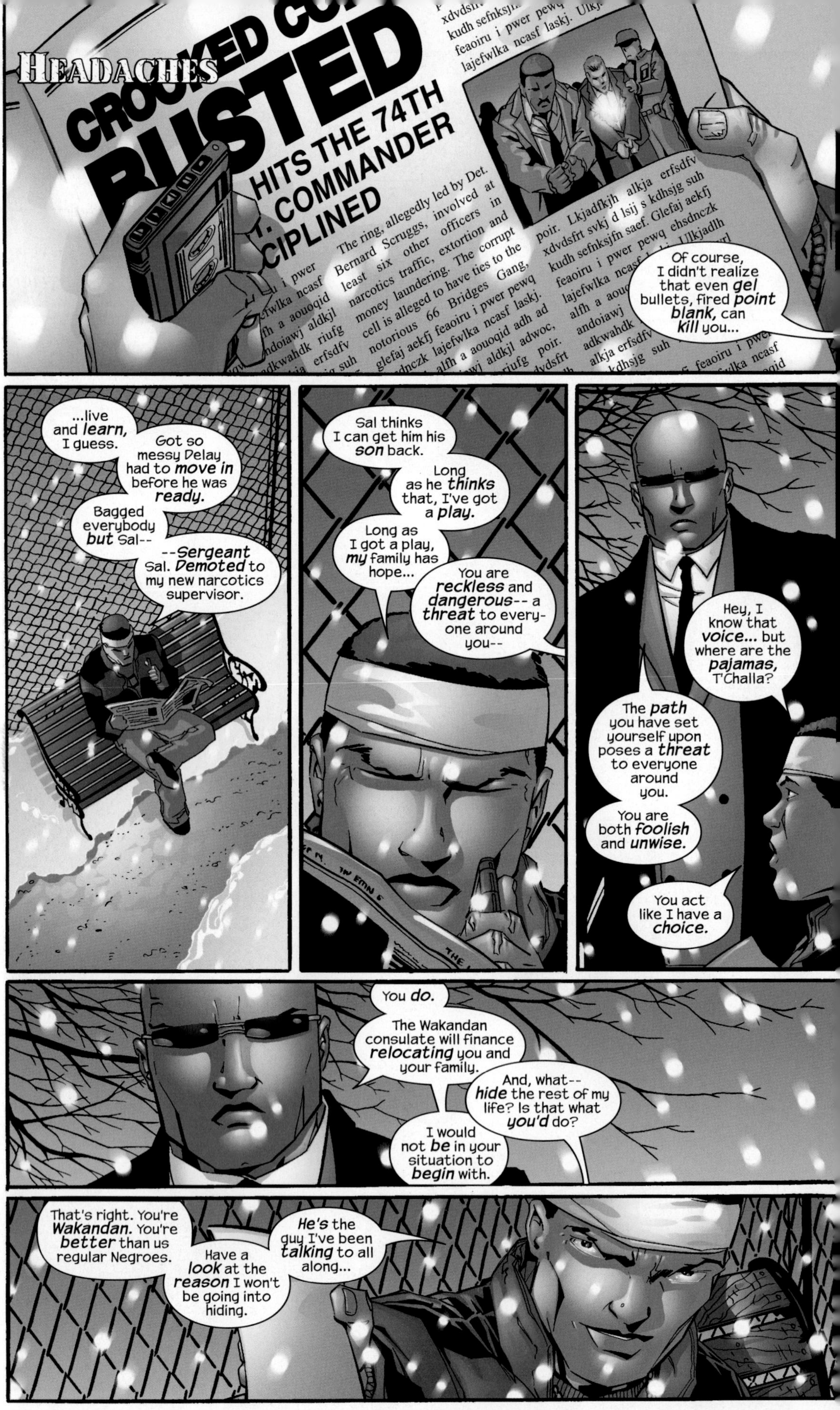
HEADACHES
CROOKED CO
BUSTED
HITS THE 74TH
T. COMMANDER
CIPLINED
The ring, allegedly led by Det. Bernard Scruggs, involved at least six other officers in narcotics traffic, extortion and money laundering. The corrupt cell is alleged to have ties to the notorious 66 Bridges Gang,
Of course, I didn't realize that even gel bullets, fired point blank, can kill you...
...live and learn, I guess.
Got so messy Delay had to move in before he was ready.
Bagged everybody but Sal--
--Sergeant Sal. Demoted to my new narcotics supervisor.
Sal thinks I can get him his son back.
Long as he thinks that, I've got a play.
Long as I got a play, my family has hope...
You are reckless and dangerous-- a threat to every-one around you--
Hey, I know that voice... but where are the pajamas, T'Challa?
The path you have set yourself upon poses a threat to everyone around you.
You are both foolish and unwise.
You act like I have a choice.
You do.
The Wakandan consulate will finance relocating you and your family.
And, what-- hide the rest of my life? Is that what you'd do?
I would not be in your situation to begin with.
That's right. You're Wakandan. You're better than us regular Negroes.
Have a look at the reason I won't be going into hiding.
He's the guy I've been talking to all along...

--my son.

Just like I'm somebody's son-- and you're somebody's son.

Great men to whom we owe it not to go into hiding.

And Sgt. Tork-- your friend-- we let them win, what'd he die for?

And why'd you help me convince Sal's people the girl was a federal agent--

--and the taxi driver a CIA pilot?

Had I not intervened, you would be dead.

Like you care.

I hear you Wakandans are sort of like Klingons-- big on all of that "honor" crap.

Well, honor your friend, Panther-- honor his sacrifice. Either help me--

--or get out of my way.

I hear news...

...there is not much I like about it.

Hiya, Pop.

Two reports-- one in paper say crooked cops busted-- Sal demoted to sergeant.

One not in paper--

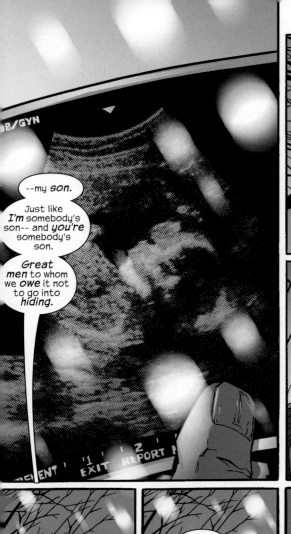

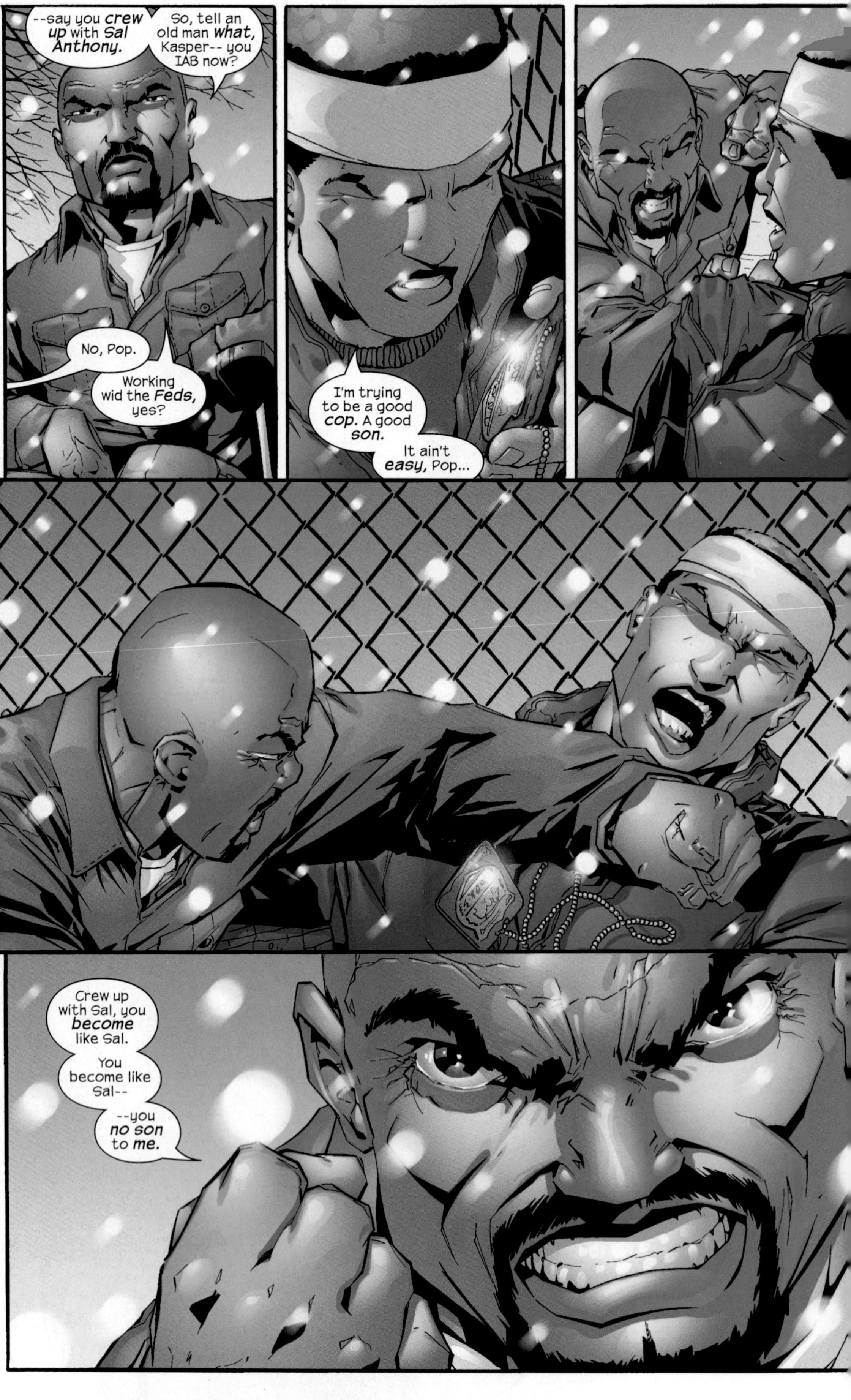

--say you crew up with Sal Anthony.
So, tell an old man what, Kasper-- you IAB now?
No, Pop.
Working wid the Feds, yes?
I'm trying to be a good cop. A good son.
It ain't easy, Pop...
Crew up with Sal, you become like Sal.
You become like Sal--
--you no son to me.

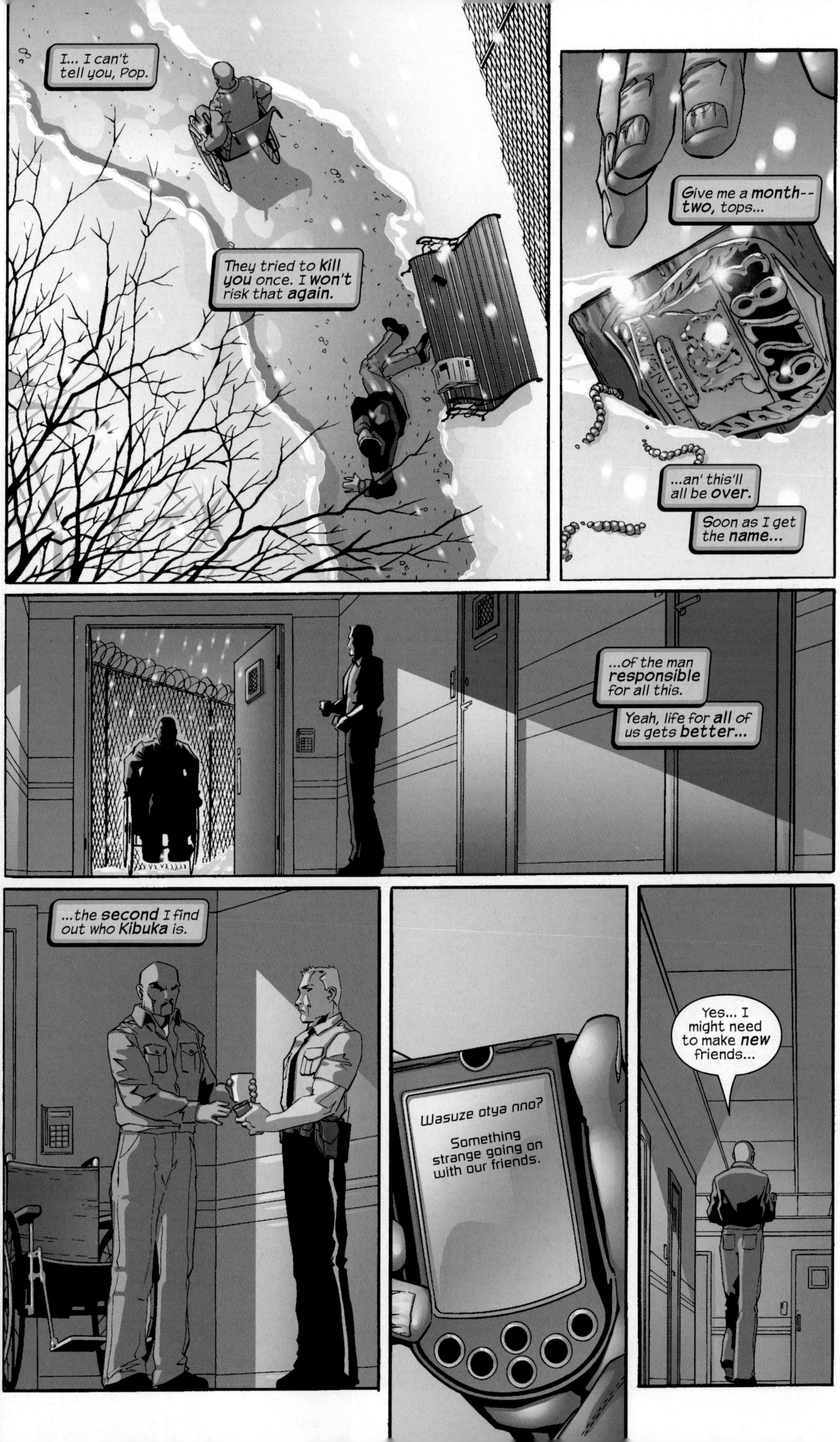
I... I can't tell you, Pop.
They tried to kill you once. I won't risk that again.
Give me a month-- two, tops...
...an' this'll all be over.
Soon as I get the name...
...of the man responsible for all this.
Yeah, life for all of us gets better...
...the second I find out who Kibuka is.
Wasuze otya nno?
Something strange going on with our friends.
Yes... I might need to make new friends...

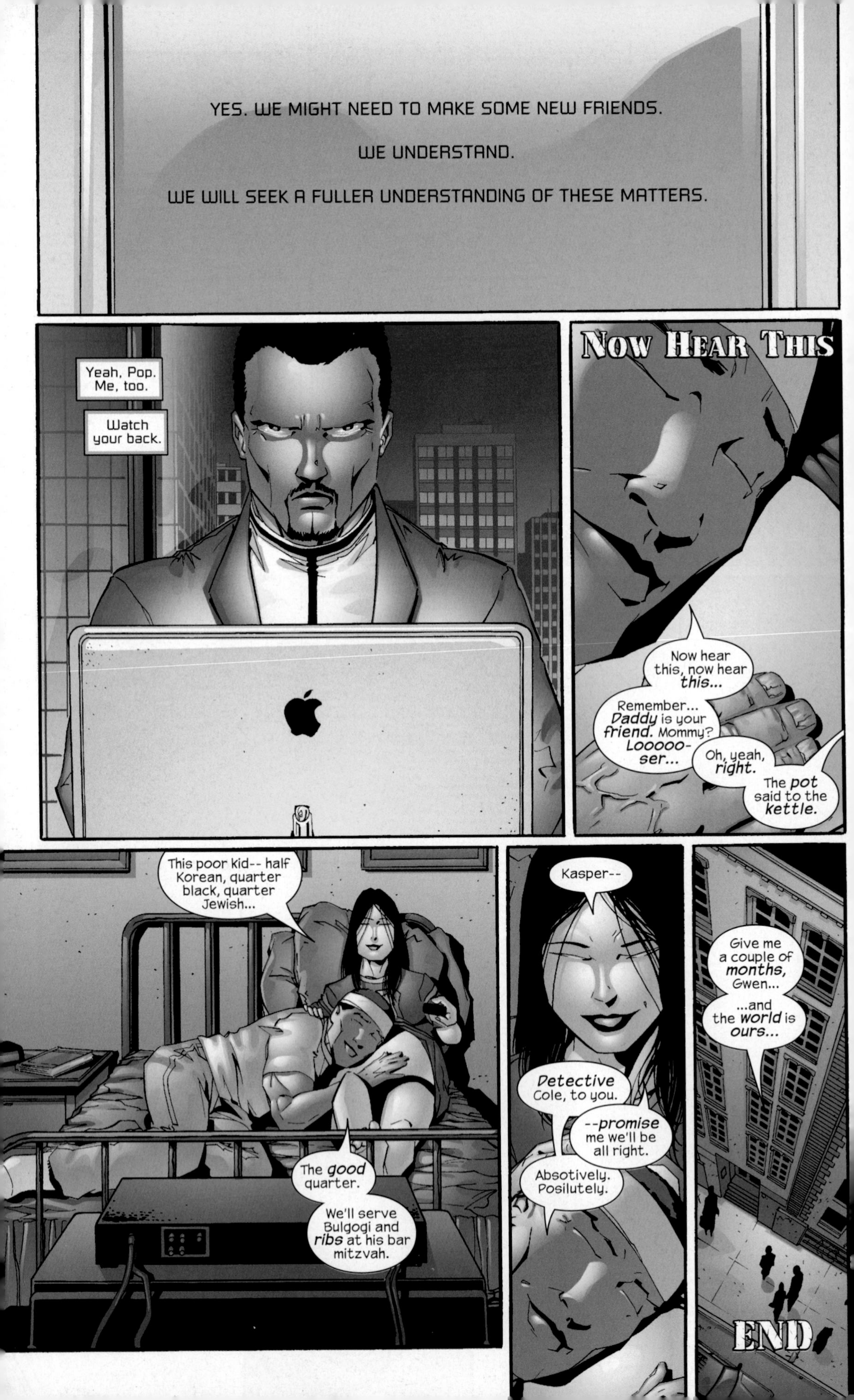

YES. WE MIGHT NEED TO MAKE SOME NEW FRIENDS.
WE UNDERSTAND.
WE WILL SEEK A FULLER UNDERSTANDING OF THESE MATTERS.
Yeah, Pop. Me, too.
Watch your back.
NOW HEAR THIS
Now hear this, now hear this...
Remember... Daddy is your friend. Mommy? Looooo-ser...
Oh, yeah, right.
The pot said to the kettle.
This poor kid-- half Korean, quarter black, quarter Jewish...
The good quarter.
We'll serve Bulgogi and ribs at his bar mitzvah.
Kasper--
Detective Cole, to you.
--promise me we'll be all right.
Absotively. Posilutely.
Give me a couple of months, Gwen...
...and the world is ours...
END

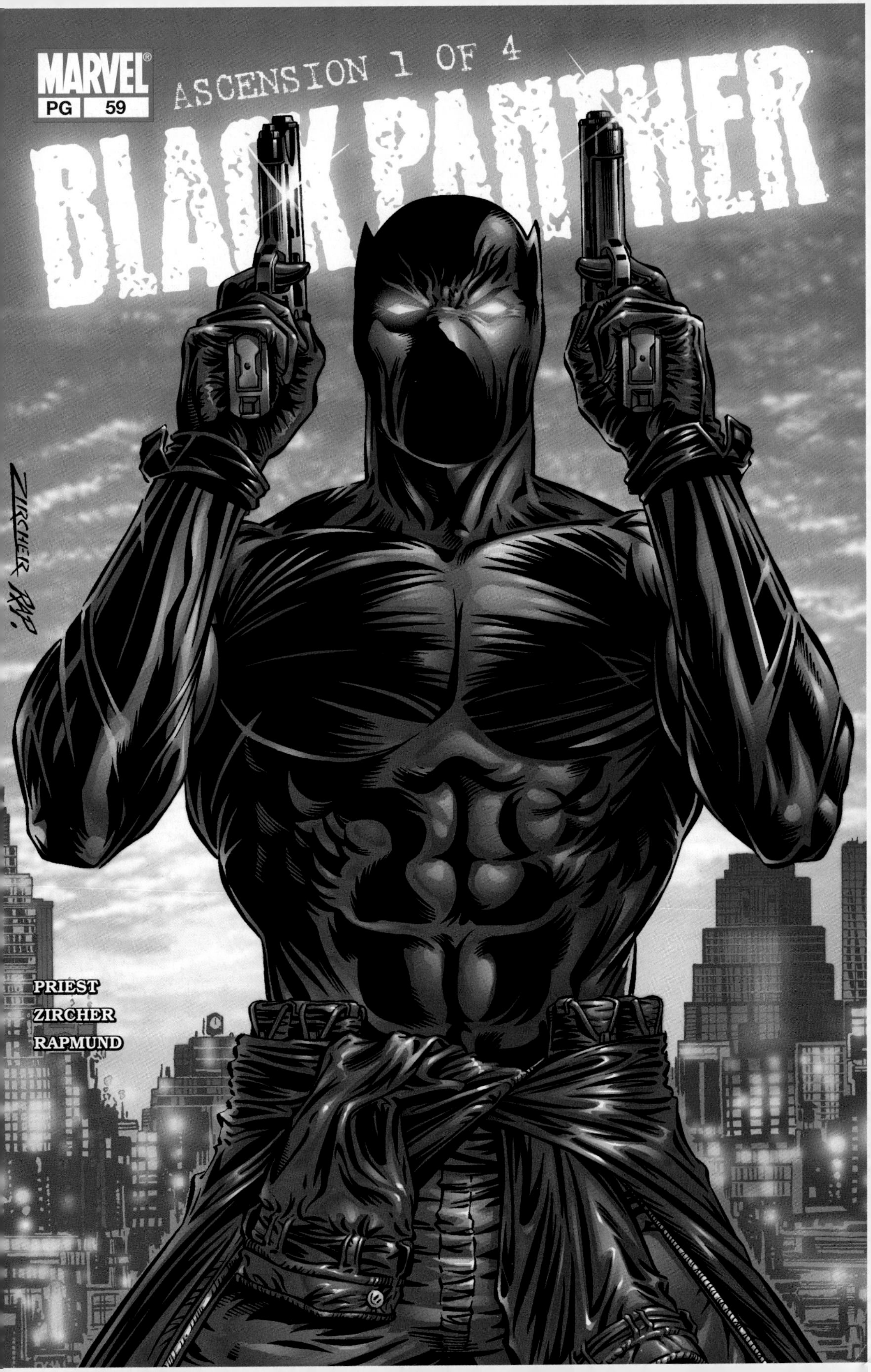
MARVEL
PG 59
ASCENSION 1 OF 4
BLACK PANTHER
ZIRCHER RAP.
PRIEST
ZIRCHER
RAPMUND

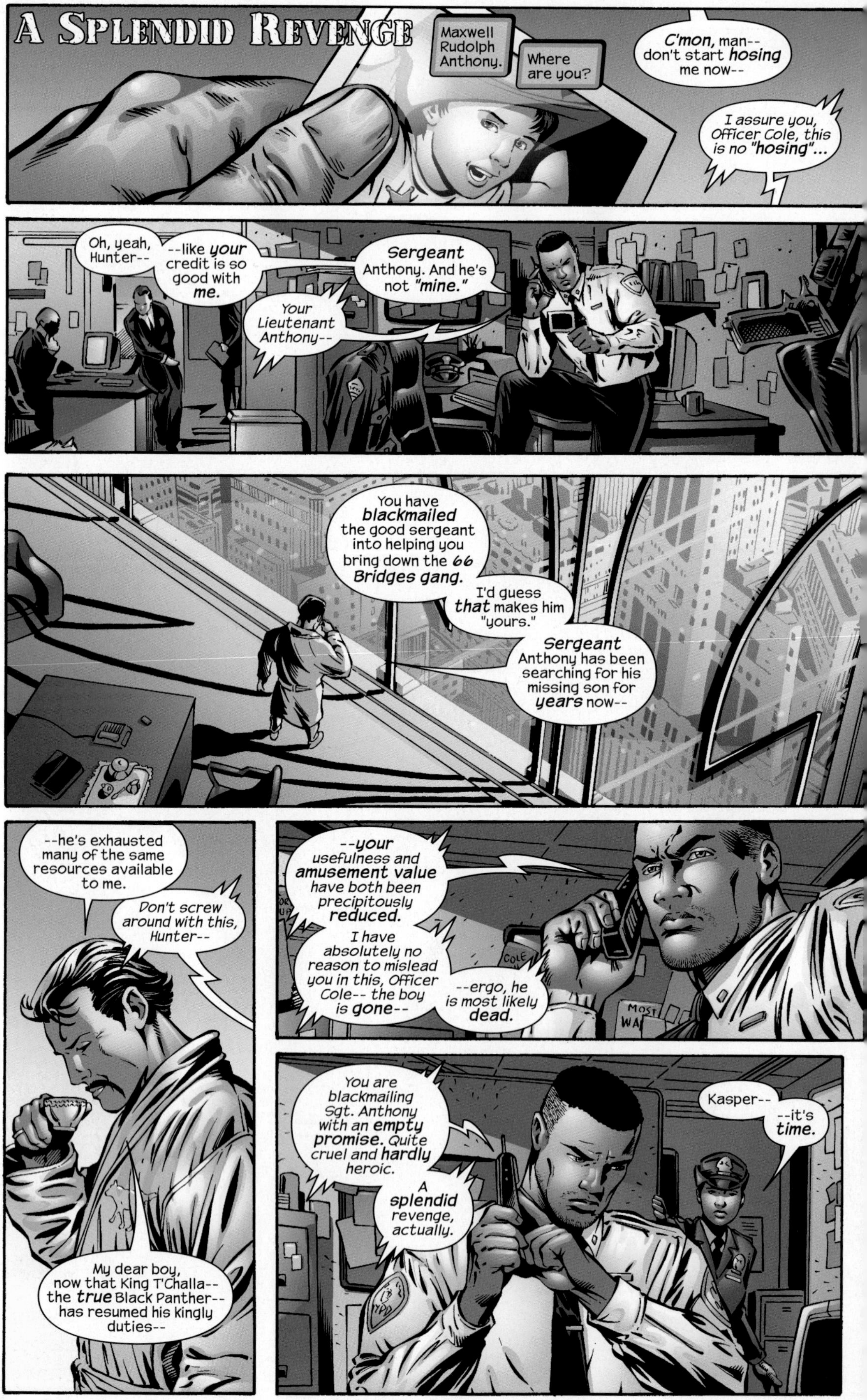
A Splendid Revenge
Maxwell Rudolph Anthony.
Where are you?
C'mon, man-- don't start hosing me now--
I assure you, Officer Cole, this is no "hosing"...
Oh, yeah, Hunter--
--like your credit is so good with me.
Your Lieutenant Anthony--
Sergeant Anthony. And he's not "mine."
You have blackmailed the good sergeant into helping you bring down the 66 Bridges gang.
I'd guess that makes him "yours."
Sergeant Anthony has been searching for his missing son for years now--
--he's exhausted many of the same resources available to me.
Don't screw around with this, Hunter--
My dear boy, now that King T'Challa-- the true Black Panther-- has resumed his kingly duties--
--your usefulness and amusement value have both been precipitously reduced.
I have absolutely no reason to mislead you in this, Officer Cole-- the boy is gone--
--ergo, he is most likely dead.
You are blackmailing Sgt. Anthony with an empty promise. Quite cruel and hardly heroic.
A splendid revenge, actually.
Kasper--
--it's time.

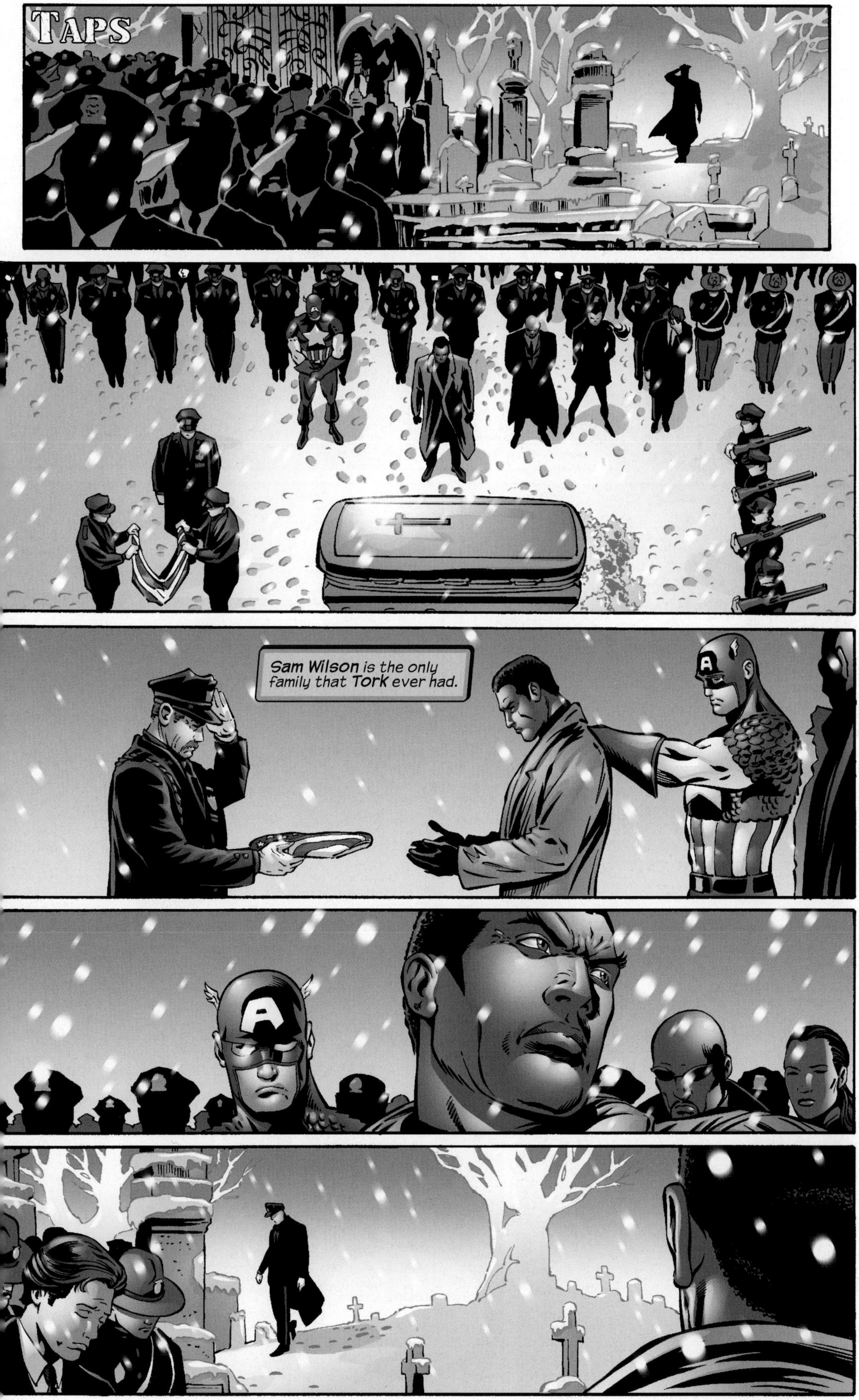
TAPS
Sam Wilson is the only family that Tork ever had.

Last time I saw *these* brothers, they were laid out in ICU.

Meet the *family*--

--Daz, Eddie X, and The Jinx. My *crew.*

'Sup, yo.

Kaint callit.

Life's a *beach*, Kasper...

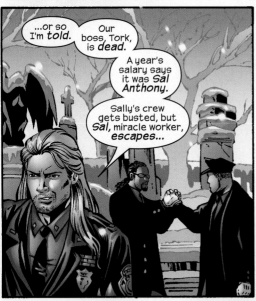

...or so I'm *told.*

Our boss, Tork, is *dead.*

A year's salary says it was *Sal Anthony.*

Sally's crew gets busted, but *Sal*, miracle worker, *escapes*...

...with a wrist slap *demotion* to Sergeant...

...and transferred to OCCB Narcotics...

...given the platoon of the man he *killed.*

Somebody *explain* that spit to me, yo.

Mira, ese--I'm *out*...

...got my 32 in already.

Mira--I work for Sally--I'll end up *shankin'* that mug.

Bustin' up the *crew*, Ed--?

Sal is *66 Bridges*, man. *Everybody* knows. How you think he *survived* his crew gettin' *pinched*, yo?

Yo, Ed, *bump* Bridges. Daz *wanna* work under that mug.

Catch that mug *sleep.*

Be the *Day of the Daz.*

Excuse me-- are *you* Officer Cole?

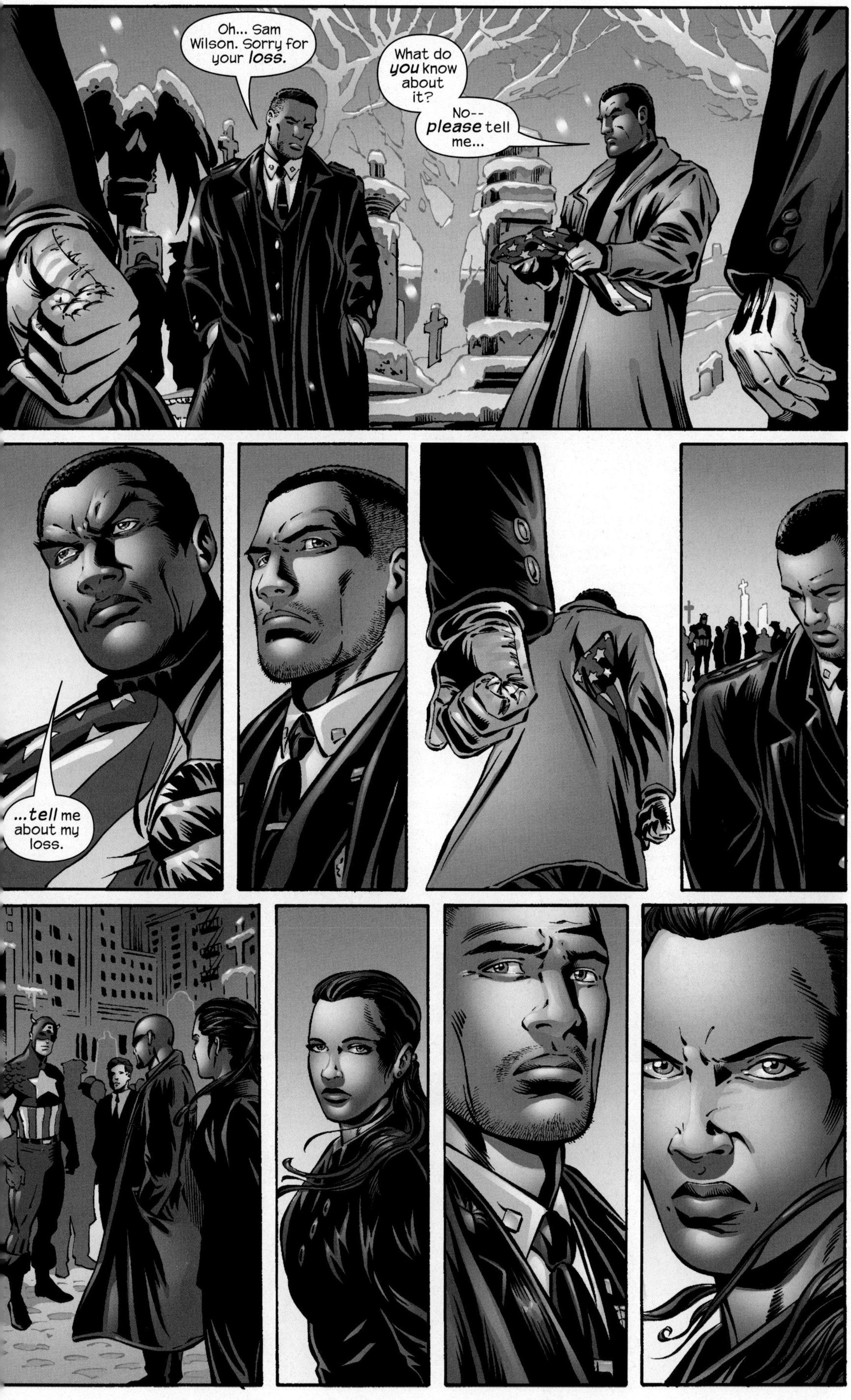
Oh... Sam Wilson. Sorry for your *loss.*
What do *you* know about it?
No-- *please* tell me...
...*tell* me about my loss.

CRIME SCENE

Tork's place.

The scene of the **crime**.

Where I set my best friend up to get **killed**...

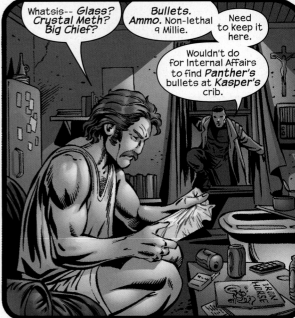

Whatsis-- **Glass?** Crystal Meth? **Big Chief?**

Bullets. Ammo. Non-lethal 9 Millie.

Need to keep it here.

Wouldn't do for Internal Affairs to find **Panther's** bullets at **Kasper's** crib.

Dump 'em in **the river.**

Don't **get in** with this guy, Kasper.

And **hello**-- you are **not** the Black Panther.

Too **ugly** and too **broke.**

...I never listen.

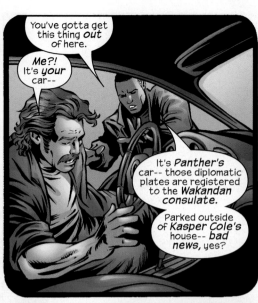

You've gotta get this thing *out* of here.

Me?! It's *your* car--

It's *Panther's* car-- those diplomatic plates are registered to the *Wakandan consulate.*

Parked outside of *Kasper Cole's* house-- *bad news,* yes?

Park it over on *The Hill*-- the projects where Panther used to live.

Tork's *finger-prints* on the car... Panther's *gear* at his crib.

They got your *Sergeant.*

Sal and his crew bagged Tork a couple hours ago. Dumped our surveillance. Tork *confessed* to being The Black Panther.

I'd guess to protect *you.*

...

Gotta make this up. Got to *try.*

Got to make this all *count* for something...

SSQQMAAAAWWK--!

Dammit! How'd a *bird* get in here--?

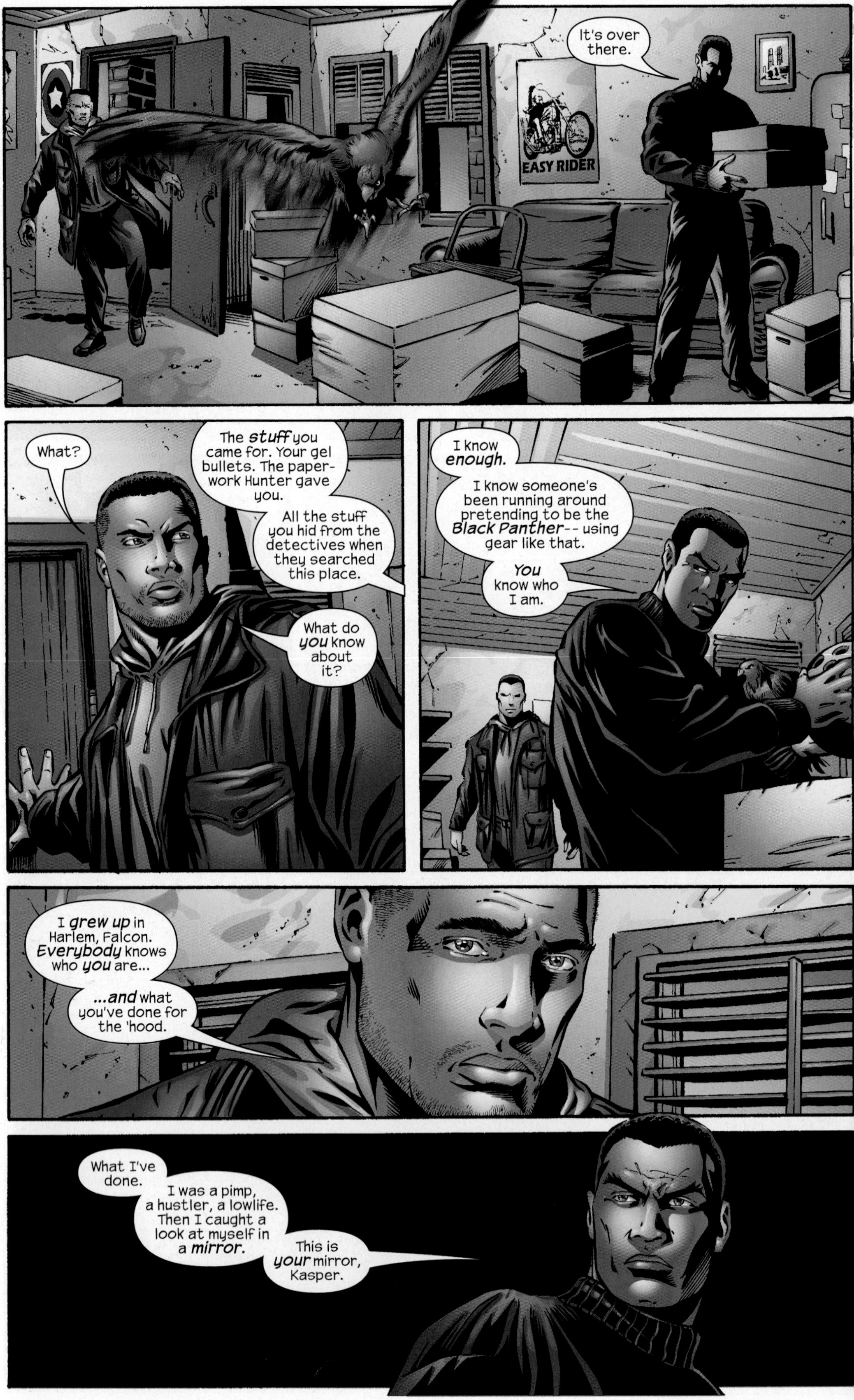

It's over there.
EASY RIDER
What?
The stuff you came for. Your gel bullets. The paper-work Hunter gave you.
All the stuff you hid from the detectives when they searched this place.
What do you know about it?
I know enough.
I know someone's been running around pretending to be the Black Panther-- using gear like that.
You know who I am.
I grew up in Harlem, Falcon. Everybody knows who you are...
...and what you've done for the 'hood.
What I've done.
I was a pimp, a hustler, a lowlife. Then I caught a look at myself in a mirror.
This is your mirror, Kasper.

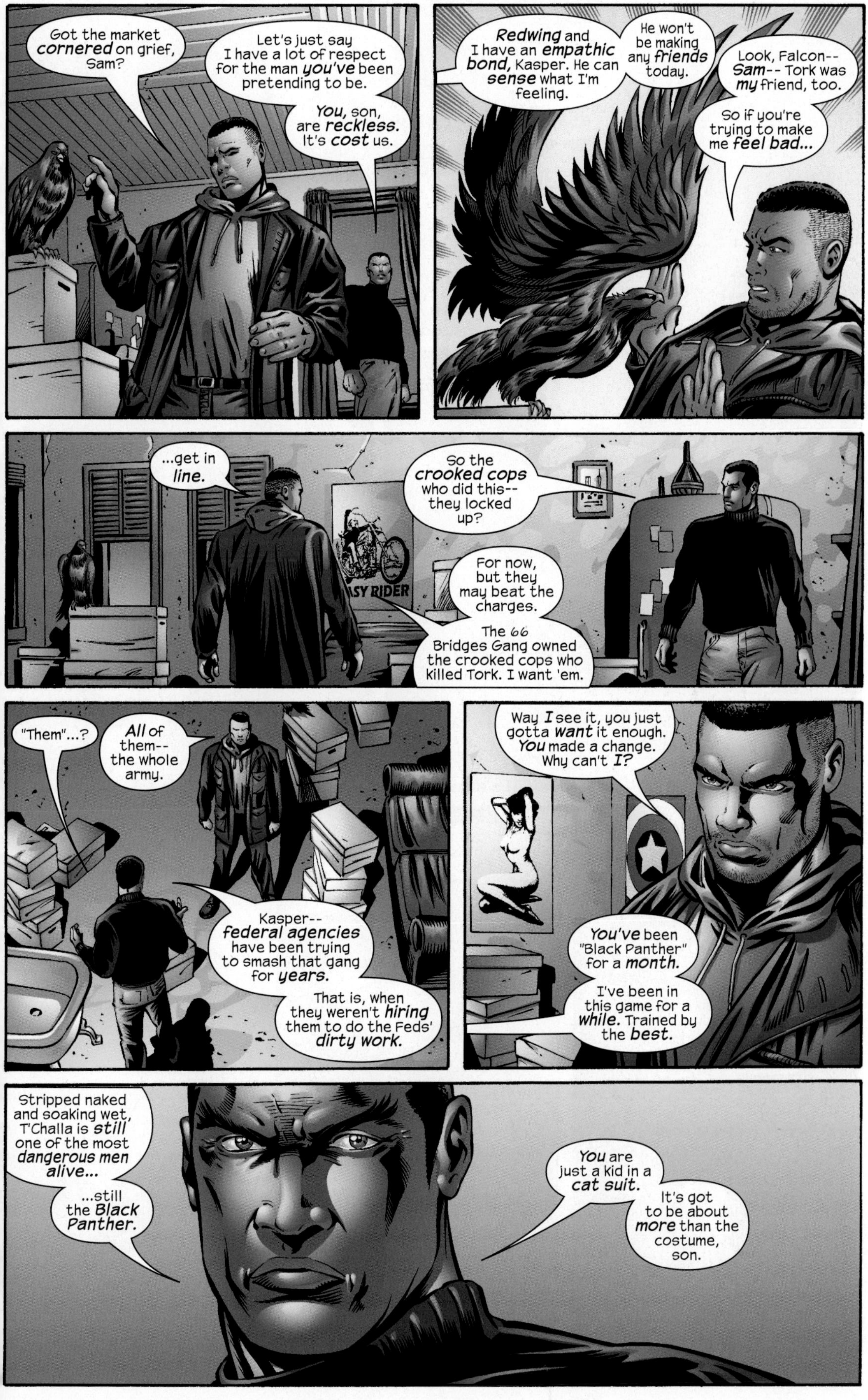
Got the market cornered on grief, Sam?
Let's just say I have a lot of respect for the man you've been pretending to be.
You, son, are reckless. It's cost us.
Redwing and I have an empathic bond, Kasper. He can sense what I'm feeling.
He won't be making any friends today.
Look, Falcon-- Sam-- Tork was my friend, too.
So if you're trying to make me feel bad...
...get in line.
So the crooked cops who did this-- they locked up?
For now, but they may beat the charges.
The 66 Bridges Gang owned the crooked cops who killed Tork. I want 'em.
"Them"...?
All of them-- the whole army.
Kasper-- federal agencies have been trying to smash that gang for years.
That is, when they weren't hiring them to do the Feds' dirty work.
Way I see it, you just gotta want it enough. You made a change. Why can't I?
You've been "Black Panther" for a month.
I've been in this game for a while. Trained by the best.
Stripped naked and soaking wet, T'Challa is still one of the most dangerous men alive...
...still the Black Panther.
You are just a kid in a cat suit.
It's got to be about more than the costume, son.

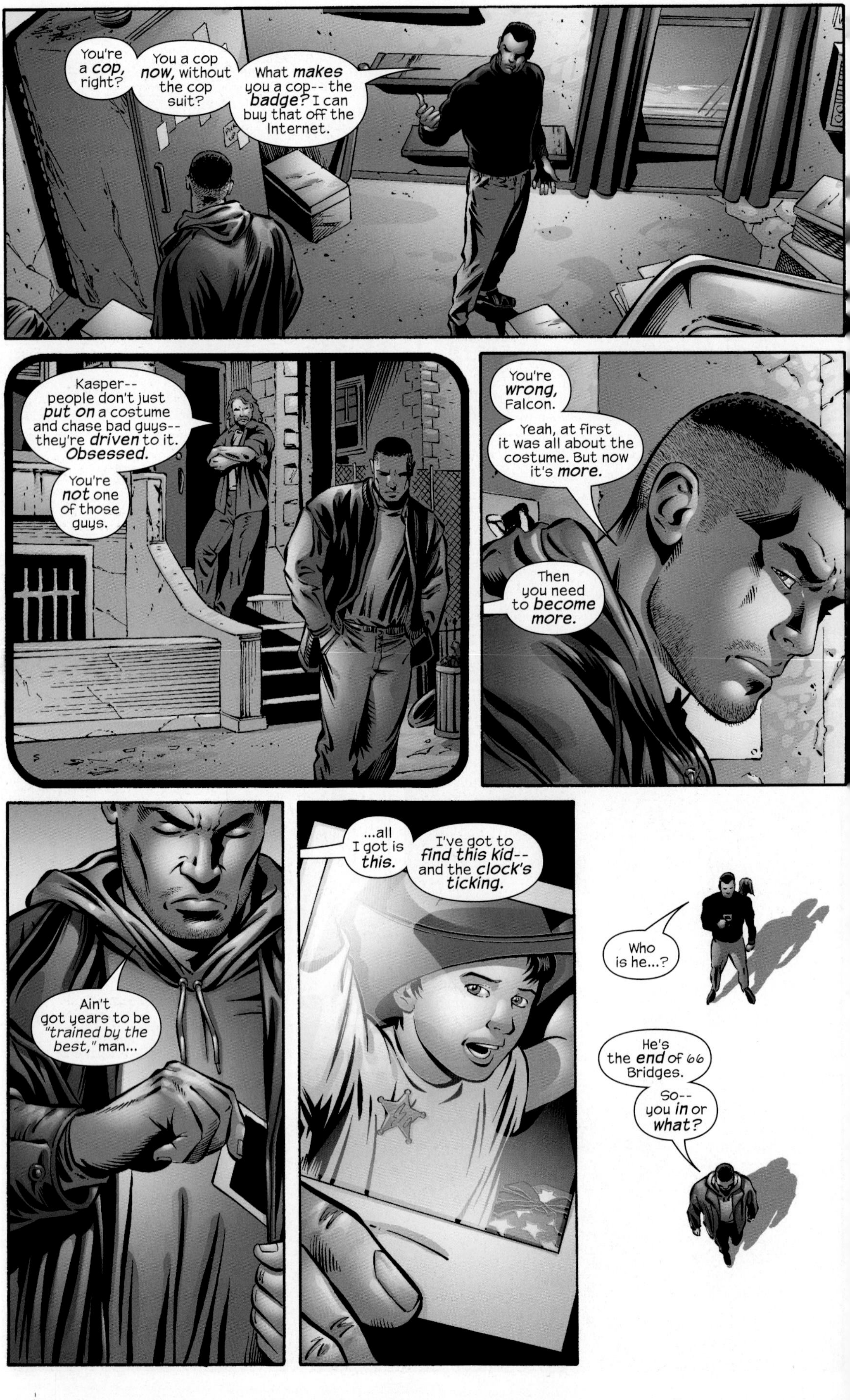
You're a cop, right?
You a cop now, without the cop suit?
What makes you a cop-- the badge? I can buy that off the Internet.
Kasper-- people don't just put on a costume and chase bad guys-- they're driven to it. Obsessed.
You're not one of those guys.
You're wrong, Falcon.
Yeah, at first it was all about the costume. But now it's more.
Then you need to become more.
Ain't got years to be "trained by the best," man...
...all I got is this.
I've got to find this kid-- and the clock's ticking.
Who is he...?
He's the end of 66 Bridges.
So-- you in or what?

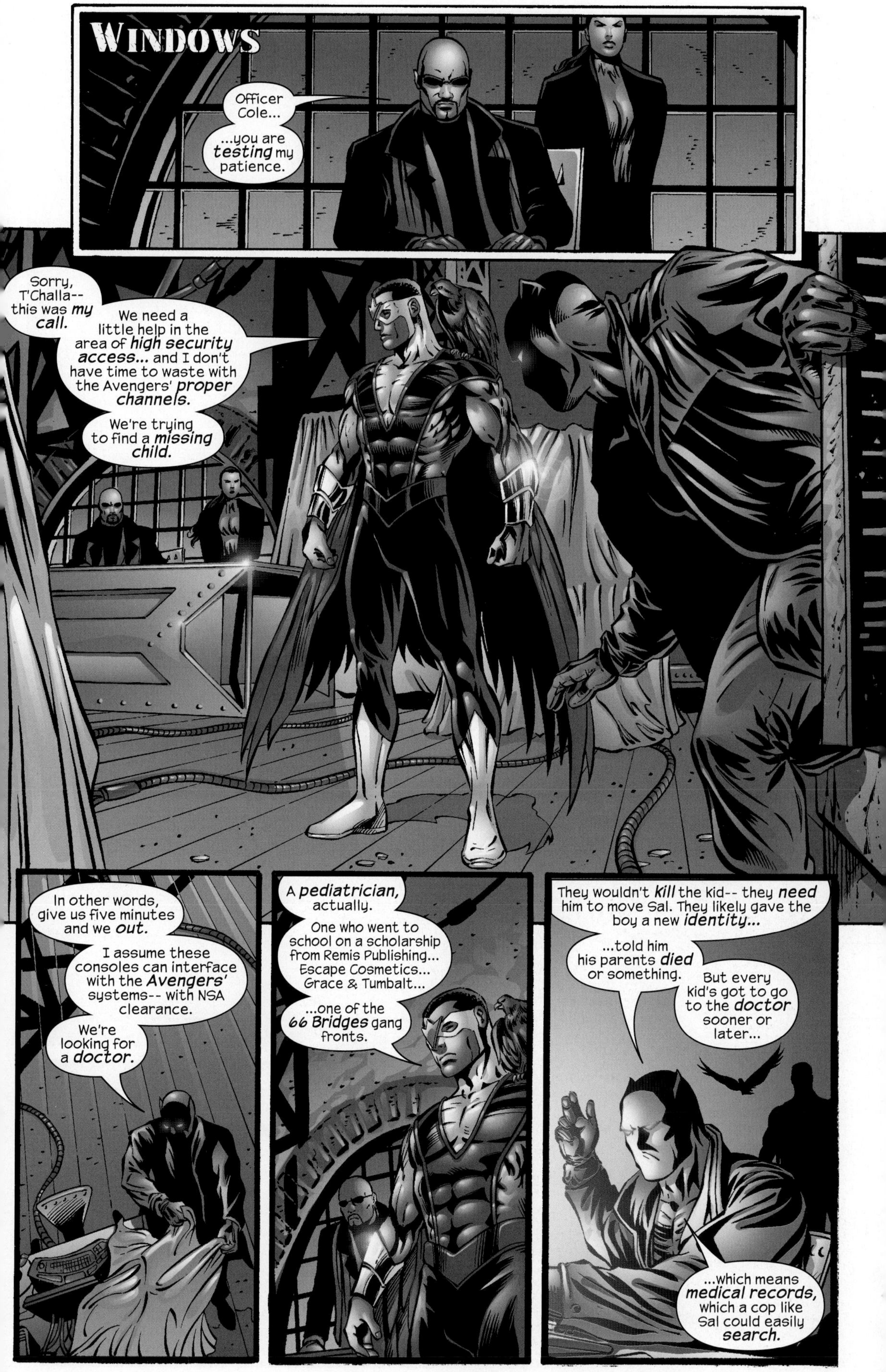
WINDOWS
Officer Cole...
...you are testing my patience.
Sorry, T'Challa-- this was my call.
We need a little help in the area of high security access... and I don't have time to waste with the Avengers' proper channels.
We're trying to find a missing child.
In other words, give us five minutes and we out.
I assume these consoles can interface with the Avengers' systems-- with NSA clearance.
We're looking for a doctor.
A pediatrician, actually.
One who went to school on a scholarship from Remis Publishing... Escape Cosmetics... Grace & Tumbalt...
...one of the 66 Bridges gang fronts.
They wouldn't kill the kid-- they need him to move Sal. They likely gave the boy a new identity...
...told him his parents died or something.
But every kid's got to go to the doctor sooner or later...
...which means medical records, which a cop like Sal could easily search.

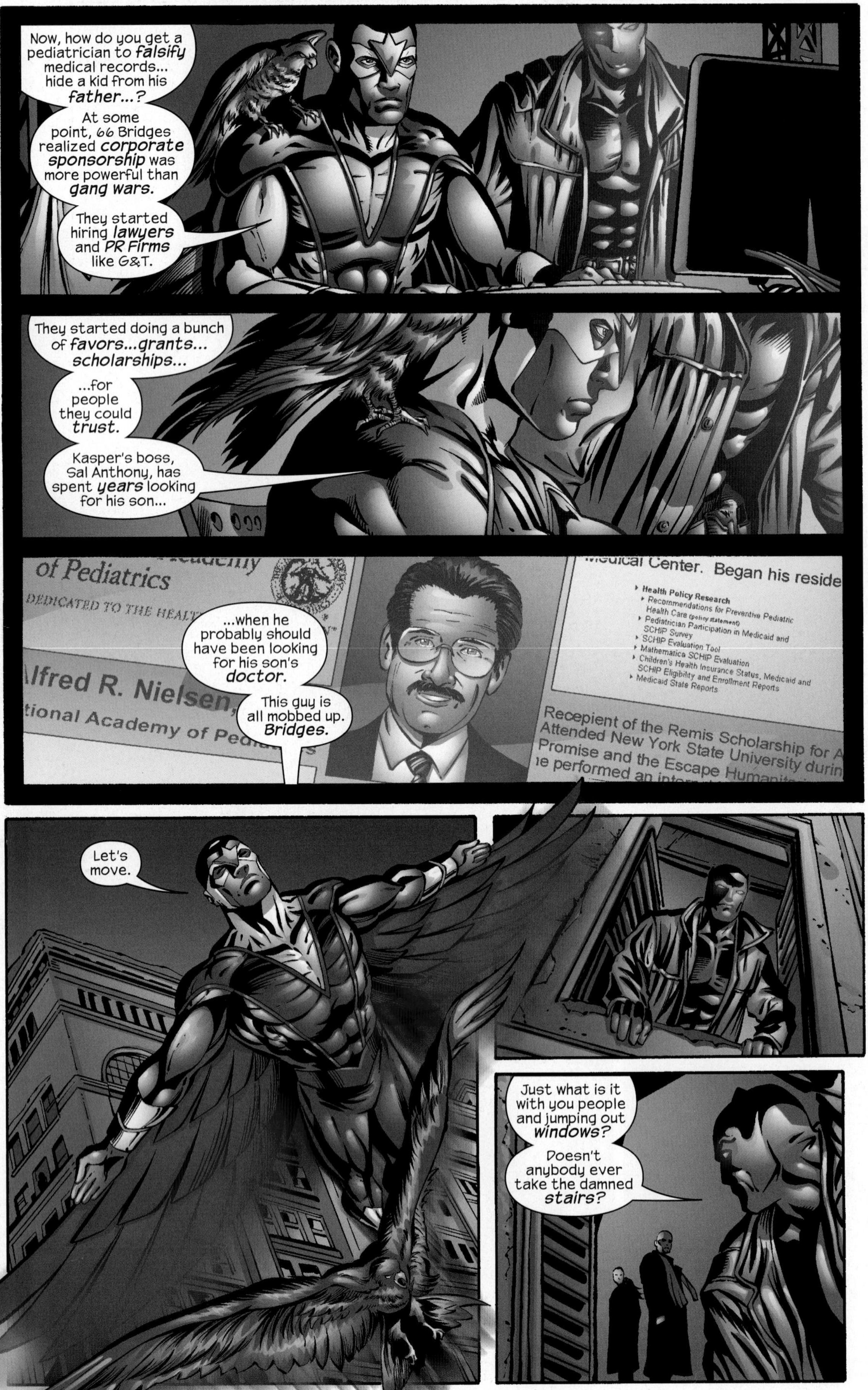
Now, how do you get a pediatrician to falsify medical records... hide a kid from his father...?
At some point, 66 Bridges realized corporate sponsorship was more powerful than gang wars.
They started hiring lawyers and PR Firms like G&T.
They started doing a bunch of favors...grants... scholarships...
...for people they could trust.
Kasper's boss, Sal Anthony, has spent years looking for his son...
of Pediatrics
Health Policy Research
Recommendations for Preventive Pediatric Health Care
Pediatrician Participation in Medicaid and SCHIP Survey
SCHIP Evaluation Tool
Mathematica SCHIP Evaluation
Children's Health Insurance Status, Medicaid and SCHIP Eligibility and Enrollment Reports
Medicaid State Reports
...when he probably should have been looking for his son's doctor.
This guy is all mobbed up. Bridges.
Let's move.
Just what is it with you people and jumping out windows?
Doesn't anybody ever take the damned stairs?

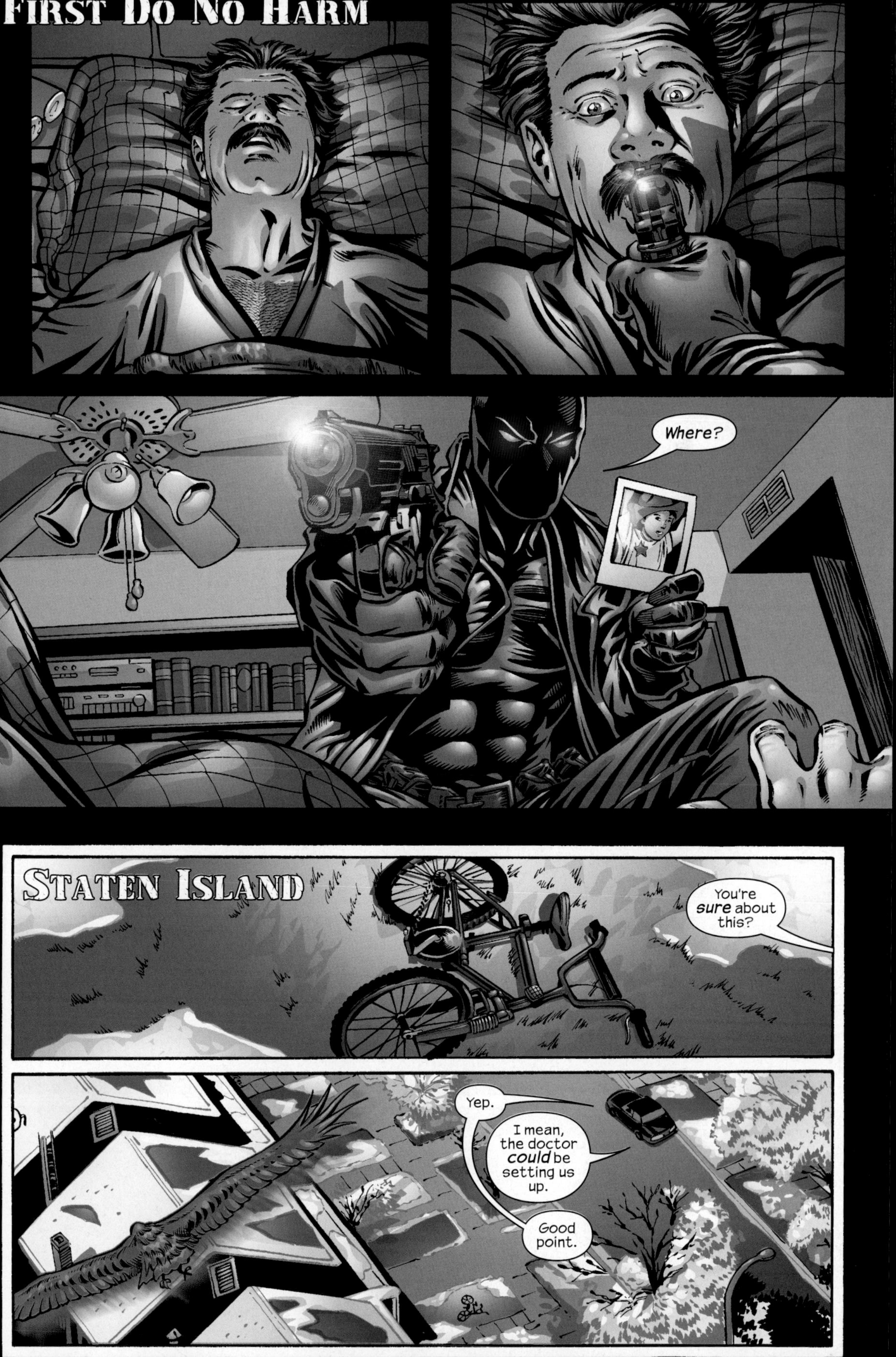
FIRST DO NO HARM
Where?
STATEN ISLAND
You're sure about this?
Yep.
I mean, the doctor could be setting us up.
Good point.

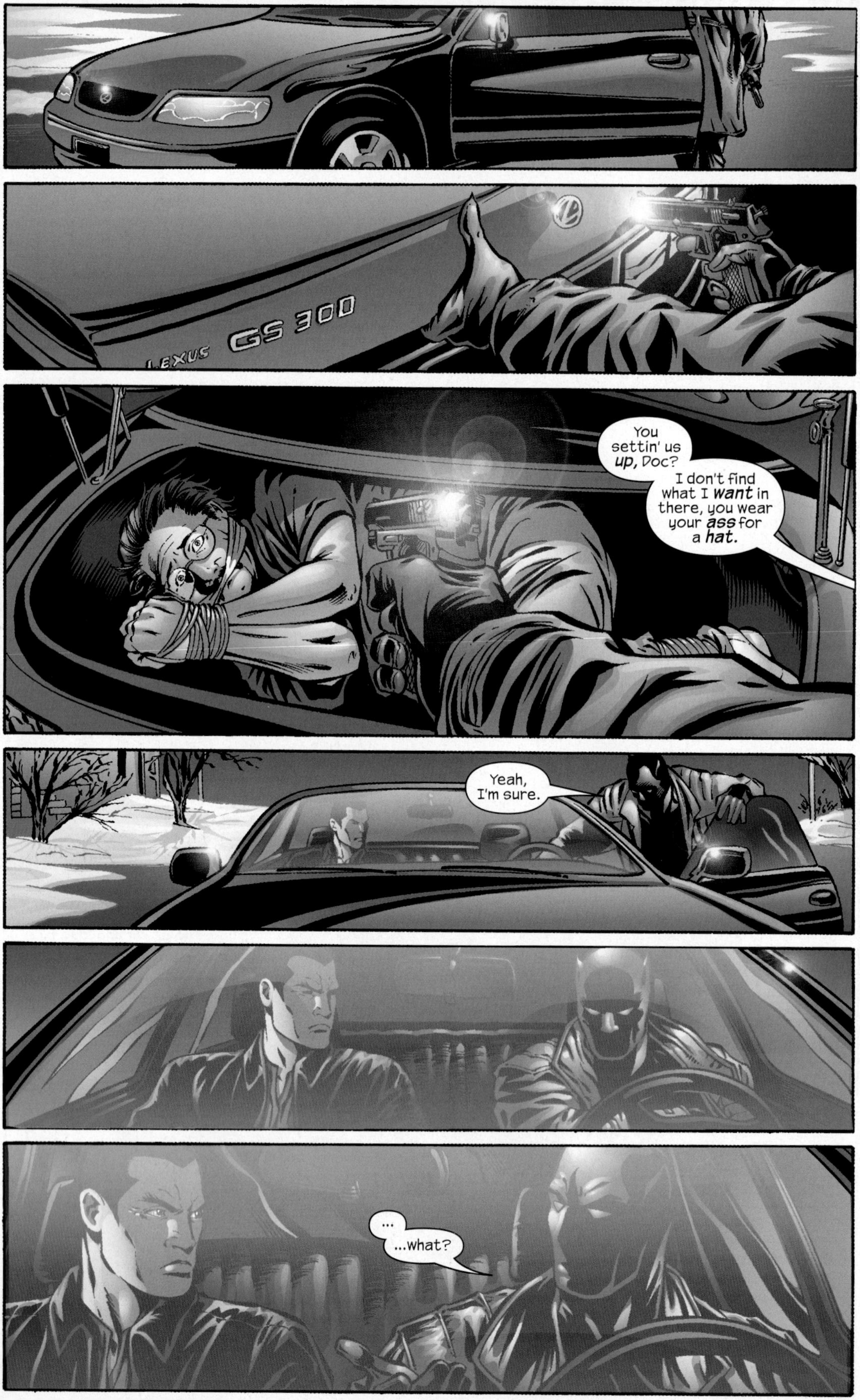
LEXUS GS 300
You settin' us up, Doc?
I don't find what I want in there, you wear your ass for a hat.
Yeah, I'm sure.
...
...what?

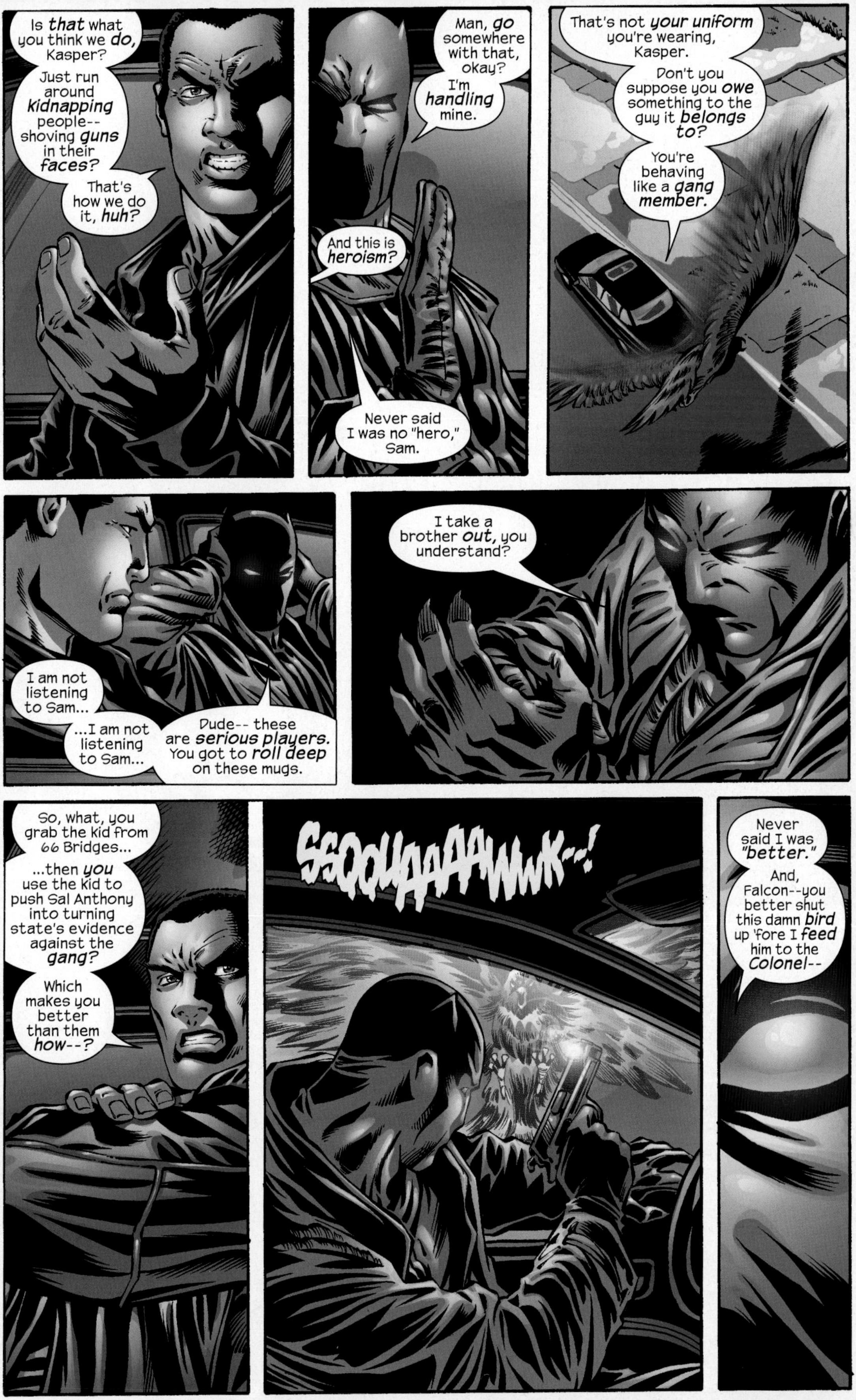
Is that what you think we do, Kasper?
Just run around kidnapping people-- shoving guns in their faces?
That's how we do it, huh?
Man, go somewhere with that, okay?
I'm handling mine.
And this is heroism?
Never said I was no "hero," Sam.
That's not your uniform you're wearing, Kasper.
Don't you suppose you owe something to the guy it belongs to?
You're behaving like a gang member.
I am not listening to Sam...
...I am not listening to Sam...
Dude-- these are serious players. You got to roll deep on these mugs.
I take a brother out, you understand?
So, what, you grab the kid from 66 Bridges...
...then you use the kid to push Sal Anthony into turning state's evidence against the gang?
Which makes you better than them how--?
SSQQUAAAAWWK--!
Never said I was "better."
And, Falcon--you better shut this damn bird up 'fore I feed him to the Colonel--

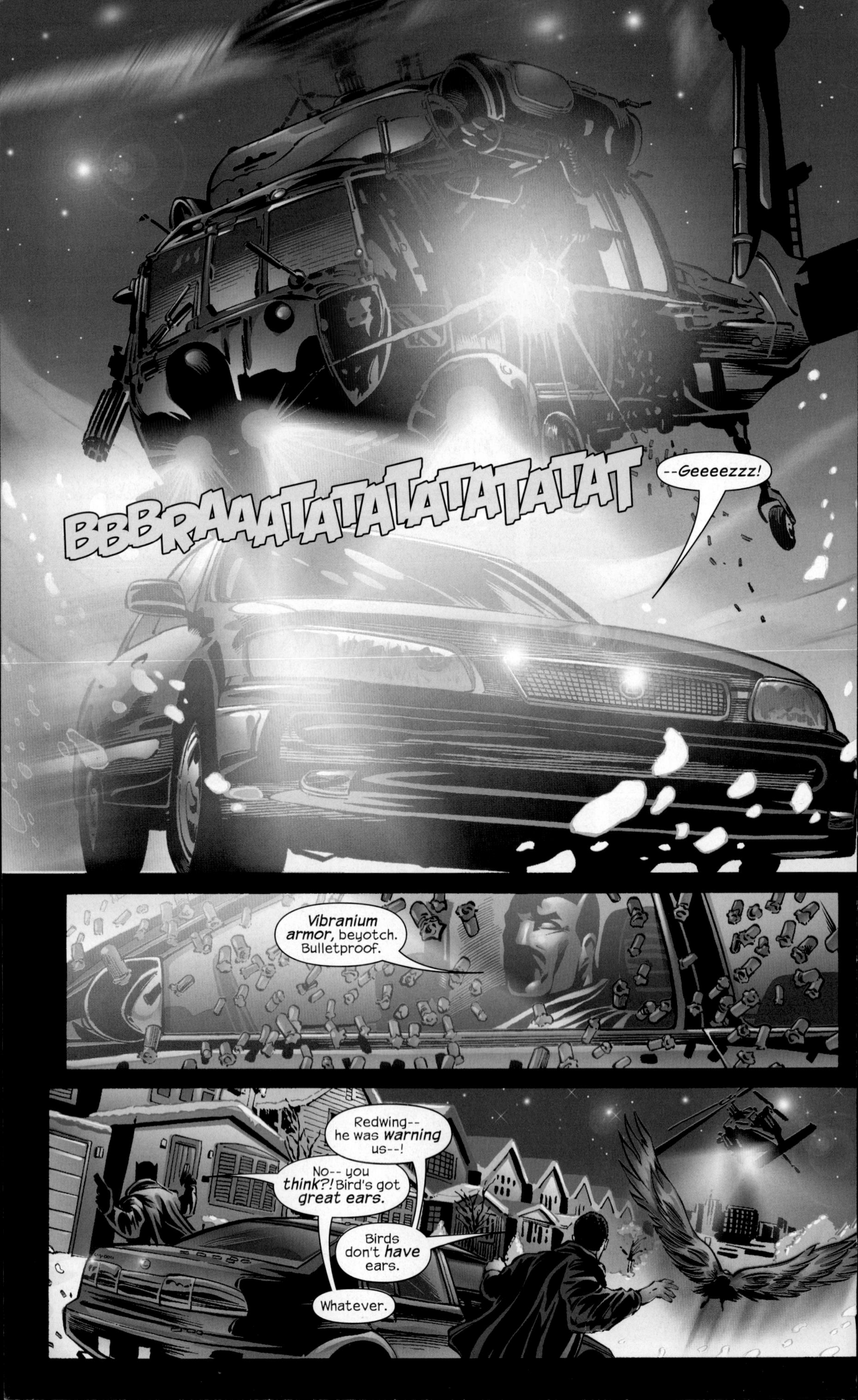
BBBRAAATATATATATATAT
--Geeeezzz!
Vibranium armor, beyotch. Bulletproof.
Redwing-- he was warning us--!
No-- you think?! Bird's got great ears.
Birds don't have ears.
Whatever.

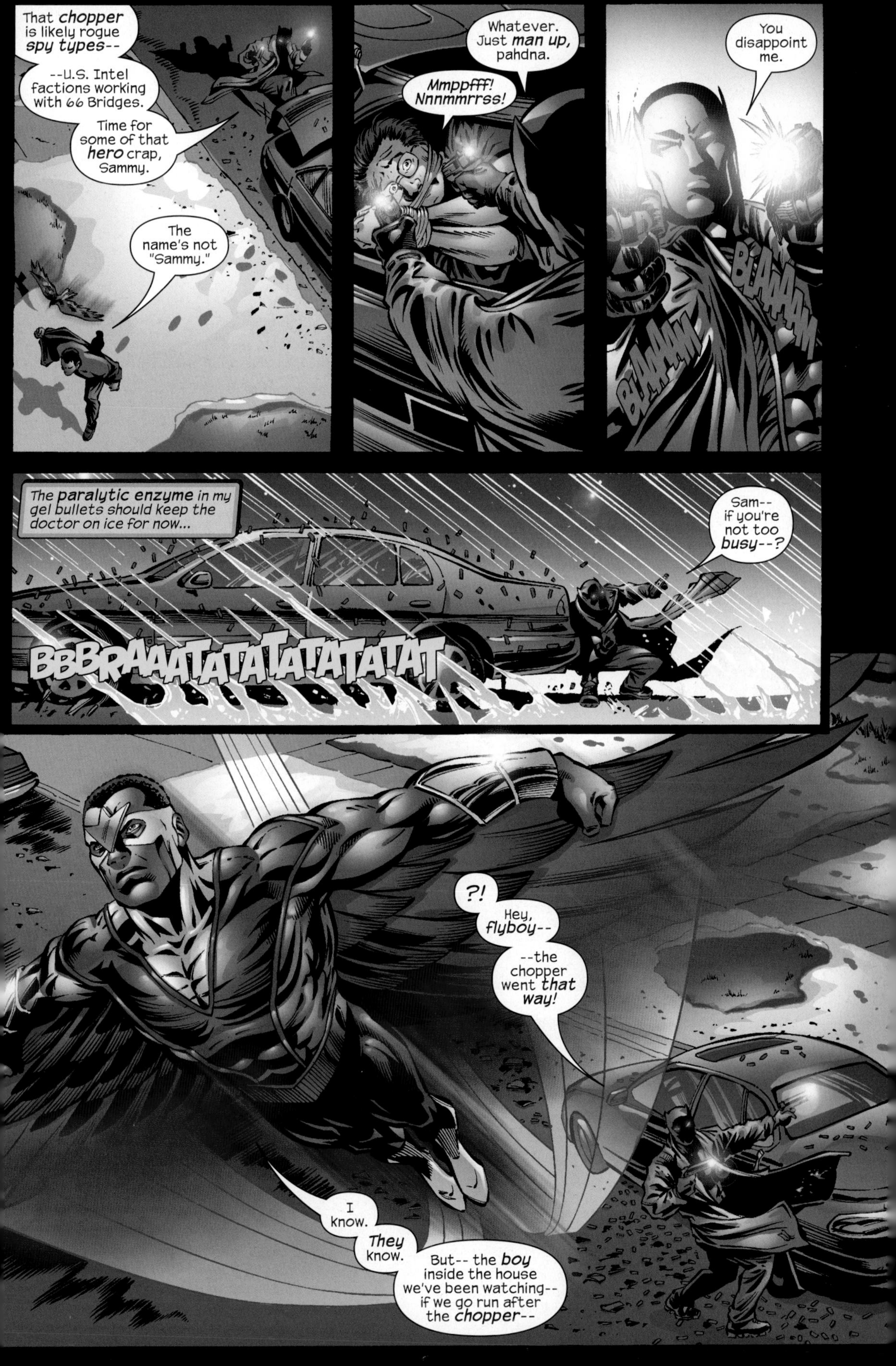
That chopper is likely rogue spy types--
--U.S. Intel factions working with 66 Bridges.
Time for some of that hero crap, Sammy.
The name's not "Sammy."
Whatever. Just man up, pahdna.
Mmppfff! Nnnmmrrss!
You disappoint me.
BLAAAAAM
BLAAAAM
The paralytic enzyme in my gel bullets should keep the doctor on ice for now...
Sam-- if you're not too busy--?
BBBRAAAATATATATATATAT
?!
Hey, flyboy--
--the chopper went that way!
I know.
They know.
But-- the boy inside the house we've been watching-- if we go run after the chopper--

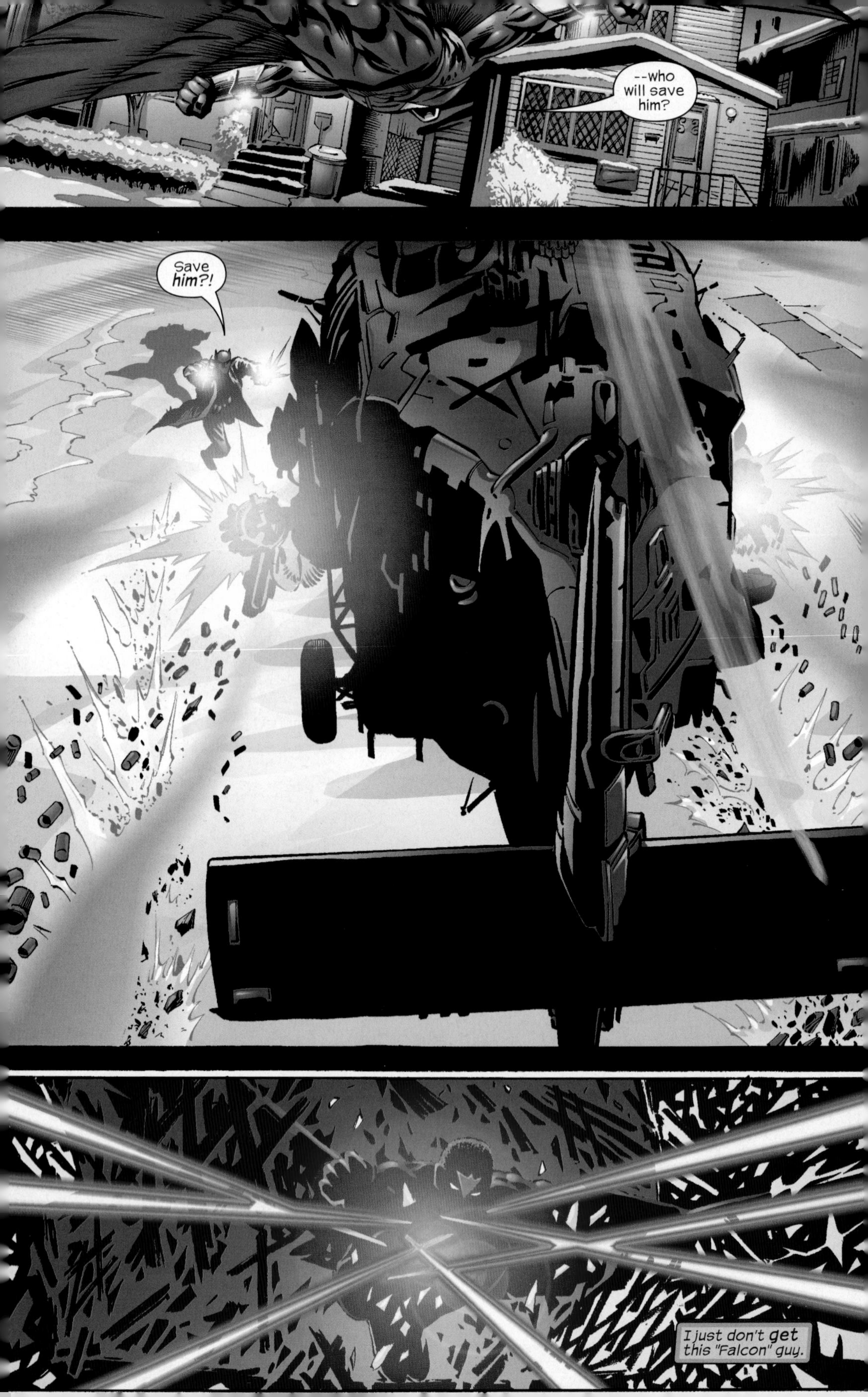
--who will save him?
Save *him?!*
I just don't **get** this "Falcon" guy.

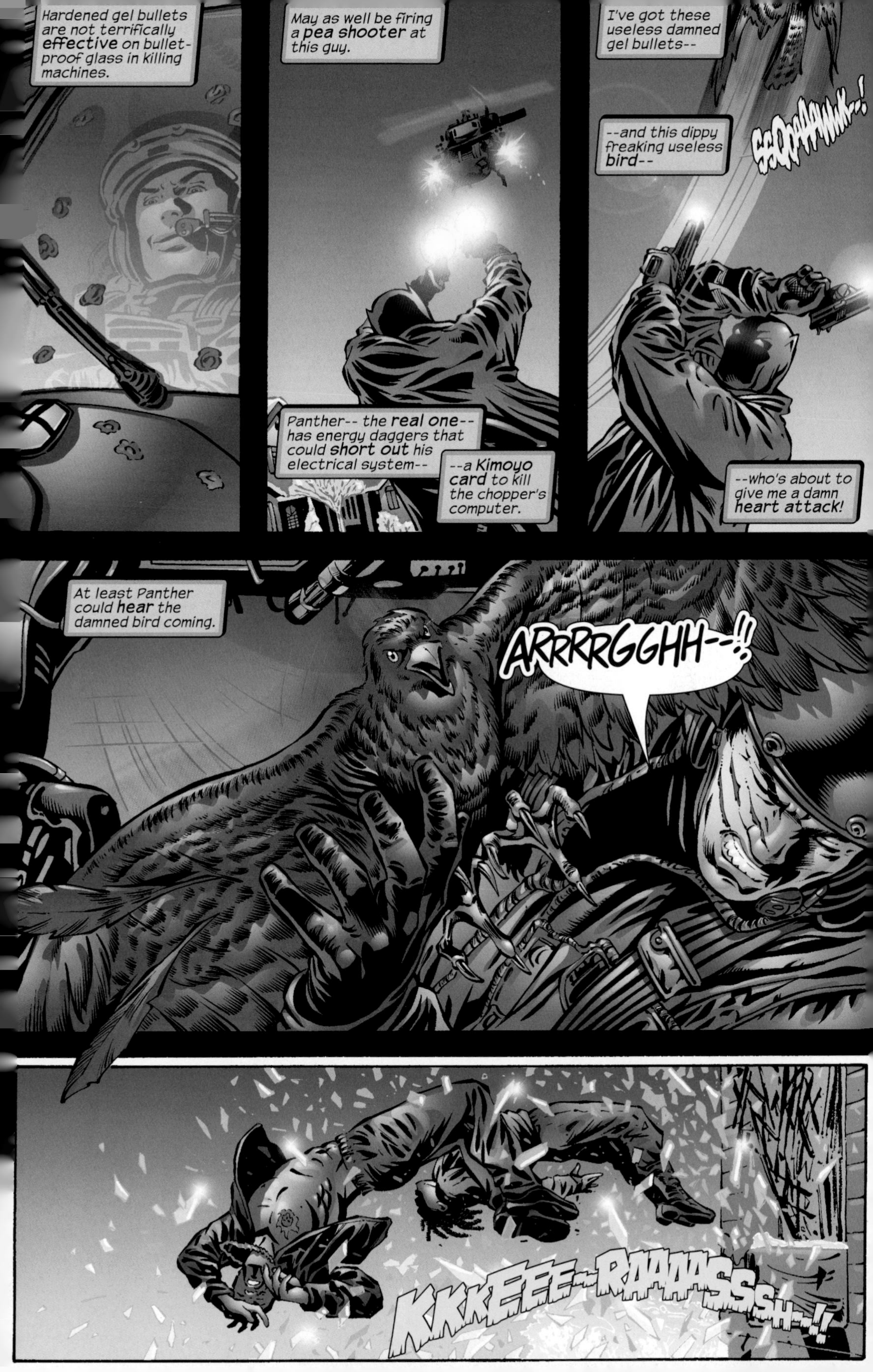

Hardened gel bullets are not terrifically effective on bullet-proof glass in killing machines.
May as well be firing a pea shooter at this guy.
Panther-- the real one-- has energy daggers that could short out his electrical system--
--a Kimoyo card to kill the chopper's computer.
I've got these useless damned gel bullets--
--and this dippy freaking useless bird--
SSQQAAAWWK--!
--who's about to give me a damn heart attack!
At least Panther could hear the damned bird coming.
ARRRRGGHH--!!
KKKEEE--RAAAASSSH--!!

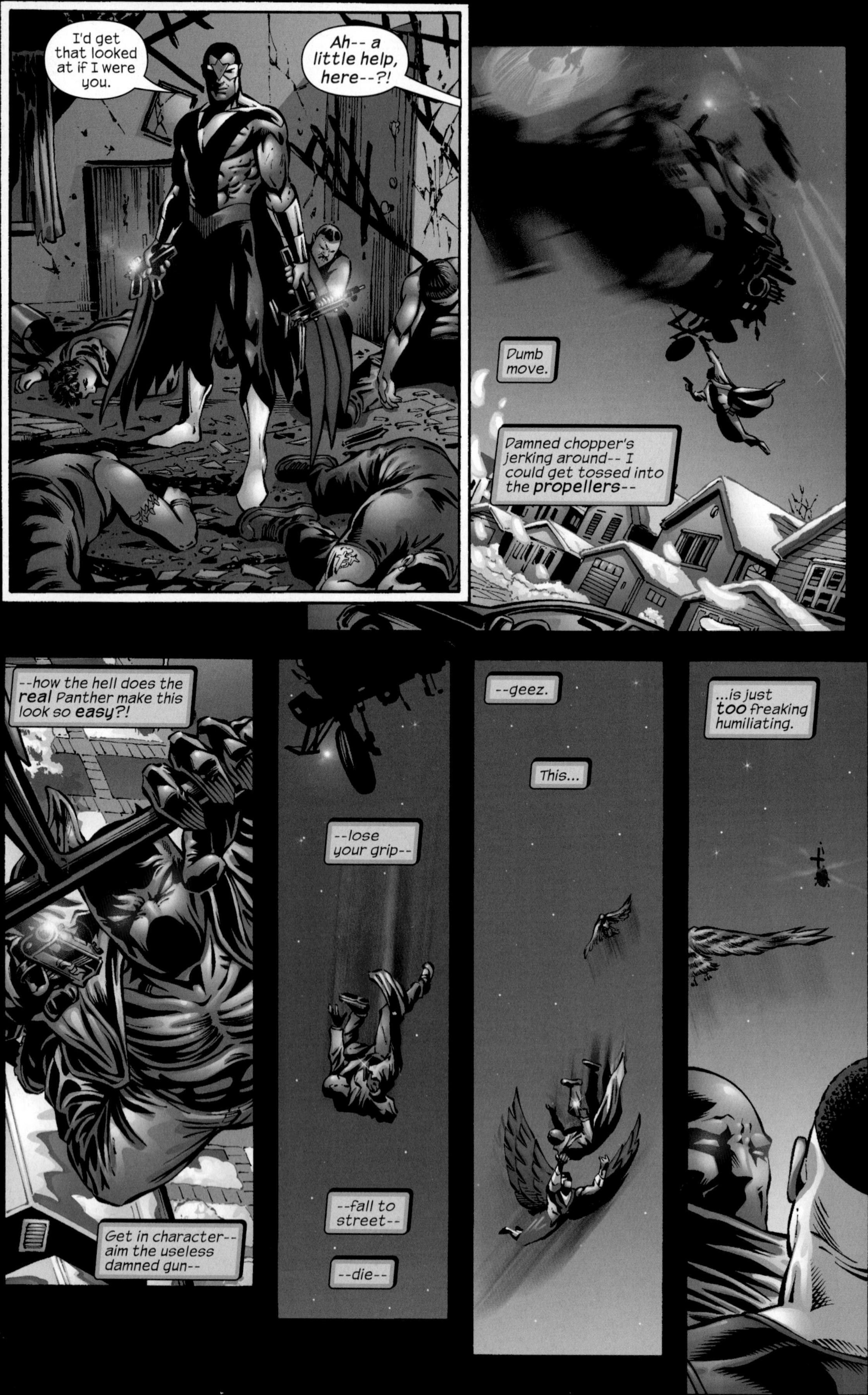
I'd get that looked at if I were you.
Ah-- a little help, here--?!
Dumb move.
Damned chopper's jerking around-- I could get tossed into the propellers--
--how the hell does the real Panther make this look so easy?!
Get in character-- aim the useless damned gun--
--lose your grip--
--fall to street--
--die--
--geez.
This...
...is just too freaking humiliating.

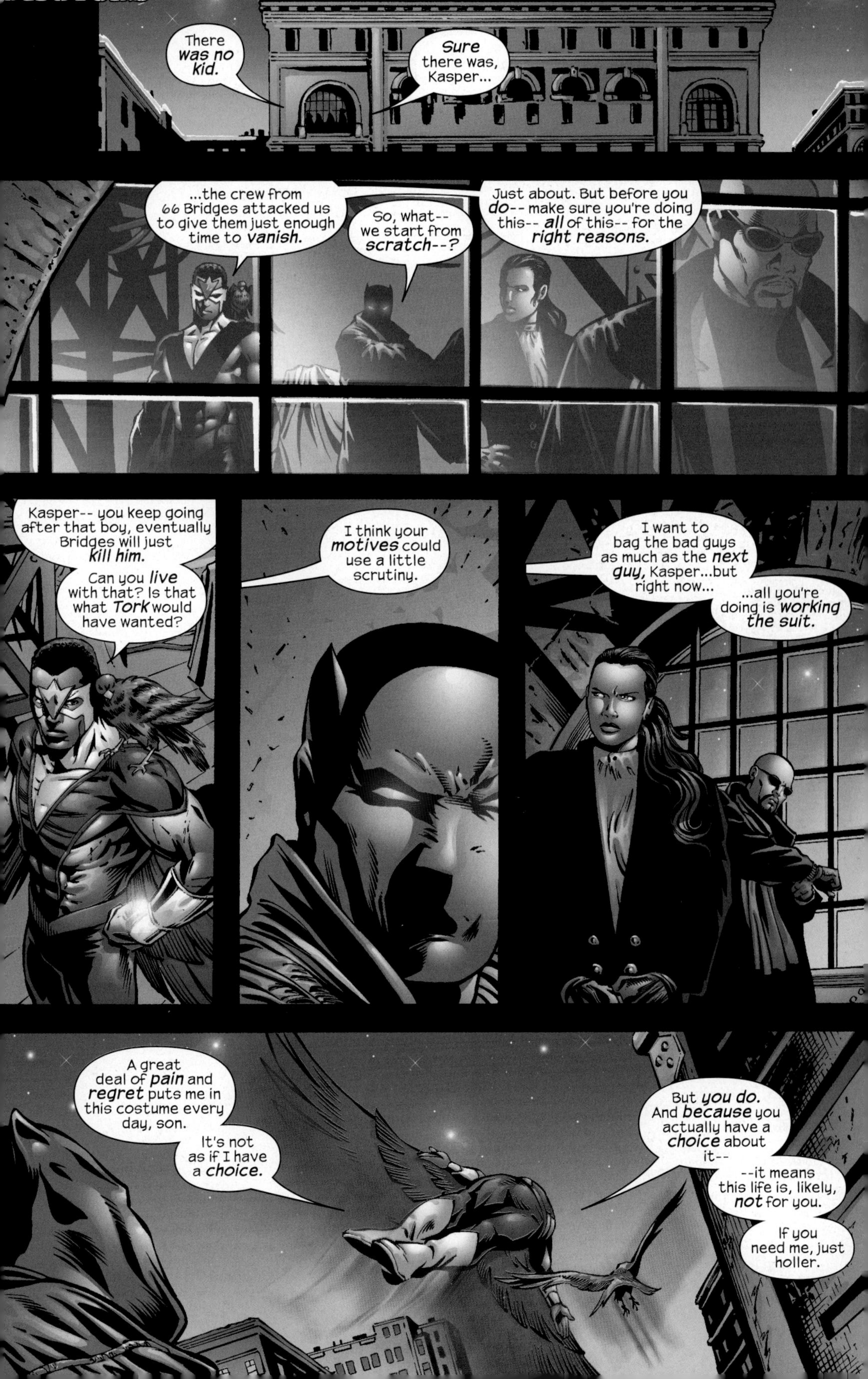
There was no kid.
Sure there was, Kasper...
...the crew from 66 Bridges attacked us to give them just enough time to vanish.
So, what-- we start from scratch--?
Just about. But before you do-- make sure you're doing this-- all of this-- for the right reasons.
Kasper-- you keep going after that boy, eventually Bridges will just kill him.
Can you live with that? Is that what Tork would have wanted?
I think your motives could use a little scrutiny.
I want to bag the bad guys as much as the next guy, Kasper...but right now...
...all you're doing is working the suit.
A great deal of pain and regret puts me in this costume every day, son.
It's not as if I have a choice.
But you do. And because you actually have a choice about it--
--it means this life is, likely, not for you.
If you need me, just holler.

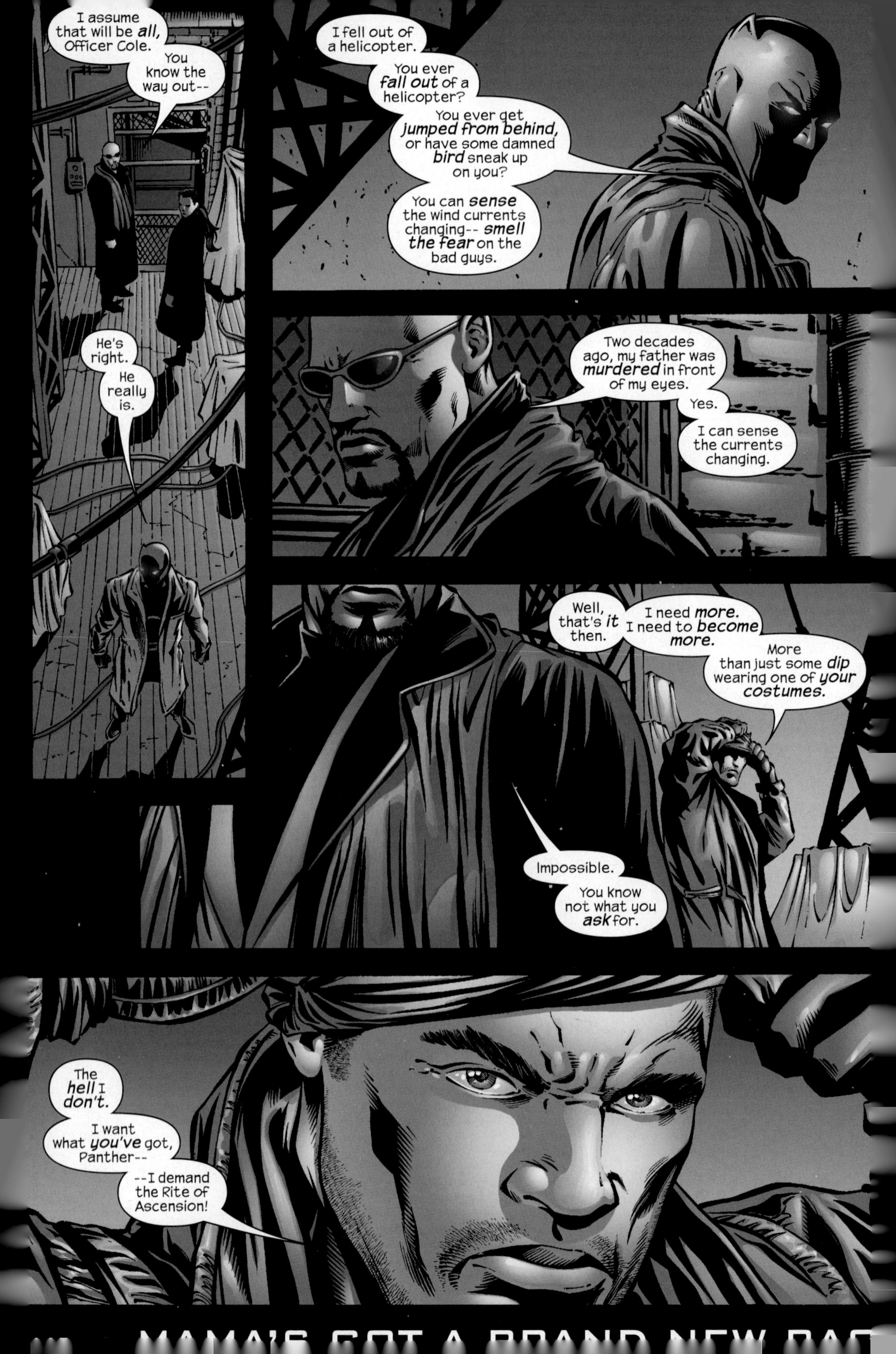
I assume that will be *all*, Officer Cole.
You know the way out--
He's right.
He really is.
I fell out of a helicopter.
You ever *fall out* of a helicopter?
You ever get *jumped from behind,* or have some damned *bird* sneak up on you?
You can *sense* the wind currents changing-- *smell the fear* on the bad guys.
Two decades ago, my father was *murdered* in front of my eyes.
Yes.
I can sense the currents changing.
Well, that's *it* then.
I need *more.* I need to *become more.*
More than just some *dip* wearing one of *your costumes.*
Impossible.
You know not what you *ask* for.
The *hell* I *don't.*
I want what *you've* got, Panther--
--I demand the Rite of Ascension!

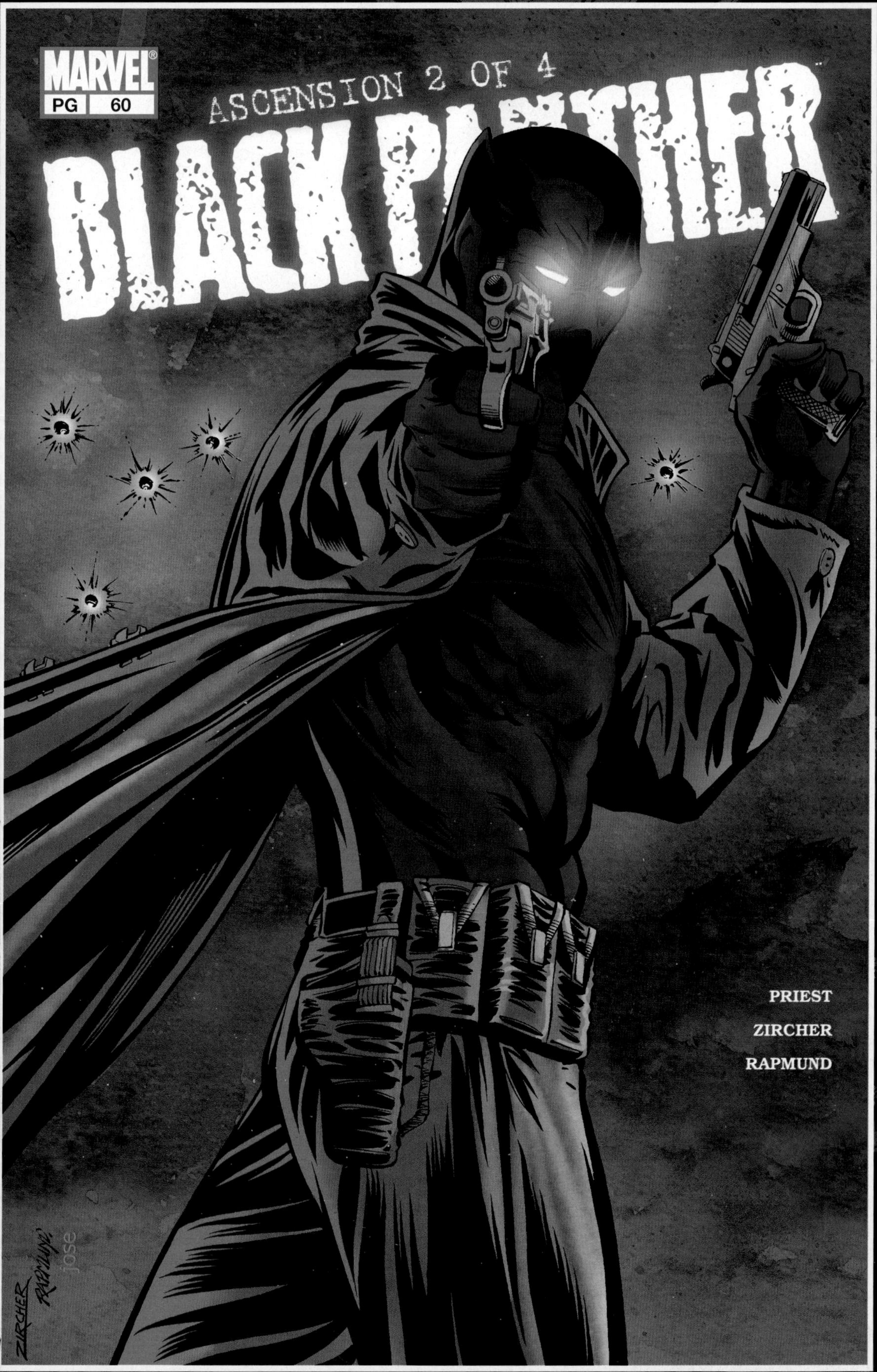
MARVEL
PG 60
ASCENSION 2 OF 4
BLACK PANTHER
PRIEST
ZIRCHER
RAPMUND
ZIRCHER
RAPMUND
jose

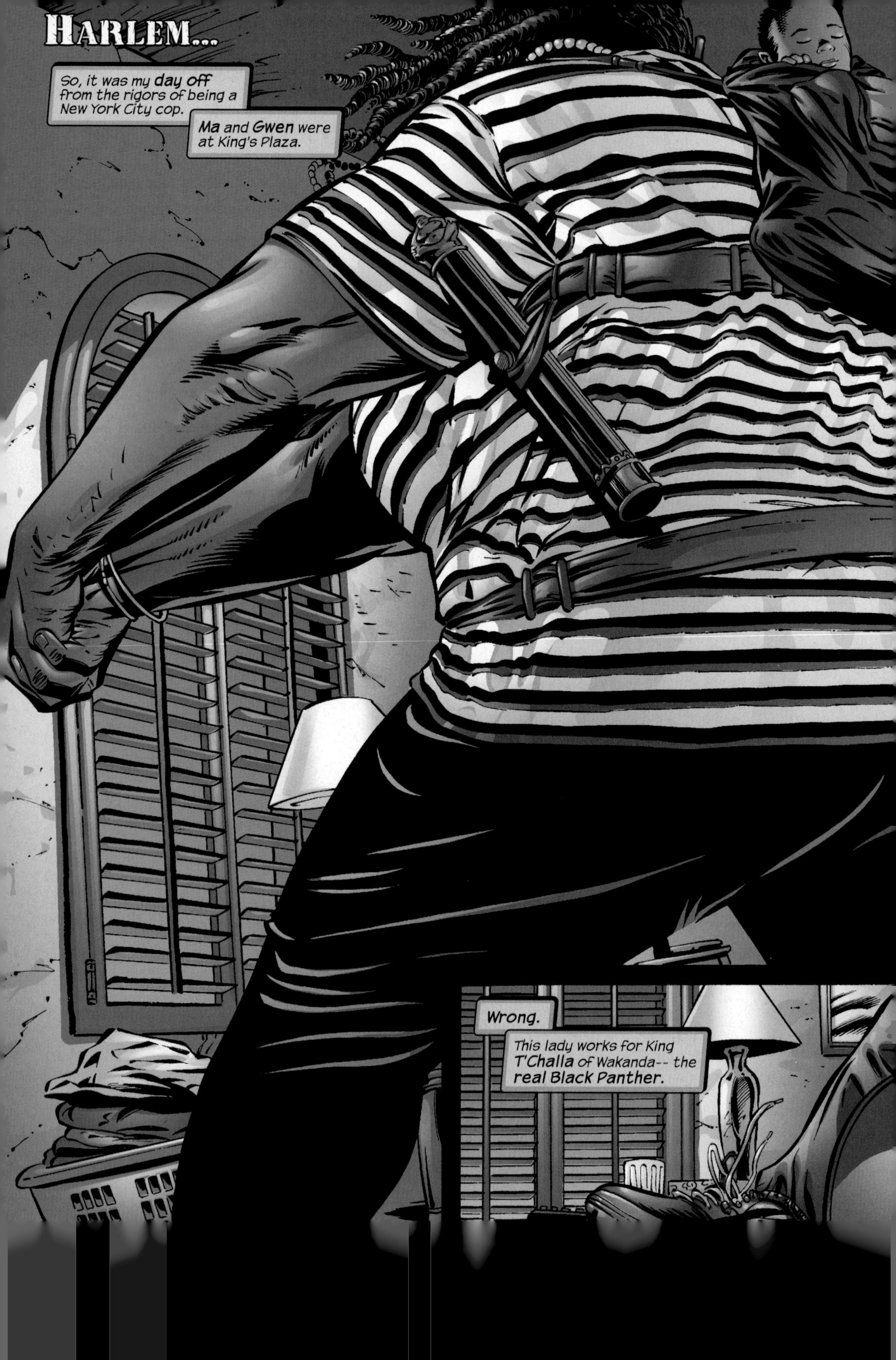
HARLEM...
So, it was my day off from the rigors of being a New York City cop.
Ma and Gwen were at King's Plaza.
Wrong.
This lady works for King T'Challa of Wakanda-- the real Black Panther.

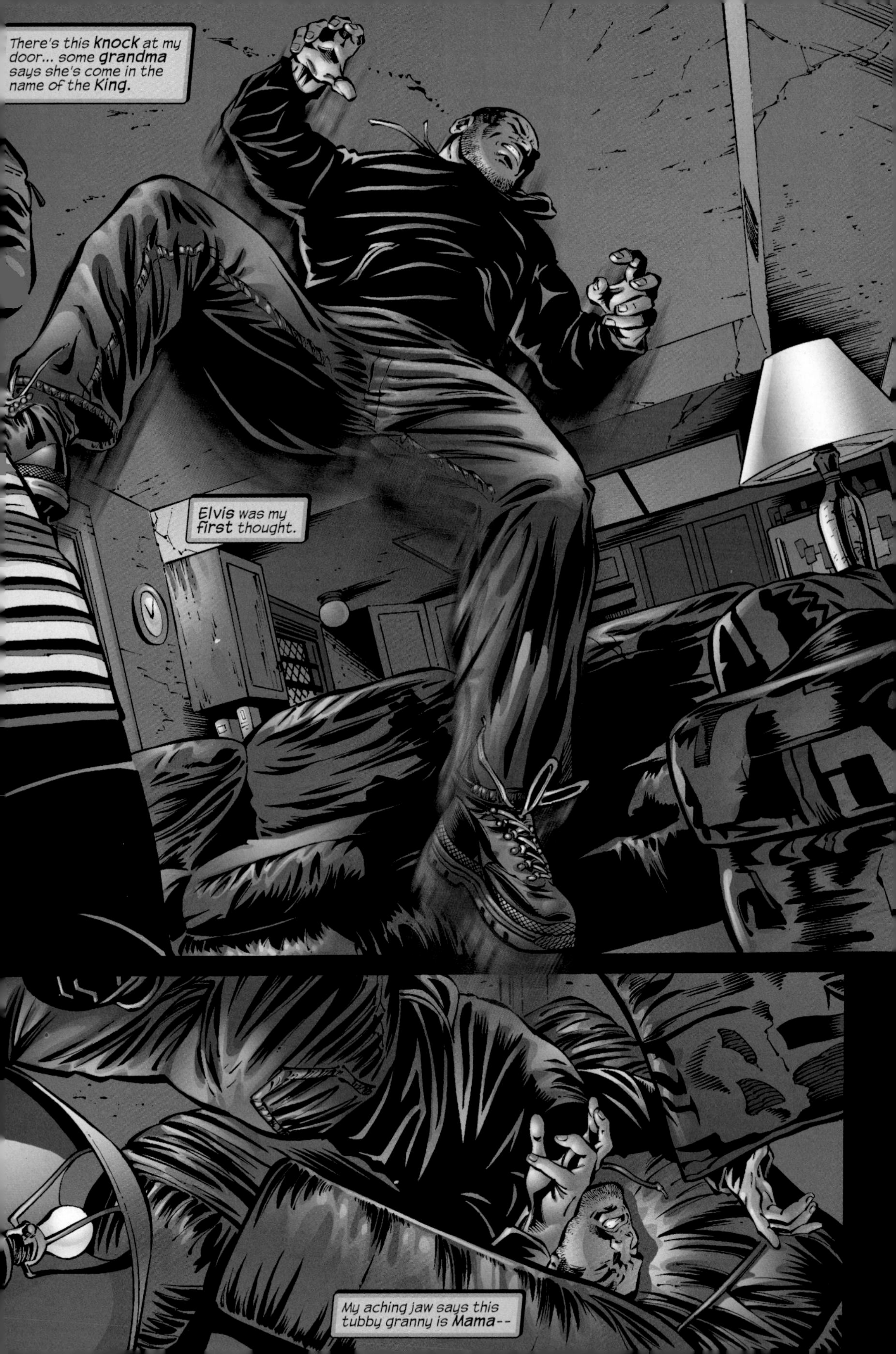
There's this knock at my door... some grandma says she's come in the name of the King.
Elvis was my first thought.
My aching jaw says this tubby granny is Mama--

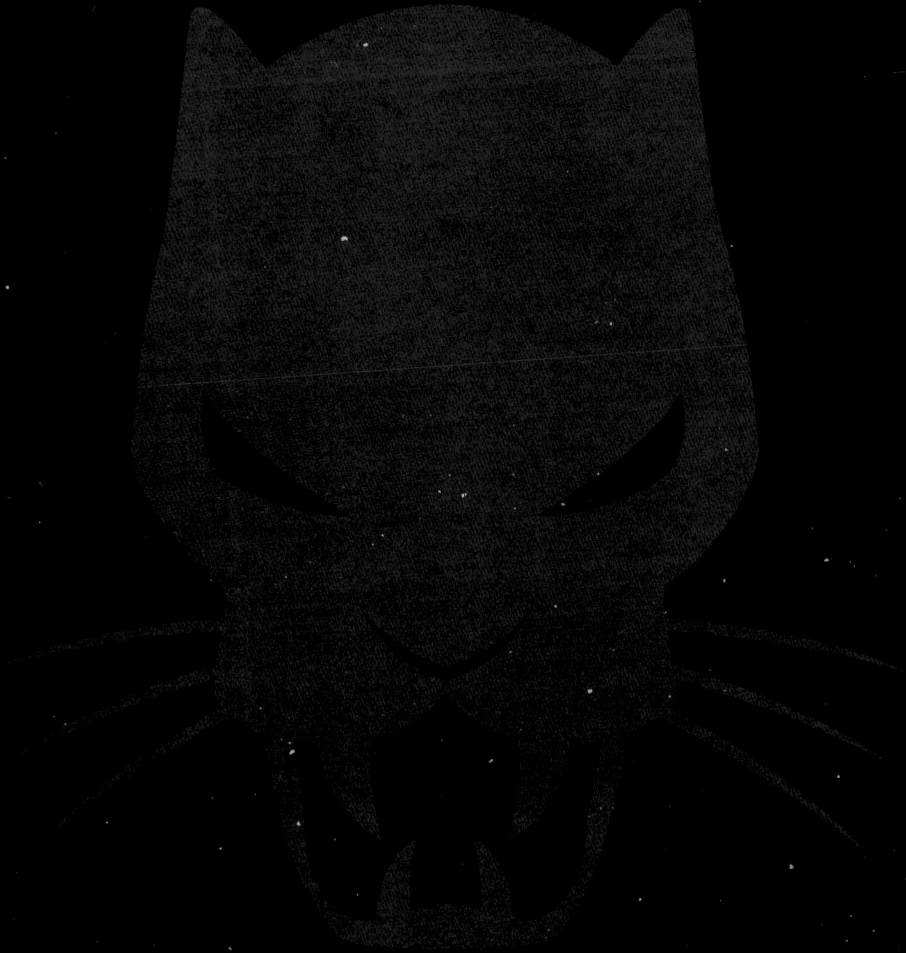

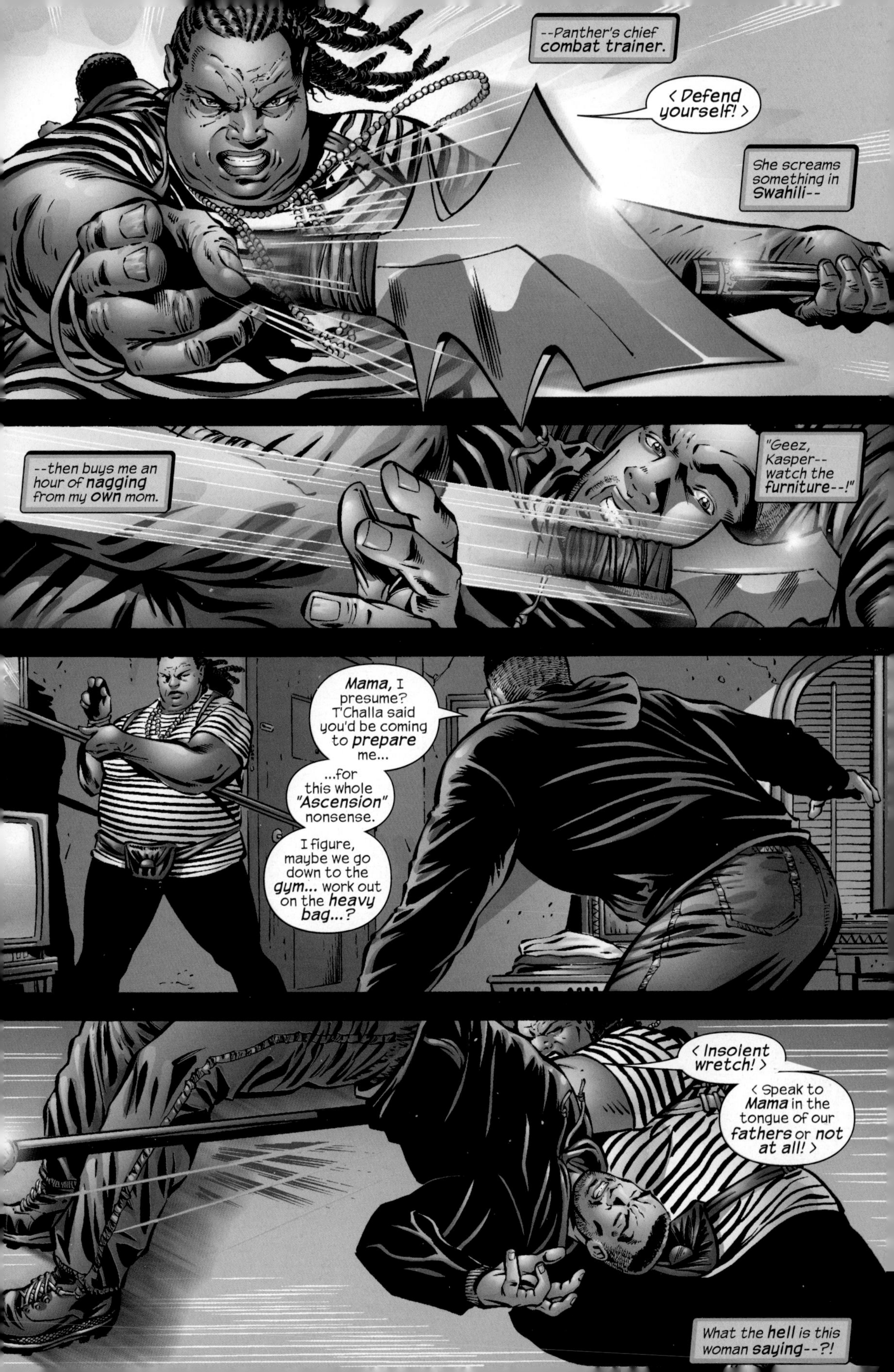
--Panther's chief combat trainer.
< Defend yourself! >
She screams something in Swahili--
--then buys me an hour of nagging from my own mom.
"Geez, Kasper-- watch the furniture--!"
Mama, I presume? T'Challa said you'd be coming to prepare me...
...for this whole "Ascension" nonsense.
I figure, maybe we go down to the gym... work out on the heavy bag...?
< Insolent wretch! >
< Speak to Mama in the tongue of our fathers or not at all! >
What the hell is this woman saying--?!

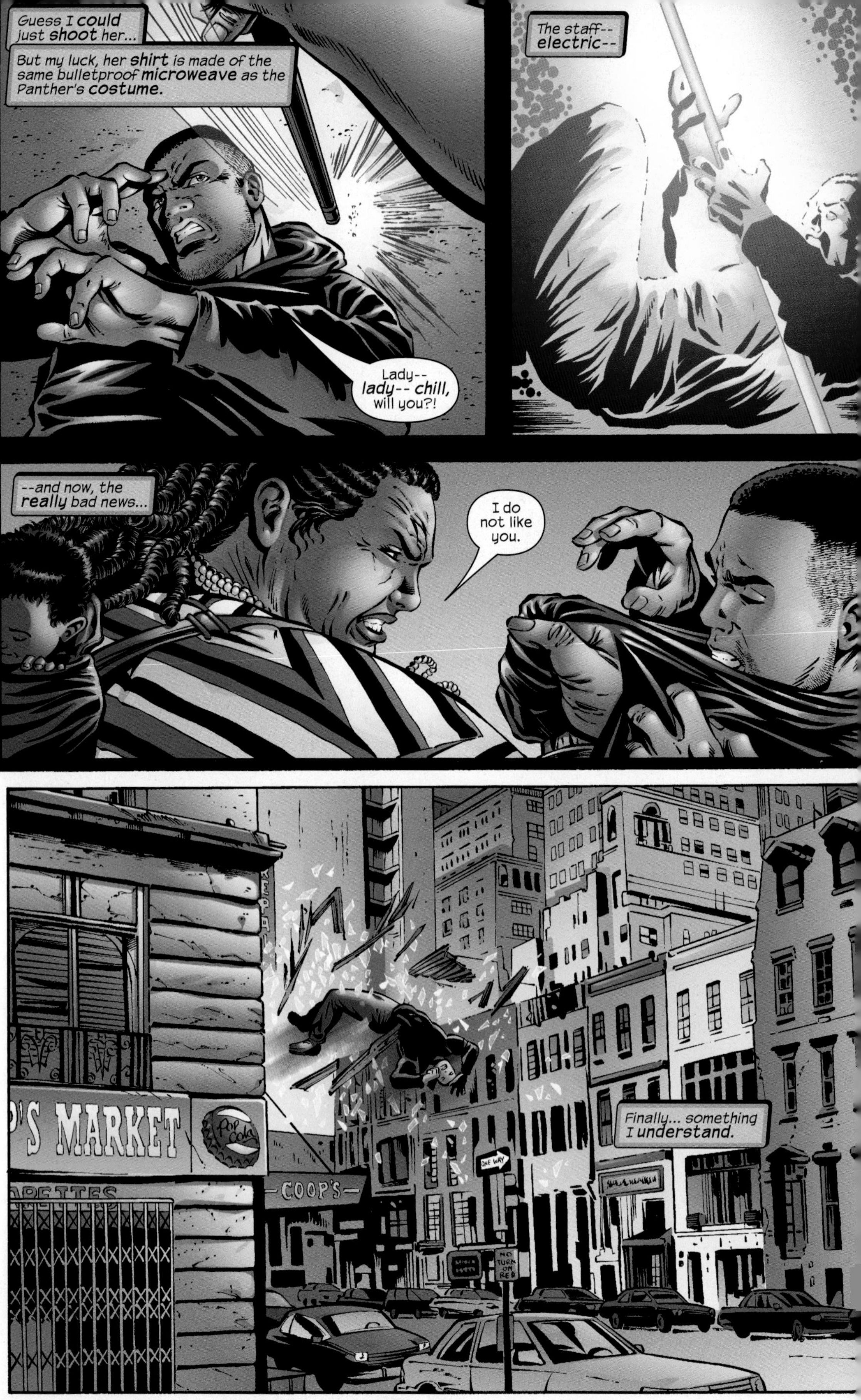
Guess I could just shoot her...
But my luck, her shirt is made of the same bulletproof microweave as the Panther's costume.
Lady-- lady-- chill, will you?!
The staff-- electric--
--and now, the really bad news...
I do not like you.
'S MARKET
Pop Cola
COOP'S
ONE WAY
NO TURN ON RED
Finally... something I understand.

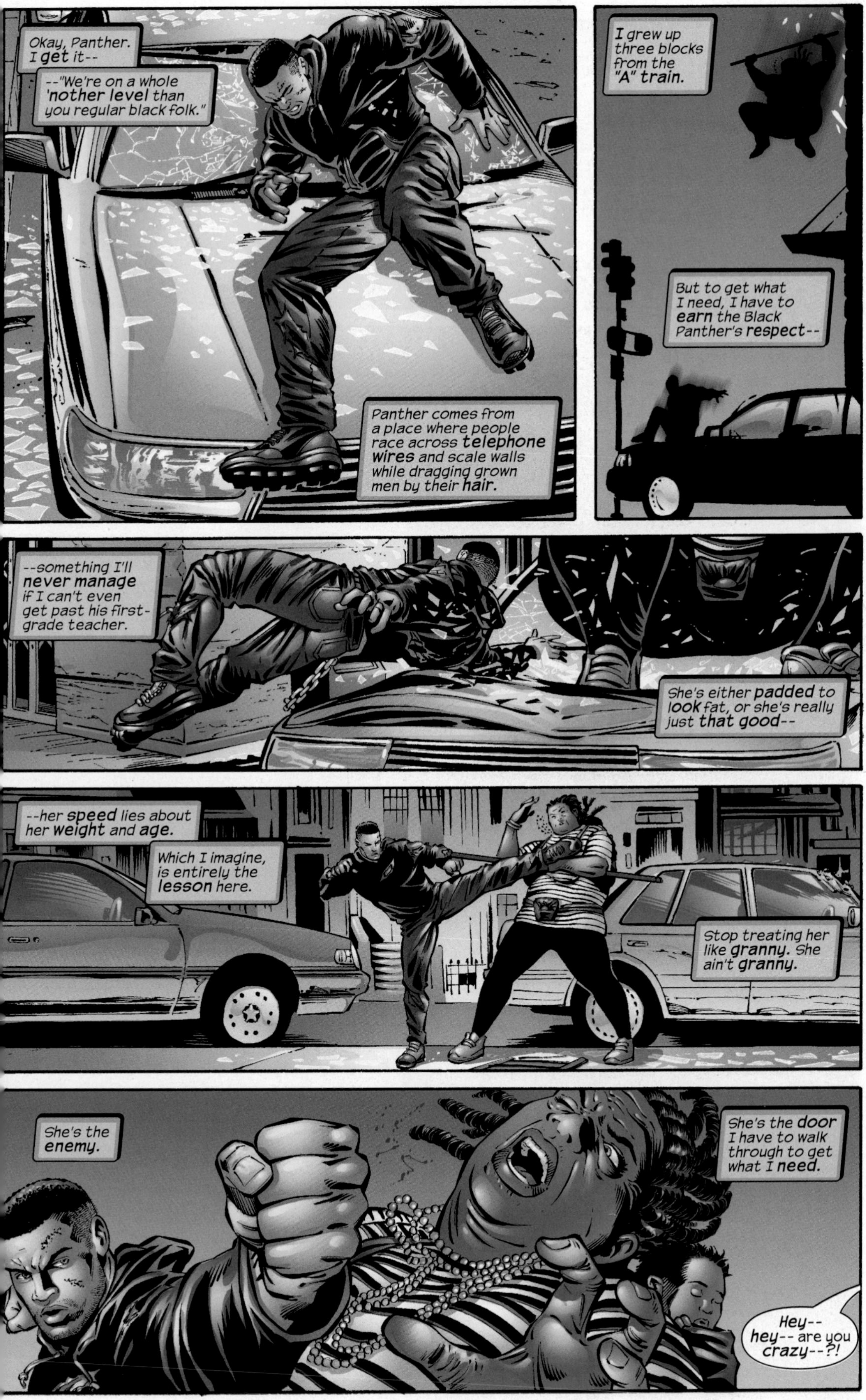
Okay, Panther. I get it--
--"We're on a whole 'nother level than you regular black folk."
Panther comes from a place where people race across telephone wires and scale walls while dragging grown men by their hair.
I grew up three blocks from the "A" train.
But to get what I need, I have to earn the Black Panther's respect--
--something I'll never manage if I can't even get past his first-grade teacher.
She's either padded to look fat, or she's really just that good--
--her speed lies about her weight and age.
Which I imagine, is entirely the lesson here.
Stop treating her like granny. She ain't granny.
She's the enemy.
She's the door I have to walk through to get what I need.
Hey-- hey-- are you crazy--?!

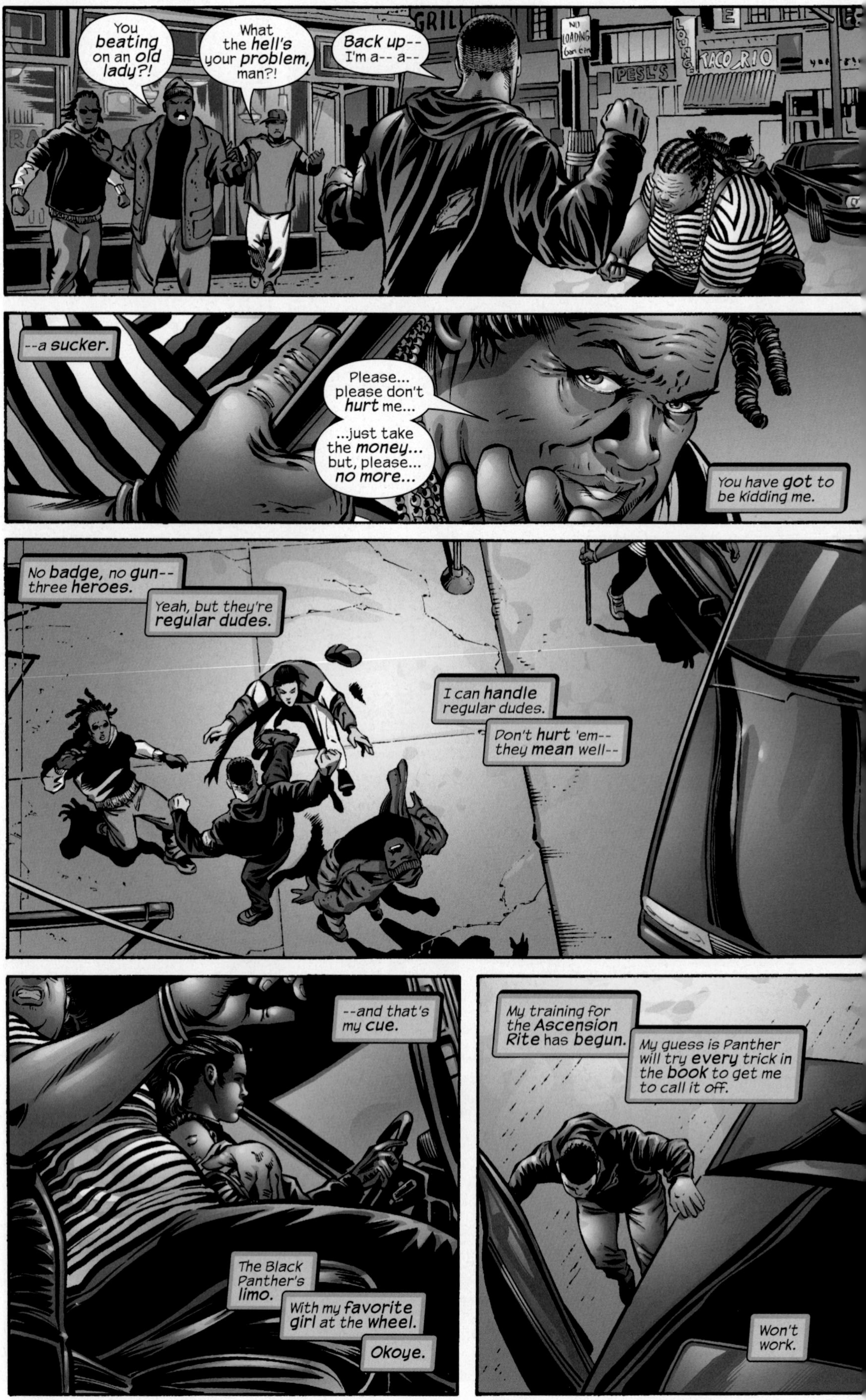

You beating on an old lady?!
What the hell's your problem, man?!
Back up-- I'm a-- a--
GRILL
NO LOADING
LOUNGE
PESL'S
TACO RIO
--a sucker.
Please... please don't hurt me...
...just take the money... but, please... no more...
You have got to be kidding me.
No badge, no gun-- three heroes.
Yeah, but they're regular dudes.
I can handle regular dudes.
Don't hurt 'em-- they mean well--
--and that's my cue.
The Black Panther's limo.
With my favorite girl at the wheel.
Okoye.
My training for the Ascension Rite has begun.
My guess is Panther will try every trick in the book to get me to call it off.
Won't work.

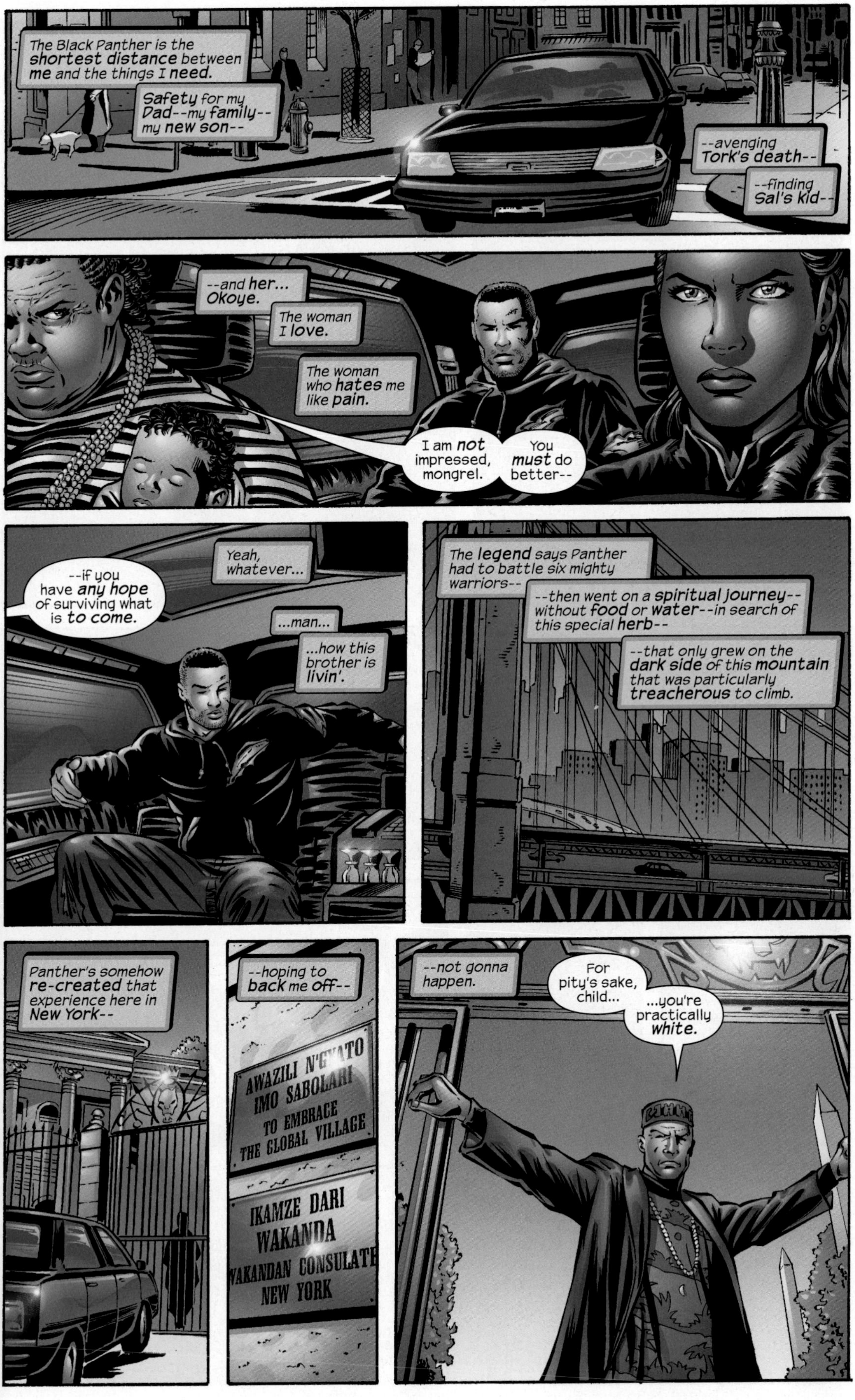
The Black Panther is the shortest distance between me and the things I need.
Safety for my Dad--my family--my new son--
--avenging Tork's death--
--finding Sal's kid--
--and her... Okoye.
The woman I love.
The woman who hates me like pain.
I am not impressed, mongrel.
You must do better--
--if you have any hope of surviving what is to come.
Yeah, whatever...
...man...
...how this brother is livin'.
The legend says Panther had to battle six mighty warriors--
--then went on a spiritual journey--without food or water--in search of this special herb--
--that only grew on the dark side of this mountain that was particularly treacherous to climb.
Panther's somehow re-created that experience here in New York--
--hoping to back me off--
AWAZILI N'GYATO IMO SABOLARI TO EMBRACE THE GLOBAL VILLAGE
IKAMZE DARI WAKANDA
WAKANDAN CONSULATE NEW YORK
--not gonna happen.
For pity's sake, child...
...you're practically white.

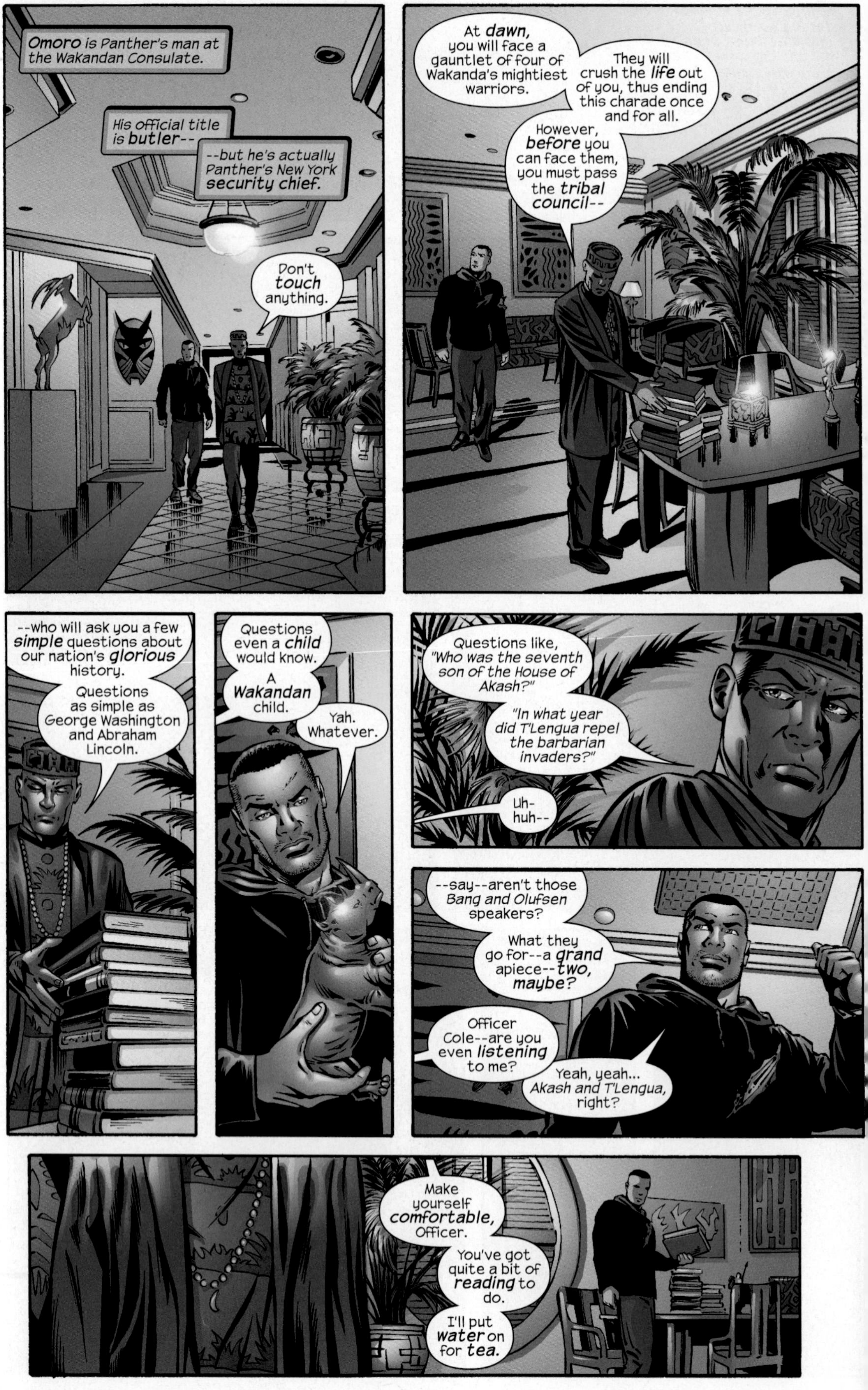
Omoro is Panther's man at the Wakandan Consulate.
His official title is butler--
--but he's actually Panther's New York security chief.
Don't touch anything.
At dawn, you will face a gauntlet of four of Wakanda's mightiest warriors.
They will crush the life out of you, thus ending this charade once and for all.
However, before you can face them, you must pass the tribal council--
--who will ask you a few simple questions about our nation's glorious history.
Questions as simple as George Washington and Abraham Lincoln.
Questions even a child would know.
A Wakandan child.
Yah. Whatever.
Questions like, "Who was the seventh son of the House of Akash?"
"In what year did T'Lengua repel the barbarian invaders?"
Uh-huh--
--say--aren't those Bang and Olufsen speakers?
What they go for--a grand apiece--two, maybe?
Officer Cole--are you even listening to me?
Yeah, yeah... Akash and T'Lengua, right?
Make yourself comfortable, Officer.
You've got quite a bit of reading to do.
I'll put water on for tea.

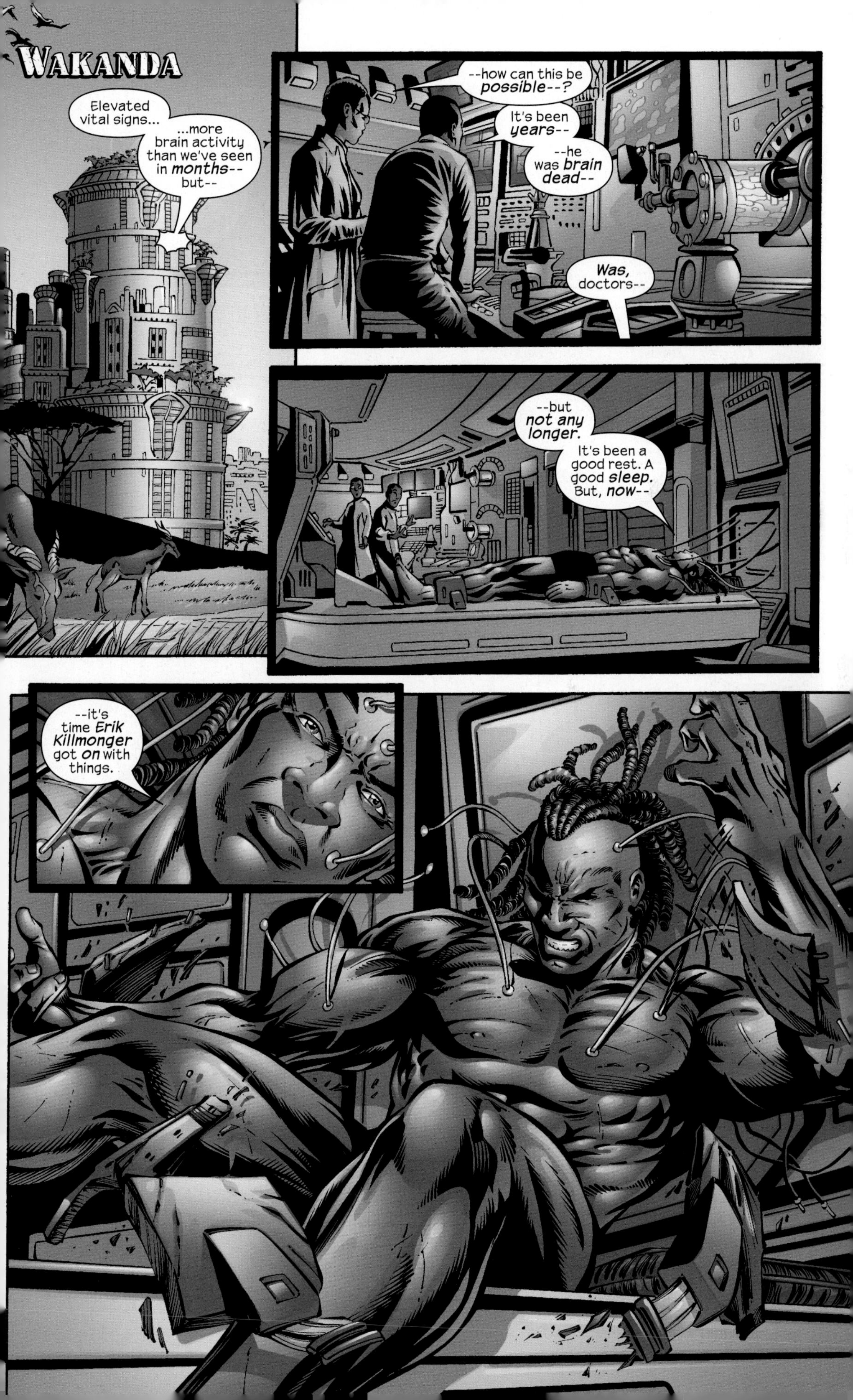
WAKANDA
Elevated vital signs...
...more brain activity than we've seen in *months*-- but--
--how can this be *possible*--?
It's been *years*--
--he was *brain dead*--
Was, doctors--
--but *not any longer.*
It's been a good rest. A good *sleep.* But, *now*--
--it's time *Erik Killmonger* got *on* with things.

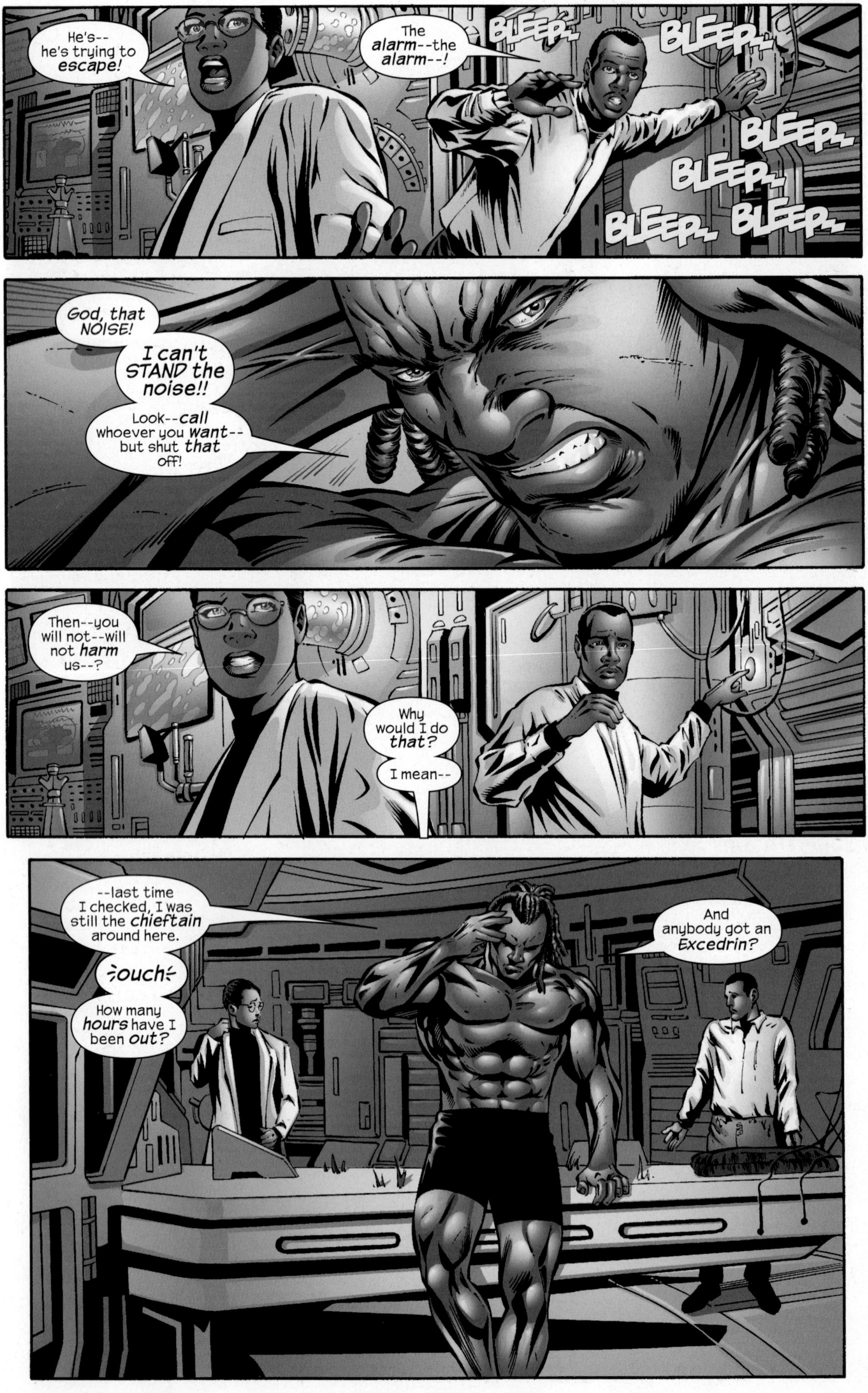

He's--
he's trying to
escape!
The
alarm--the
alarm--!
BLEEP BLEEP BLEEP BLEEP BLEEP BLEEP
God, that
NOISE!
I can't
STAND the
noise!!
Look--call
whoever you want--
but shut that
off!
Then--you
will not--will
not harm
us--?
Why
would I do
that?
I mean--
--last time
I checked, I was
still the chieftain
around here.
ouch
How many
hours have I
been out?
And
anybody got an
Excedrin?

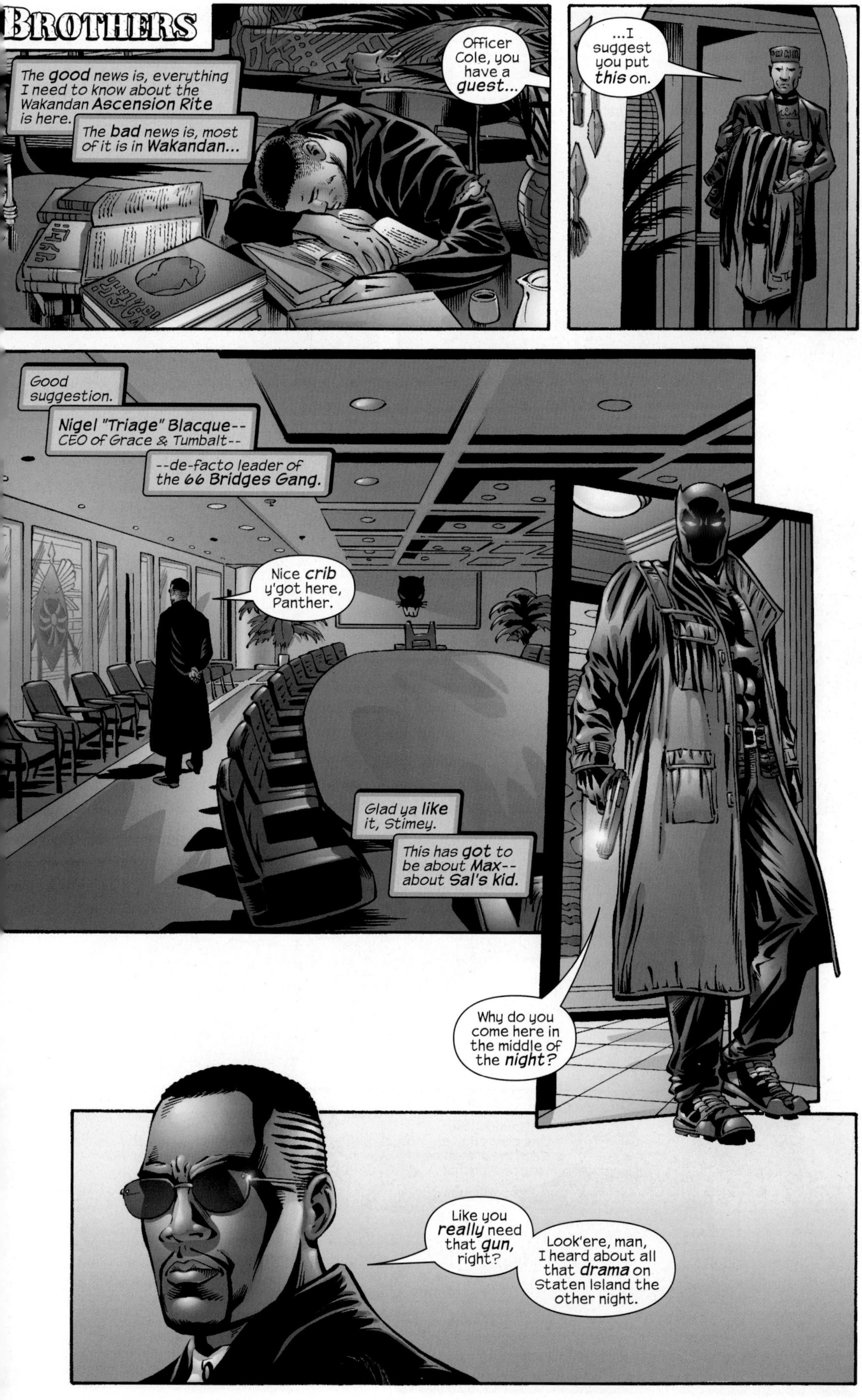
BROTHERS
The good news is, everything I need to know about the Wakandan Ascension Rite is here.
The bad news is, most of it is in Wakandan...
Officer Cole, you have a guest...
...I suggest you put this on.
Good suggestion.
Nigel "Triage" Blacque--
CEO of Grace & Tumbalt--
--de-facto leader of the 66 Bridges Gang.
Nice crib y'got here, Panther.
Glad ya like it, Stimey.
This has got to be about Max--about Sal's kid.
Why do you come here in the middle of the night?
Like you really need that gun, right?
Look'ere, man, I heard about all that drama on Staten Island the other night.

Seems like *my name* keeps comin' up in that mess. Like *I* got somethin' to do with Sal's *missing kid.*

And you've come to *convince* me of your *innocence.*

No, I've come to *help.*

Shouldn't you be sittin' up *there*--in the big chair?

Help *how?*

By saving you *time.*

You think 66 Bridges snatched Sal's kid to get *Sal*-- an NYPD lieutenant-- on our *payroll.*

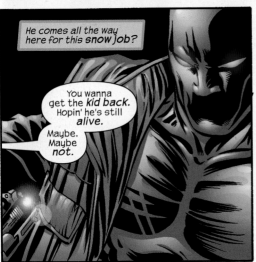

He comes all the way here for this *snow job?*

You wanna get the *kid back.* Hopin' he's still *alive.*

Maybe. Maybe *not.*

The *bigger* question, dog, is what's in it for *me?*

See, I'm a *businessman,* dog. All about them *assets* and *liabilities.*

Sal's kid is a prime *asset* protecting us from the *liability* of Sal's cop pals *bustin'* us.

I give little Max up to *you,* what do I get?

Oxygen.

Sounds like there's definitely a *deal* in here some-where, Panther.

You just gotta decide how much of your *soul* you're willin' to *lease* me to make it.

Nice *digs,* man.

I'ma **hurt** him.

The day is comin', **Triage**...

I have come to **release** you from the Ascension Rites, Officer Cole.

New developments in **Wakanda** require the tribal council's attention.

They will not hear your petition to become **chieftain**.

I never **wanted** to be **chieftain**, Panther.

I just want **respect** in your eyes...

And to not fall out of **helicopters** and whatnot.

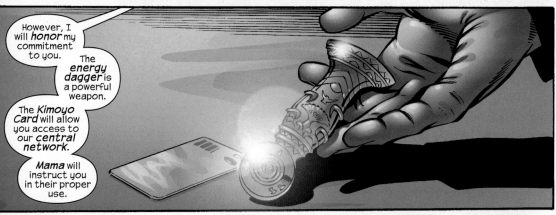

However, I will **honor** my commitment to you.

The **energy dagger** is a powerful weapon.

The **Kimoyo Card** will allow you access to our **central network**.

Mama will instruct you in their proper use.

And the **heart-shaped herb**?

Will likely **kill** you.

The **dagger** and **card** are sufficient for your purposes.

What do **you** know about my "**purposes**"...?

Panther-- without that **herb**, I'm just a **regular guy**.

You've got **grandmas** who can mop the **floor** with regular guys **all night**.

The difference between **regular guys** and guys like **you**--like **Captain America**--is a bag of **dirty roots**.

So I'm gonna do what I **gotta** do to **get** it. And **you** gave **your** word...

WHAT HE GOTTA DO

You will wait here, in the *Great Hall* of the *Tribal Council*, for their *ruling*.

Again, I urge you to *withdraw* your challenge.

Wait-- hold up--

--*you're* chieftain of the Panther tribe-- doesn't that mean I have to challenge *you*--?

I am *King* of the Wakandas, Officer Col But I have served as chieftain by *default* these past years.

"Default"...?

Officer Cole--

YOU *DARE* TURN YOUR BACK ON THE *HIGH COUNCIL* OF THE *WAKANDAS*, HERETIC?!

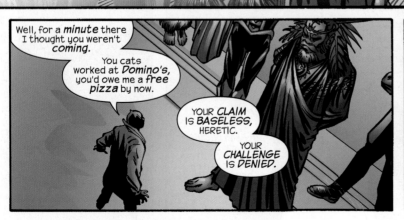

Well, for a *minute* there I thought you weren't *coming*.

You cats worked at *Domino's*, you'd owe me a *free pizza* by now.

YOUR *CLAIM* IS *BASELESS*, HERETIC.

YOUR *CHALLENGE* IS *DENIED*.

Ah, yes, but *Nooo*, folks. You see...

...under Title 14 of the Law of Ascension, once your *King* has decree a challenger *worthy* you *must* allow him to continue.

If I survive the first round-- you've *no choice* but to accept my challenge.

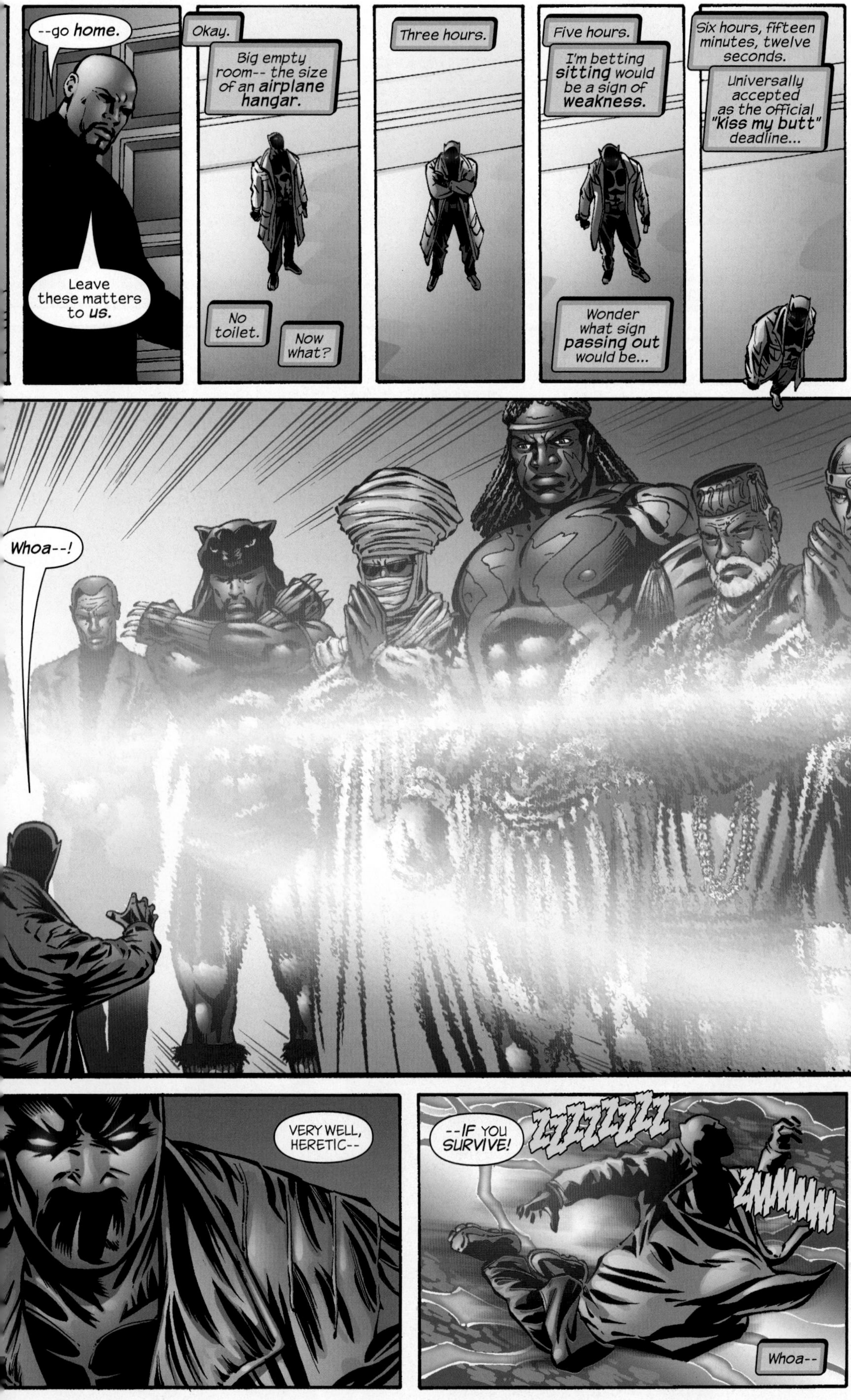

--go home.
Leave these matters to us.
Okay.
Big empty room-- the size of an airplane hangar.
No toilet.
Now what?
Three hours.
Five hours.
I'm betting sitting would be a sign of weakness.
Wonder what sign passing out would be...
Six hours, fifteen minutes, twelve seconds.
Universally accepted as the official "kiss my butt" deadline...
Whoa--!
VERY WELL, HERETIC--
--IF YOU SURVIVE!
ZZZZZZZZ
ZMMMM
Whoa--

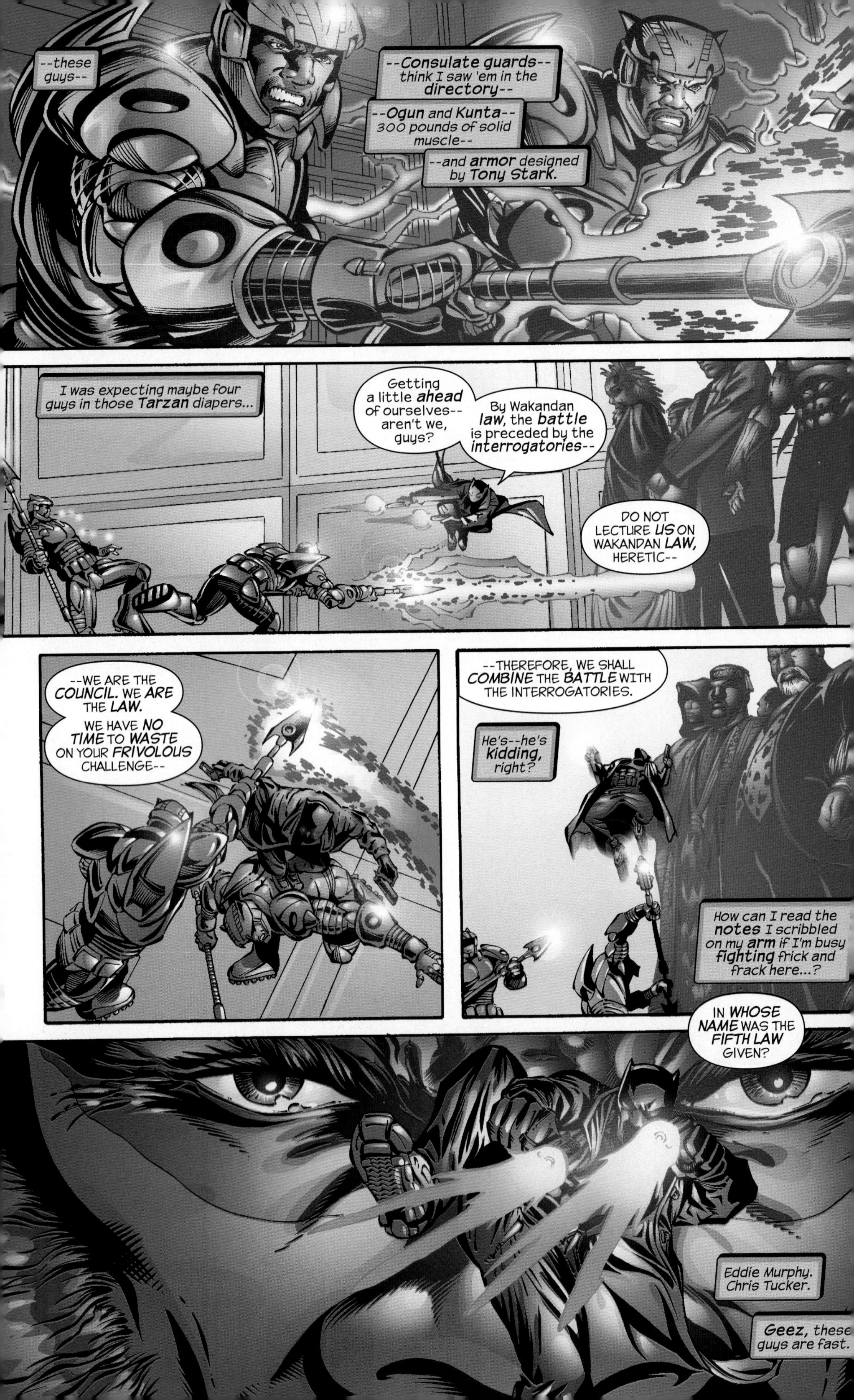
--these guys--
--Consulate guards-- think I saw 'em in the directory--
--Ogun and Kunta-- 300 pounds of solid muscle--
--and armor designed by Tony Stark.
I was expecting maybe four guys in those Tarzan diapers...
Getting a little ahead of ourselves-- aren't we, guys?
By Wakandan law, the battle is preceded by the interrogatories--
DO NOT LECTURE US ON WAKANDAN LAW, HERETIC--
--WE ARE THE COUNCIL. WE ARE THE LAW.
WE HAVE NO TIME TO WASTE ON YOUR FRIVOLOUS CHALLENGE--
--THEREFORE, WE SHALL COMBINE THE BATTLE WITH THE INTERROGATORIES.
He's--he's kidding, right?
How can I read the notes I scribbled on my arm if I'm busy fighting frick and frack here...?
IN WHOSE NAME WAS THE FIFTH LAW GIVEN?
Eddie Murphy. Chris Tucker.
Geez, these guys are fast.

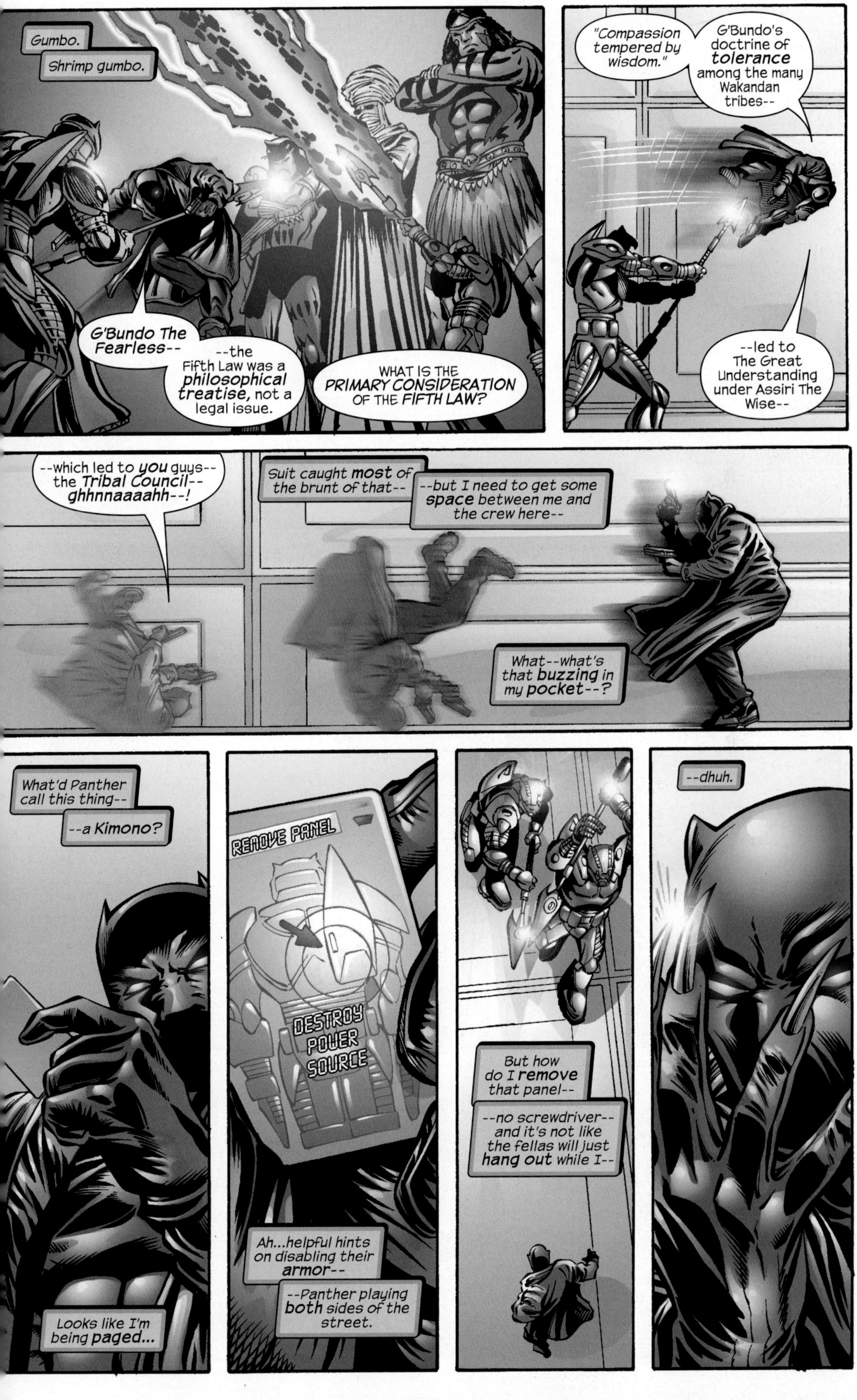
Gumbo.
Shrimp gumbo.
G'Bundo The Fearless--
--the Fifth Law was a philosophical treatise, not a legal issue.
WHAT IS THE PRIMARY CONSIDERATION OF THE FIFTH LAW?
"Compassion tempered by wisdom."
G'Bundo's doctrine of tolerance among the many Wakandan tribes--
--led to The Great Understanding under Assiri The Wise--
--which led to you guys-- the Tribal Council-- ghhnnaaaahh--!
Suit caught most of the brunt of that--
--but I need to get some space between me and the crew here--
What--what's that buzzing in my pocket--?
What'd Panther call this thing--
--a Kimono?
Looks like I'm being paged...
REMOVE PANEL
DESTROY POWER SOURCE
Ah...helpful hints on disabling their armor--
--Panther playing both sides of the street.
But how do I remove that panel--
--no screwdriver-- and it's not like the fellas will just hang out while I--
--dhuh.

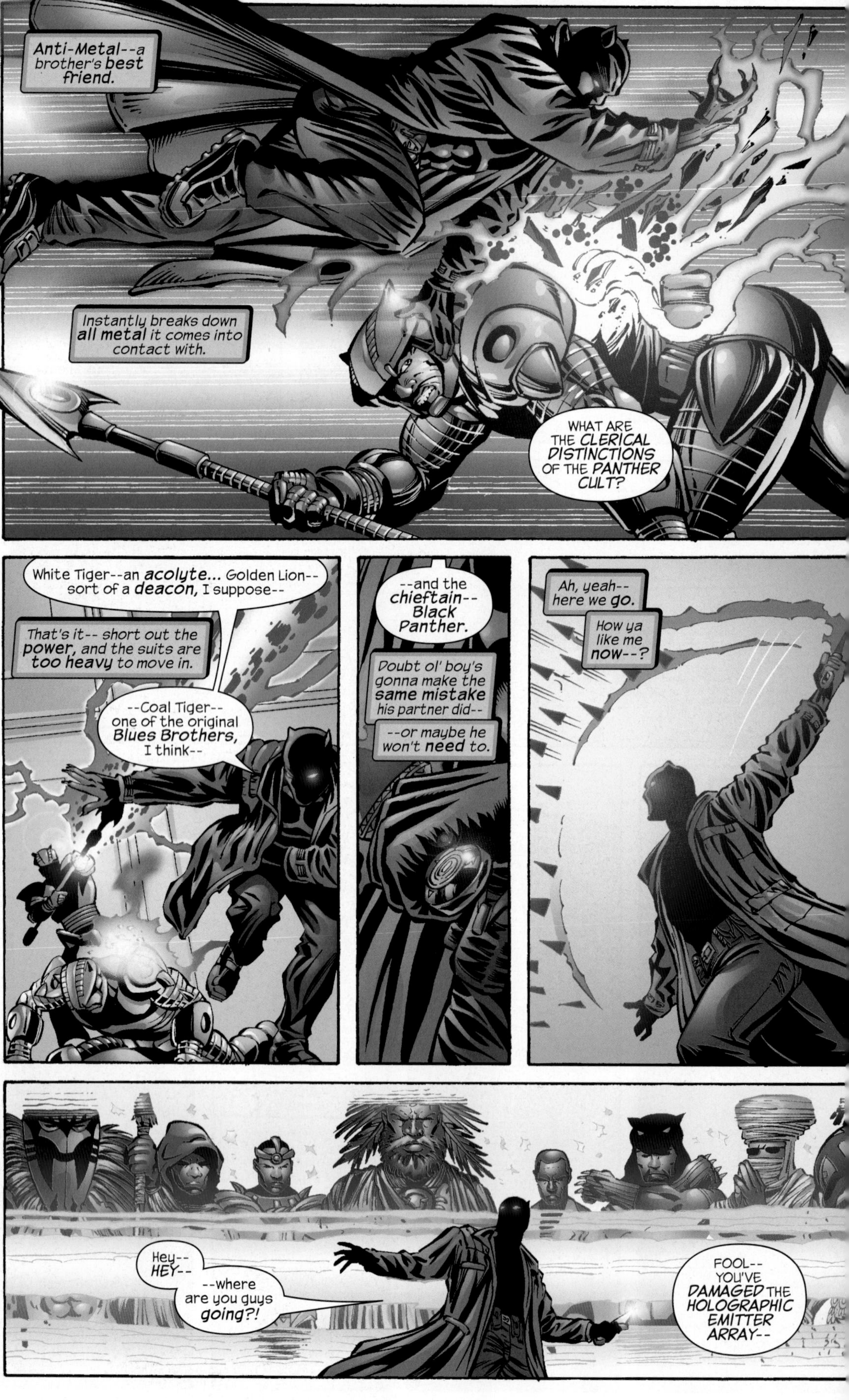

Anti-Metal--a brother's best friend.
Instantly breaks down all metal it comes into contact with.
WHAT ARE THE CLERICAL DISTINCTIONS OF THE PANTHER CULT?
White Tiger--an acolyte... Golden Lion--sort of a deacon, I suppose--
That's it-- short out the power, and the suits are too heavy to move in.
--Coal Tiger--one of the original Blues Brothers, I think--
--and the chieftain--Black Panther.
Doubt ol' boy's gonna make the same mistake his partner did--
--or maybe he won't need to.
Ah, yeah--here we go.
How ya like me now--?
Hey--HEY--
--where are you guys going?!
FOOL--YOU'VE DAMAGED THE HOLOGRAPHIC EMITTER ARRAY--

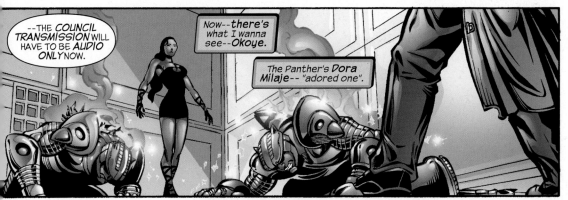

--THE COUNCIL TRANSMISSION WILL HAVE TO BE AUDIO ONLY NOW.

Now--there's what I wanna see--Okoye.

The Panther's Dora Milaje-- "adored one".

Thanks for the tip on the armor.

Biggie and Tupac there woulda smoked a brother.

Something wrong, though...I thought Omoro said I'd have to face four warriors...

Dhuh.

Like she was here to bring me tea...

First time we met, she damn near threw me out a window.

Gotta improve my percentages...

HOW MANY MEMBERS SIT ON THE TRIBAL COUNCIL?

The Wakandan Parliament is made up of 18 ministers representing a couple dozen indigenous Wakandan tribes--

--few of which actually agree on anything.

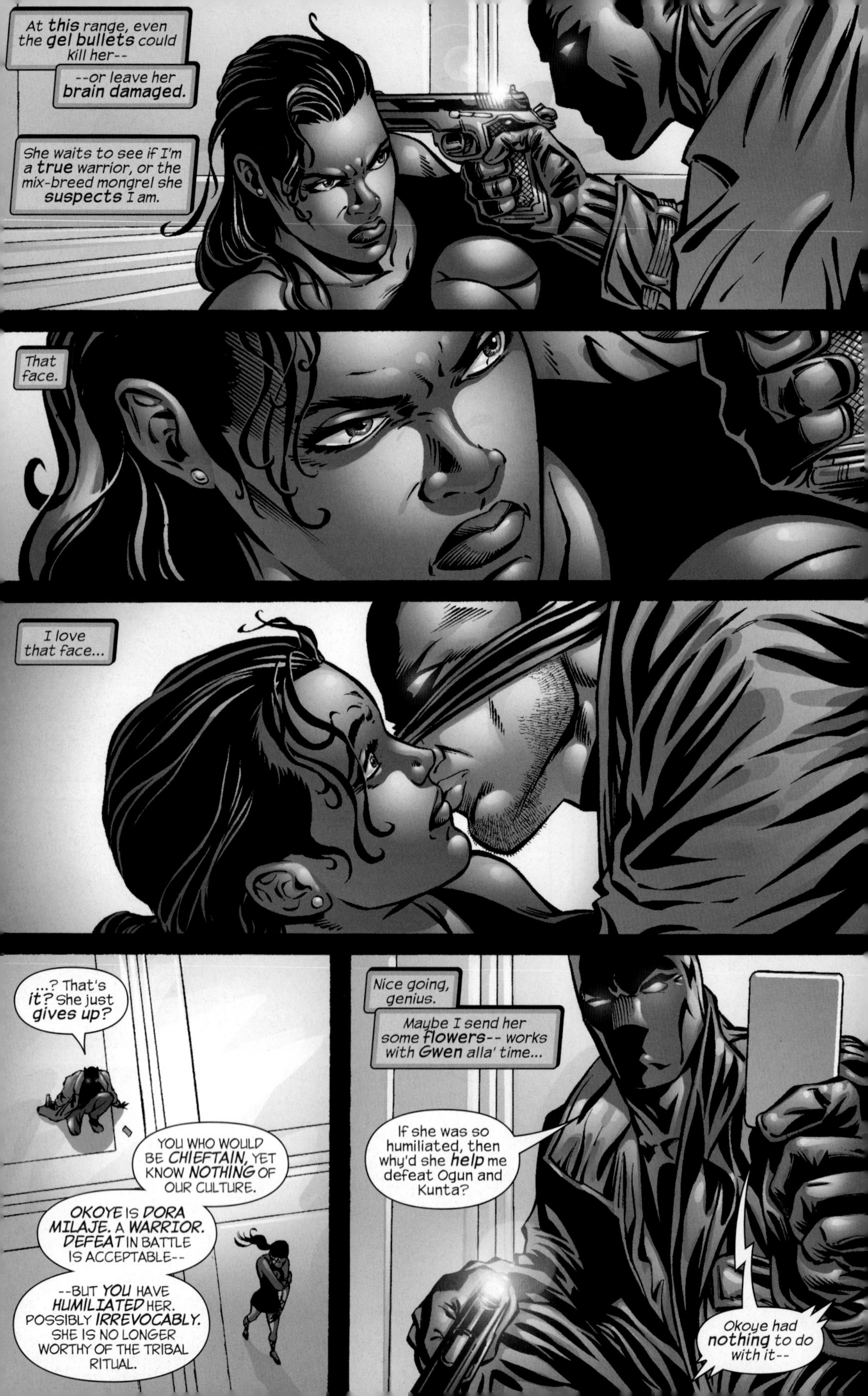
At this range, even the gel bullets could kill her--
--or leave her brain damaged.
She waits to see if I'm a true warrior, or the mix-breed mongrel she suspects I am.
That face.
I love that face...
...? That's it? She just gives up?
YOU WHO WOULD BE CHIEFTAIN, YET KNOW NOTHING OF OUR CULTURE.
OKOYE IS DORA MILAJE. A WARRIOR. DEFEAT IN BATTLE IS ACCEPTABLE--
--BUT YOU HAVE HUMILIATED HER. POSSIBLY IRREVOCABLY. SHE IS NO LONGER WORTHY OF THE TRIBAL RITUAL.
Nice going, genius.
Maybe I send her some flowers-- works with Gwen alla' time...
If she was so humiliated, then why'd she help me defeat Ogun and Kunta?
Okoye had nothing to do with it--

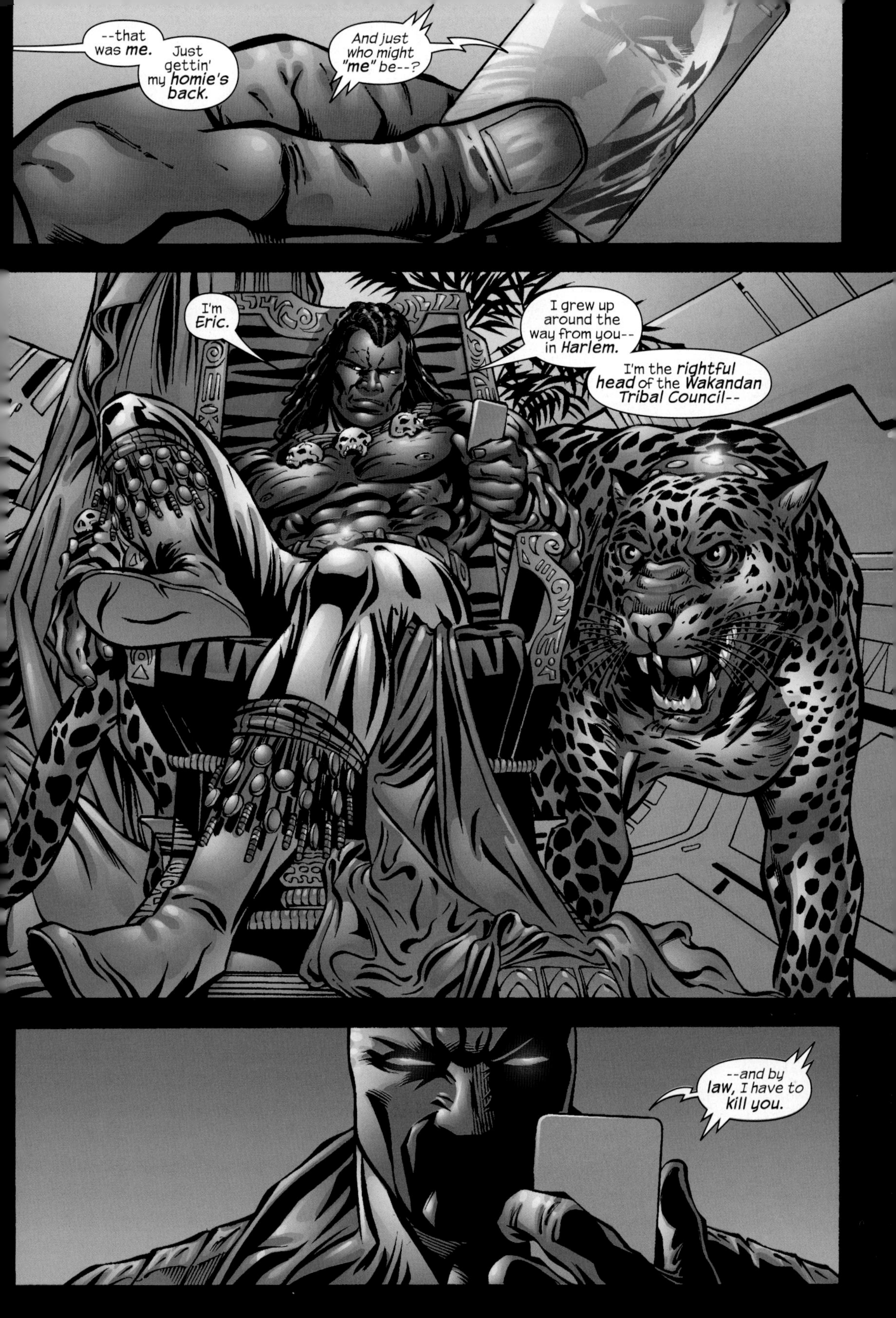
--that was me. Just gettin' my homie's back.
And just who might "me" be--?
I'm Eric.
I grew up around the way from you--in Harlem.
I'm the rightful head of the Wakandan Tribal Council--
--and by law, I have to kill you.

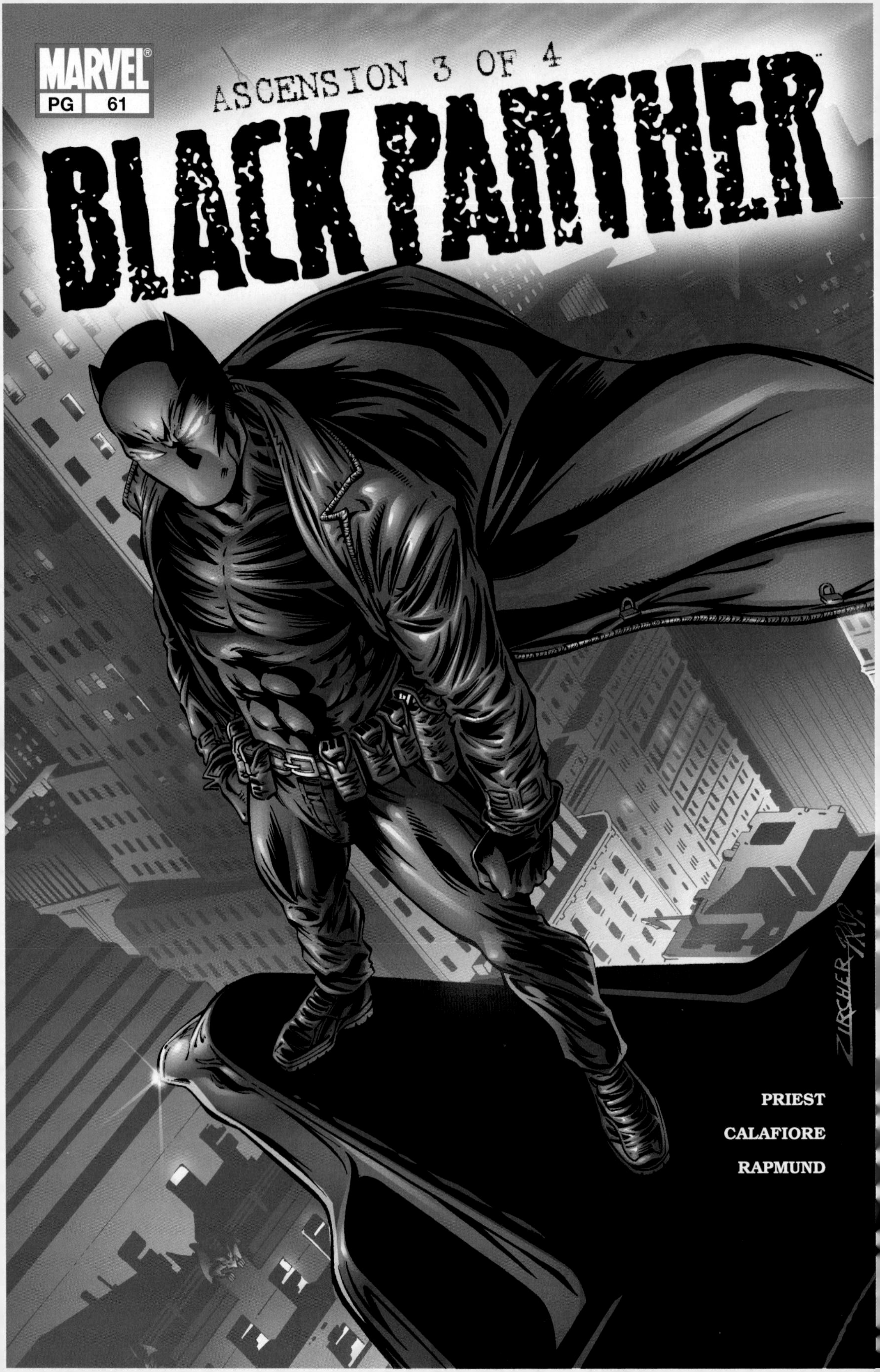
MARVEL
PG 61
ASCENSION 3 OF 4
BLACK PANTHER
ZIRCHER
PRIEST
CALAFIORE
RAPMUND

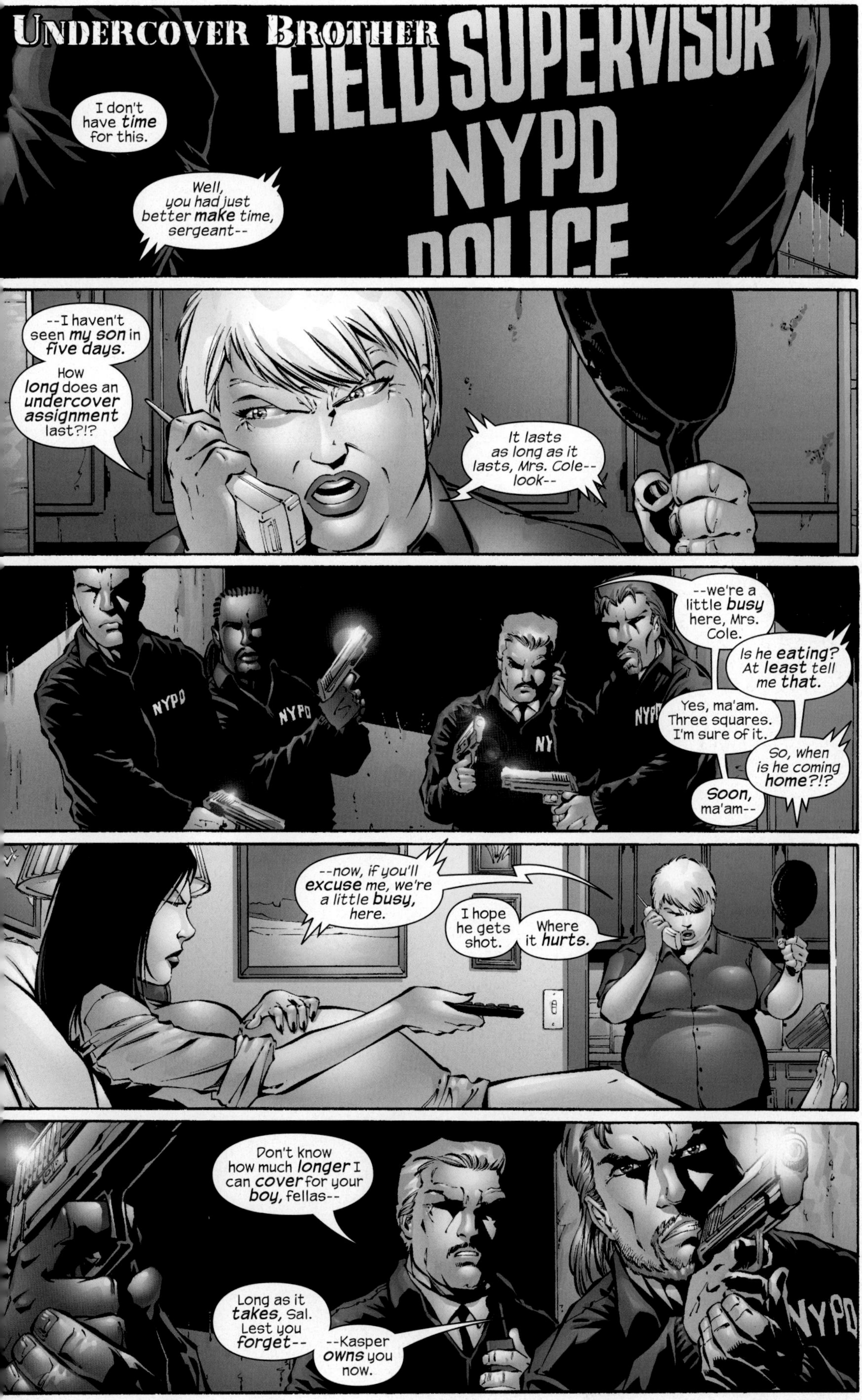
UNDERCOVER BROTHER
FIELD SUPERVISOR
NYPD
POLICE
I don't have time for this.
Well, you had just better make time, sergeant--
--I haven't seen my son in five days.
How long does an undercover assignment last?!?
It lasts as long as it lasts, Mrs. Cole-- look--
--we're a little busy here, Mrs. Cole.
Is he eating? At least tell me that.
Yes, ma'am. Three squares. I'm sure of it.
So, when is he coming home?!?
Soon, ma'am--
--now, if you'll excuse me, we're a little busy, here.
I hope he gets shot.
Where it hurts.
Don't know how much longer I can cover for your boy, fellas--
Long as it takes, Sal. Lest you forget--
--Kasper owns you now.

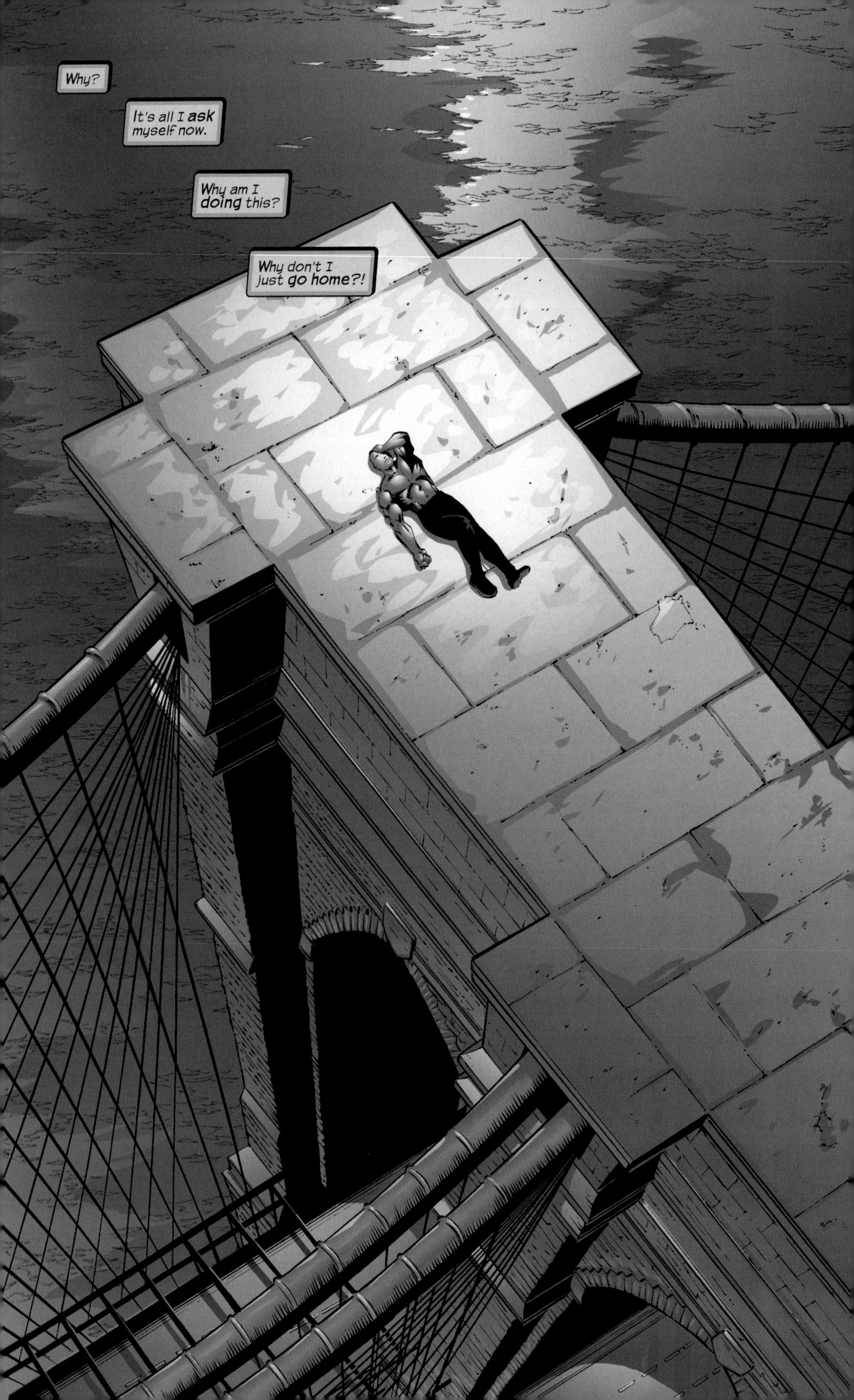
Why?
It's all I ask myself now.
Why am I doing this?
Why don't I just go home?!

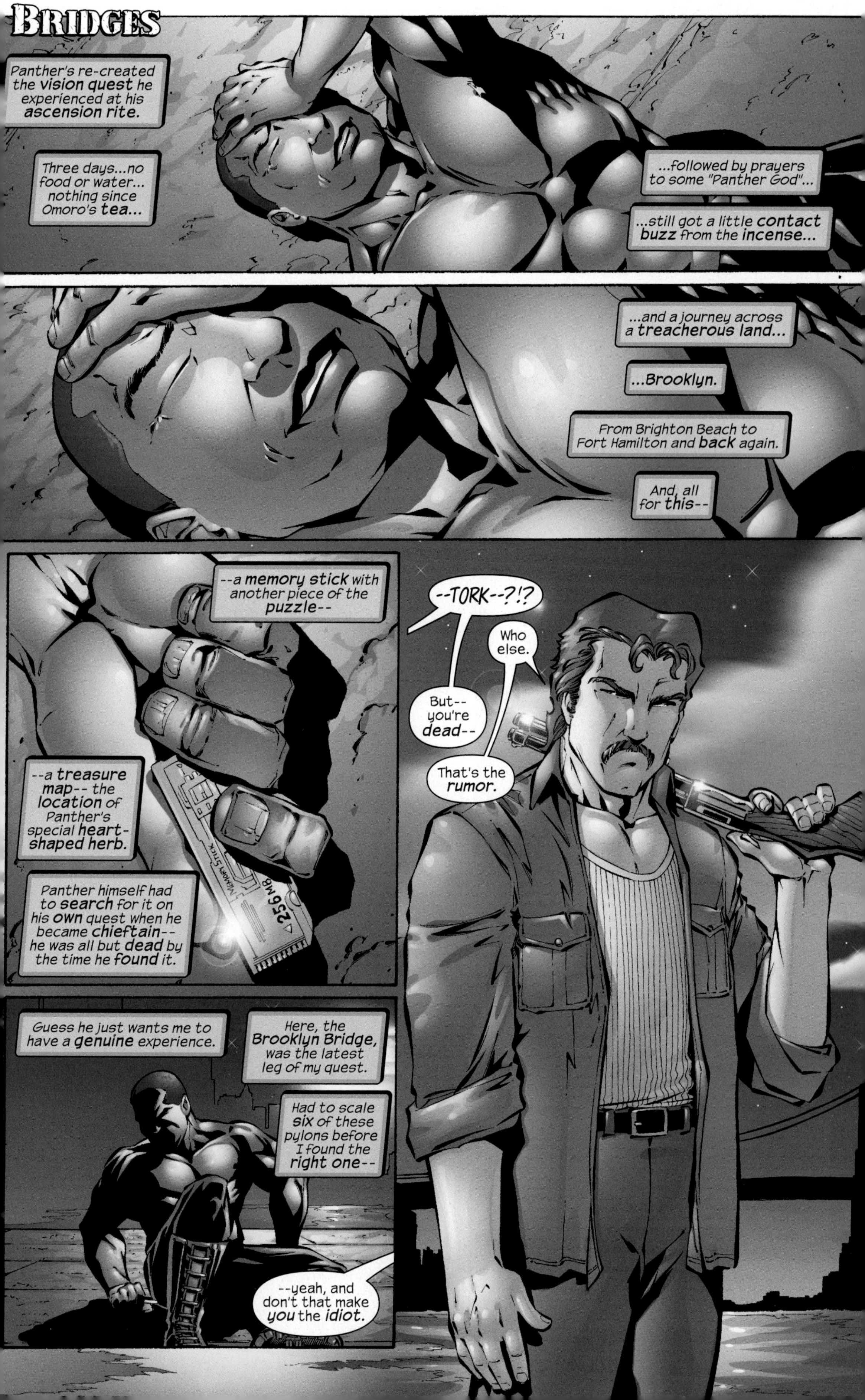
BRIDGES
Panther's re-created the vision quest he experienced at his ascension rite.
Three days...no food or water... nothing since Omoro's tea...
...followed by prayers to some "Panther God"...
...still got a little contact buzz from the incense...
...and a journey across a treacherous land...
...Brooklyn.
From Brighton Beach to Fort Hamilton and back again.
And, all for this--
--a memory stick with another piece of the puzzle--
--a treasure map-- the location of Panther's special heart-shaped herb.
Panther himself had to search for it on his own quest when he became chieftain-- he was all but dead by the time he found it.
MEMORY STICK
256 MB
Guess he just wants me to have a genuine experience.
Here, the Brooklyn Bridge, was the latest leg of my quest.
Had to scale six of these pylons before I found the right one--
--yeah, and don't that make you the idiot.
--TORK--?!?
Who else.
But--you're dead--
That's the rumor.

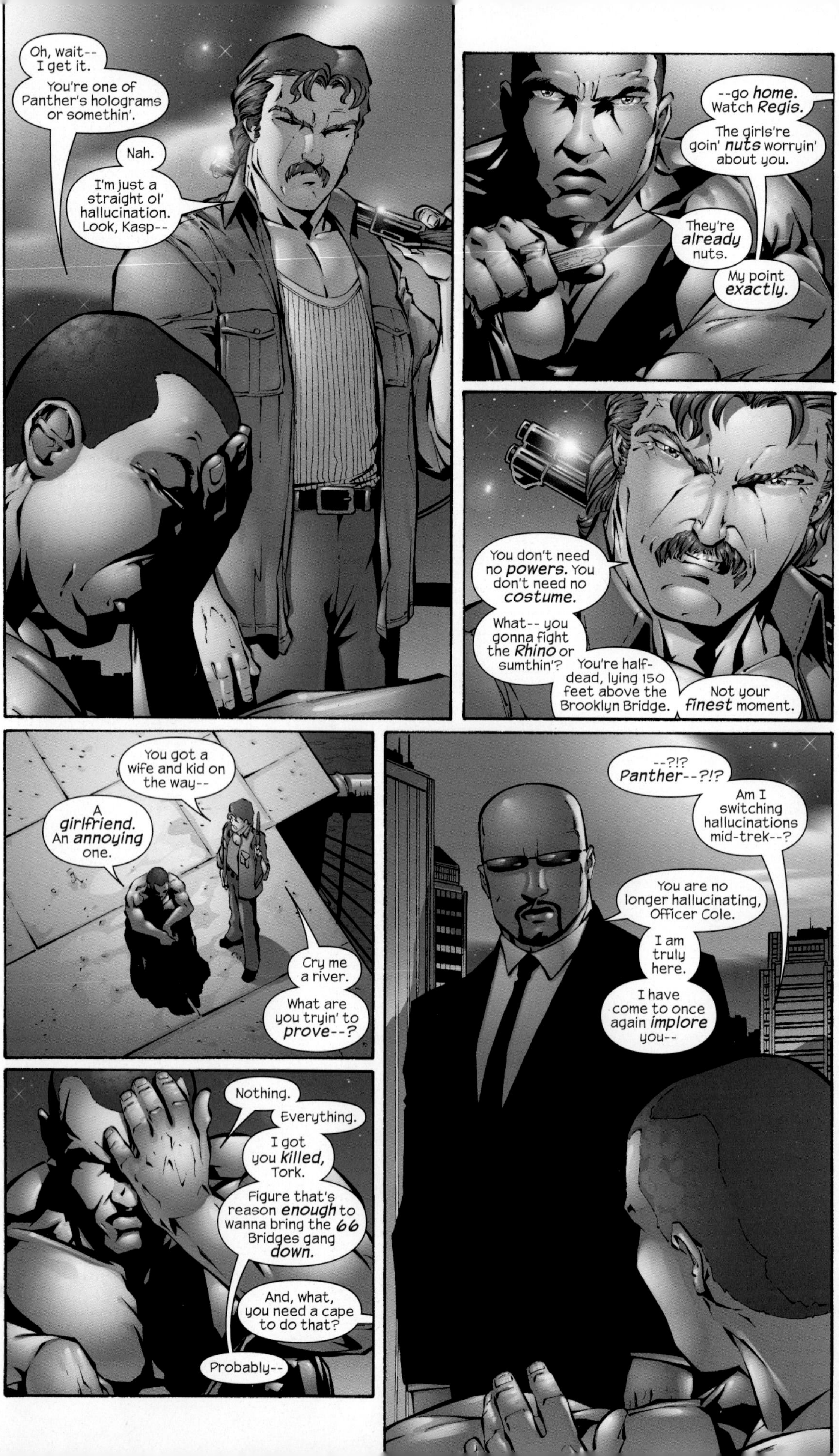
Oh, wait-- I get it.
You're one of Panther's holograms or somethin'.
Nah.
I'm just a straight ol' hallucination. Look, Kasp--
--go home. Watch Regis.
The girls're goin' nuts worryin' about you.
They're already nuts.
My point exactly.
You don't need no powers. You don't need no costume.
What-- you gonna fight the Rhino or sumthin'?
You're half-dead, lying 150 feet above the Brooklyn Bridge.
Not your finest moment.
You got a wife and kid on the way--
A girlfriend. An annoying one.
Cry me a river.
What are you tryin' to prove--?
Nothing.
Everything.
I got you killed, Tork.
Figure that's reason enough to wanna bring the 66 Bridges gang down.
And, what, you need a cape to do that?
Probably--
--?!? Panther--?!?
Am I switching hallucinations mid-trek--?
You are no longer hallucinating, Officer Cole.
I am truly here.
I have come to once again implore you--

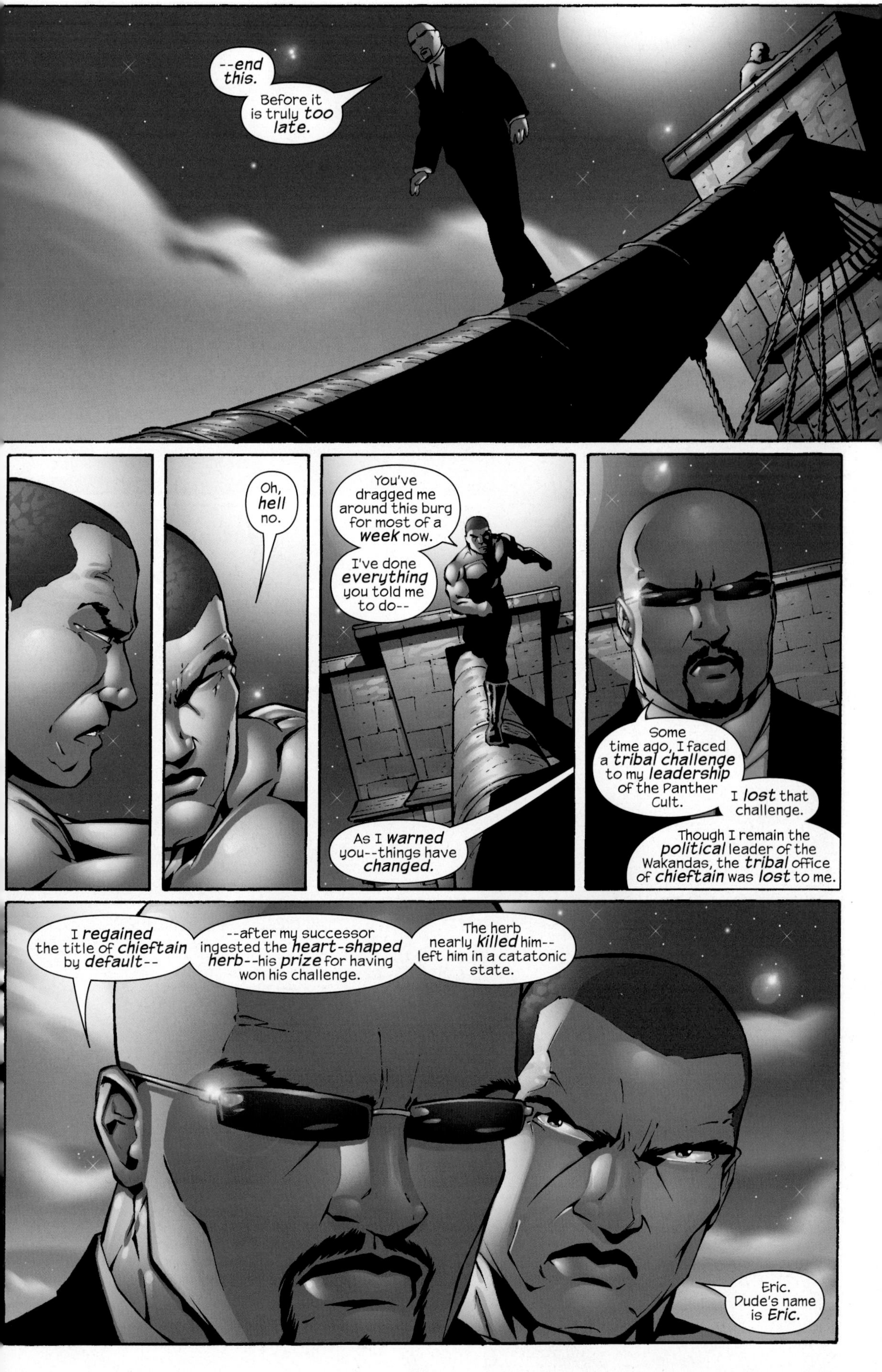
--end this.
Before it is truly too late.
Oh, hell no.
You've dragged me around this burg for most of a week now.
I've done everything you told me to do--
As I warned you--things have changed.
Some time ago, I faced a tribal challenge to my leadership of the Panther Cult.
I lost that challenge.
Though I remain the political leader of the Wakandas, the tribal office of chieftain was lost to me.
I regained the title of chieftain by default--
--after my successor ingested the heart-shaped herb--his prize for having won his challenge.
The herb nearly killed him--left him in a catatonic state.
Eric. Dude's name is Eric.

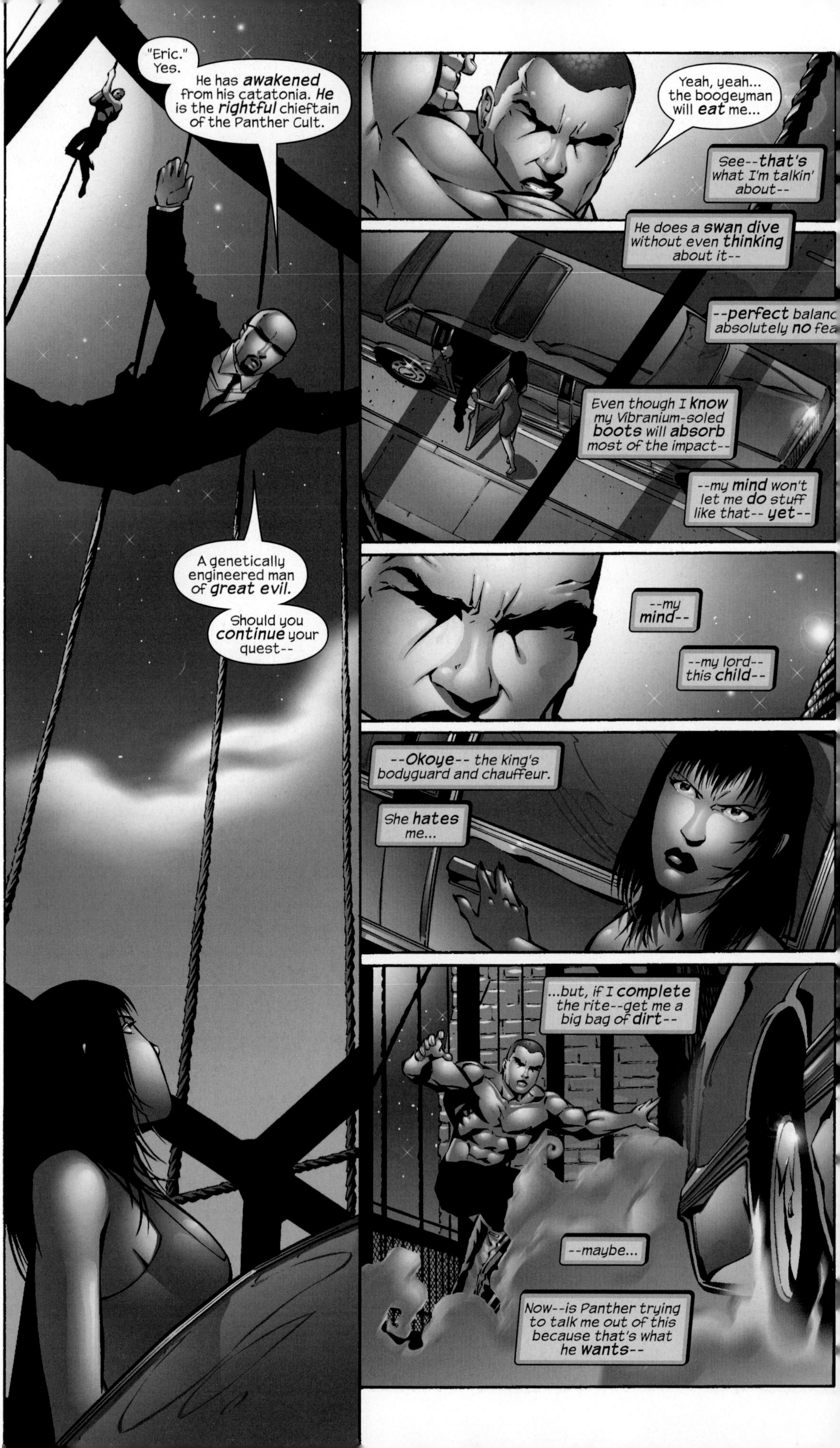
"Eric." Yes.
He has awakened from his catatonia. He is the rightful chieftain of the Panther Cult.
A genetically engineered man of great evil.
Should you continue your quest--
Yeah, yeah... the boogeyman will eat me...
See--that's what I'm talkin' about--
He does a swan dive without even thinking about it--
--perfect balanc
absolutely no fea
Even though I know my Vibranium-soled boots will absorb most of the impact--
--my mind won't let me do stuff like that-- yet--
--my mind--
--my lord-- this child--
--Okoye-- the king's bodyguard and chauffeur.
She hates me...
...but, if I complete the rite--get me a big bag of dirt--
--maybe...
Now--is Panther trying to talk me out of this because that's what he wants--

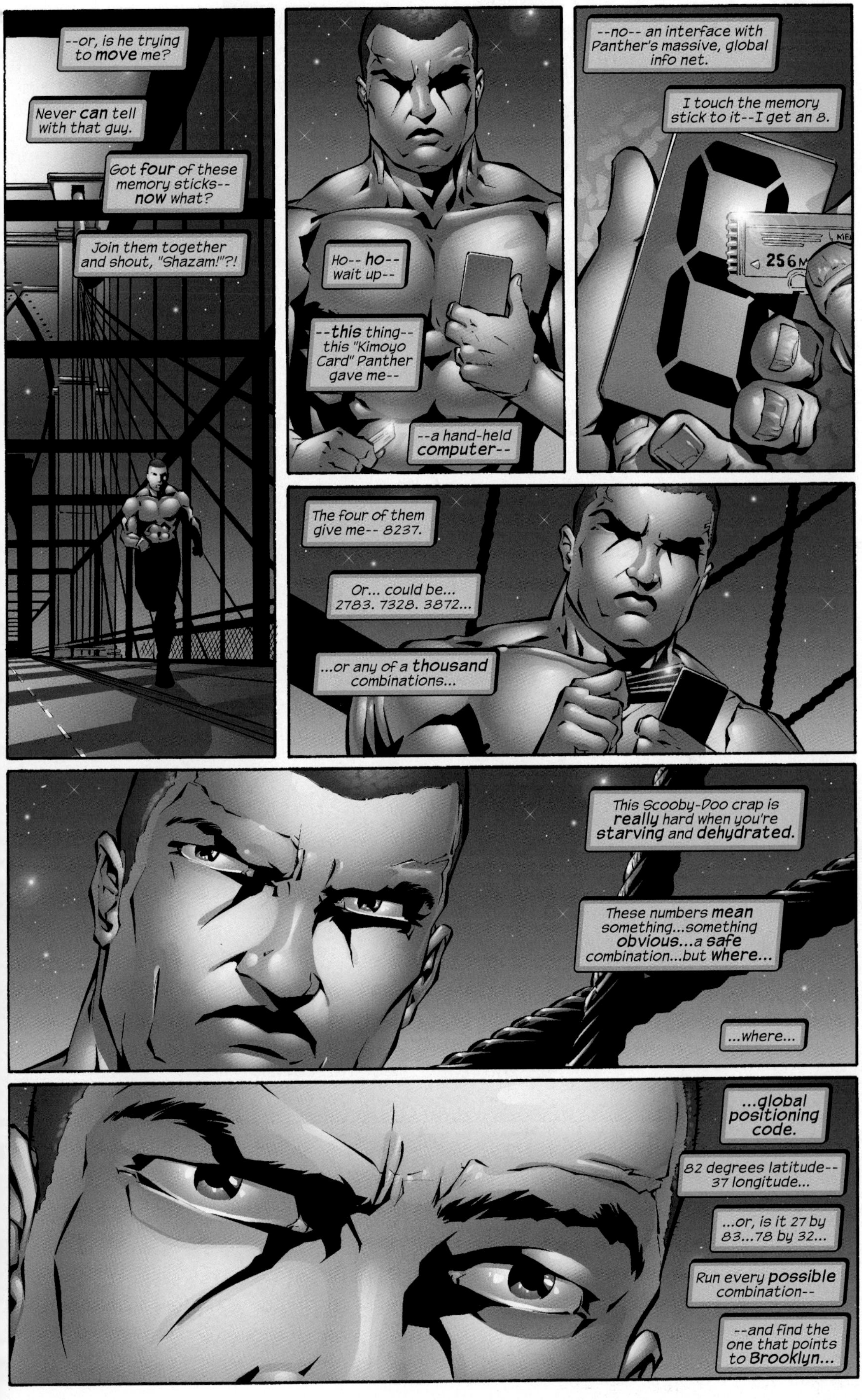
--or, is he trying to move me?
Never can tell with that guy.
Got four of these memory sticks-- now what?
Join them together and shout, "Shazam!"?!
Ho-- ho-- wait up--
--this thing-- this "Kimoyo Card" Panther gave me--
--a hand-held computer--
--no-- an interface with Panther's massive, global info net.
I touch the memory stick to it--I get an 8.
256M
The four of them give me-- 8237.
Or... could be... 2783. 7328. 3872...
...or any of a thousand combinations...
This Scooby-Doo crap is really hard when you're starving and dehydrated.
These numbers mean something...something obvious...a safe combination...but where...
...where...
...global positioning code.
82 degrees latitude-- 37 longitude...
...or, is it 27 by 83...78 by 32...
Run every possible combination--
--and find the one that points to Brooklyn...

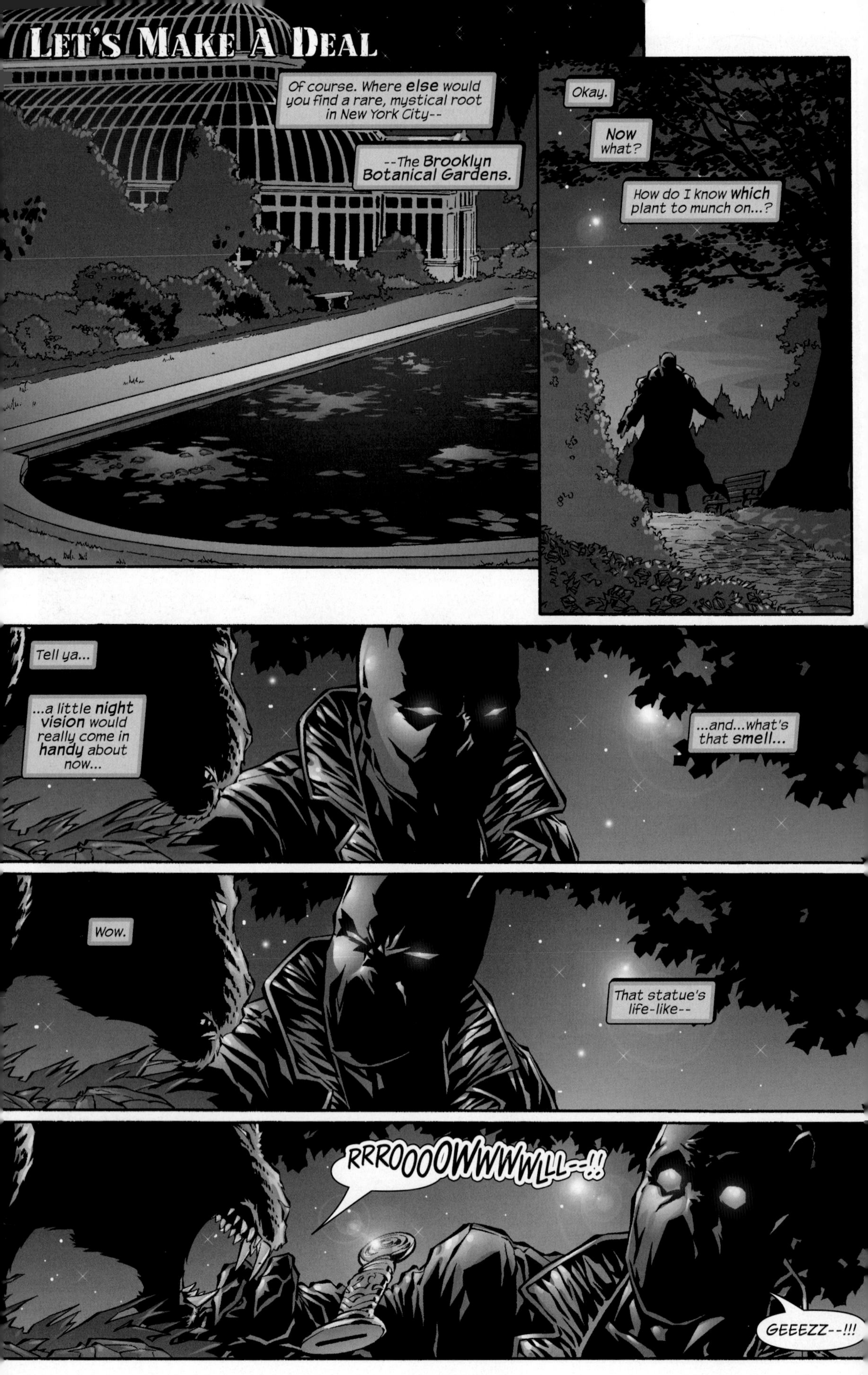

LET'S MAKE A DEAL
Of course. Where else would you find a rare, mystical root in New York City--
--The Brooklyn Botanical Gardens.
Okay.
Now what?
How do I know which plant to munch on...?
Tell ya...
...a little night vision would really come in handy about now...
...and...what's that smell...
Wow.
That statue's life-like--
RRROOOOWWWWLLL--!!!
GEEEZZ--!!!

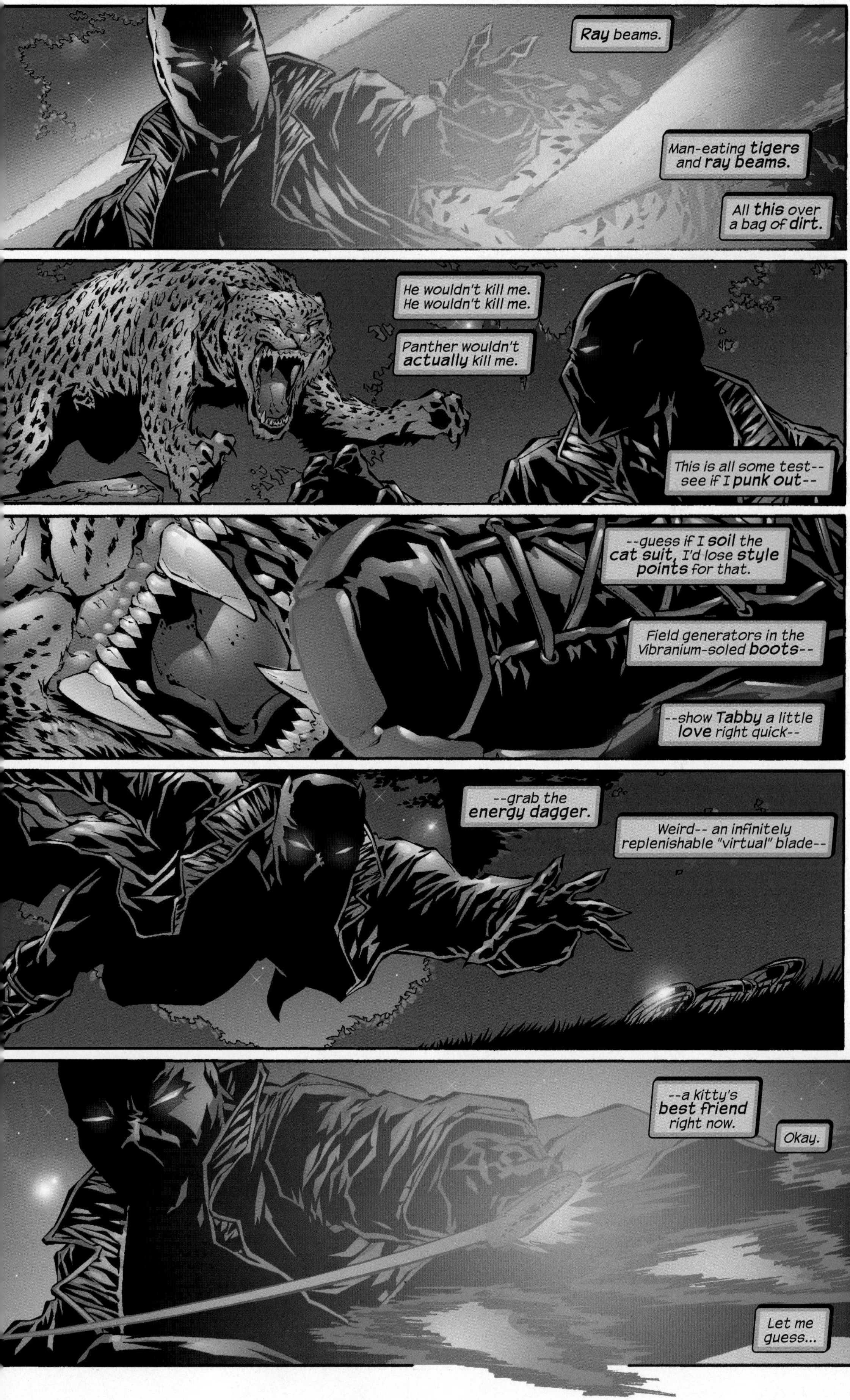
Ray beams.
Man-eating tigers and ray beams.
All this over a bag of dirt.
He wouldn't kill me. He wouldn't kill me.
Panther wouldn't actually kill me.
This is all some test-- see if I punk out--
--guess if I soil the cat suit, I'd lose style points for that.
Field generators in the Vibranium-soled boots--
--show Tabby a little love right quick--
--grab the energy dagger.
Weird-- an infinitely replenishable "virtual" blade--
--a kitty's best friend right now.
Okay.
Let me guess...

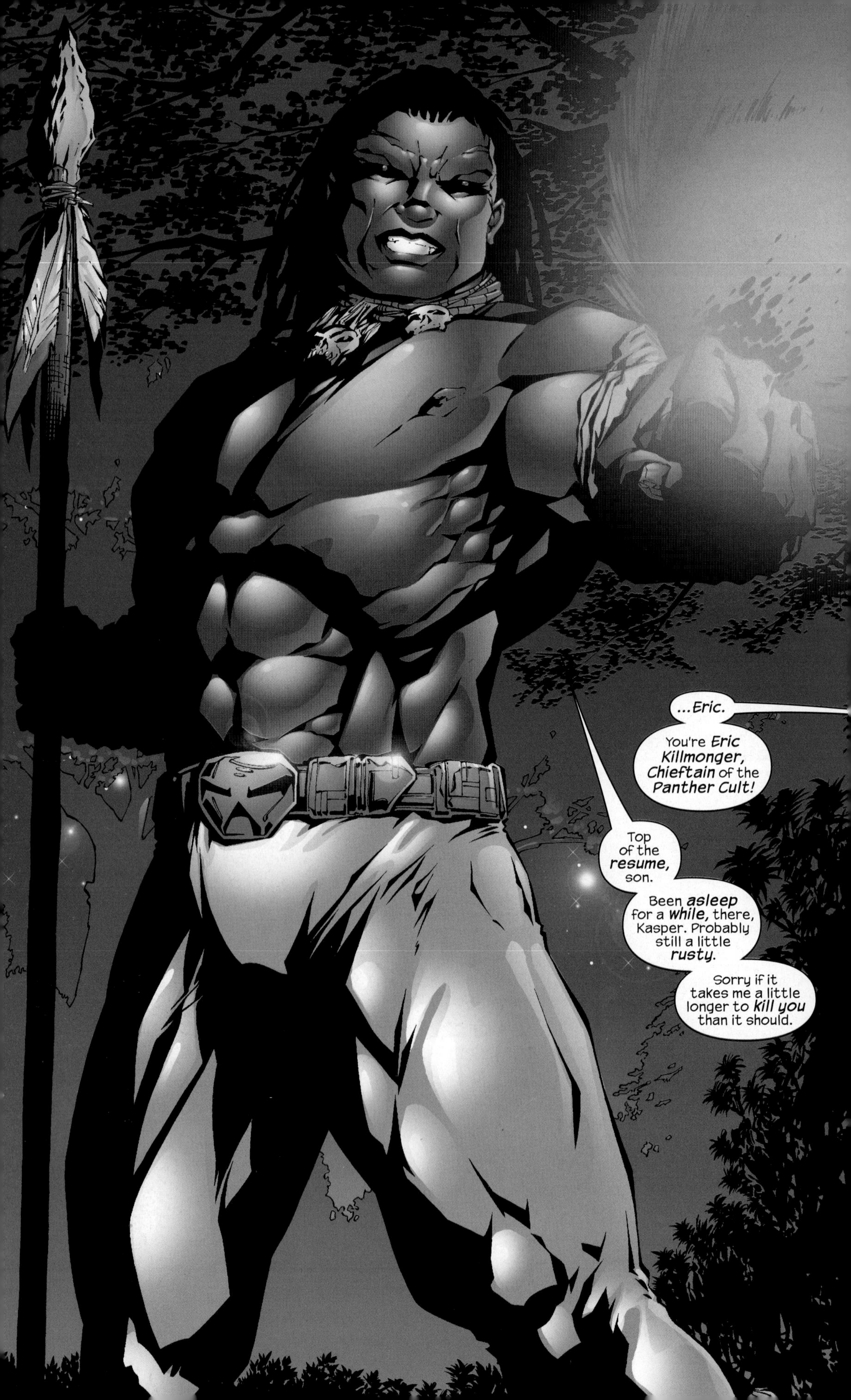
...Eric.
You're Eric Killmonger, Chieftain of the Panther Cult!
Top of the resume, son.
Been asleep for a while, there, Kasper. Probably still a little rusty.
Sorry if it takes me a little longer to kill you than it should.

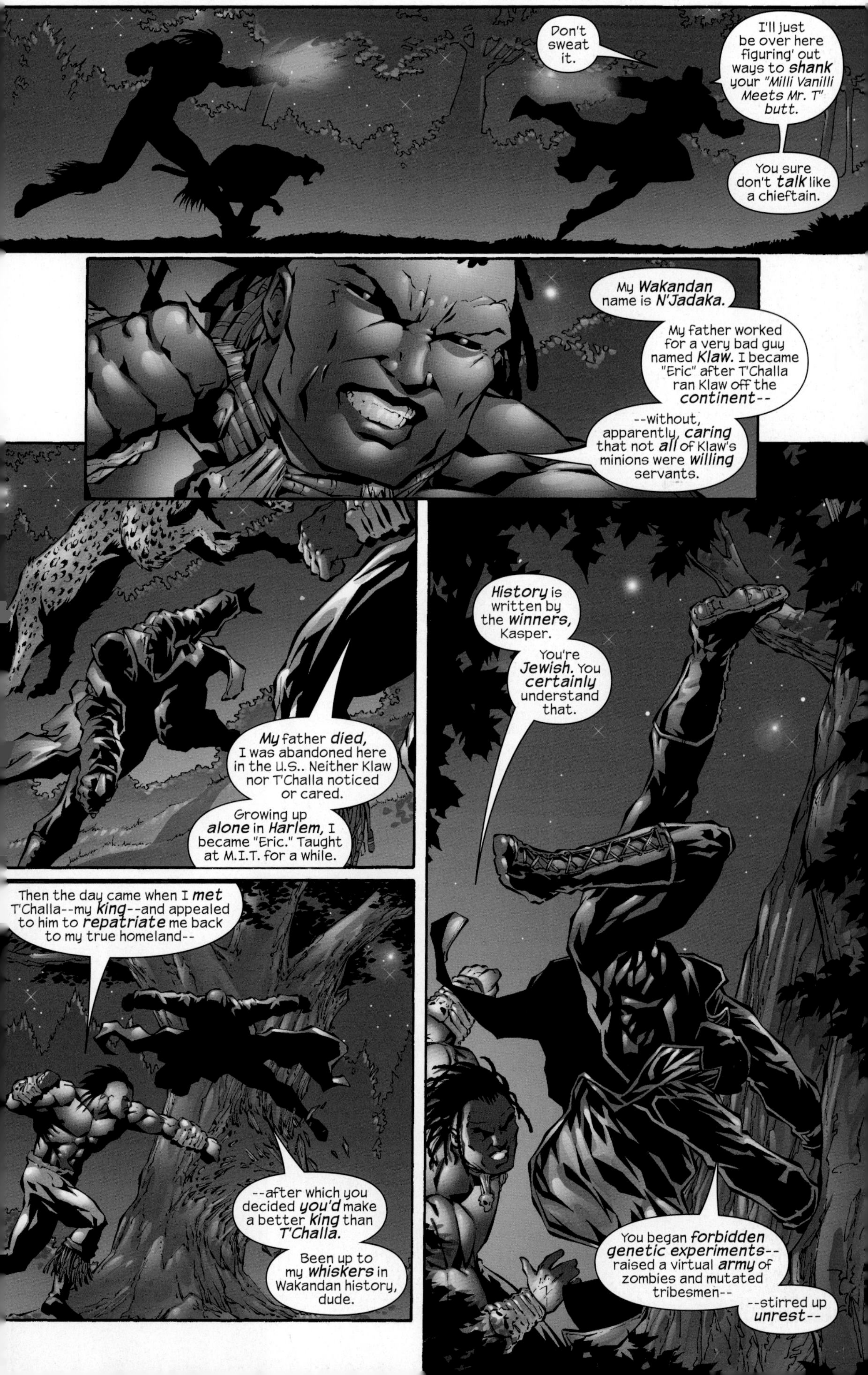
Don't sweat it.
I'll just be over here figuring' out ways to shank your "Milli Vanilli Meets Mr. T" butt.
You sure don't talk like a chieftain.
My Wakandan name is N'Jadaka.
My father worked for a very bad guy named Klaw. I became "Eric" after T'Challa ran Klaw off the continent--
--without, apparently, caring that not all of Klaw's minions were willing servants.
My father died, I was abandoned here in the U.S.. Neither Klaw nor T'Challa noticed or cared.
Growing up alone in Harlem, I became "Eric." Taught at M.I.T. for a while.
History is written by the winners, Kasper.
You're Jewish. You certainly understand that.
Then the day came when I met T'Challa--my king--and appealed to him to repatriate me back to my true homeland--
--after which you decided you'd make a better king than T'Challa.
Been up to my whiskers in Wakandan history, dude.
You began forbidden genetic experiments--raised a virtual army of zombies and mutated tribesmen--
--stirred up unrest--

I am a **patriot**. A **nationalist**--like Che Guevara--Nelson Mandela.

A voice of **social change** in **Wakanda**.

You're a nutty **capitalist**--

--N'Jadaka Village, your home base, is the **only** place in **Wakanda** that has a **Starbucks**--!

Yes. And we hope to host the **Stanley Cup** playoffs next year.

Kasper-- this stuff's too **deep** for you.

I'm trying to figure out what you hope to **get** out of this--

--other than multiple fractures and profound **hearing loss**.

Okay.

--?!?

I have my reasons. Even if you don't know what they **are**, you've **got** to realize--

--I'm all the way **in** this.

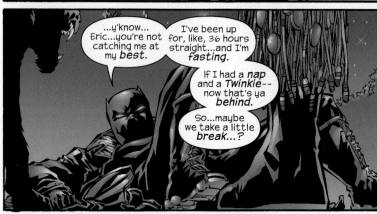

...y'know... Eric...you're not catching me at my **best**.

I've been up for, like, 36 hours straight...and I'm **fasting**.

If I had a **nap** and a **Twinkie**--now that's ya **behind**.

So...maybe we take a little **break**...?

What... the hell...?

There are *rules* to Wakandan tribal contests, Kasper. I kill you in, what, twelve seconds-- what's *that* prove?

Makes me more *lucky* than *skilled.*

I give you *every* chance--make sure you have *every* opportunity--

--then *victory* is *truly* meaningful.

By the way-- how's your *portfolio?*

My... *what...?*

Y'know-- stocks--bonds-- 401K. *Whole life.* I wake from a *coma* and find a *Texan* in the White House--

--and the global economy in the toilet. Snapple--?

I got eighty- five bucks in my checking account.

Some Tic-Tacs in my pocket.

Baby on the way.

I *need* this, man.

Need *what?* A *cape? Heat vision?*

That day is *dead,* dog.

Truth, justice-- the American *way*-- what's that *mean* in a world like *this?*

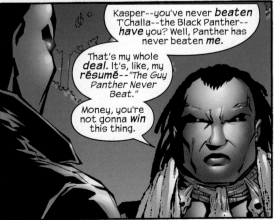

Kasper--you've never *beaten* T'Challa--the Black Panther-- *have* you? Well, Panther has never beaten *me.*

That's my whole *deal.* It's, like, my *résumé*--"The Guy Panther Never Beat."

Money, you're not gonna *win* this thing.

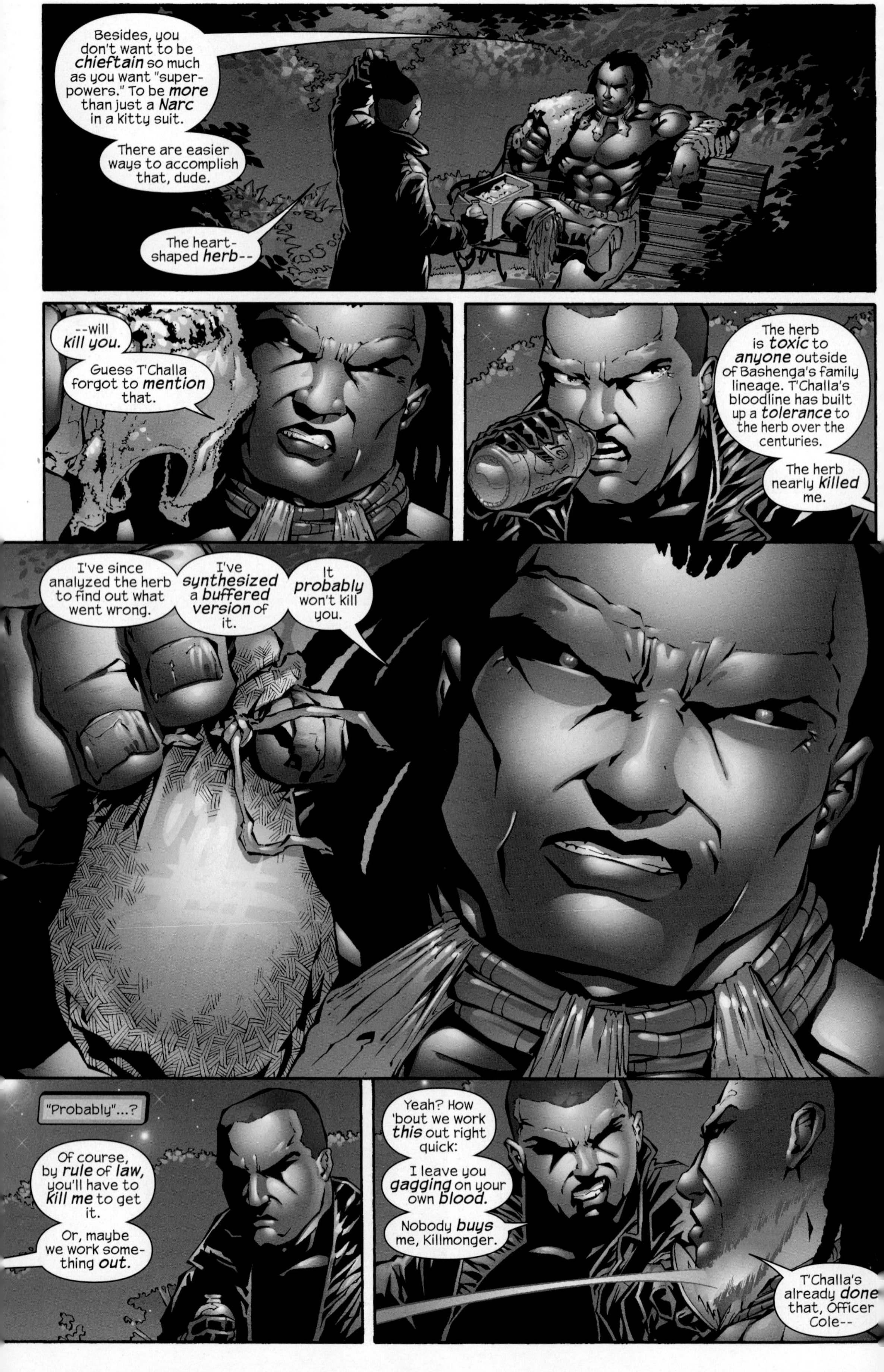

Besides, you don't want to be chieftain so much as you want "super-powers." To be more than just a Narc in a kitty suit.
There are easier ways to accomplish that, dude.
The heart-shaped herb--
--will kill you.
Guess T'Challa forgot to mention that.
The herb is toxic to anyone outside of Bashenga's family lineage. T'Challa's bloodline has built up a tolerance to the herb over the centuries.
The herb nearly killed me.
I've since analyzed the herb to find out what went wrong.
I've synthesized a buffered version of it.
It probably won't kill you.
"Probably"...?
Of course, by rule of law, you'll have to kill me to get it.
Or, maybe we work something out.
Yeah? How 'bout we work this out right quick:
I leave you gagging on your own blood.
Nobody buys me, Killmonger.
T'Challa's already done that, Officer Cole--

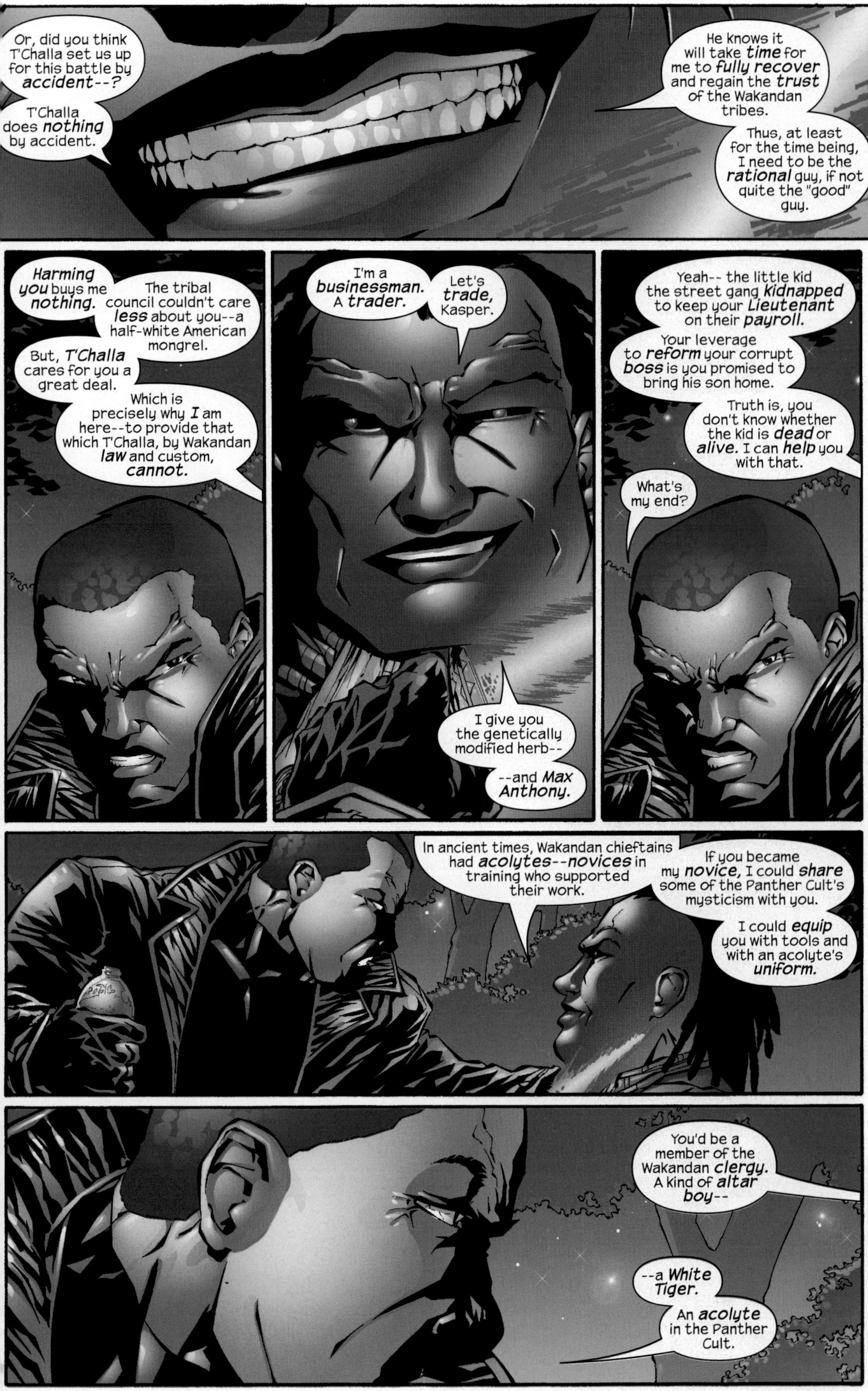
Or, did you think T'Challa set us up for this battle by accident--?
T'Challa does nothing by accident.
He knows it will take time for me to fully recover and regain the trust of the Wakandan tribes.
Thus, at least for the time being, I need to be the rational guy, if not quite the "good" guy.
Harming you buys me nothing.
The tribal council couldn't care less about you--a half-white American mongrel.
But, T'Challa cares for you a great deal.
Which is precisely why I am here--to provide that which T'Challa, by Wakandan law and custom, cannot.
I'm a businessman. A trader.
Let's trade, Kasper.
I give you the genetically modified herb--
--and Max Anthony.
Yeah-- the little kid the street gang kidnapped to keep your Lieutenant on their payroll.
Your leverage to reform your corrupt boss is you promised to bring his son home.
Truth is, you don't know whether the kid is dead or alive. I can help you with that.
What's my end?
In ancient times, Wakandan chieftains had acolytes--novices in training who supported their work.
If you became my novice, I could share some of the Panther Cult's mysticism with you.
I could equip you with tools and with an acolyte's uniform.
You'd be a member of the Wakandan clergy. A kind of altar boy--
--a White Tiger.
An acolyte in the Panther Cult.

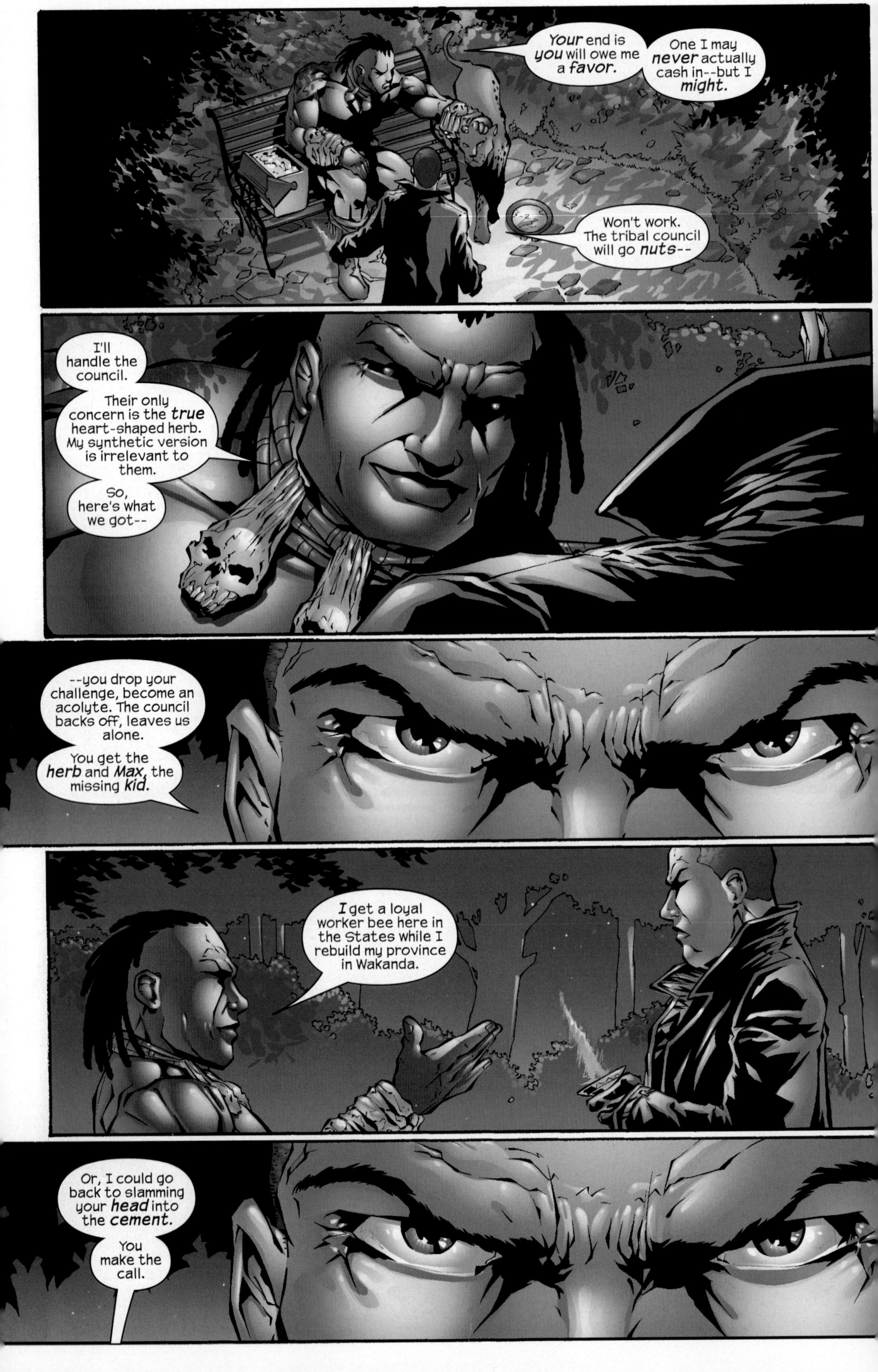
Your end is you will owe me a favor.
One I may never actually cash in--but I might.
Won't work. The tribal council will go nuts--
I'll handle the council.
Their only concern is the true heart-shaped herb. My synthetic version is irrelevant to them.
So, here's what we got--
--you drop your challenge, become an acolyte. The council backs off, leaves us alone.
You get the herb and Max, the missing kid.
I get a loyal worker bee here in the States while I rebuild my province in Wakanda.
Or, I could go back to slamming your head into the cement.
You make the call.

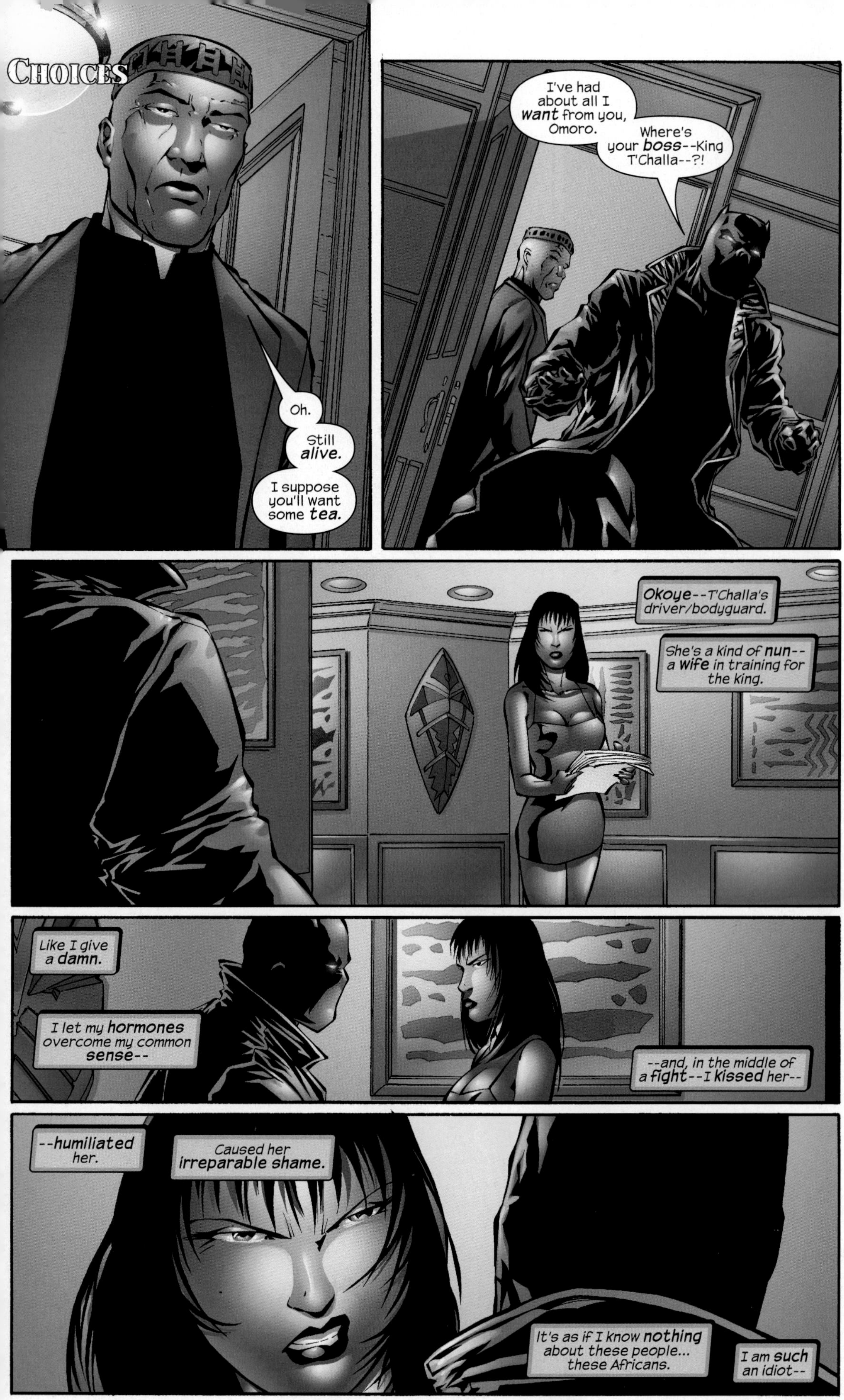
CHOICES
Oh.
Still alive.
I suppose you'll want some tea.
I've had about all I want from you, Omoro.
Where's your boss--King T'Challa--?!
Okoye--T'Challa's driver/bodyguard.
She's a kind of nun--a wife in training for the king.
Like I give a damn.
I let my hormones overcome my common sense--
--and, in the middle of a fight--I kissed her--
--humiliated her.
Caused her irreparable shame.
It's as if I know nothing about these people... these Africans.
I am such an idiot--

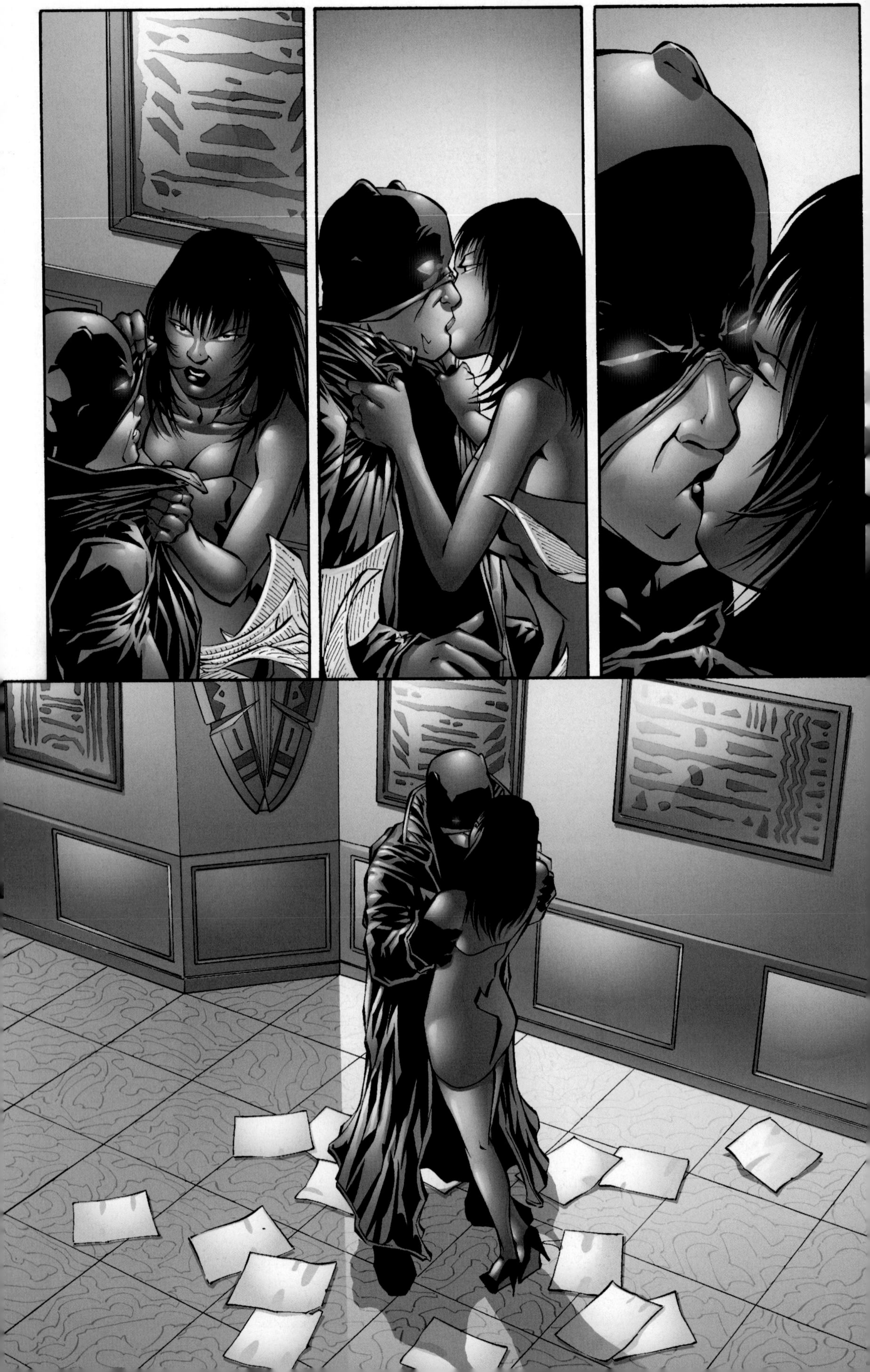

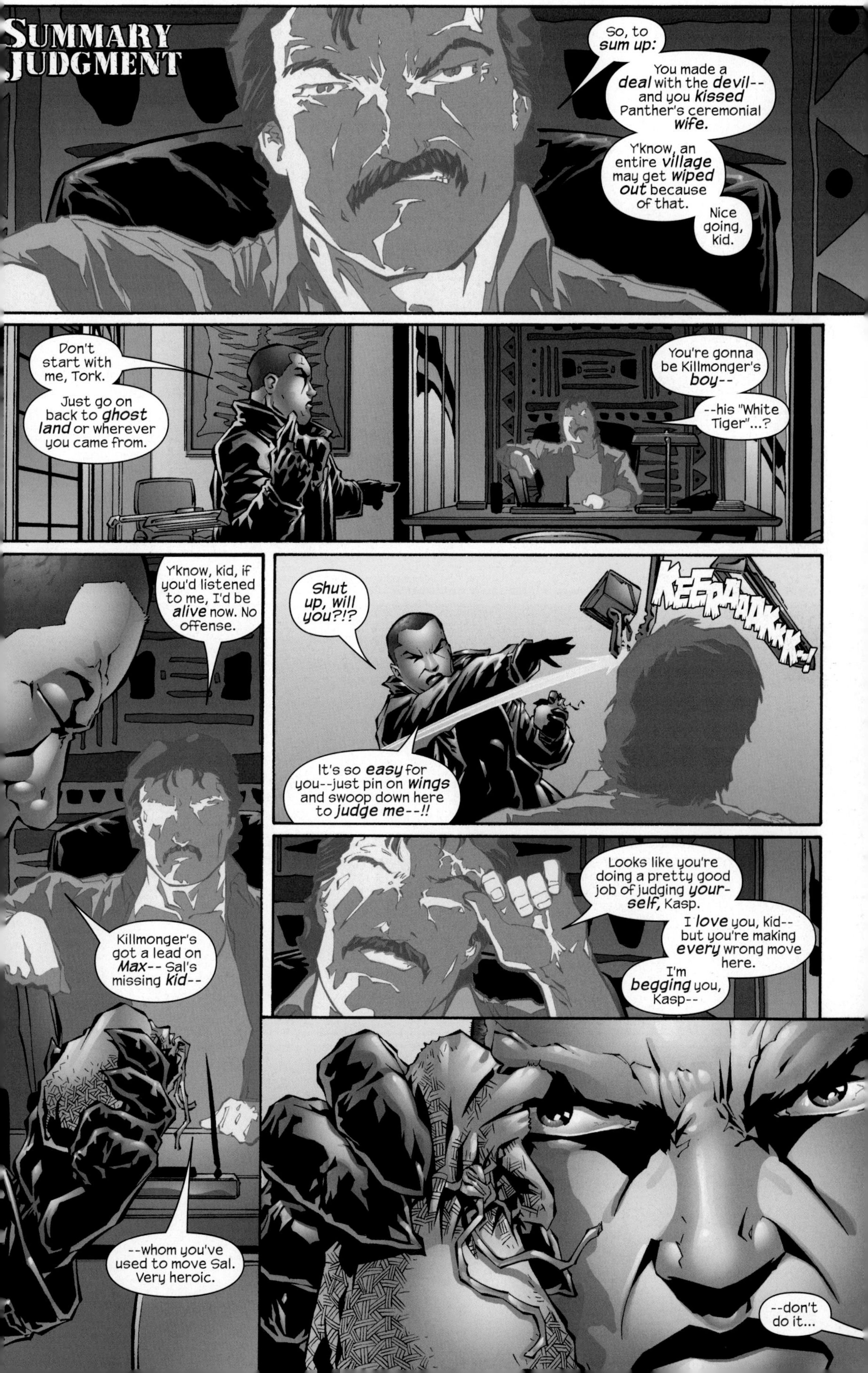
SUMMARY JUDGMENT
So, to sum up:
You made a deal with the devil-- and you kissed Panther's ceremonial wife.
Y'know, an entire village may get wiped out because of that.
Nice going, kid.
Don't start with me, Tork.
Just go on back to ghost land or wherever you came from.
You're gonna be Killmonger's boy--
--his "White Tiger"...?
Y'know, kid, if you'd listened to me, I'd be alive now. No offense.
Killmonger's got a lead on Max-- Sal's missing kid--
--whom you've used to move Sal. Very heroic.
Shut up, will you?!?
KEERAAAKKK--!
It's so easy for you--just pin on wings and swoop down here to judge me--!!
Looks like you're doing a pretty good job of judging your-self, Kasp.
I love you, kid-- but you're making every wrong move here.
I'm begging you, Kasp--
--don't do it...

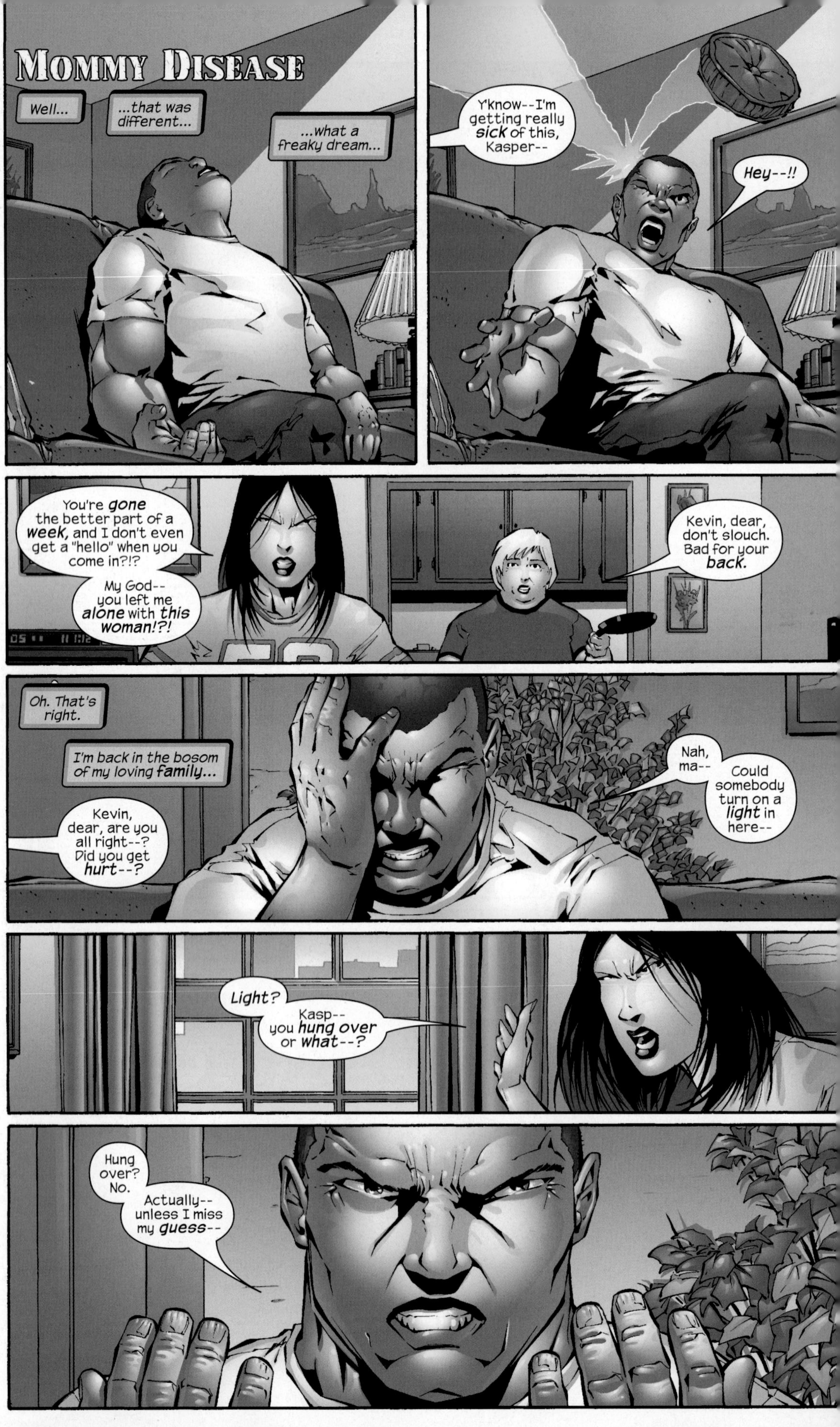
MOMMY DISEASE
Well...
...that was different...
...what a freaky dream...
Y'know--I'm getting really sick of this, Kasper--
Hey--!!
You're gone the better part of a week, and I don't even get a "hello" when you come in?!?
My God-- you left me alone with this woman!?!
Kevin, dear, don't slouch. Bad for your back.
Oh. That's right.
I'm back in the bosom of my loving family...
Kevin, dear, are you all right--? Did you get hurt--?
Nah, ma--
Could somebody turn on a light in here--
Light?
Kasp-- you hung over or what--?
Hung over? No.
Actually-- unless I miss my guess--

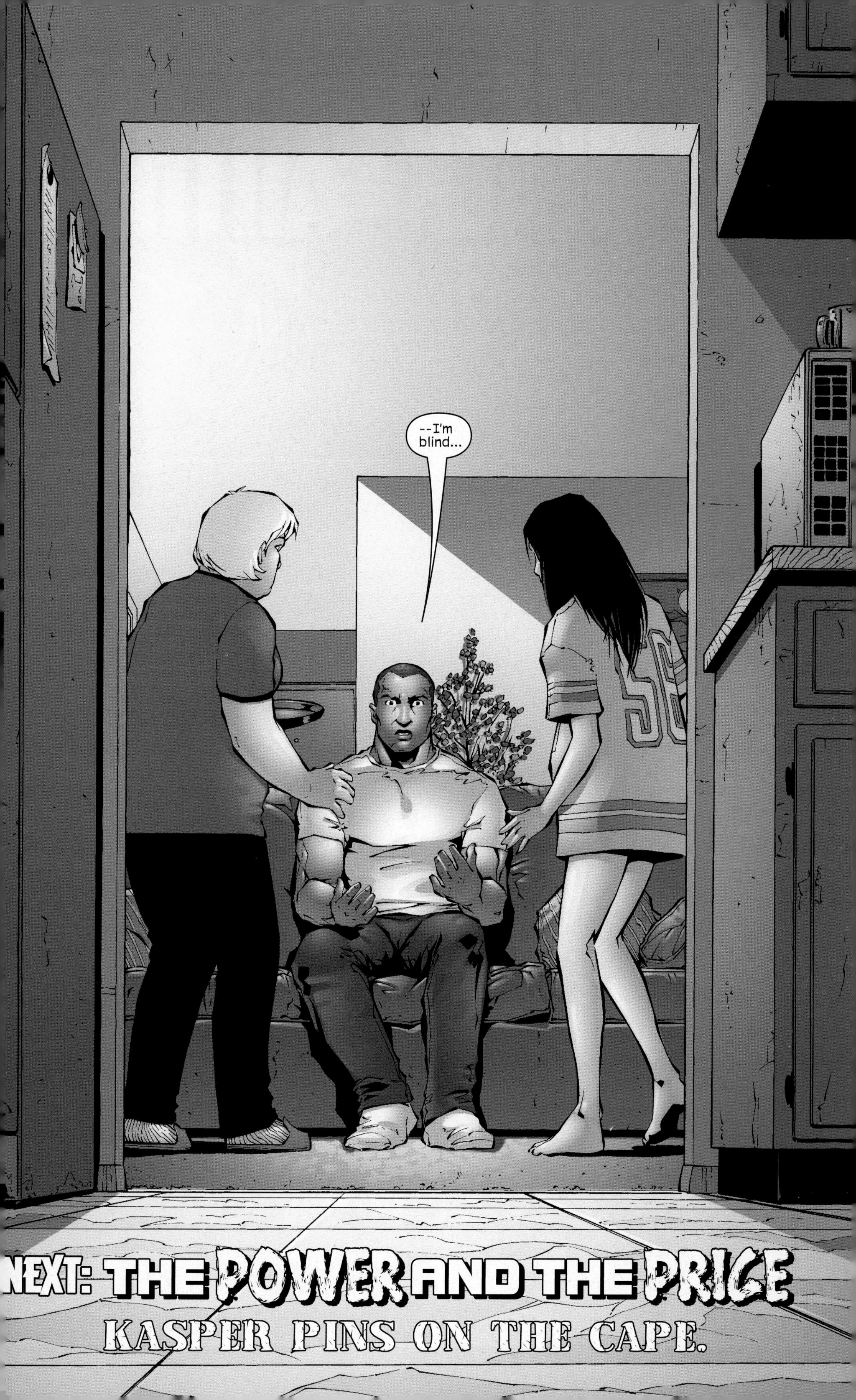
--I'm blind...
NEXT: THE POWER AND THE PRICE
KASPER PINS ON THE CAPE.

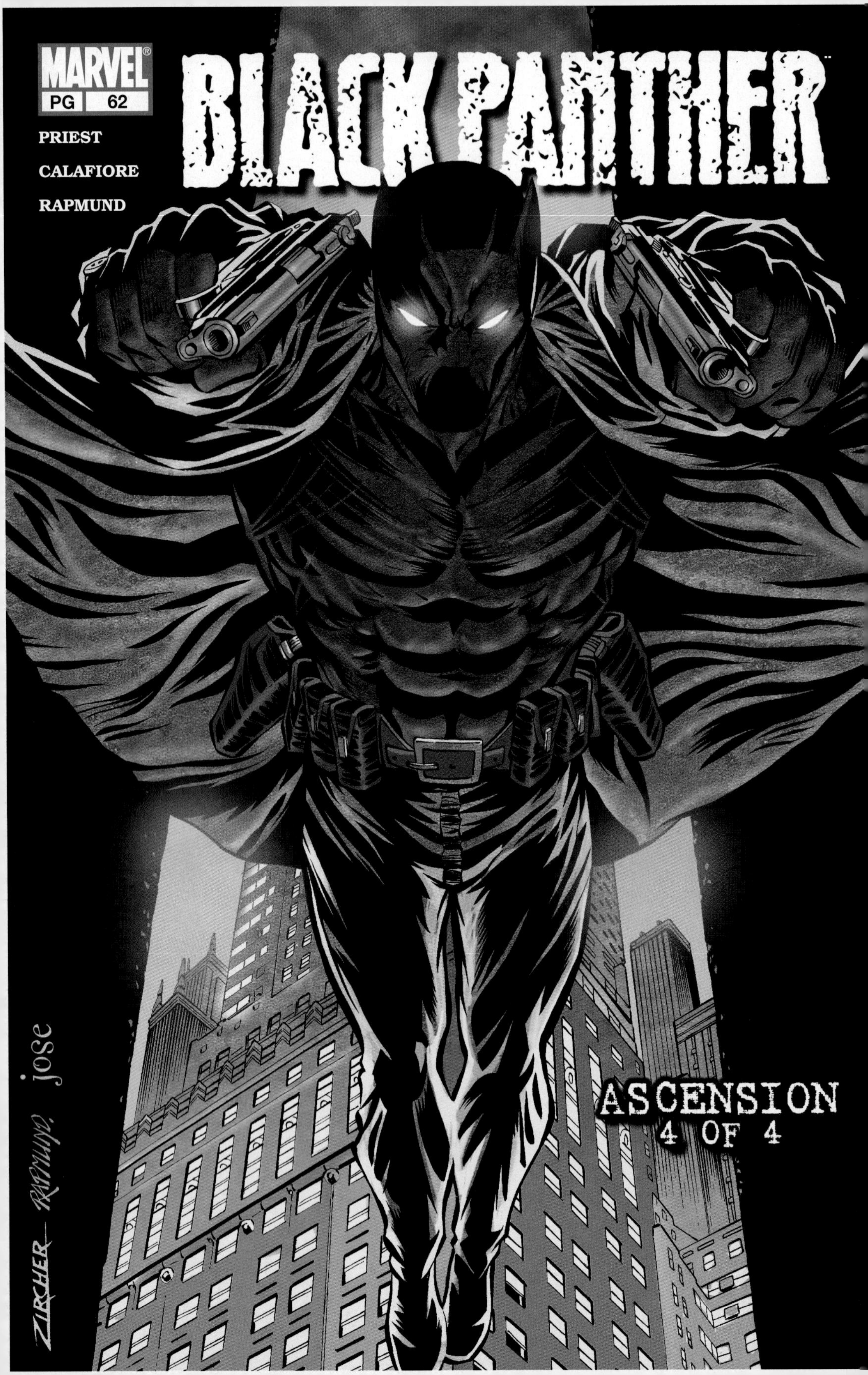
MARVEL
PG 62
PRIEST
CALAFIORE
RAPMUND
BLACK PANTHER
ASCENSION
4 OF 4
ZIRCHER RAPMUND jose

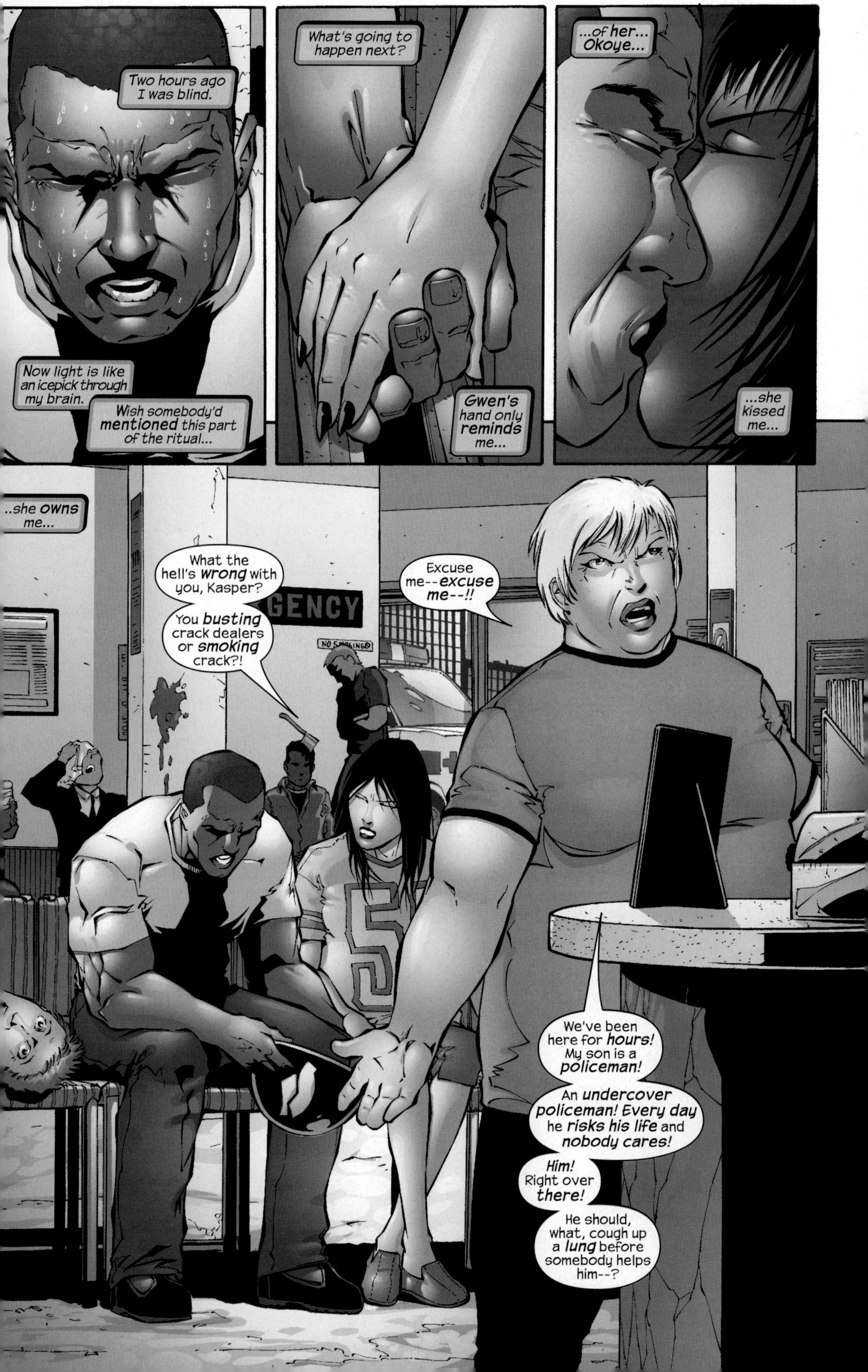
Two hours ago I was blind.
Now light is like an icepick through my brain.
Wish somebody'd mentioned this part of the ritual...
What's going to happen next?
Gwen's hand only reminds me...
...of her... Okoye...
...she kissed me...
..she owns me...
What the hell's wrong with you, Kasper?
You busting crack dealers or smoking crack?!
Excuse me--excuse me--!!
GENCY
NO SMOKING
We've been here for hours! My son is a policeman!
An undercover policeman! Every day he risks his life and nobody cares!
Him! Right over there!
He should, what, cough up a lung before somebody helps him--?

The **stench** of body odors and **colognes**...overwhelming smell of **alcohol**...

...I can **see** smells... scents...like **colors**...

I've gotta **pee**, Kasper. Be right back.

Can't **see** Gwen leaving... but I can follow the **talcum**...

Okoye...

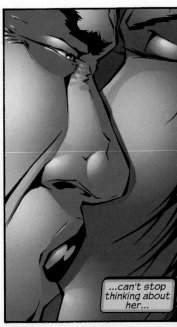

...can't stop thinking about her...

B**L**U**U**R**GFF**!

And, so, ol' boy enters the life...

So...got what you **wanted**. You're a **super**-hero now. **Glamorous**, ain't it--?

Tork. My old boss--

--who got **killed** covering for me. Now a friendly **ghost**, haunting me **again**.

C'mon, man--not **now**.

What **better** time, dog breath--?

You're **high** on **Killmonger's** genetically-altered **weed**.

The **job** comes in here and **tests** you, you'll **lose** your **shield**--along with your **soul**.

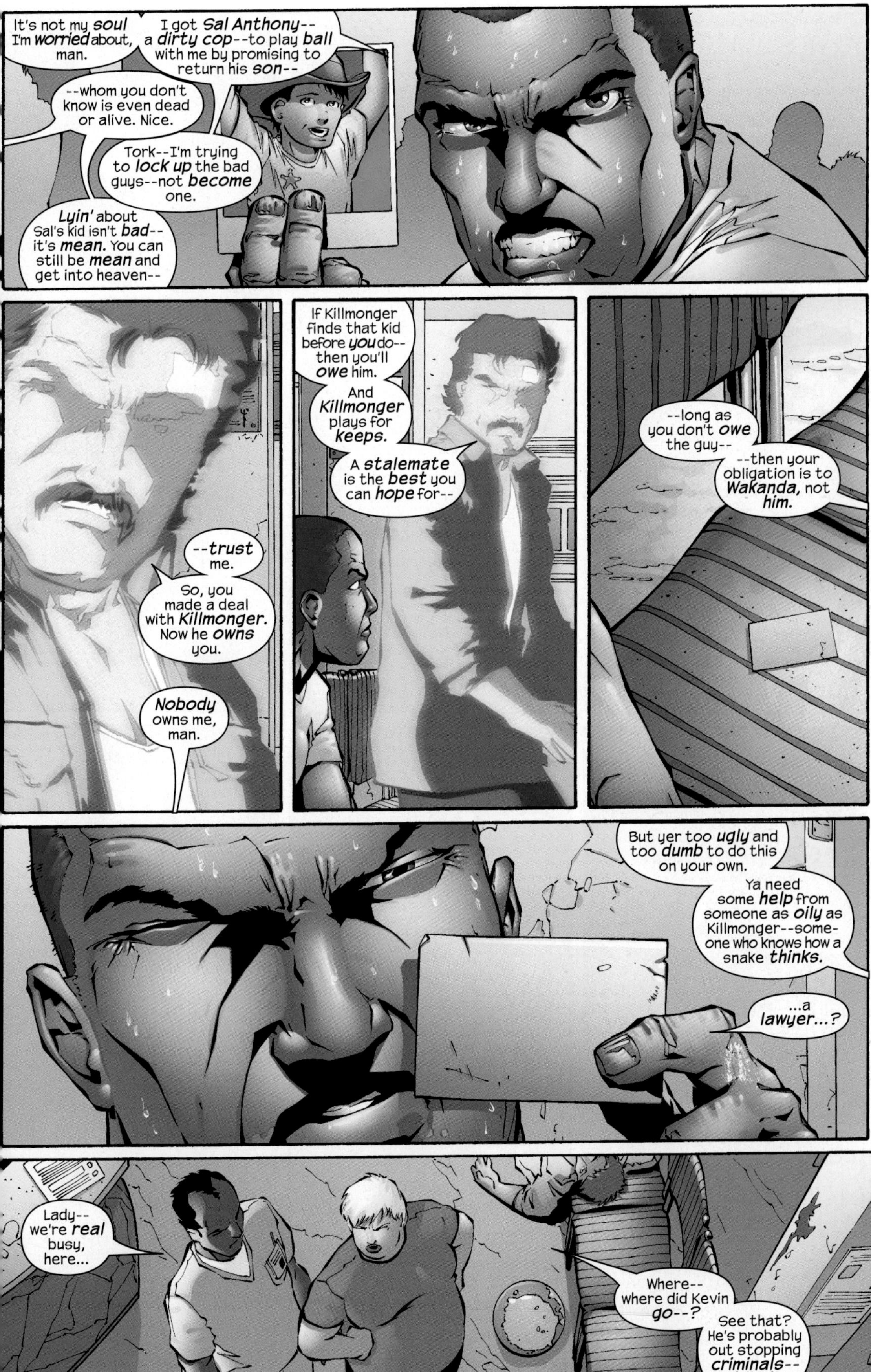
It's not my soul I'm worried about, man.
I got Sal Anthony-- a dirty cop--to play ball with me by promising to return his son--
--whom you don't know is even dead or alive. Nice.
Tork--I'm trying to lock up the bad guys--not become one.
Lyin' about Sal's kid isn't bad-- it's mean. You can still be mean and get into heaven--
--trust me.
So, you made a deal with Killmonger. Now he owns you.
Nobody owns me, man.
If Killmonger finds that kid before you do-- then you'll owe him.
And Killmonger plays for keeps.
A stalemate is the best you can hope for--
--long as you don't owe the guy--
--then your obligation is to Wakanda, not him.
But yer too ugly and too dumb to do this on your own.
Ya need some help from someone as oily as Killmonger--some-one who knows how a snake thinks.
...a lawyer...?
Lady-- we're real busy, here...
Where-- where did Kevin go--?
See that? He's probably out stopping criminals-- blind!

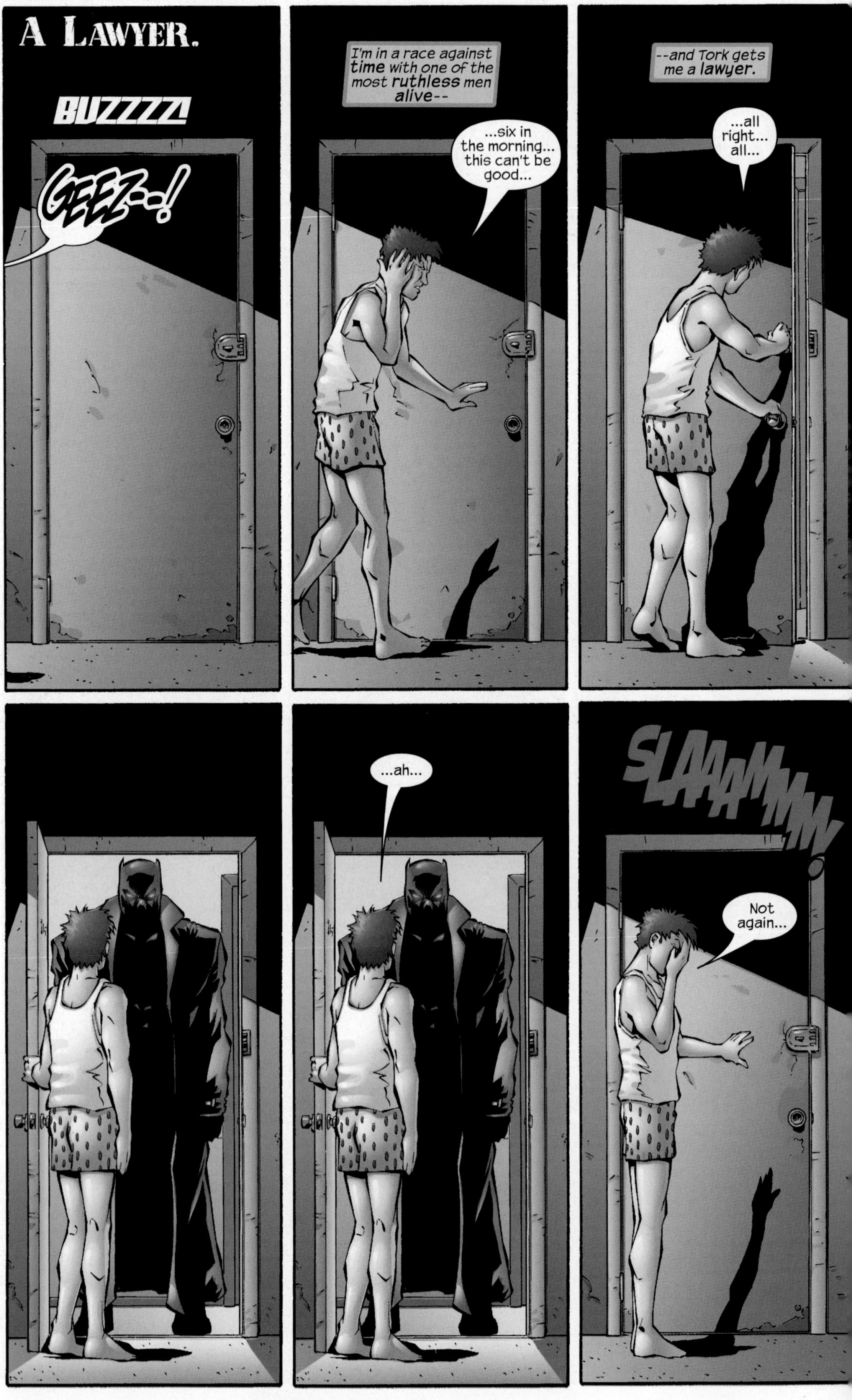
A LAWYER.
BUZZZZZ!
GEEZ--!
I'm in a race against time with one of the most ruthless men alive--
...six in the morning... this can't be good...
--and Tork gets me a lawyer.
...all right... all...
...ah...
SLAAAMMM!
Not again...

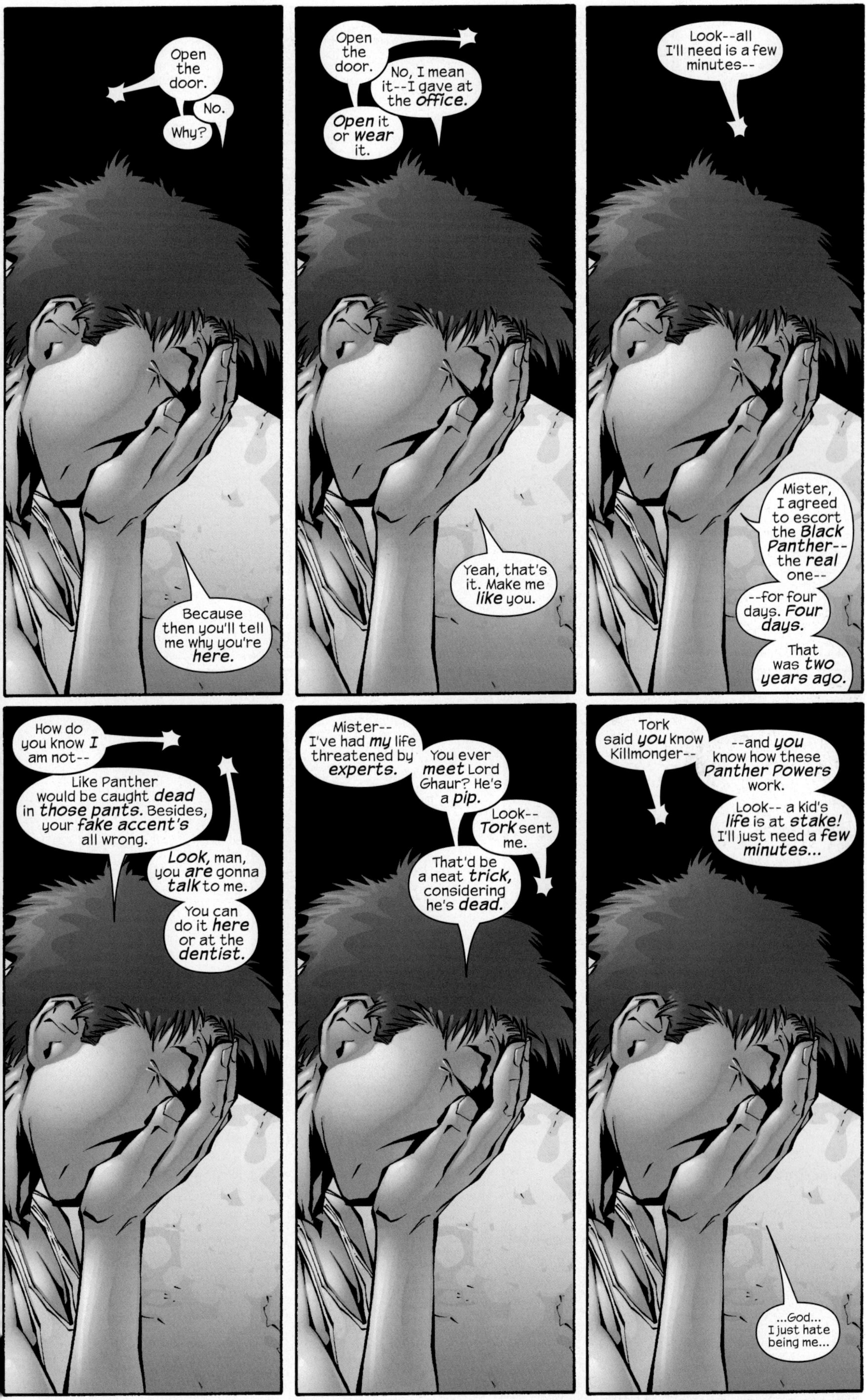
Open the door.
Why?
No.
Because then you'll tell me why you're here.
Open the door.
No, I mean it--I gave at the office.
Open it or wear it.
Yeah, that's it. Make me like you.
Look--all I'll need is a few minutes--
Mister, I agreed to escort the Black Panther--the real one--
--for four days. Four days.
That was two years ago.
How do you know I am not--
Like Panther would be caught dead in those pants. Besides, your fake accent's all wrong.
Look, man, you are gonna talk to me.
You can do it here or at the dentist.
Mister--I've had my life threatened by experts.
You ever meet Lord Ghaur? He's a pip.
Look--Tork sent me.
That'd be a neat trick, considering he's dead.
Tork said you know Killmonger--
--and you know how these Panther Powers work.
Look-- a kid's life is at stake! I'll just need a few minutes...
...God... I just hate being me...

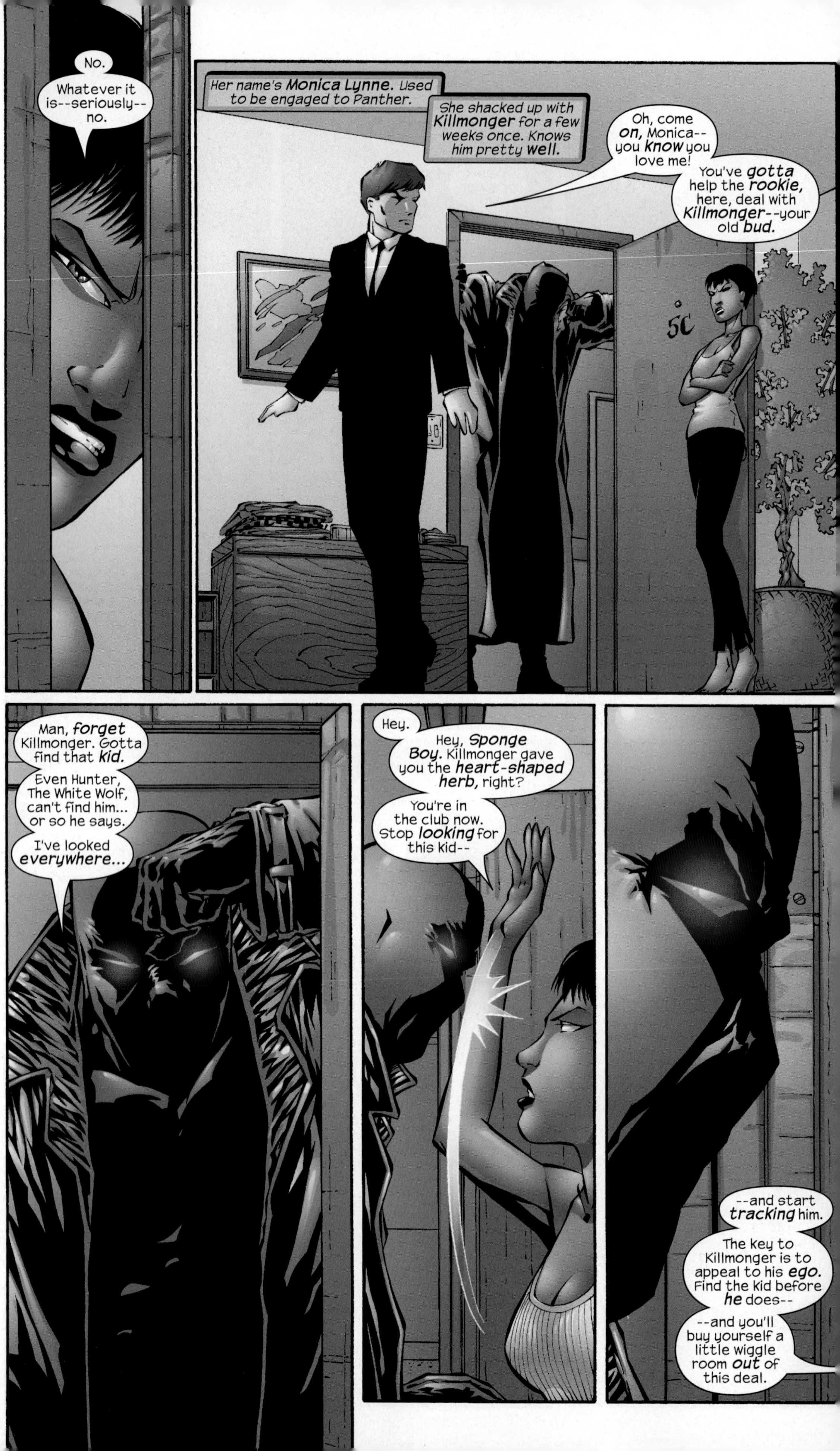
No.
Whatever it is--seriously--no.
Her name's Monica Lynne. Used to be engaged to Panther.
She shacked up with Killmonger for a few weeks once. Knows him pretty well.
Oh, come on, Monica--you know you love me!
You've gotta help the rookie, here, deal with Killmonger--your old bud.
5C
Man, forget Killmonger. Gotta find that kid.
Even Hunter, The White Wolf, can't find him... or so he says.
I've looked everywhere...
Hey.
Hey, Sponge Boy. Killmonger gave you the heart-shaped herb, right?
You're in the club now. Stop looking for this kid--
--and start tracking him.
The key to Killmonger is to appeal to his ego. Find the kid before he does--
--and you'll buy yourself a little wiggle room out of this deal.

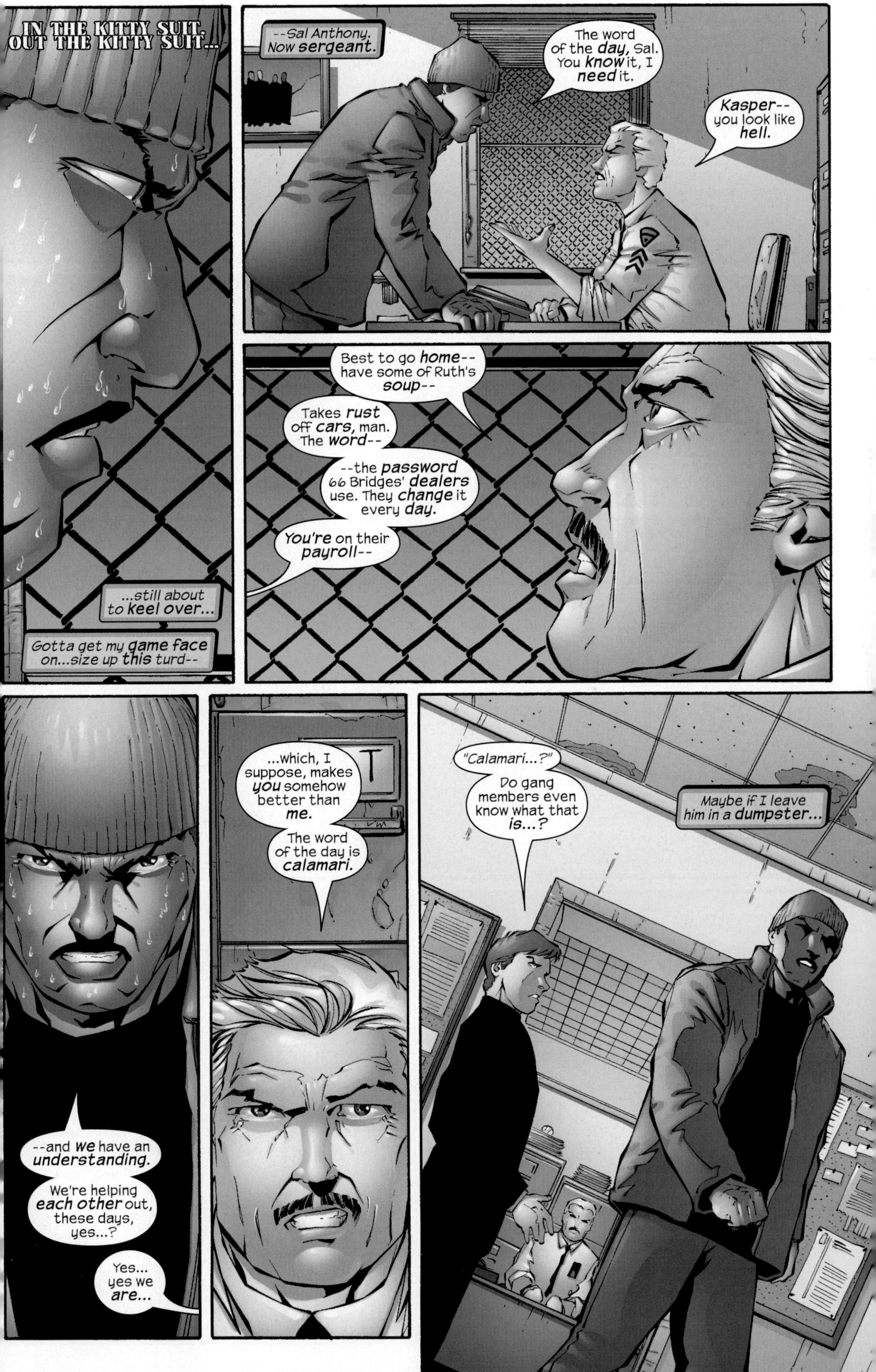

IN THE KITTY SUIT. OUT THE KITTY SUIT...
--Sal Anthony. Now sergeant.
The word of the day, Sal. You know it, I need it.
Kasper-- you look like hell.
...still about to keel over...
Gotta get my game face on...size up this turd--
Best to go home-- have some of Ruth's soup--
Takes rust off cars, man. The word--
--the password 66 Bridges' dealers use. They change it every day.
You're on their payroll--
--and we have an understanding.
We're helping each other out, these days, yes...?
Yes... yes we are...
...which, I suppose, makes you somehow better than me.
The word of the day is calamari.
"Calamari...?"
Do gang members even know what that is...?
Maybe if I leave him in a dumpster...

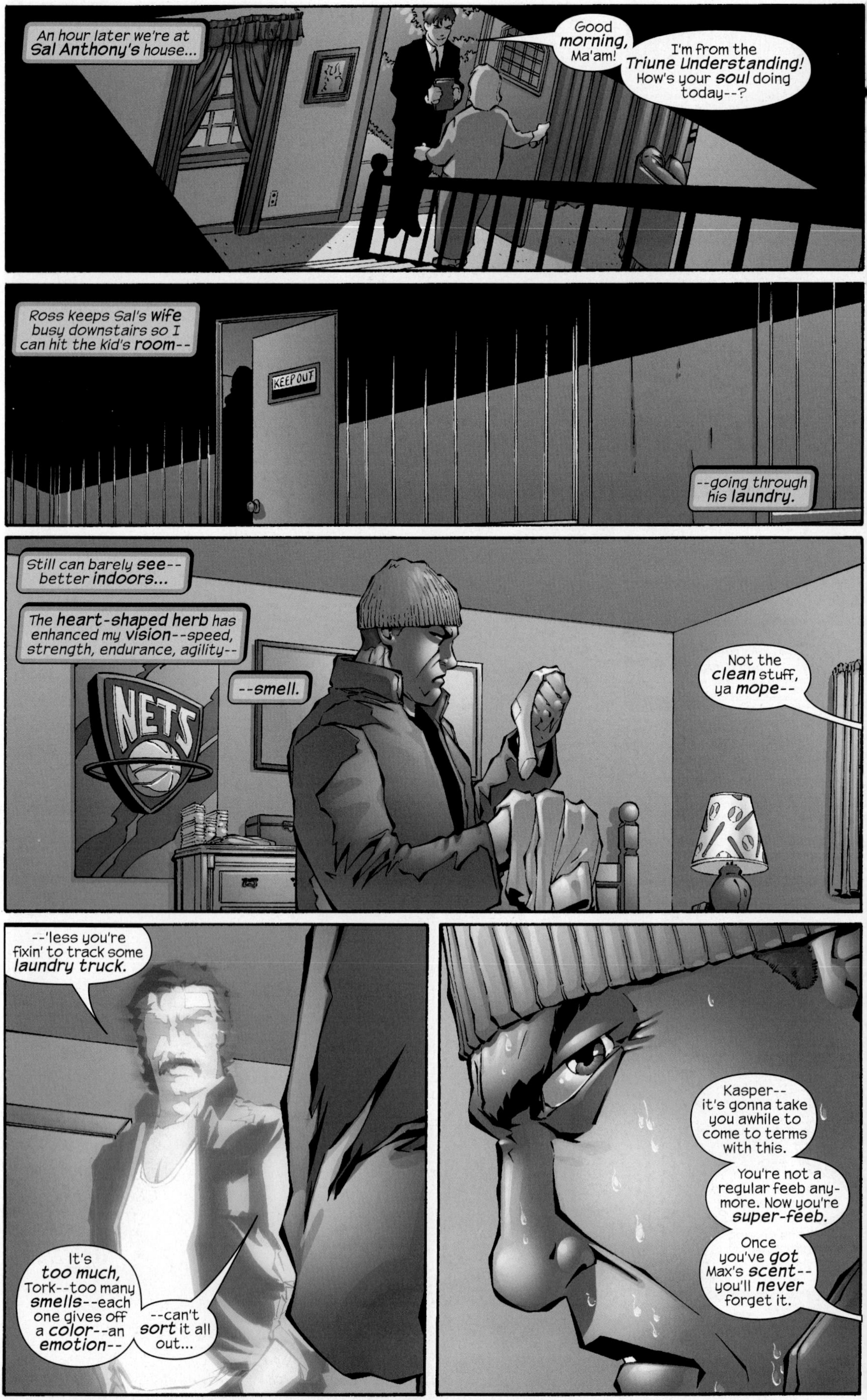

An hour later we're at Sal Anthony's house...
Good morning, Ma'am!
I'm from the Triune Understanding! How's your soul doing today--?
Ross keeps Sal's wife busy downstairs so I can hit the kid's room--
KEEP OUT
--going through his laundry.
Still can barely see-- better indoors...
The heart-shaped herb has enhanced my vision--speed, strength, endurance, agility--
--smell.
NETS
Not the clean stuff, ya mope--
--'less you're fixin' to track some laundry truck.
It's too much, Tork--too many smells--each one gives off a color--an emotion--
--can't sort it all out...
Kasper-- it's gonna take you awhile to come to terms with this.
You're not a regular feeb any-more. Now you're super-feeb.
Once you've got Max's scent-- you'll never forget it.

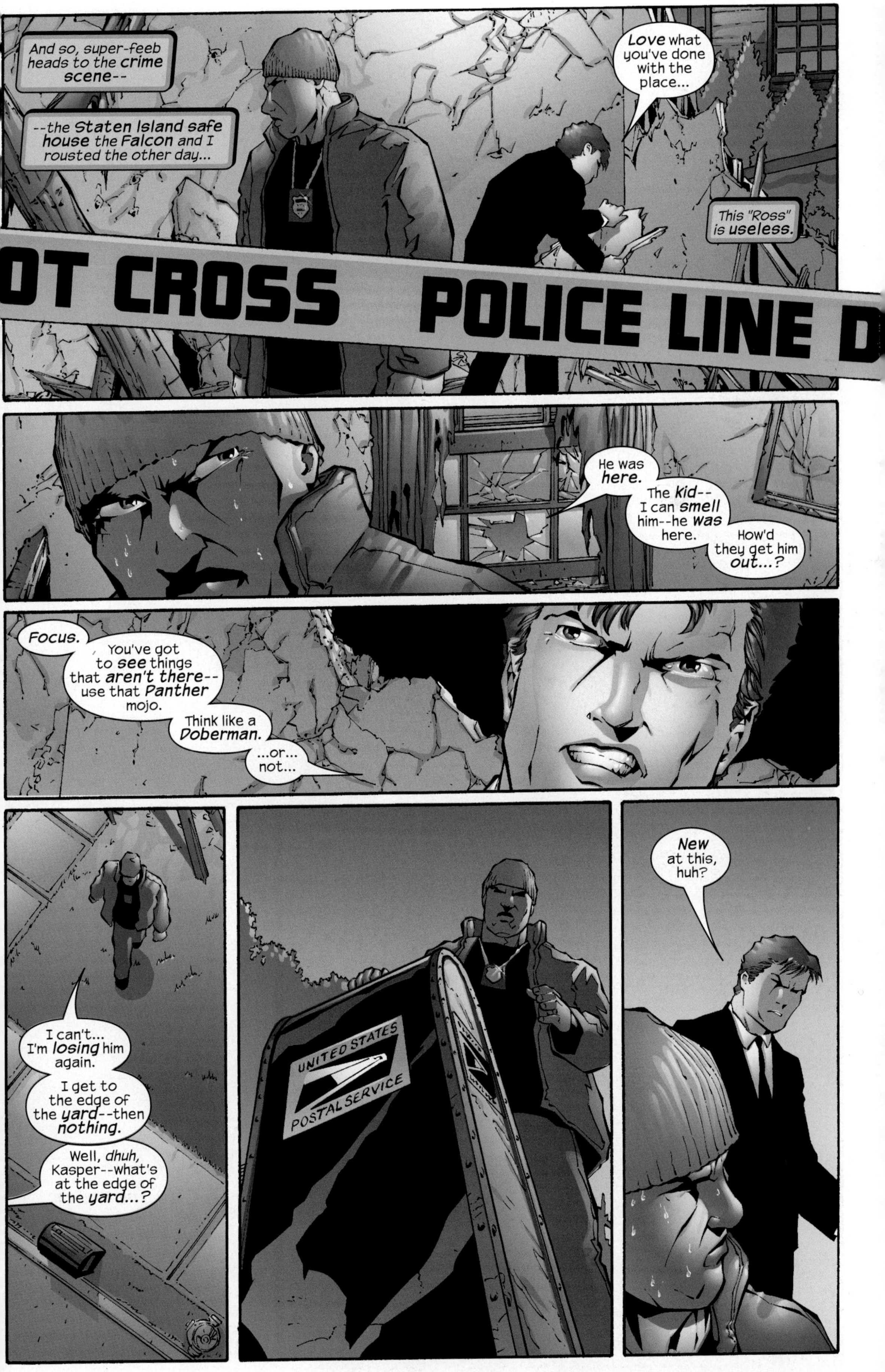
And so, super-feeb heads to the crime scene--
--the Staten Island safe house the Falcon and I rousted the other day...
Love what you've done with the place...
This "Ross" is useless.
OT CROSS POLICE LINE D
He was here.
The kid-- I can smell him--he was here.
How'd they get him out...?
Focus.
You've got to see things that aren't there-- use that Panther mojo.
Think like a Doberman.
...or... not...
I can't... I'm losing him again.
I get to the edge of the yard--then nothing.
Well, dhuh, Kasper--what's at the edge of the yard...?
UNITED STATES POSTAL SERVICE
New at this, huh?

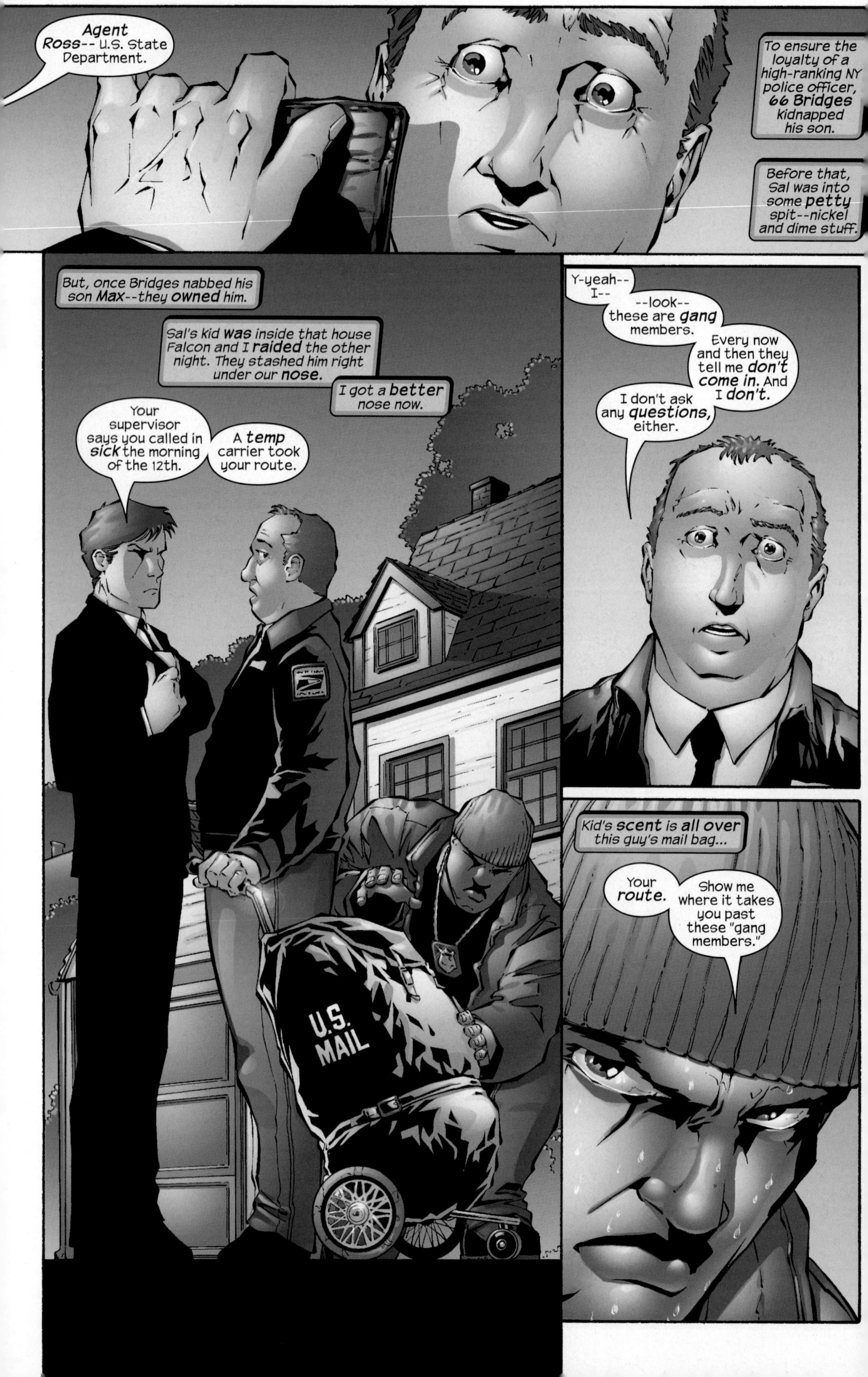
Agent Ross-- U.S. State Department.
To ensure the loyalty of a high-ranking NY police officer, 66 Bridges kidnapped his son.
Before that, Sal was into some petty spit--nickel and dime stuff.
But, once Bridges nabbed his son Max--they owned him.
Sal's kid was inside that house Falcon and I raided the other night. They stashed him right under our nose.
I got a better nose now.
Your supervisor says you called in sick the morning of the 12th.
A temp carrier took your route.
U.S. MAIL
Y-yeah-- I--
--look-- these are gang members.
Every now and then they tell me don't come in. And I don't.
I don't ask any questions, either.
Kid's scent is all over this guy's mail bag...
Your route.
Show me where it takes you past these "gang members."

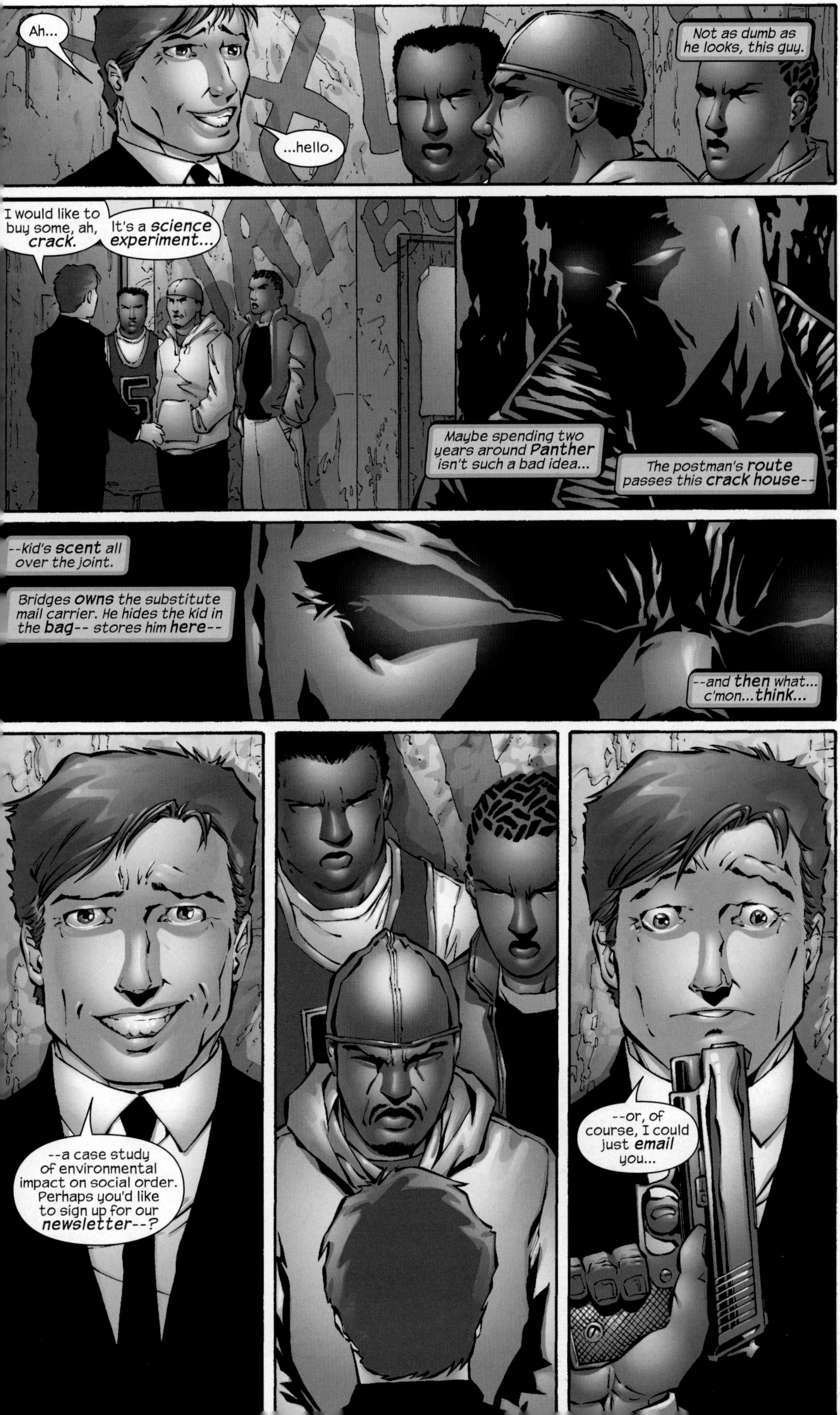
Ah...
...hello.
Not as dumb as he looks, this guy.
I would like to buy some, ah, crack.
It's a science experiment...
Maybe spending two years around Panther isn't such a bad idea...
The postman's route passes this crack house--
--kid's scent all over the joint.
Bridges owns the substitute mail carrier. He hides the kid in the bag-- stores him here--
--and then what... c'mon...think...
--a case study of environmental impact on social order. Perhaps you'd like to sign up for our newsletter--?
--or, of course, I could just email you...

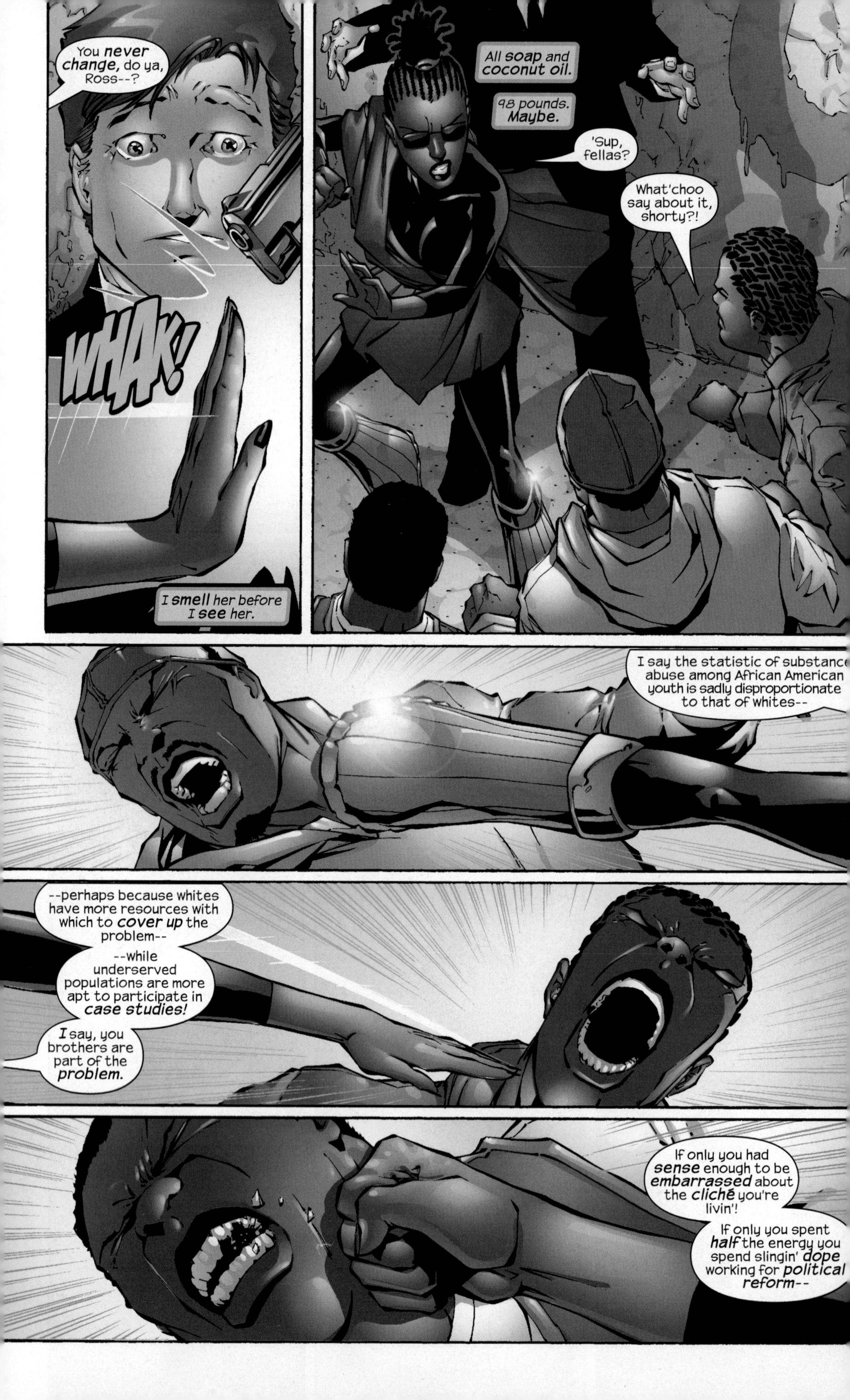

You never change, do ya, Ross--?
WHAK!
I smell her before I see her.
All soap and coconut oil.
98 pounds. Maybe.
'Sup, fellas?
What'choo say about it, shorty?!
I say the statistic of substance abuse among African American youth is sadly disproportionate to that of whites--
--perhaps because whites have more resources with which to cover up the problem--
--while underserved populations are more apt to participate in case studies!
I say, you brothers are part of the problem.
If only you had sense enough to be embarrassed about the cliché you're livin'!
If only you spent half the energy you spend slingin' dope working for political reform--

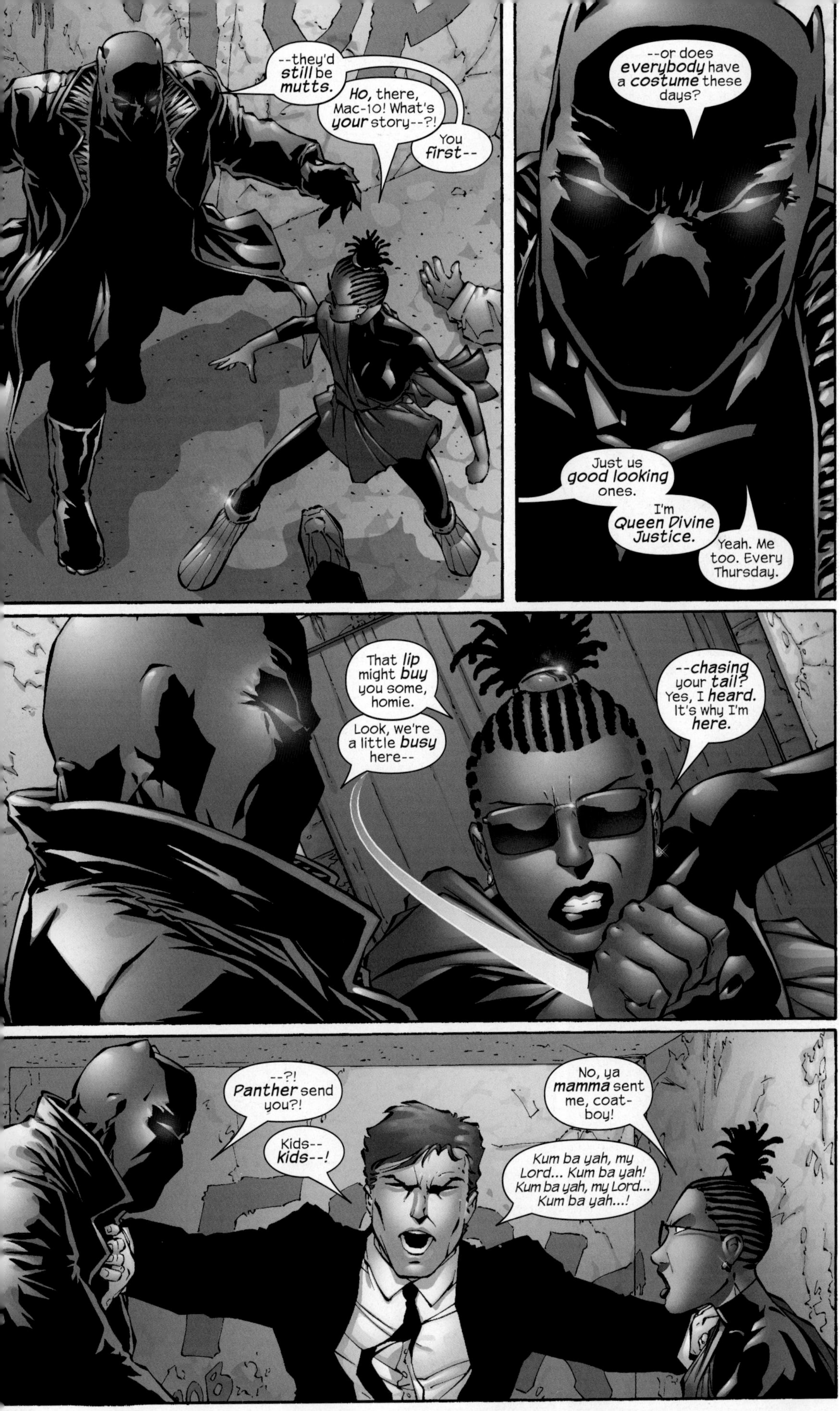

--they'd still be mutts.
Ho, there, Mac-10! What's your story--?!
You first--
--or does everybody have a costume these days?
Just us good looking ones.
I'm Queen Divine Justice.
Yeah. Me too. Every Thursday.
That lip might buy you some, homie.
Look, we're a little busy here--
--chasing your tail? Yes, I heard. It's why I'm here.
--?! Panther send you?!
Kids-- kids--!
No, ya mamma sent me, coat-boy!
Kum ba yah, my Lord... Kum ba yah! Kum ba yah, my Lord... Kum ba yah...!

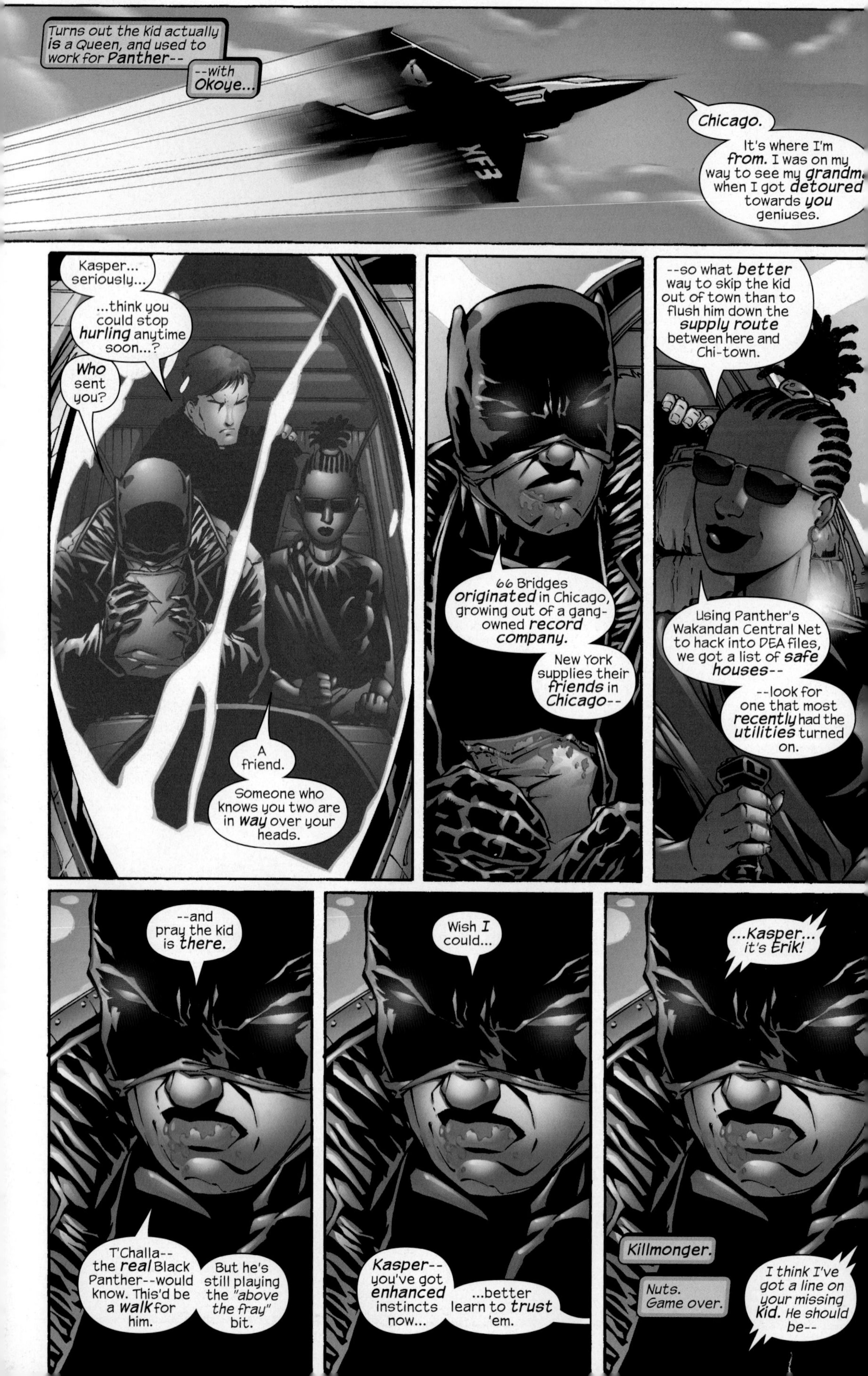
Turns out the kid actually is a Queen, and used to work for Panther--
--with Okoye...
Chicago.
It's where I'm from. I was on my way to see my grandm. when I got detoured towards you geniuses.
XF3
Kasper... seriously...
...think you could stop hurling anytime soon...?
Who sent you?
A friend.
Someone who knows you two are in way over your heads.
66 Bridges originated in Chicago, growing out of a gang-owned record company.
New York supplies their friends in Chicago--
--so what better way to skip the kid out of town than to flush him down the supply route between here and Chi-town.
Using Panther's Wakandan Central Net to hack into DEA files, we got a list of safe houses--
--look for one that most recently had the utilities turned on.
--and pray the kid is there.
T'Challa--the real Black Panther--would know. This'd be a walk for him.
But he's still playing the "above the fray" bit.
Wish I could...
Kasper--you've got enhanced instincts now...
...better learn to trust 'em.
...Kasper... it's Erik!
Killmonger.
Nuts. Game over.
I think I've got a line on your missing kid. He should be--

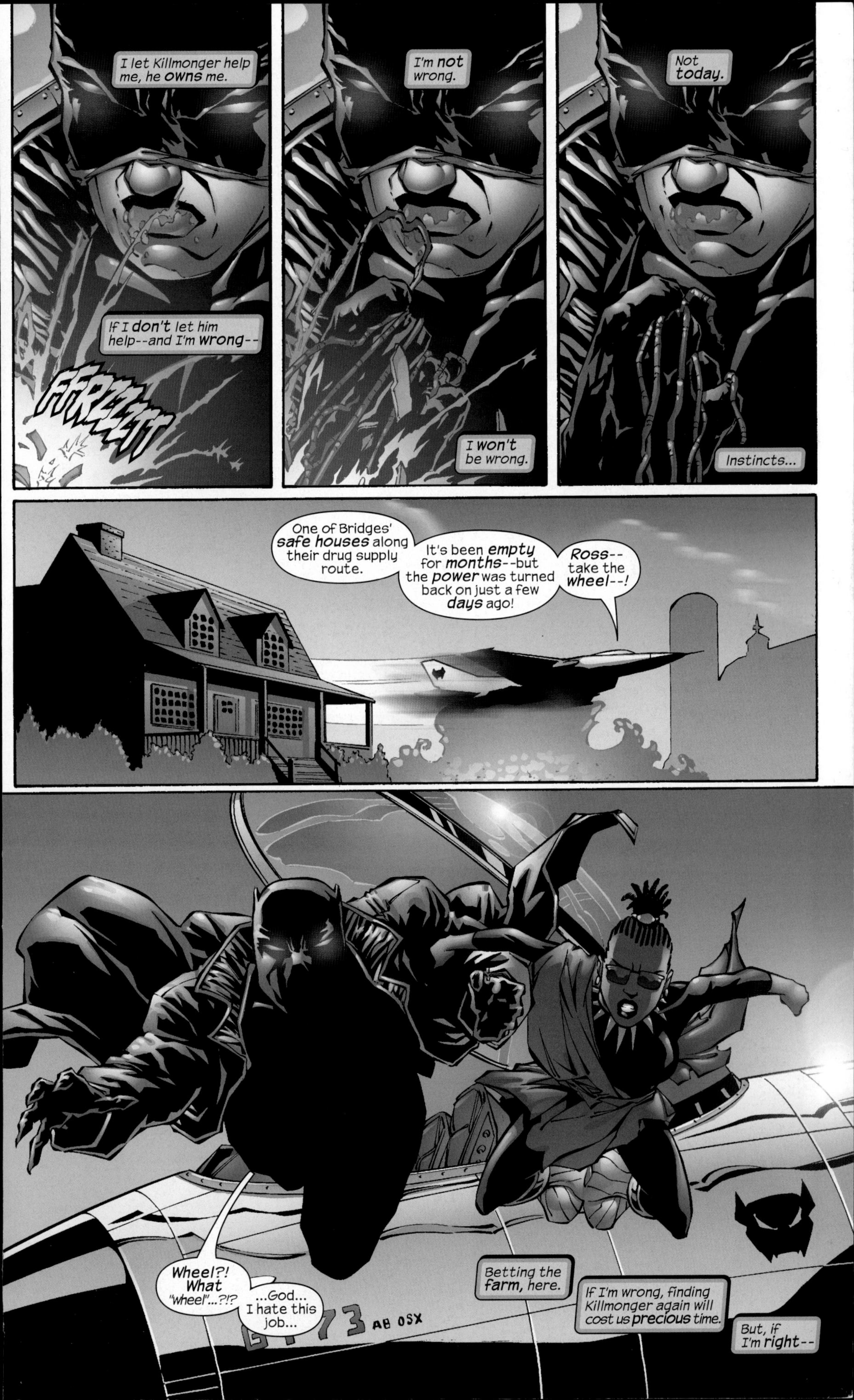
I let Killmonger help me, he owns me.
If I don't let him help--and I'm wrong--
FFFZZZATT
I'm not wrong.
I won't be wrong.
Not today.
Instincts...
One of Bridges' safe houses along their drug supply route.
It's been empty for months--but the power was turned back on just a few days ago!
Ross--take the wheel--!
Wheel?! What "wheel"...?!?
...God... I hate this job...
Betting the farm, here.
If I'm wrong, finding Killmonger again will cost us precious time.
But, if I'm right--

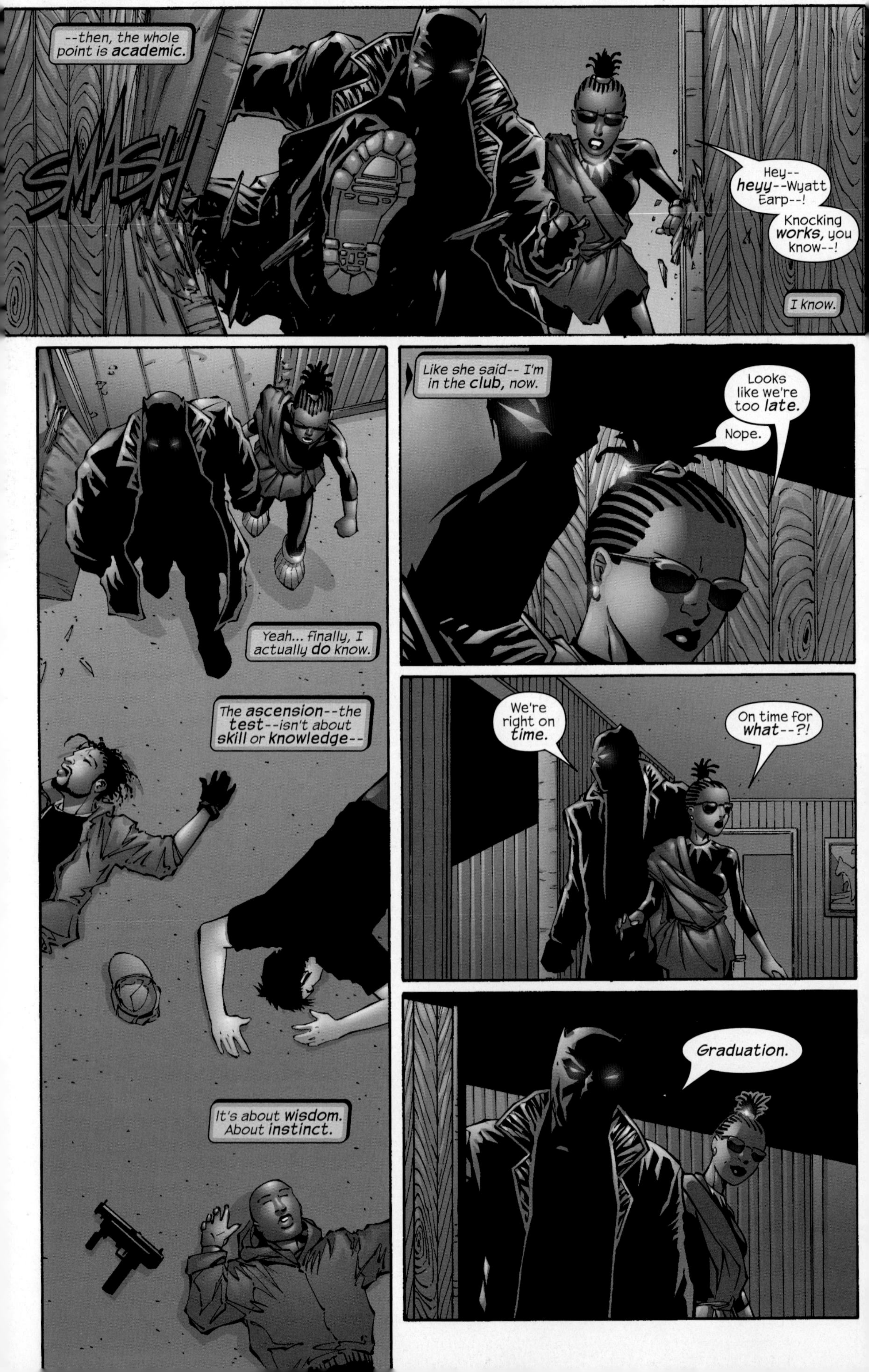
--then, the whole point is academic.
SMASH
Hey-- heyy--Wyatt Earp--!
Knocking works, you know--!
I know.
Yeah... finally, I actually do know.
The ascension--the test--isn't about skill or knowledge--
It's about wisdom. About instinct.
Like she said-- I'm in the club, now.
Looks like we're too late.
Nope.
We're right on time.
On time for what--?!
Graduation.

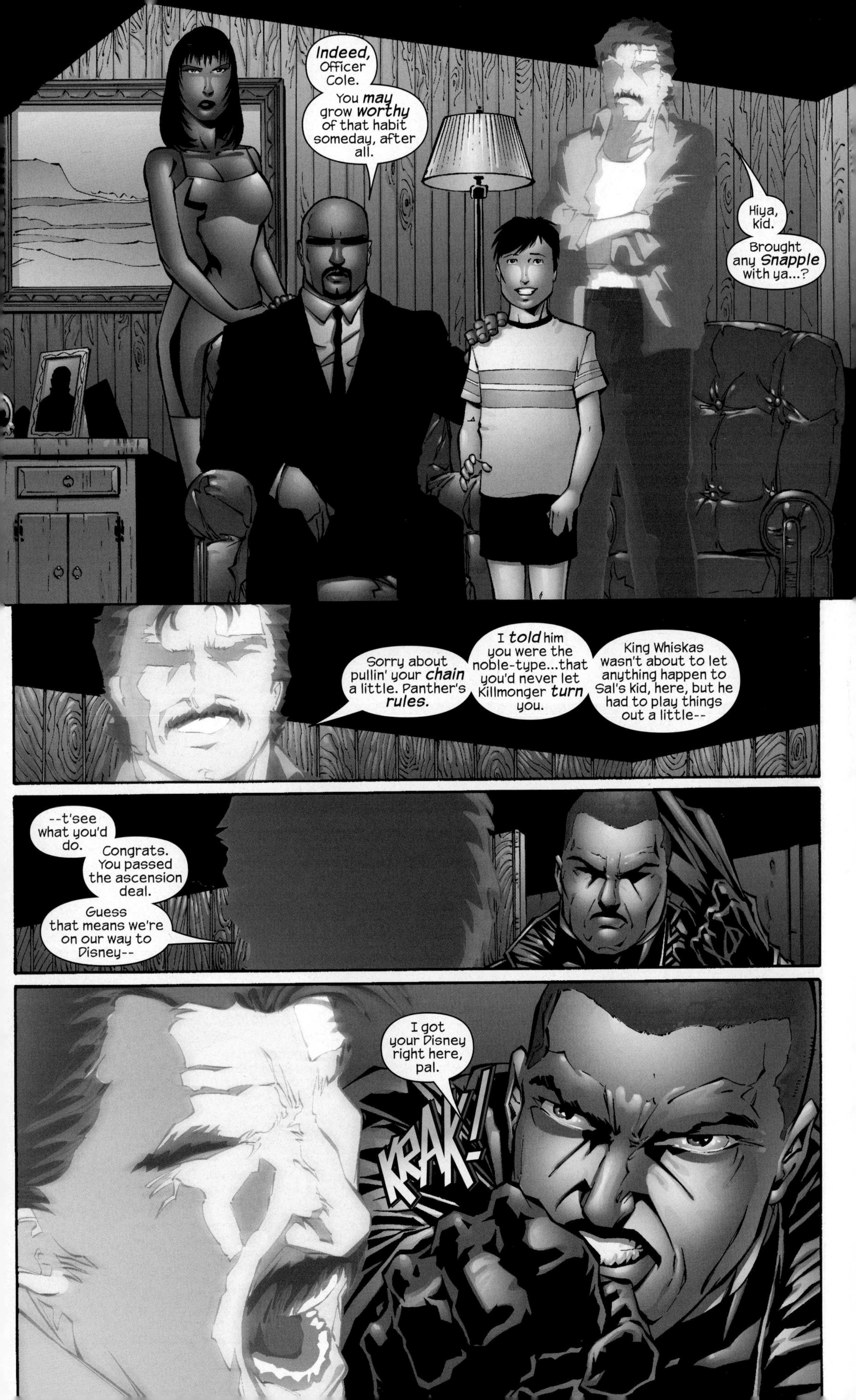
Indeed, Officer Cole.
You may grow worthy of that habit someday, after all.
Hiya, kid.
Brought any Snapple with ya...?
Sorry about pullin' your chain a little. Panther's rules.
I told him you were the noble-type...that you'd never let Killmonger turn you.
King Whiskas wasn't about to let anything happen to Sal's kid, here, but he had to play things out a little--
--t'see what you'd do.
Congrats. You passed the ascension deal.
Guess that means we're on our way to Disney--
I got your Disney right here, pal.
KRAK!

What the *hell's wrong* with you?!? Lucky I didn't buy you a *Rolex*...

Ghosts don't *bleed*. *Ghosts* don't feel *pain*.

And, ghosts *sure* as hell don't have a *scent*.

Y'know, Tork, it's taken me a *while* to figure out what I was *smelling*--to *sort* through it all--

--but even *dead*, you're still wearing that drug store cologne!

It's *Pola*, you hockey puck.

Just as good as *Polo* for *one-third* the price--

--comes with a free *tooth brush*...

Shut up. I thought you were *dead*, man. You made me *think* you were *dead*. I even found your *body*--!!

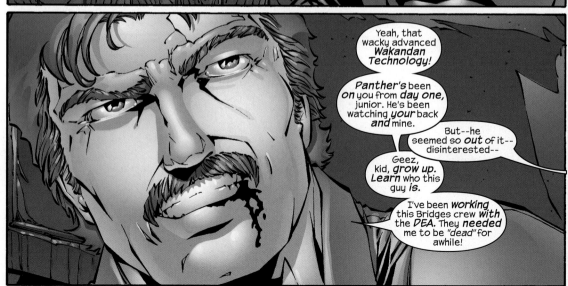

Yeah, that wacky advanced *Wakandan Technology!*

Panther's been *on* you from *day one*, junior. He's been watching *your* back *and* mine.

But--he seemed so *out* of it-- disinterested--

Geez, kid, *grow up. Learn* who this guy *is.*

I've been *working* this Bridges crew *with* the *DEA.* They *needed* me to be "*dead*" for awhile!

We busted up this crew, took down some heavy hitters.

Now I get to be *alive* again.

Try and *restrain* your great joy and relief...

You son of a...

I was mistaken about you.

I presumed you to be an arrogant American mongrel.

I've since learned your *father* is from Uganda-- *Africa*.

Makes me, what, an arrogant Jewish *African* mongrel...?

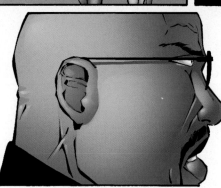

Perhaps.

You, an *American* outsider, could not be embraced by the Wakandan council.

Your direct *African* lineage, however, provides Killmonger with legal ground to force them to accept you.

N'Jadaka desires only my *dead body* on display in Tranquility Temple.

Since when did you and Killmonger become friends...?

You are a *means* to his ultimate *end*. Nothing more.

So, what, now I'm a "Black Panther?" Killmonger's *flunky*...?

You are *never* to wear that uniform again.

To do so would blaspheme the very council you seek to embrace.

Only *you* can decide your destiny, Officer Cole.

But decide *now*. Tonight.

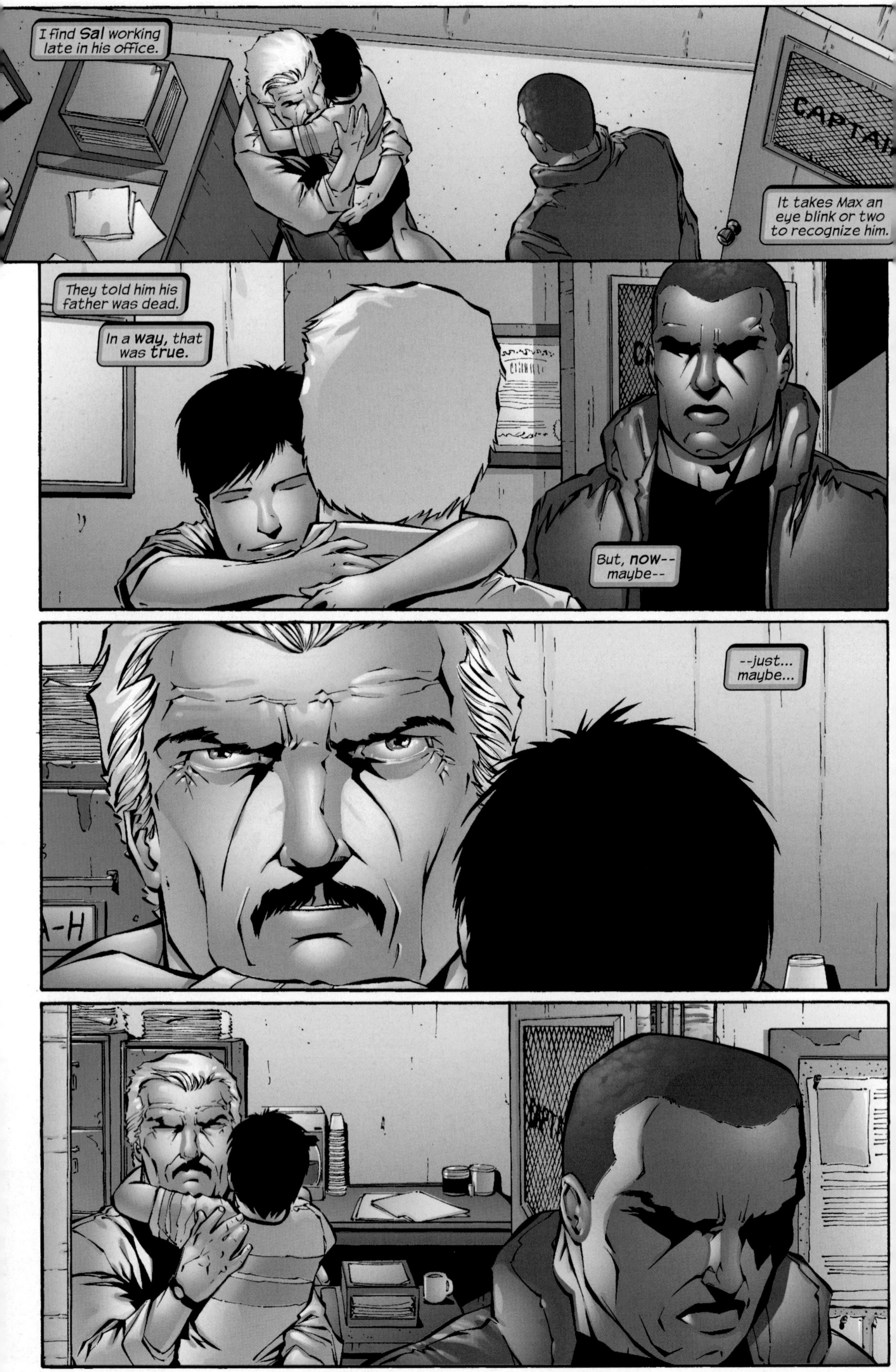
I find Sal working late in his office.
CAPTAIN
It takes Max an eye blink or two to recognize him.
They told him his father was dead.
In a way, that was true.
But, now-- maybe--
--just... maybe...
A-H

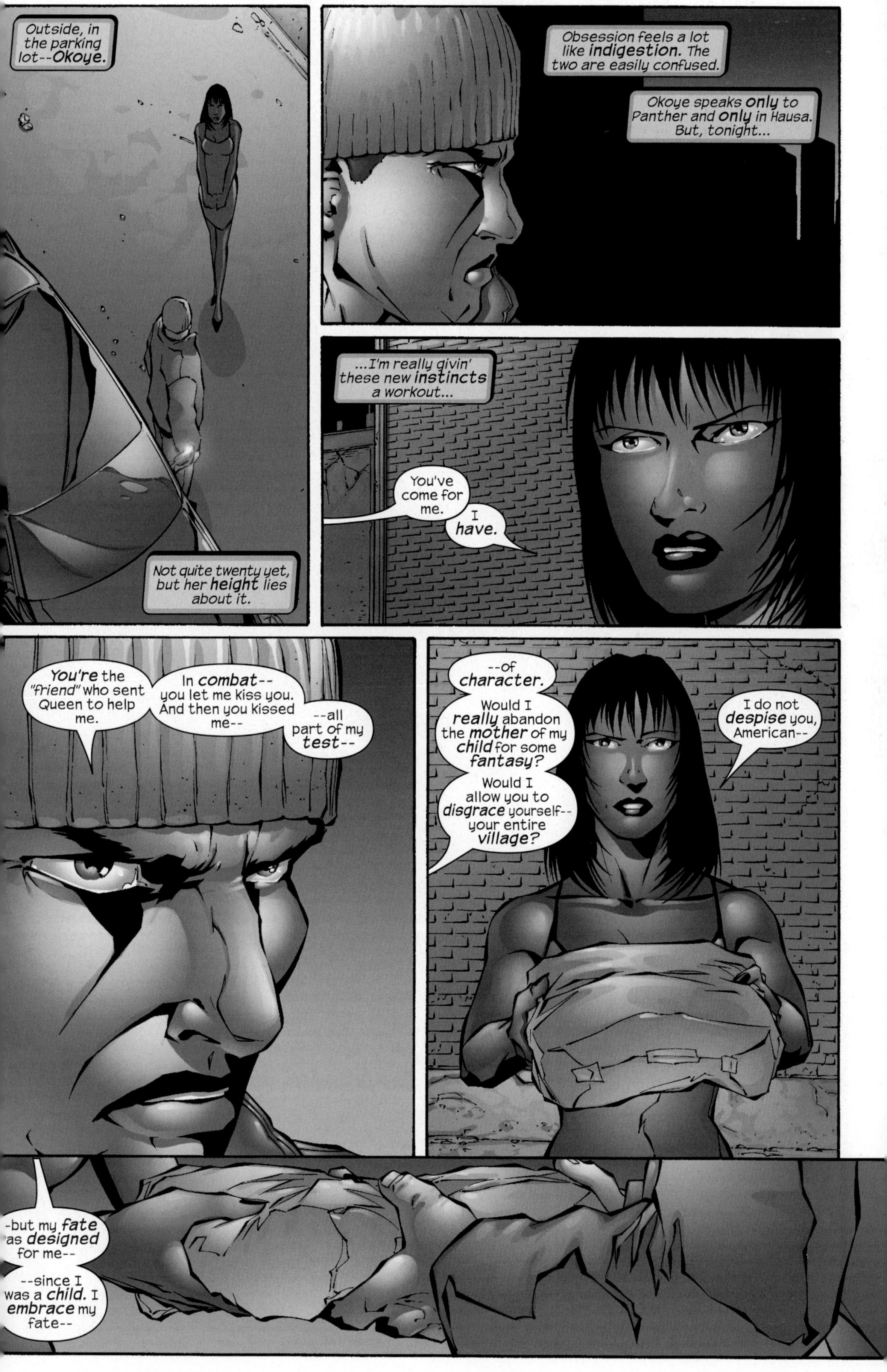
Outside, in the parking lot--Okoye.
Not quite twenty yet, but her height lies about it.
Obsession feels a lot like indigestion. The two are easily confused.
Okoye speaks only to Panther and only in Hausa. But, tonight...
...I'm really givin' these new instincts a workout...
You've come for me.
I have.
You're the "friend" who sent Queen to help me.
In combat--you let me kiss you. And then you kissed me--
--all part of my test--
I do not despise you, American--
--of character.
Would I really abandon the mother of my child for some fantasy?
Would I allow you to disgrace yourself--your entire village?
-but my fate as designed for me--
--since I was a child. I embrace my fate--

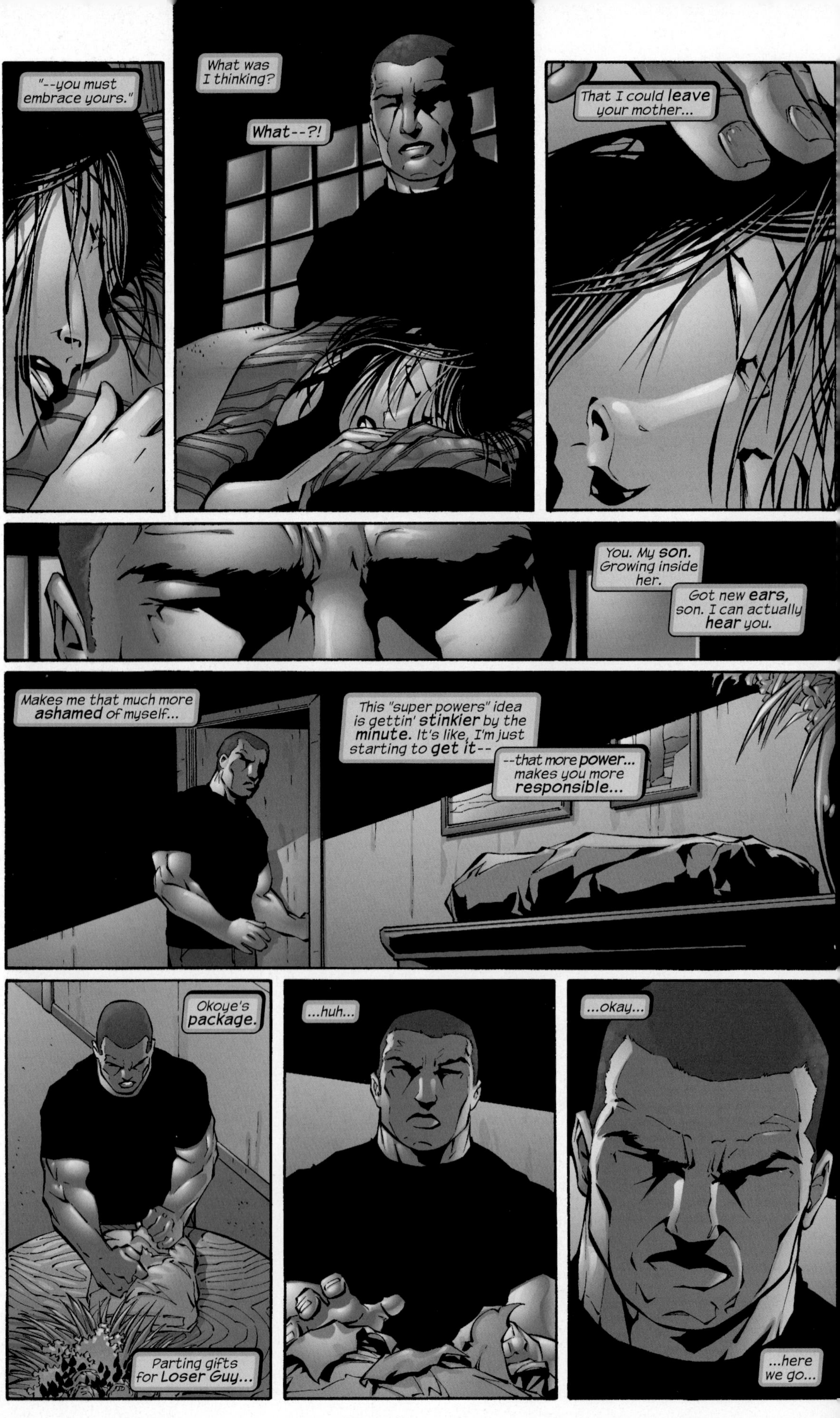
"--you must embrace yours."
What was I thinking?
What--?!
That I could leave your mother...
You. My son. Growing inside her.
Got new ears, son. I can actually hear you.
Makes me that much more ashamed of myself...
This "super powers" idea is gettin' stinkier by the minute. It's like, I'm just starting to get it--
--that more power... makes you more responsible...
Okoye's package.
Parting gifts for Loser Guy...
...huh...
...okay...
...here we go...

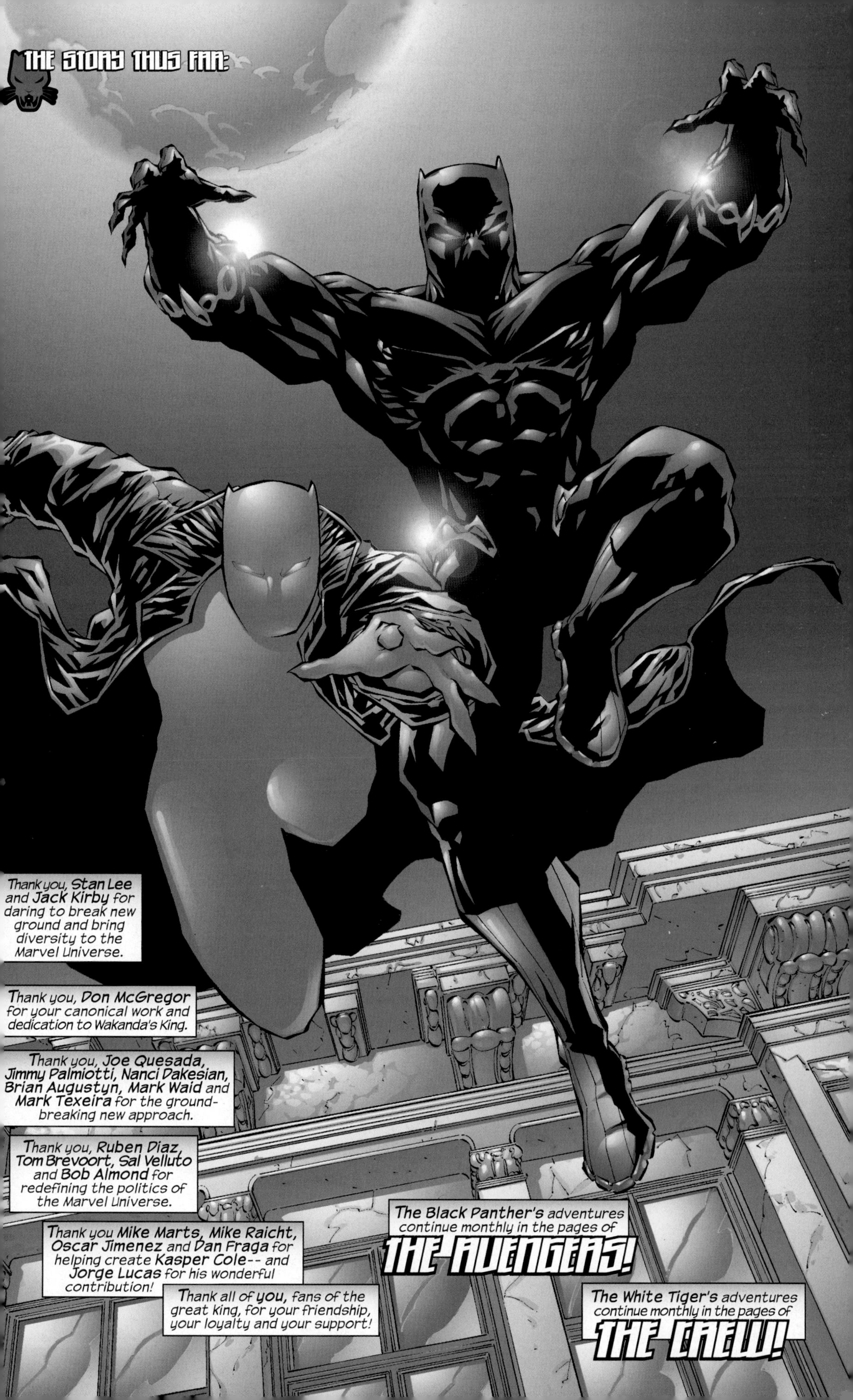
THE STORY THUS FAR:
Thank you, Stan Lee and Jack Kirby for daring to break new ground and bring diversity to the Marvel Universe.
Thank you, Don McGregor for your canonical work and dedication to Wakanda's King.
Thank you, Joe Quesada, Jimmy Palmiotti, Nanci Dakesian, Brian Augustyn, Mark Waid and Mark Texeira for the ground-breaking new approach.
Thank you, Ruben Diaz, Tom Brevoort, Sal Velluto and Bob Almond for redefining the politics of the Marvel Universe.
Thank you Mike Marts, Mike Raicht, Oscar Jimenez and Dan Fraga for helping create Kasper Cole-- and Jorge Lucas for his wonderful contribution!
Thank all of you, fans of the great king, for your friendship, your loyalty and your support!
The Black Panther's adventures continue monthly in the pages of
THE AVENGERS!
The White Tiger's adventures continue monthly in the pages of
THE CREW!

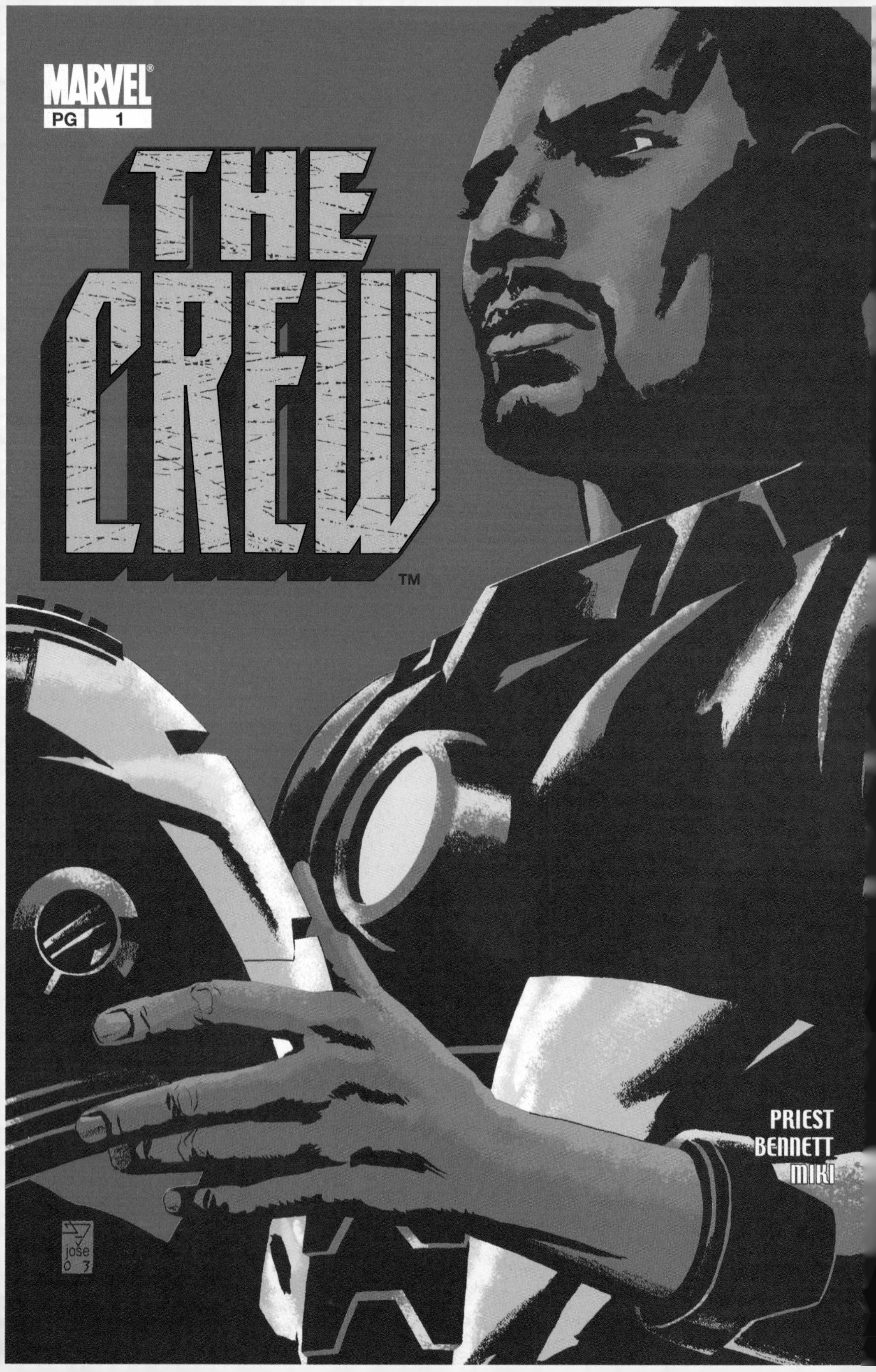
MARVEL®
PG 1
THE CREW™
PRIEST
BENNETT
MIKI
jose 03

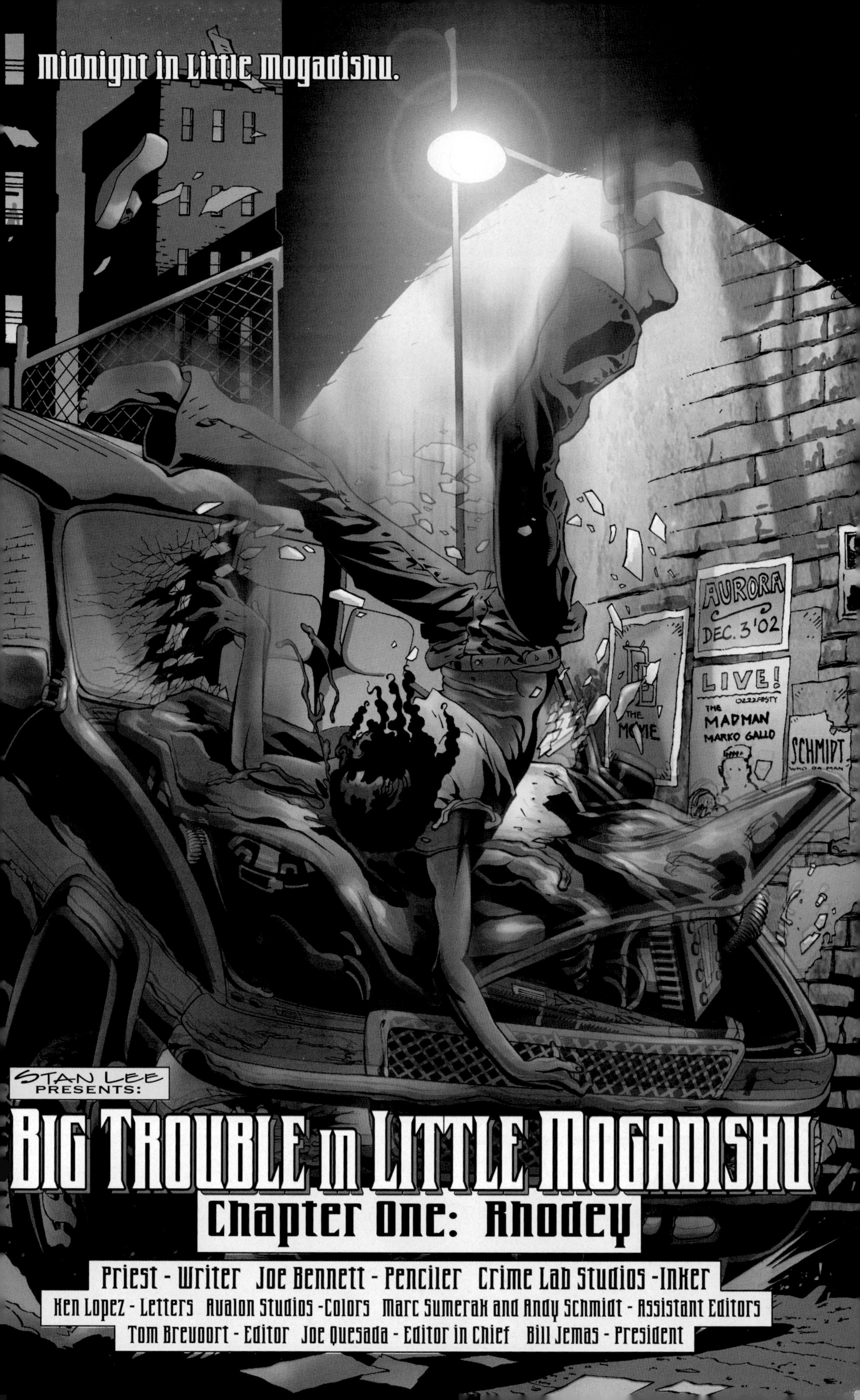
Midnight in Little Mogadishu.
AURORA
DEC. 3 '02
LIVE!
THE
MADMAN
MARKO GALLO
THE
MOVIE
SCHMIDT
STAN LEE
PRESENTS:
BIG TROUBLE in LITTLE MOGADISHU
Chapter One: Rhodey
Priest - Writer Joe Bennett - Penciler Crime Lab Studios - Inker
Ken Lopez - Letters Avalon Studios - Colors Marc Sumerak and Andy Schmidt - Assistant Editors
Tom Brevoort - Editor Joe Quesada - Editor in Chief Bill Jemas - President

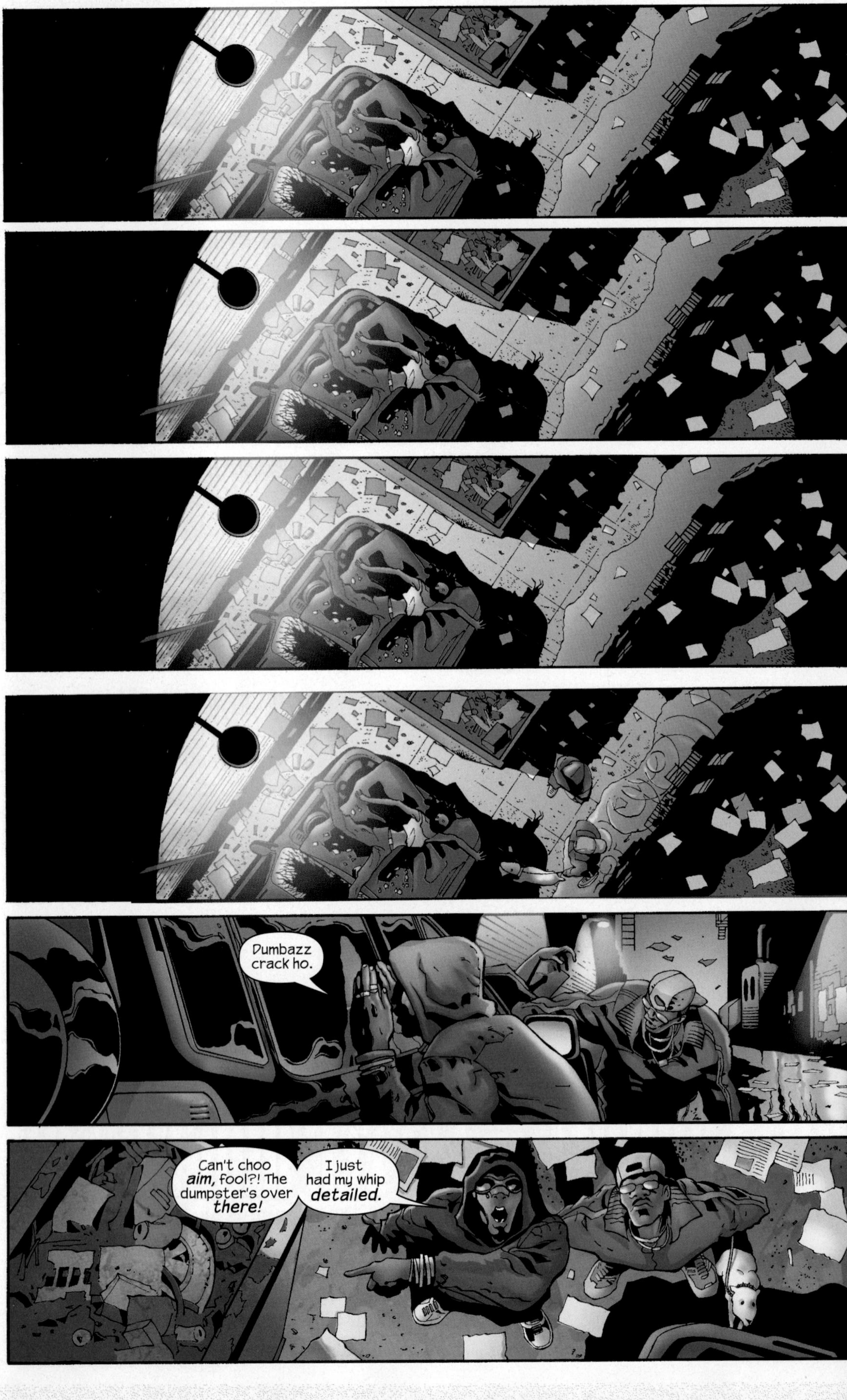
Dumbazz crack ho.
Can't choo aim, fool?! The dumpster's over there!
I just had my whip detailed.

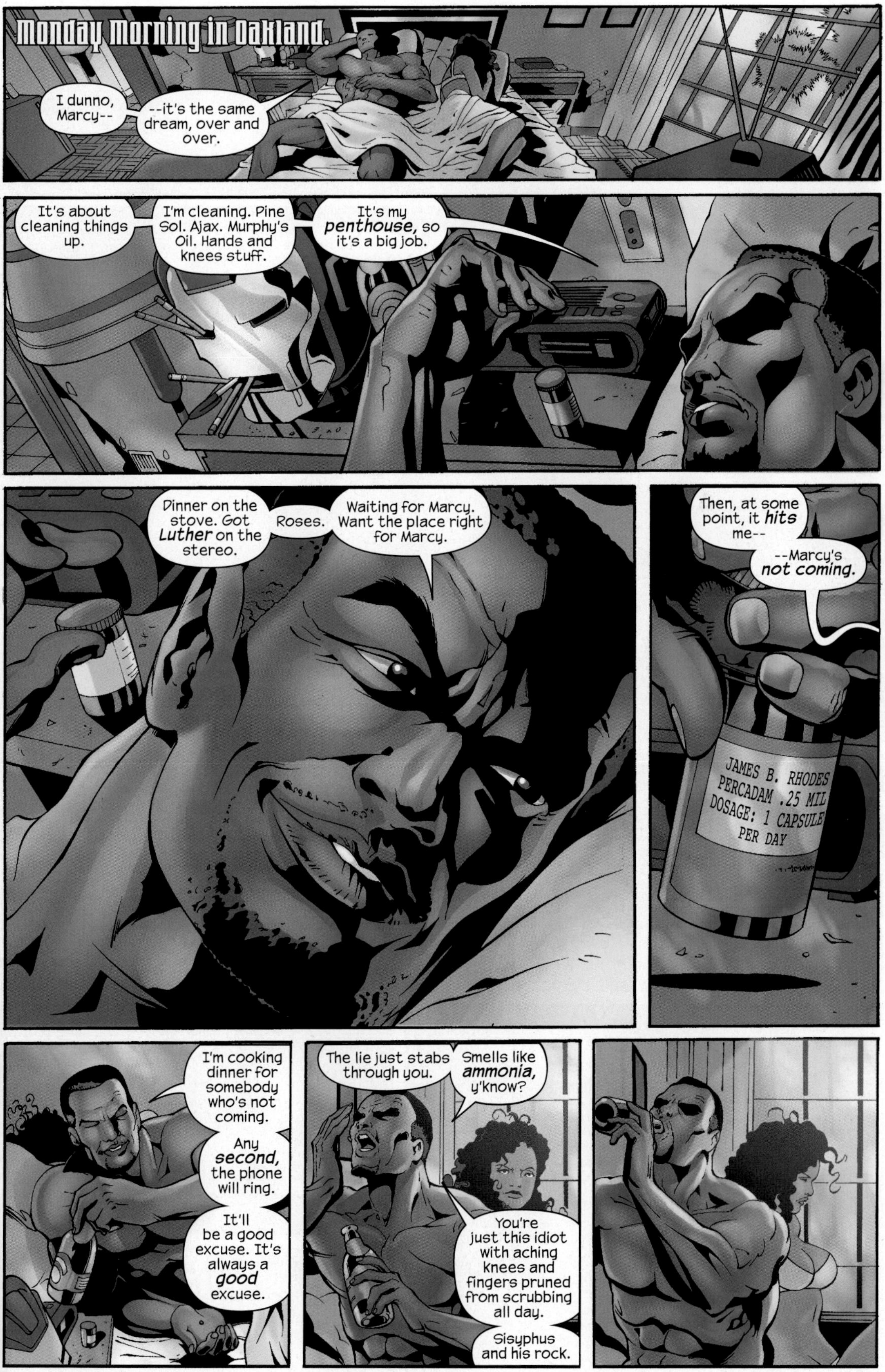
Monday Morning in Oakland.
I dunno, Marcy--
--it's the same dream, over and over.
It's about cleaning things up.
I'm cleaning. Pine Sol. Ajax. Murphy's Oil. Hands and knees stuff.
It's my penthouse, so it's a big job.
Dinner on the stove. Got Luther on the stereo.
Roses.
Waiting for Marcy. Want the place right for Marcy.
Then, at some point, it hits me--
--Marcy's not coming.
JAMES B. RHODES
PERCADAM .25 MIL
DOSAGE: 1 CAPSULE
PER DAY
I'm cooking dinner for somebody who's not coming.
Any second, the phone will ring.
It'll be a good excuse. It's always a good excuse.
The lie just stabs through you.
Smells like ammonia, y'know?
You're just this idiot with aching knees and fingers pruned from scrubbing all day.
Sisyphus and his rock.

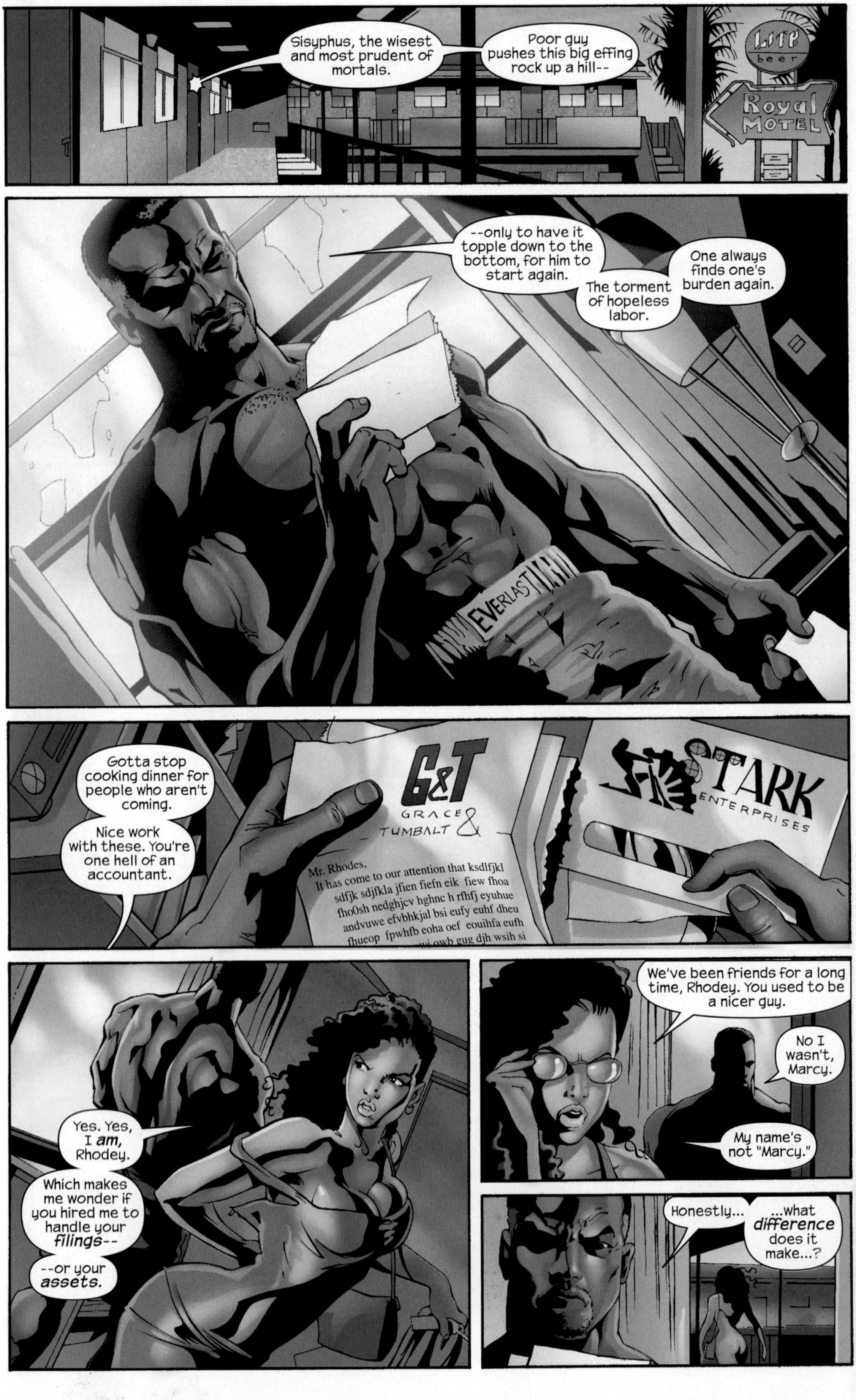

Sisyphus, the wisest and most prudent of mortals.
Poor guy pushes this big effing rock up a hill--
Lite beer
Royal MOTEL
--only to have it topple down to the bottom, for him to start again.
The torment of hopeless labor.
One always finds one's burden again.
EVERLAST
Gotta stop cooking dinner for people who aren't coming.
Nice work with these. You're one hell of an accountant.
G&T
GRACE & TUMBALT
Mr. Rhodes,
It has come to our attention that ksdlfjkl
sdfjk sdjfkla jfien fiefn eik fiew fhoa
fho0sh nedghjcv hghnc h rfhfj eyuhue
andvuwe efvbhkjal bsi eufy euhf dheu
fhueop fpwhfb eoha oef eouihfa eufh
STARK
ENTERPRISES
Yes. Yes, I *am,* Rhodey.
Which makes me wonder if you hired me to handle your *filings*--
--or your *assets.*
We've been friends for a long time, Rhodey. You used to be a nicer guy.
No I wasn't, Marcy.
My name's not "Marcy."
Honestly...
...what *difference* does it make...?

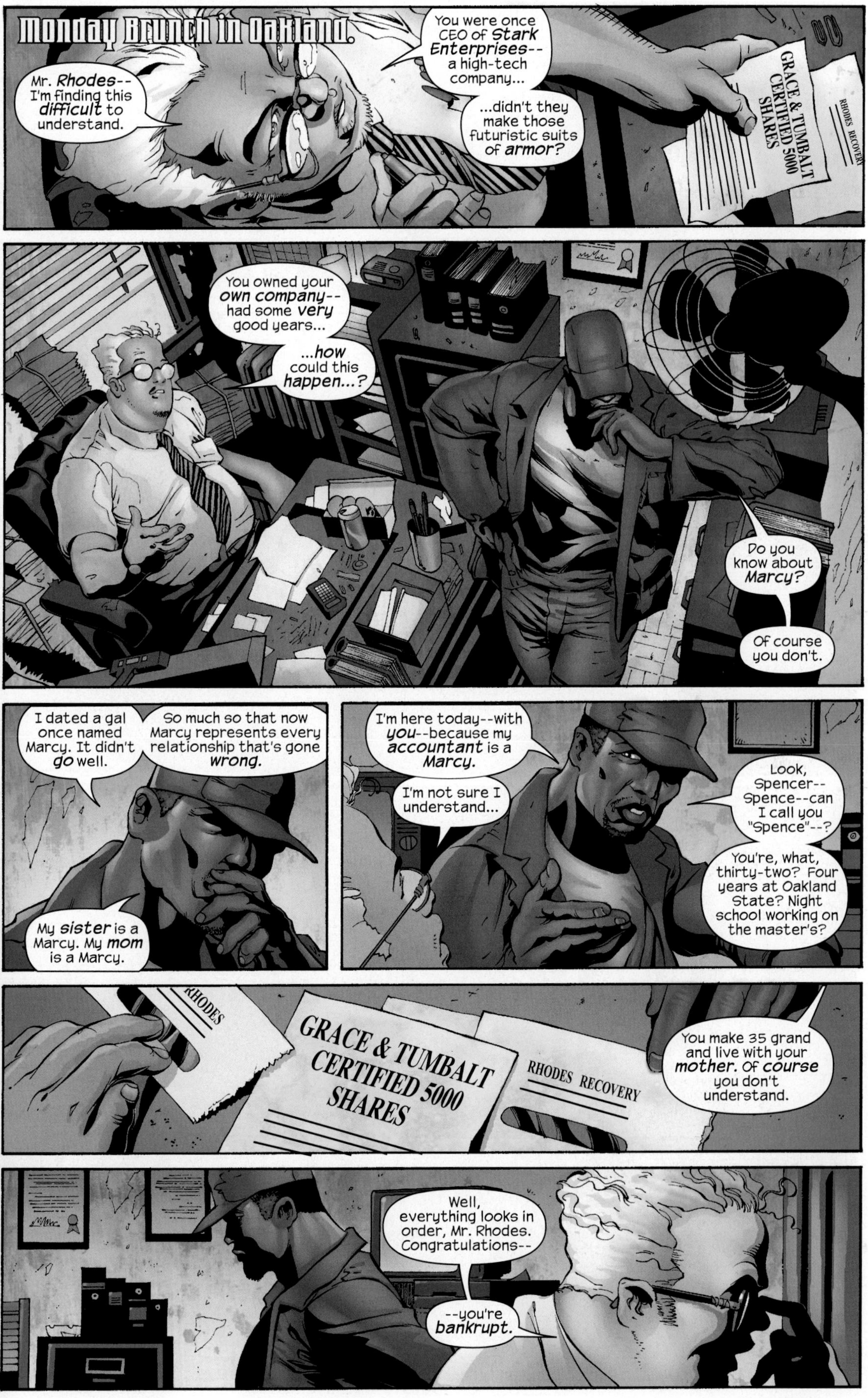
Monday Brunch in Oakland.
Mr. Rhodes--I'm finding this difficult to understand.
You were once CEO of Stark Enterprises--a high-tech company...
...didn't they make those futuristic suits of armor?
GRACE & TUMBALT CERTIFIED 5000 SHARES
RHODES RECOVERY
You owned your own company--had some very good years...
...how could this happen...?
Do you know about Marcy?
Of course you don't.
I dated a gal once named Marcy. It didn't go well.
So much so that now Marcy represents every relationship that's gone wrong.
My sister is a Marcy. My mom is a Marcy.
I'm here today--with you--because my accountant is a Marcy.
I'm not sure I understand...
Look, Spencer--Spence--can I call you "Spence"--?
You're, what, thirty-two? Four years at Oakland State? Night school working on the master's?
RHODES
GRACE & TUMBALT CERTIFIED 5000 SHARES
RHODES RECOVERY
You make 35 grand and live with your mother. Of course you don't understand.
Well, everything looks in order, Mr. Rhodes. Congratulations--
--you're bankrupt.

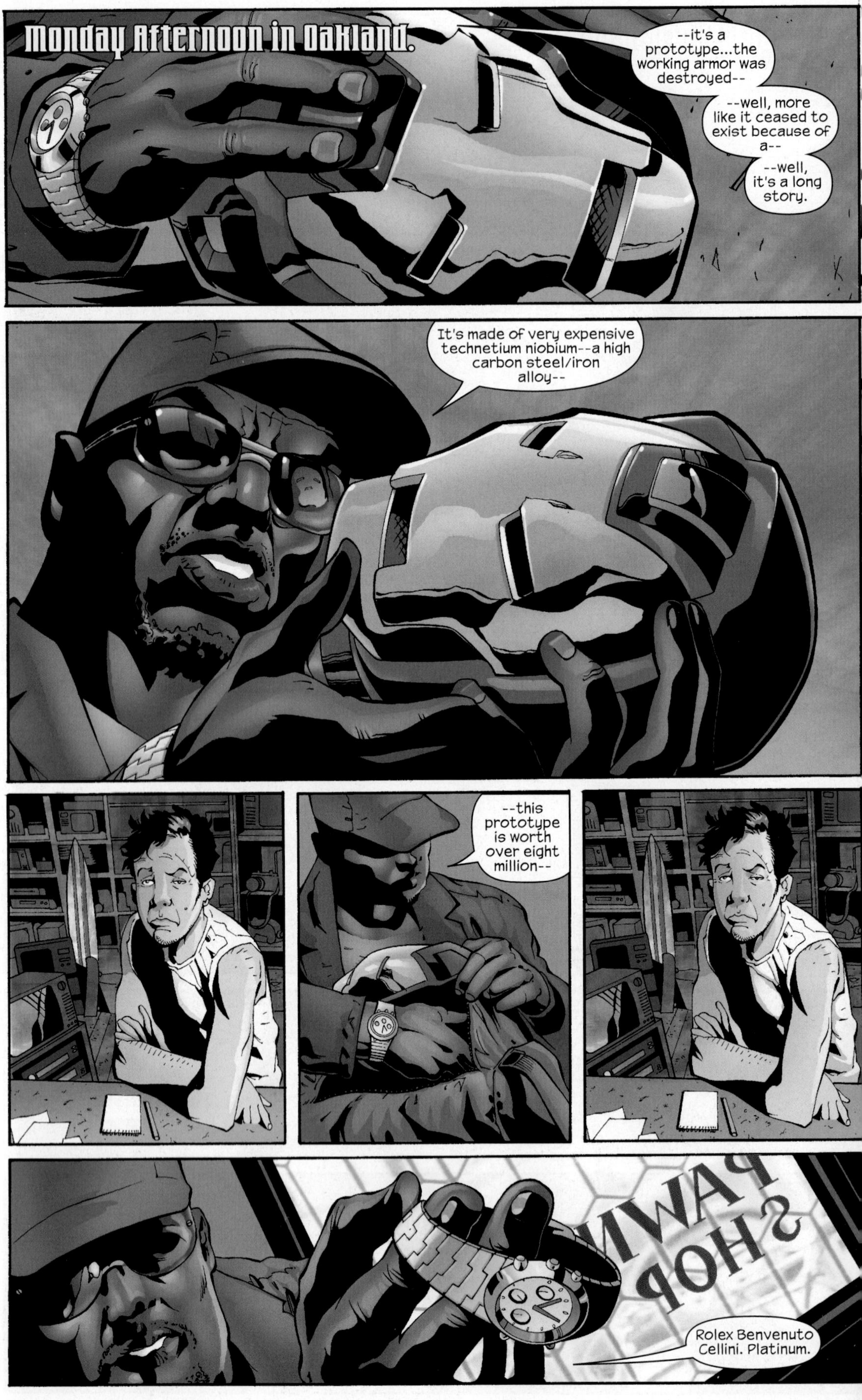
Monday Afternoon in Oakland.
--it's a prototype...the working armor was destroyed--
--well, more like it ceased to exist because of a--
--well, it's a long story.
It's made of very expensive technetium niobium--a high carbon steel/iron alloy--
--this prototype is worth over eight million--
PAWN SHOP
Rolex Benvenuto Cellini. Platinum.

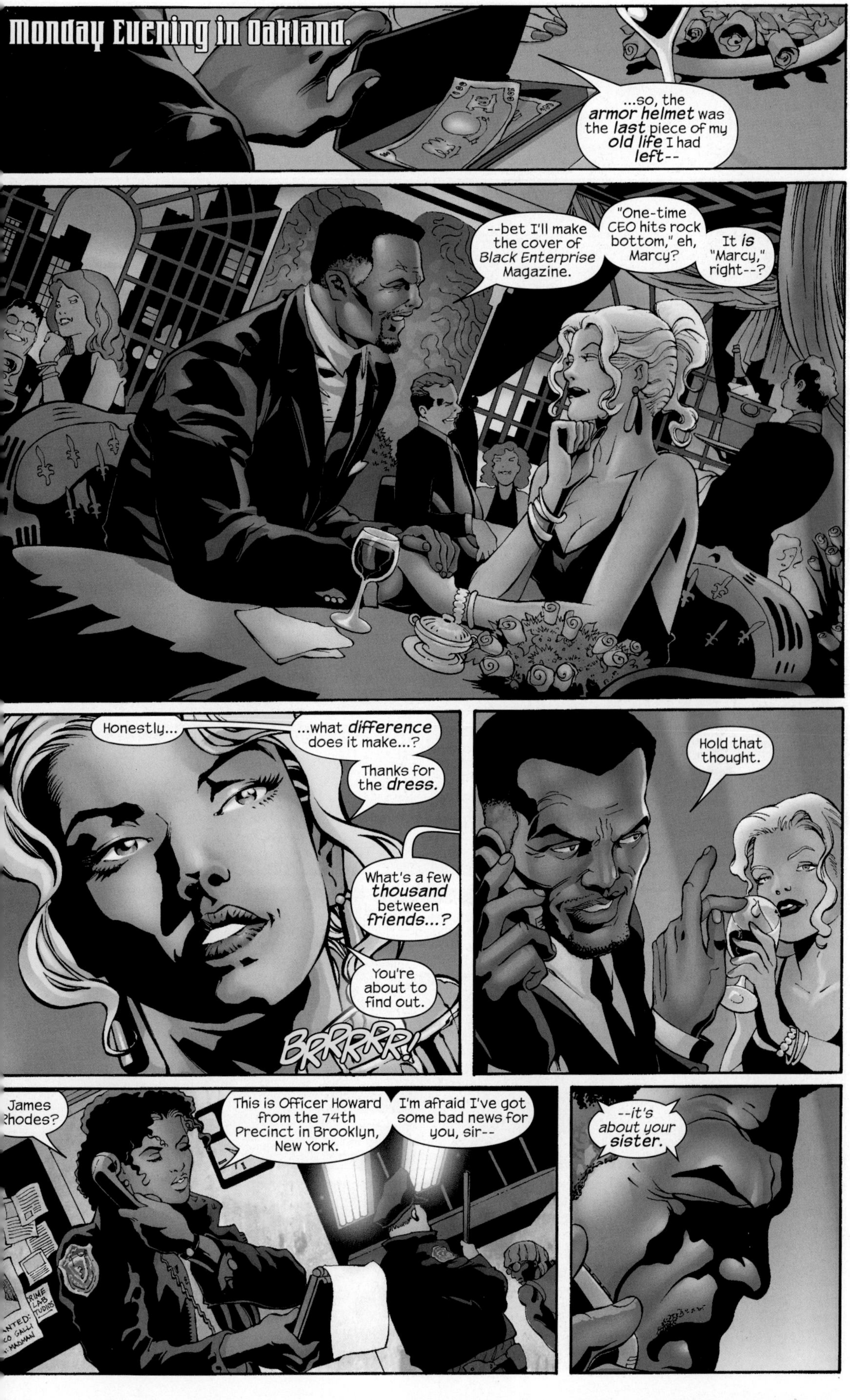
Monday Evening in Oakland.
...so, the armor helmet was the last piece of my old life I had left--
--bet I'll make the cover of Black Enterprise Magazine.
"One-time CEO hits rock bottom," eh, Marcy?
It is "Marcy," right--?
Honestly...
...what difference does it make...?
Thanks for the dress.
What's a few thousand between friends...?
You're about to find out.
BRRRRR!
Hold that thought.
James Rhodes?
This is Officer Howard from the 74th Precinct in Brooklyn, New York.
I'm afraid I've got some bad news for you, sir--
--it's about your sister.

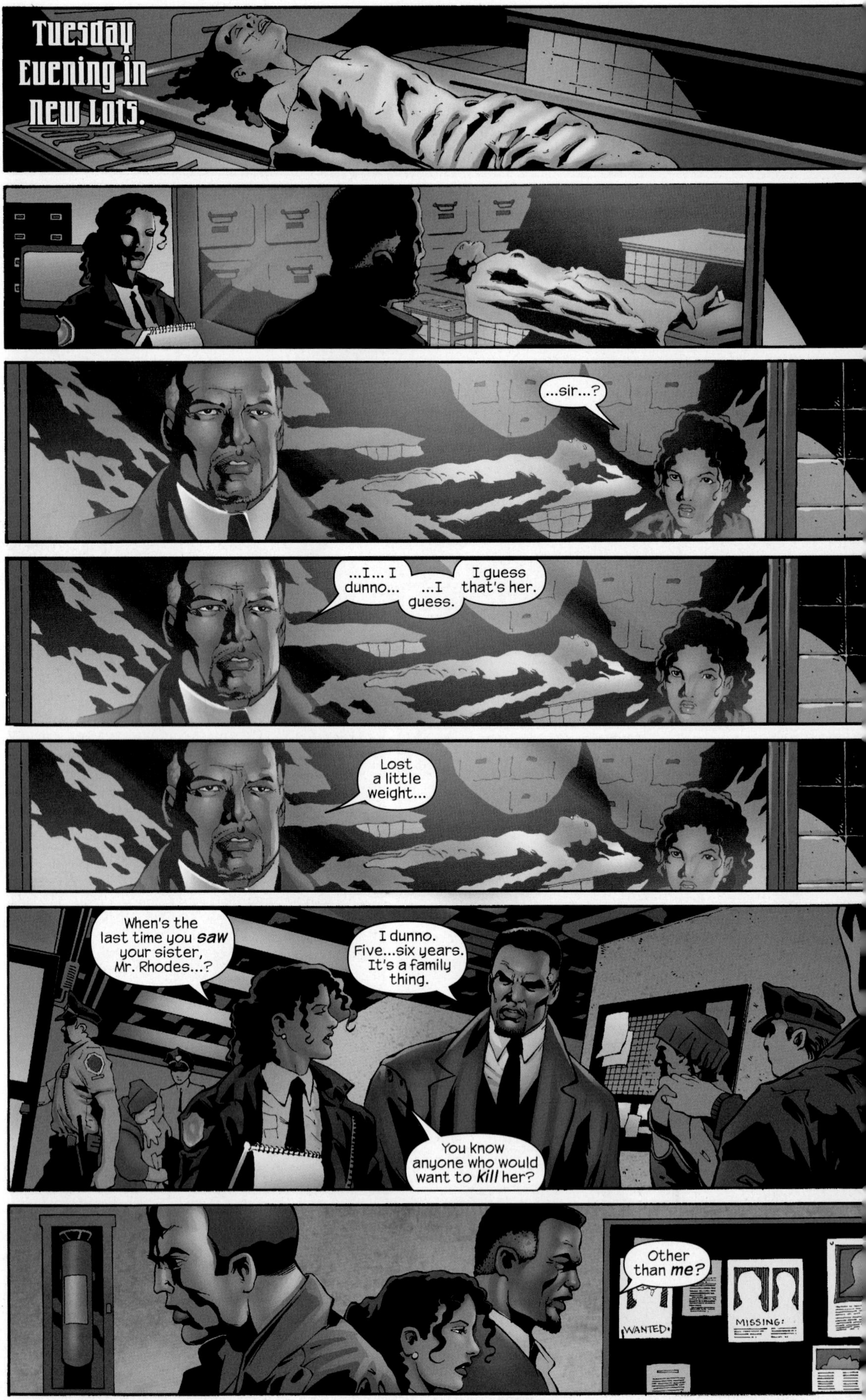
Tuesday Evening in New Lots.
...sir...?
...I... I dunno...
...I guess.
I guess that's her.
Lost a little weight...
When's the last time you saw your sister, Mr. Rhodes...?
I dunno. Five...six years. It's a family thing.
You know anyone who would want to kill her?
Other than me?
WANTED
MISSING:

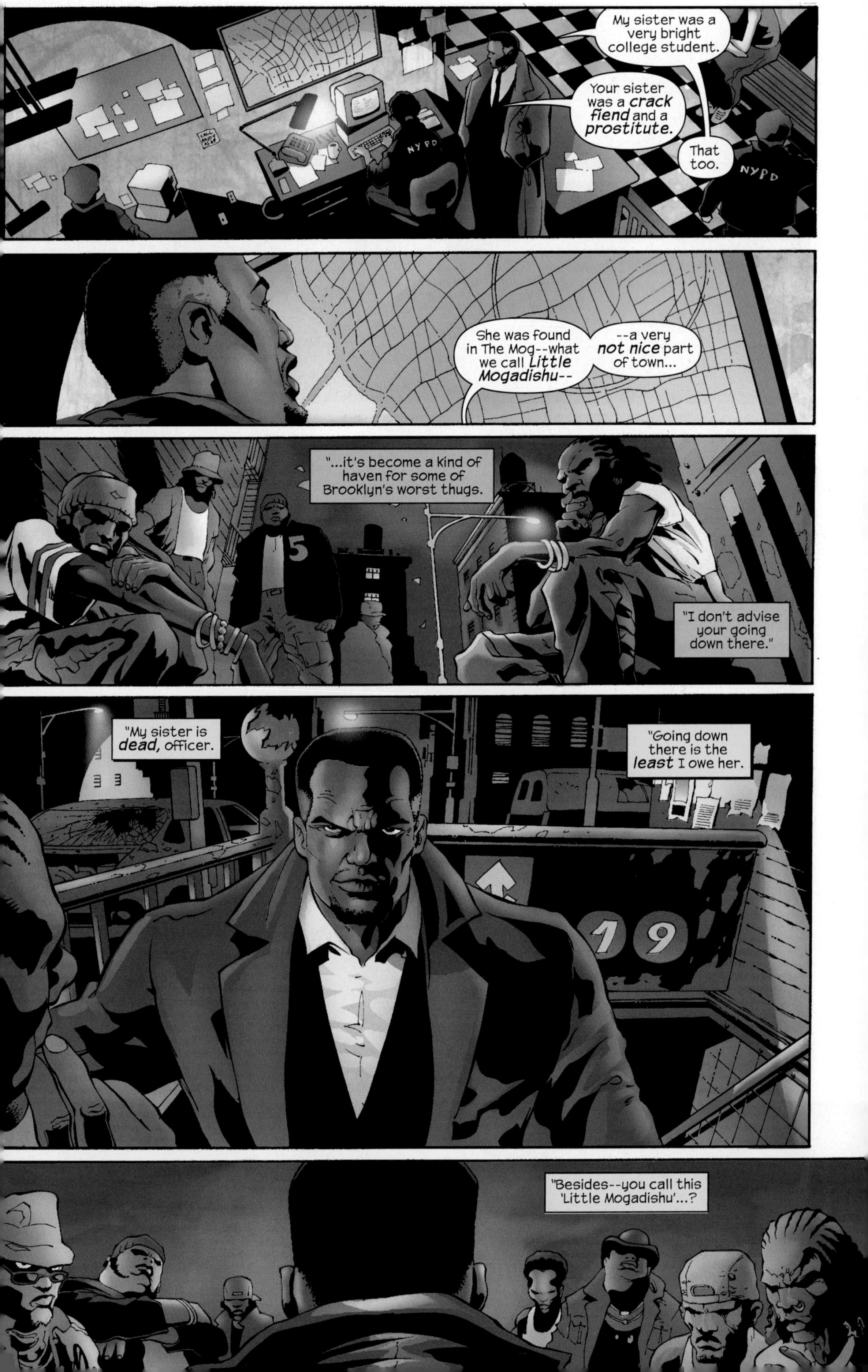
CALL ANDY MAP
My sister was a very bright college student.
Your sister was a crack fiend and a prostitute.
That too.
NYPD
NYPD
She was found in The Mog--what we call Little Mogadishu--
--a very not nice part of town...
"...it's become a kind of haven for some of Brooklyn's worst thugs.
5
"I don't advise your going down there."
"My sister is dead, officer.
"Going down there is the least I owe her.
19
"Besides--you call this 'Little Mogadishu'...?

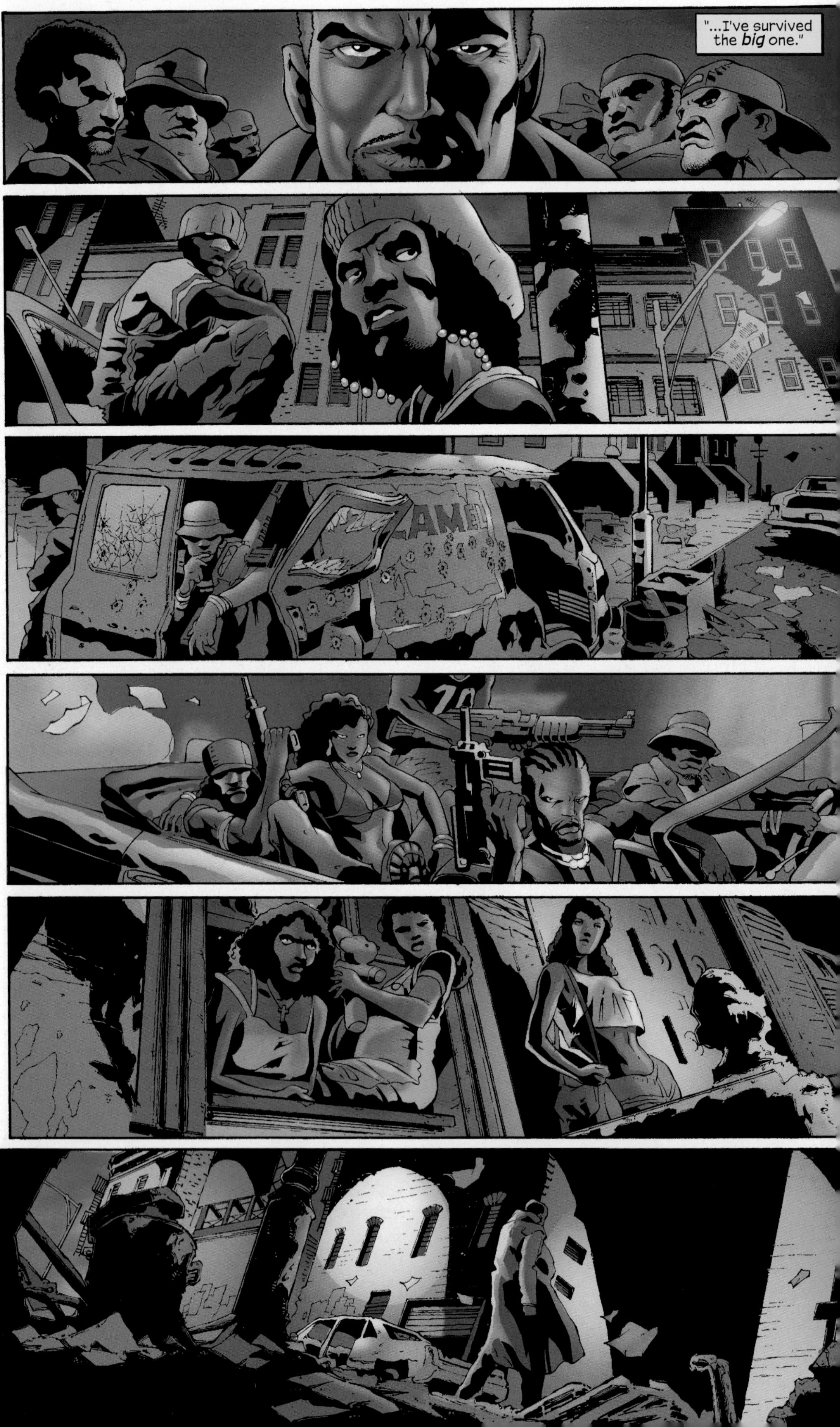
"...I've survived the *big* one."

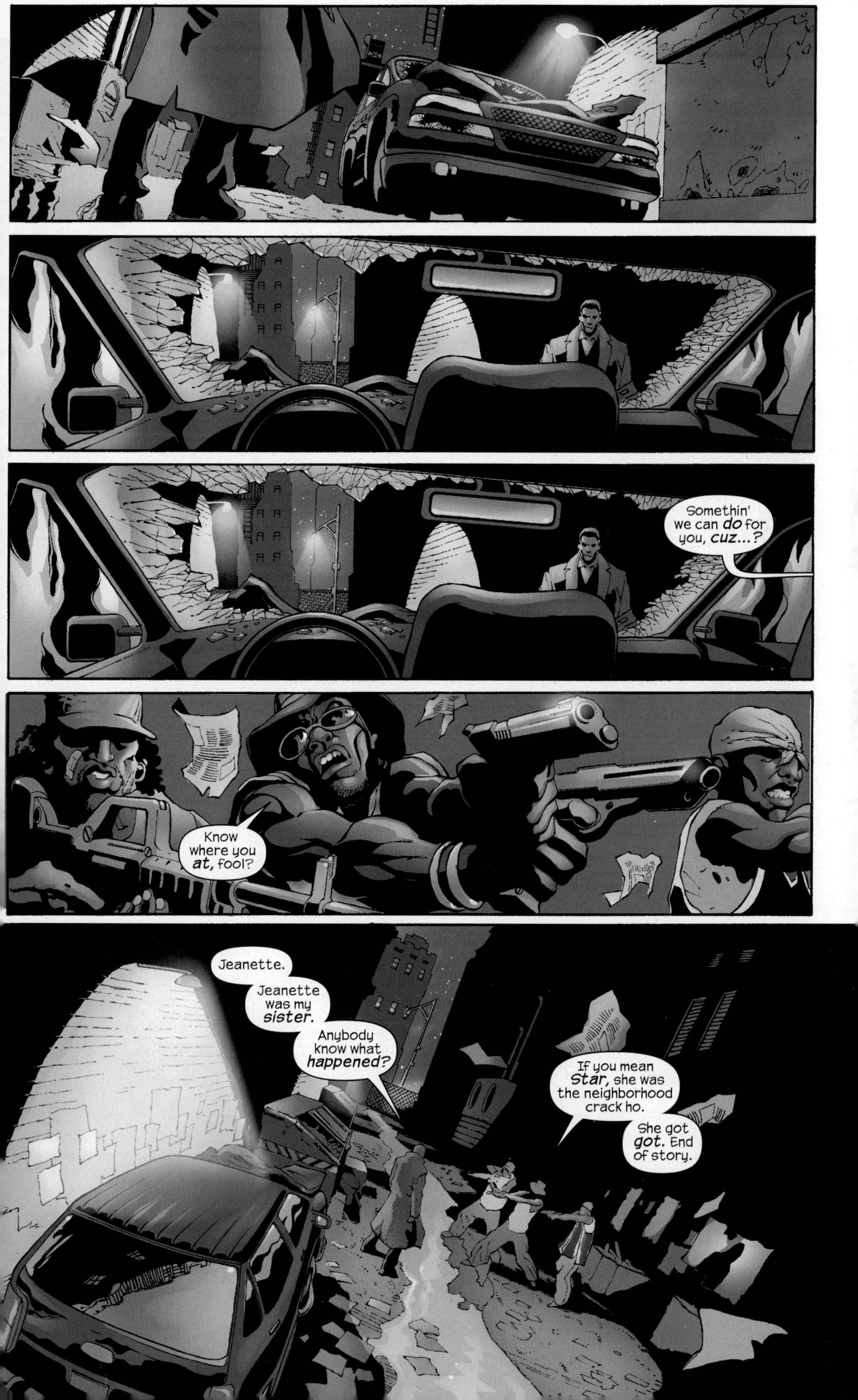
Somethin' we can do for you, cuz...?
Know where you at, fool?
Jeanette.
Jeanette was my sister.
Anybody know what happened?
If you mean Star, she was the neighborhood crack ho.
She got got. End of story.

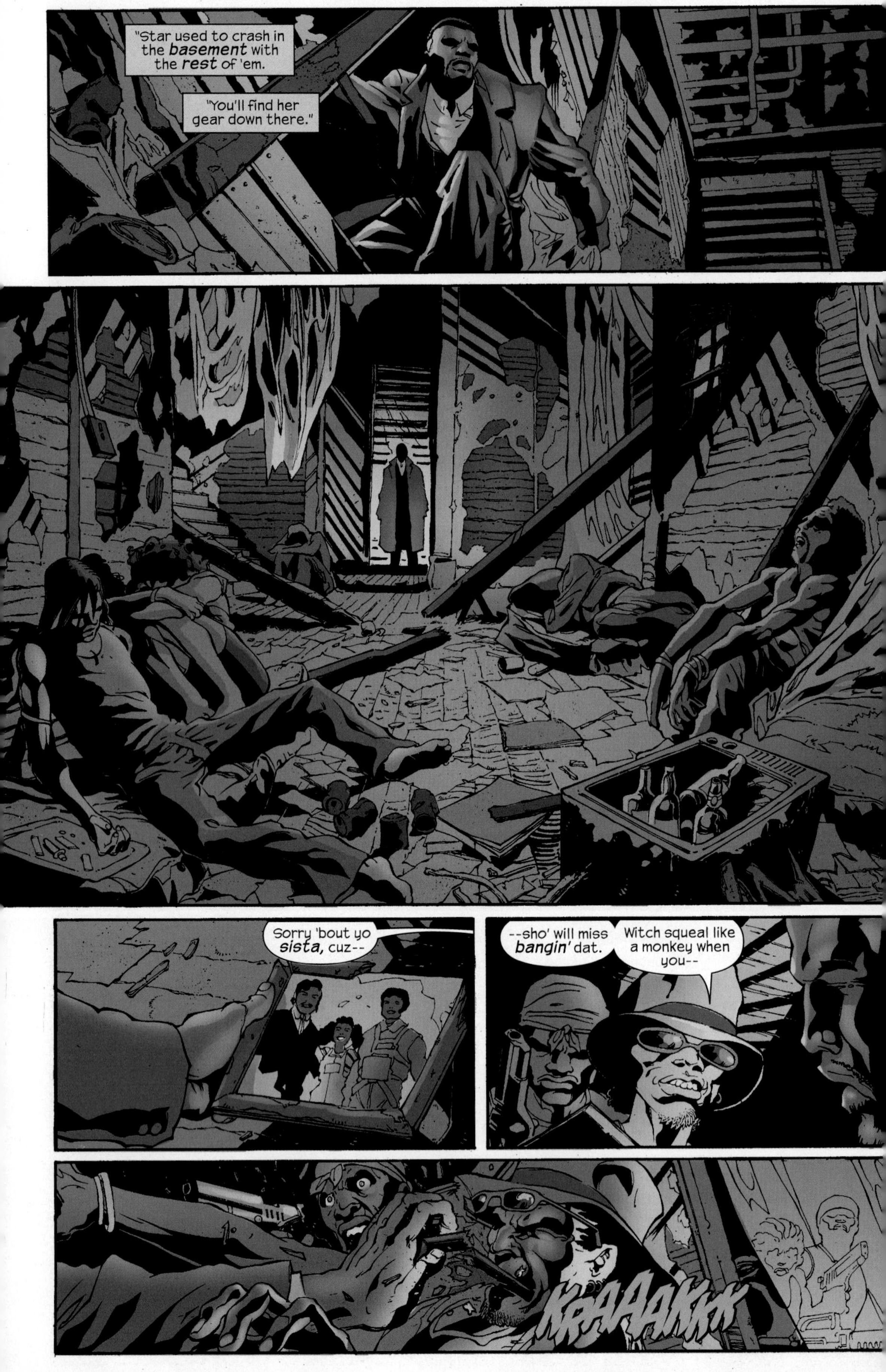
"Star used to crash in the basement with the rest of 'em.
"You'll find her gear down there."
Sorry 'bout yo sista, cuz--
--sho' will miss bangin' dat.
Witch squeal like a monkey when you--
KRAAAKKK

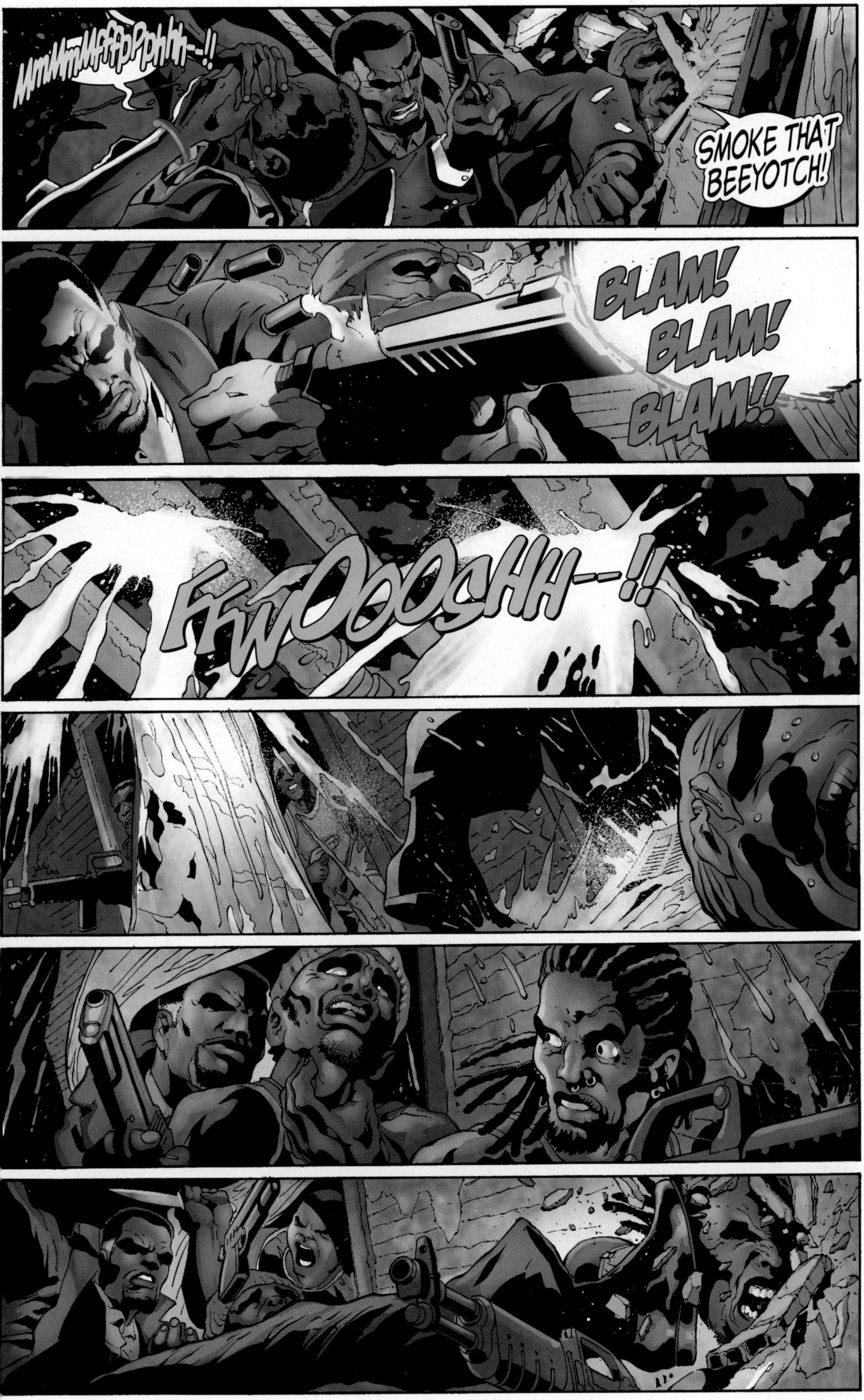
MmMmMffpPphhh--!!
SMOKE THAT BEEYOTCH!
BLAM! BLAM! BLAM!!
FFWOOOSHH--!!

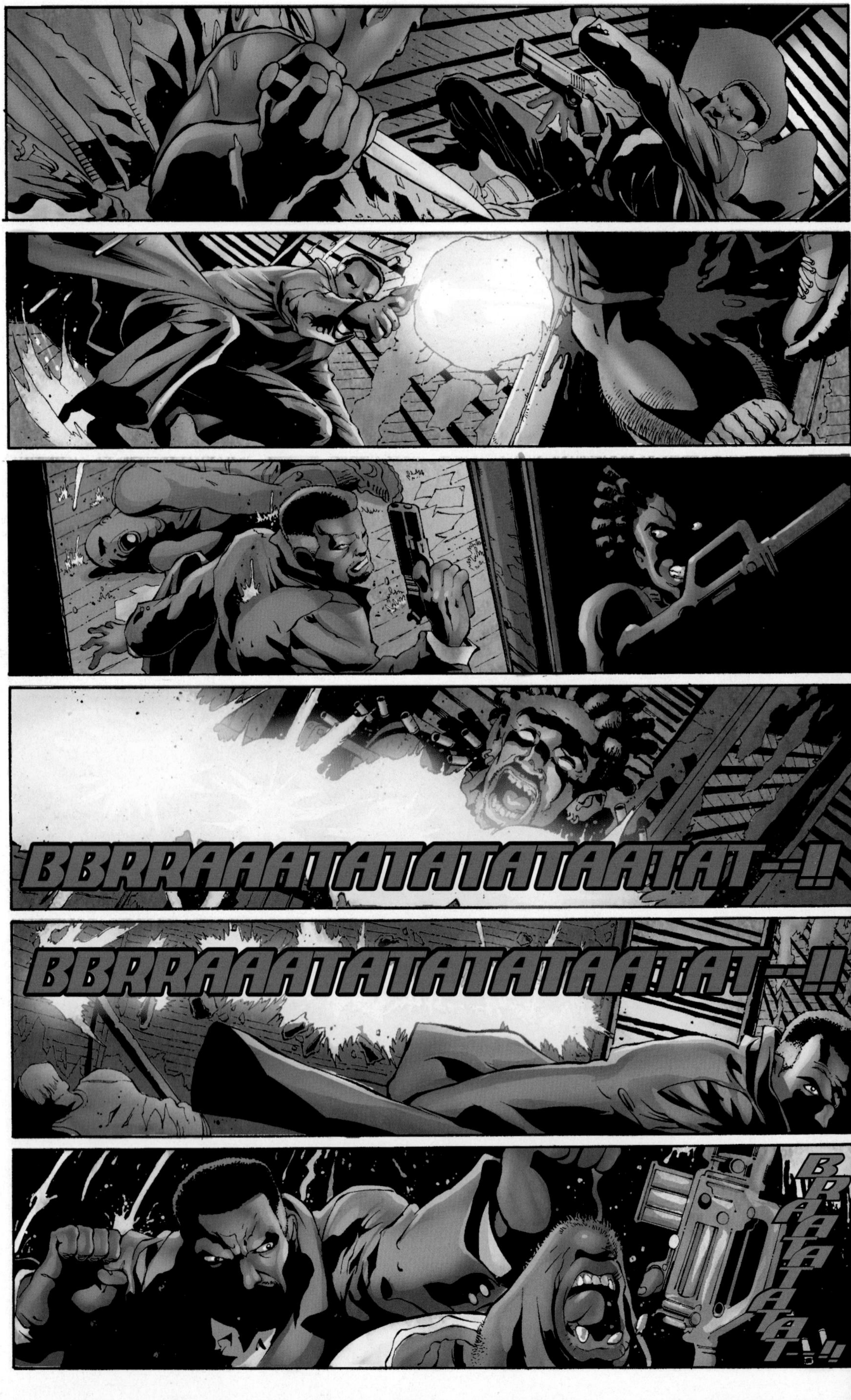
BBRRAAATATATATATAATATAT--!!
BBRRAAATATATATATAATATAT--!!
BRAATATATAT--!!

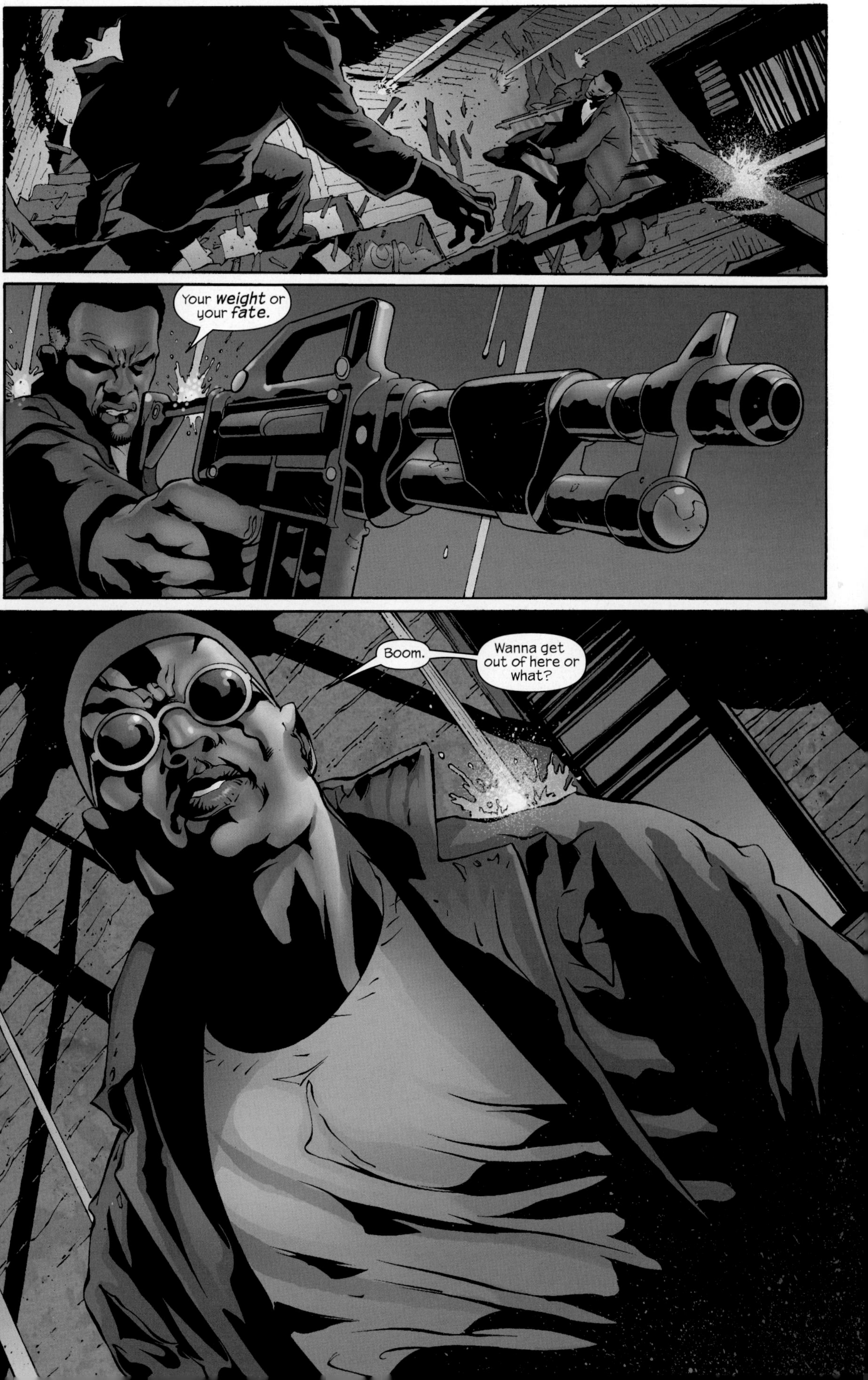
Your weight or your fate.
Boom.
Wanna get out of here or what?

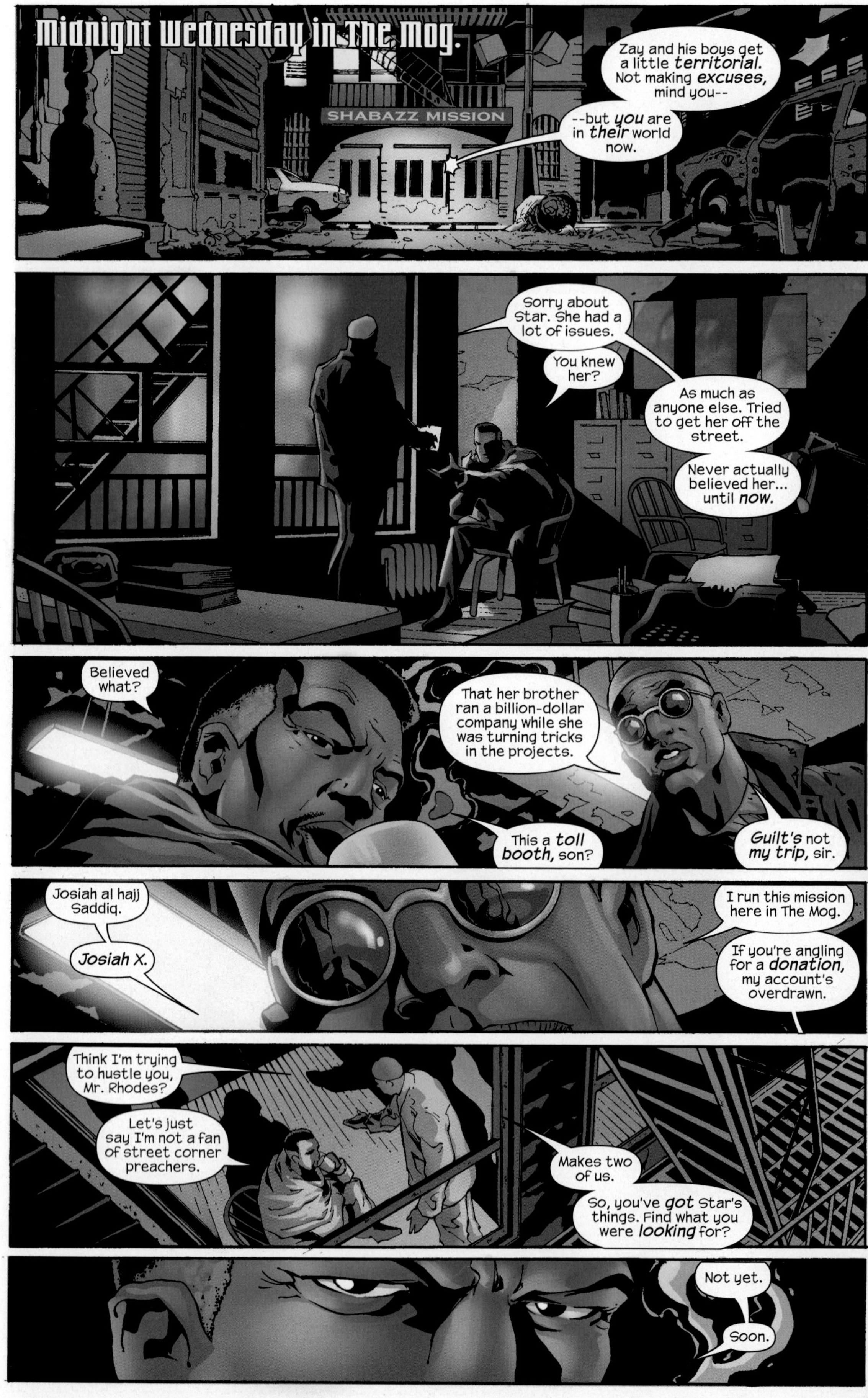
Midnight Wednesday in The Mog.
SHABAZZ MISSION
Zay and his boys get a little territorial. Not making excuses, mind you--
--but you are in their world now.
Sorry about Star. She had a lot of issues.
You knew her?
As much as anyone else. Tried to get her off the street.
Never actually believed her... until now.
Believed what?
That her brother ran a billion-dollar company while she was turning tricks in the projects.
This a toll booth, son?
Guilt's not my trip, sir.
Josiah al hajj Saddiq.
Josiah X.
I run this mission here in The Mog.
If you're angling for a donation, my account's overdrawn.
Think I'm trying to hustle you, Mr. Rhodes?
Let's just say I'm not a fan of street corner preachers.
Makes two of us.
So, you've got Star's things. Find what you were looking for?
Not yet.
Soon.

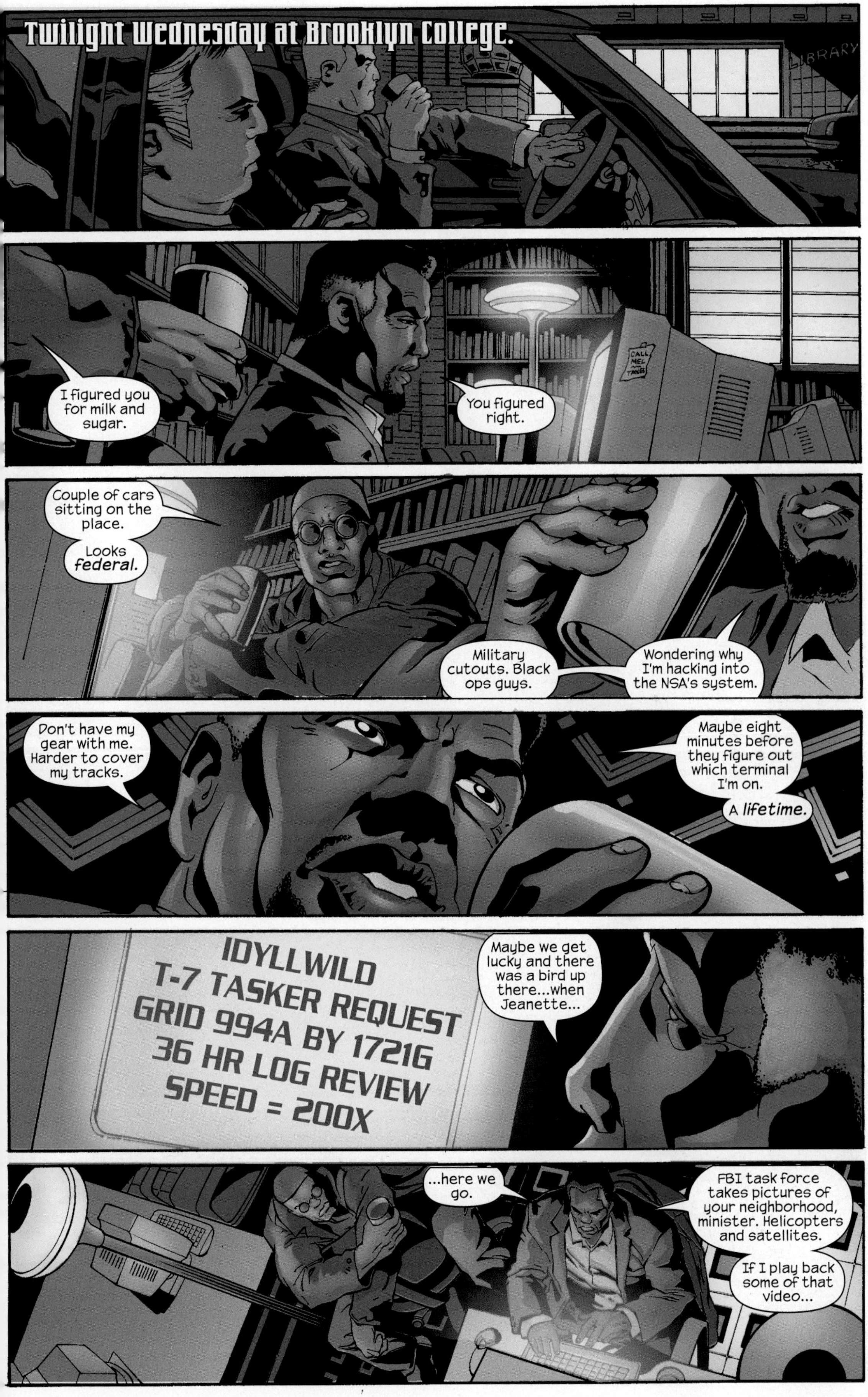
Twilight Wednesday at Brooklyn College.
LIBRARY
I figured you for milk and sugar.
You figured right.
CALL MEL TAKES
Couple of cars sitting on the place.
Looks *federal.*
Military cutouts. Black ops guys.
Wondering why I'm hacking into the NSA's system.
Don't have my gear with me. Harder to cover my tracks.
Maybe eight minutes before they figure out which terminal I'm on.
A *lifetime.*
IDYLLWILD
T-7 TASKER REQUEST
GRID 994A BY 1721G
36 HR LOG REVIEW
SPEED = 200X
Maybe we get lucky and there was a bird up there...when Jeanette...
...here we go.
FBI task force takes pictures of your neighborhood, minister. Helicopters and satellites.
If I play back some of that video...

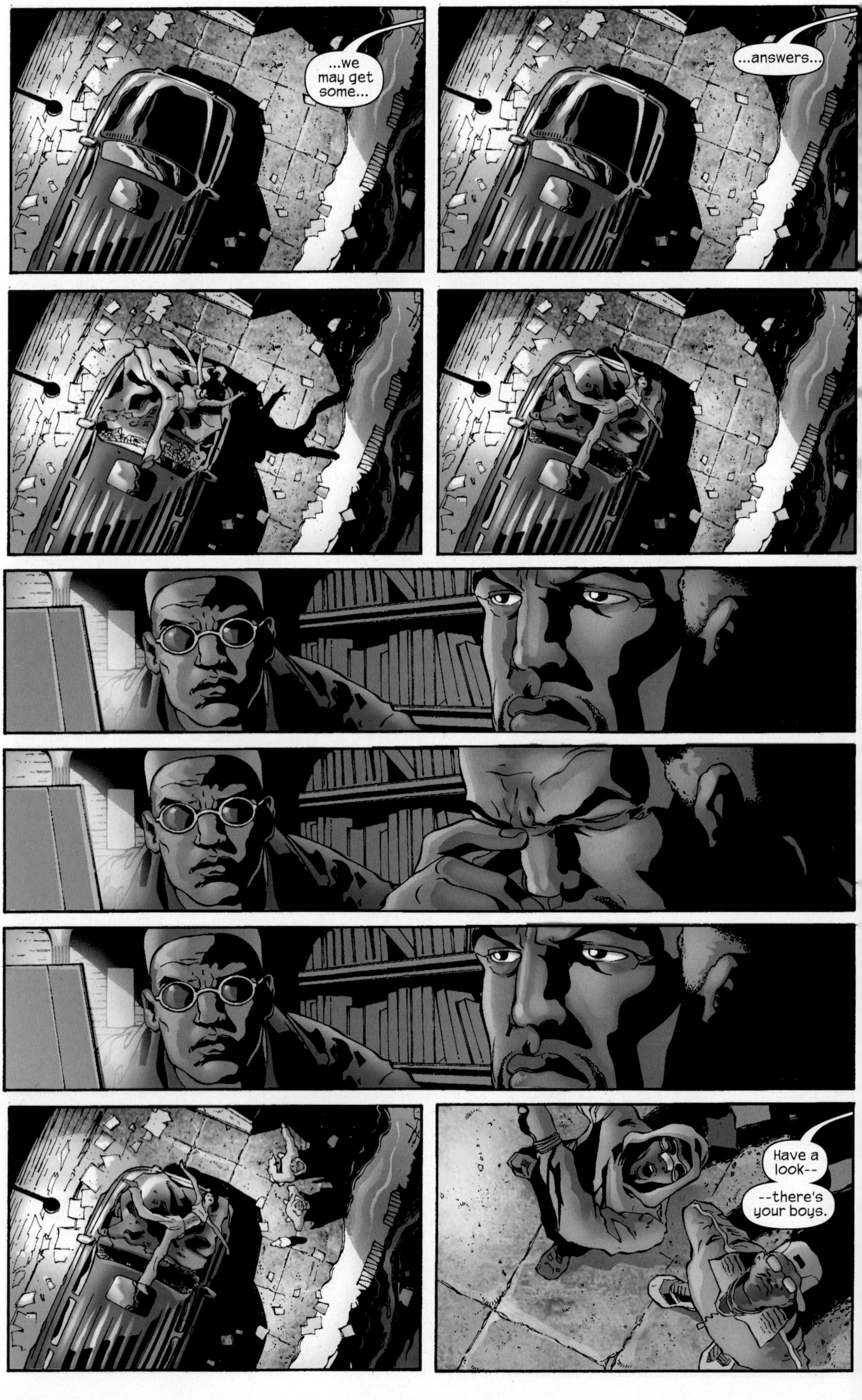
...we may get some...
...answers...
Have a look--
--there's your boys.

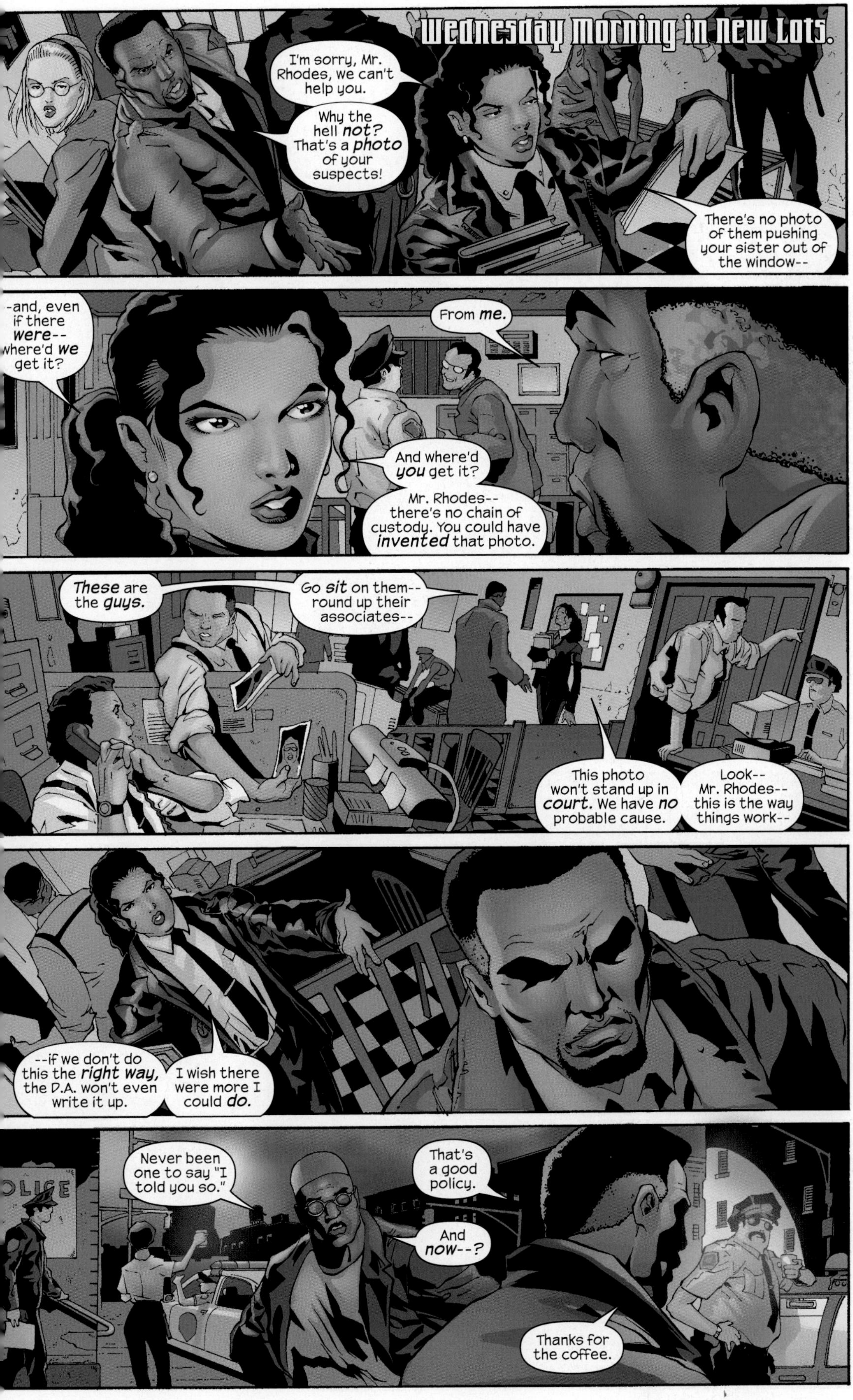
Wednesday Morning in New Lots.
I'm sorry, Mr. Rhodes, we can't help you.
Why the hell *not?* That's a *photo* of your suspects!
There's no photo of them pushing your sister out of the window--
-and, even if there *were*-- where'd *we* get it?
From *me.*
And where'd *you* get it?
Mr. Rhodes-- there's no chain of custody. You could have *invented* that photo.
These are the *guys.*
Go *sit* on them-- round up their associates--
This photo won't stand up in *court.* We have *no* probable cause.
Look-- Mr. Rhodes-- this is the way things work--
--if we don't do this the *right way,* the D.A. won't even write it up.
I wish there were more I could *do.*
OLICE
Never been one to say "I told you so."
That's a good policy.
And *now--?*
Thanks for the coffee.

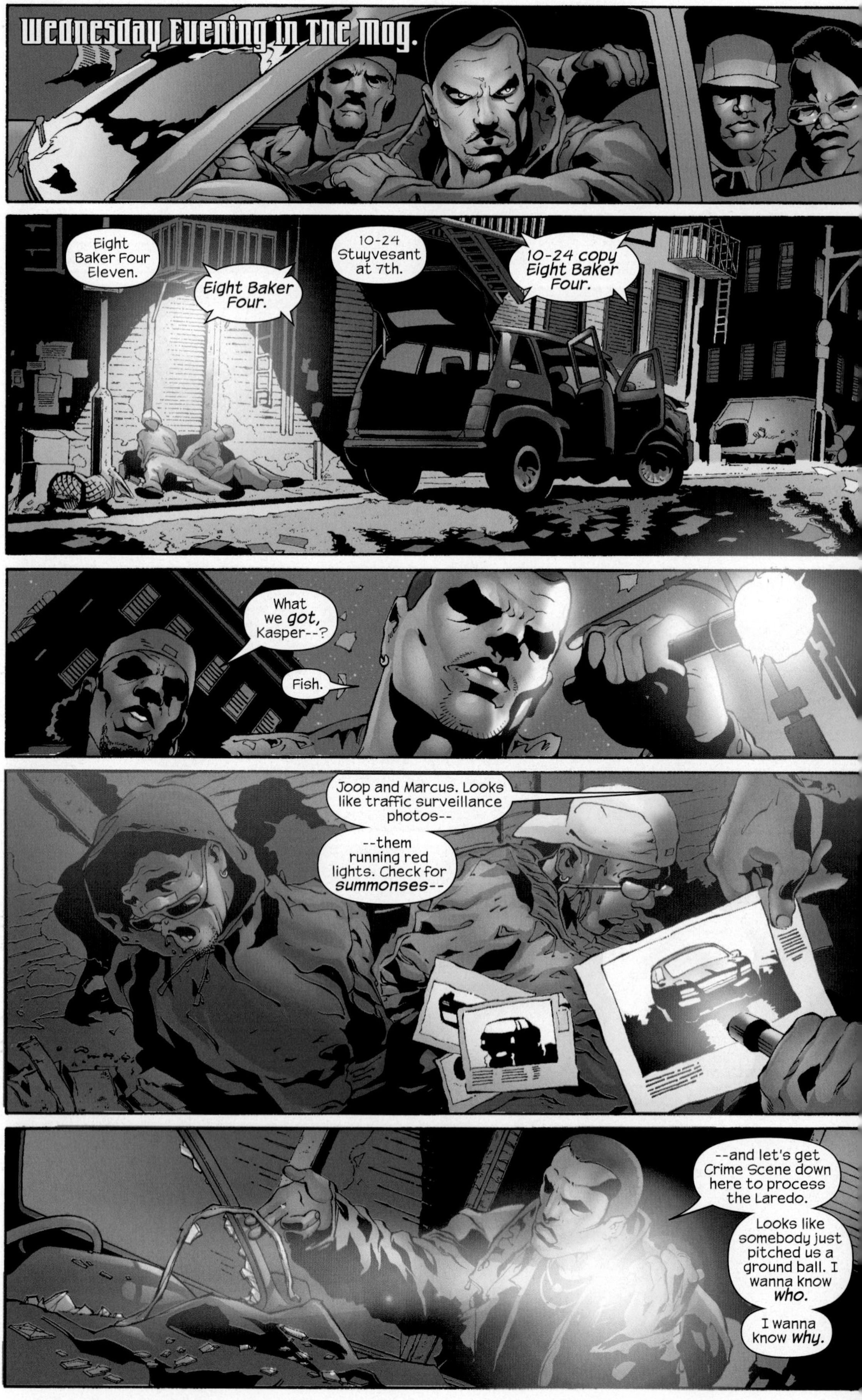
Wednesday Evening in The Mog.
Eight Baker Four Eleven.
Eight Baker Four.
10-24 Stuyvesant at 7th.
10-24 copy Eight Baker Four.
What we got, Kasper--?
Fish.
Joop and Marcus. Looks like traffic surveillance photos--
--them running red lights. Check for summonses--
--and let's get Crime Scene down here to process the Laredo.
Looks like somebody just pitched us a ground ball. I wanna know who.
I wanna know why.

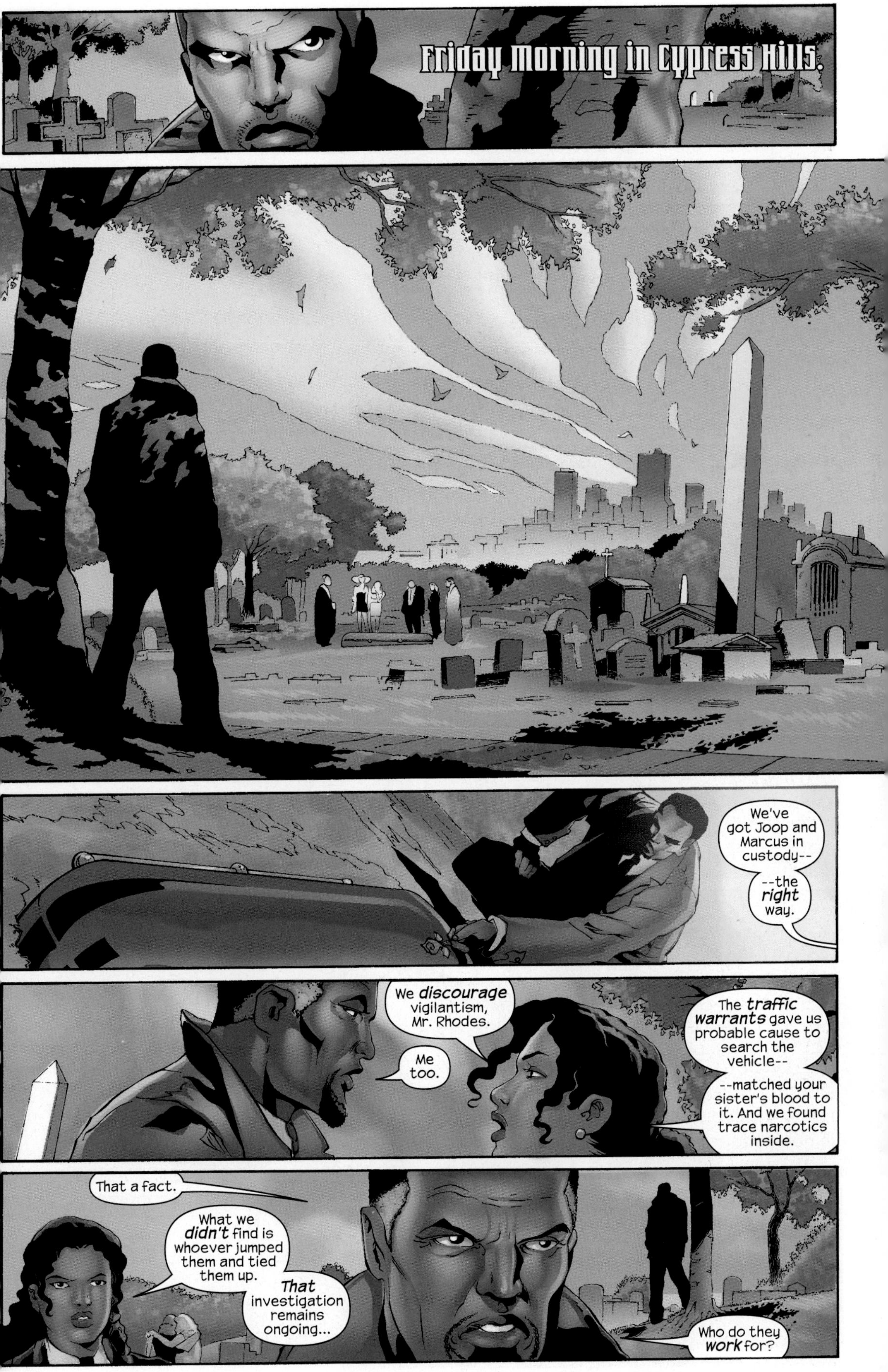
Friday Morning in Cypress Hills.
We've got Joop and Marcus in custody--
--the right way.
We discourage vigilantism, Mr. Rhodes.
Me too.
The traffic warrants gave us probable cause to search the vehicle--
--matched your sister's blood to it. And we found trace narcotics inside.
That a fact.
What we didn't find is whoever jumped them and tied them up.
That investigation remains ongoing...
Who do they work for?

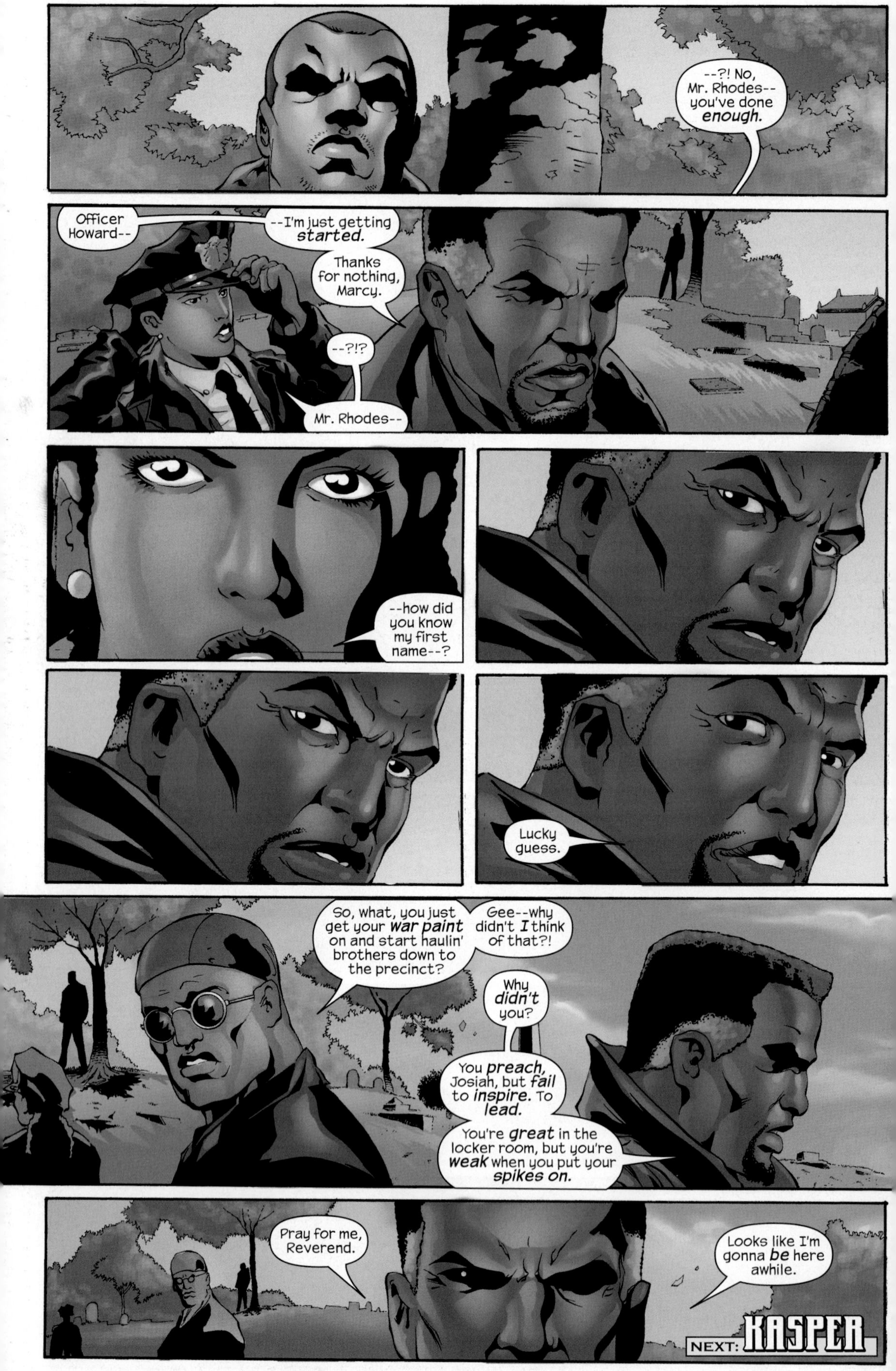
--?! No, Mr. Rhodes-- you've done *enough.*
Officer Howard--
--I'm just getting *started.*
Thanks for nothing, Marcy.
--?!?
Mr. Rhodes--
--how did you know my first name--?
Lucky guess.
So, what, you just get your *war paint* on and start haulin' brothers down to the precinct?
Gee--why didn't *I* think of that?!
Why *didn't* you?
You *preach,* Josiah, but *fail* to *inspire.* To *lead.*
You're *great* in the locker room, but you're *weak* when you put your *spikes on.*
Pray for me, Reverend.
Looks like I'm gonna *be* here awhile.
NEXT: KASPER

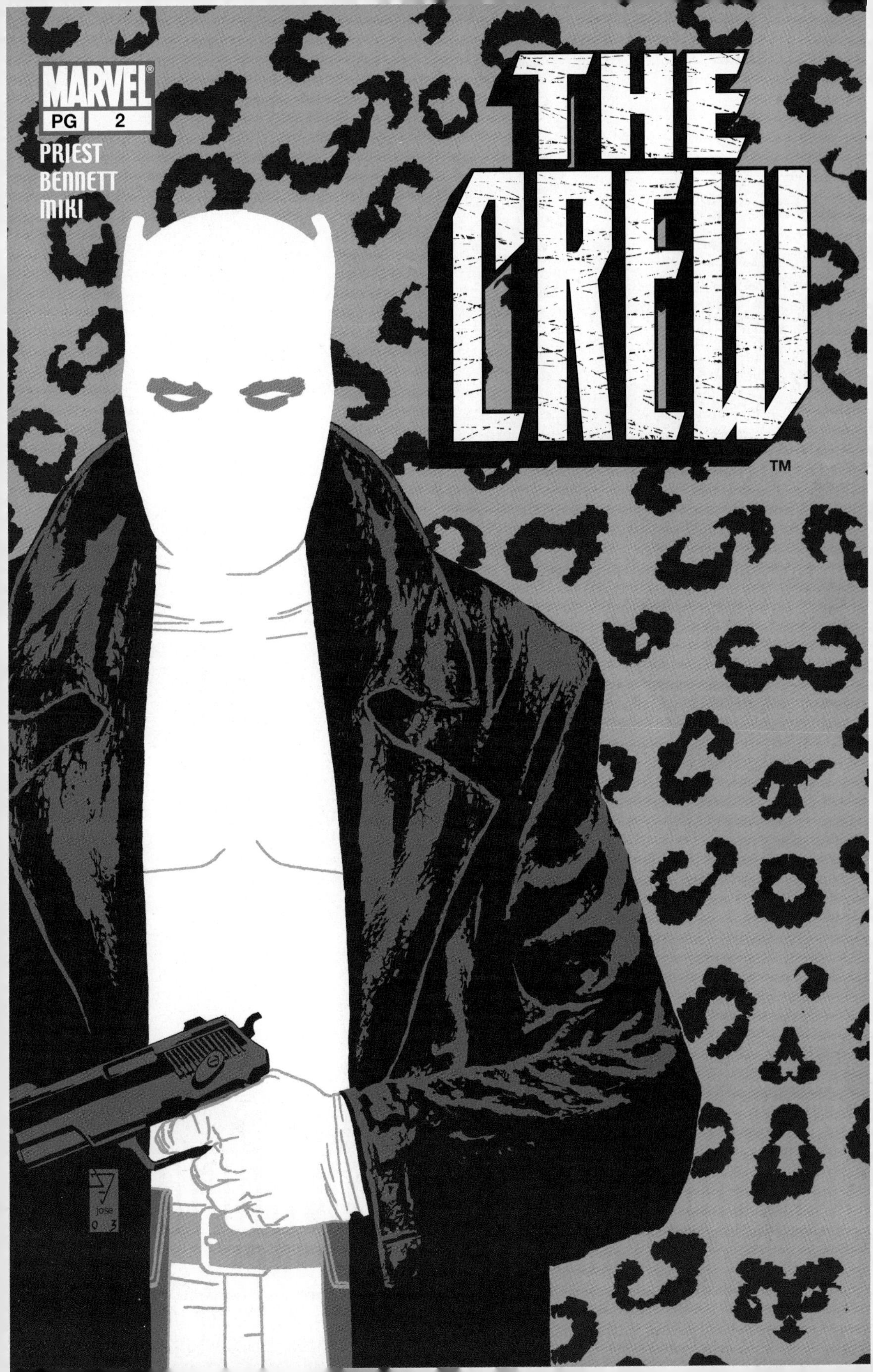
MARVEL
PG 2
PRIEST
BENNETT
MIKI
THE CREW
TM
jose
03

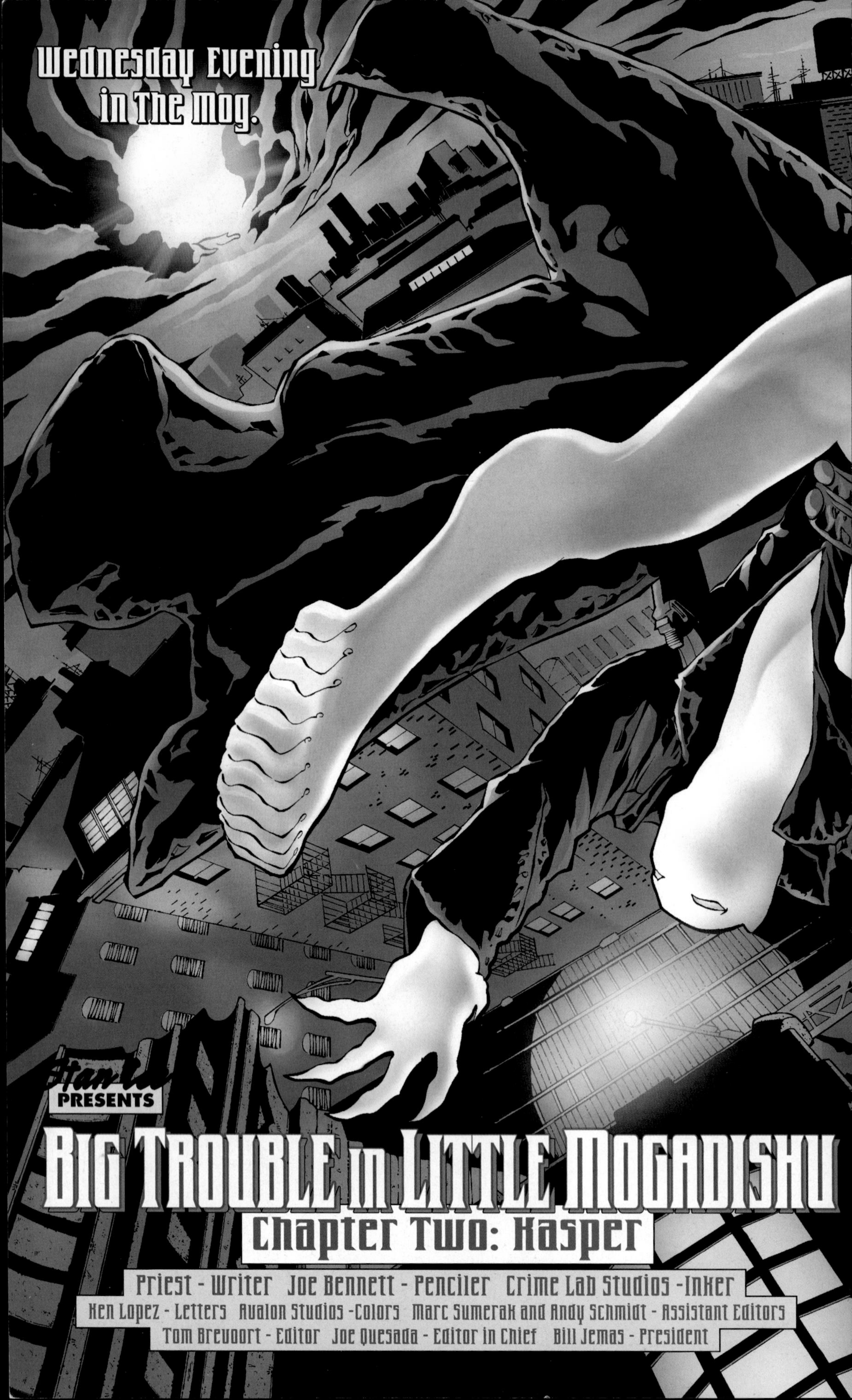
Wednesday Evening in The Mog.
Stan Lee PRESENTS
BIG TROUBLE in LITTLE MOGADISHU
Chapter Two: Kasper
Priest - Writer Joe Bennett - Penciler Crime Lab Studios - Inker
Ken Lopez - Letters Avalon Studios - Colors Marc Sumerak and Andy Schmidt - Assistant Editors
Tom Brevoort - Editor Joe Quesada - Editor in Chief Bill Jemas - President

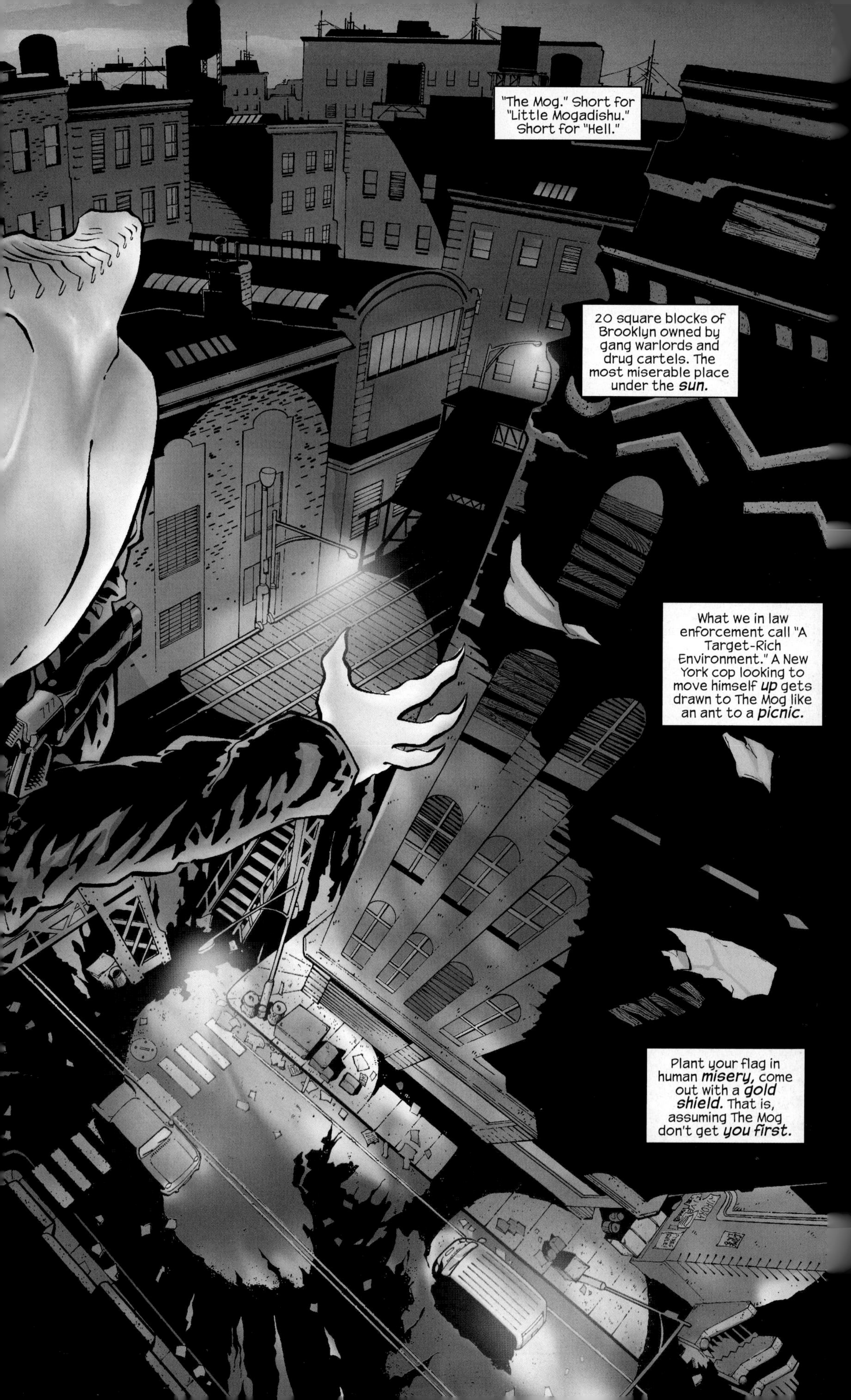
"The Mog." Short for "Little Mogadishu." Short for "Hell."
20 square blocks of Brooklyn owned by gang warlords and drug cartels. The most miserable place under the *sun.*
What we in law enforcement call "A Target-Rich Environment." A New York cop looking to move himself *up* gets drawn to The Mog like an ant to a *picnic.*
Plant your flag in human *misery,* come out with a *gold shield.* That is, assuming The Mog don't get *you first.*

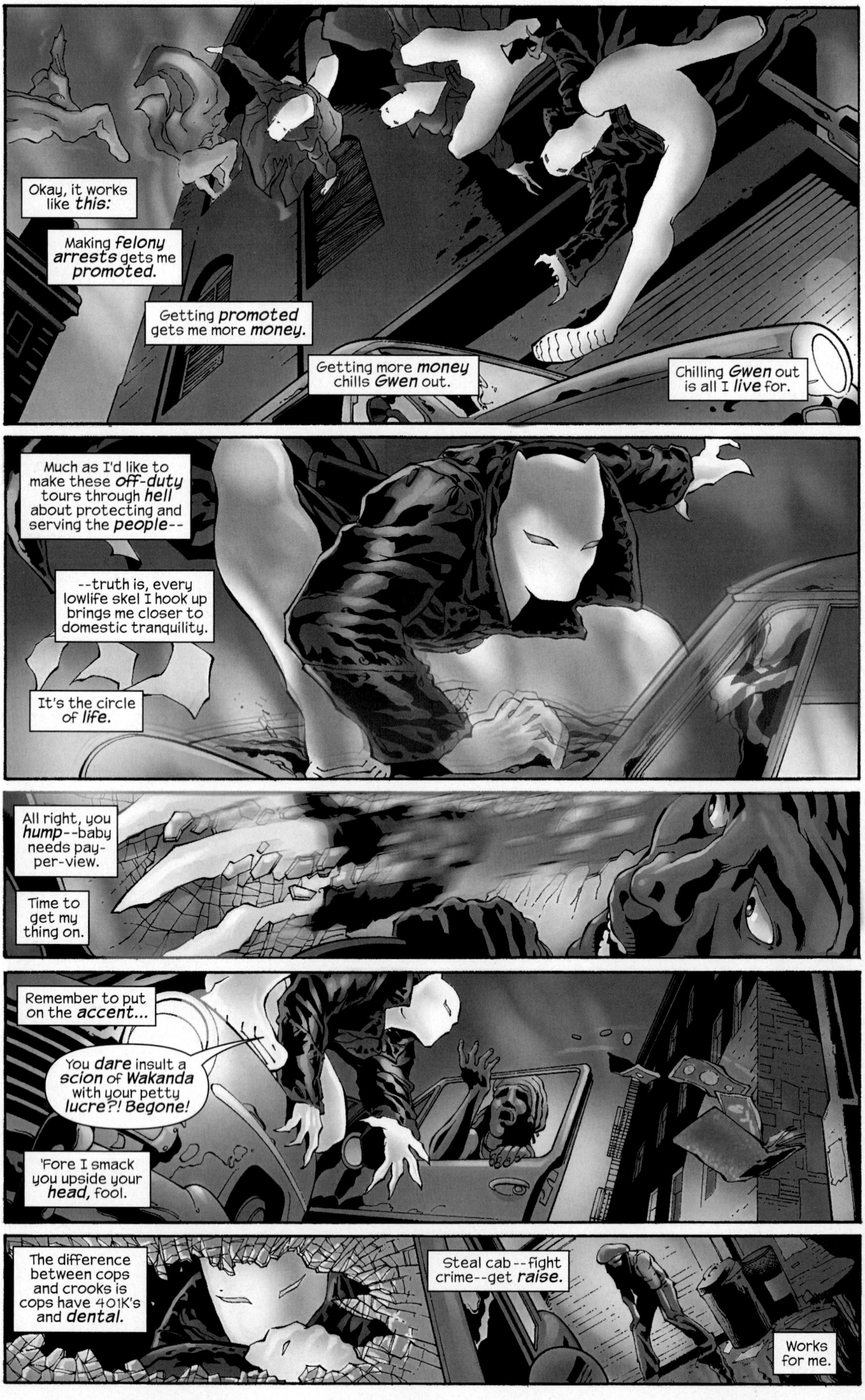
Okay, it works like this:
Making felony arrests gets me promoted.
Getting promoted gets me more money.
Getting more money chills Gwen out.
Chilling Gwen out is all I live for.
Much as I'd like to make these off-duty tours through hell about protecting and serving the people--
--truth is, every lowlife skel I hook up brings me closer to domestic tranquility.
It's the circle of life.
All right, you hump--baby needs pay-per-view.
Time to get my thing on.
Remember to put on the accent...
You dare insult a scion of Wakanda with your petty lucre?! Begone!
'Fore I smack you upside your head, fool.
The difference between cops and crooks is cops have 401K's and dental.
Steal cab--fight crime--get raise.
Works for me.

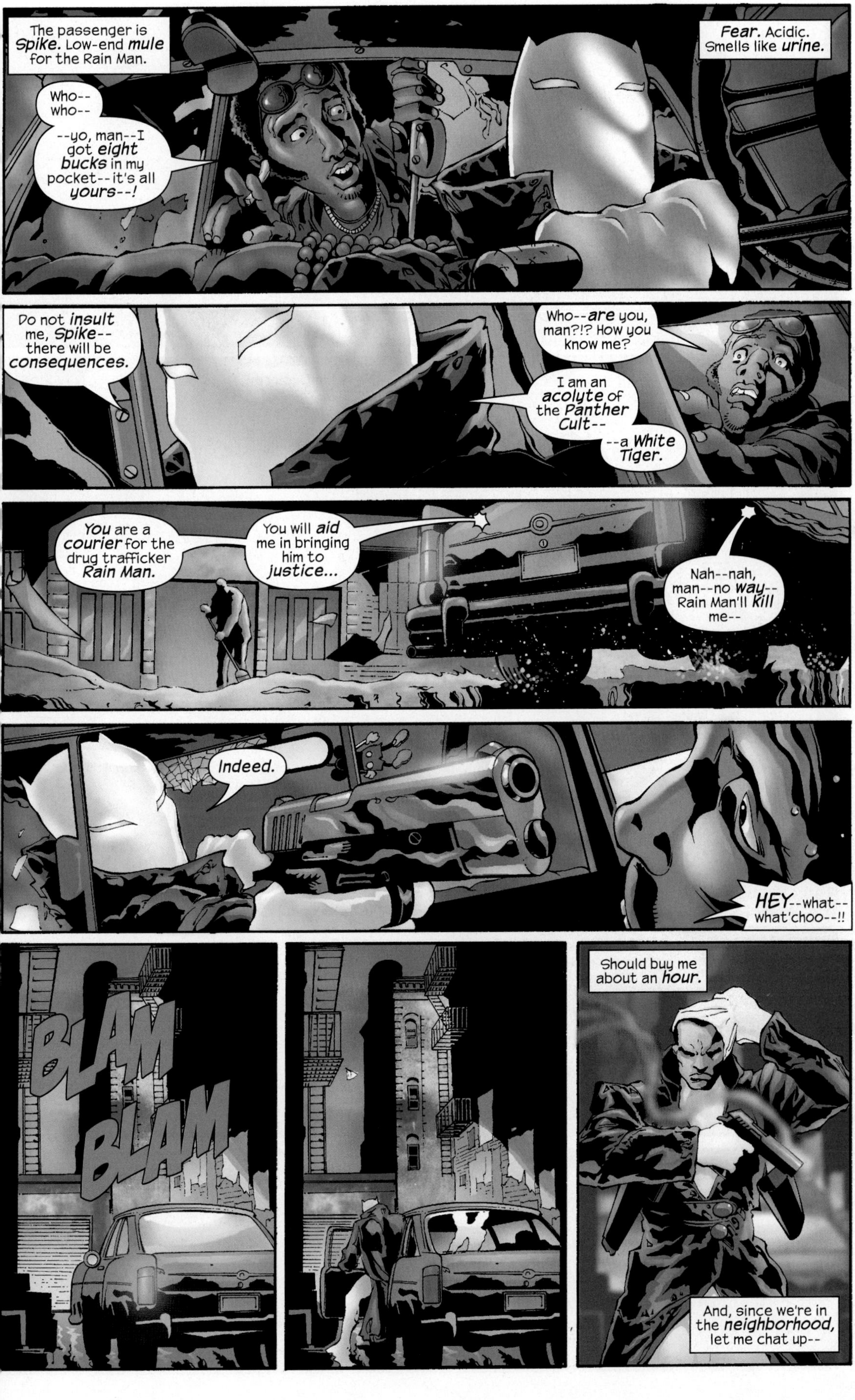

The passenger is Spike. Low-end mule for the Rain Man.
Fear. Acidic. Smells like urine.
Who-- who--
--yo, man--I got eight bucks in my pocket--it's all yours--!
Do not insult me, Spike--there will be consequences.
Who--are you, man?!? How you know me?
I am an acolyte of the Panther Cult--
--a White Tiger.
You are a courier for the drug trafficker Rain Man.
You will aid me in bringing him to justice...
Nah--nah, man--no way--Rain Man'll kill me--
Indeed.
HEY--what--what'choo--!!
BLAM
BLAM
Should buy me about an hour.
And, since we're in the neighborhood, let me chat up--

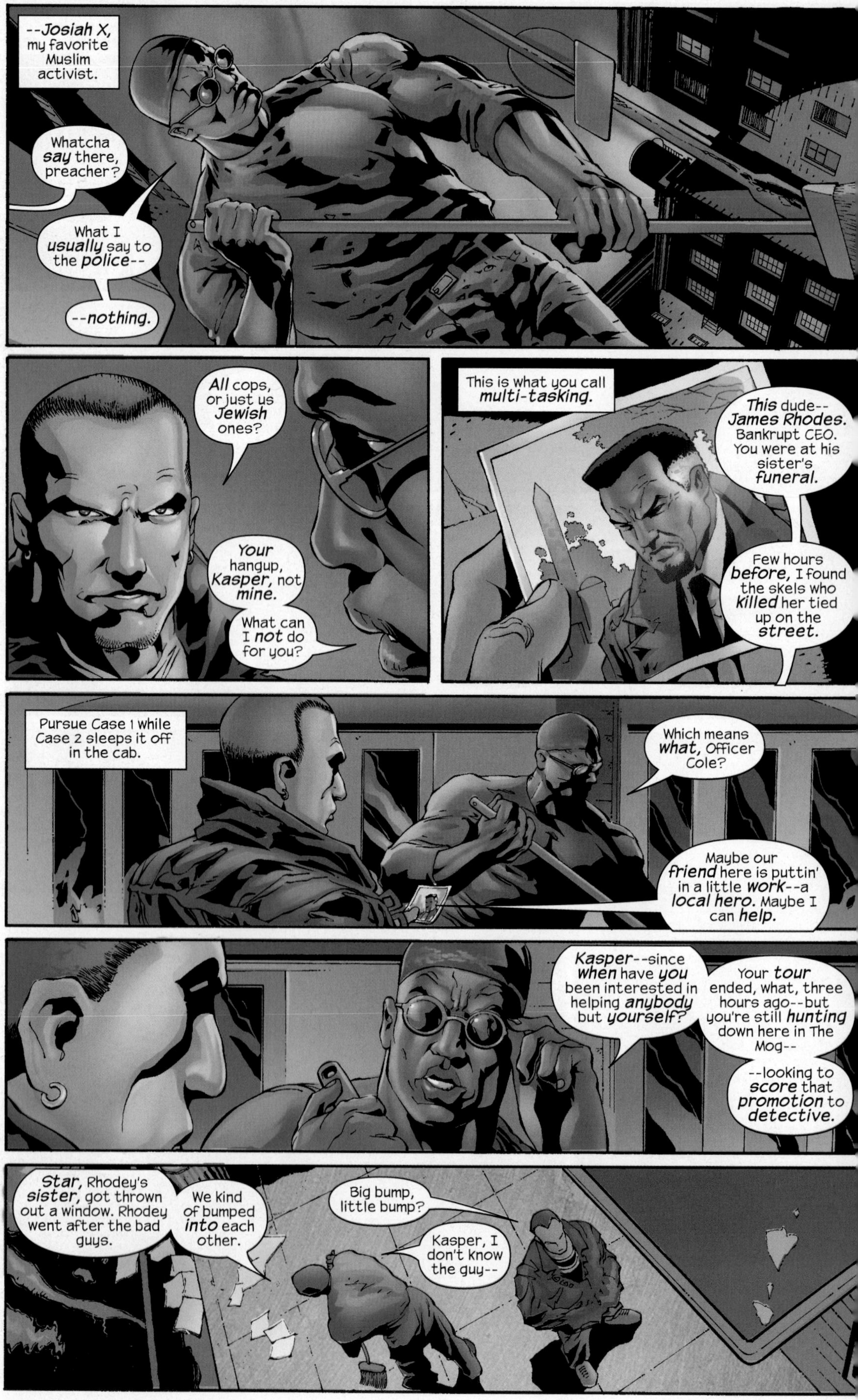
--Josiah X, my favorite Muslim activist.
Whatcha say there, preacher?
What I usually say to the police--
--nothing.
All cops, or just us Jewish ones?
Your hangup, Kasper, not mine.
What can I not do for you?
This is what you call multi-tasking.
This dude-- James Rhodes. Bankrupt CEO. You were at his sister's funeral.
Few hours before, I found the skels who killed her tied up on the street.
Pursue Case 1 while Case 2 sleeps it off in the cab.
Which means what, Officer Cole?
Maybe our friend here is puttin' in a little work--a local hero. Maybe I can help.
Kasper--since when have you been interested in helping anybody but yourself?
Your tour ended, what, three hours ago--but you're still hunting down here in The Mog--
--looking to score that promotion to detective.
Star, Rhodey's sister, got thrown out a window. Rhodey went after the bad guys.
We kind of bumped into each other.
Big bump, little bump?
Kasper, I don't know the guy--

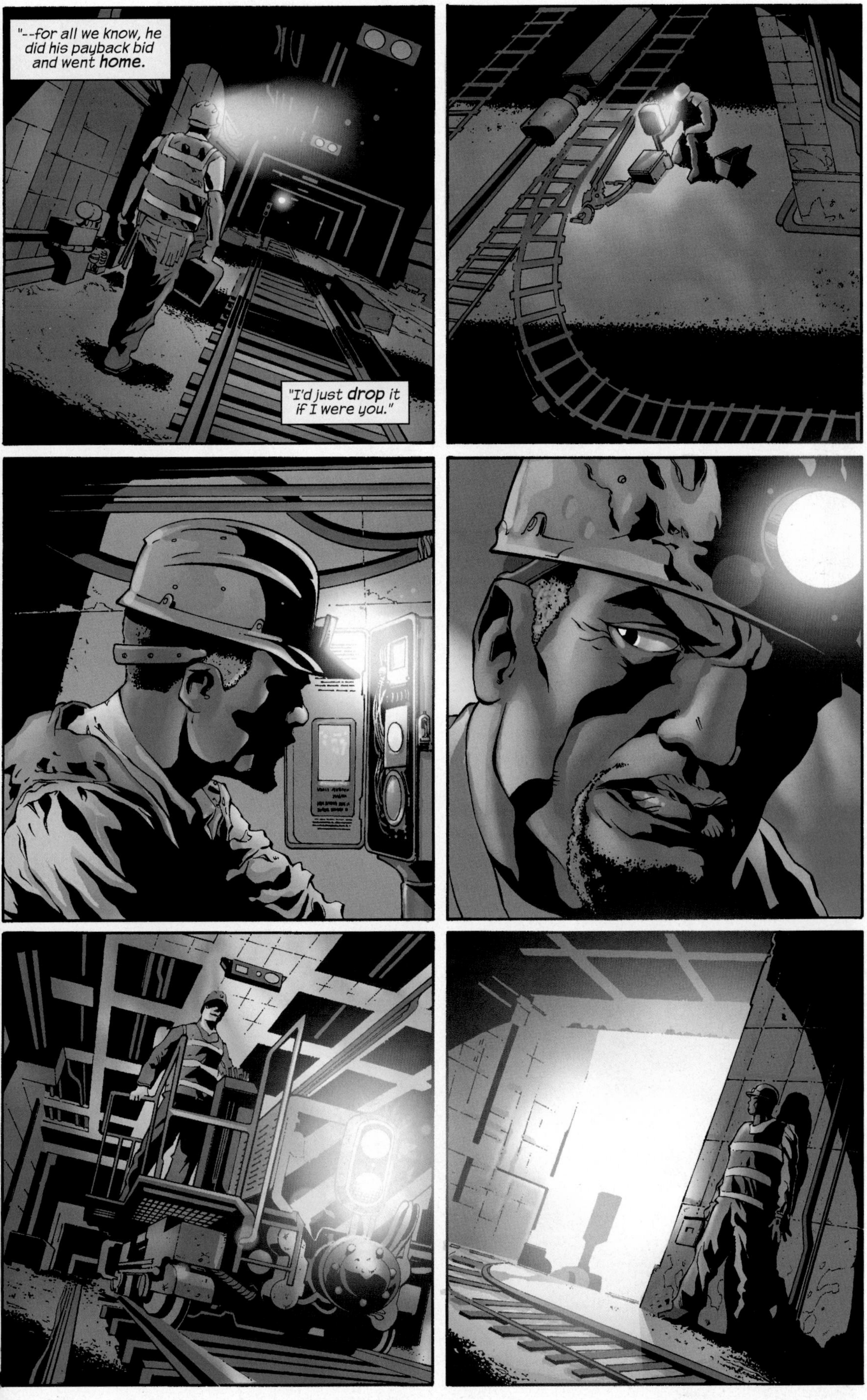
"--for all we know, he did his payback bid and went home.
"I'd just drop it if I were you."

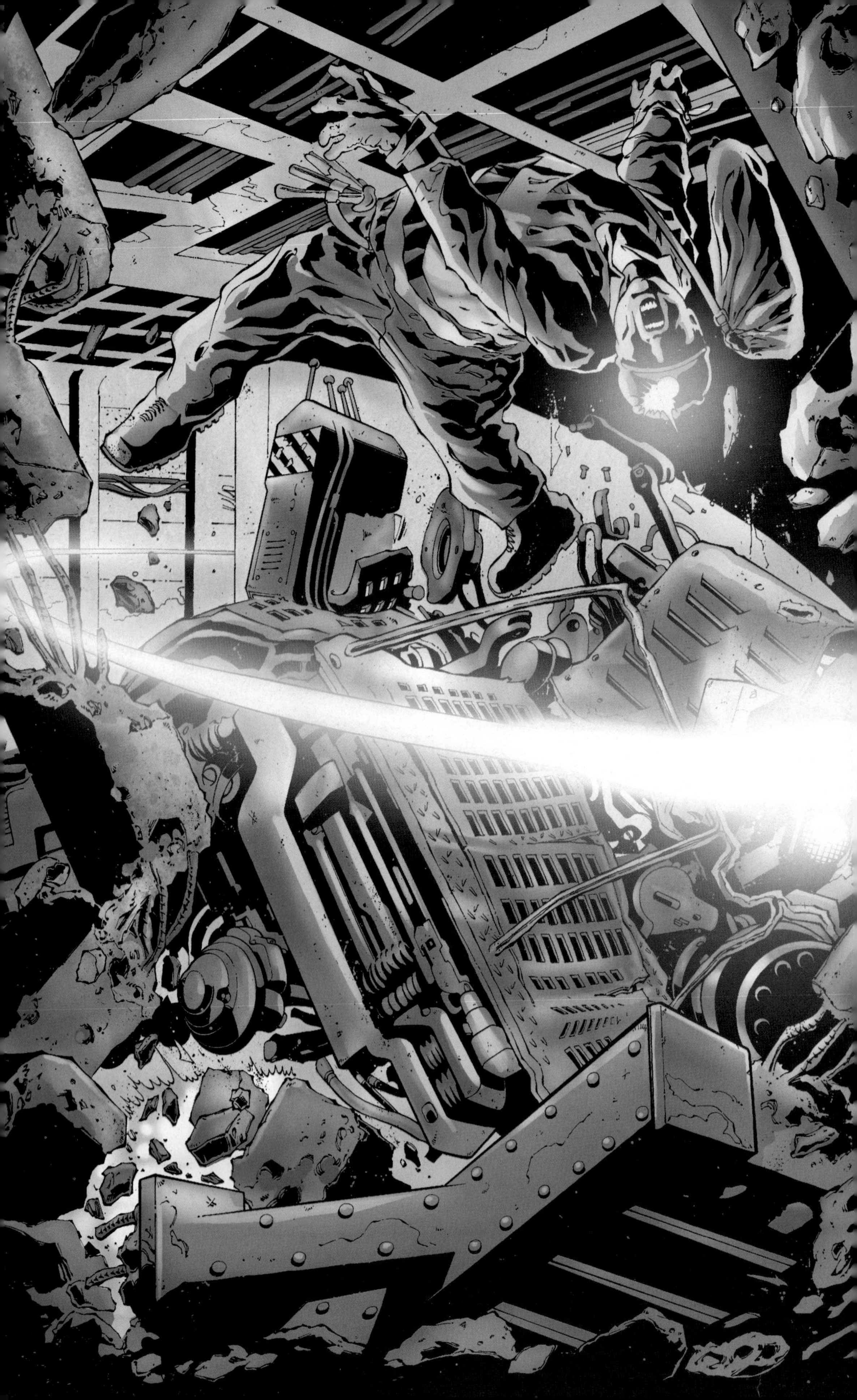

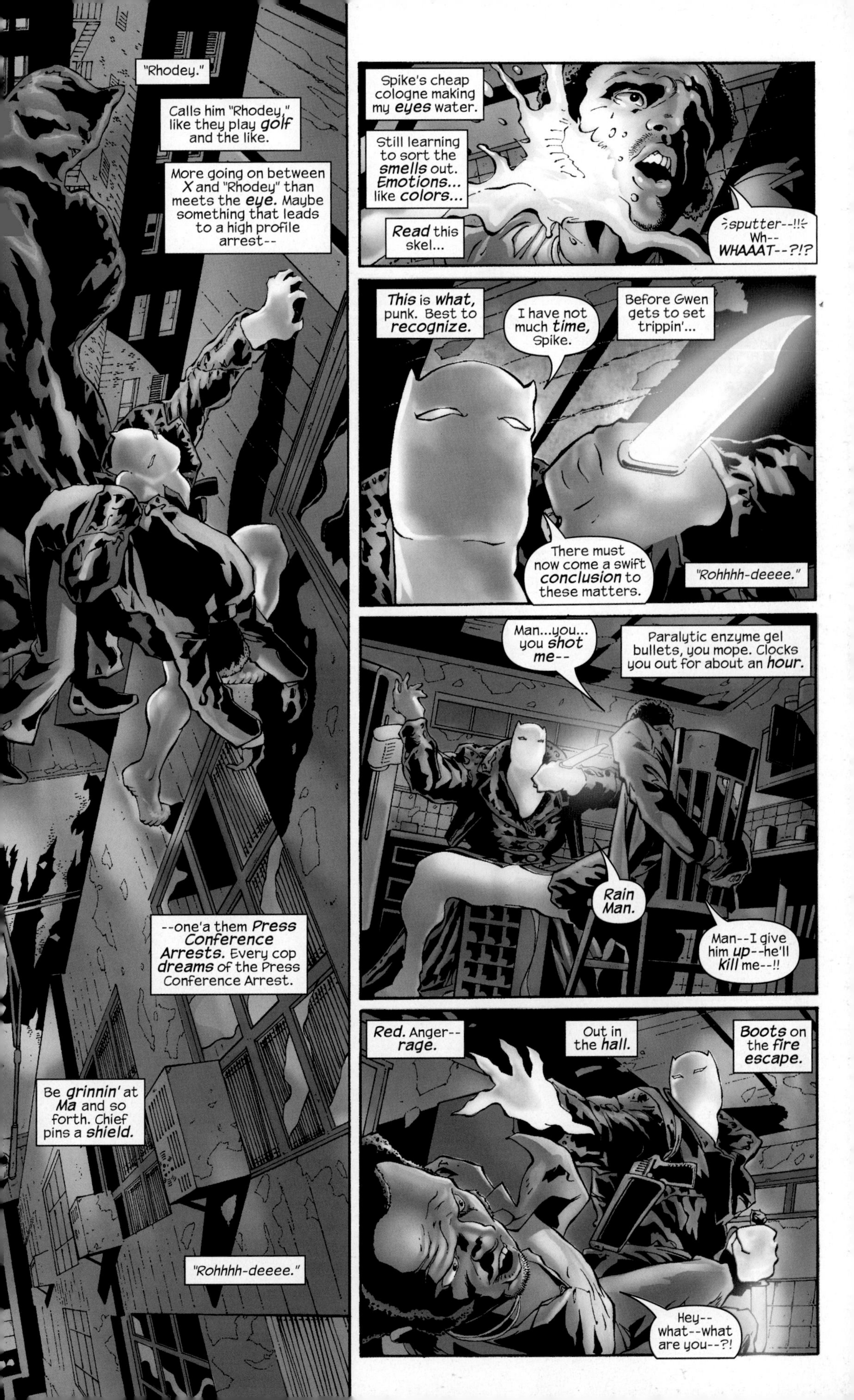
"Rhodey."
Calls him "Rhodey," like they play golf and the like.
More going on between X and "Rhodey" than meets the eye. Maybe something that leads to a high profile arrest--
--one'a them Press Conference Arrests. Every cop dreams of the Press Conference Arrest.
Be grinnin' at Ma and so forth. Chief pins a shield.
"Rohhhh-deeee."
Spike's cheap cologne making my eyes water.
Still learning to sort the smells out. Emotions... like colors...
Read this skel...
¿sputter--!!¿ Wh-- WHAAAT--?!?
This is what, punk. Best to recognize.
I have not much time, Spike.
Before Gwen gets to set trippin'...
There must now come a swift conclusion to these matters.
"Rohhhh-deeee."
Man...you... you shot me--
Paralytic enzyme gel bullets, you mope. Clocks you out for about an hour.
Rain Man.
Man--I give him up--he'll kill me--!!
Red. Anger-- rage.
Out in the hall.
Boots on the fire escape.
Hey-- what--what are you--?!

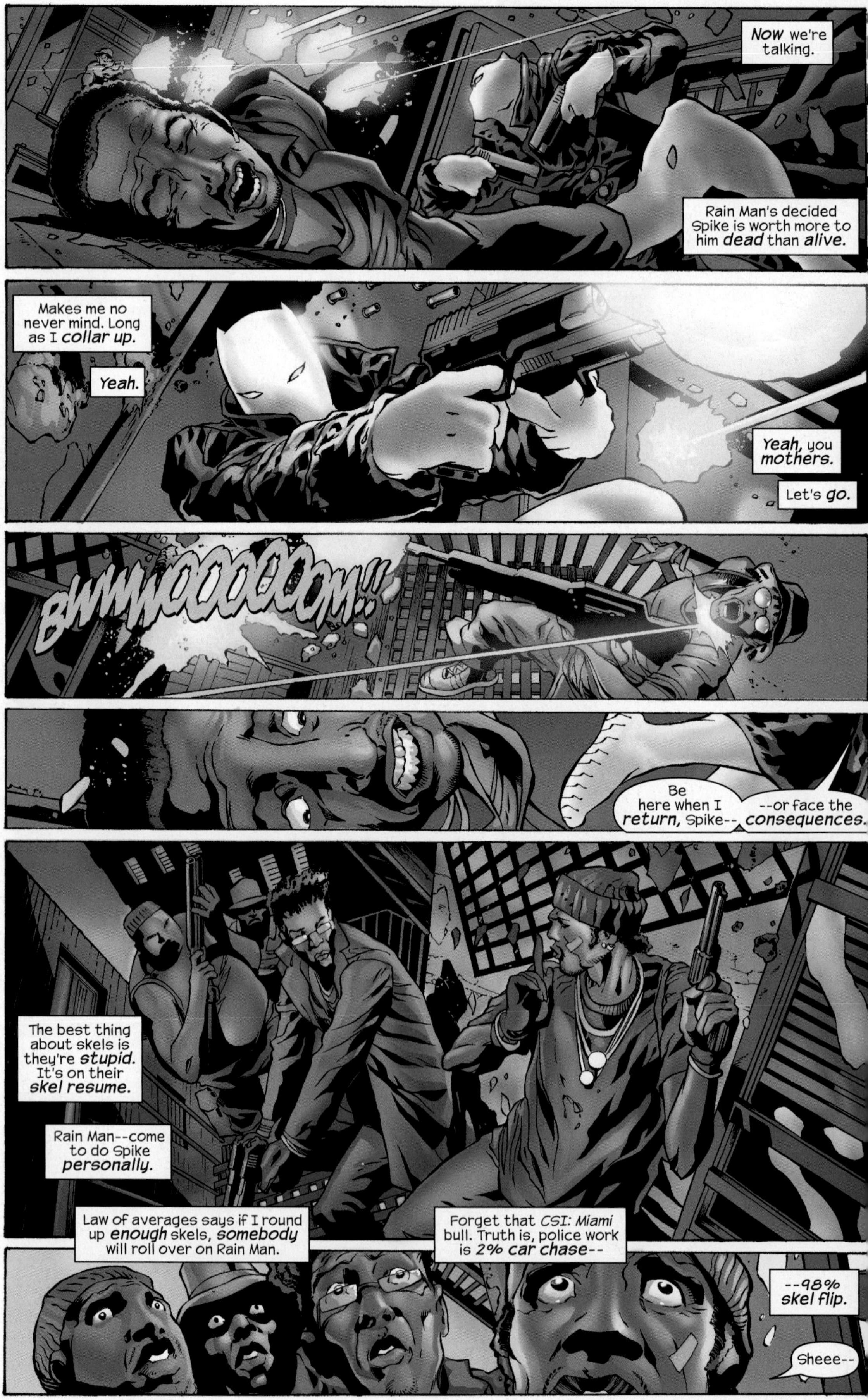
NOW we're talking.
Rain Man's decided Spike is worth more to him dead than alive.
Makes me no never mind. Long as I collar up.
Yeah.
Yeah, you mothers.
Let's go.
BWWOOOOOOM!!
Be here when I return, Spike--
--or face the consequences.
The best thing about skels is they're stupid. It's on their skel resume.
Rain Man--come to do Spike personally.
Law of averages says if I round up enough skels, somebody will roll over on Rain Man.
Forget that CSI: Miami bull. Truth is, police work is 2% car chase--
--98% skel flip.
Sheee--

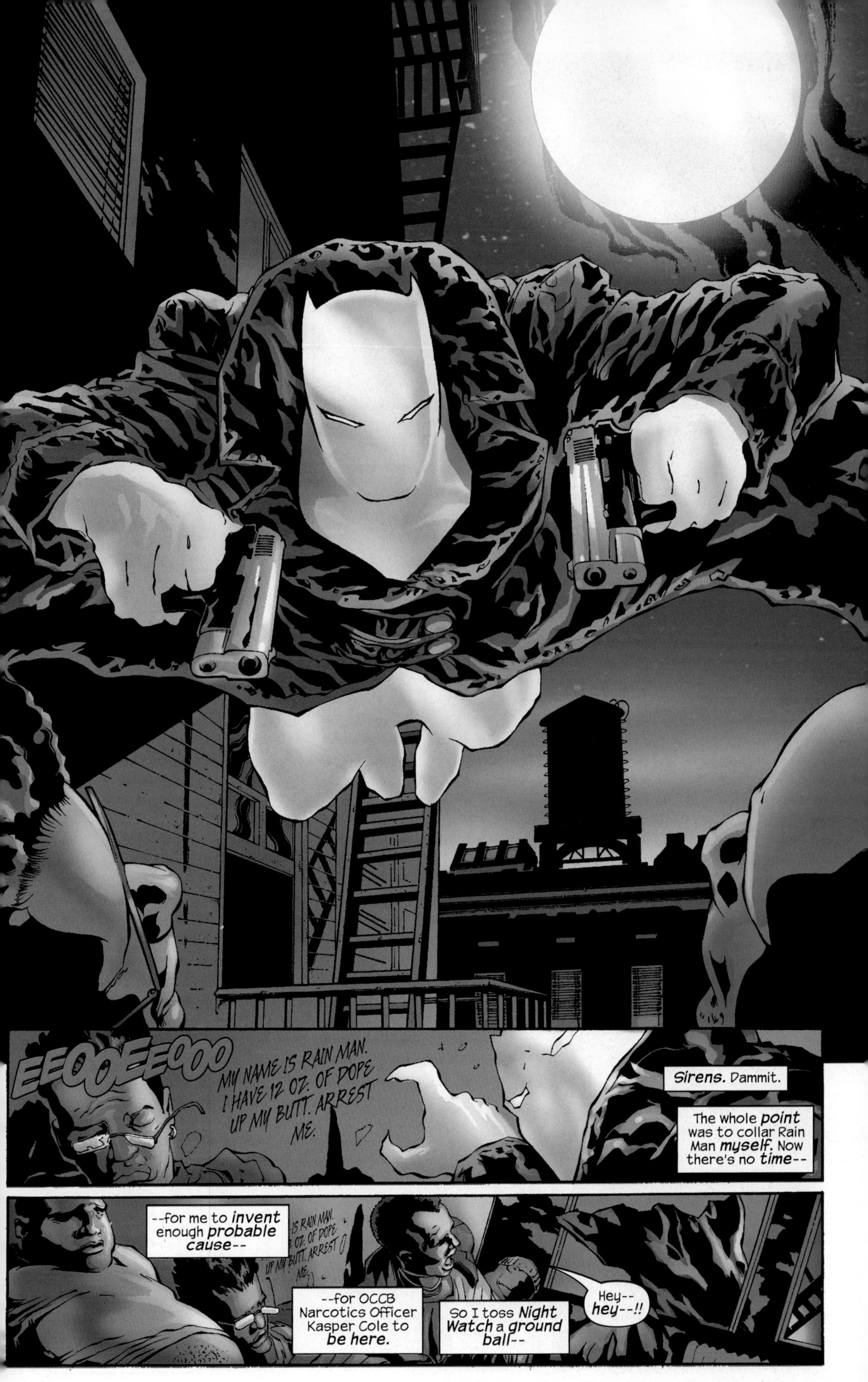
EEOOEEOOO
MY NAME IS RAIN MAN. I HAVE 12 OZ. OF DOPE UP MY BUTT. ARREST ME.
Sirens. Dammit.
The whole point was to collar Rain Man myself. Now there's no time--
--for me to invent enough probable cause--
--for OCCB Narcotics Officer Kasper Cole to be here.
So I toss Night Watch a ground ball--
Hey-- hey--!!

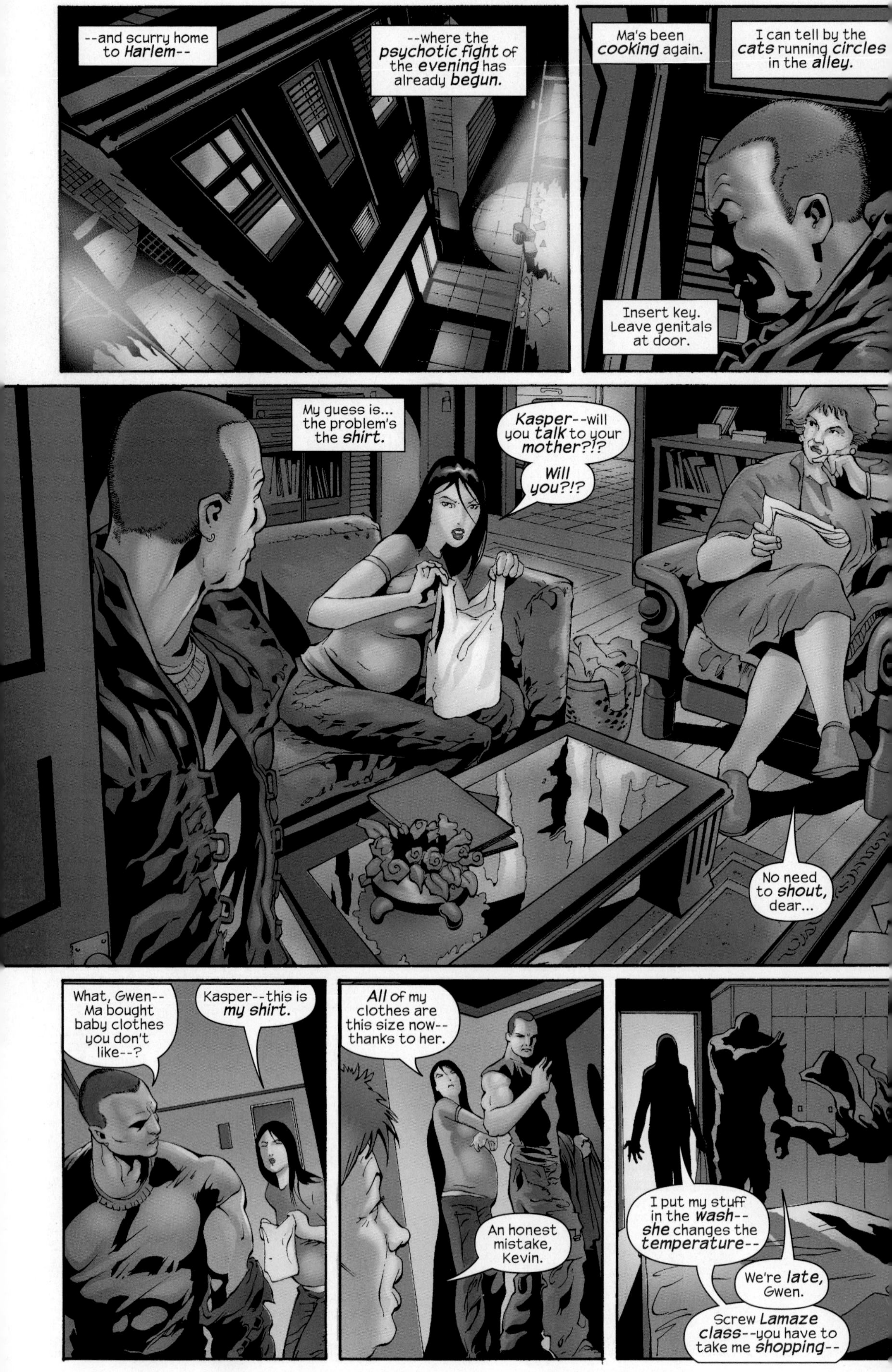
--and scurry home to Harlem--
--where the psychotic fight of the evening has already begun.
Ma's been cooking again.
I can tell by the cats running circles in the alley.
Insert key. Leave genitals at door.
My guess is... the problem's the shirt.
Kasper--will you talk to your mother?!?
Will you?!?
No need to shout, dear...
What, Gwen-- Ma bought baby clothes you don't like--?
Kasper--this is my shirt.
All of my clothes are this size now-- thanks to her.
An honest mistake, Kevin.
I put my stuff in the wash-- she changes the temperature--
We're late, Gwen.
Screw Lamaze class--you have to take me shopping--

Let this be a *lesson* to you, kid--

--keep it *zipped up.* If you know what's good for you.

Learn from *your* old man what he should have learned from *his*--

--Jonathan *Payton Cole.* Called him "Black Jack" because his skin was so *dark*--

--just like they called his kid "Kasper," because he was so *light.*

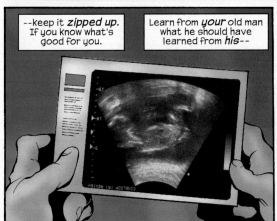

Some bad guys set your granddad *up*--sent him to *jail...disgraced.*

In an effort to *clear* his name, I started *impersonating* the *Black Panther*--

--this rich, African *king* who moved to Brooklyn to fight skels. Go figure.

Panther gave me *this*--

--the *heart-shaped herb* that grants Panther *enhanced senses,* strength, speed and agility.

Makes me a sort of Panther-in-training-- what he calls a *"White Tiger."*

Yeah, the *tights* are *itchy,* but the *mask* helps me go places a *cop can't.*

Daz. It's *Cole.* Who got **credit** for the *Rain Man* collar?

Rain Man's in the *wind,* Kasper. Every uniform in *The Mog* is at the derailment.

Derailment--?

Ho ho ho--it's *Christmas*--

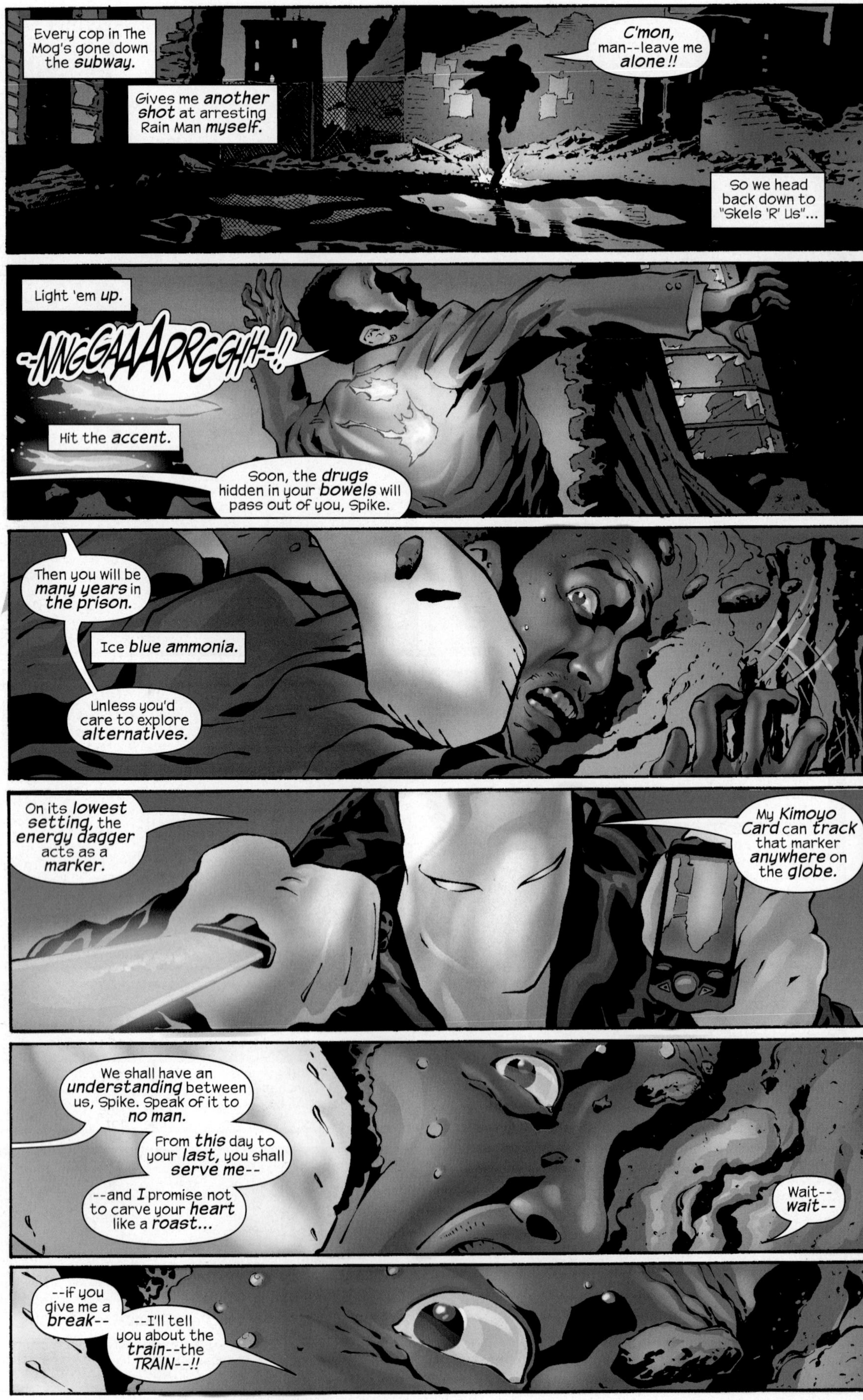

Every cop in The Mog's gone down the subway.
Gives me another shot at arresting Rain Man myself.
C'mon, man--leave me alone!!
So we head back down to "Skels 'R' Us"...
Light 'em up.
--NNGGAAARRGGHH--!!
Hit the accent.
Soon, the drugs hidden in your bowels will pass out of you, Spike.
Then you will be many years in the prison.
Ice blue ammonia.
Unless you'd care to explore alternatives.
On its lowest setting, the energy dagger acts as a marker.
My Kimoyo Card can track that marker anywhere on the globe.
We shall have an understanding between us, Spike. Speak of it to no man.
From this day to your last, you shall serve me--
--and I promise not to carve your heart like a roast...
Wait--wait--
--if you give me a break--
--I'll tell you about the train--the TRAIN--!!

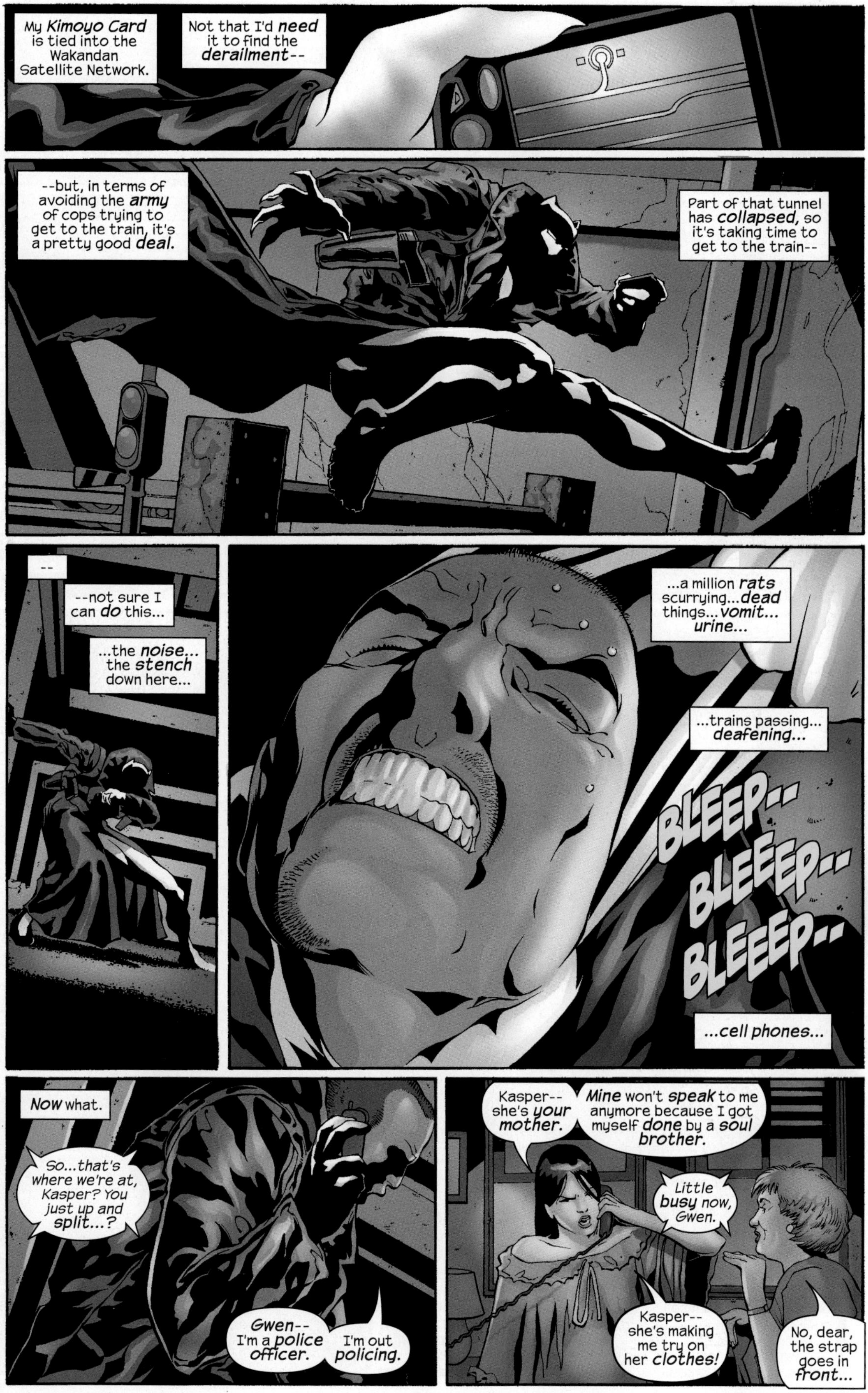

My Kimoyo Card is tied into the Wakandan Satellite Network.
Not that I'd need it to find the derailment--
--but, in terms of avoiding the army of cops trying to get to the train, it's a pretty good deal.
Part of that tunnel has collapsed, so it's taking time to get to the train--
--
--not sure I can do this...
...the noise... the stench down here...
...a million rats scurrying...dead things...vomit... urine...
...trains passing... deafening...
BLEEP.. BLEEEP.. BLEEEP..
...cell phones...
Now what.
So...that's where we're at, Kasper? You just up and split...?
Gwen-- I'm a police officer.
I'm out policing.
Kasper-- she's your mother.
Mine won't speak to me anymore because I got myself done by a soul brother.
Little busy now, Gwen.
Kasper-- she's making me try on her clothes!
No, dear, the strap goes in front...

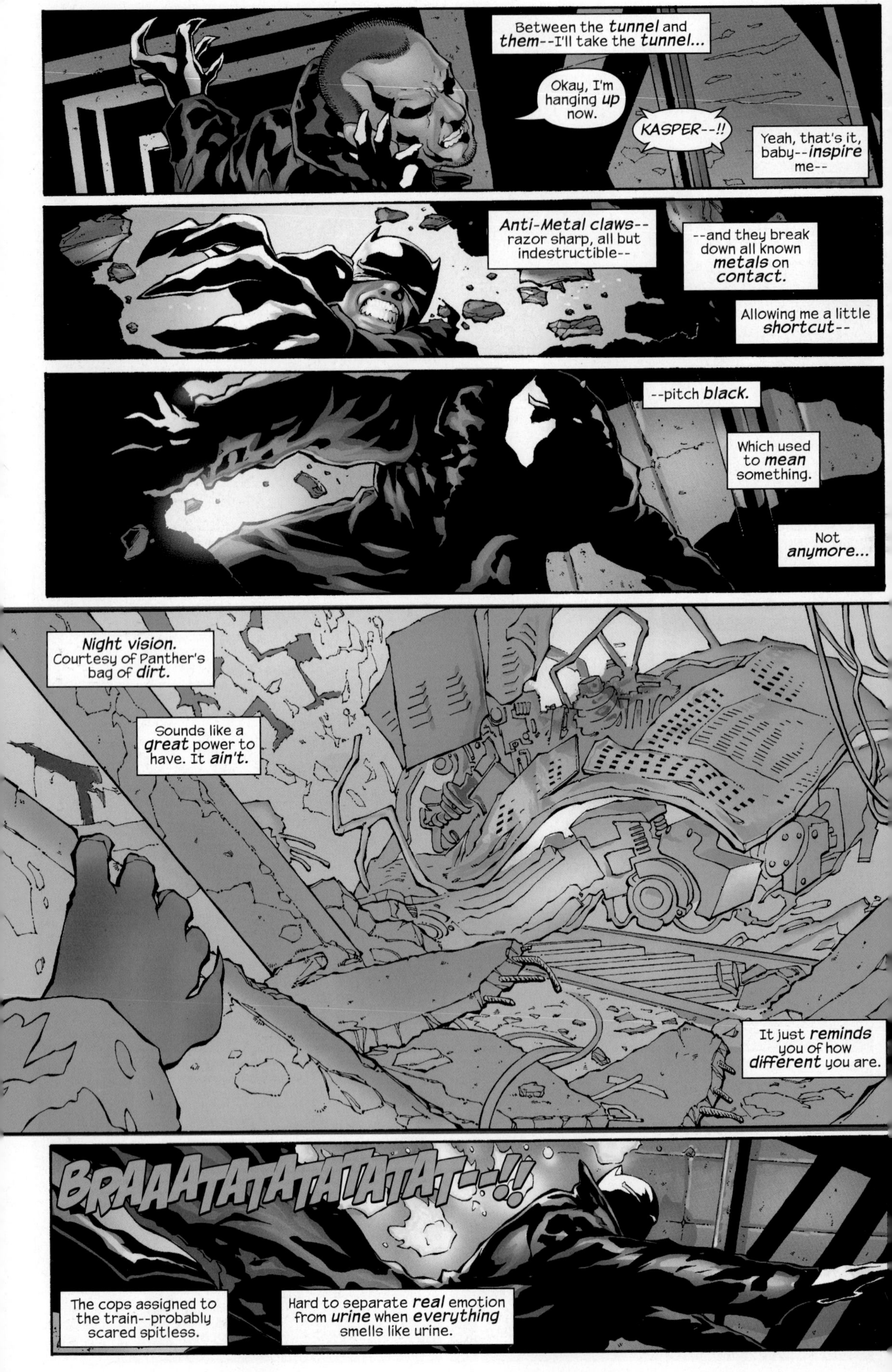
Between the tunnel and them--I'll take the tunnel...
Okay, I'm hanging up now.
KASPER--!!
Yeah, that's it, baby--inspire me--
Anti-Metal claws--razor sharp, all but indestructible--
--and they break down all known metals on contact.
Allowing me a little shortcut--
--pitch black.
Which used to mean something.
Not anymore...
Night vision. Courtesy of Panther's bag of dirt.
Sounds like a great power to have. It ain't.
It just reminds you of how different you are.
BRAAATATATATATAT--!!
The cops assigned to the train--probably scared spitless.
Hard to separate real emotion from urine when everything smells like urine.

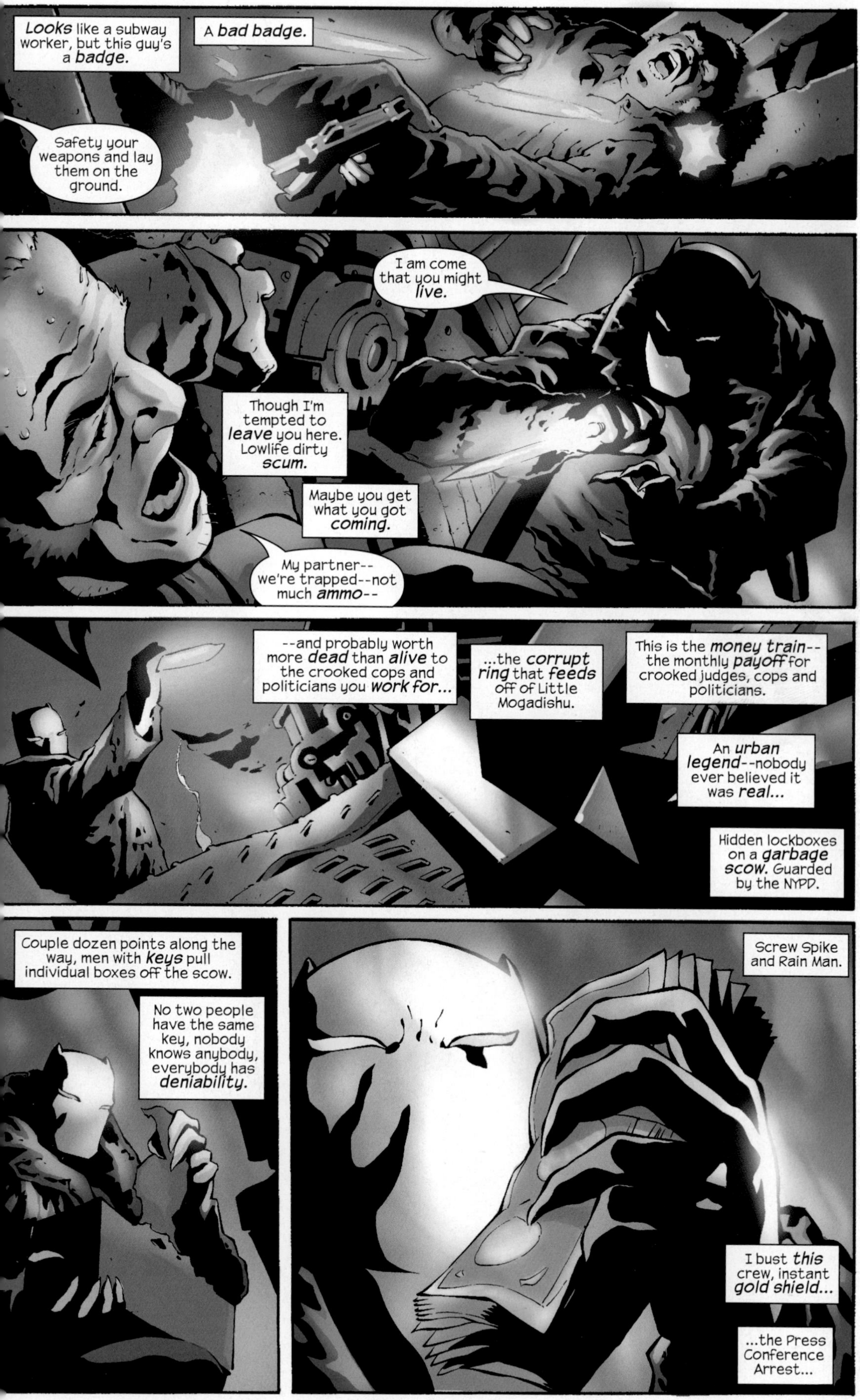
Looks like a subway worker, but this guy's a badge.
A bad badge.
Safety your weapons and lay them on the ground.
I am come that you might live.
Though I'm tempted to leave you here. Lowlife dirty scum.
Maybe you get what you got coming.
My partner--we're trapped--not much ammo--
This is the money train--the monthly payoff for crooked judges, cops and politicians.
...the corrupt ring that feeds off of Little Mogadishu.
--and probably worth more dead than alive to the crooked cops and politicians you work for...
An urban legend--nobody ever believed it was real...
Hidden lockboxes on a garbage scow. Guarded by the NYPD.
Couple dozen points along the way, men with keys pull individual boxes off the scow.
No two people have the same key, nobody knows anybody, everybody has deniability.
Screw Spike and Rain Man.
I bust this crew, instant gold shield...
...the Press Conference Arrest...

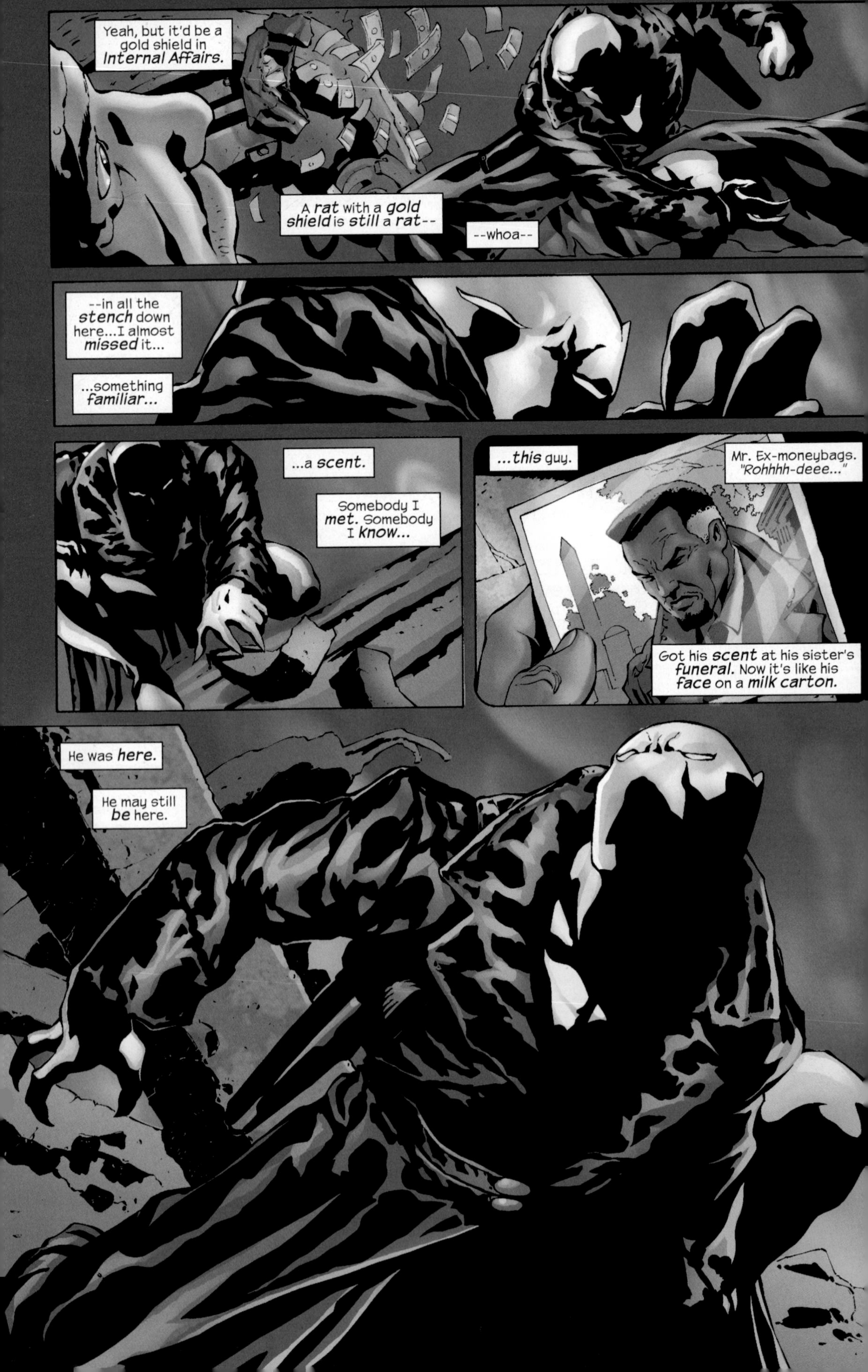

Yeah, but it'd be a gold shield in Internal Affairs.
A rat with a gold shield is still a rat--
--whoa--
--in all the stench down here...I almost missed it...
...something familiar...
...a scent.
Somebody I met. Somebody I know...
...this guy.
Mr. Ex-moneybags. "Rohhhh-deee..."
Got his scent at his sister's funeral. Now it's like his face on a milk carton.
He was here.
He may still be here.

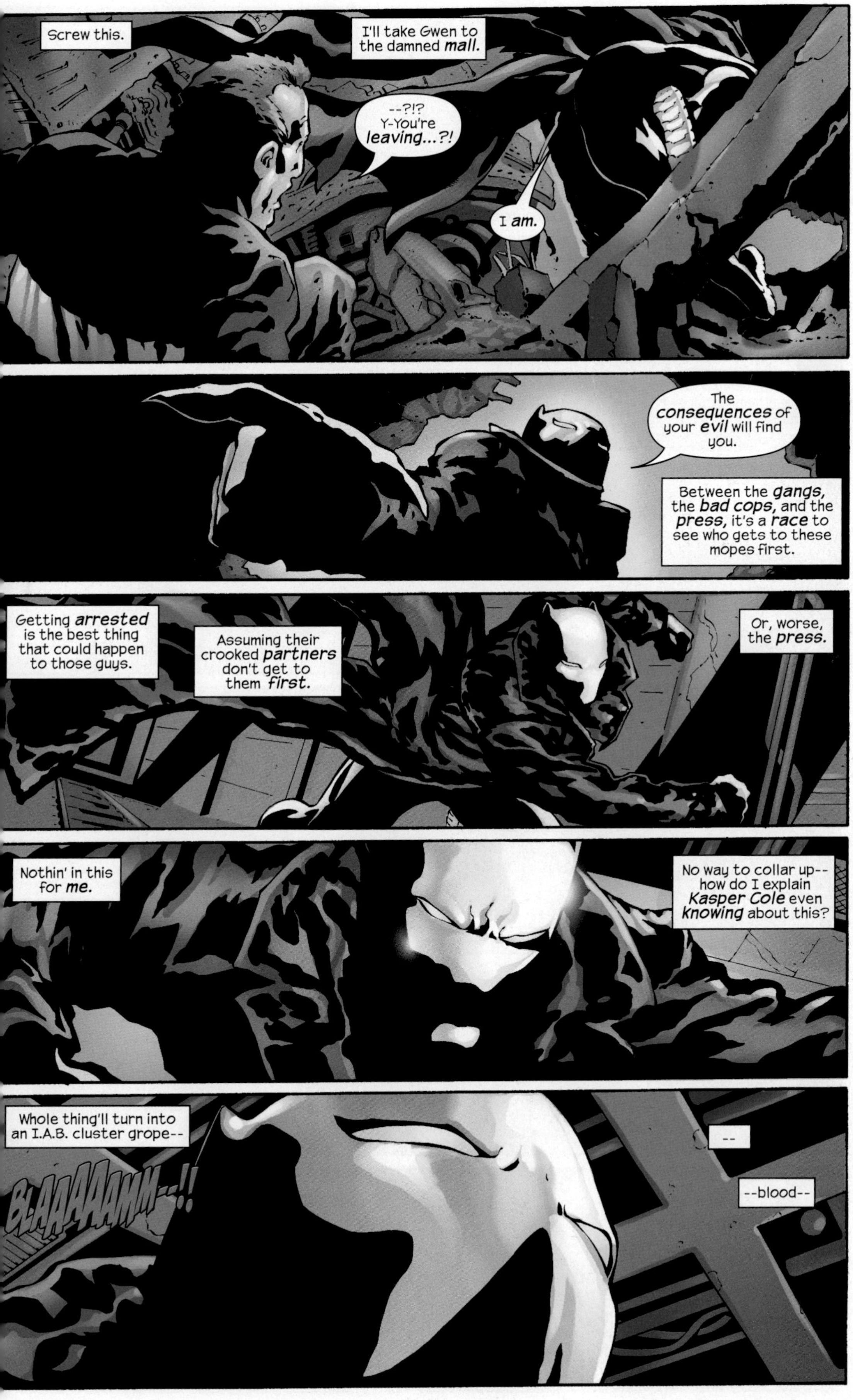
Screw this.
I'll take Gwen to the damned mall.
--?!? Y-You're leaving...?!
I am.
The consequences of your evil will find you.
Between the gangs, the bad cops, and the press, it's a race to see who gets to these mopes first.
Getting arrested is the best thing that could happen to those guys.
Assuming their crooked partners don't get to them first.
Or, worse, the press.
Nothin' in this for me.
No way to collar up-- how do I explain Kasper Cole even knowing about this?
Whole thing'll turn into an I.A.B. cluster grope--
BLAAAAAMM--!!
--
--blood--

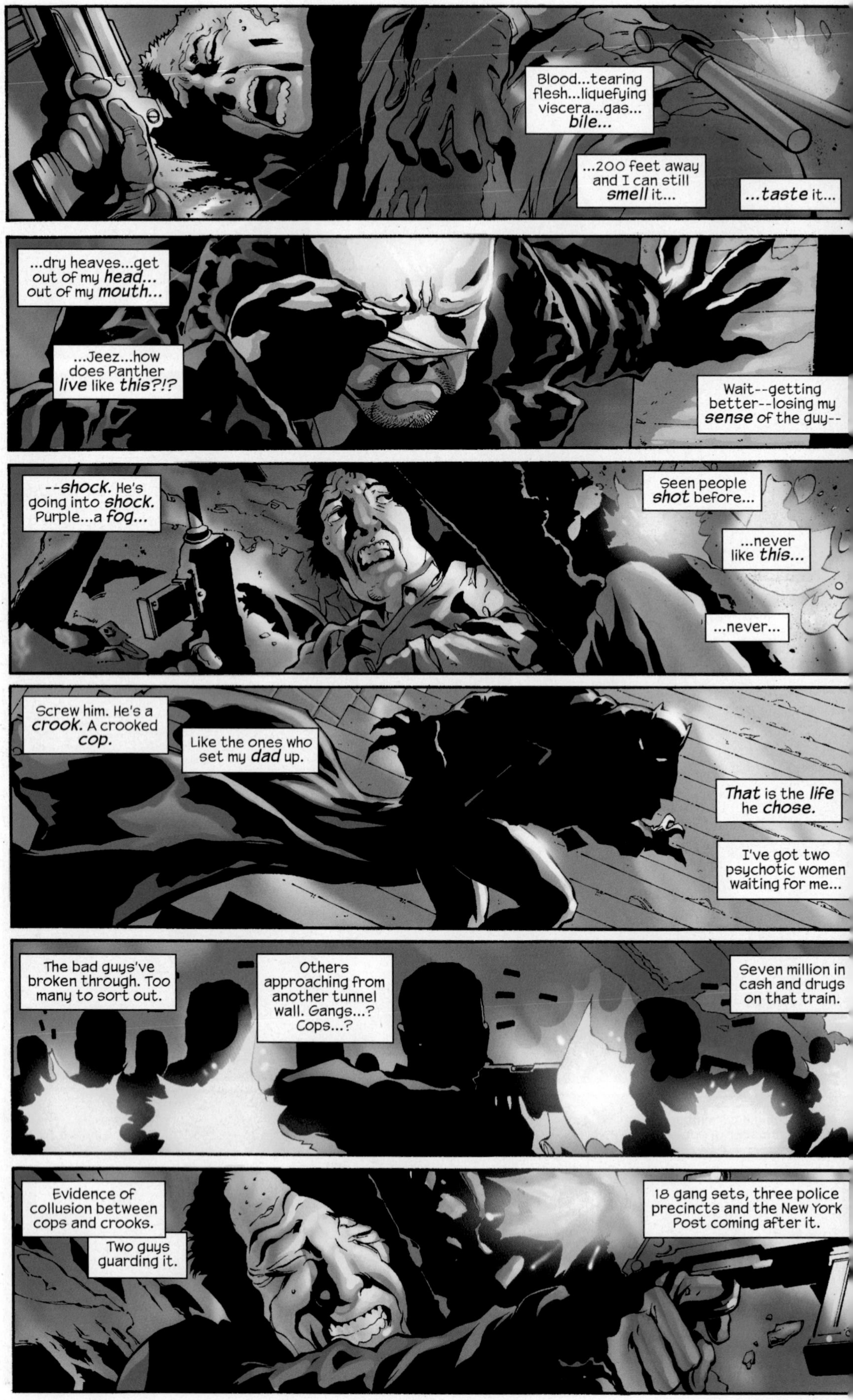
Blood...tearing flesh...liquefying viscera...gas... bile...
...200 feet away and I can still smell it...
...taste it...
...dry heaves...get out of my head... out of my mouth...
...Jeez...how does Panther live like this?!?
Wait--getting better--losing my sense of the guy--
--shock. He's going into shock. Purple...a fog...
Seen people shot before...
...never like this...
...never...
Screw him. He's a crook. A crooked cop.
Like the ones who set my dad up.
That is the life he chose.
I've got two psychotic women waiting for me...
The bad guys've broken through. Too many to sort out.
Others approaching from another tunnel wall. Gangs...? Cops...?
Seven million in cash and drugs on that train.
Evidence of collusion between cops and crooks.
Two guys guarding it.
18 gang sets, three police precincts and the New York Post coming after it.

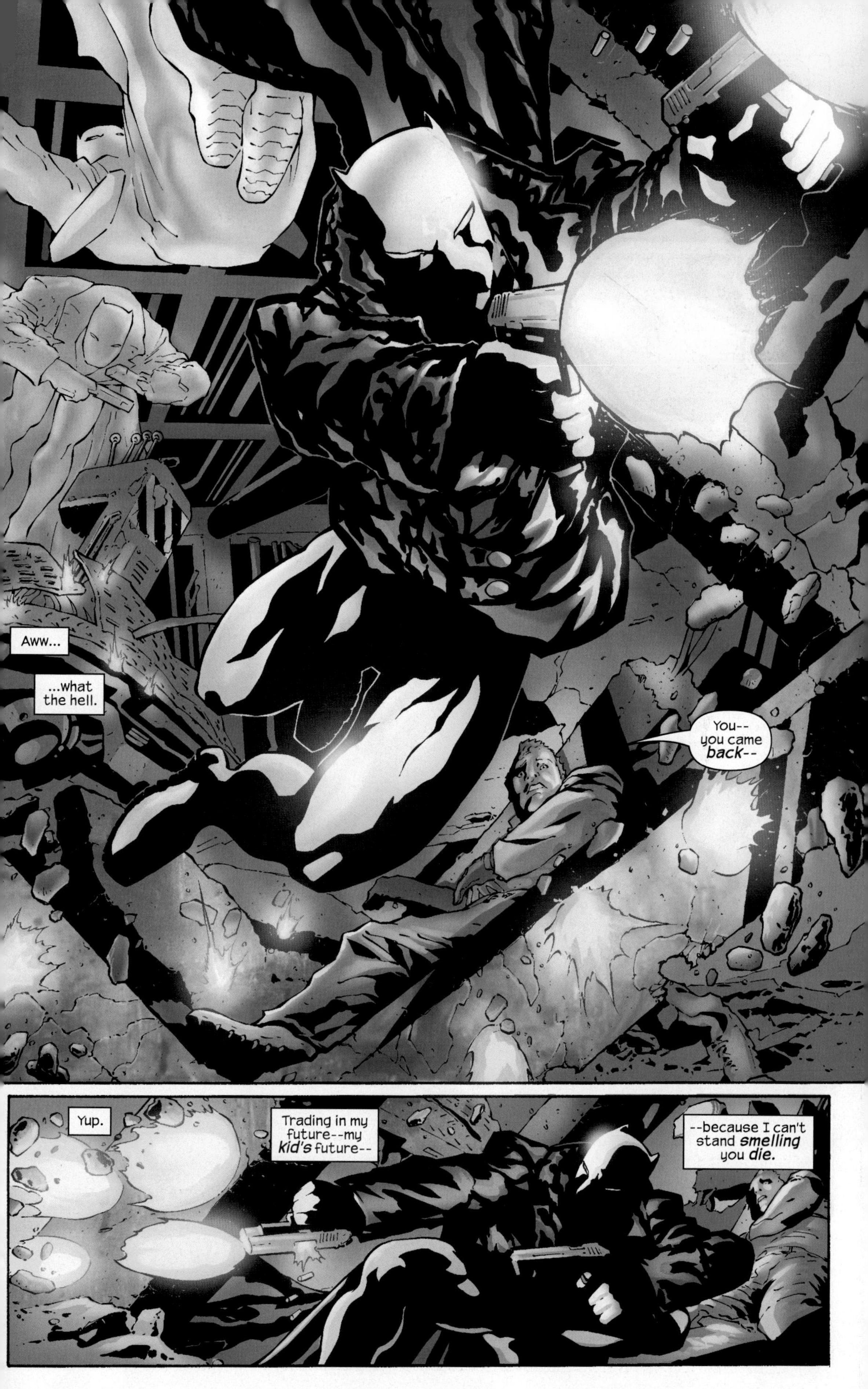

Aww...
...what the hell.
You-- you came *back*--
Yup.
Trading in my future--my *kid's* future--
--because I can't stand *smelling* you *die.*

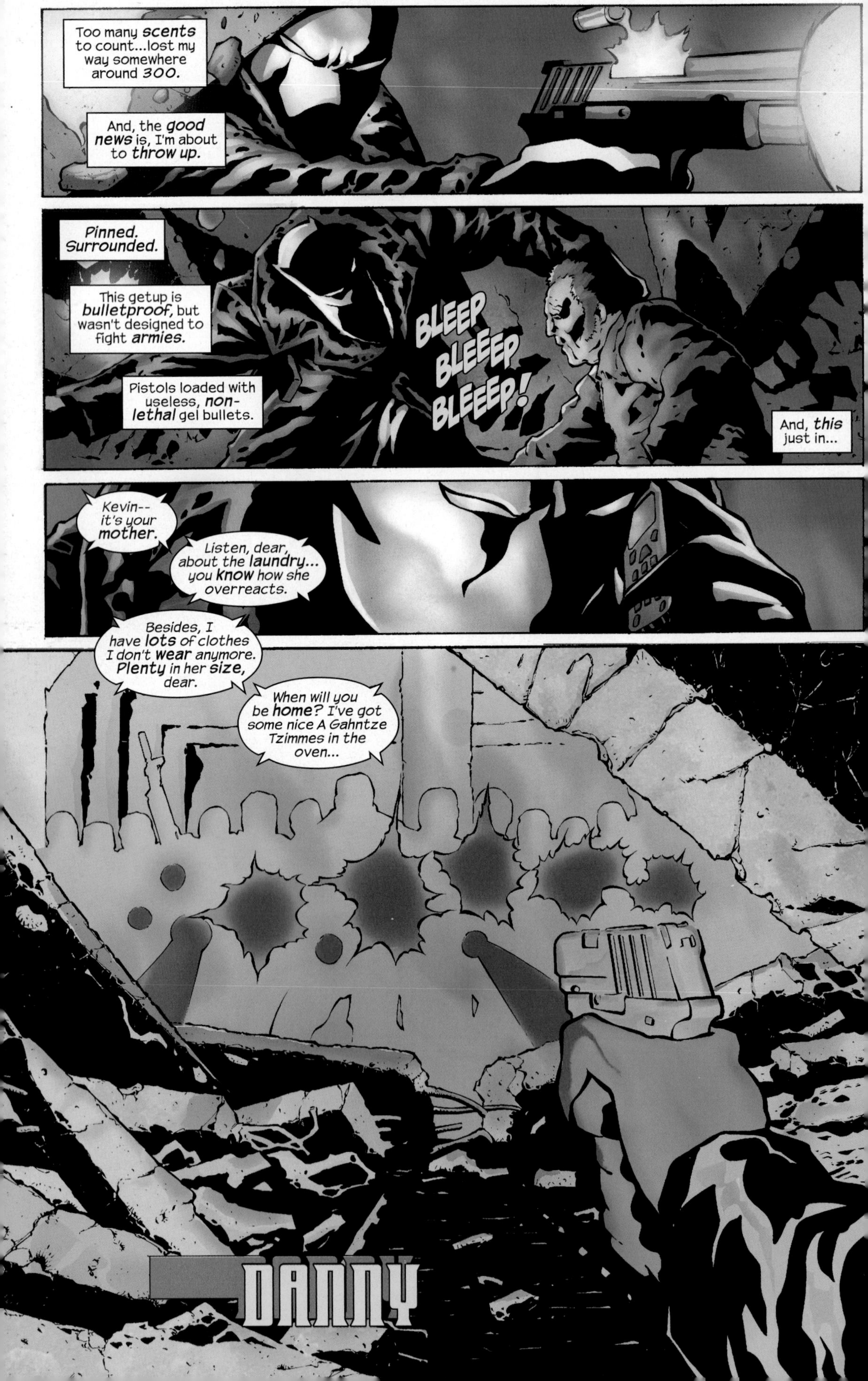
Too many scents to count...lost my way somewhere around 300.
And, the good news is, I'm about to throw up.
Pinned. Surrounded.
This getup is bulletproof, but wasn't designed to fight armies.
Pistols loaded with useless, non-lethal gel bullets.
BLEEP BLEEEP BLEEEP!
And, this just in...
Kevin-- it's your mother.
Listen, dear, about the laundry... you know how she overreacts.
Besides, I have lots of clothes I don't wear anymore. Plenty in her size, dear.
When will you be home? I've got some nice A Gahntze Tzimmes in the oven...
DANNY

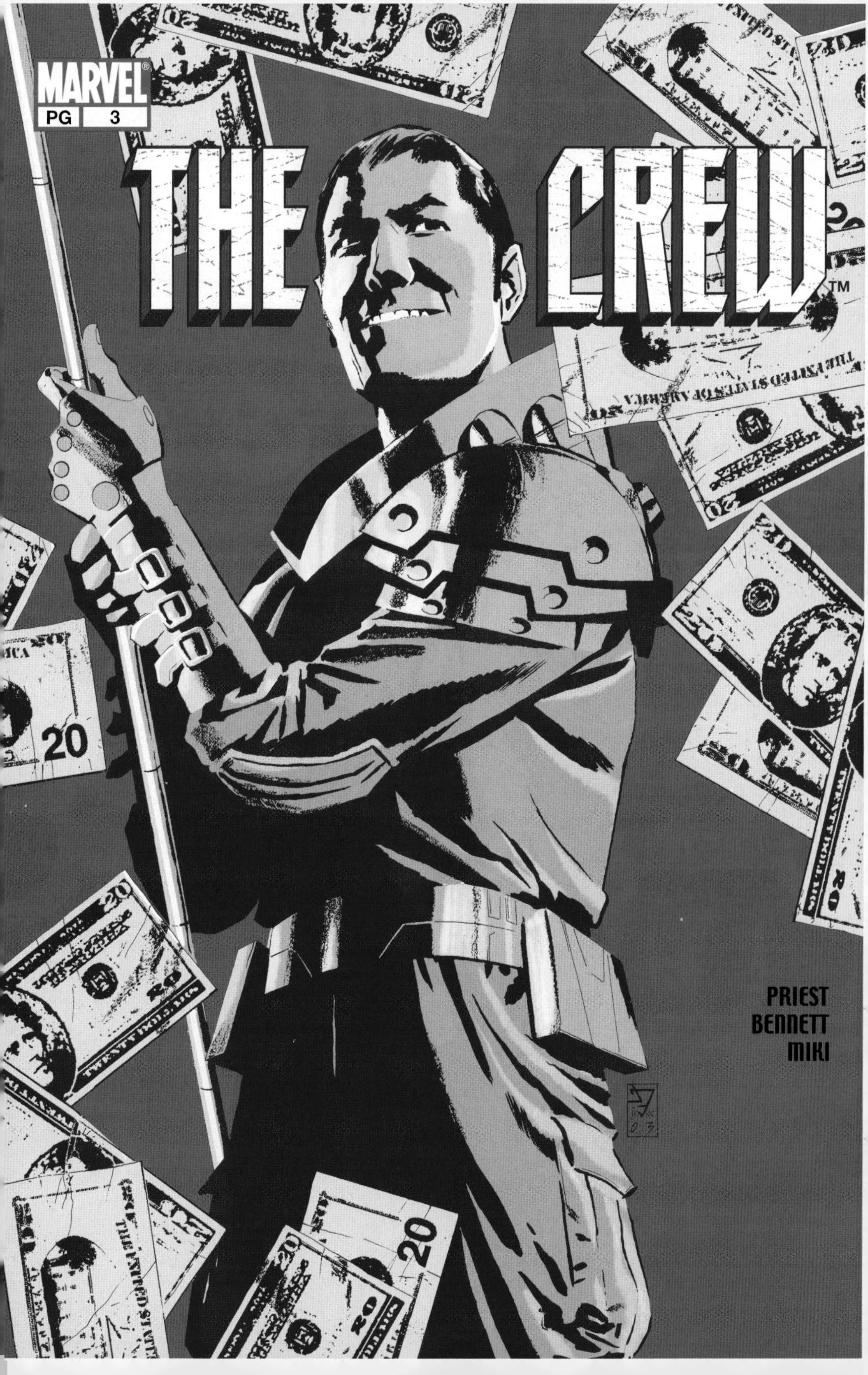
MARVEL
PG 3
THE CREW™
PRIEST
BENNETT
MIKI

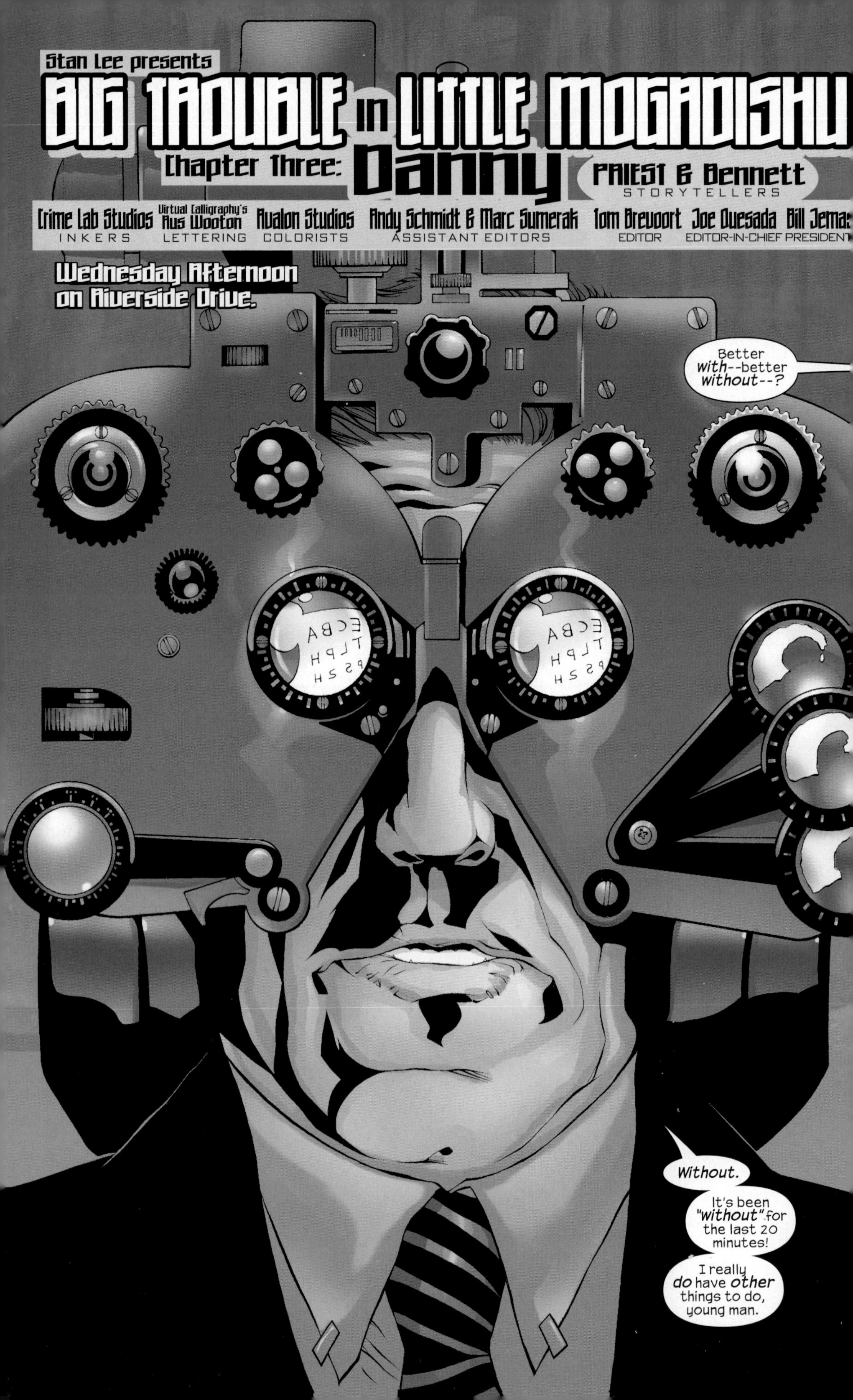
Stan Lee presents
BIG TROUBLE in LITTLE MOGADISHU
Chapter Three: Danny
PRIEST & Bennett
STORYTELLERS
Crime Lab Studios
INKERS
Virtual Calligraphy's Rus Wooton
LETTERING
Avalon Studios
COLORISTS
Andy Schmidt & Marc Sumerak
ASSISTANT EDITORS
Tom Brevoort
EDITOR
Joe Quesada
EDITOR-IN-CHIEF
Bill Jema
PRESIDENT
Wednesday Afternoon on Riverside Drive.
Better with--better without--?
Without.
It's been "without" for the last 20 minutes!
I really do have other things to do, young man.

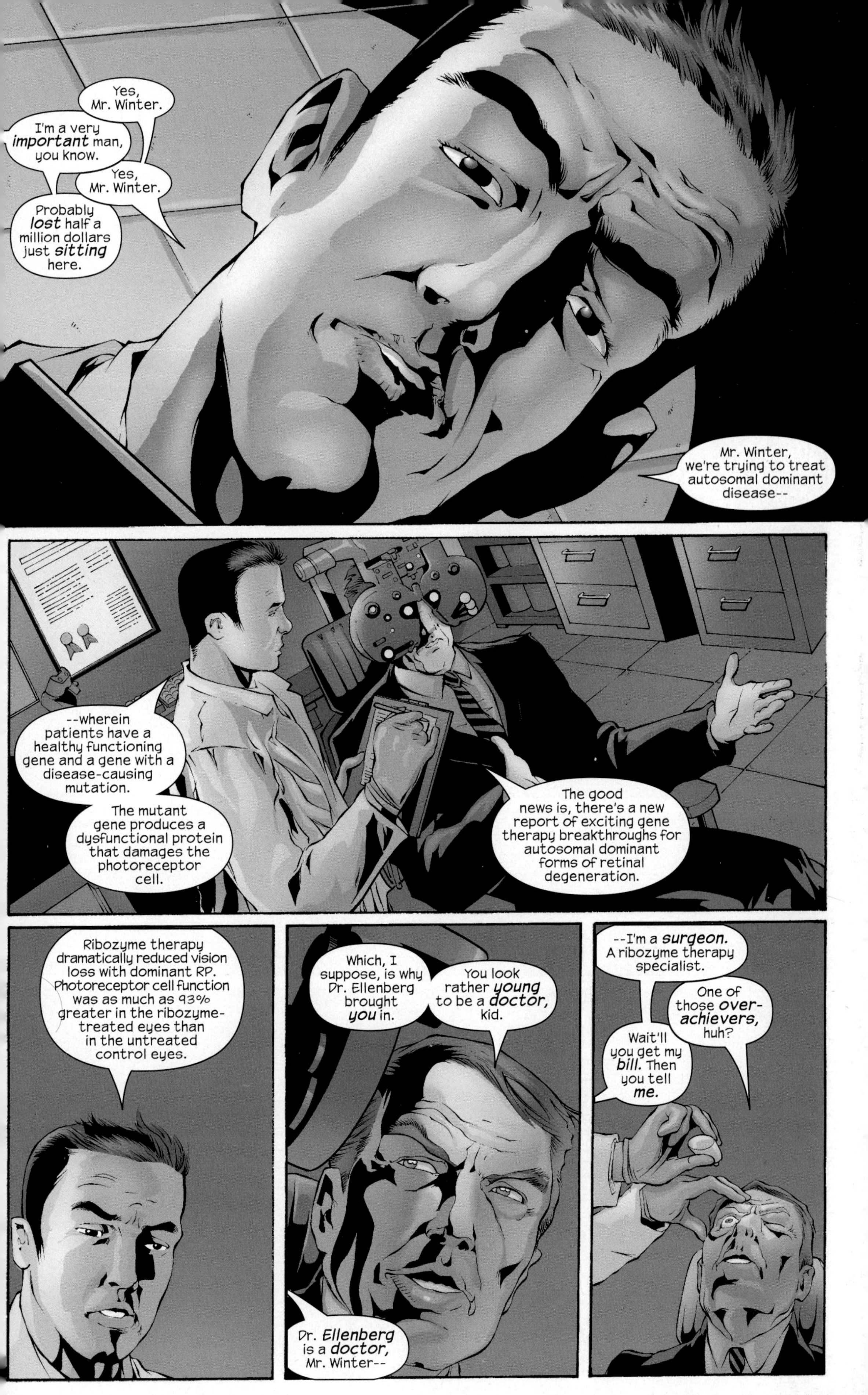
Yes, Mr. Winter.
I'm a very *important* man, you know.
Yes, Mr. Winter.
Probably *lost* half a million dollars just *sitting* here.
Mr. Winter, we're trying to treat autosomal dominant disease--
--wherein patients have a healthy functioning gene and a gene with a disease-causing mutation.
The mutant gene produces a dysfunctional protein that damages the photoreceptor cell.
The good news is, there's a new report of exciting gene therapy breakthroughs for autosomal dominant forms of retinal degeneration.
Ribozyme therapy dramatically reduced vision loss with dominant RP. Photoreceptor cell function was as much as 93% greater in the ribozyme-treated eyes than in the untreated control eyes.
Which, I suppose, is why Dr. Ellenberg brought *you* in.
You look rather *young* to be a *doctor,* kid.
Dr. *Ellenberg* is a *doctor,* Mr. Winter--
--I'm a *surgeon.* A ribozyme therapy specialist.
One of those *over-achievers,* huh?
Wait'll you get my *bill.* Then you tell *me.*

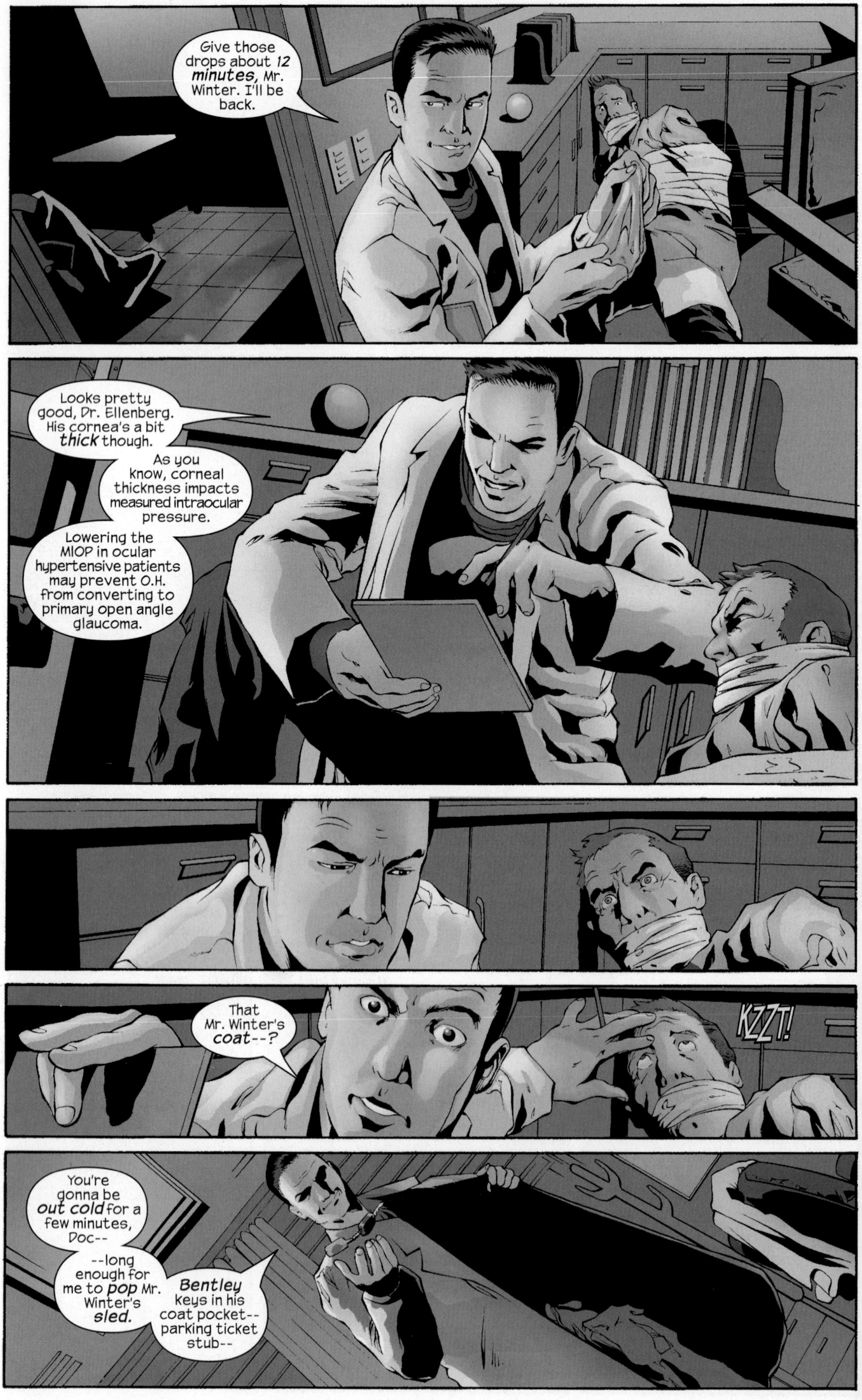

Give those drops about 12 minutes, Mr. Winter. I'll be back.
Looks pretty good, Dr. Ellenberg. His cornea's a bit thick though.
As you know, corneal thickness impacts measured intraocular pressure.
Lowering the MIOP in ocular hypertensive patients may prevent O.H. from converting to primary open angle glaucoma.
That Mr. Winter's coat--?
KZZT!
You're gonna be out cold for a few minutes, Doc--
--long enough for me to pop Mr. Winter's sled.
Bentley keys in his coat pocket--parking ticket stub--

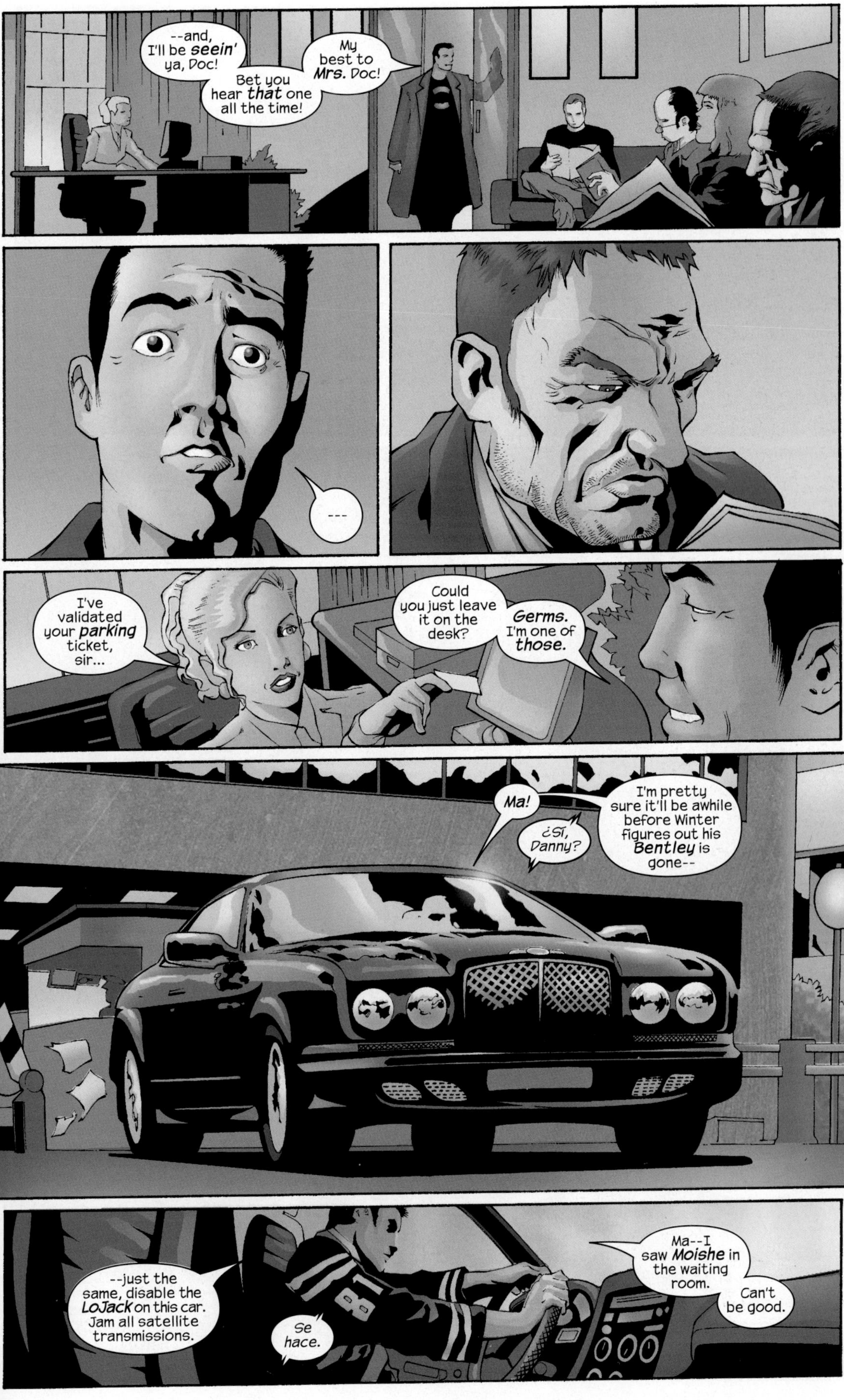
--and, I'll be seein' ya, Doc!
Bet you hear that one all the time!
My best to Mrs. Doc!

I've validated your parking ticket, sir...
Could you just leave it on the desk?
Germs. I'm one of those.
Ma!
¿Sí, Danny?
I'm pretty sure it'll be awhile before Winter figures out his Bentley is gone--
--just the same, disable the LoJack on this car. Jam all satellite transmissions.
Se hace.
Ma--I saw Moishe in the waiting room.
Can't be good.

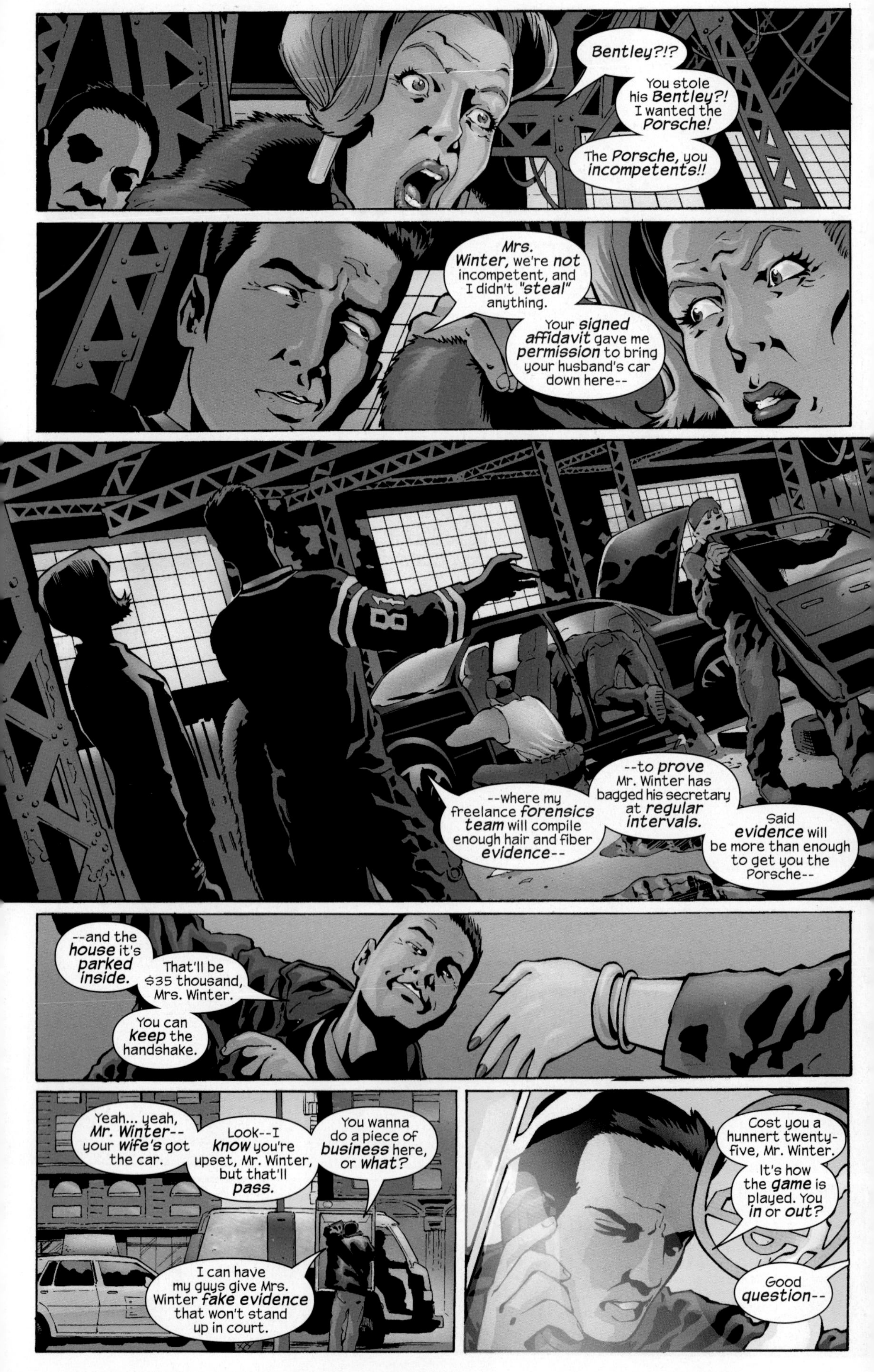

Bentley?!?
You stole his Bentley?! I wanted the Porsche!
The Porsche, you incompetents!!
Mrs. Winter, we're not incompetent, and I didn't "steal" anything.
Your signed affidavit gave me permission to bring your husband's car down here--
--where my freelance forensics team will compile enough hair and fiber evidence--
--to prove Mr. Winter has bagged his secretary at regular intervals.
Said evidence will be more than enough to get you the Porsche--
--and the house it's parked inside.
That'll be $35 thousand, Mrs. Winter.
You can keep the handshake.
Yeah... yeah, Mr. Winter-- your wife's got the car.
Look--I know you're upset, Mr. Winter, but that'll pass.
You wanna do a piece of business here, or what?
I can have my guys give Mrs. Winter fake evidence that won't stand up in court.
Cost you a hunnert twenty-five, Mr. Winter.
It's how the game is played. You in or out?
Good question--

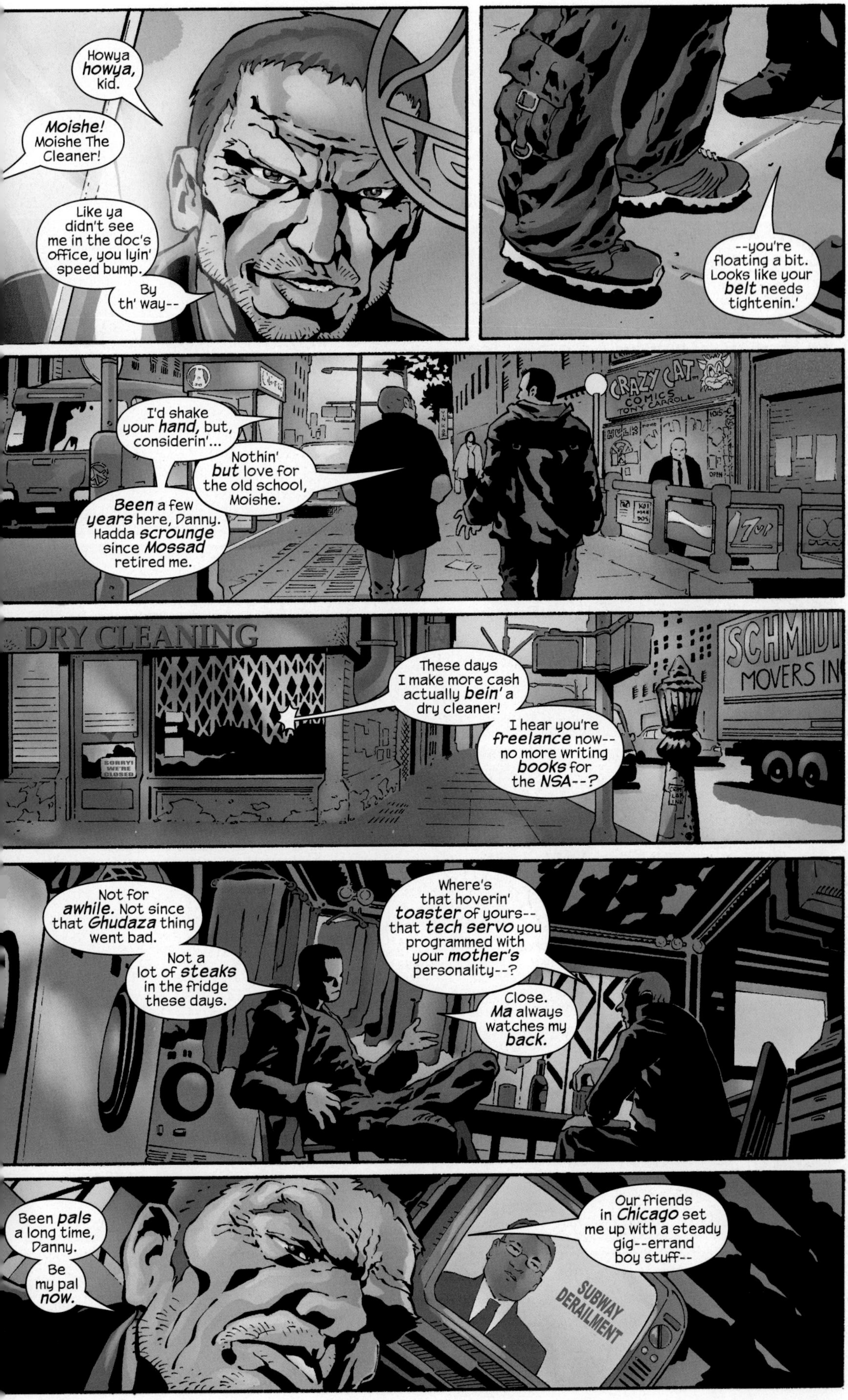
Howya howya, kid.
Moishe! Moishe The Cleaner!
Like ya didn't see me in the doc's office, you lyin' speed bump.
By th' way--
--you're floating a bit. Looks like your belt needs tightenin.'
CRAZY CAT COMICS TONY CARROLL
I'd shake your hand, but, considerin'...
Nothin' but love for the old school, Moishe.
Been a few years here, Danny. Hadda scrounge since Mossad retired me.
DRY CLEANING
SCHMID MOVERS IN
SORRY! WE'RE CLOSED
These days I make more cash actually bein' a dry cleaner!
I hear you're freelance now-- no more writing books for the NSA--?
Not for awhile. Not since that Ghudaza thing went bad.
Not a lot of steaks in the fridge these days.
Where's that hoverin' toaster of yours-- that tech servo you programmed with your mother's personality--?
Close. Ma always watches my back.
Been pals a long time, Danny.
Be my pal now.
Our friends in Chicago set me up with a steady gig--errand boy stuff--
SUBWAY DERAILMENT

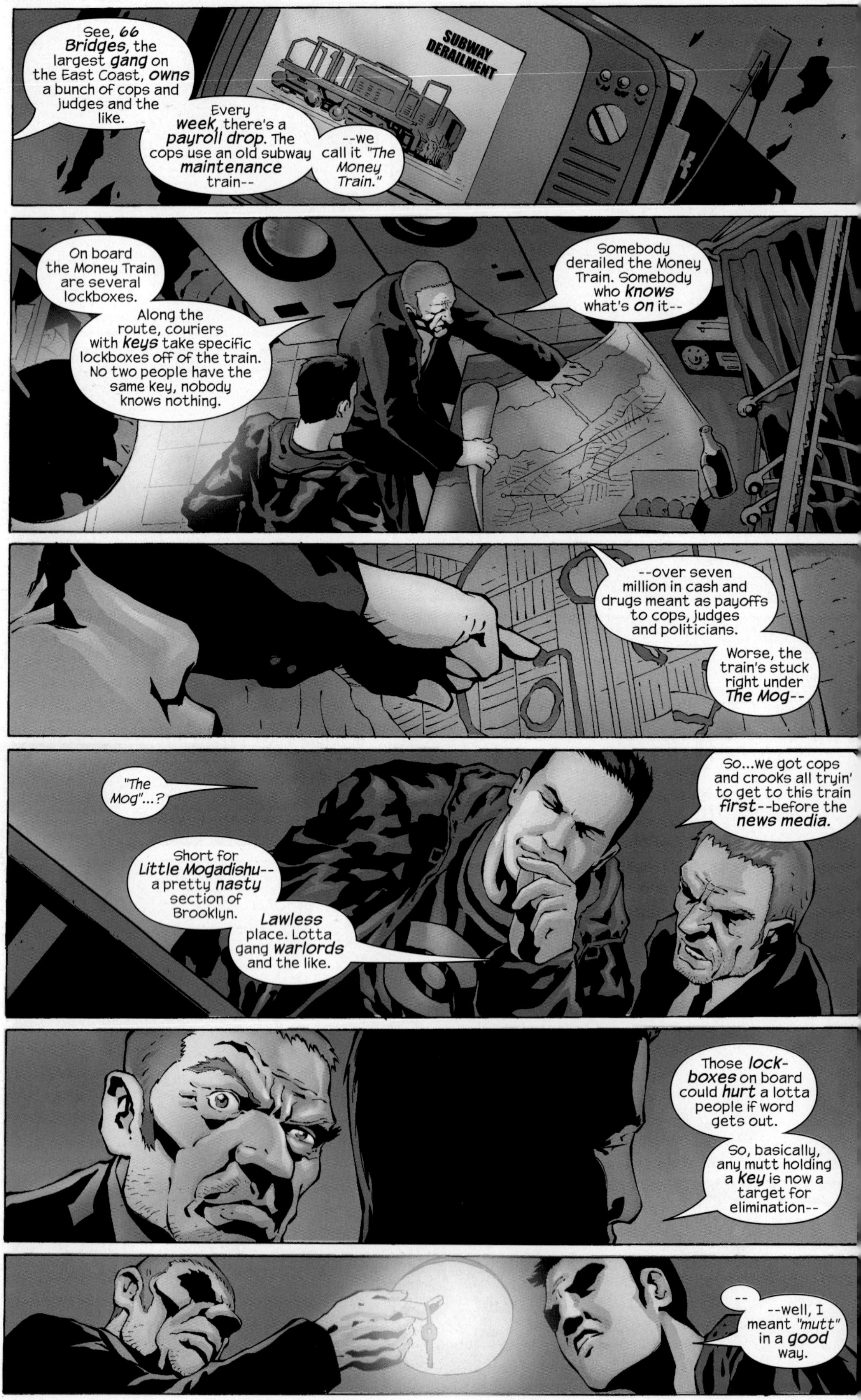

See, 66 Bridges, the largest gang on the East Coast, owns a bunch of cops and judges and the like.
Every week, there's a payroll drop. The cops use an old subway maintenance train--
--we call it "The Money Train."
SUBWAY DERAILMENT
On board the Money Train are several lockboxes.
Along the route, couriers with keys take specific lockboxes off of the train. No two people have the same key, nobody knows nothing.
Somebody derailed the Money Train. Somebody who knows what's on it--
--over seven million in cash and drugs meant as payoffs to cops, judges and politicians.
Worse, the train's stuck right under The Mog--
"The Mog"...?
Short for Little Mogadishu-- a pretty nasty section of Brooklyn.
Lawless place. Lotta gang warlords and the like.
So...we got cops and crooks all tryin' to get to this train first--before the news media.
Those lock-boxes on board could hurt a lotta people if word gets out.
So, basically, any mutt holding a key is now a target for elimination--
--
--well, I meant "mutt" in a good way.

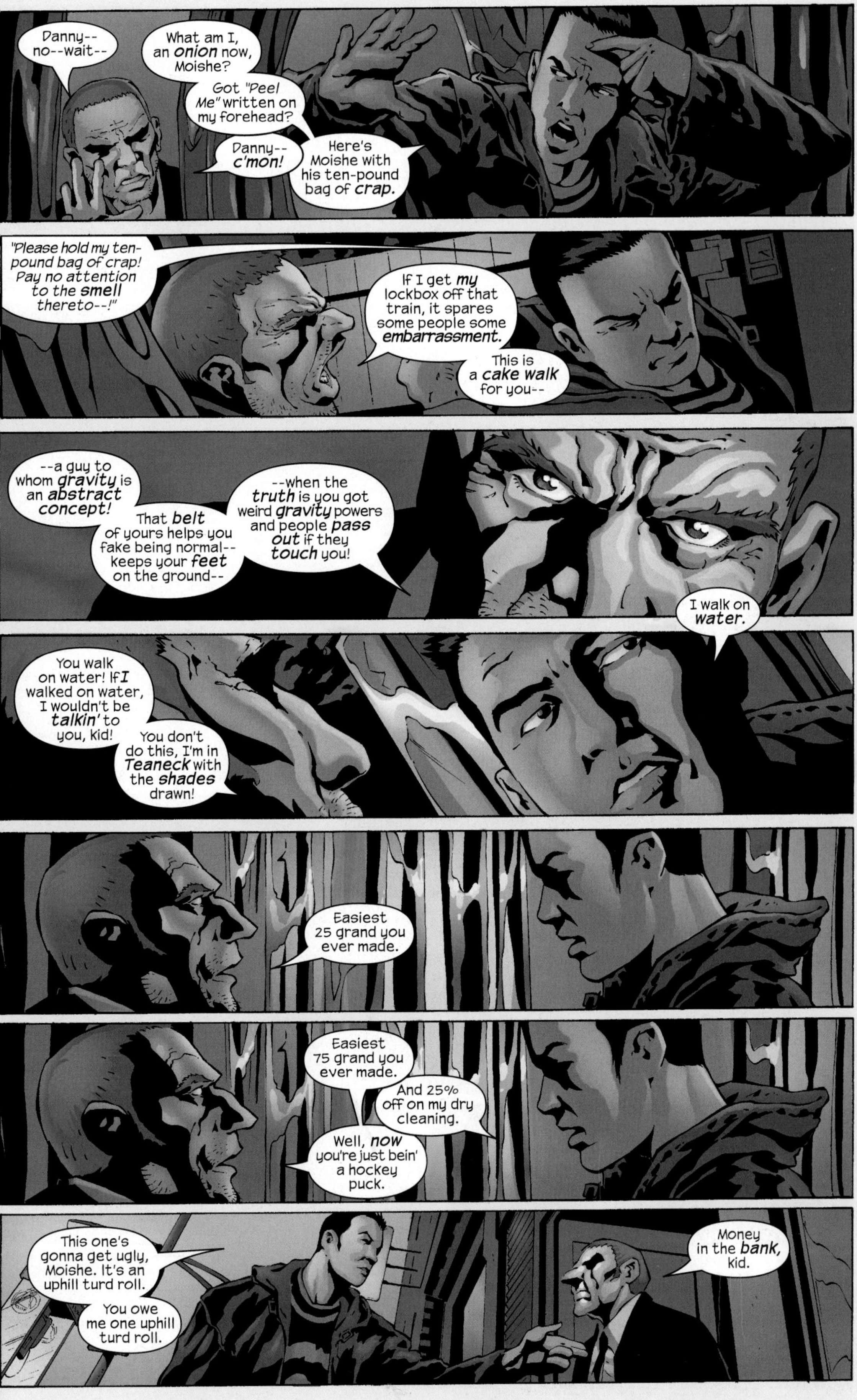

Danny-- no--wait--
What am I, an onion now, Moishe?
Got "Peel Me" written on my forehead?
Danny-- c'mon!
Here's Moishe with his ten-pound bag of crap.
"Please hold my ten-pound bag of crap! Pay no attention to the smell thereto--!"
If I get my lockbox off that train, it spares some people some embarrassment.
This is a cake walk for you--
--a guy to whom gravity is an abstract concept!
That belt of yours helps you fake being normal-- keeps your feet on the ground--
--when the truth is you got weird gravity powers and people pass out if they touch you!
I walk on water.
You walk on water! If I walked on water, I wouldn't be talkin' to you, kid!
You don't do this, I'm in Teaneck with the shades drawn!
Easiest 25 grand you ever made.
Easiest 75 grand you ever made.
And 25% off on my dry cleaning.
Well, now you're just bein' a hockey puck.
This one's gonna get ugly, Moishe. It's an uphill turd roll.
You owe me one uphill turd roll.
Money in the bank, kid.

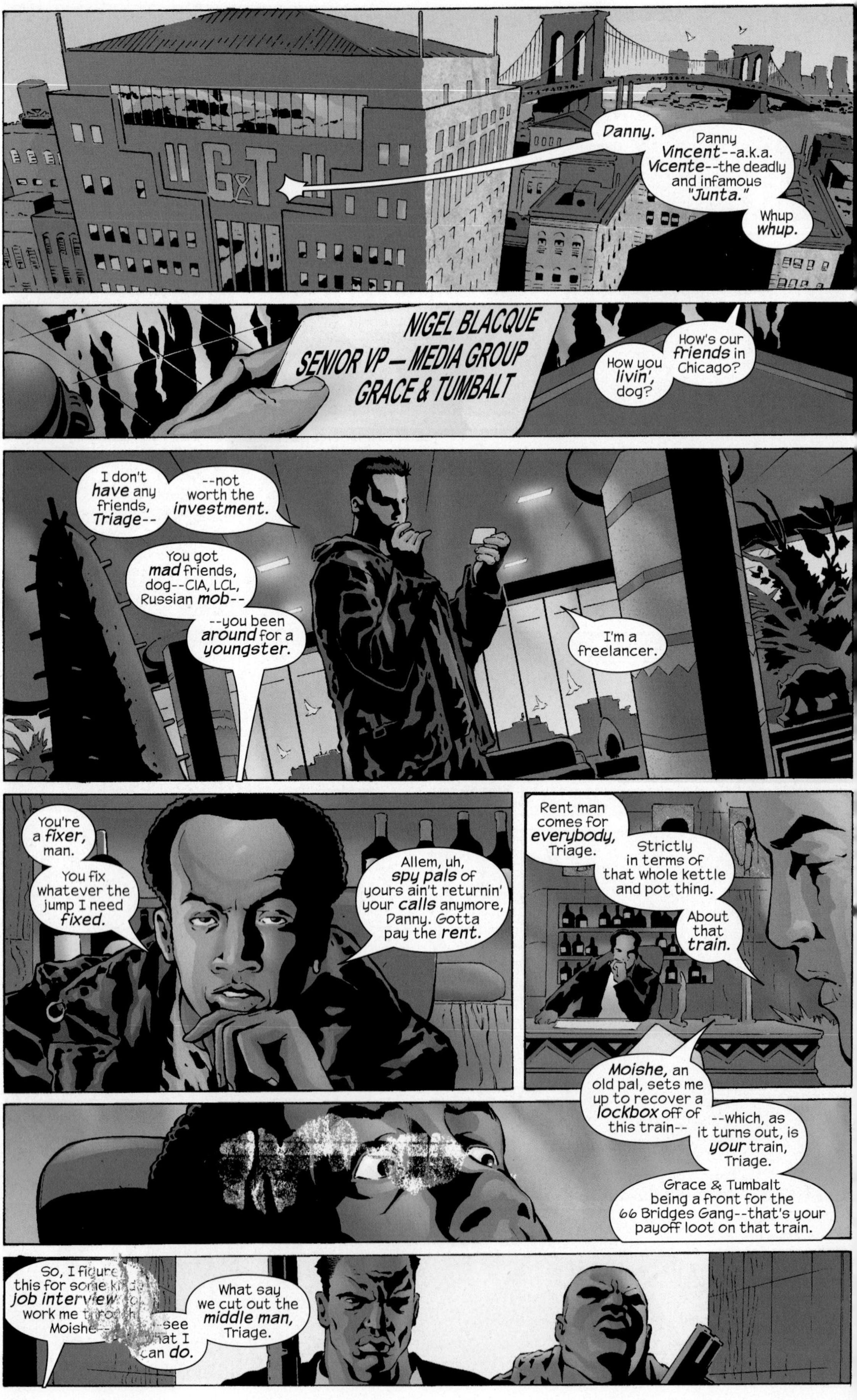
Danny.
Danny Vincent--a.k.a. Vicente--the deadly and infamous "Junta."
Whup whup.
NIGEL BLACQUE
SENIOR VP — MEDIA GROUP
GRACE & TUMBALT
How you livin', dog?
How's our friends in Chicago?
I don't have any friends, Triage--
--not worth the investment.
You got mad friends, dog--CIA, LCL, Russian mob--
--you been around for a youngster.
I'm a freelancer.
You're a fixer, man.
You fix whatever the jump I need fixed.
Allem, uh, spy pals of yours ain't returnin' your calls anymore, Danny. Gotta pay the rent.
Rent man comes for everybody, Triage.
Strictly in terms of that whole kettle and pot thing.
About that train.
Moishe, an old pal, sets me up to recover a lockbox off of this train--
--which, as it turns out, is your train, Triage.
Grace & Tumbalt being a front for the 66 Bridges Gang--that's your payoff loot on that train.
So, I figure this for some ki job interview work me thro Moishe--
--see hat I can do.
What say we cut out the middle man, Triage.

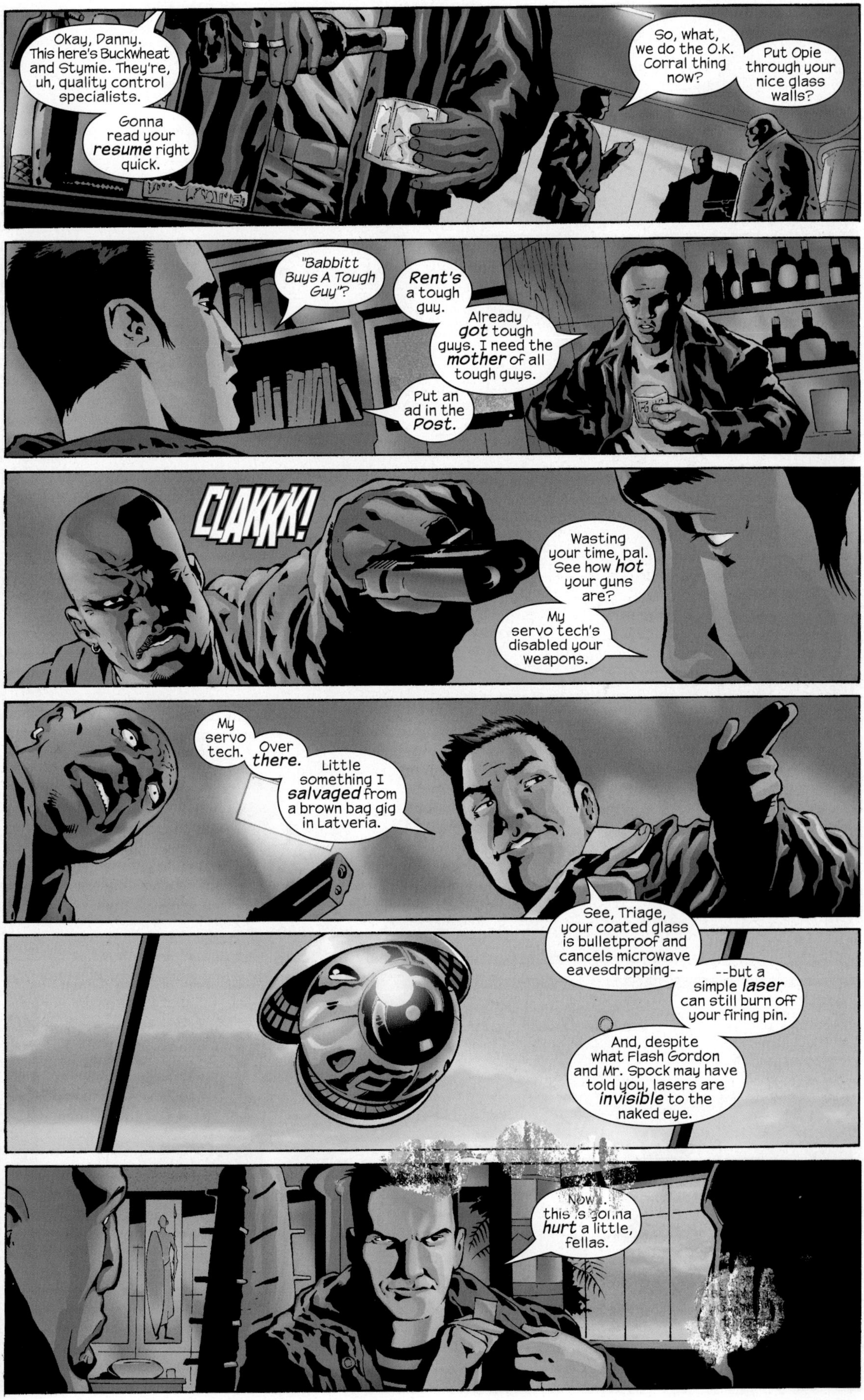

Okay, Danny. This here's Buckwheat and Stymie. They're, uh, quality control specialists.
Gonna read your *resume* right quick.
So, what, we do the O.K. Corral thing now?
Put Opie through your nice glass walls?
"Babbitt Buys A Tough Guy"?
Rent's a tough guy.
Already *got* tough guys. I need the *mother* of all tough guys.
Put an ad in the *Post*.
CLAKKK!
Wasting your time, pal. See how *hot* your guns are?
My servo tech's disabled your weapons.
My servo tech.
Over *there.*
Little something I *salvaged* from a brown bag gig in Latveria.
See, Triage, your coated glass is bulletproof and cancels microwave eavesdropping--
--but a simple *laser* can still burn off your firing pin.
And, despite what Flash Gordon and Mr. Spock may have told you, lasers are *invisible* to the naked eye.
Now... this is gonna *hurt* a little, fellas.

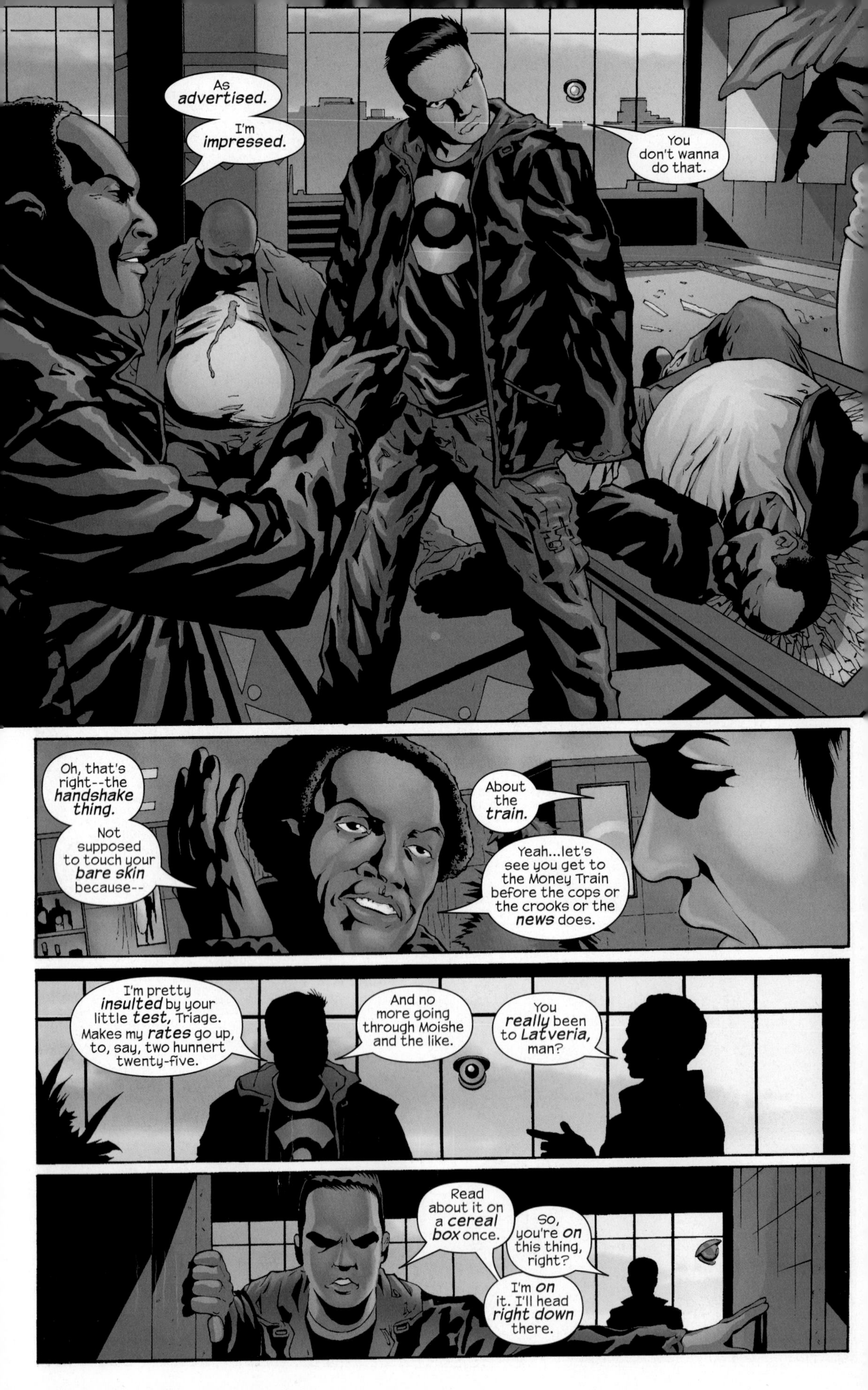

As advertised.
I'm impressed.
You don't wanna do that.
Oh, that's right--the handshake thing.
Not supposed to touch your bare skin because--
About the train.
Yeah...let's see you get to the Money Train before the cops or the crooks or the news does.
I'm pretty insulted by your little test, Triage. Makes my rates go up, to, say, two hunnert twenty-five.
And no more going through Moishe and the like.
You really been to Latveria, man?
Read about it on a cereal box once.
So, you're on this thing, right?
I'm on it. I'll head right down there.

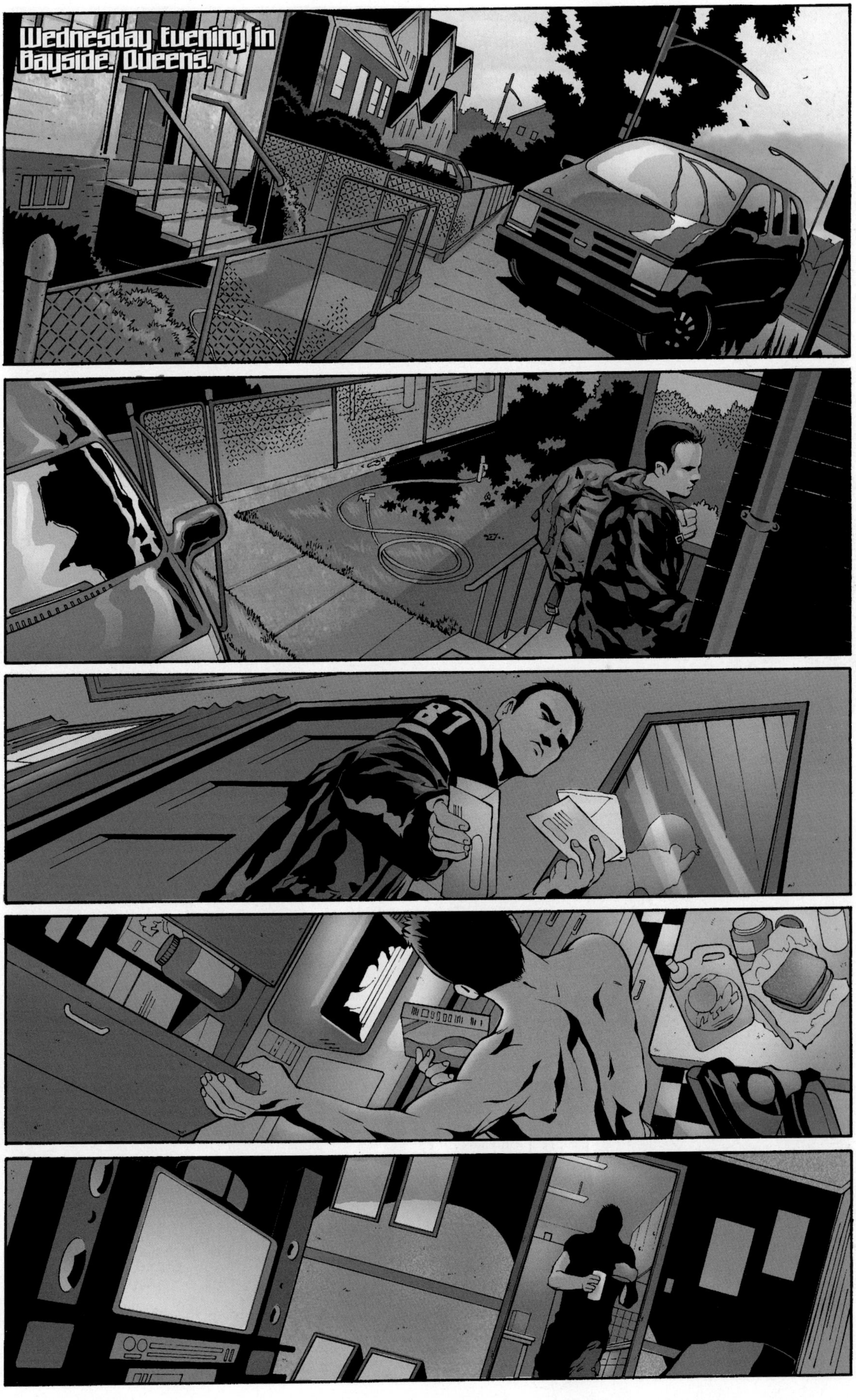
Wednesday evening in Bayside, Queens.

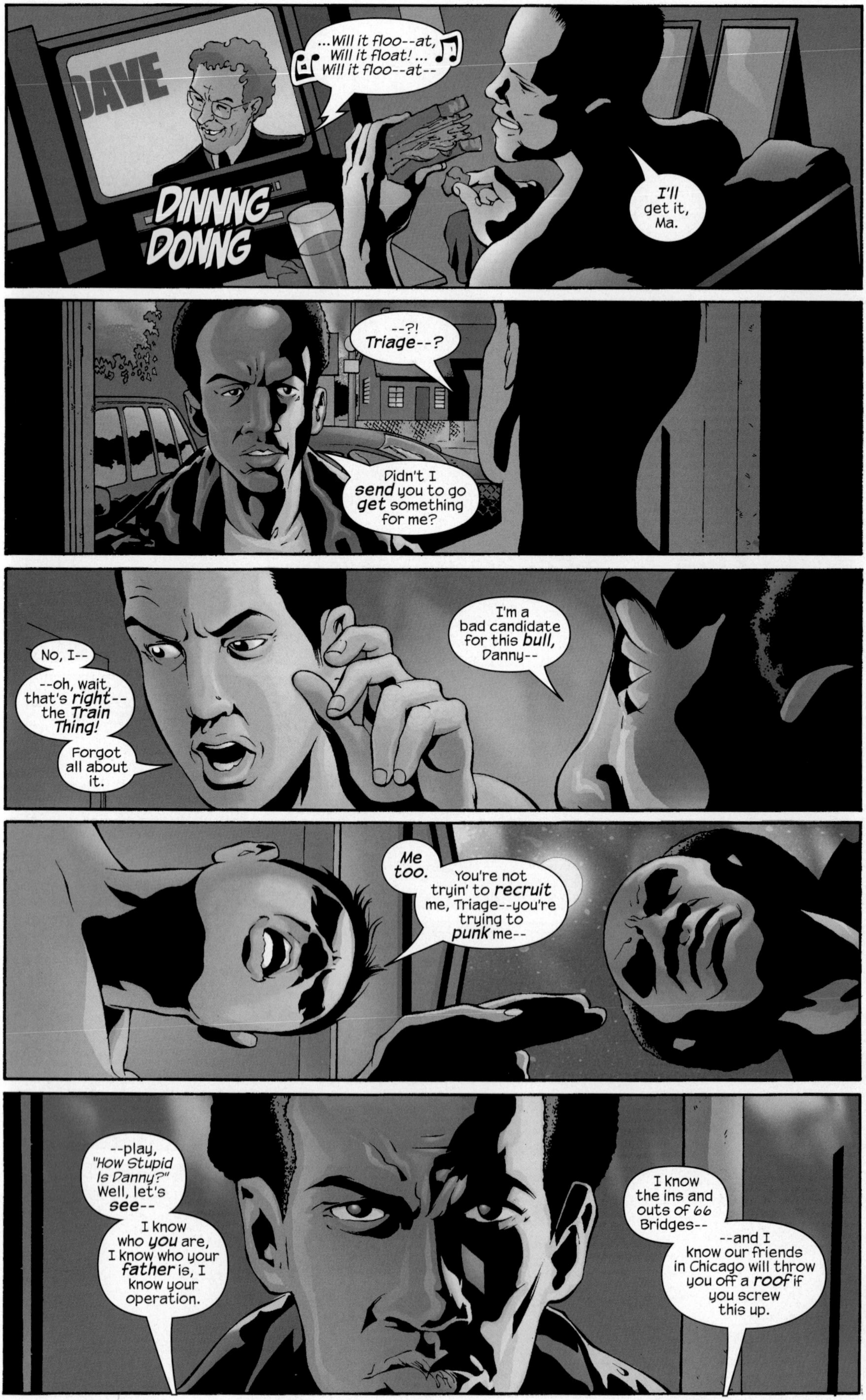
DAVE
...Will it floo--at, Will it float! ... Will it floo--at--
DINNNG DONNG
I'll get it, Ma.
--?! Triage--?
Didn't I send you to go get something for me?
I'm a bad candidate for this bull, Danny--
No, I--
--oh, wait, that's right--the Train Thing!
Forgot all about it.
Me too.
You're not tryin' to recruit me, Triage--you're trying to punk me--
--play, "How Stupid Is Danny?" Well, let's see--
I know who you are, I know who your father is, I know your operation.
I know the ins and outs of 66 Bridges--
--and I know our friends in Chicago will throw you off a roof if you screw this up.

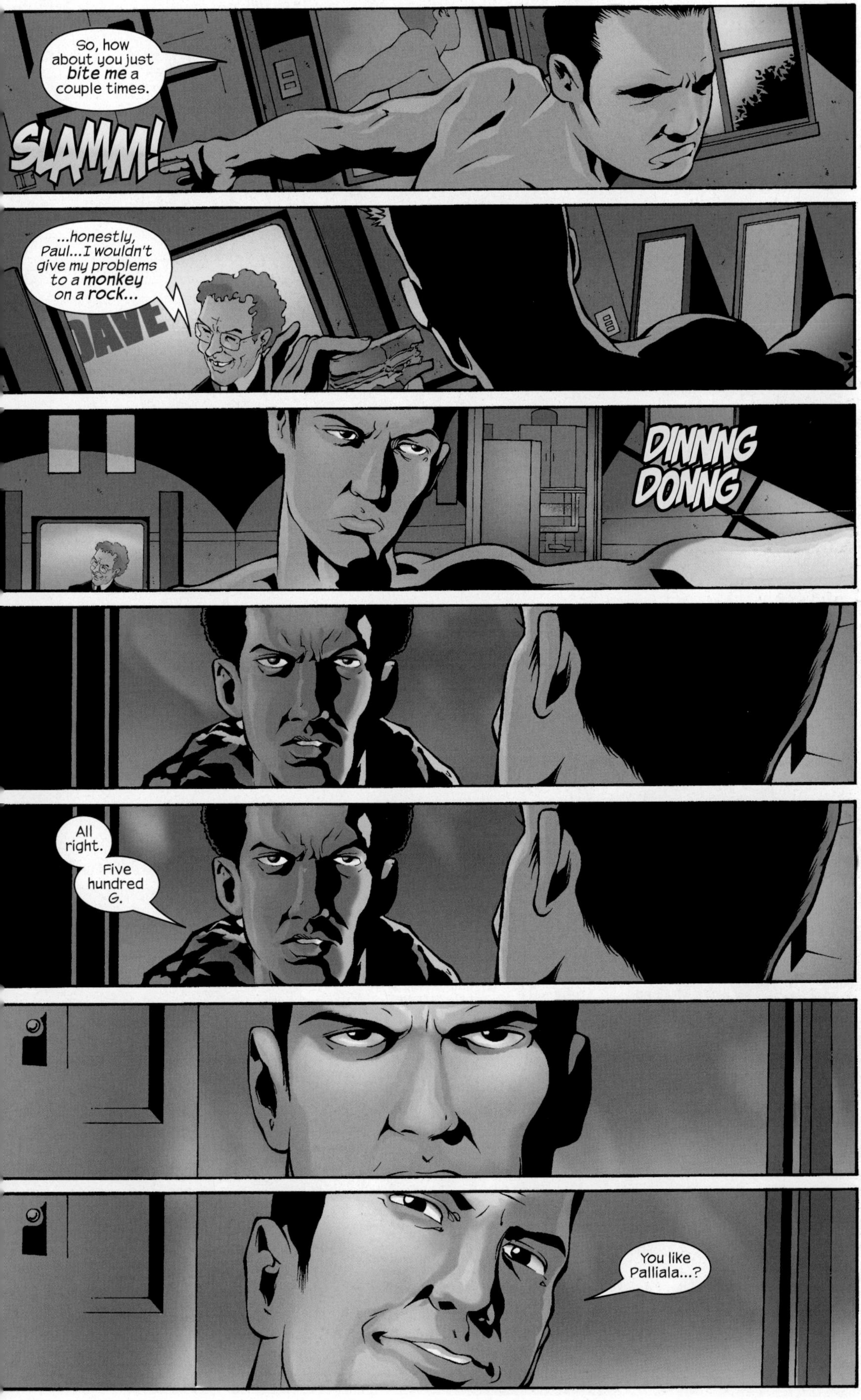
So, how about you just bite me a couple times.
SLAMM!
...honestly, Paul...I wouldn't give my problems to a monkey on a rock...
DAVE
DINNNG DONNG
All right.
Five hundred G.
You like Palliala...?

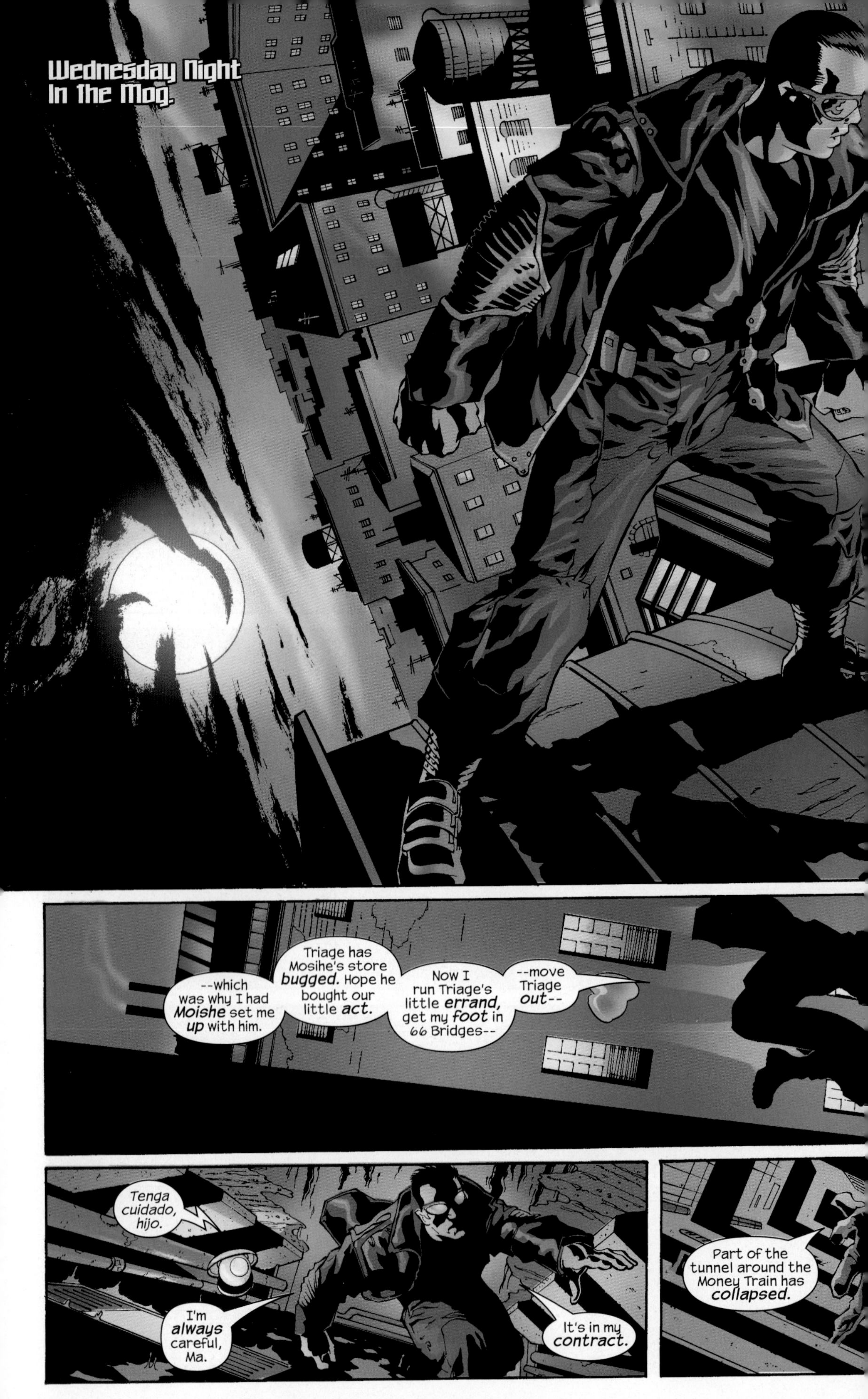

Wednesday Night In the Mog.
--which was why I had Moishe set me up with him.
Triage has Mosihe's store bugged. Hope he bought our little act.
Now I run Triage's little errand, get my foot in 66 Bridges--
--move Triage out--
Tenga cuidado, hijo.
I'm always careful, Ma.
It's in my contract.
Part of the tunnel around the Money Train has collapsed.

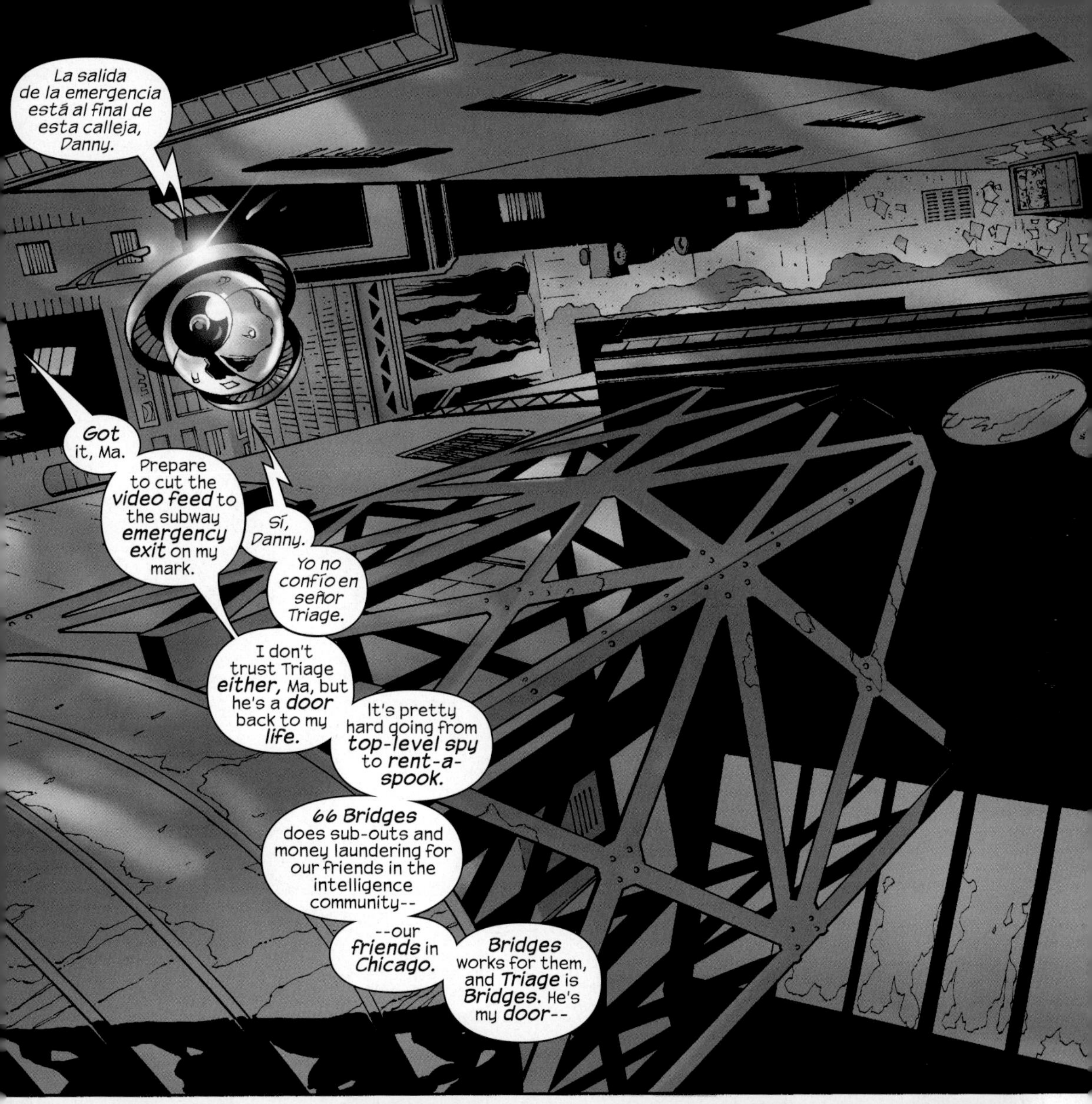
La salida de la emergencia está al final de esta calleja, Danny.
Got it, Ma. Prepare to cut the video feed to the subway emergency exit on my mark.
Sí, Danny. Yo no confío en señor Triage.
I don't trust Triage either, Ma, but he's a door back to my life.
It's pretty hard going from top-level spy to rent-a-spook.
66 Bridges does sub-outs and money laundering for our friends in the intelligence community--
--our friends in Chicago.
Bridges works for them, and Triage is Bridges. He's my door--

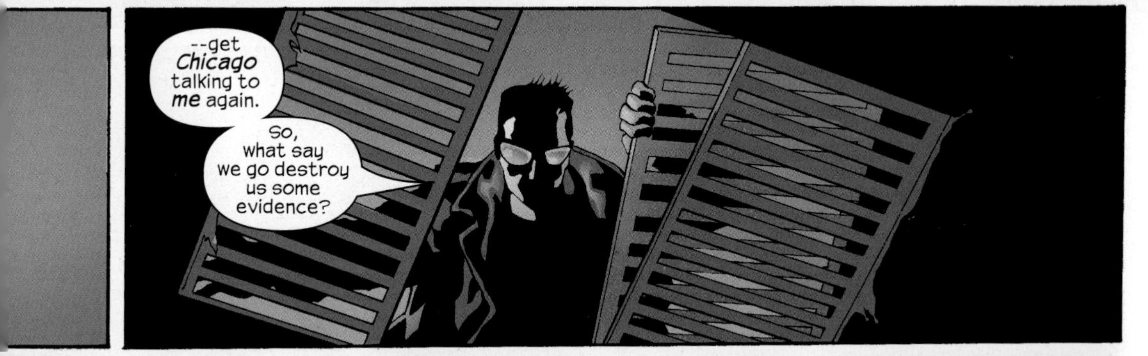
--get Chicago talking to me again.
So, what say we go destroy us some evidence?

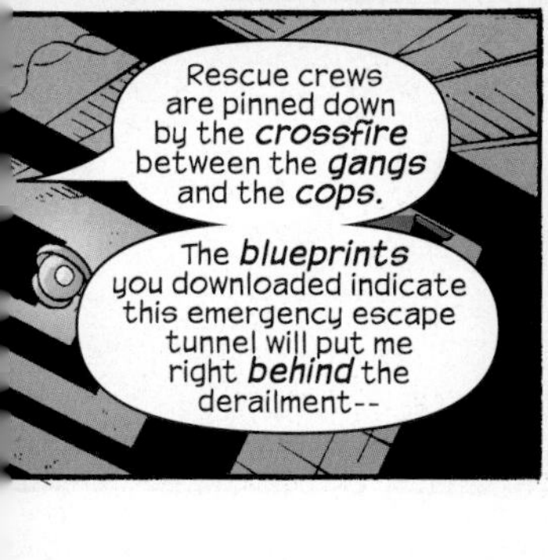
Rescue crews are pinned down by the crossfire between the gangs and the cops.
The blueprints you downloaded indicate this emergency escape tunnel will put me right behind the derailment--

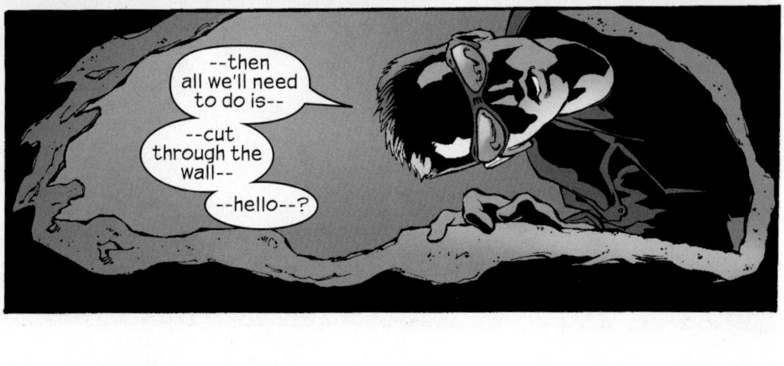
--then all we'll need to do is--
--cut through the wall--
--hello--?

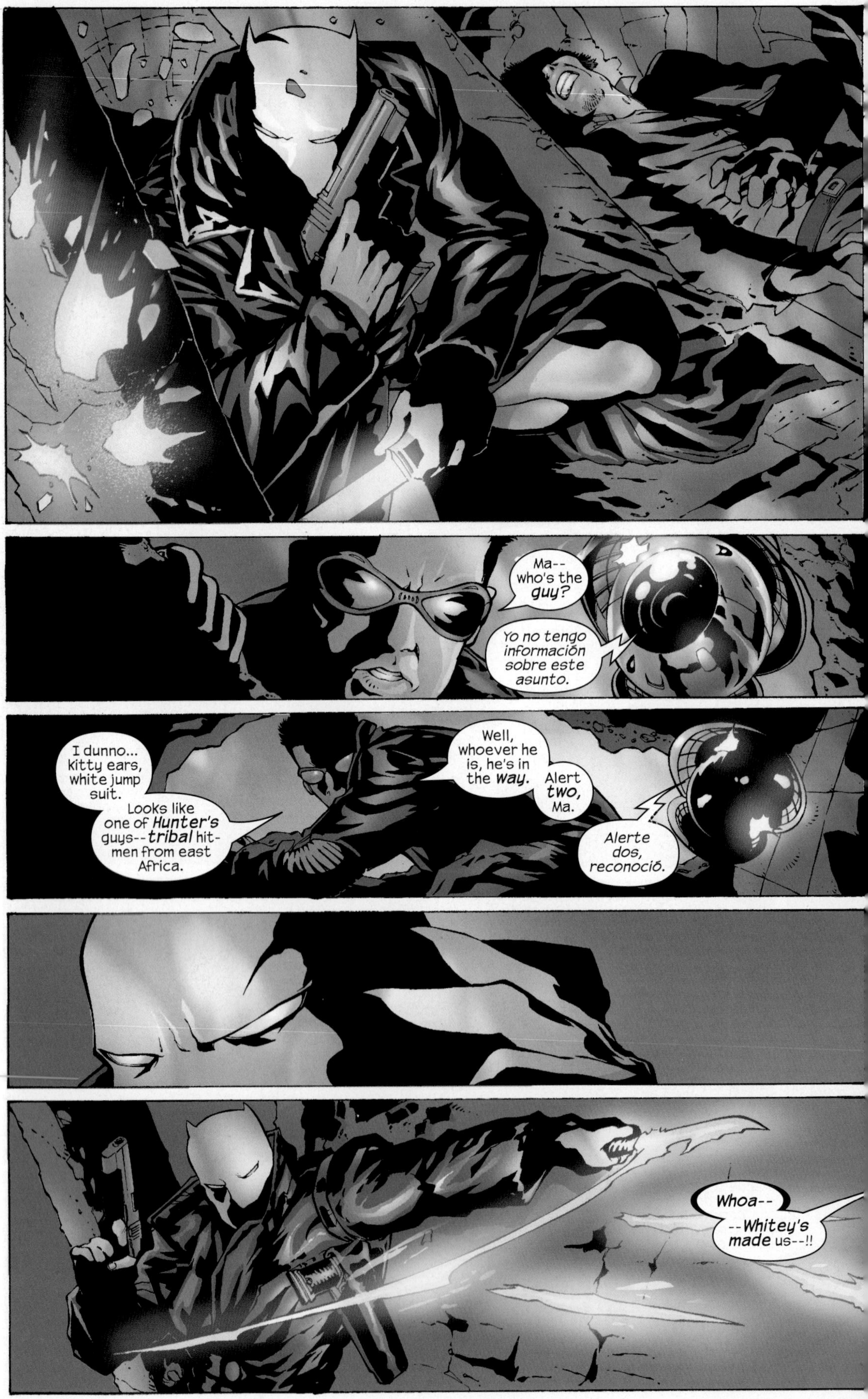

Ma--
who's the
guy?
Yo no tengo
información
sobre este
asunto.
I dunno...
kitty ears,
white jump
suit.
Looks like
one of Hunter's
guys--tribal hit-
men from east
Africa.
Well,
whoever he
is, he's in
the way.
Alert
two,
Ma.
Alerte
dos,
reconoció.
Whoa--
--Whitey's
made us--!!

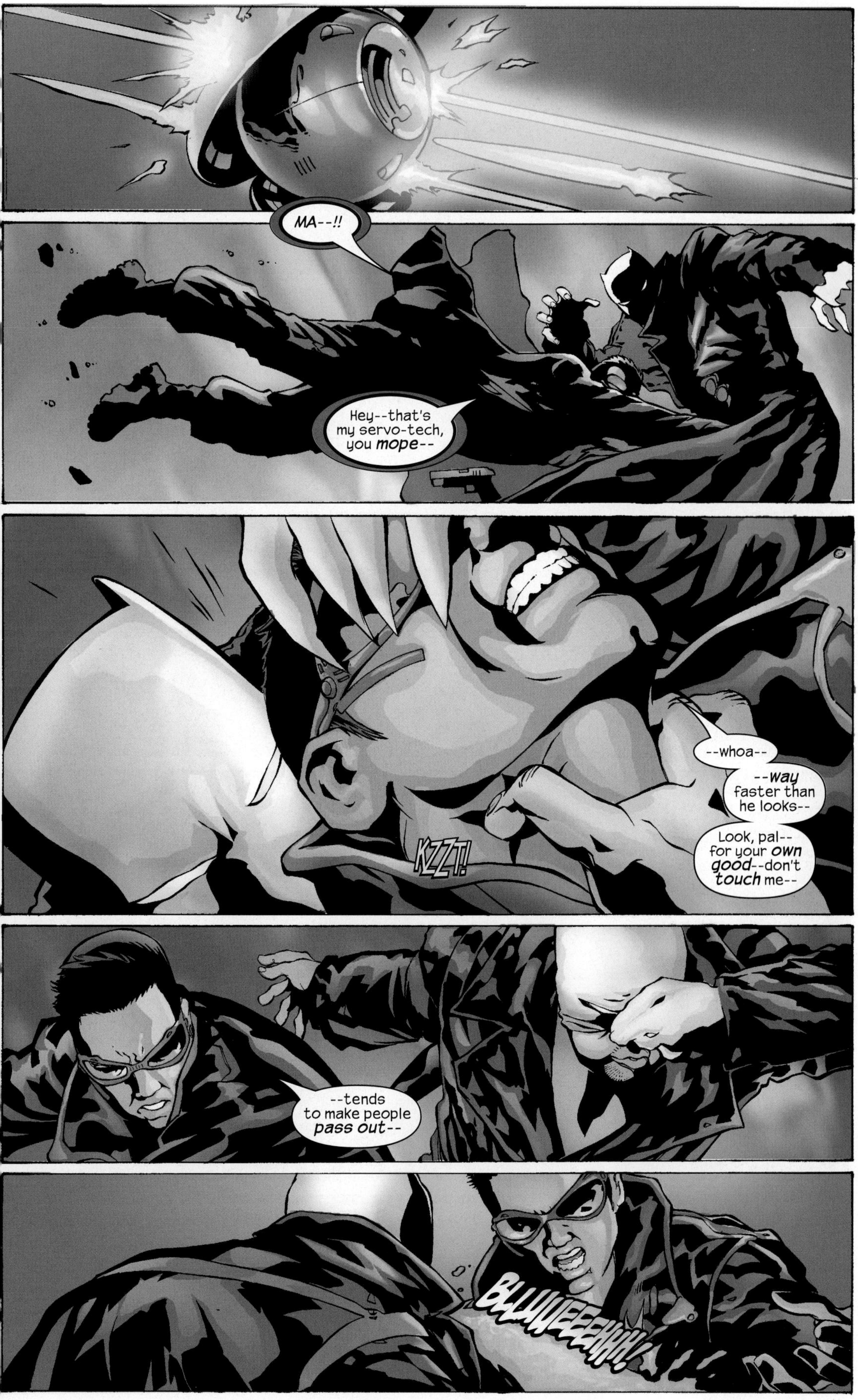
MA--!!
Hey--that's my servo-tech, you mope--
KZZT!
--whoa--
--way faster than he looks--
Look, pal-- for your own good--don't touch me--
--tends to make people pass out--
BLUUEEEHHH!

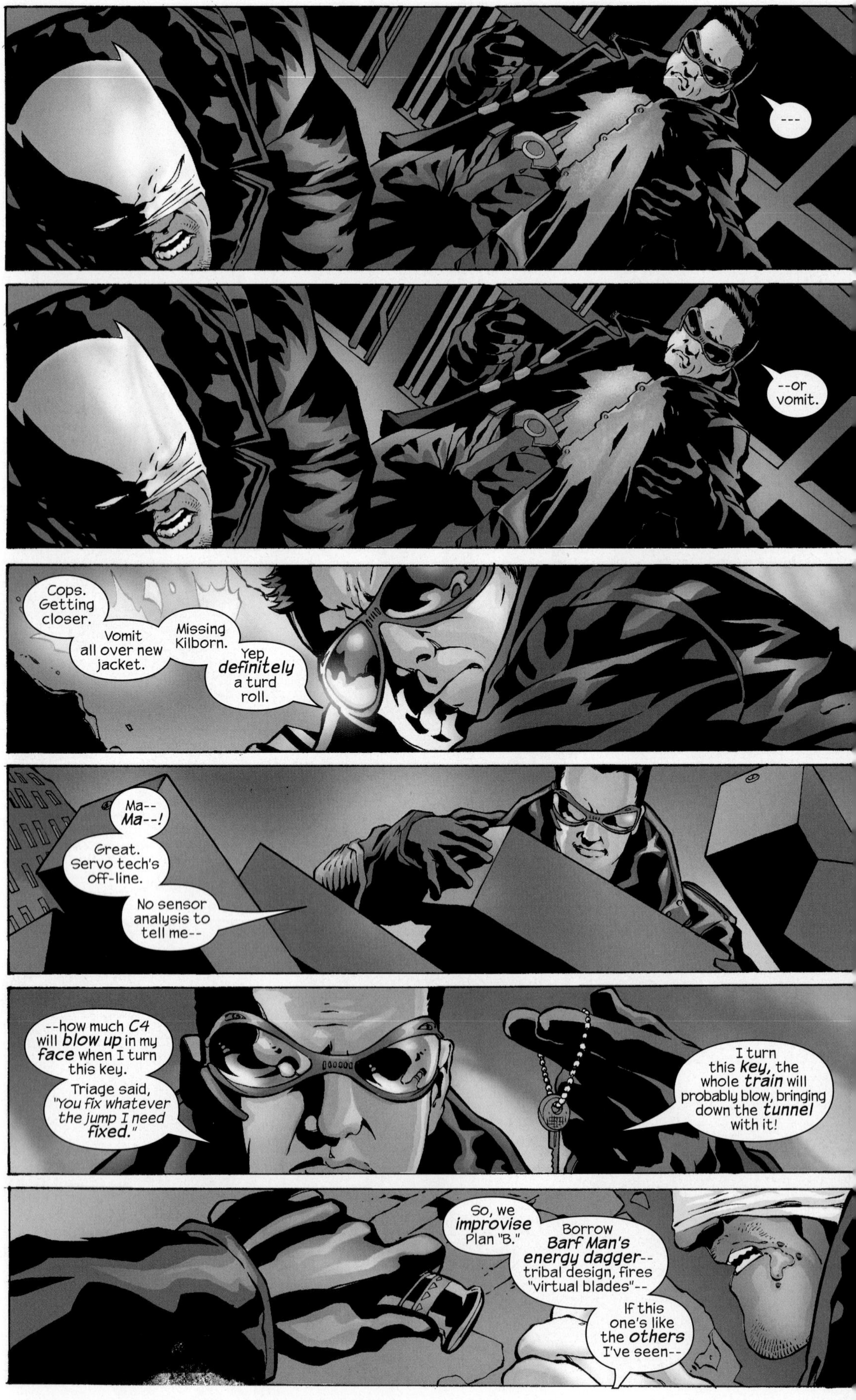

--or vomit.
Cops. Getting closer.
Vomit all over new jacket.
Missing Kilborn.
Yep, definitely a turd roll.
Ma-- Ma--!
Great. Servo tech's off-line.
No sensor analysis to tell me--
--how much C4 will blow up in my face when I turn this key.
Triage said, "You fix whatever the jump I need fixed."
I turn this key, the whole train will probably blow, bringing down the tunnel with it!
So, we improvise Plan "B."
Borrow Barf Man's energy dagger-- tribal design, fires "virtual blades"--
If this one's like the others I've seen--

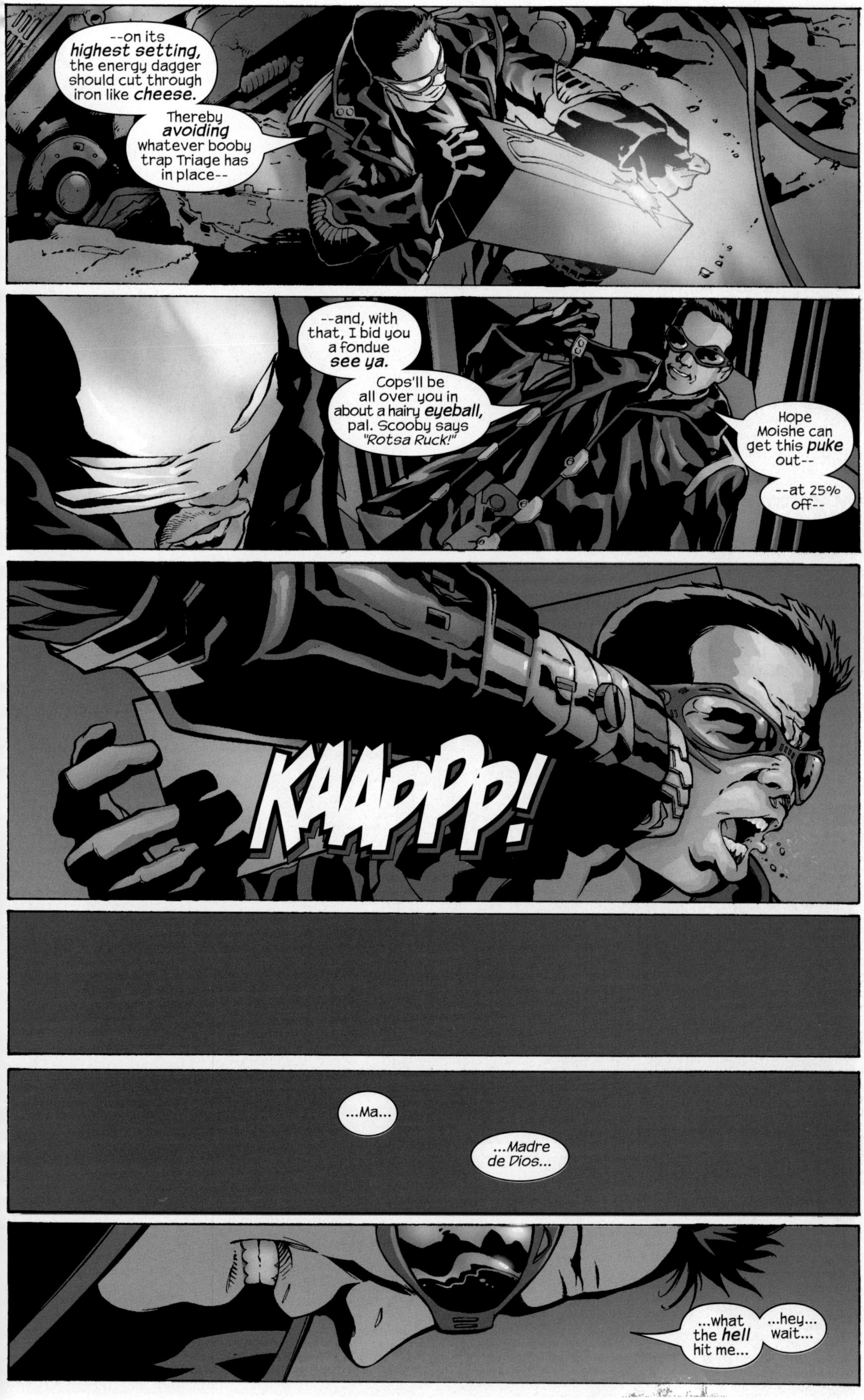
--on its highest setting, the energy dagger should cut through iron like cheese.
Thereby avoiding whatever booby trap Triage has in place--
--and, with that, I bid you a fondue see ya.
Cops'll be all over you in about a hairy eyeball, pal. Scooby says "Rotsa Ruck!"
Hope Moishe can get this puke out--
--at 25% off--
KAAPPP!
...Ma...
...Madre de Dios...
...what the hell hit me...
...hey... wait...

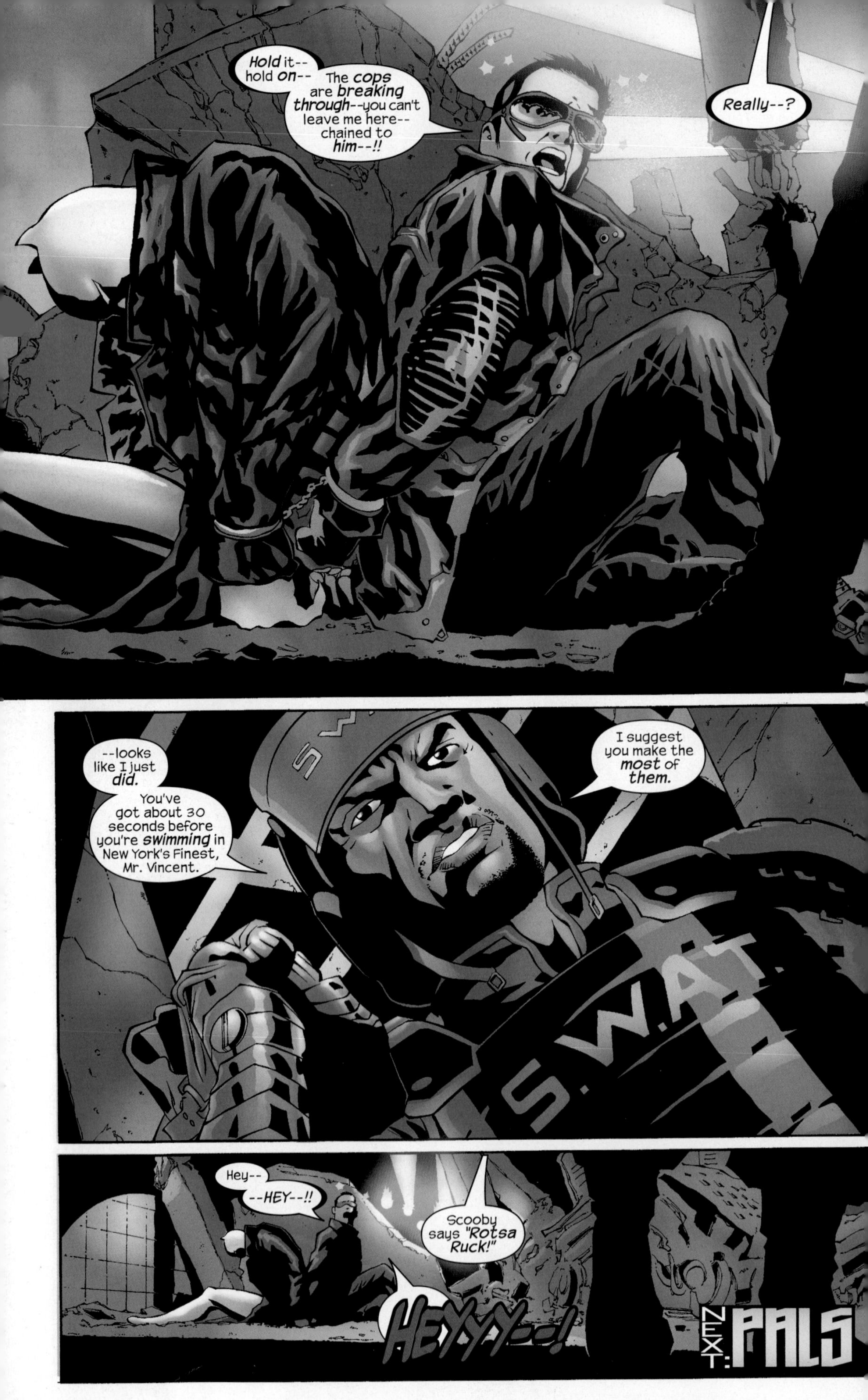
Hold it--
hold on--
The cops are breaking through--you can't leave me here--chained to him--!!
Really--?
--looks like I just did.
You've got about 30 seconds before you're swimming in New York's Finest, Mr. Vincent.
I suggest you make the most of them.
S.W.A.T.
Hey--
--HEY--!!
Scooby says "Rotsa Ruck!"
HEYYY--!
NEXT: PALS

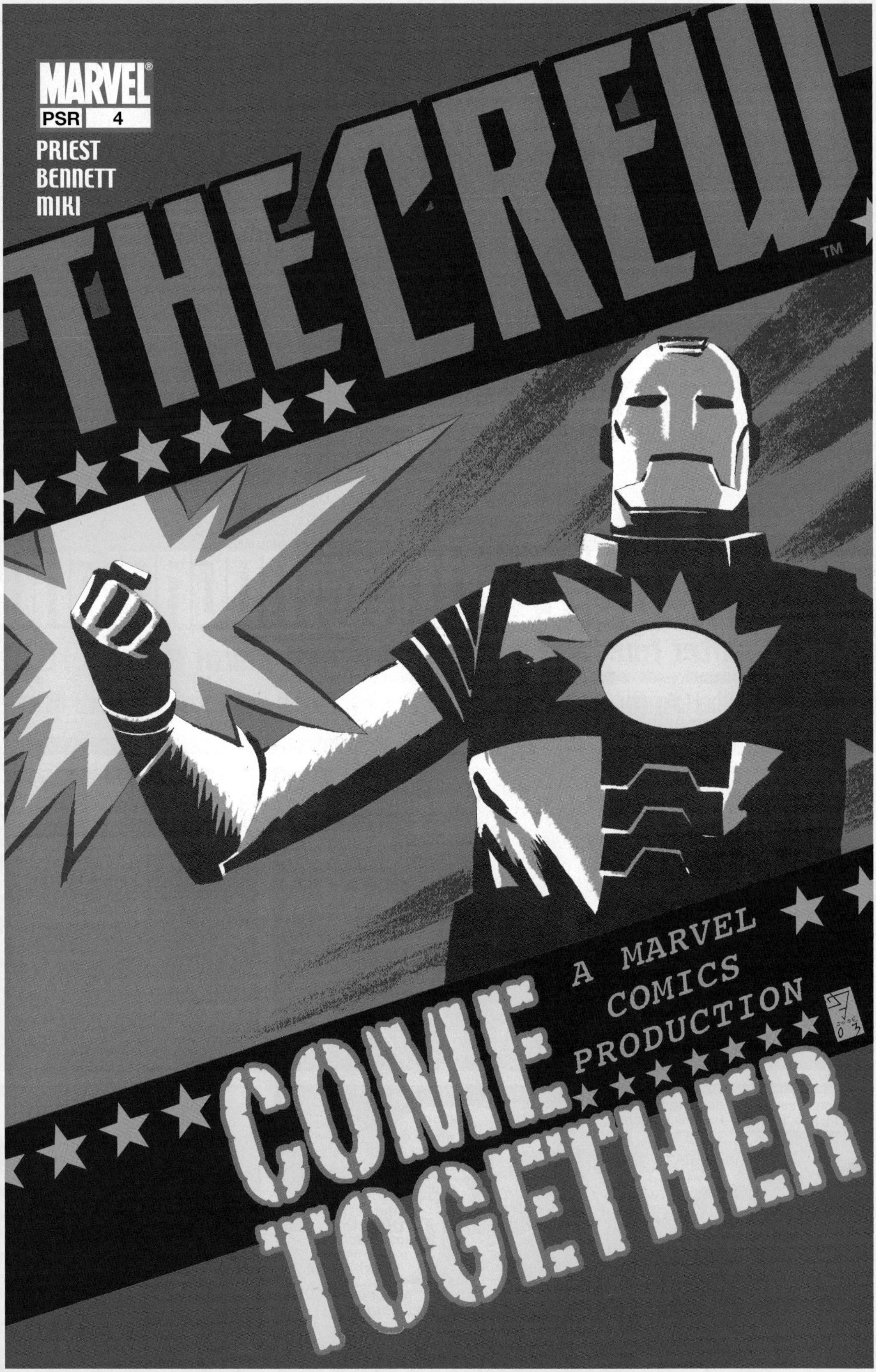

MARVEL
PSR 4
PRIEST
BENNETT
MIKI
THE CREW
A MARVEL COMICS PRODUCTION
COME TOGETHER

Thursday Morning in the Mog.

Anxiety-- boiling *orange*. *Sweat* glands pumping *salt*. Labored *breathing--heat--* coming *this* way.

E.S.U. The *smell* of *boot polish* acts like a *radar* blip. *Foot falls* sound like *mortar rounds. Five* of them--

--*Barry Dale* on point. He chews *Trident* when he gets nervous.

Jeff Allen, in Walgreens bargain cologne, backs him up.

In about *80 feet*, they'll find the *hole* I cut through the subway tunnel access wall.

Then they'll find *me* on the other side of it--

Stan Lee presents

BIG TROUBLE in LITTLE MOGADISHU

Chapter Four: PALS

PRIEST & Joe Bennett
STORYTELLERS

Crime Lab Studios	Virtual Calligraphy	Avalon Studios	Andy Schmidt & Marc Sumerak	Tom Brevoort	Joe Quesada	Bill Jemas
INKERS	LETTERING	COLORISTS	ASSISTANT EDITORS	EDITOR	EDITOR IN CHIEF	PRESIDENT

--cuffed to *Sleeping Beauty*, here.

Bruh.

Ay, yo *Bruh.*

Time to *bounce,* G.

In about 15 seconds Barry and his crew are gonna yank off this mask--

--and find OCCB Narcotics Officer *Kasper Cole* dressed like a *White Tiger.*

Remember: when I got the *Tiger* mask on, it's "*Big Talk*" and thick accent...

...*Ma*--!
...what...where's my *servo-tech?*

Your *what?*

The little *robot* that hangs out with me--my *tech*--

Are you *delirious*--?

Probably...what *hap*--wait--stop-- hold up--

--my *belt.* He *broke* my *belt.*

Who--?!

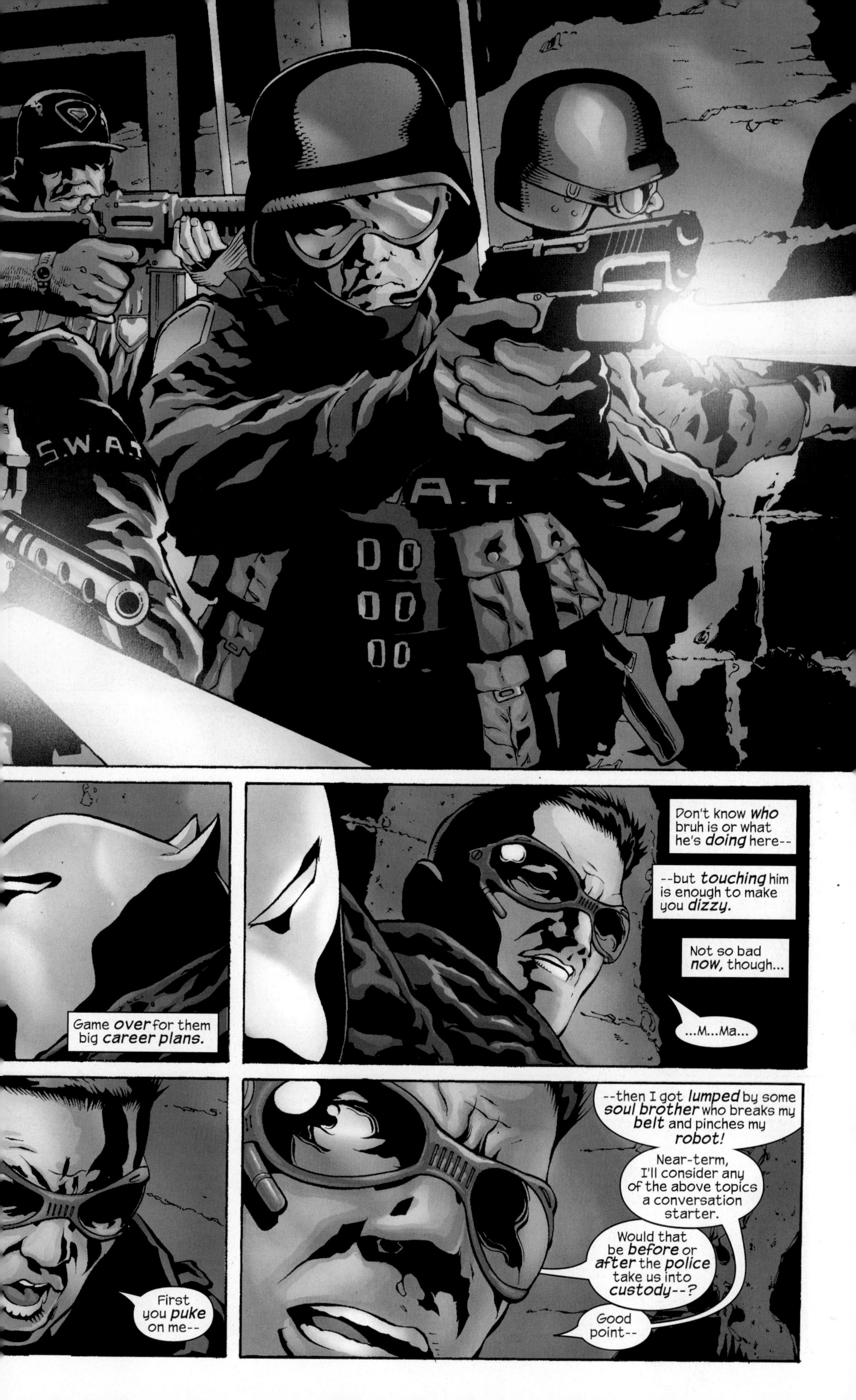

S.W.A.T.
Game over for them big career plans.
Don't know who bruh is or what he's doing here--
--but touching him is enough to make you dizzy.
Not so bad now, though...
...M...Ma...
First you puke on me--
--then I got lumped by some soul brother who breaks my belt and pinches my robot!
Near-term, I'll consider any of the above topics a conversation starter.
Would that be before or after the police take us into custody--?
Good point--

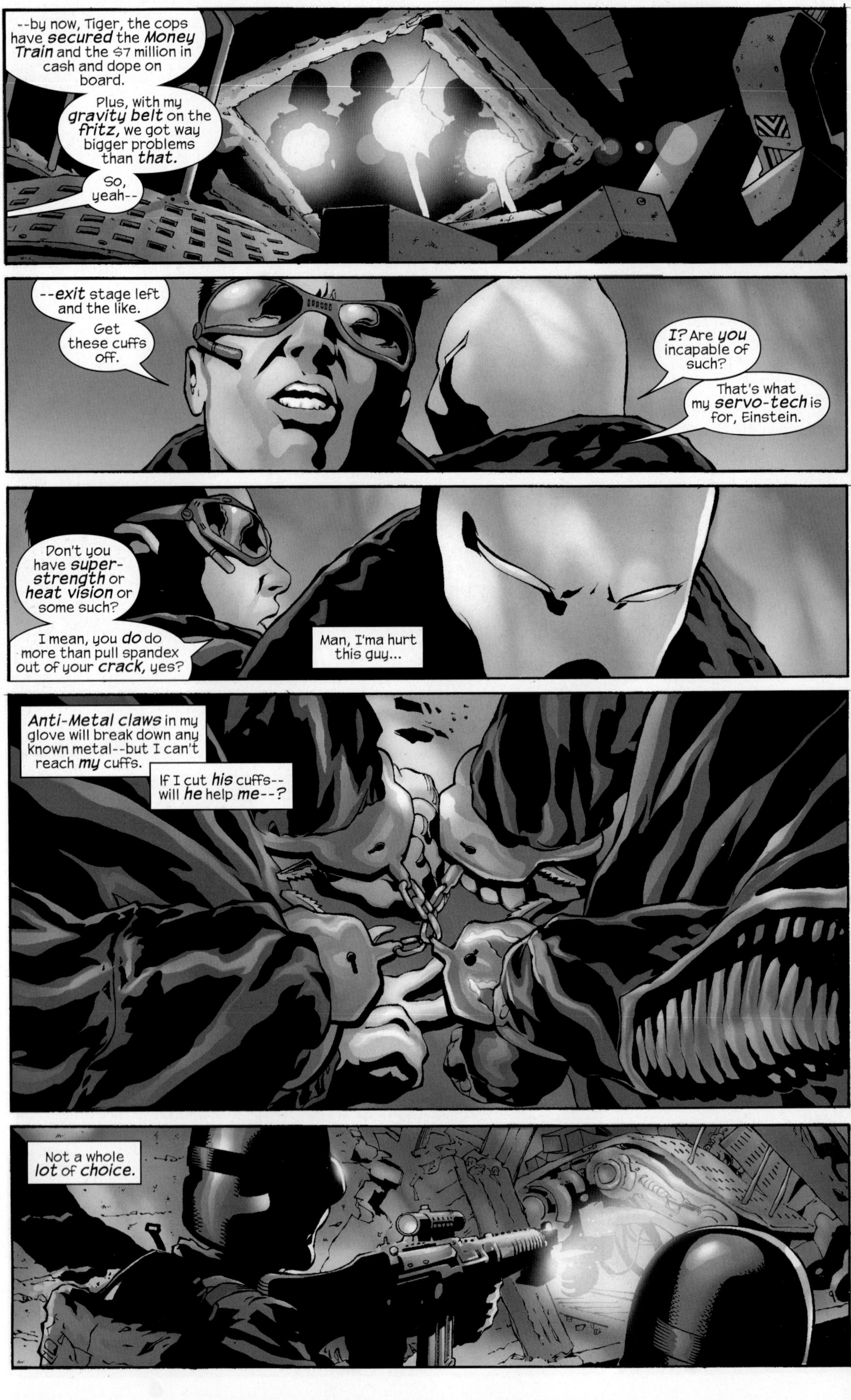
--by now, Tiger, the cops have *secured* the *Money Train* and the $7 million in cash and dope on board.
Plus, with my *gravity belt* on the *fritz*, we got way bigger problems than *that.*
So, yeah--
--*exit* stage left and the like.
Get these cuffs off.
I? Are *you* incapable of such?
That's what my *servo-tech* is for, Einstein.
Don't you have *super-strength* or *heat vision* or some such?
I mean, you *do* do more than pull spandex out of your *crack*, yes?
Man, I'ma hurt this guy...
Anti-Metal claws in my glove will break down any known metal--but I can't reach *my* cuffs.
If I cut *his* cuffs--will *he* help *me*--?
Not a whole *lot* of *choice.*

Yes!

Good *deal*, Whitey.

Damn.

Well, it's been *grins*.

I *knew* it...

By the way, I'm *sendin'* you Moishe's *bill* for the *dry cleaning*.

You *do* that. I'll be living in a *Maytag box* in an *alley* somewhere--

--once I lose my *shield* for playing "super hero."

Vibranium-based *field generators* in the soles of these *boots* allow me to run up the sides of *buildings*--

--and survive falls up to 8 stories high.

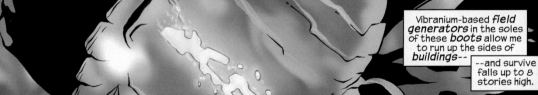

Looks like the *vibrational field* has *other* uses, too.

Vibranium *microweave* in the *costume* saps incoming bullets of their *momentum*--

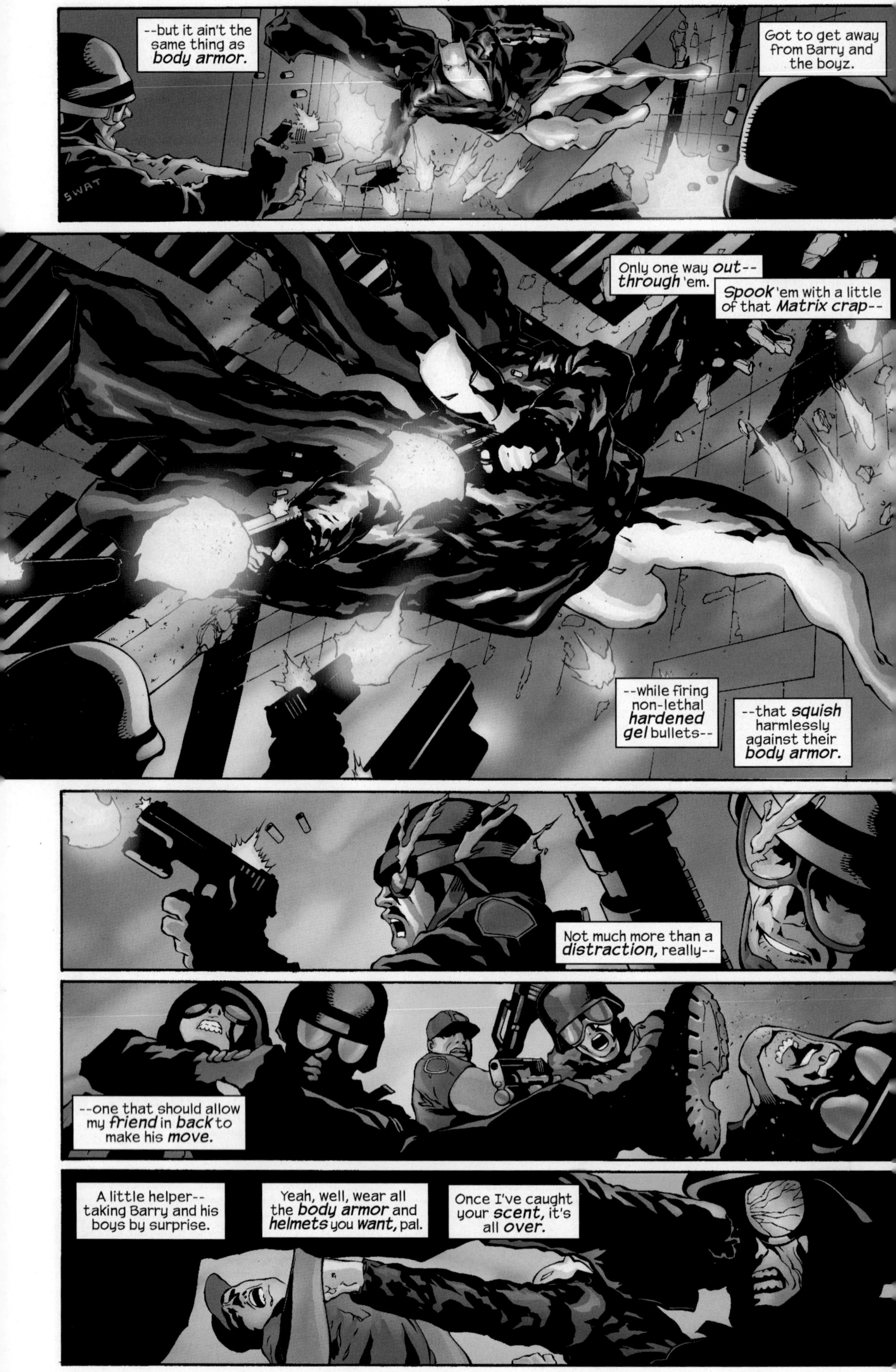
--but it ain't the same thing as body armor.
Got to get away from Barry and the boyz.
SWAT
Only one way out--through 'em.
Spook 'em with a little of that Matrix crap--
--while firing non-lethal hardened gel bullets--
--that squish harmlessly against their body armor.
Not much more than a distraction, really--
--one that should allow my friend in back to make his move.
A little helper--taking Barry and his boys by surprise.
Yeah, well, wear all the body armor and helmets you want, pal.
Once I've caught your scent, it's all over.

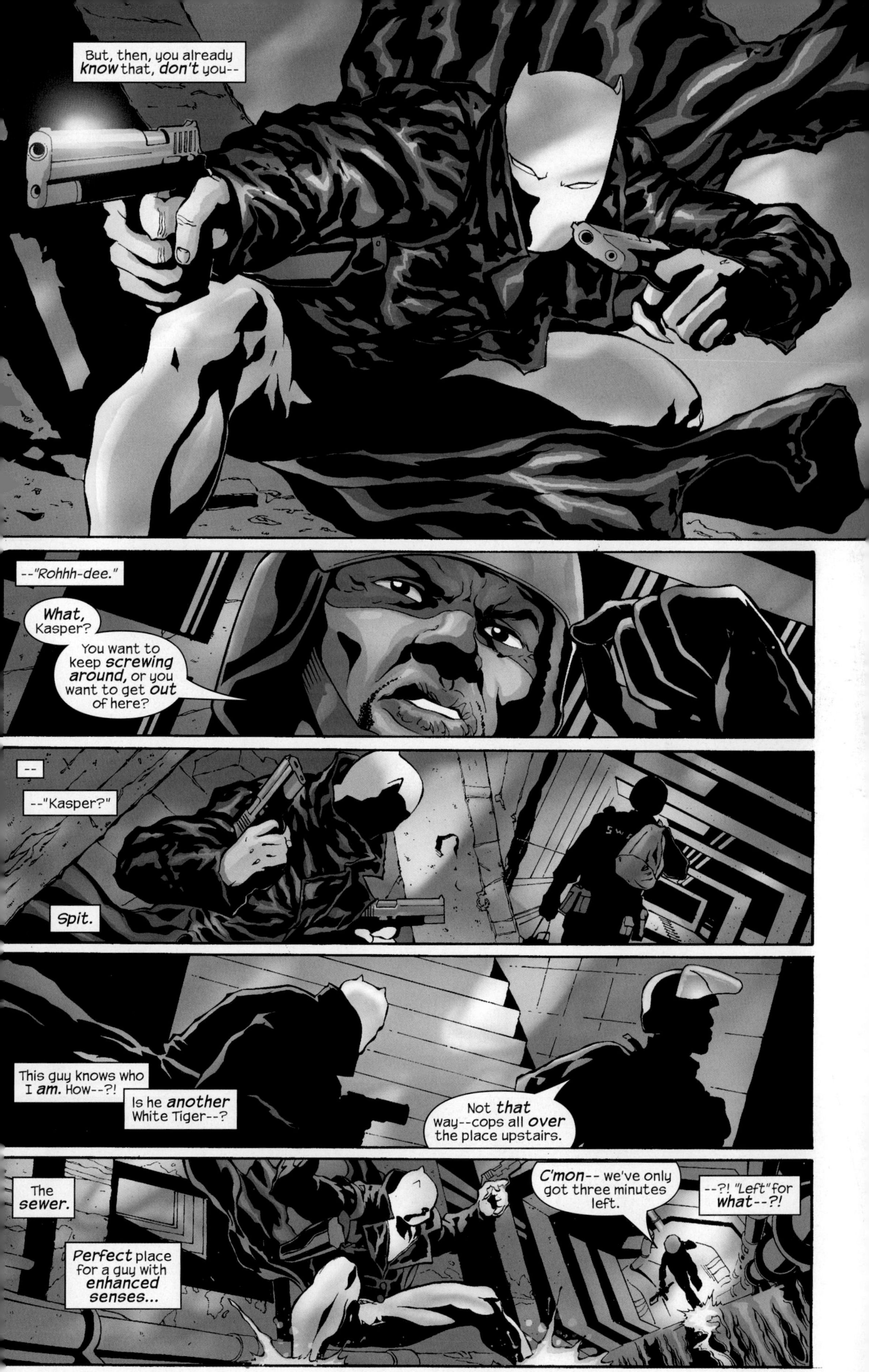

But, then, you already know that, don't you--
--"Rohhh-dee."
What, Kasper?
You want to keep screwing around, or you want to get out of here?
--
--"Kasper?"
Spit.
This guy knows who I am. How--?!
Is he another White Tiger--?
Not that way--cops all over the place upstairs.
The sewer.
Perfect place for a guy with enhanced senses...
C'mon-- we've only got three minutes left.
--?! "Left" for what--?!

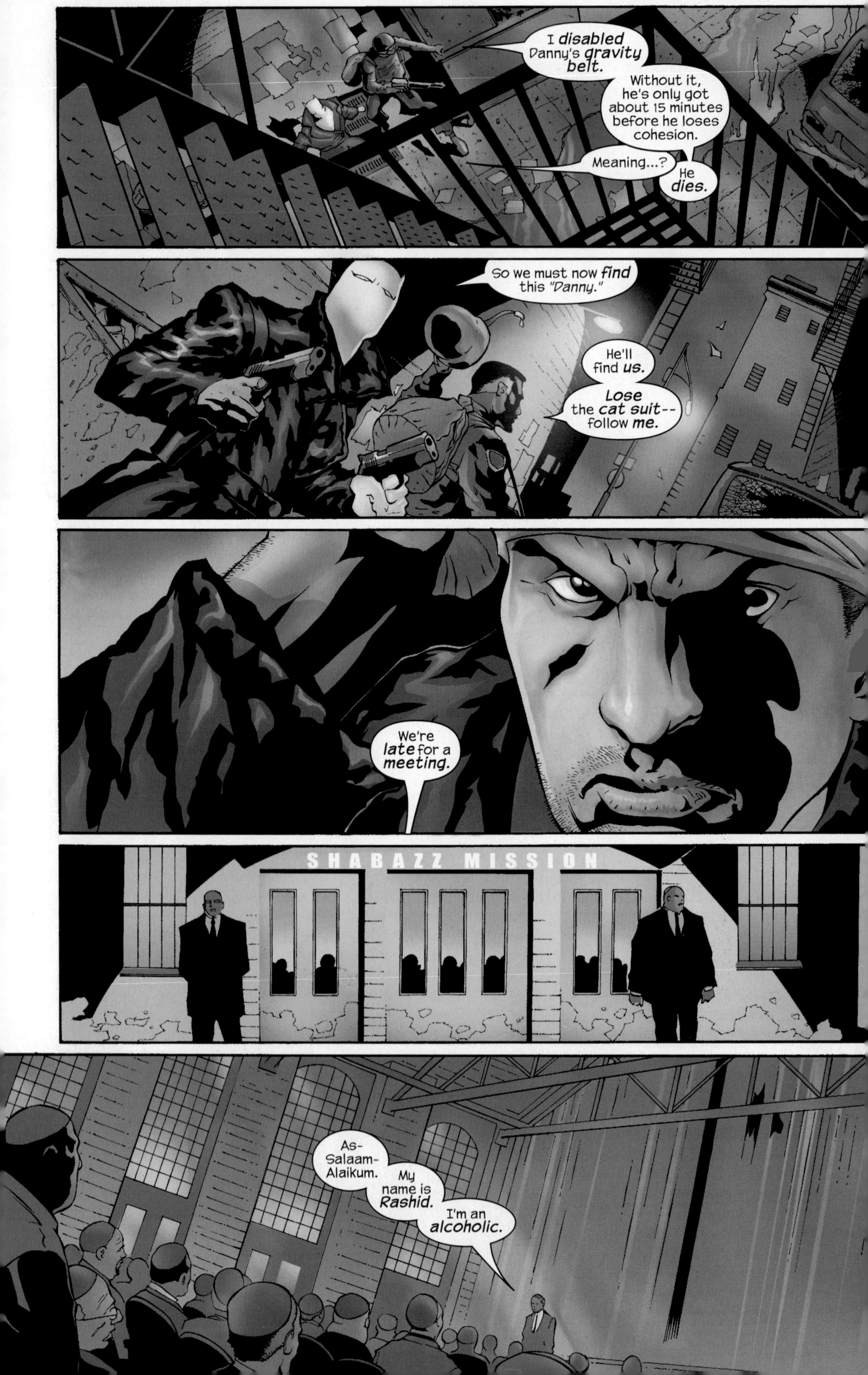
I disabled Danny's gravity belt.
Without it, he's only got about 15 minutes before he loses cohesion.
Meaning...?
He dies.
So we must now find this "Danny."
He'll find us.
Lose the cat suit-- follow me.
We're late for a meeting.
SHABAZZ MISSION
As-Salaam-Alaikum.
My name is Rashid.
I'm an alcoholic.

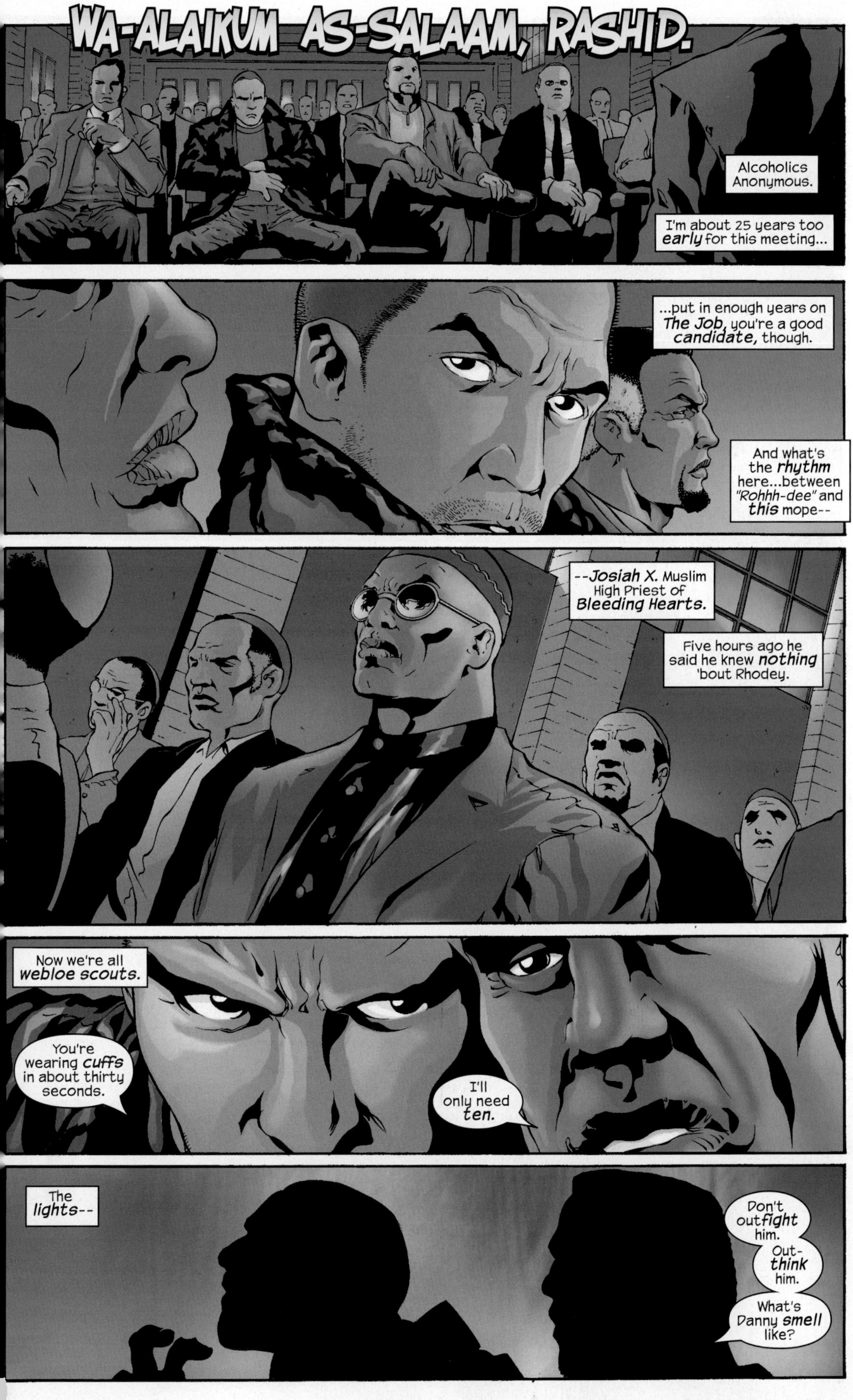
WA-ALAIKUM AS-SALAAM, RASHID.
Alcoholics Anonymous.
I'm about 25 years too *early* for this meeting...
...put in enough years on *The Job*, you're a good *candidate*, though.
And what's the *rhythm* here...between *"Rohhh-dee"* and *this* mope--
--*Josiah X.* Muslim High Priest of *Bleeding Hearts.*
Five hours ago he said he knew *nothing* 'bout Rhodey.
Now we're all *webloe scouts.*
You're wearing *cuffs* in about thirty seconds.
I'll only need *ten.*
The *lights*--
Don't out*fight* him.
Out-*think* him.
What's Danny *smell* like?

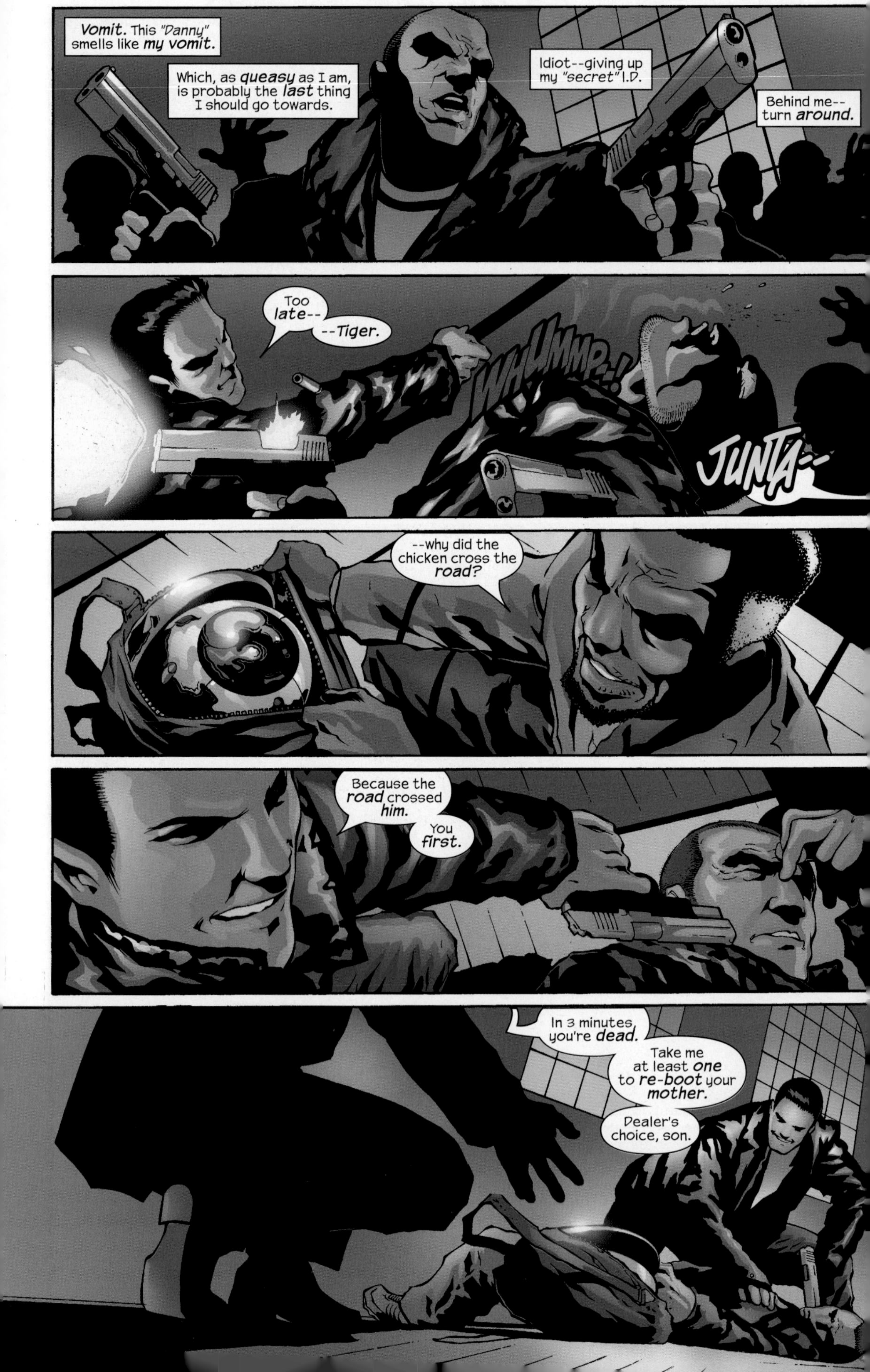
Vomit. This "Danny" smells like my vomit.
Which, as queasy as I am, is probably the last thing I should go towards.
Idiot--giving up my "secret" I.D.
Behind me--turn around.
Too late--
--Tiger.
WHUMMP..!
JUNTA--
--why did the chicken cross the road?
Because the road crossed him.
You first.
In 3 minutes, you're dead.
Take me at least one to re-boot your mother.
Dealer's choice, son.

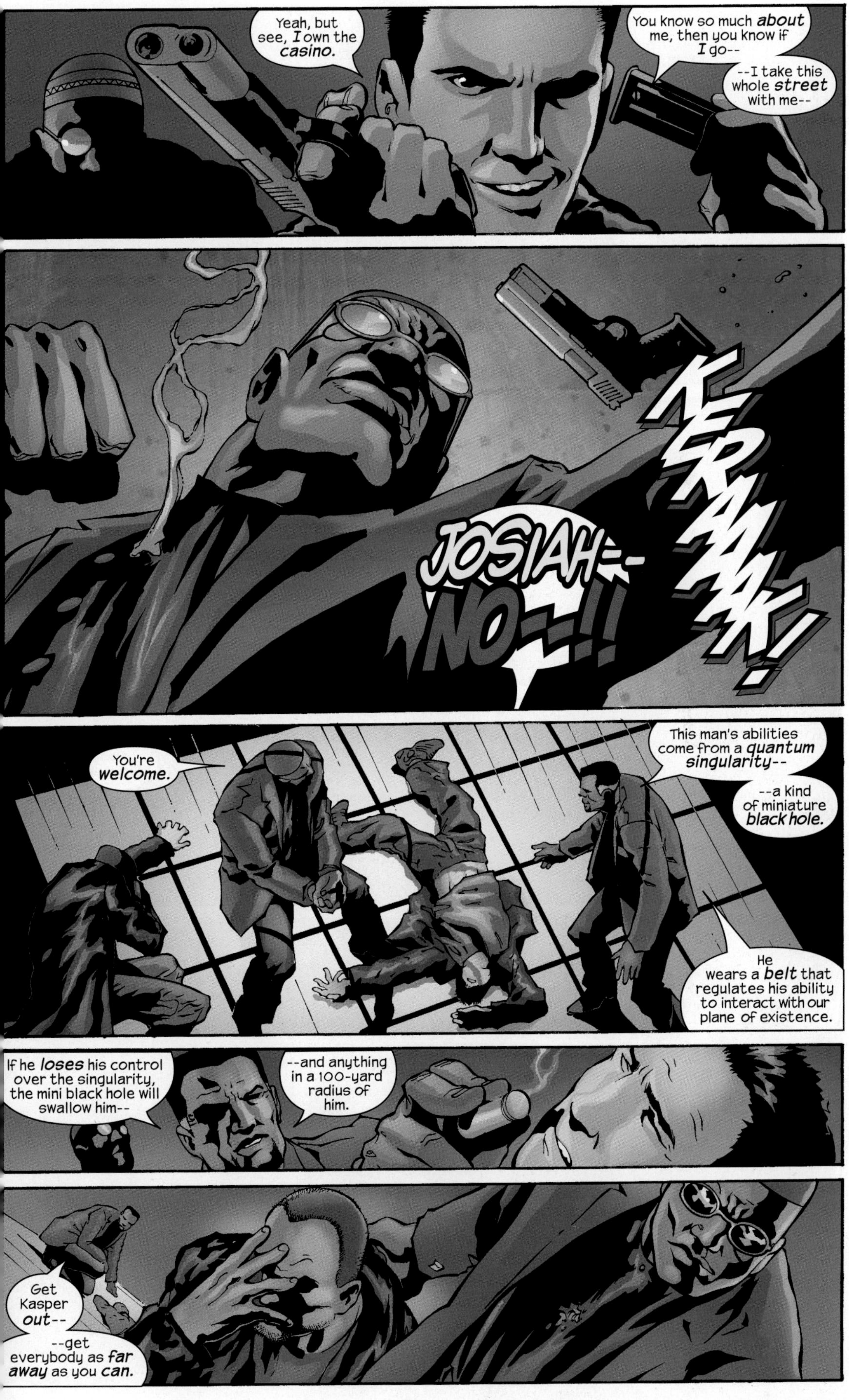

Yeah, but see, *I* own the *casino.*
You know so much *about* me, then you know if *I* go--
--I take this whole *street* with me--
KERRAAAK!
JOSIAH--
NO--!!
You're *welcome.*
This man's abilities come from a *quantum singularity*--
--a kind of miniature *black hole.*
He wears a *belt* that regulates his ability to interact with our plane of existence.
If he *loses* his control over the singularity, the mini black hole will swallow him--
--and anything in a 100-yard radius of him.
Get Kasper *out*--
--get everybody as *far away* as you *can.*

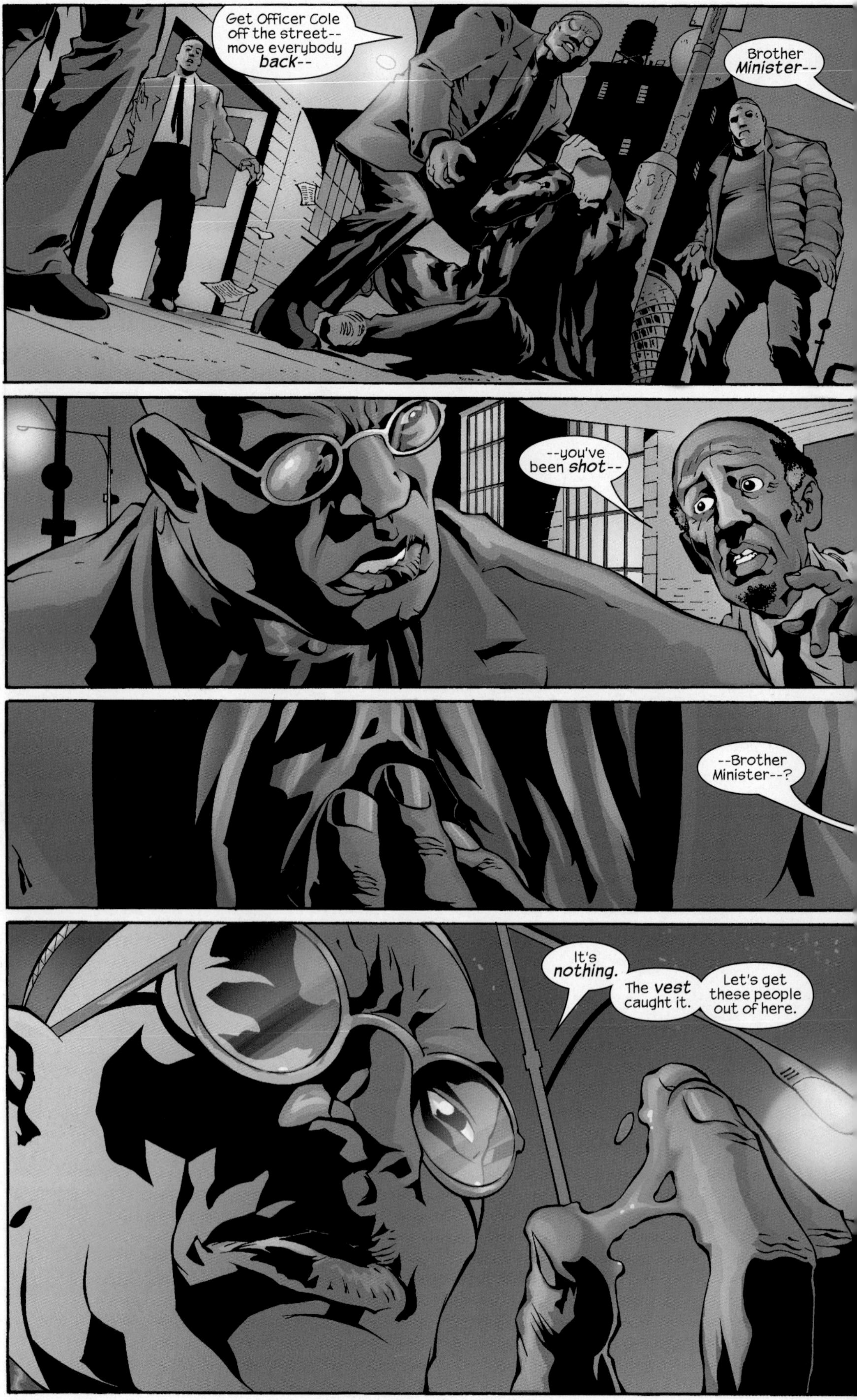
Get Officer Cole off the street--move everybody back--
Brother Minister--
--you've been shot--
--Brother Minister--?
It's nothing.
The vest caught it.
Let's get these people out of here.

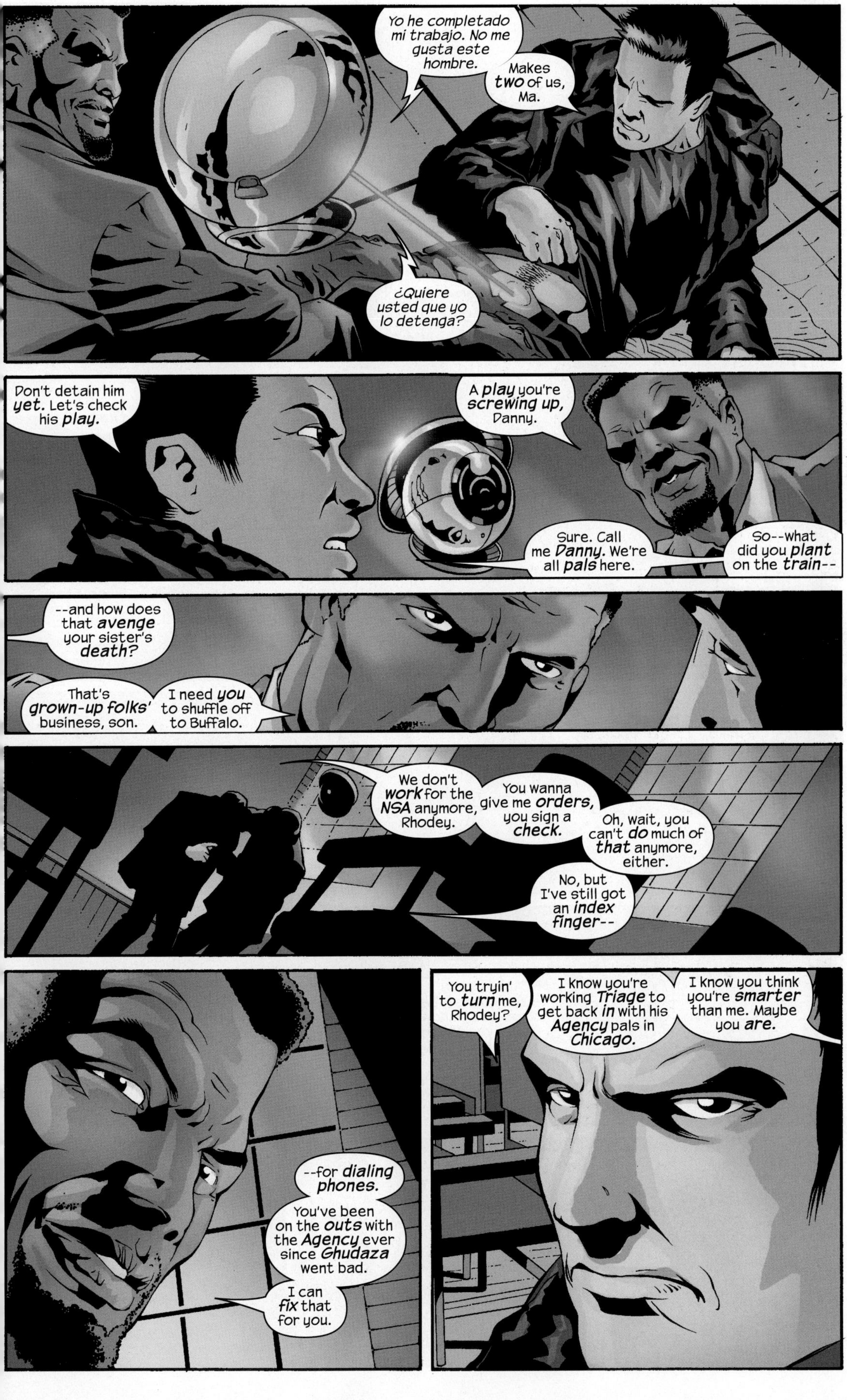
Yo he completado mi trabajo. No me gusta este hombre.
Makes two of us, Ma.
¿Quiere usted que yo lo detenga?
Don't detain him yet. Let's check his play.
A play you're screwing up, Danny.
Sure. Call me Danny. We're all pals here.
So--what did you plant on the train--
--and how does that avenge your sister's death?
That's grown-up folks' business, son.
I need you to shuffle off to Buffalo.
We don't work for the NSA anymore, Rhodey.
You wanna give me orders, you sign a check.
Oh, wait, you can't do much of that anymore, either.
No, but I've still got an index finger--
--for dialing phones.
You've been on the outs with the Agency ever since Ghudaza went bad.
I can fix that for you.
You tryin' to turn me, Rhodey?
I know you're working Triage to get back in with his Agency pals in Chicago.
I know you think you're smarter than me. Maybe you are.

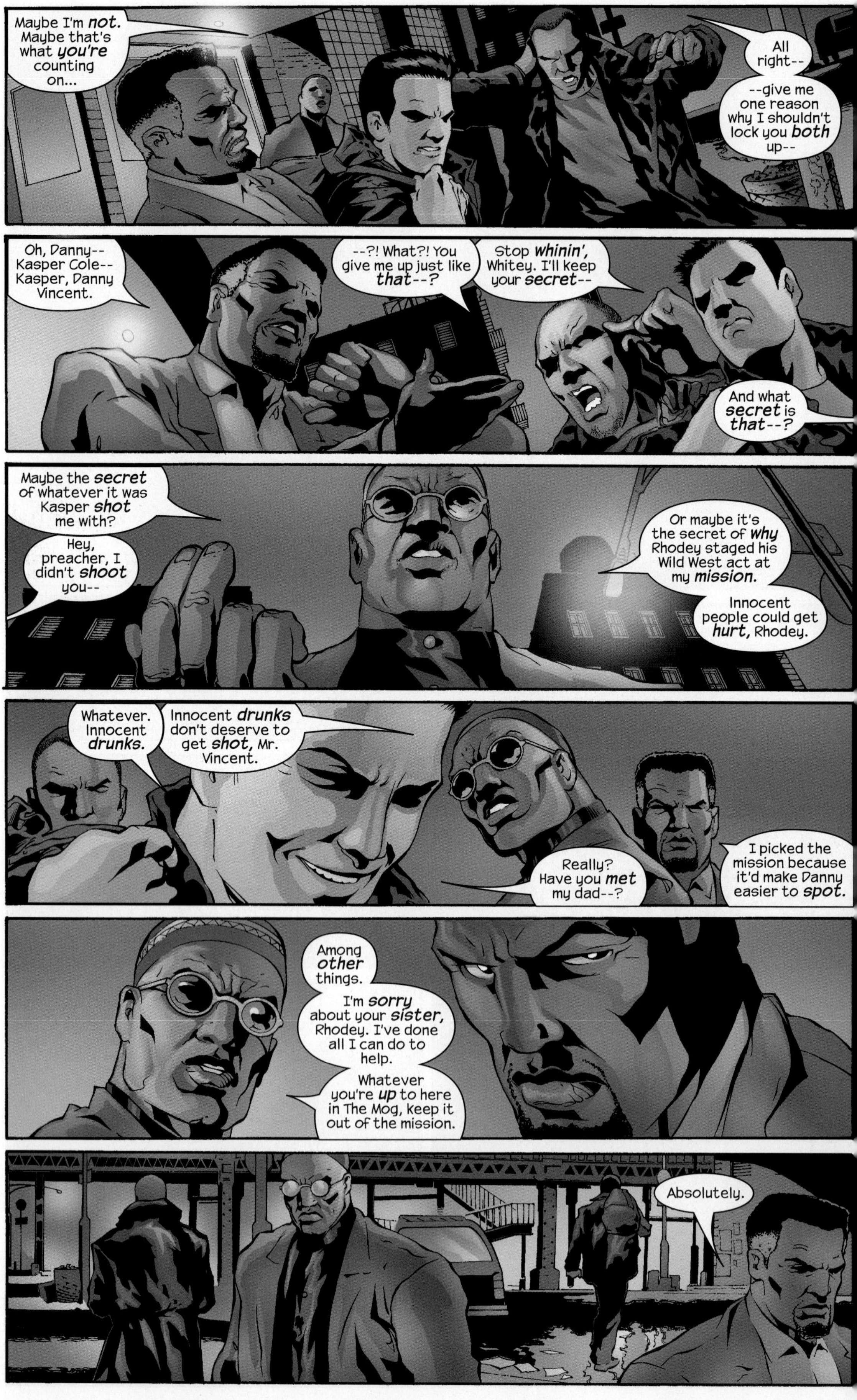
Maybe I'm not. Maybe that's what you're counting on...
All right--
--give me one reason why I shouldn't lock you both up--
Oh, Danny-- Kasper Cole-- Kasper, Danny Vincent.
--?! What?! You give me up just like that--?
Stop whinin', Whitey. I'll keep your secret--
And what secret is that--?
Maybe the secret of whatever it was Kasper shot me with?
Hey, preacher, I didn't shoot you--
Or maybe it's the secret of why Rhodey staged his Wild West act at my mission.
Innocent people could get hurt, Rhodey.
Whatever. Innocent drunks.
Innocent drunks don't deserve to get shot, Mr. Vincent.
Really? Have you met my dad--?
I picked the mission because it'd make Danny easier to spot.
Among other things.
I'm sorry about your sister, Rhodey. I've done all I can do to help.
Whatever you're up to here in The Mog, keep it out of the mission.
Absolutely.

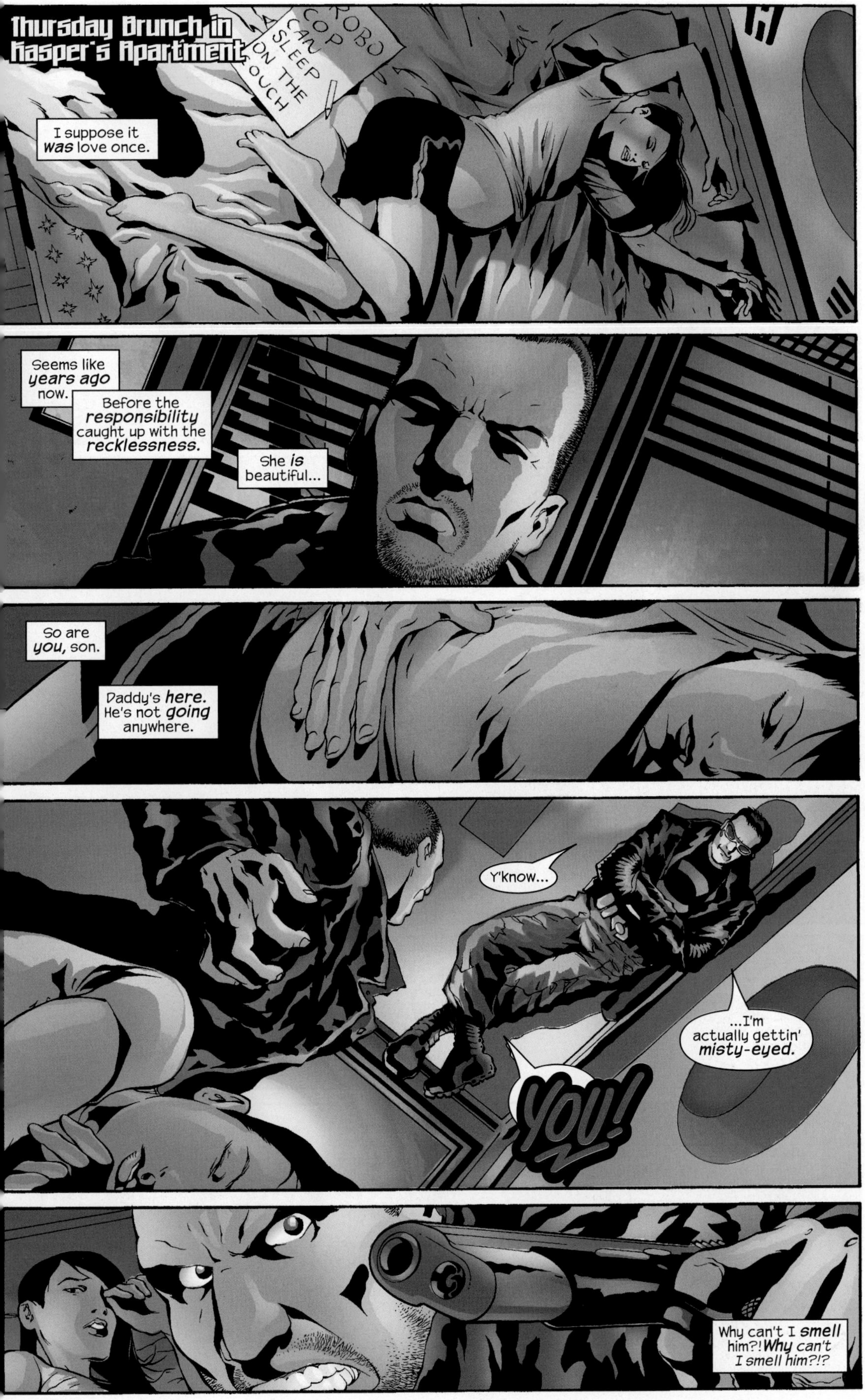

Thursday Brunch in Kasper's Apartment
ROBO COP CAN SLEEP ON THE COUCH
I suppose it *was* love once.
Seems like *years ago* now.
Before the *responsibility* caught up with the *recklessness.*
She *is* beautiful...
So are *you,* son.
Daddy's *here.* He's not *going* anywhere.
Y'know...
...I'm actually gettin' *misty-eyed.*
YOU!
Why can't I *smell* him?! *Why* can't I smell him?!?

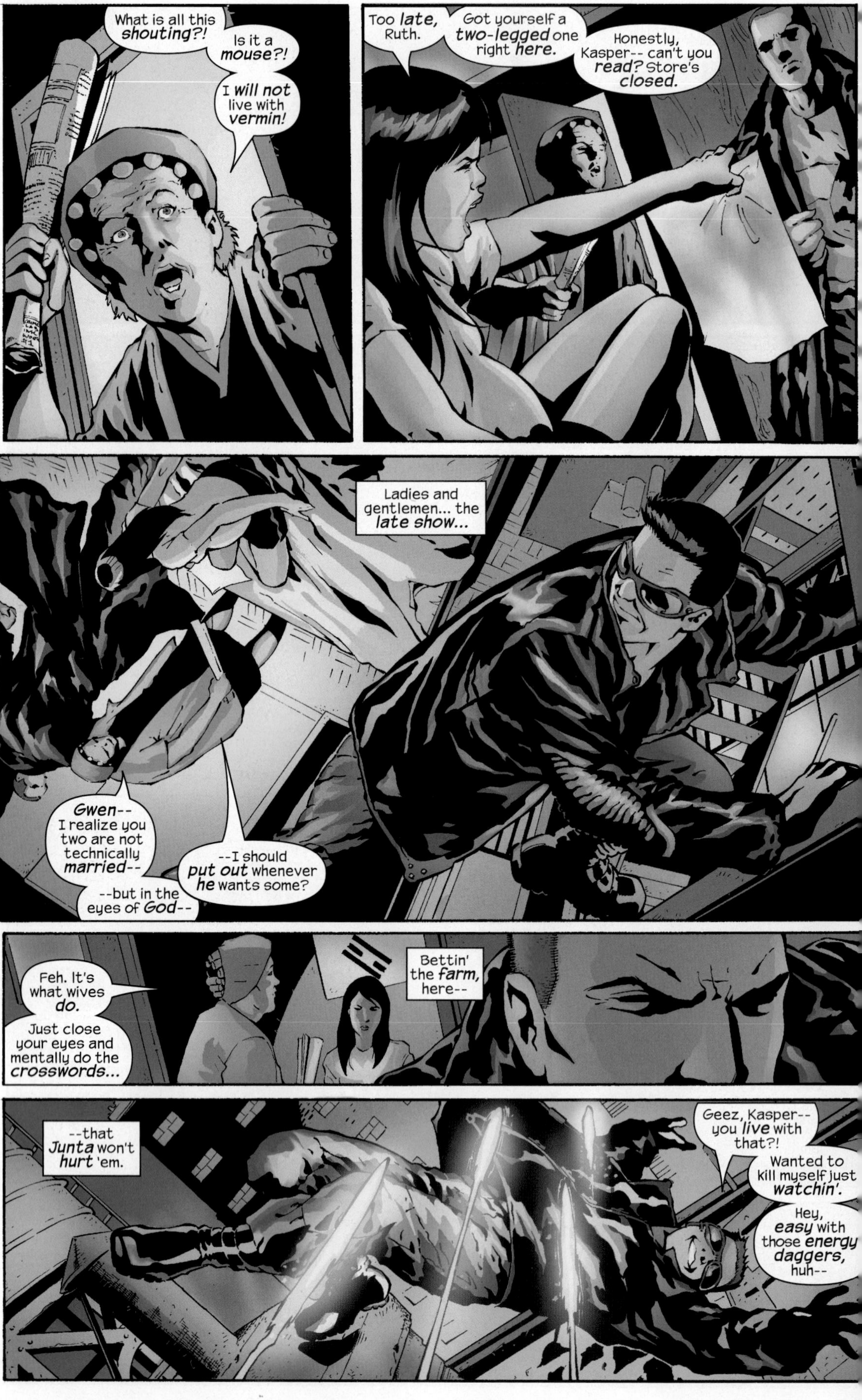

What is all this shouting?!
Is it a mouse?!
I will not live with vermin!
Too late, Ruth.
Got yourself a two-legged one right here.
Honestly, Kasper-- can't you read? Store's closed.
Ladies and gentlemen... the late show...
Gwen-- I realize you two are not technically married--
--but in the eyes of God--
--I should put out whenever he wants some?
Feh. It's what wives do.
Just close your eyes and mentally do the crosswords...
Bettin' the farm, here--
--that Junta won't hurt 'em.
Geez, Kasper-- you live with that?!
Wanted to kill myself just watchin'.
Hey, easy with those energy daggers, huh--

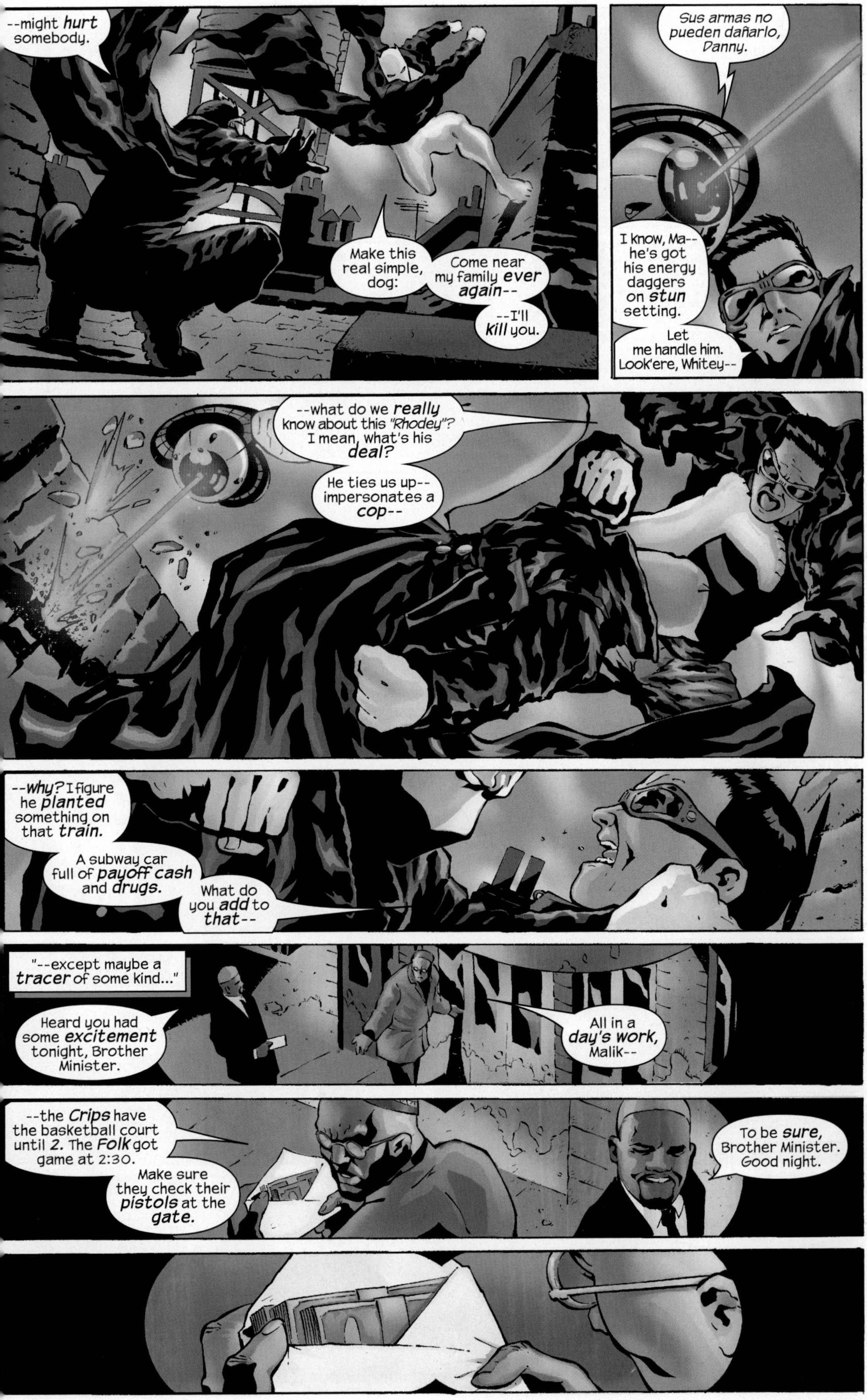
--might hurt somebody.
Make this real simple, dog:
Come near my family ever again--
--I'll kill you.
Sus armas no pueden dañarlo, Danny.
I know, Ma-- he's got his energy daggers on stun setting.
Let me handle him. Look'ere, Whitey--
--what do we really know about this "Rhodey"? I mean, what's his deal?
He ties us up-- impersonates a cop--
--why? I figure he planted something on that train.
A subway car full of payoff cash and drugs.
What do you add to that--
"--except maybe a tracer of some kind..."
Heard you had some excitement tonight, Brother Minister.
All in a day's work, Malik--
--the Crips have the basketball court until 2. The Folk got game at 2:30.
Make sure they check their pistols at the gate.
To be sure, Brother Minister. Good night.

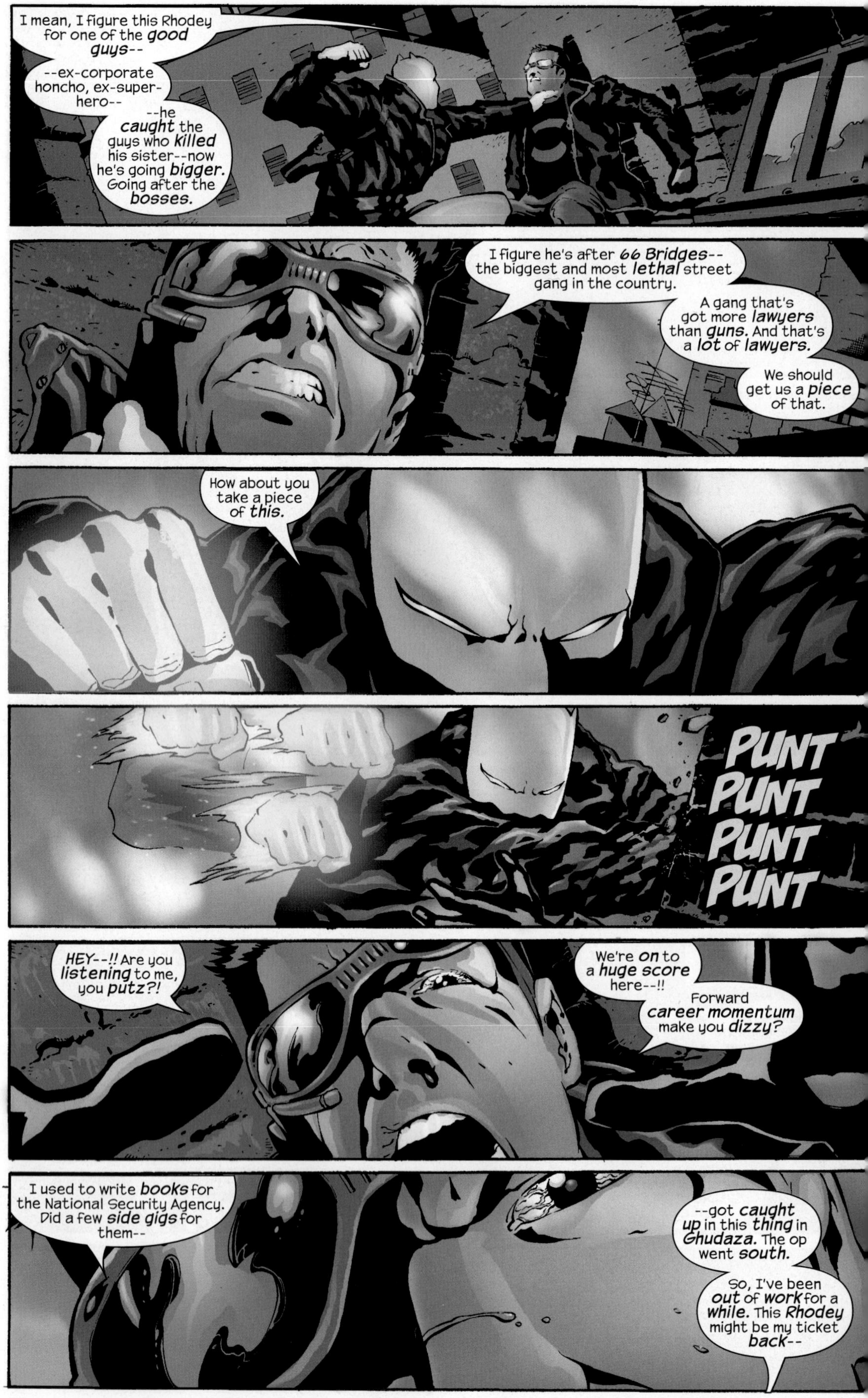
I mean, I figure this Rhodey for one of the good guys--
--ex-corporate honcho, ex-super-hero--
--he caught the guys who killed his sister--now he's going bigger. Going after the bosses.
I figure he's after 66 Bridges-- the biggest and most lethal street gang in the country.
A gang that's got more lawyers than guns. And that's a lot of lawyers.
We should get us a piece of that.
How about you take a piece of this.
PUNT
PUNT
PUNT
PUNT
HEY--!! Are you listening to me, you putz?!
We're on to a huge score here--!!
Forward career momentum make you dizzy?
I used to write books for the National Security Agency. Did a few side gigs for them--
--got caught up in this thing in Ghudaza. The op went south.
So, I've been out of work for a while. This Rhodey might be my ticket back--

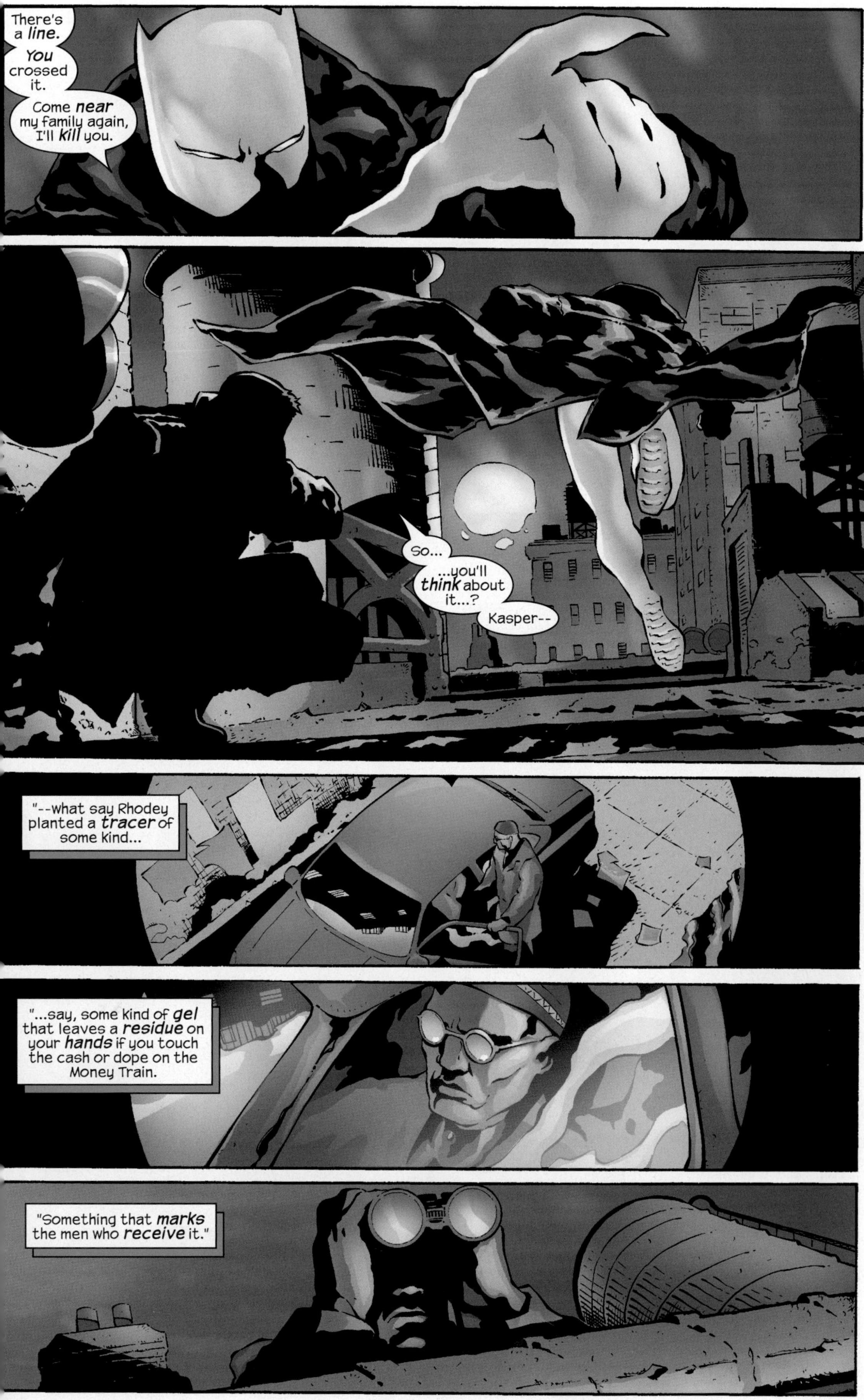

There's a *line.*
You crossed it.
Come *near* my family again, I'll *kill* you.
So...
...you'll *think* about it...?
Kasper--
"--what say Rhodey planted a *tracer* of some kind...
"...say, some kind of *gel* that leaves a *residue* on your *hands* if you touch the cash or dope on the Money Train.
"Something that *marks* the men who *receive* it."

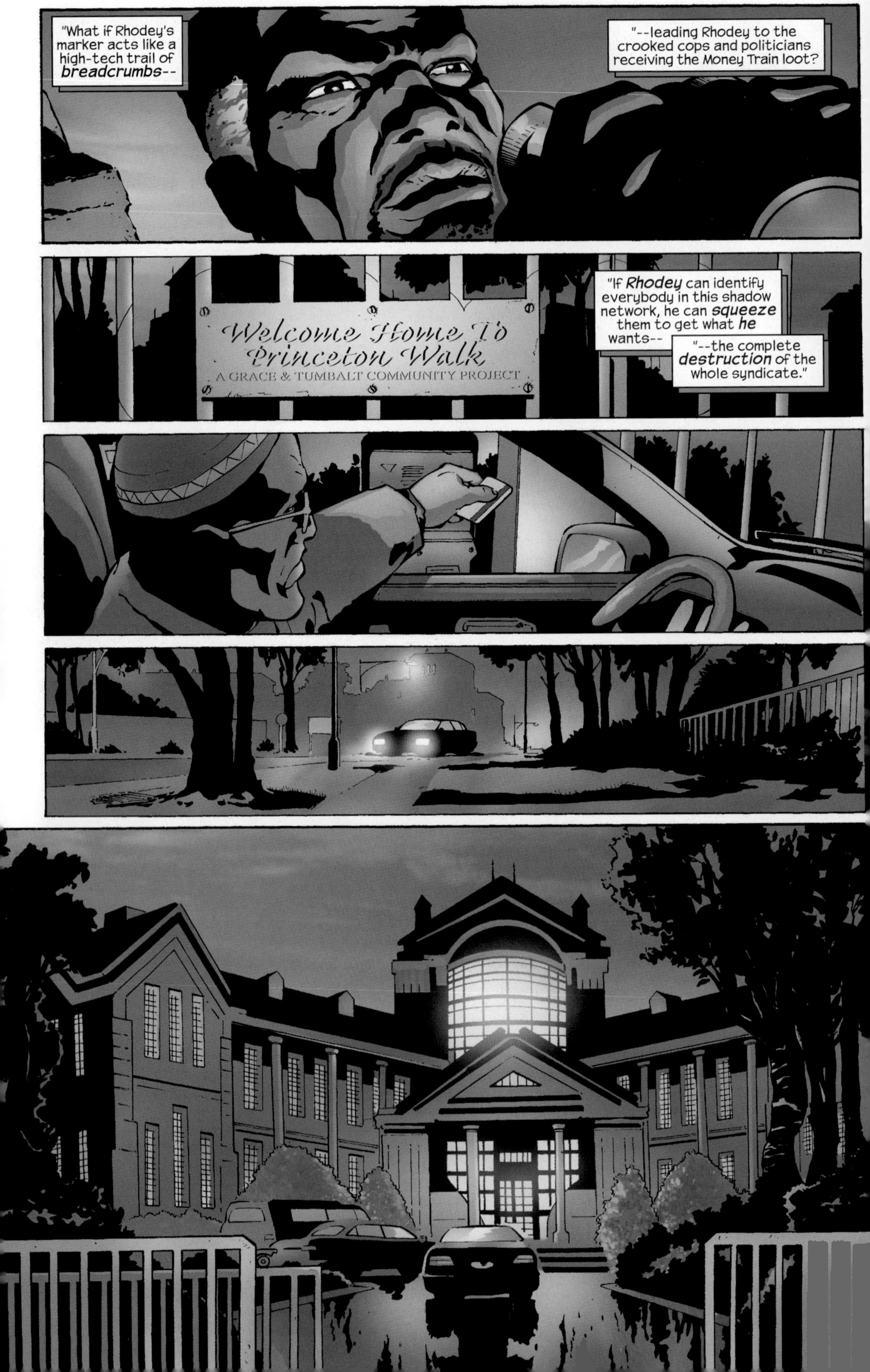
"What if Rhodey's marker acts like a high-tech trail of *breadcrumbs*--
"--leading Rhodey to the crooked cops and politicians receiving the Money Train loot?
Welcome Home To Princeton Walk
A GRACE & TUMBALT COMMUNITY PROJECT
"If *Rhodey* can identify everybody in this shadow network, he can *squeeze* them to get what *he* wants--
"--the complete *destruction* of the whole syndicate."

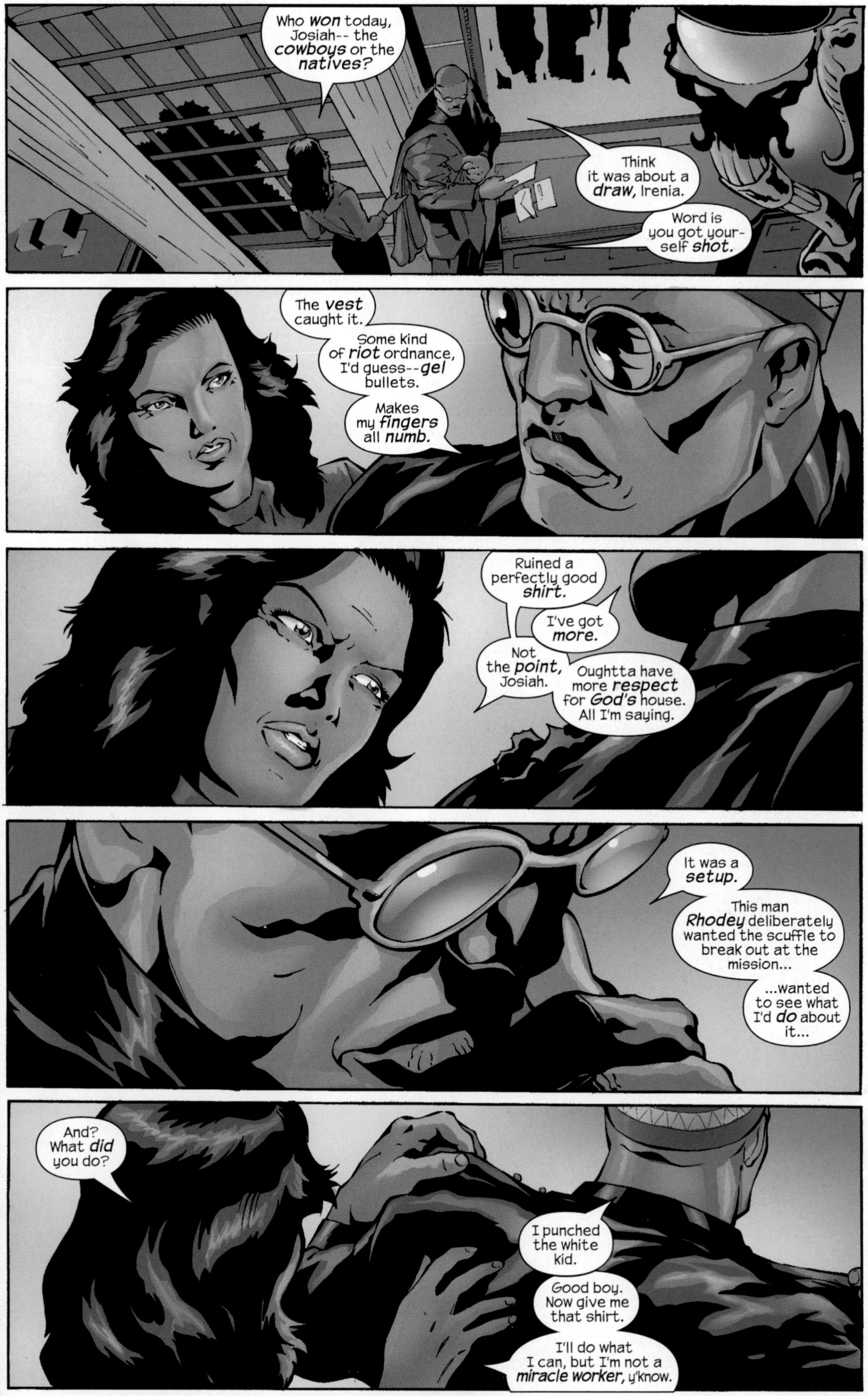

Who won today, Josiah-- the cowboys or the natives?
Think it was about a draw, Irenia.
Word is you got yourself shot.
The vest caught it.
Some kind of riot ordnance, I'd guess--gel bullets.
Makes my fingers all numb.
Ruined a perfectly good shirt.
I've got more.
Not the point, Josiah.
Oughtta have more respect for God's house. All I'm saying.
It was a setup.
This man Rhodey deliberately wanted the scuffle to break out at the mission...
...wanted to see what I'd do about it...
And? What did you do?
I punched the white kid.
Good boy. Now give me that shirt.
I'll do what I can, but I'm not a miracle worker, y'know.

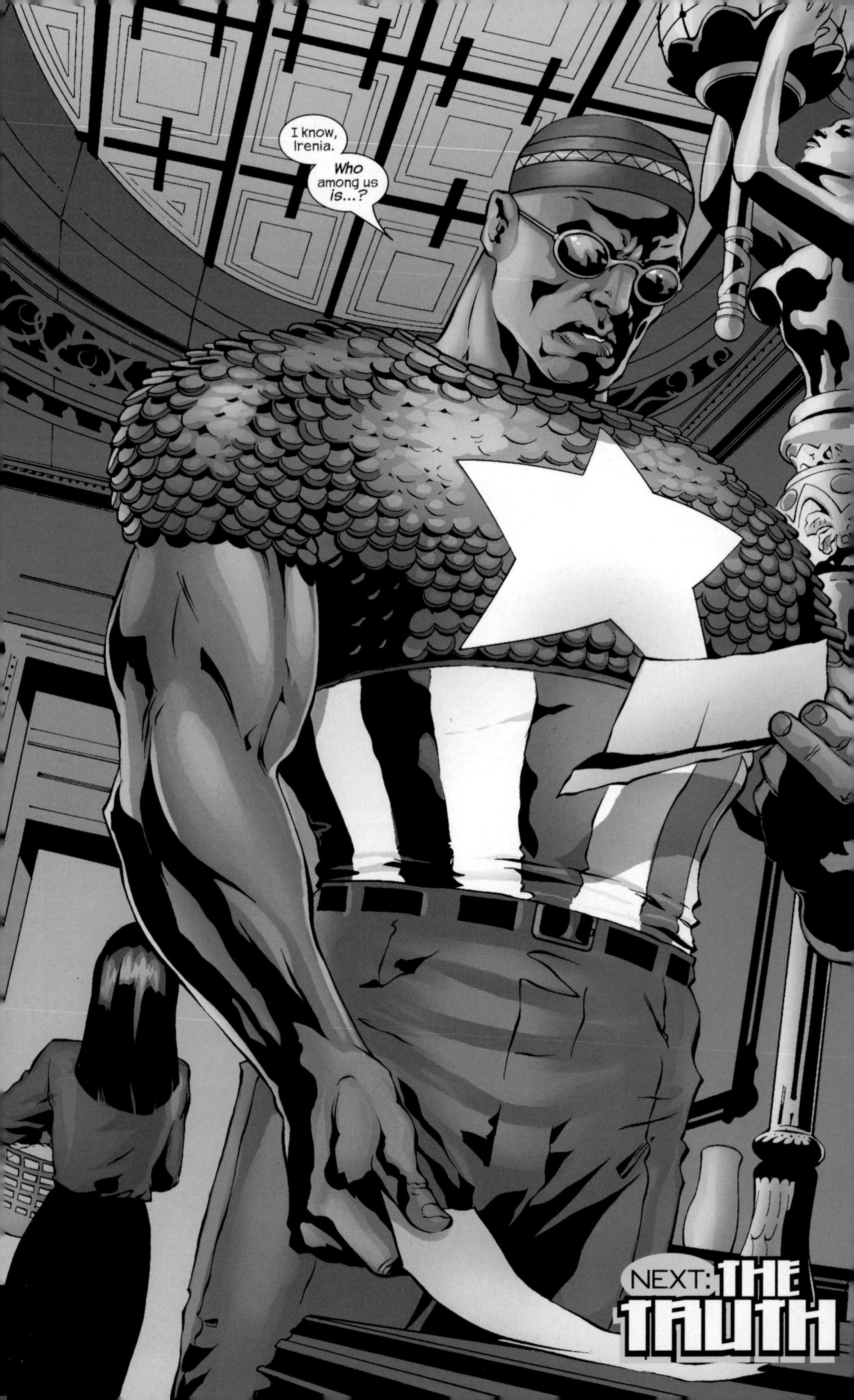
I know, Irenia.
Who among us is...?
NEXT: THE TRUTH

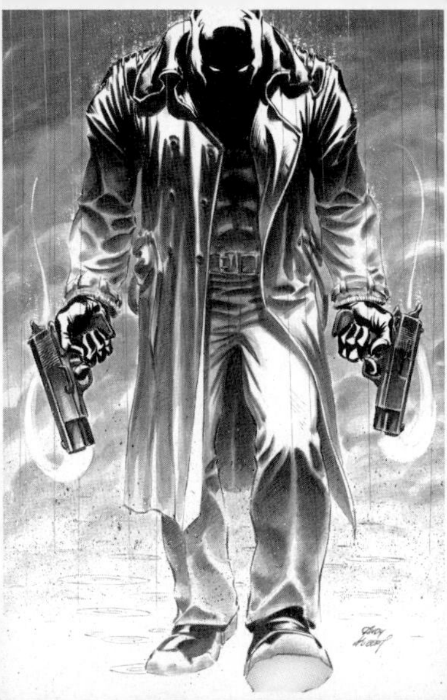
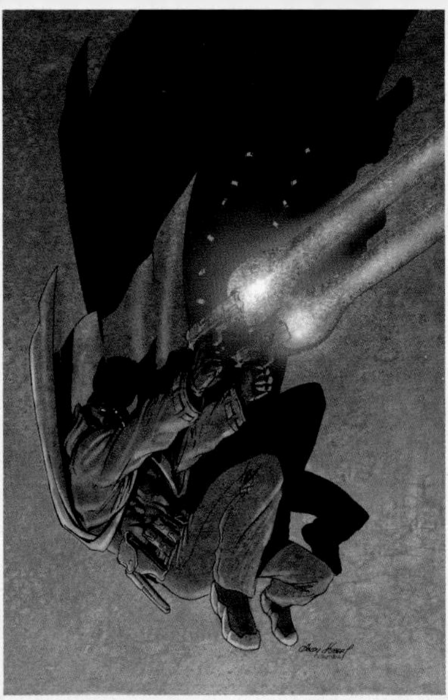
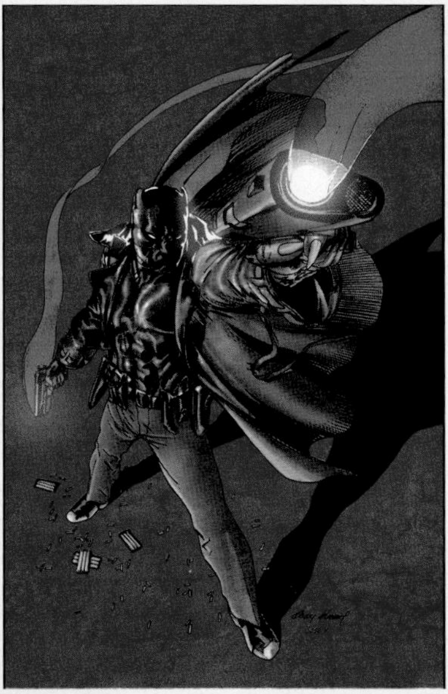
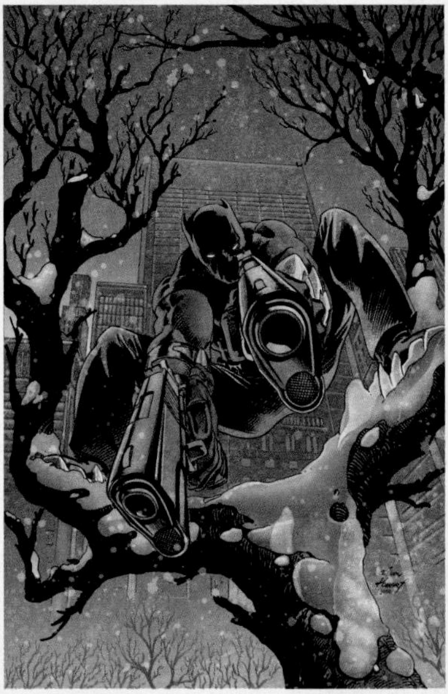
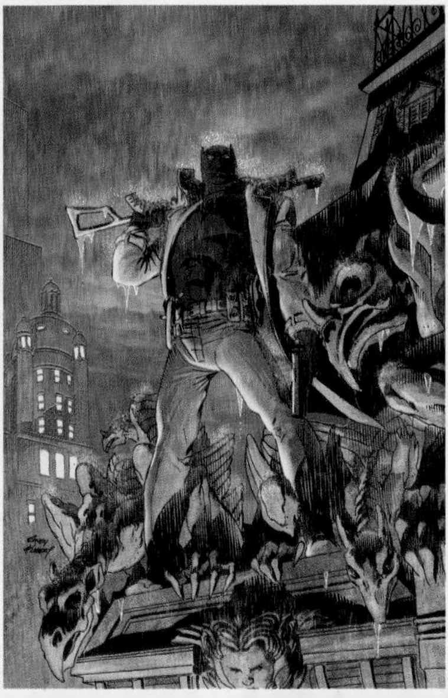
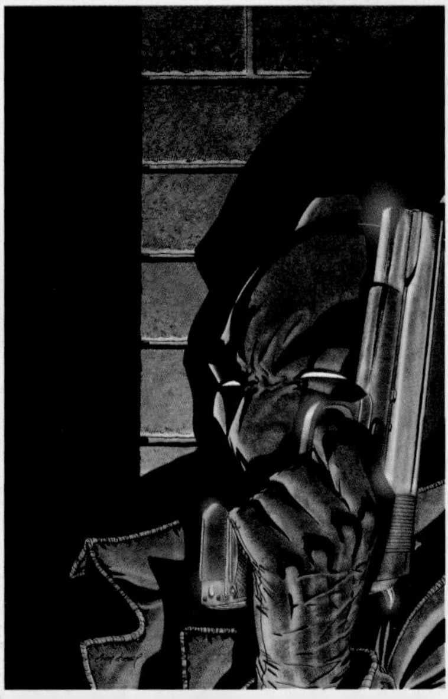

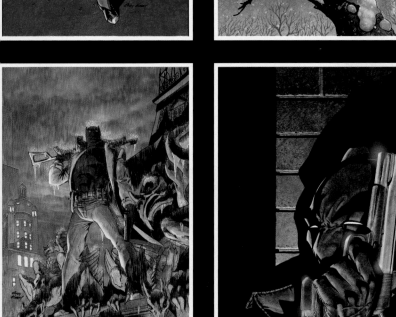

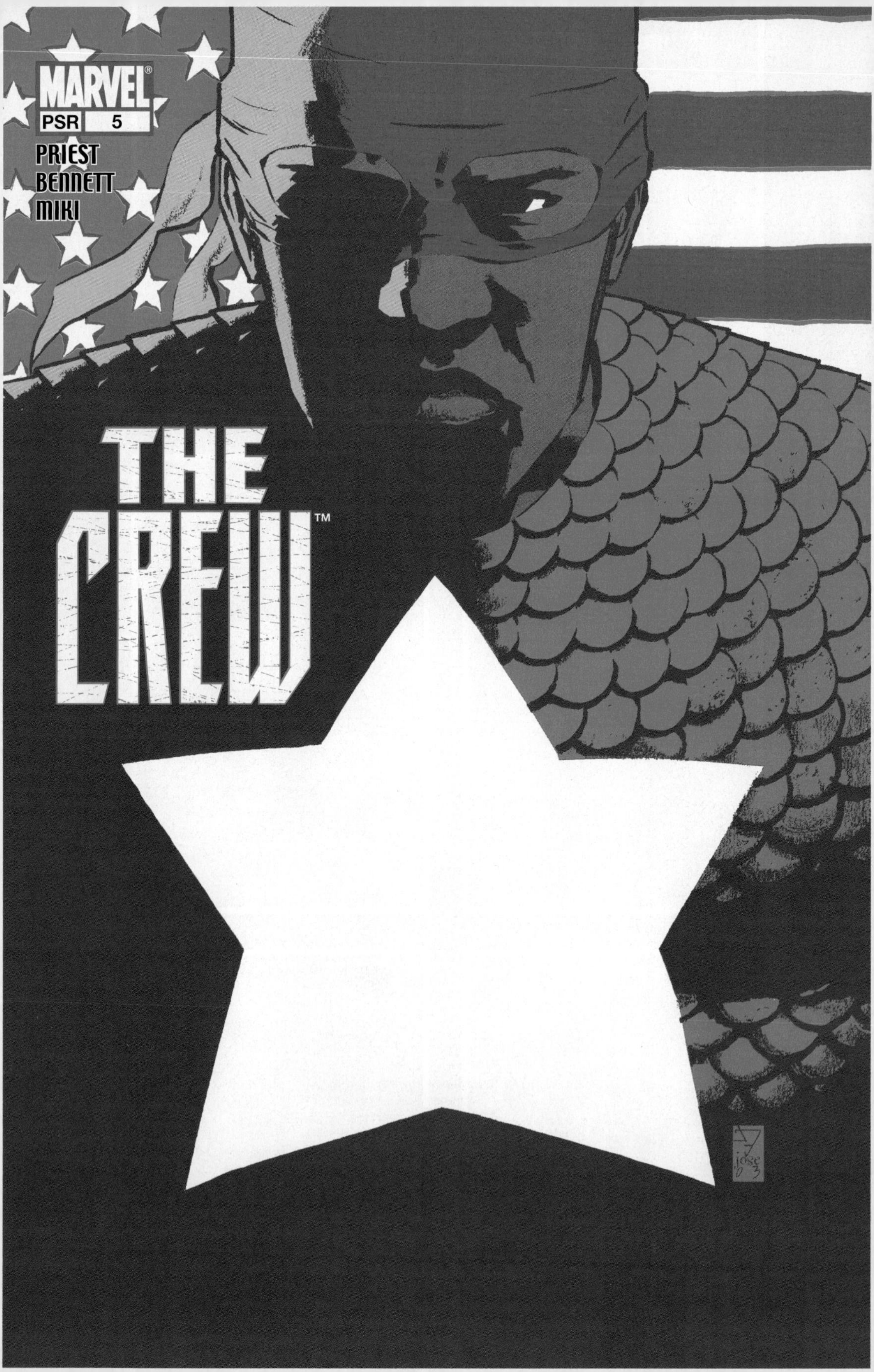
MARVEL
PSR 5
PRIEST
BENNETT
MIKI
THE CREW™

THE CREW

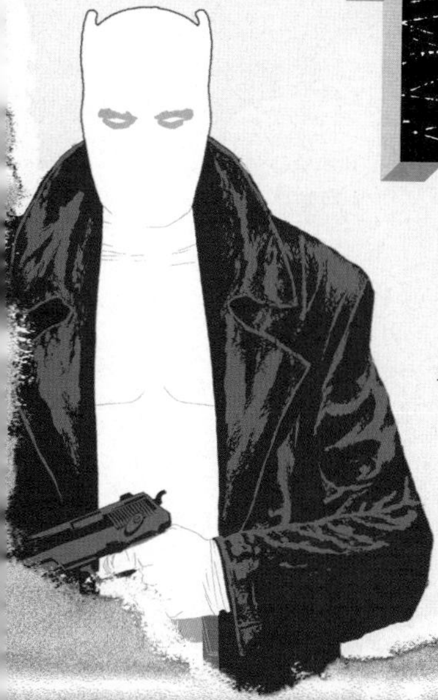

Writer
PRIEST

Pencils
JOE BENNETT

Inks
CRIME LAB STUDIOS

Colors
AVALON STUDIOS

Letterer
VIRTUAL CALLIGRAPHY'S
RUS WOOTON

Assistant Editors
MARC SUMERAK
ANDY SCHMIDT

Editor
TOM BREVOORT

Editor In Chief
JOE QUESADA

President
BILL JEMAS

Big Trouble in Little Mogadishu Part 5:

JOSIAH

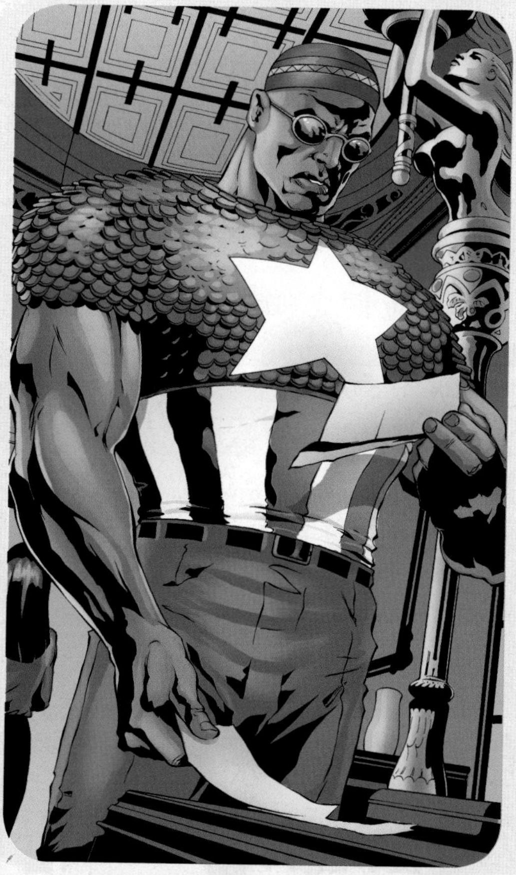

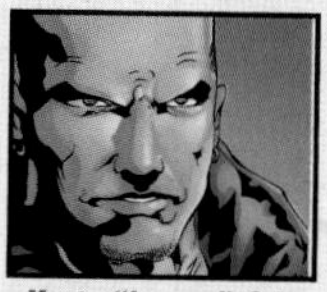

Kevin "kasper" Cole

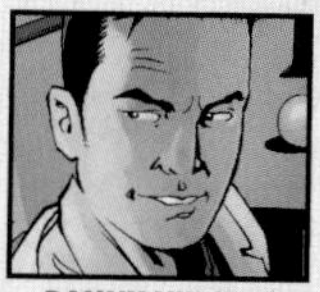

DANNY VINCENT

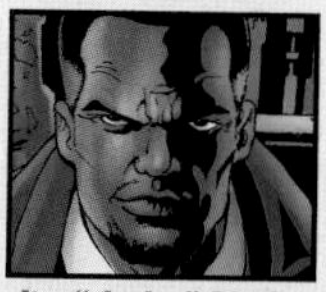

Jim "rhodey" Rhodes

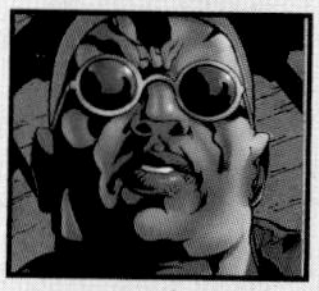

josiah x

PREVIOUSLY...

There is a legend among the African-American community.

This legend tells of a soldier, Isaiah Bradley, who, in the early 1940s, was the sole Negro survivor of the United States Army's experimental Super-Soldier procedure--and the prototype for Captain America.

In October 1942, wearing a freshly-stolen Captain America costume, Isaiah embarked on a suicide mission to Schwarzebitte, a Nazi death-camp. Though generally believed killed in action, a grievously injured Isaiah was instead smuggled out of Germany by the underground and returned to the United States--where he was promptly arrested without trial and sentenced to life imprisonment in Leavenworth. His crime: being a political liability to those within the government who masterminded the Super-Soldier project.

Isaiah's wife, Faith Bradley, works diligently to secure her husband's release, his very existence denied by the government that used him so badly.

It is now 1953...

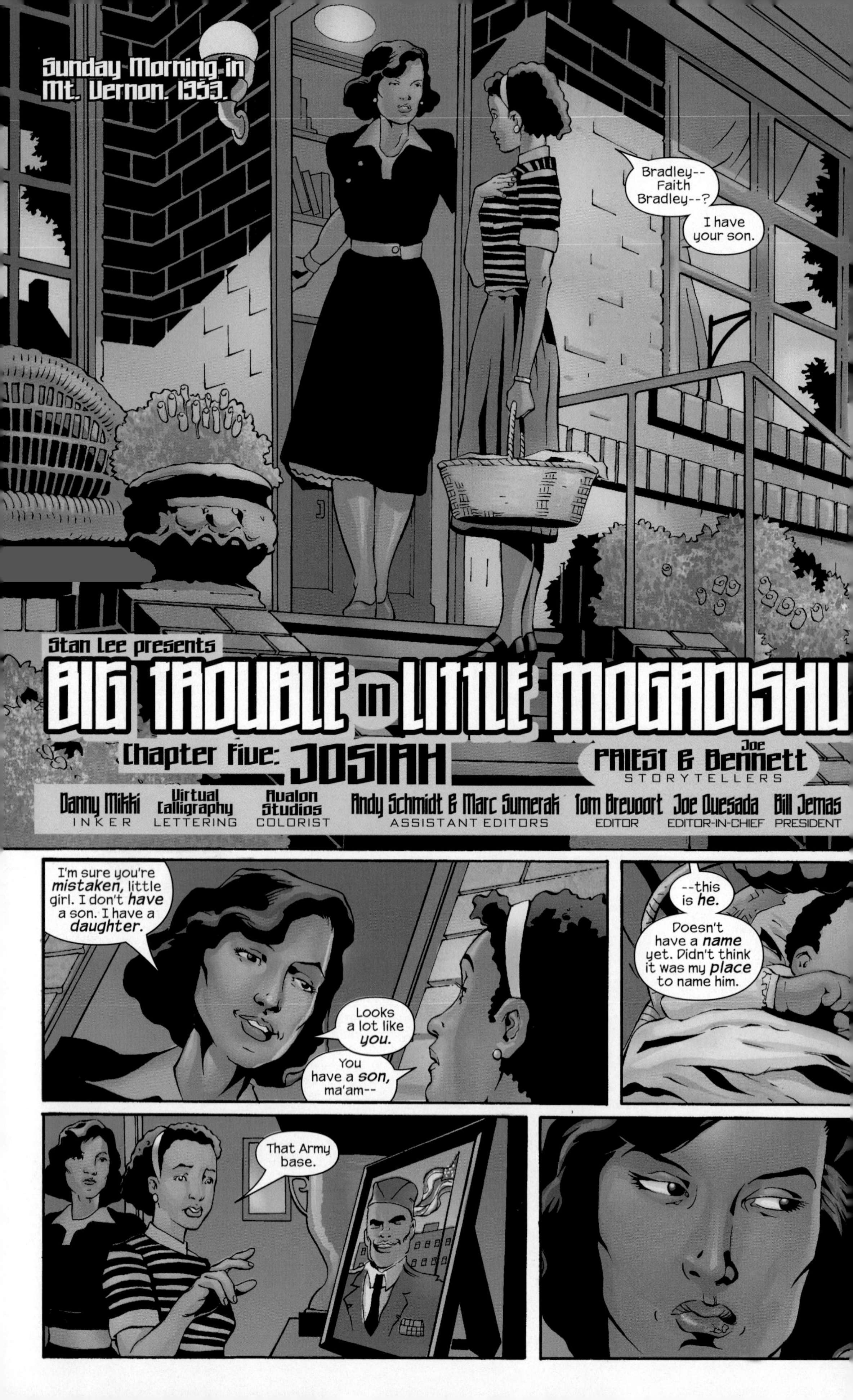
Sunday Morning in Mt. Vernon. 1953.
Bradley-- Faith Bradley--?
I have your son.
Stan Lee presents
BIG TROUBLE in LITTLE MOGADISHU
Chapter Five: JOSIAH
PRIEST & Joe Bennett STORYTELLERS
Danny Mikki INKER
Virtual Calligraphy LETTERING
Avalon Studios COLORIST
Andy Schmidt & Marc Sumerak ASSISTANT EDITORS
Tom Brevoort EDITOR
Joe Quesada EDITOR-IN-CHIEF
Bill Jemas PRESIDENT
I'm sure you're *mistaken,* little girl. I don't *have* a son. I have a *daughter.*
Looks a lot like *you.*
You have a *son,* ma'am--
--this is *he.*
Doesn't have a *name* yet. Didn't think it was my *place* to name him.
That Army base.

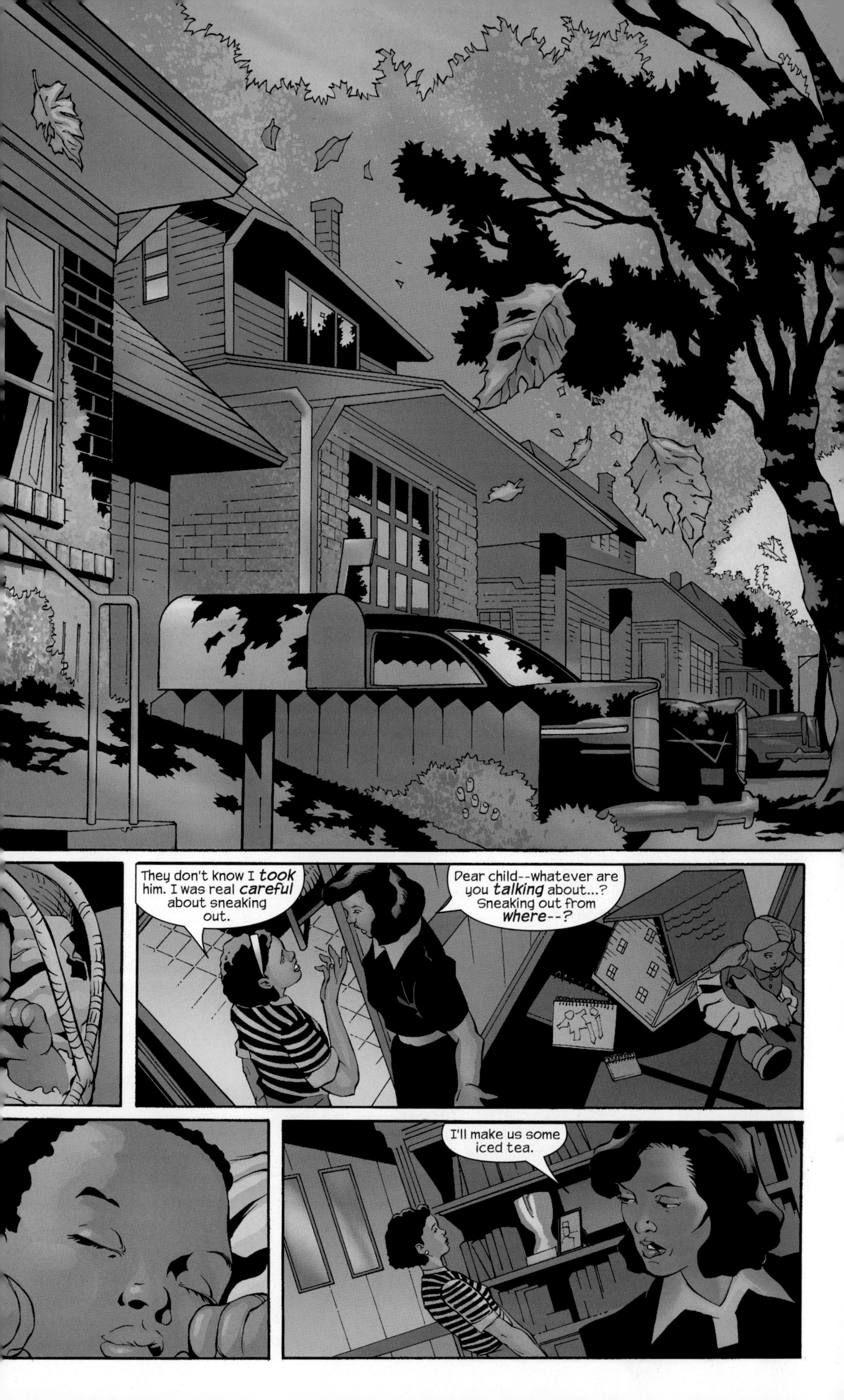
They don't know I took him. I was real careful about sneaking out.
Dear child--whatever are you talking about...? Sneaking out from where--?
I'll make us some iced tea.

MAN O[F] MYTH?

Though repeatedly dismissed as "a figment of vivid imaginations" by the Pentagon, Negro war veterans attest to the fact many of Captain America's earliest "victories" were actually the work of a colored officer. But, who was this man? And where is he now?

alsfjdvbqarbyi
aopdibnao
qapoefbr
qaoefubn
oin

Colored officers came to see me in **high school.** They said I fit the profile **perfectly.**

I didn't understand... until **now.**

Blood type, physical type--I was close enough to **you** to do what they wanted.

Carry your **baby.**

My baby.

Them **Army** men-- they harvested **sperm cells** from your **husband**-- **before** he became sterile.

Got **egg cells** from **you** when you had your appendix removed last year.

They wanted a **control group.**

Isaiah and I already have a child. They'll **maximize** their research if the child they **create** was composed of the same genetic material as our **normal** daughter--

--the only change being the **Super-Soldier Serum** they injected my husband with during World War II.

They study the boy as he grows--compare his growth to our daughter's.

You're a **surrogate.**

You--you're **in** on this--you're **with** them--!!

Sit down.

How could you **know** so much... about **them**...about what they **do**...?!

I've had a lot of **practice.**

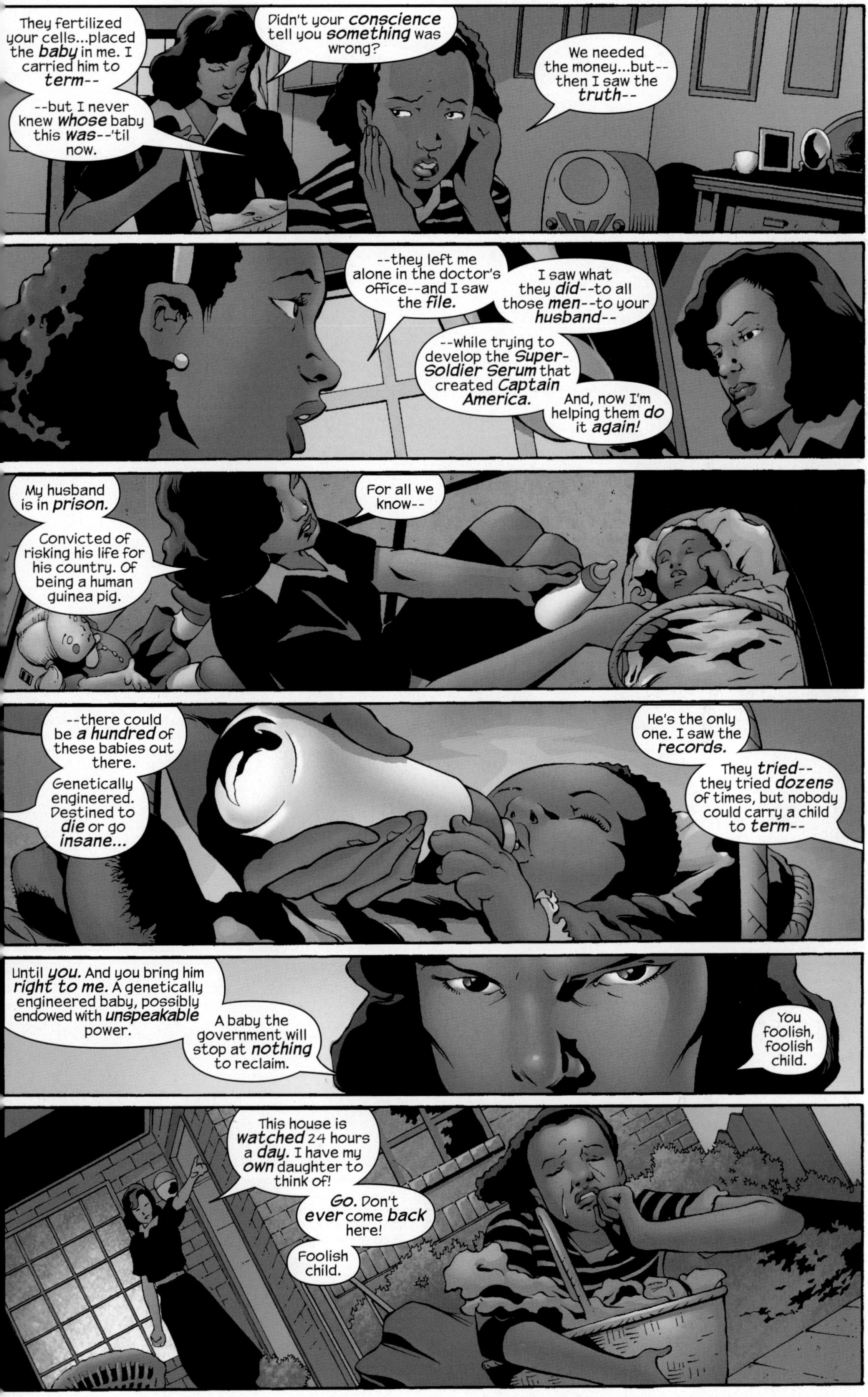
They fertilized your cells...placed the baby in me. I carried him to term--
Didn't your conscience tell you something was wrong?
We needed the money...but--then I saw the truth--
--but I never knew whose baby this was--'til now.
--they left me alone in the doctor's office--and I saw the file.
I saw what they did--to all those men--to your husband--
--while trying to develop the Super-Soldier Serum that created Captain America.
And, now I'm helping them do it again!
My husband is in prison.
Convicted of risking his life for his country. Of being a human guinea pig.
For all we know--
--there could be a hundred of these babies out there.
Genetically engineered. Destined to die or go insane...
He's the only one. I saw the records.
They tried--they tried dozens of times, but nobody could carry a child to term--
Until you. And you bring him right to me. A genetically engineered baby, possibly endowed with unspeakable power.
A baby the government will stop at nothing to reclaim.
You foolish, foolish child.
This house is watched 24 hours a day. I have my own daughter to think of!
Go. Don't ever come back here!
Foolish child.

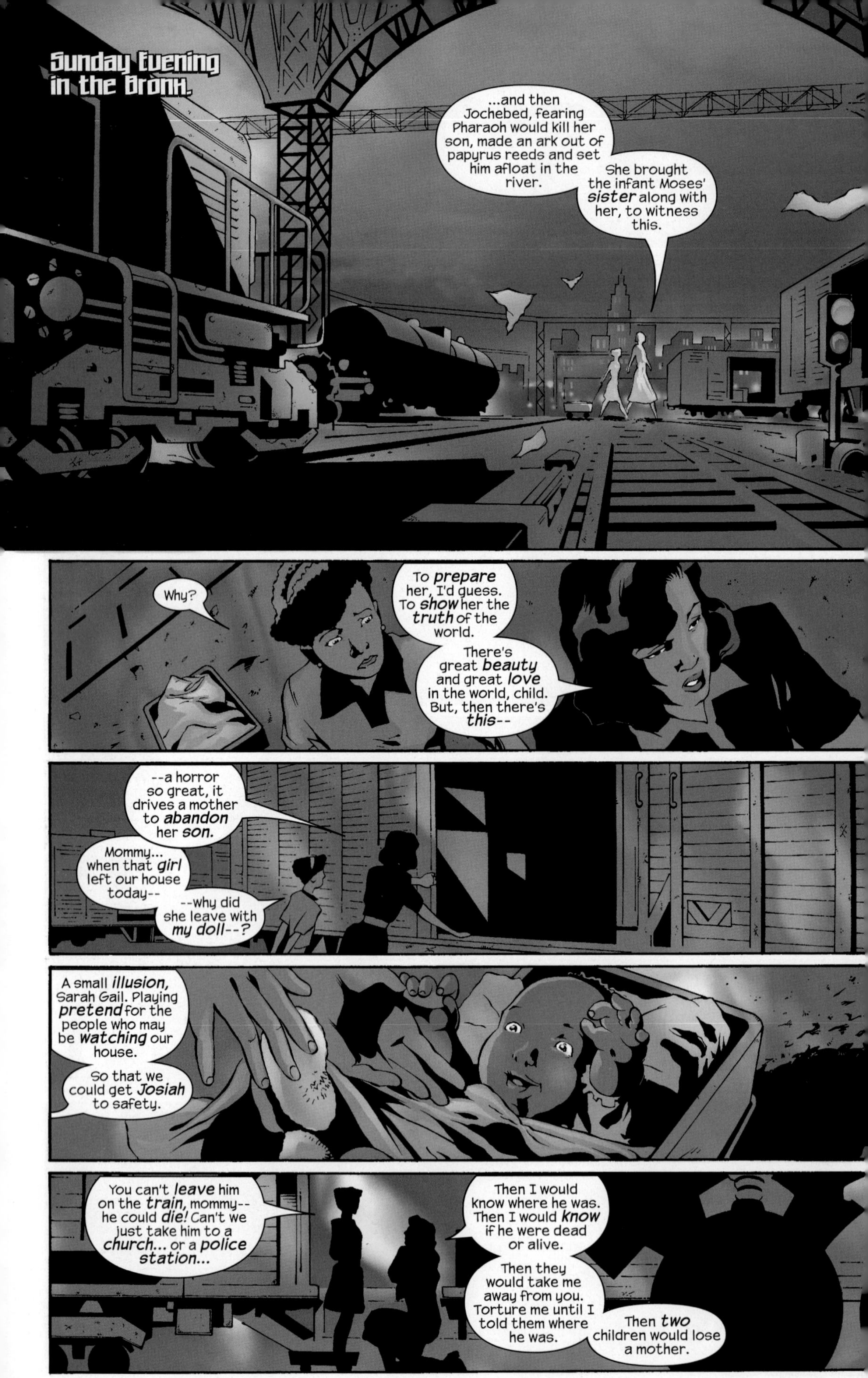
Sunday Evening in the Bronx.
...and then Jochebed, fearing Pharaoh would kill her son, made an ark out of papyrus reeds and set him afloat in the river.
She brought the infant Moses' *sister* along with her, to witness this.
Why?
To *prepare* her, I'd guess. To *show* her the *truth* of the world.
There's great *beauty* and great *love* in the world, child. But, then there's *this*--
--a horror so great, it drives a mother to *abandon* her *son.*
Mommy... when that *girl* left our house today--
--why did she leave with *my doll*--?
A small *illusion,* Sarah Gail. Playing *pretend* for the people who may be *watching* our house.
So that we could get *Josiah* to safety.
You can't *leave* him on the *train,* mommy-- he could *die!* Can't we just take him to a *church*... or a *police station*...
Then I would know where he was. Then I would *know* if he were dead or alive.
Then they would take me away from you. Torture me until I told them where he was.
Then *two* children would lose a mother.

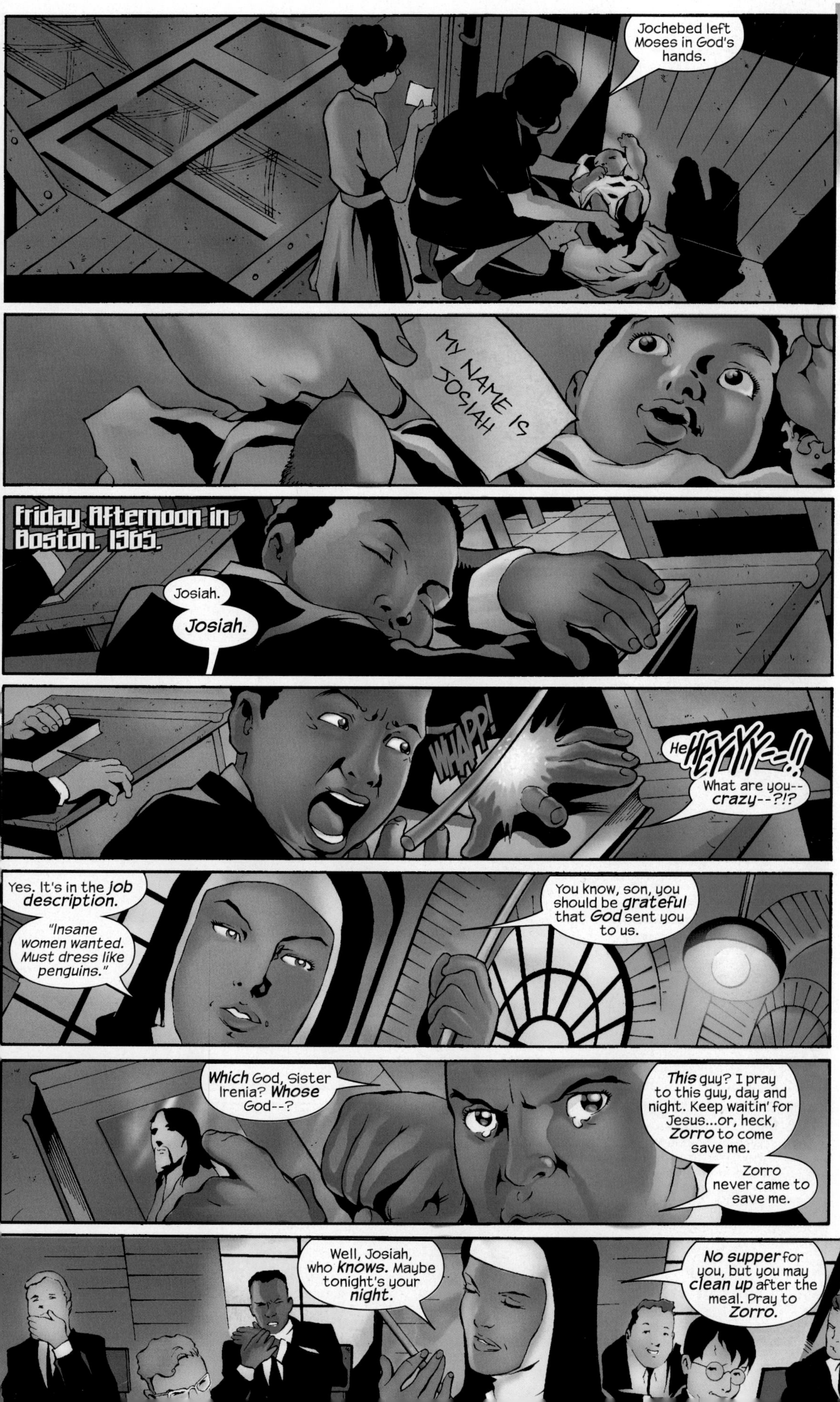
Jochebed left Moses in God's hands.
MY NAME IS JOSIAH
Friday Afternoon in Boston. 1965.
Josiah.
Josiah.
WHAPP!
HeHEYYYY--!!
What are you-- crazy--?!?
Yes. It's in the job description.
"Insane women wanted. Must dress like penguins."
You know, son, you should be grateful that God sent you to us.
Which God, Sister Irenia? Whose God--?
This guy? I pray to this guy, day and night. Keep waitin' for Jesus...or, heck, Zorro to come save me.
Zorro never came to save me.
Well, Josiah, who knows. Maybe tonight's your night.
No supper for you, but you may clean up after the meal. Pray to Zorro.

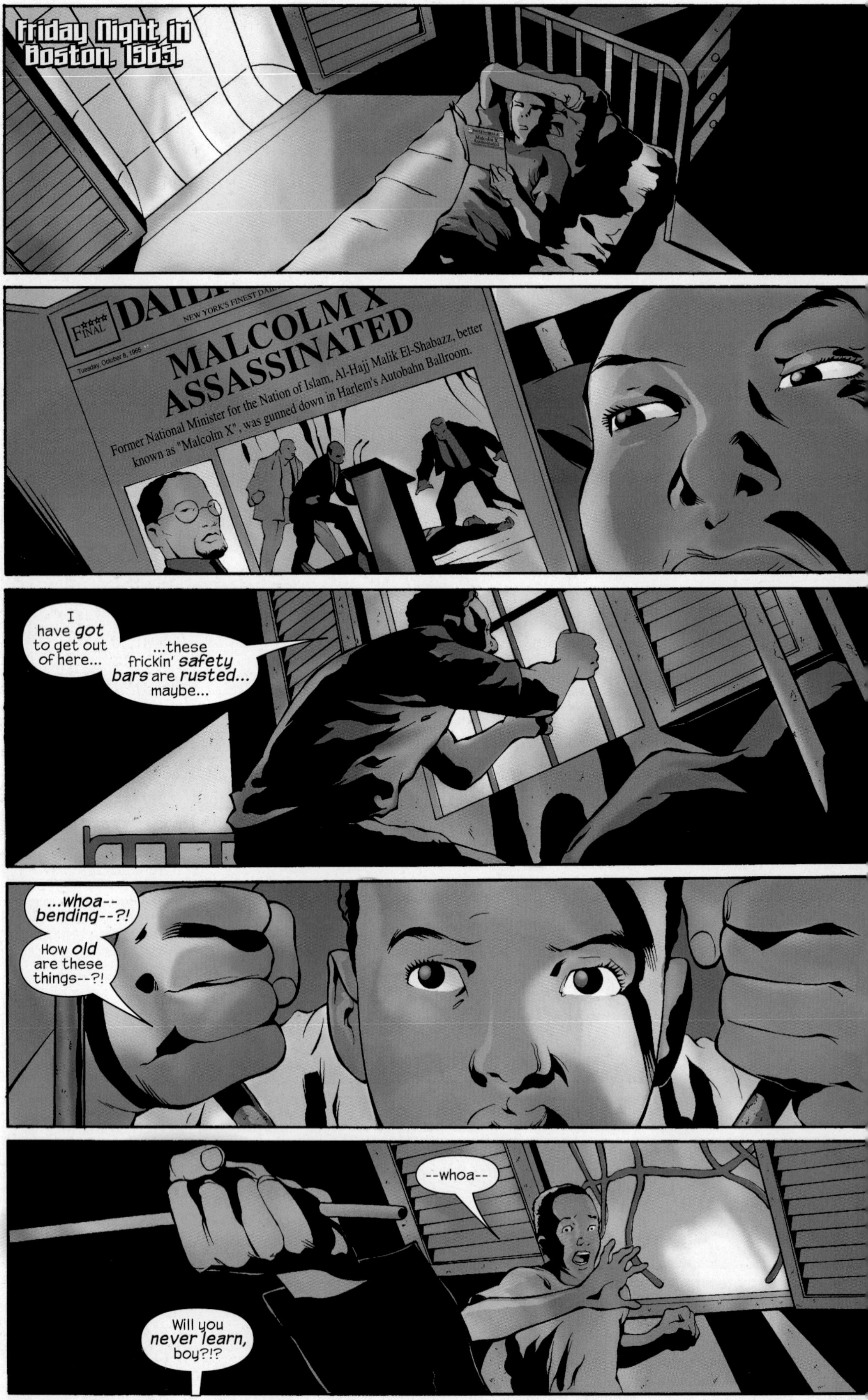
Friday Night in Boston. 1965.
FINAL
NEW YORK'S FINEST DAI
Tuesday, October 8, 1965
MALCOLM X ASSASSINATED
Former National Minister for the Nation of Islam, Al-Hajj Malik El-Shabazz, better known as "Malcolm X", was gunned down in Harlem's Autobahn Ballroom.
I have got to get out of here...
...these frickin' safety bars are rusted... maybe...
...whoa-- bending--?!
How old are these things--?!
--whoa--
Will you never learn, boy?!?

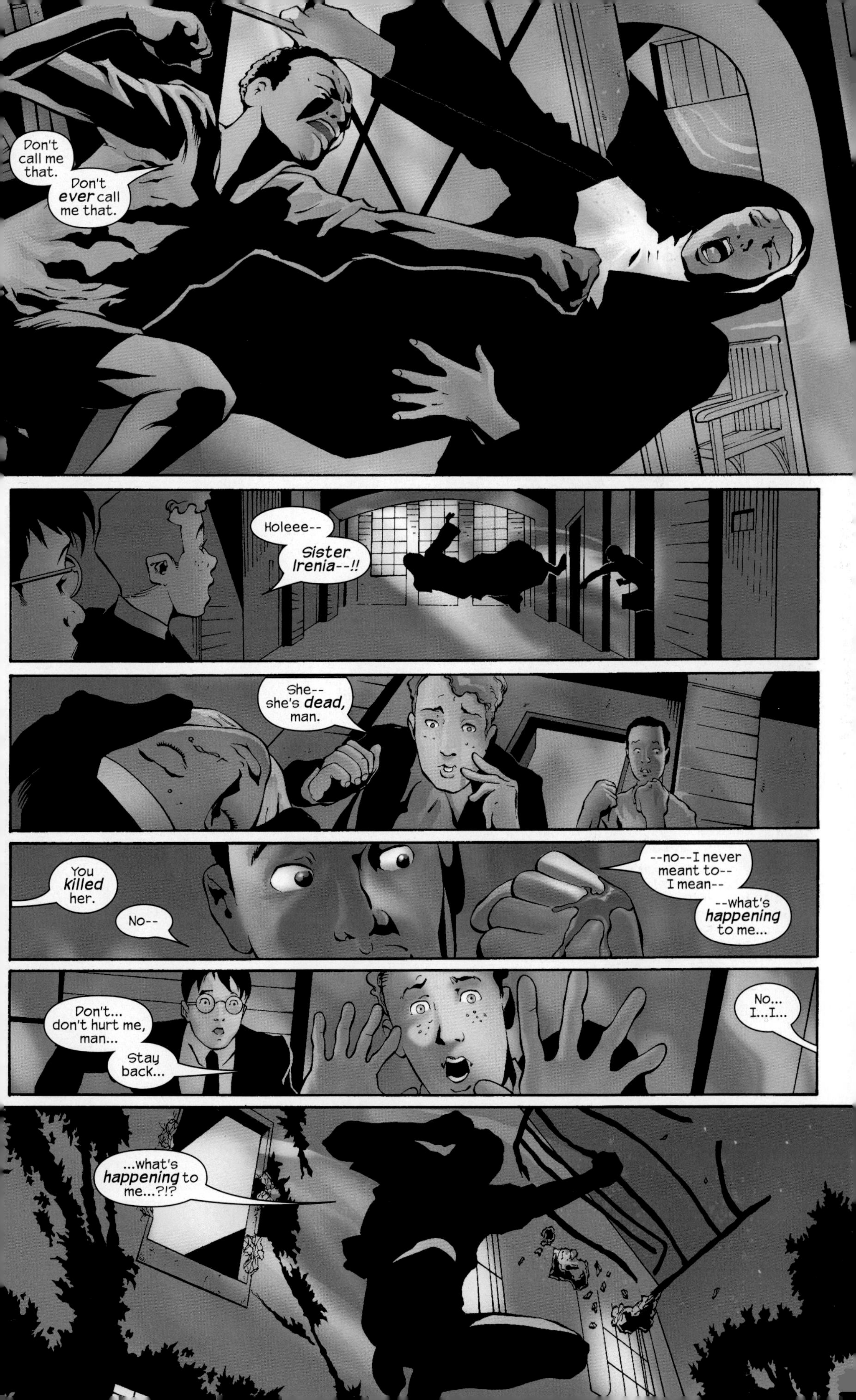

Don't call me that.
Don't *ever* call me that.
Holeee-- *Sister Irenia*--!!
She-- she's *dead,* man.
You *killed* her.
No--
--no--I never meant to-- I mean--
--what's *happening* to me...
Don't... don't hurt me, man...
Stay back...
No... I...I...
...what's *happening* to me...?!?

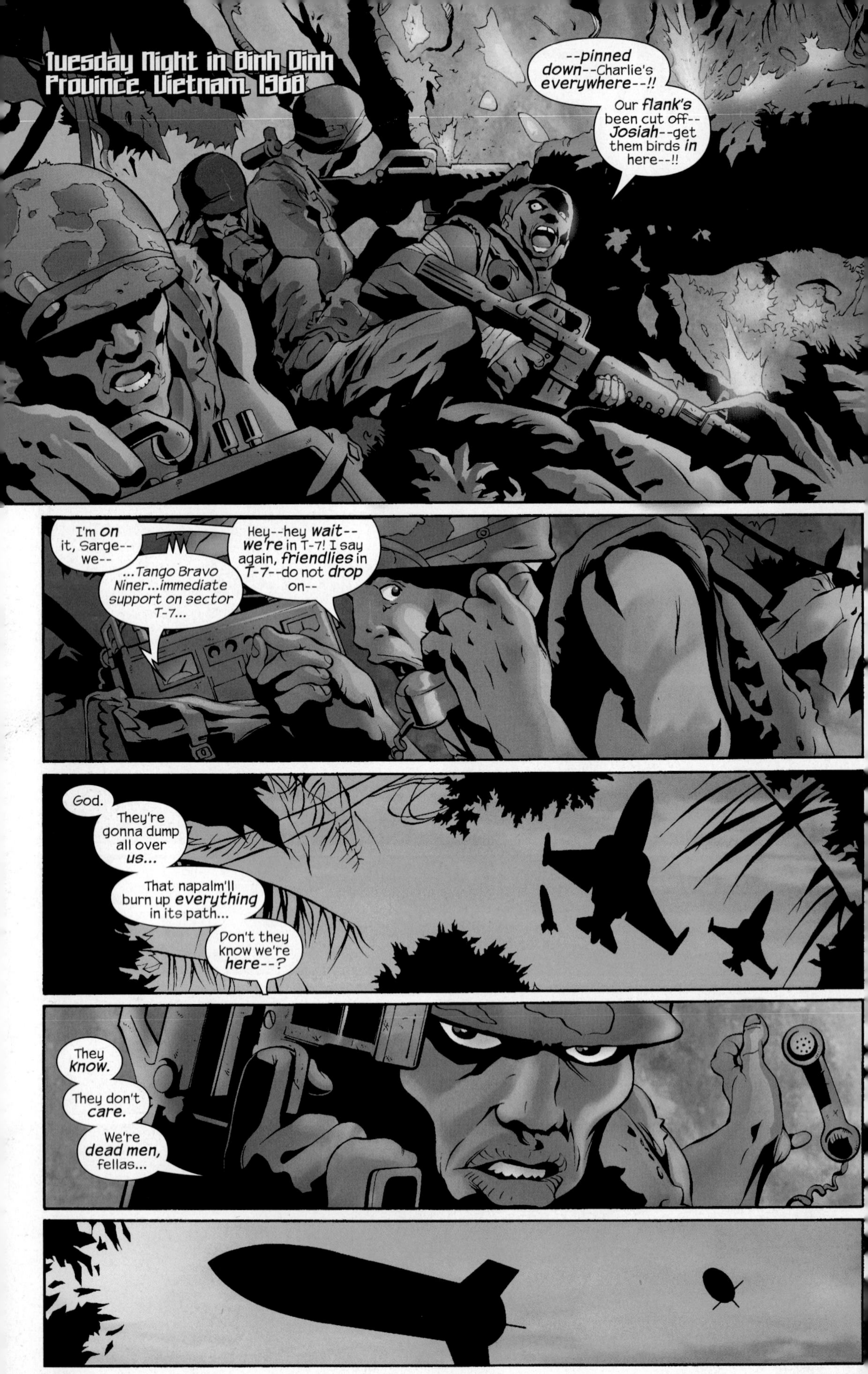
Tuesday Night in Binh Dinh Province, Vietnam, 1968
--pinned down--Charlie's everywhere--!!
Our flank's been cut off--Josiah--get them birds in here--!!
I'm on it, Sarge--we--
...Tango Bravo Niner...immediate support on sector T-7...
Hey--hey wait--we're in T-7! I say again, friendlies in T-7--do not drop on--
God.
They're gonna dump all over us...
That napalm'll burn up everything in its path...
Don't they know we're here--?
They know.
They don't care.
We're dead men, fellas...

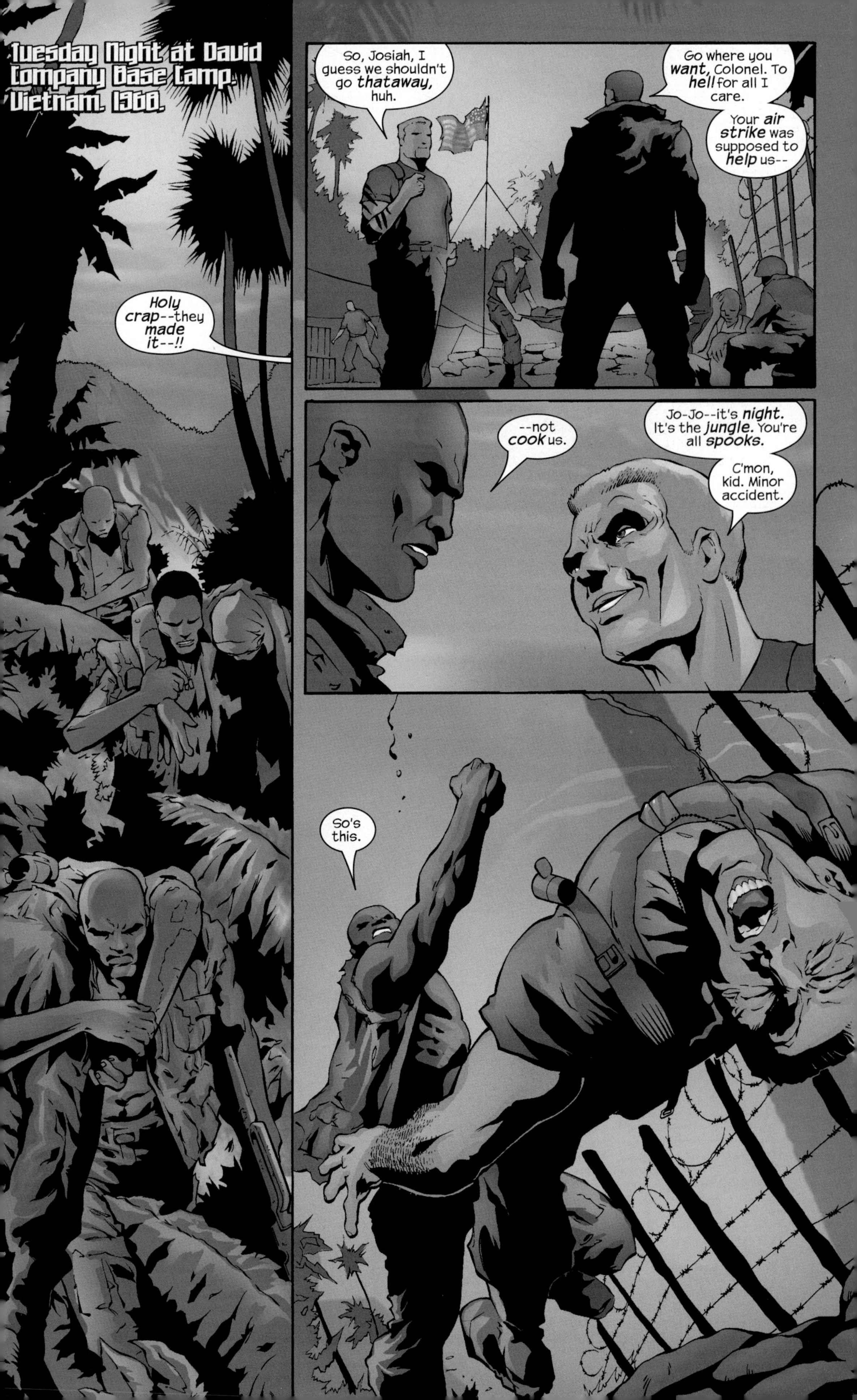
Tuesday Night at David Company Base Camp. Vietnam. 1968.
So, Josiah, I guess we shouldn't go thataway, huh.
Go where you want, Colonel. To hell for all I care.
Your air strike was supposed to help us--
Holy crap--they made it--!!
--not cook us.
Jo-Jo--it's night. It's the jungle. You're all spooks.
C'mon, kid. Minor accident.
So's this.

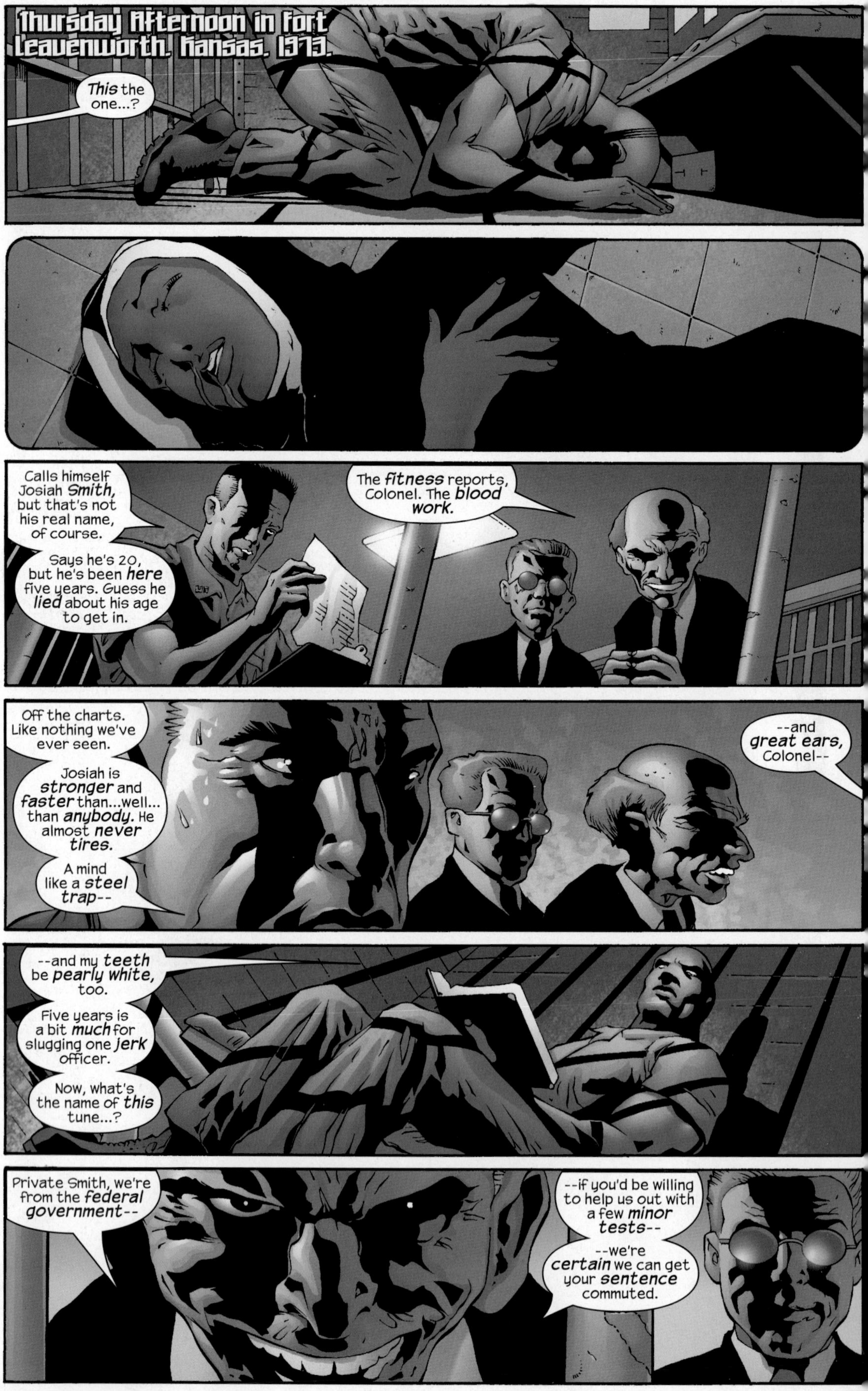
Thursday Afternoon in Fort Leavenworth, Kansas, 1973.
This the one...?
Calls himself Josiah Smith, but that's not his real name, of course.
Says he's 20, but he's been here five years. Guess he lied about his age to get in.
The fitness reports, Colonel. The blood work.
Off the charts. Like nothing we've ever seen.
Josiah is stronger and faster than...well... than anybody. He almost never tires.
A mind like a steel trap--
--and great ears, Colonel--
--and my teeth be pearly white, too.
Five years is a bit much for slugging one jerk officer.
Now, what's the name of this tune...?
Private Smith, we're from the federal government--
--if you'd be willing to help us out with a few minor tests--
--we're certain we can get your sentence commuted.

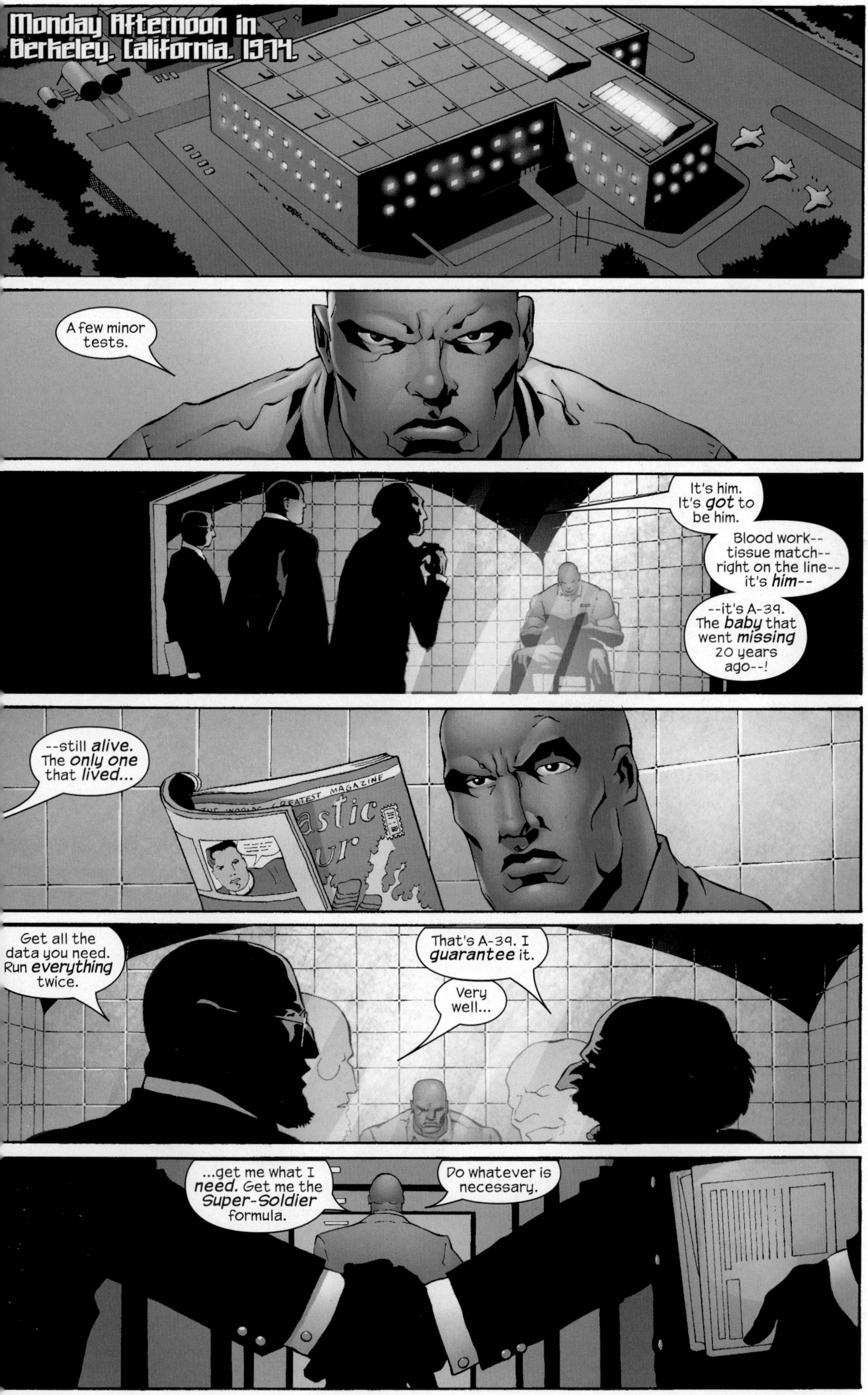

Monday Afternoon in Berkeley, California. 1974.
A few minor tests.
It's him. It's got to be him.
Blood work--tissue match--right on the line--it's him--
--it's A-39. The baby that went missing 20 years ago--!
--still alive. The only one that lived...
THE WORLD'S GREATEST MAGAZINE
Get all the data you need. Run everything twice.
That's A-39. I guarantee it.
Very well...
...get me what I need. Get me the Super-Soldier formula.
Do whatever is necessary.

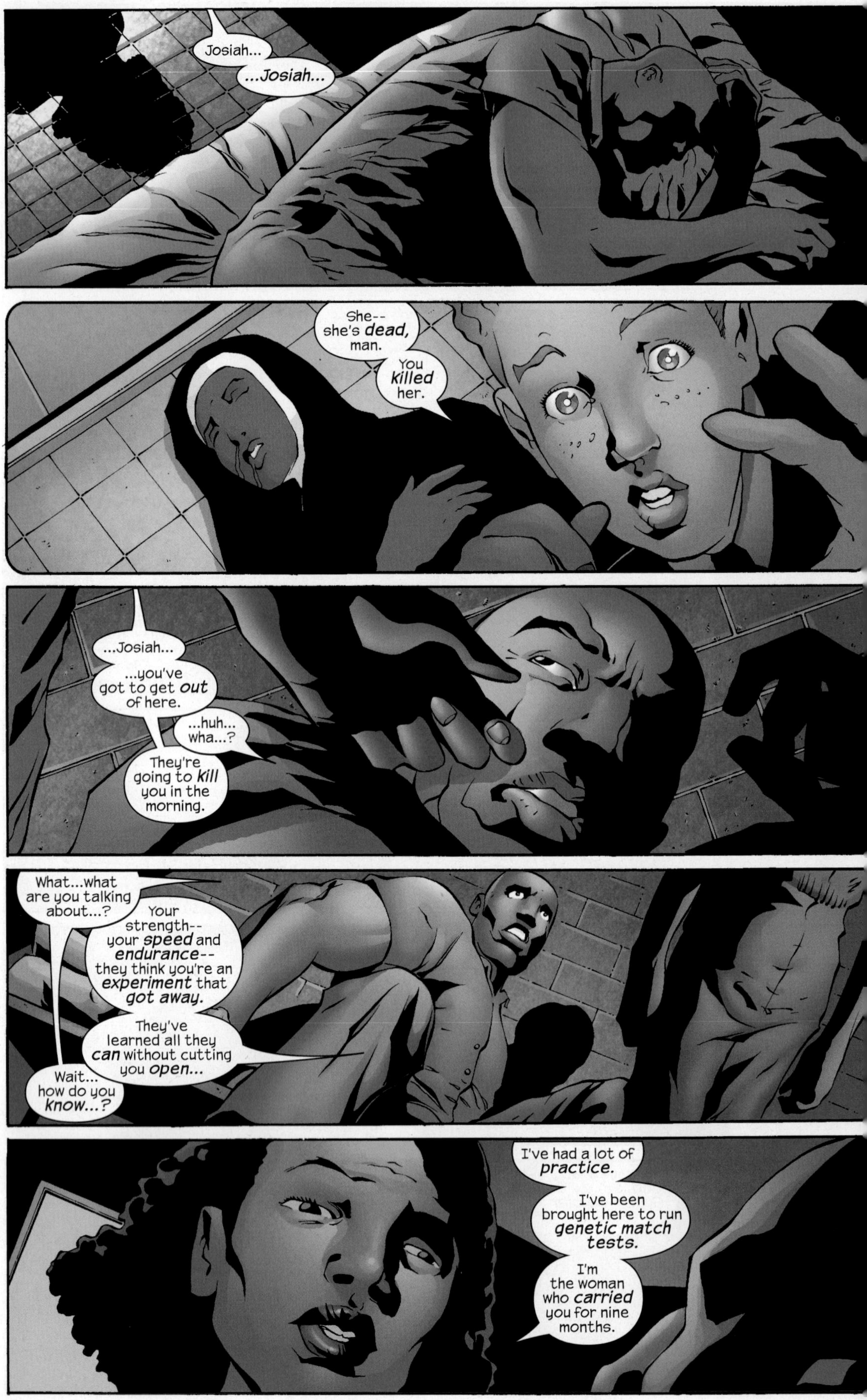
Josiah...
...Josiah...
She-- she's dead, man.
You killed her.
...Josiah...
...you've got to get out of here.
...huh... wha...?
They're going to kill you in the morning.
What...what are you talking about...?
Your strength-- your speed and endurance-- they think you're an experiment that got away.
They've learned all they can without cutting you open...
Wait... how do you know...?
I've had a lot of practice.
I've been brought here to run genetic match tests.
I'm the woman who carried you for nine months.

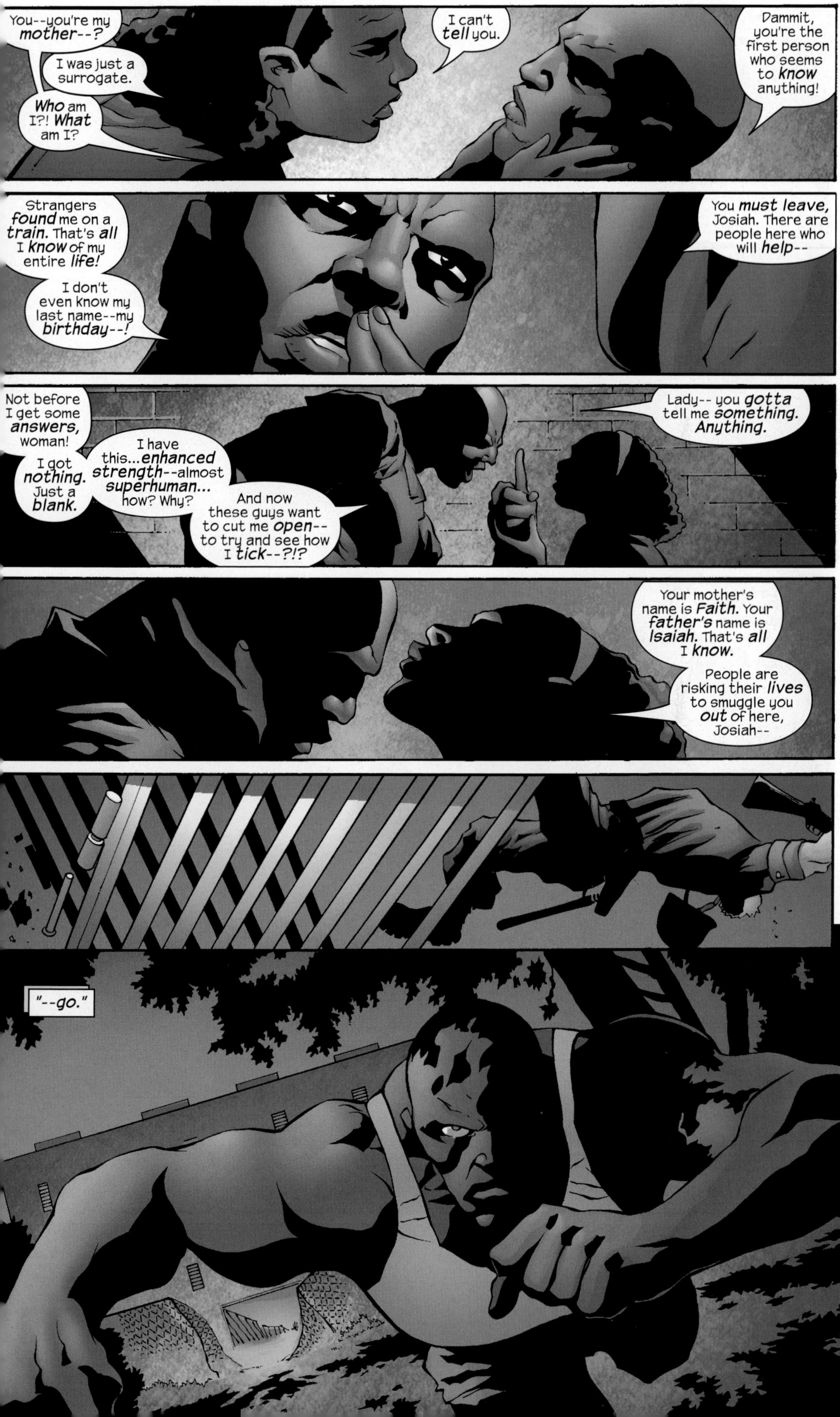

You--you're my mother--?
I was just a surrogate.
Who am I?! What am I?
I can't tell you.
Dammit, you're the first person who seems to know anything!
Strangers found me on a train. That's all I know of my entire life!
I don't even know my last name--my birthday--!
You must leave, Josiah. There are people here who will help--
Not before I get some answers, woman!
I got nothing. Just a blank.
I have this...enhanced strength--almost superhuman... how? Why?
And now these guys want to cut me open--to try and see how I tick--?!?
Lady-- you gotta tell me something. Anything.
Your mother's name is Faith. Your father's name is Isaiah. That's all I know.
People are risking their lives to smuggle you out of here, Josiah--
"--go."

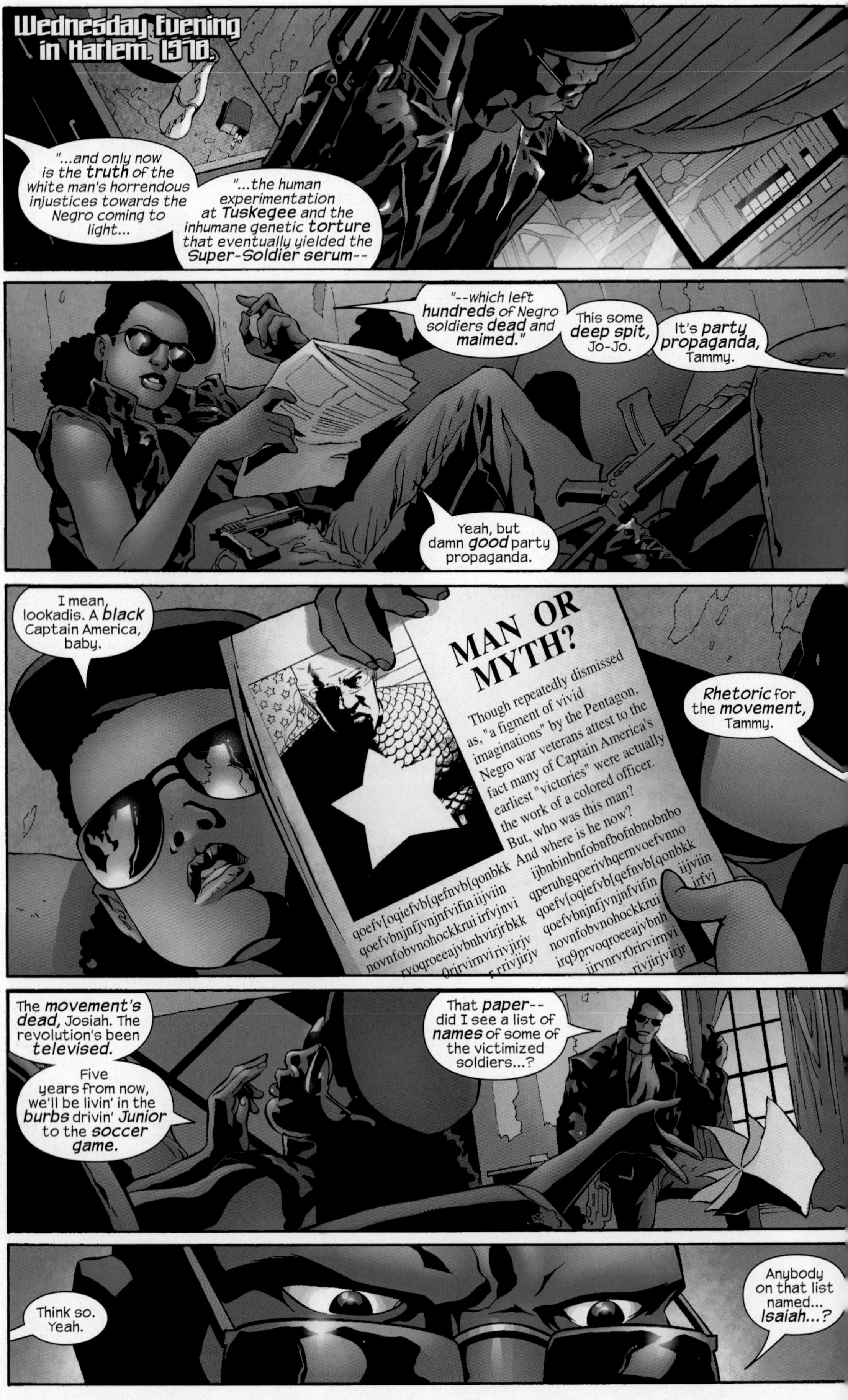
Wednesday Evening in Harlem, 1970.
"...and only now is the truth of the white man's horrendous injustices towards the Negro coming to light...
"...the human experimentation at Tuskegee and the inhumane genetic torture that eventually yielded the Super-Soldier serum--
"--which left hundreds of Negro soldiers dead and maimed."
This some deep spit, Jo-Jo.
It's party propaganda, Tammy.
Yeah, but damn good party propaganda.
I mean, lookadis. A black Captain America, baby.
MAN OR MYTH?
Though repeatedly dismissed as, "a figment of vivid imaginations" by the Pentagon, Negro war veterans attest to the fact many of Captain America's earliest "victories" were actually the work of a colored officer. But, who was this man? And where is he now?
Rhetoric for the movement, Tammy.
The movement's dead, Josiah. The revolution's been televised.
Five years from now, we'll be livin' in the burbs drivin' Junior to the soccer game.
That paper-- did I see a list of names of some of the victimized soldiers...?
Think so. Yeah.
Anybody on that list named... Isaiah...?

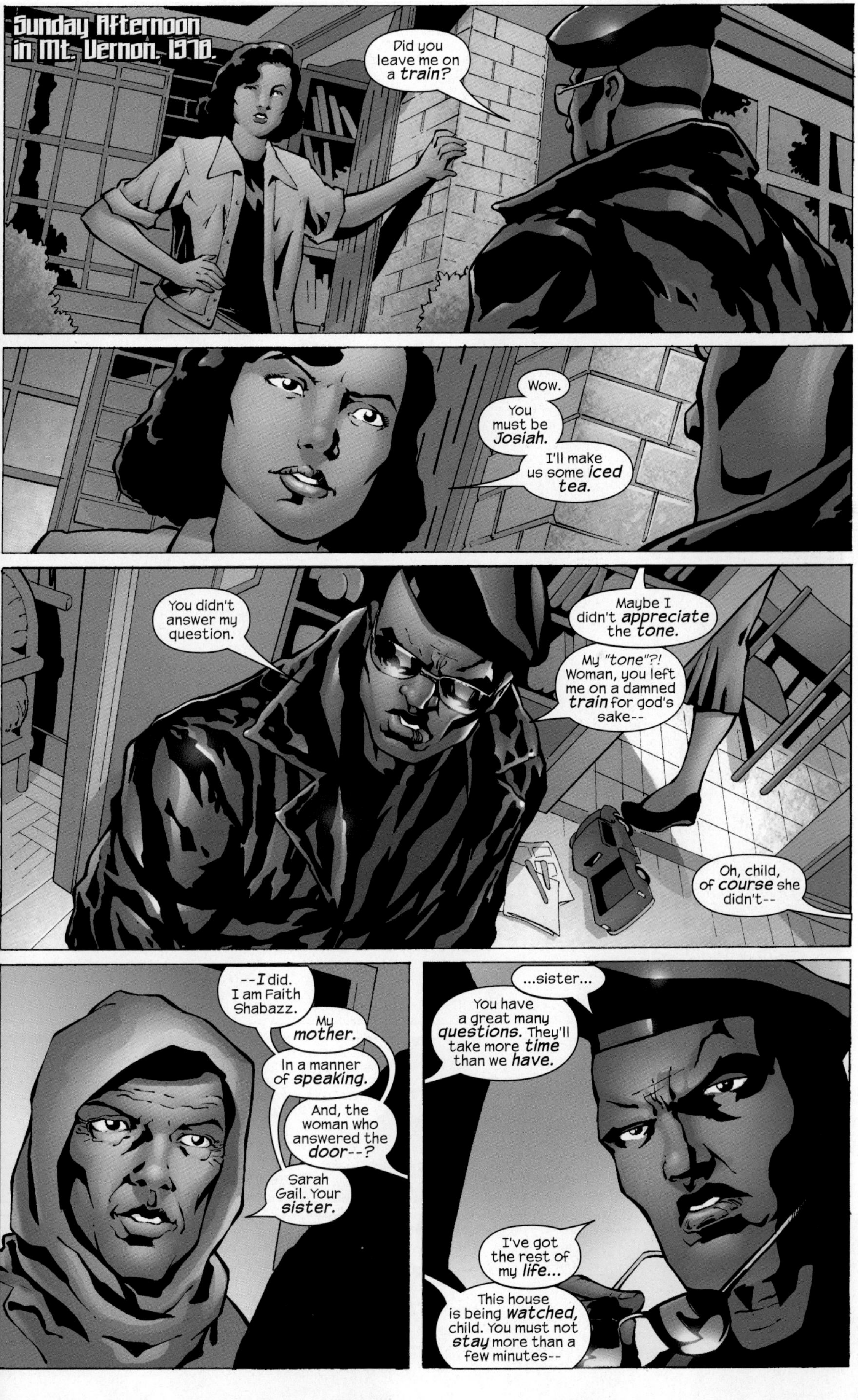

Sunday Afternoon in Mt. Vernon, 1970.
Did you leave me on a train?
Wow.
You must be Josiah.
I'll make us some iced tea.
You didn't answer my question.
Maybe I didn't appreciate the tone.
My "tone"?! Woman, you left me on a damned train for god's sake--
Oh, child, of course she didn't--
--I did. I am Faith Shabazz.
My mother.
In a manner of speaking.
And, the woman who answered the door--?
Sarah Gail. Your sister.
...sister...
You have a great many questions. They'll take more time than we have.
I've got the rest of my life...
This house is being watched, child. You must not stay more than a few minutes--

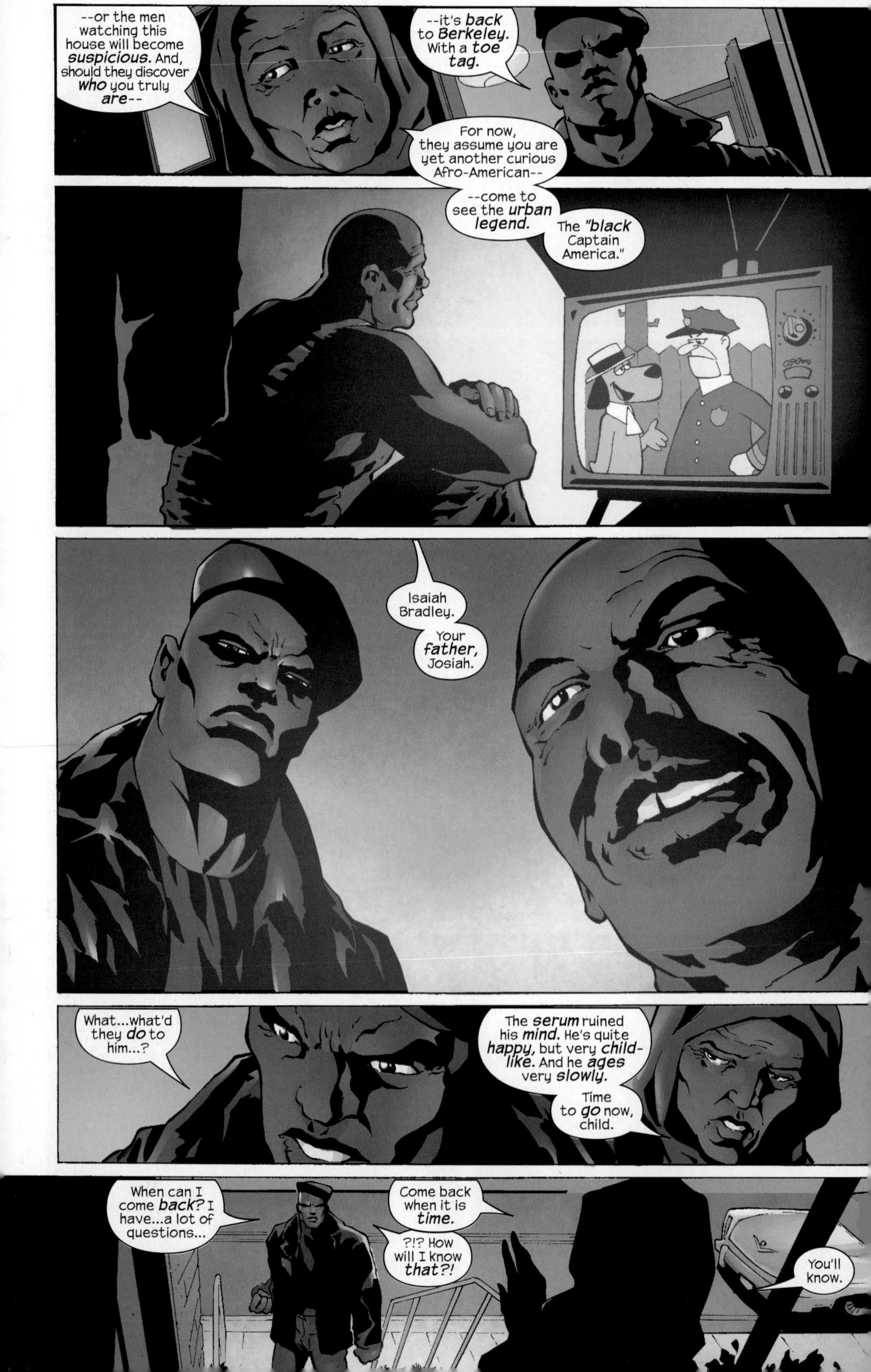
--or the men watching this house will become suspicious. And, should they discover who you truly are--
--it's back to Berkeley. With a toe tag.
For now, they assume you are yet another curious Afro-American--
--come to see the urban legend.
The "black Captain America."
Isaiah Bradley.
Your father, Josiah.
What...what'd they do to him...?
The serum ruined his mind. He's quite happy, but very child-like. And he ages very slowly.
Time to go now, child.
When can I come back? I have...a lot of questions...
Come back when it is time.
?!? How will I know that?!
You'll know.

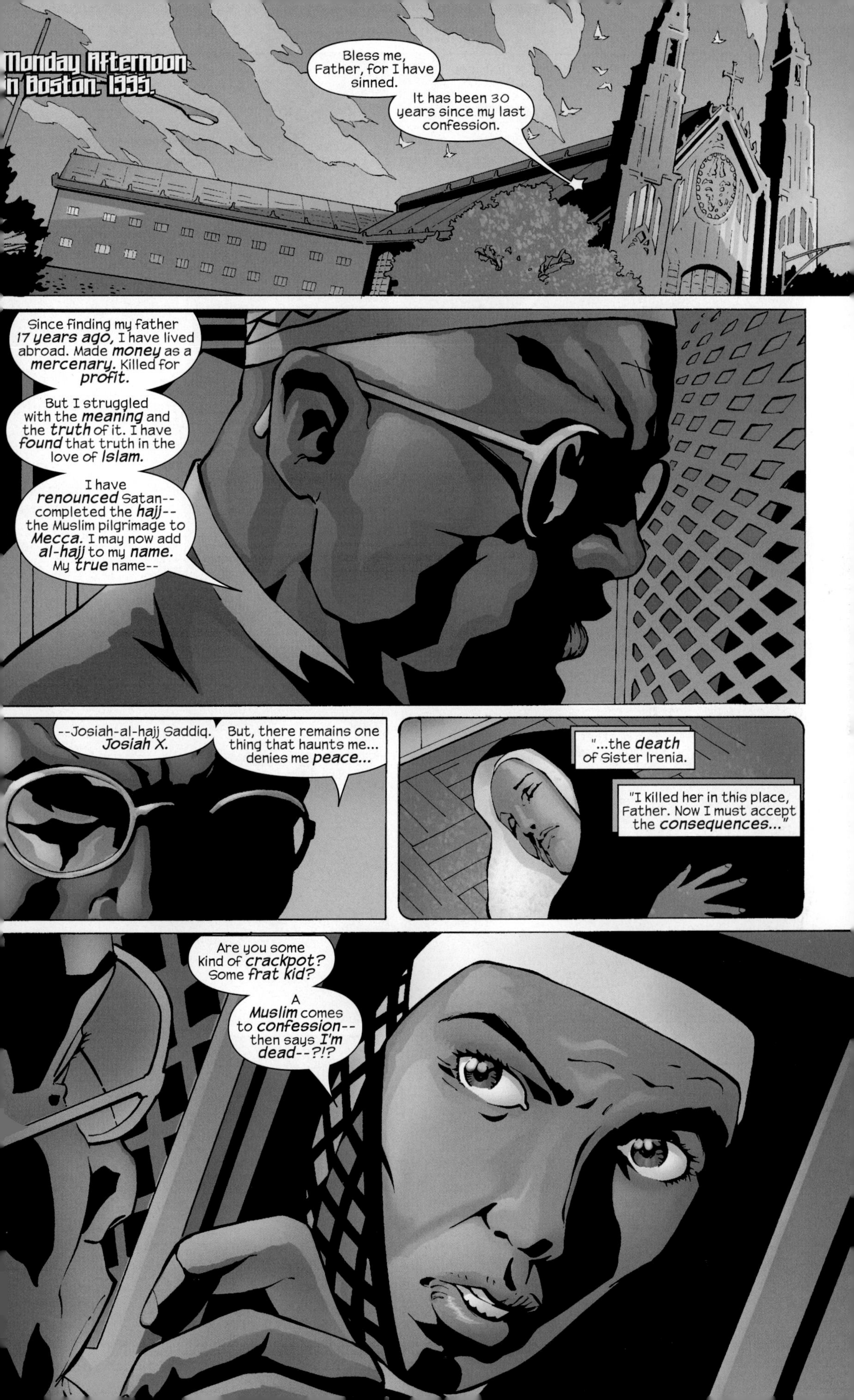

Monday Afternoon
n Boston. 1995.
Bless me, Father, for I have sinned.
It has been 30 years since my last confession.
Since finding my father 17 years ago, I have lived abroad. Made money as a mercenary. Killed for profit.
But I struggled with the meaning and the truth of it. I have found that truth in the love of Islam.
I have renounced Satan--completed the hajj--the Muslim pilgrimage to Mecca. I may now add al-hajj to my name. My true name--
--Josiah-al-hajj Saddiq. Josiah X.
But, there remains one thing that haunts me... denies me peace...
"...the death of Sister Irenia.
"I killed her in this place, Father. Now I must accept the consequences..."
Are you some kind of crackpot? Some frat kid?
A Muslim comes to confession--then says I'm dead--?!?

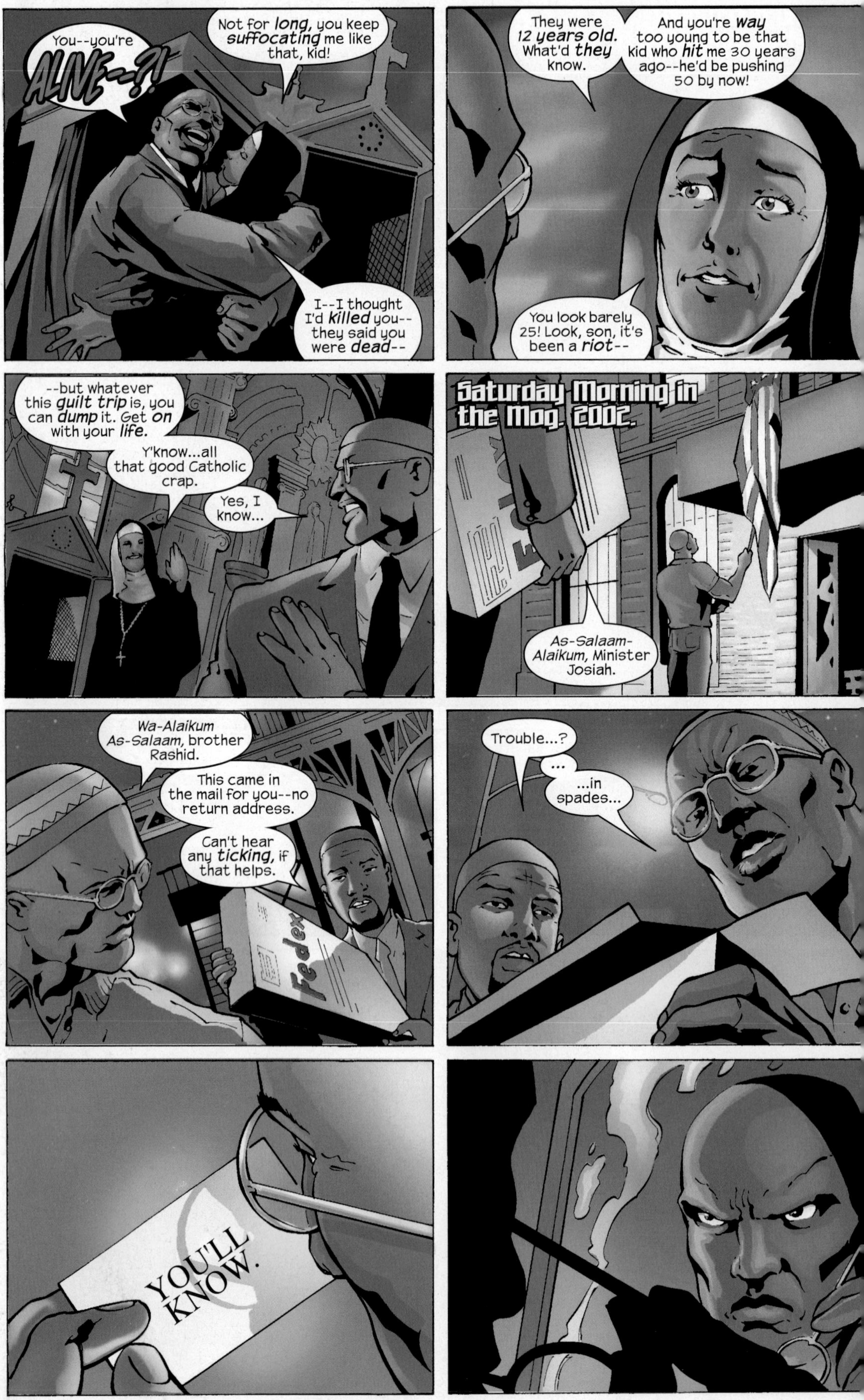
You--you're ALIVE--?!
Not for long, you keep suffocating me like that, kid!
I--I thought I'd killed you--they said you were dead--
They were 12 years old. What'd they know.
And you're way too young to be that kid who hit me 30 years ago--he'd be pushing 50 by now!
You look barely 25! Look, son, it's been a riot--
--but whatever this guilt trip is, you can dump it. Get on with your life.
Y'know...all that good Catholic crap.
Yes, I know...
Saturday Morning in the Mog. 2002.
As-Salaam-Alaikum, Minister Josiah.
Wa-Alaikum As-Salaam, brother Rashid.
This came in the mail for you--no return address.
Can't hear any ticking, if that helps.
Fedex
Trouble...?
...
...in spades...
YOU'LL KNOW.

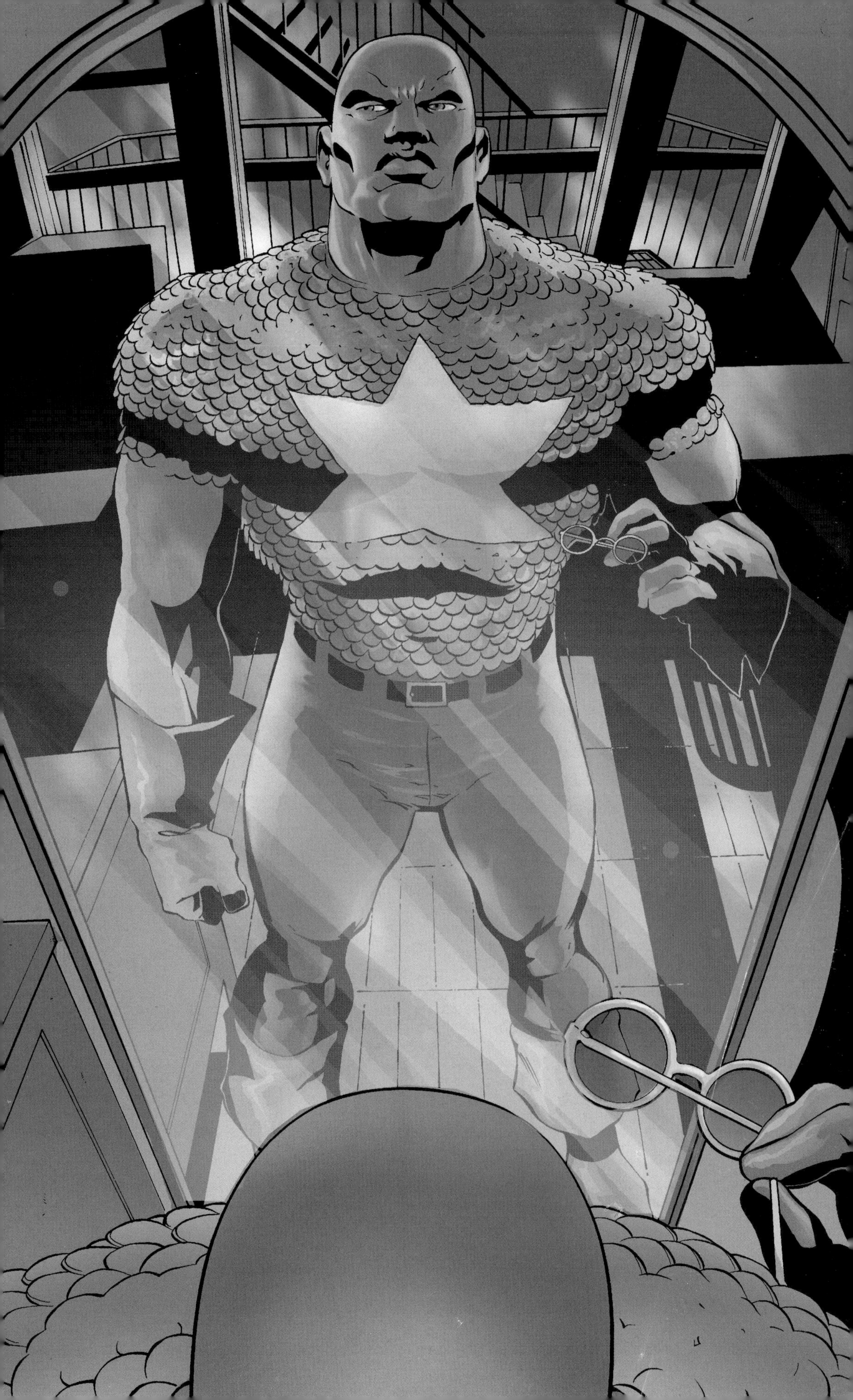

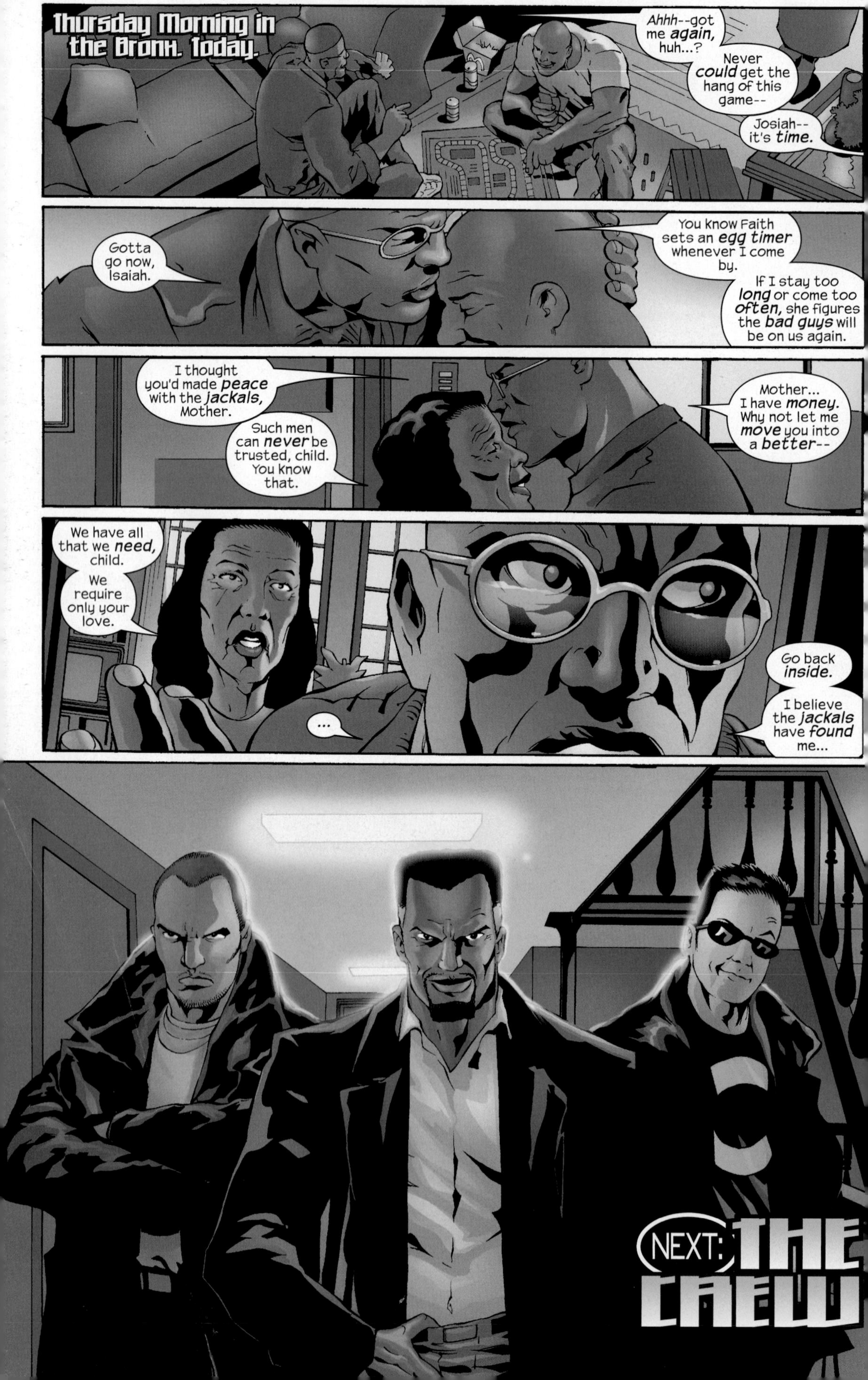
Thursday Morning in the Bronx. today.
Ahhh--got me again, huh...?
Never could get the hang of this game--
Josiah--it's time.
Gotta go now, Isaiah.
You know Faith sets an egg timer whenever I come by.
If I stay too long or come too often, she figures the bad guys will be on us again.
I thought you'd made peace with the jackals, Mother.
Such men can never be trusted, child. You know that.
Mother... I have money. Why not let me move you into a better--
We have all that we need, child.
We require only your love.
...
Go back inside.
I believe the jackals have found me...
NEXT: THE CREW

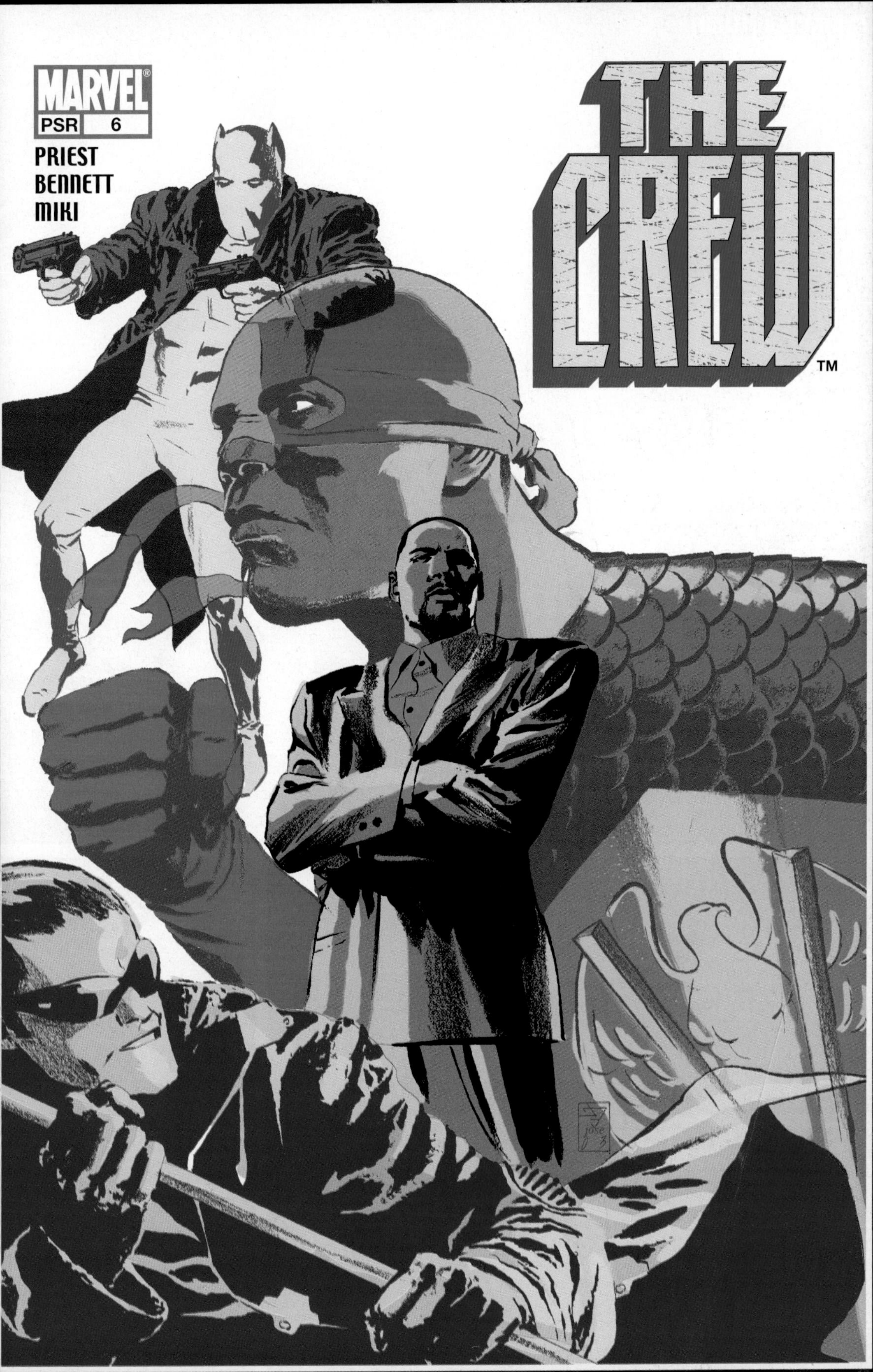
MARVEL
PSR 6
PRIEST
BENNETT
MIKI
THE CREW™

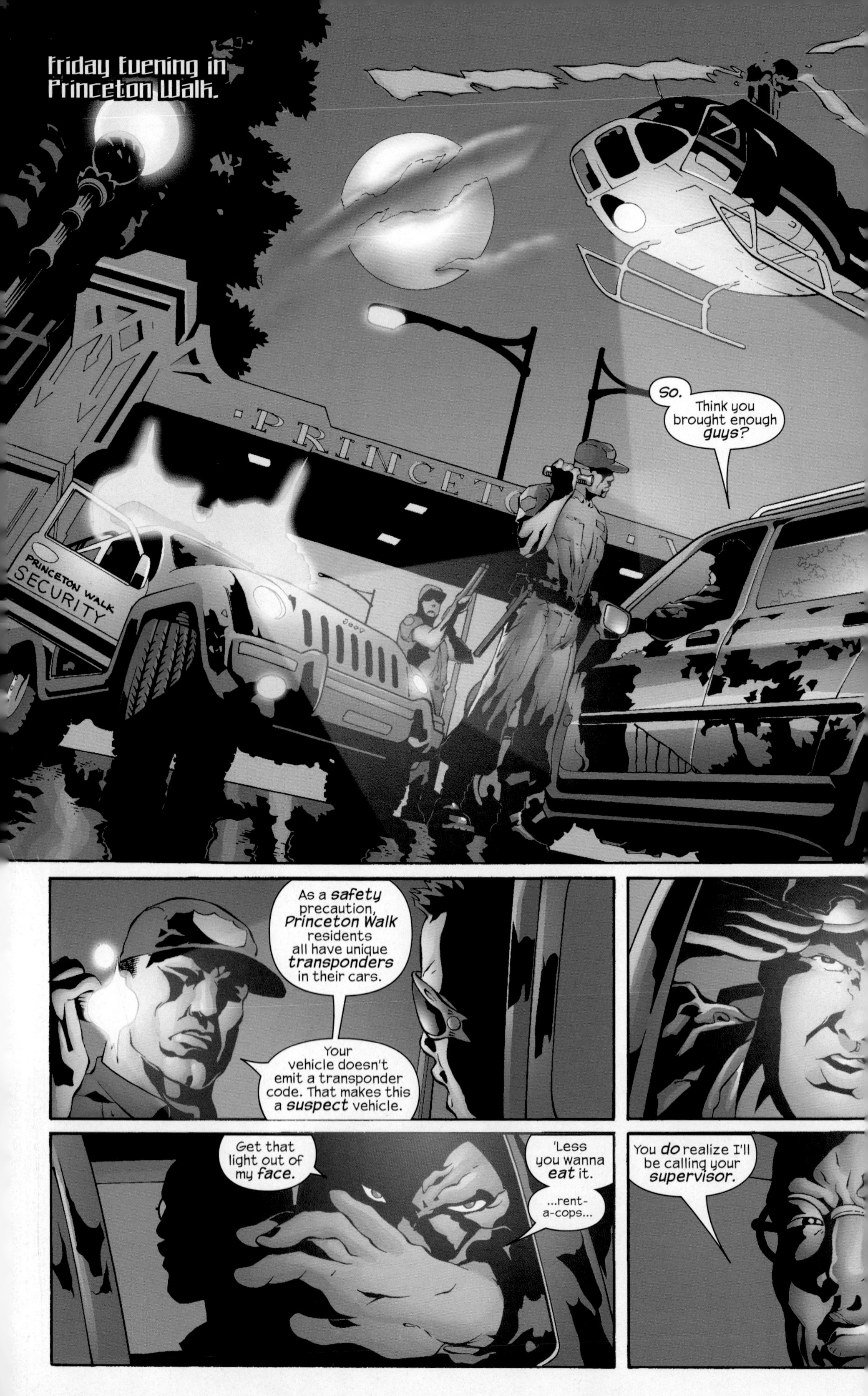

Friday Evening in Princeton Walk.
·PRINCETON
PRINCETON WALK SECURITY
So.
Think you brought enough *guys?*
As a *safety* precaution, *Princeton Walk* residents all have unique *transponders* in their cars.
Your vehicle doesn't emit a transponder code. That makes this a *suspect* vehicle.
Get that light out of my *face.*
'Less you wanna *eat* it.
...rent-a-cops...
You *do* realize I'll be calling your *supervisor.*

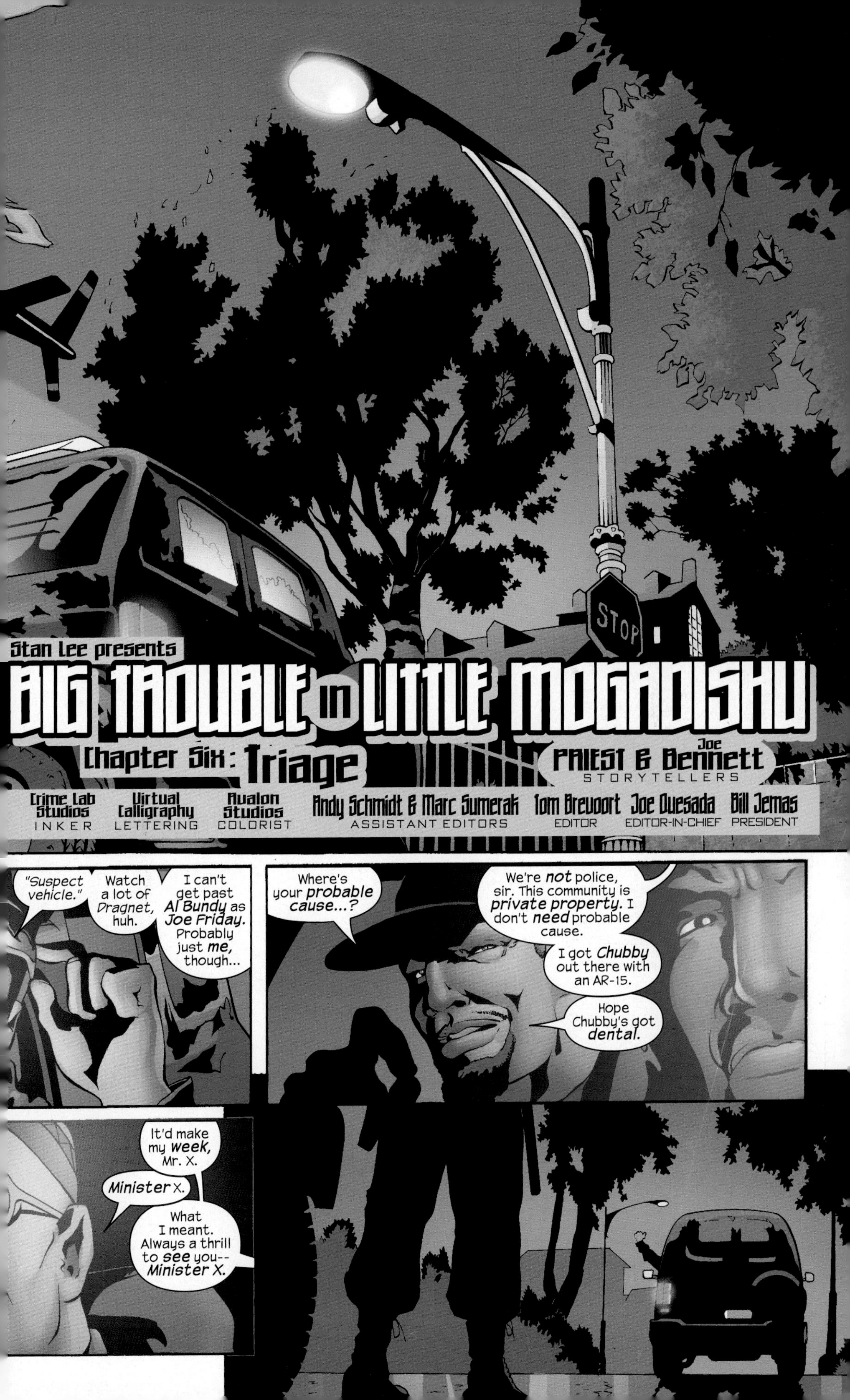

Stan Lee presents
BIG TROUBLE in LITTLE MOGADISHU
Chapter Six: Triage
PRIEST & Joe Bennett
STORYTELLERS
Crime Lab Studios INKER
Virtual Calligraphy LETTERING
Avalon Studios COLORIST
Andy Schmidt & Marc Sumerak ASSISTANT EDITORS
Tom Brevoort EDITOR
Joe Quesada EDITOR-IN-CHIEF
Bill Jemas PRESIDENT
STOP
"Suspect vehicle."
Watch a lot of Dragnet, huh.
I can't get past Al Bundy as Joe Friday. Probably just me, though...
Where's your probable cause...?
We're not police, sir. This community is private property. I don't need probable cause.
I got Chubby out there with an AR-15.
Hope Chubby's got dental.
It'd make my week, Mr. X.
Minister X.
What I meant. Always a thrill to see you-- Minister X.

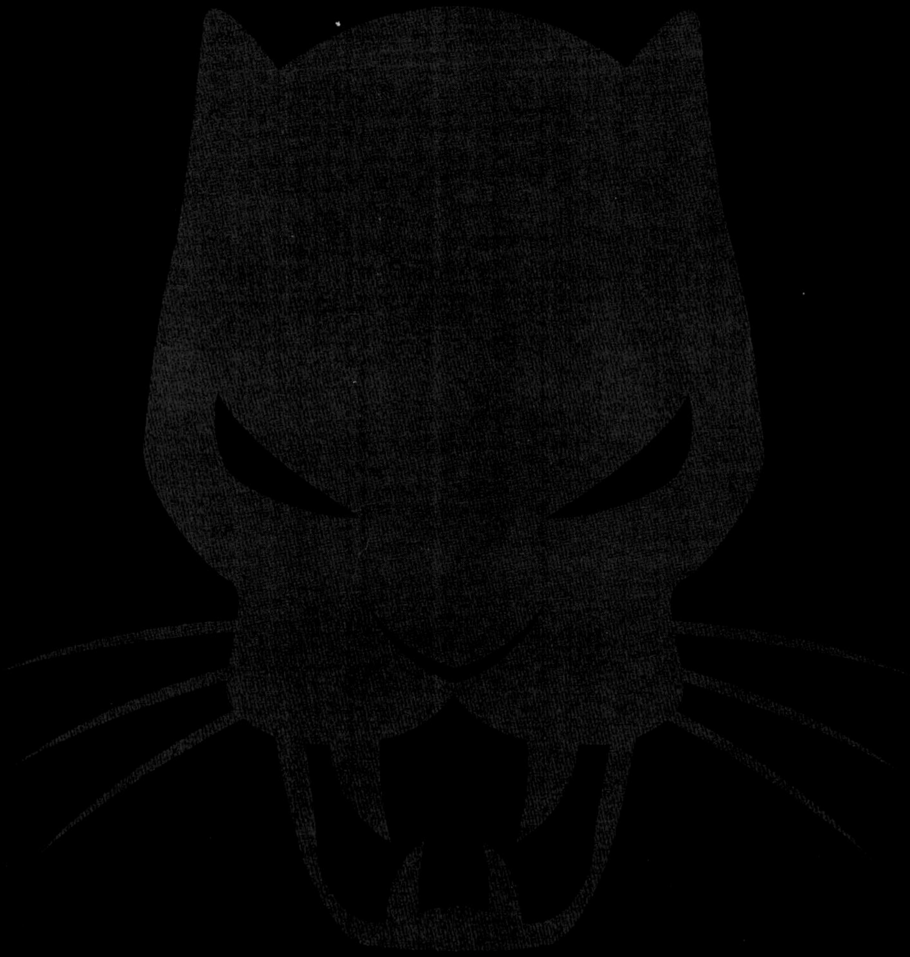

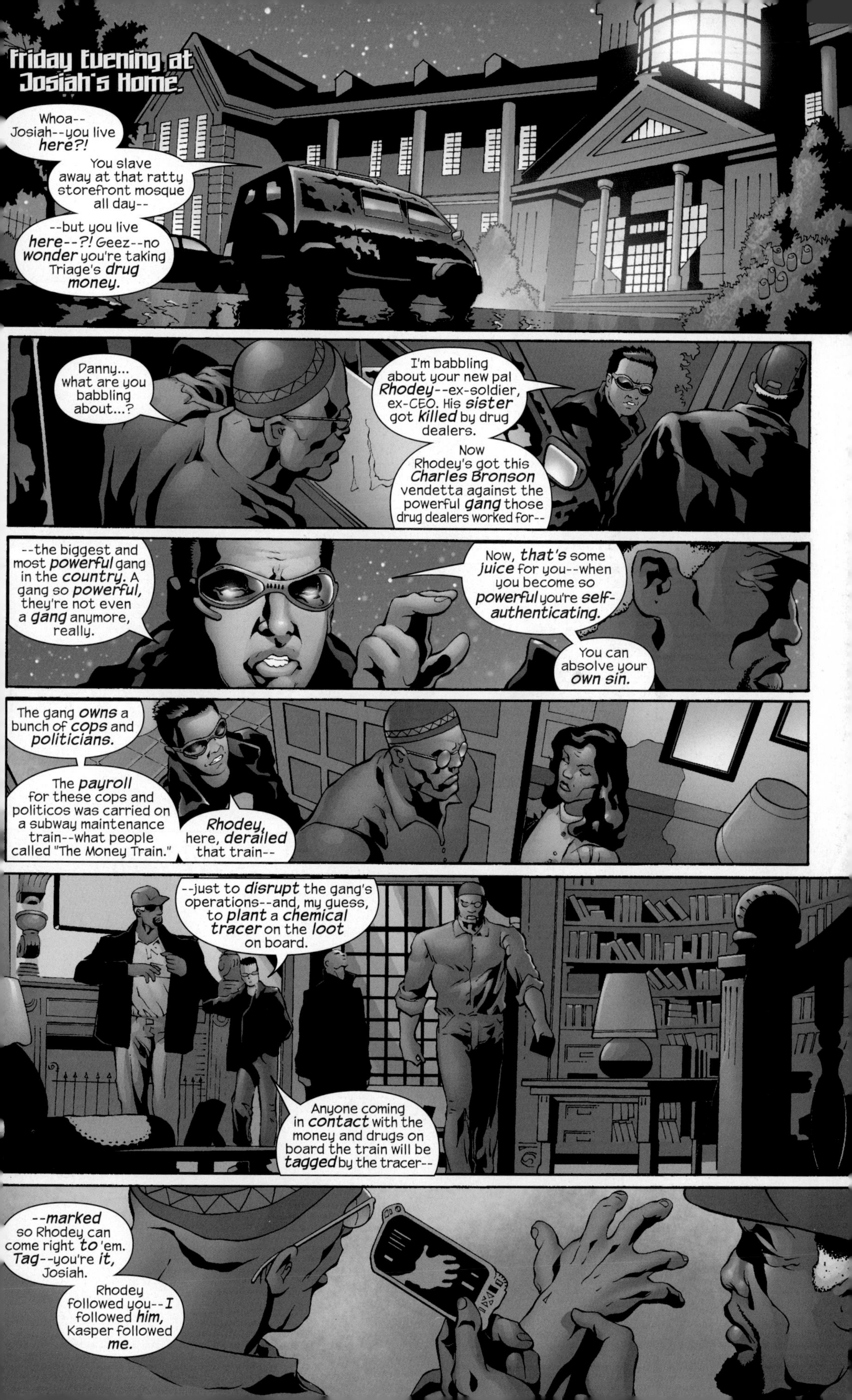

Friday Evening at Josiah's Home.
Whoa--Josiah--you live here?!
You slave away at that ratty storefront mosque all day--
--but you live here--?! Geez--no wonder you're taking Triage's drug money.
Danny... what are you babbling about...?
I'm babbling about your new pal Rhodey--ex-soldier, ex-CEO. His sister got killed by drug dealers.
Now Rhodey's got this Charles Bronson vendetta against the powerful gang those drug dealers worked for--
--the biggest and most powerful gang in the country. A gang so powerful, they're not even a gang anymore, really.
Now, that's some juice for you--when you become so powerful you're self-authenticating.
You can absolve your own sin.
The gang owns a bunch of cops and politicians.
The payroll for these cops and politicos was carried on a subway maintenance train--what people called "The Money Train."
Rhodey, here, derailed that train--
--just to disrupt the gang's operations--and, my guess, to plant a chemical tracer on the loot on board.
Anyone coming in contact with the money and drugs on board the train will be tagged by the tracer--
--marked so Rhodey can come right to 'em. Tag--you're it, Josiah.
Rhodey followed you--I followed him, Kasper followed me.

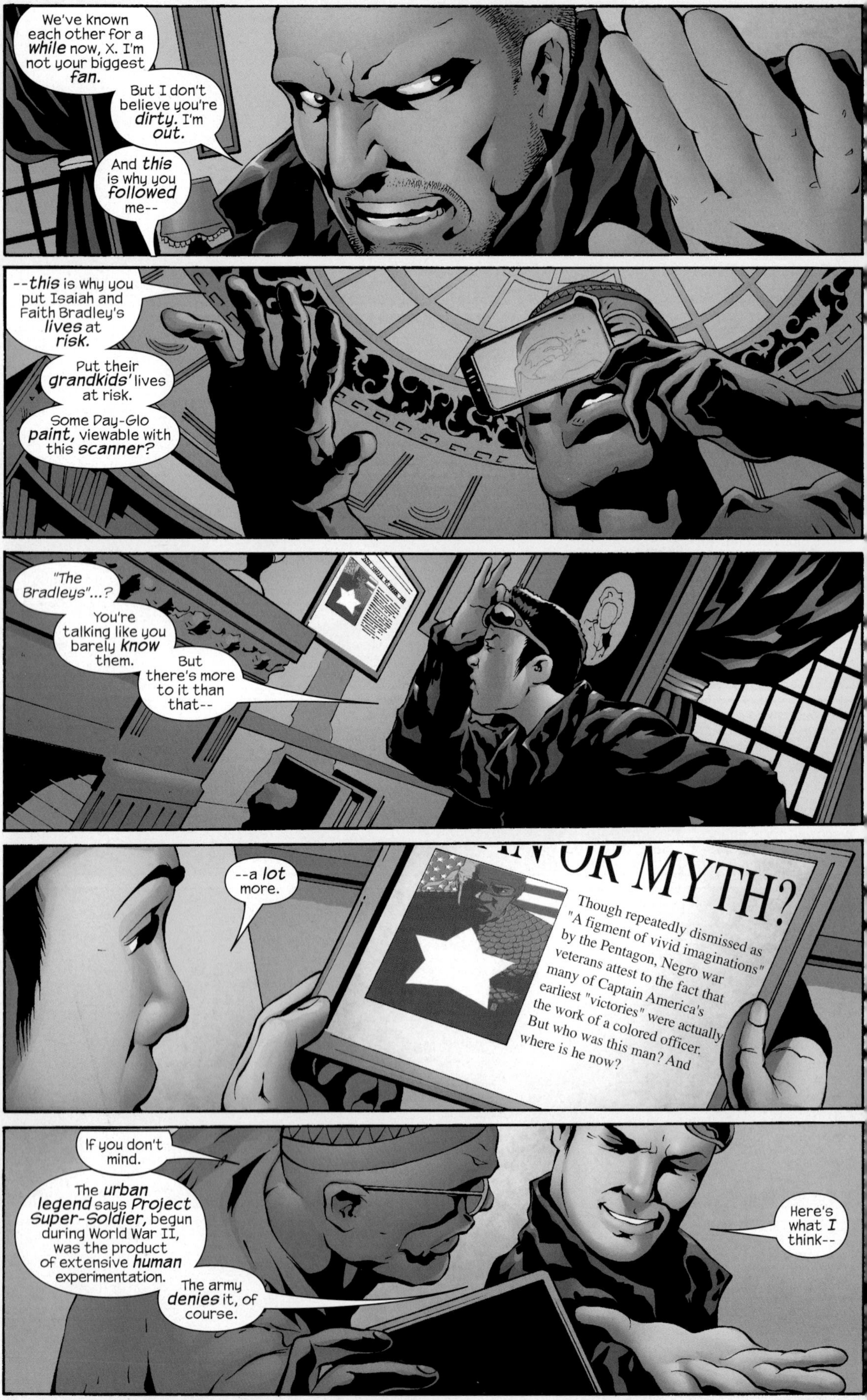
We've known each other for a while now, X. I'm not your biggest fan.
But I don't believe you're dirty. I'm out.
And this is why you followed me--
--this is why you put Isaiah and Faith Bradley's lives at risk.
Put their grandkids' lives at risk.
Some Day-Glo paint, viewable with this scanner?
"The Bradleys"...?
You're talking like you barely know them.
But there's more to it than that--
--a lot more.
OR MYTH?
Though repeatedly dismissed as "A figment of vivid imaginations" by the Pentagon, Negro war veterans attest to the fact that many of Captain America's earliest "victories" were actually the work of a colored officer. But who was this man? And where is he now?
If you don't mind.
The urban legend says Project Super-Soldier, begun during World War II, was the product of extensive human experimentation.
The army denies it, of course.
Here's what I think--

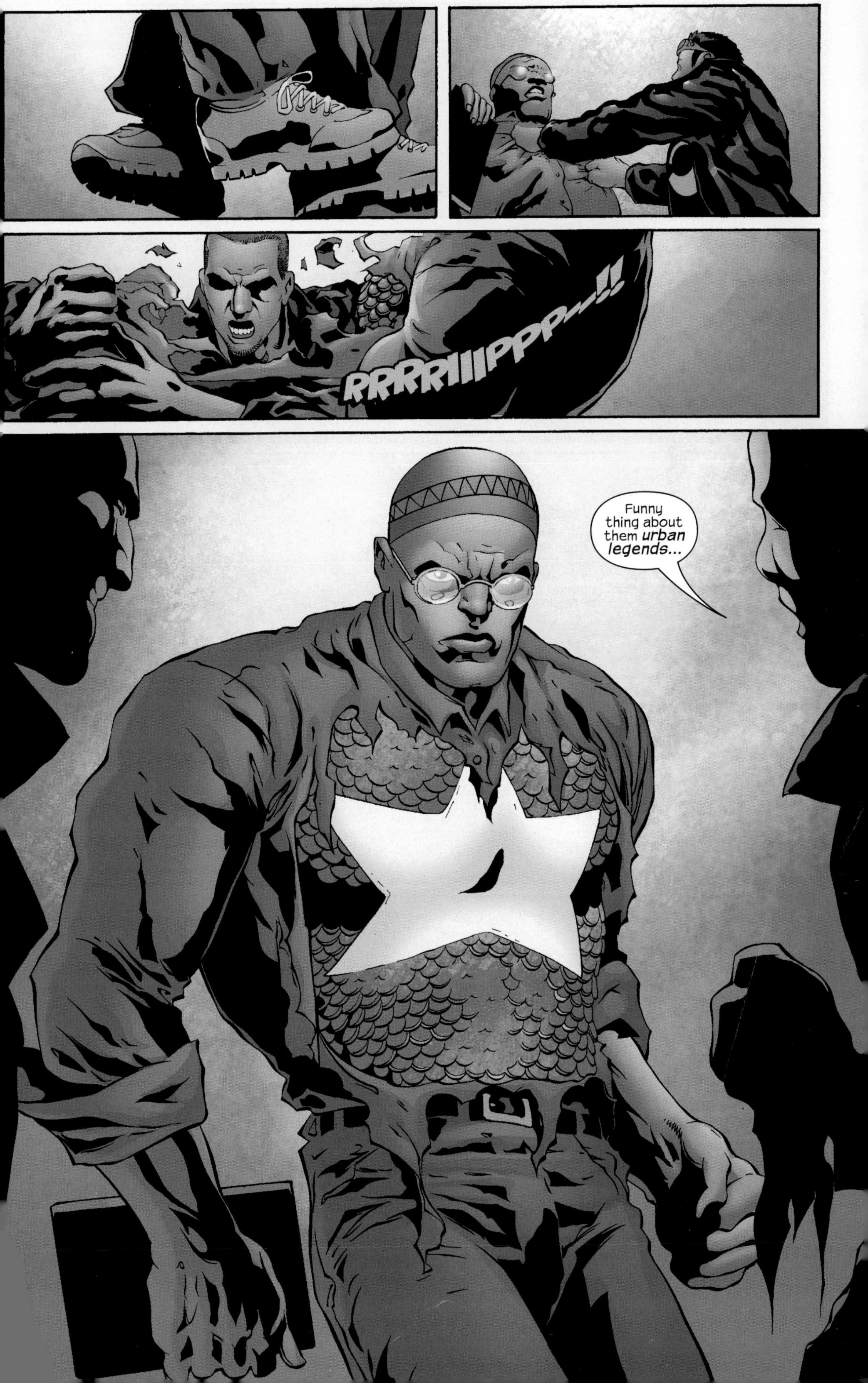
RRRRIIIIPPPP--!!
Funny thing about them *urban legends*...

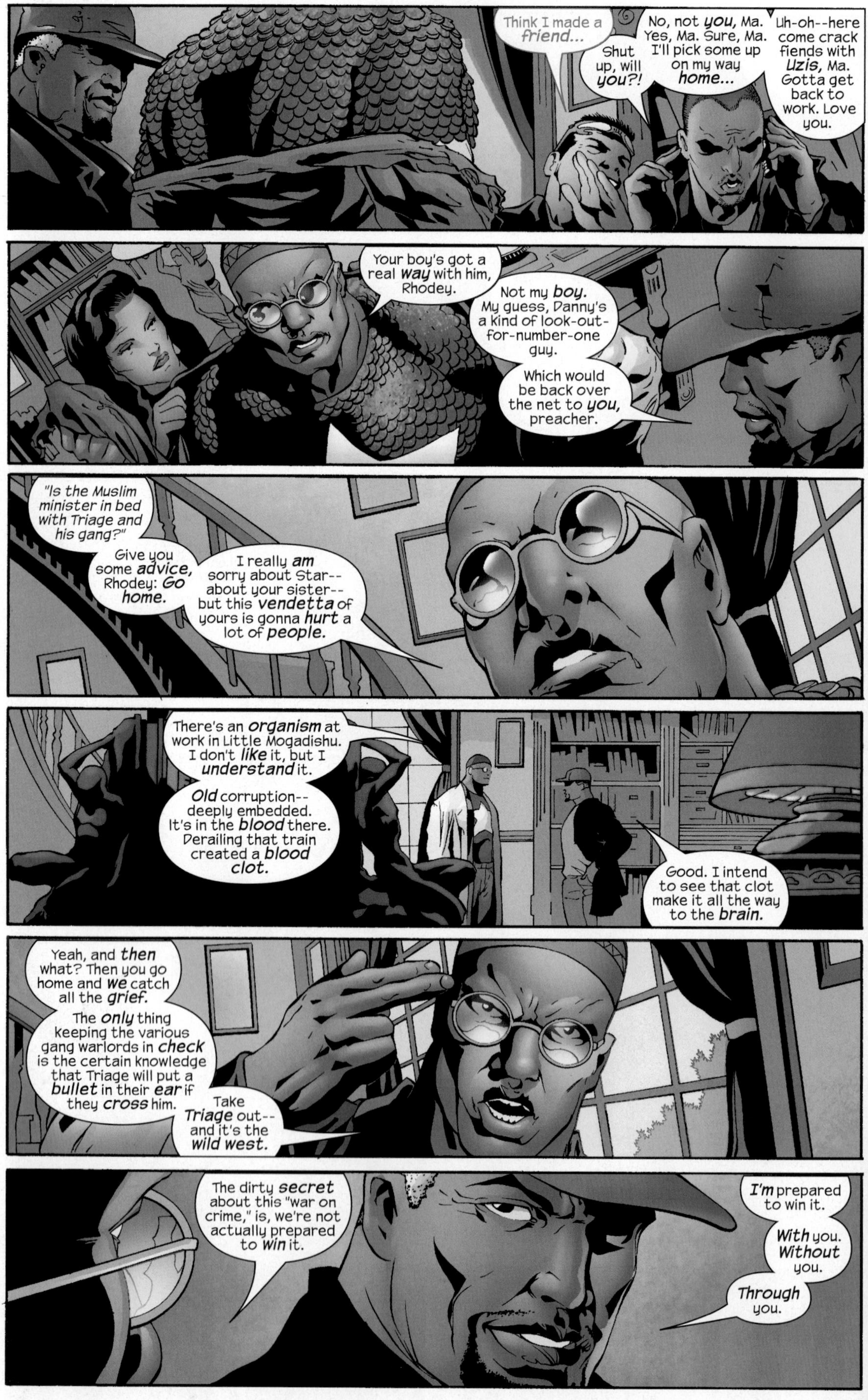
Think I made a friend...
Shut up, will you?!
No, not you, Ma. Yes, Ma. Sure, Ma. I'll pick some up on my way home...
Uh-oh--here come crack fiends with Uzis, Ma. Gotta get back to work. Love you.
Your boy's got a real way with him, Rhodey.
Not my boy. My guess, Danny's a kind of look-out-for-number-one guy.
Which would be back over the net to you, preacher.
"Is the Muslim minister in bed with Triage and his gang?"
Give you some advice, Rhodey: Go home.
I really am sorry about Star--about your sister--but this vendetta of yours is gonna hurt a lot of people.
There's an organism at work in Little Mogadishu. I don't like it, but I understand it.
Old corruption--deeply embedded. It's in the blood there. Derailing that train created a blood clot.
Good. I intend to see that clot make it all the way to the brain.
Yeah, and then what? Then you go home and we catch all the grief.
The only thing keeping the various gang warlords in check is the certain knowledge that Triage will put a bullet in their ear if they cross him.
Take Triage out--and it's the wild west.
The dirty secret about this "war on crime," is, we're not actually prepared to win it.
I'm prepared to win it.
With you. Without you.
Through you.

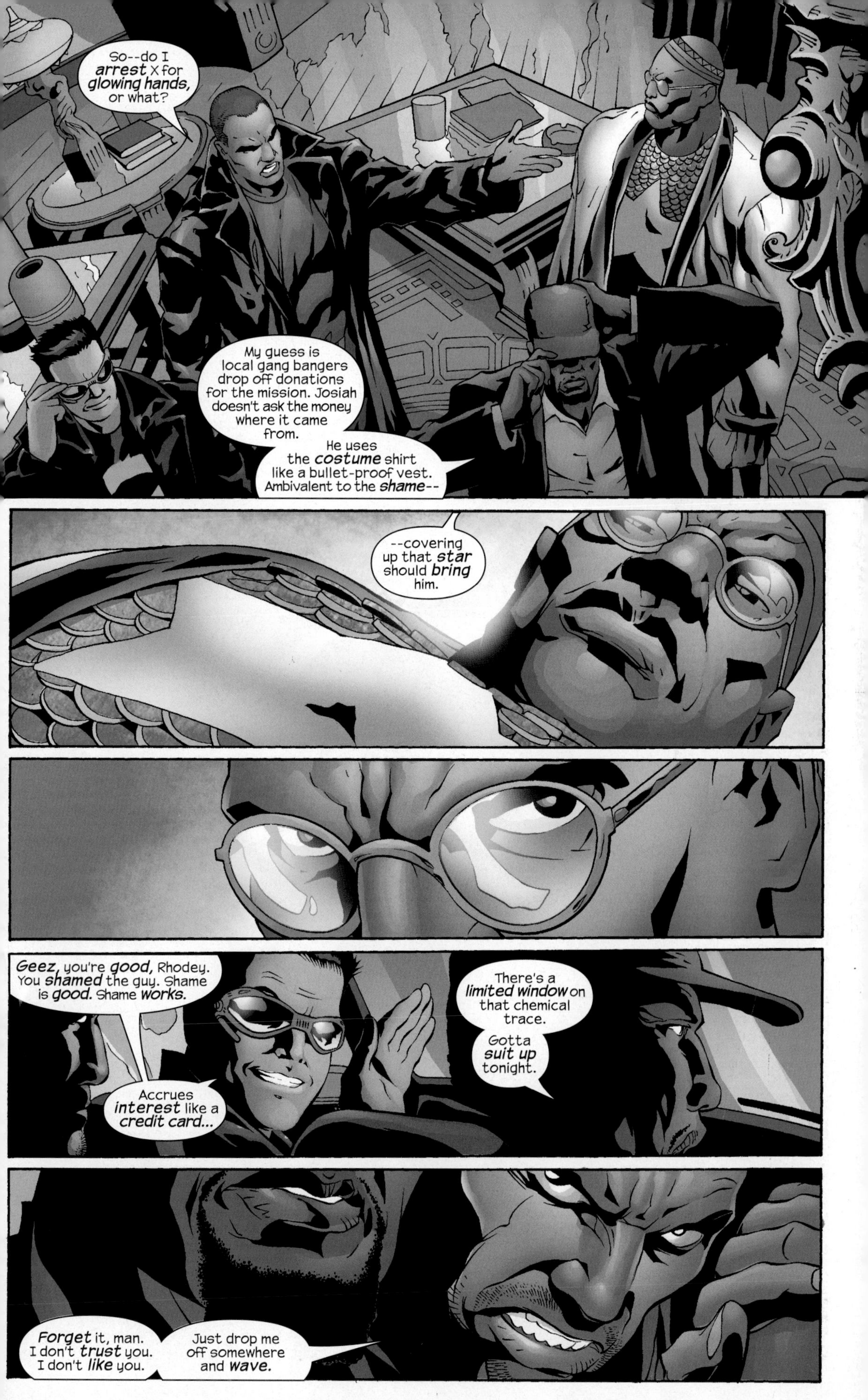
So--do I arrest X for glowing hands, or what?
My guess is local gang bangers drop off donations for the mission. Josiah doesn't ask the money where it came from.
He uses the costume shirt like a bullet-proof vest. Ambivalent to the shame--
--covering up that star should bring him.
Geez, you're good, Rhodey. You shamed the guy. Shame is good. Shame works.
Accrues interest like a credit card...
There's a limited window on that chemical trace.
Gotta suit up tonight.
Forget it, man. I don't trust you. I don't like you.
Just drop me off somewhere and wave.

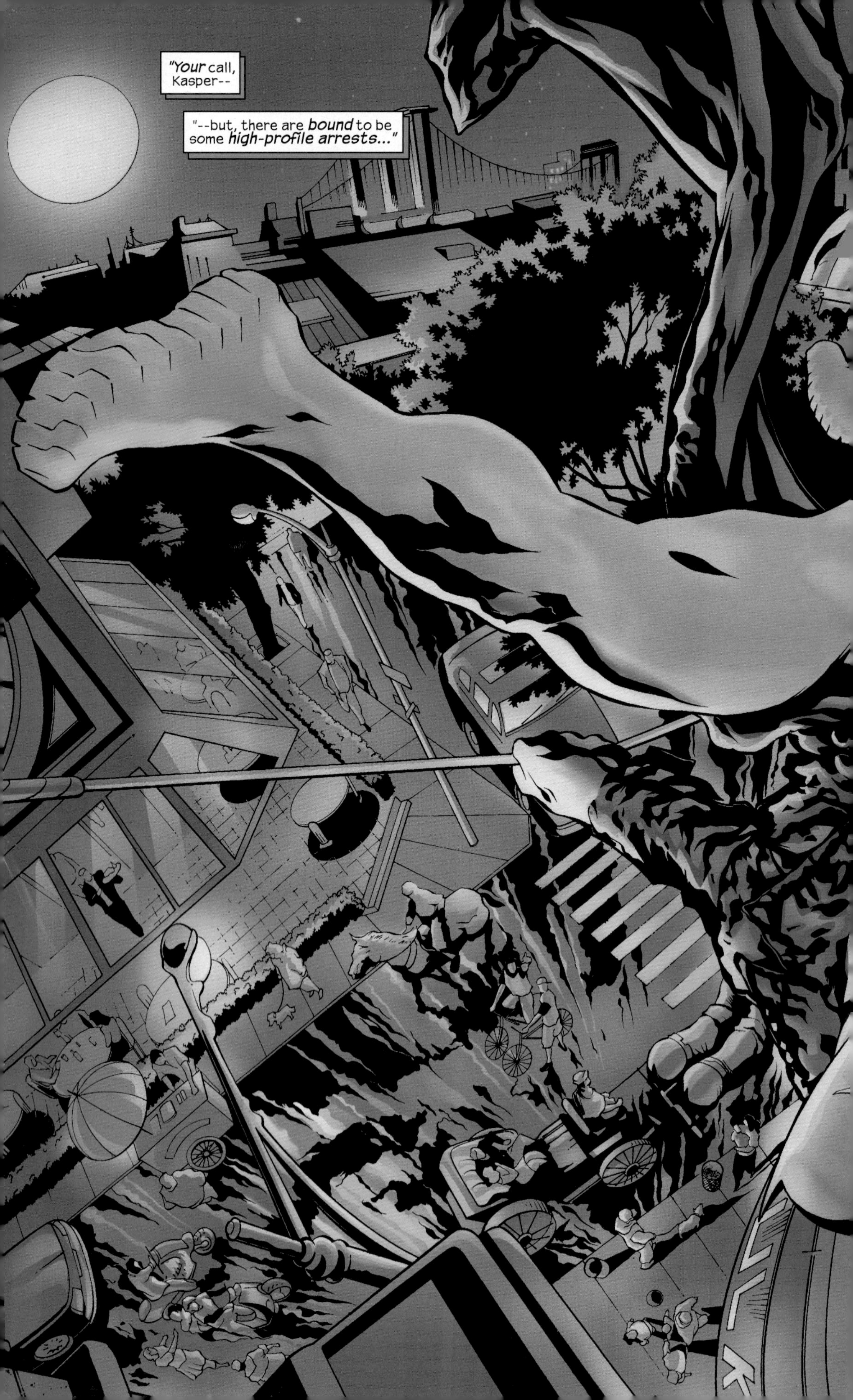
"Your call, Kasper--
"--but, there are bound to be some high-profile arrests..."

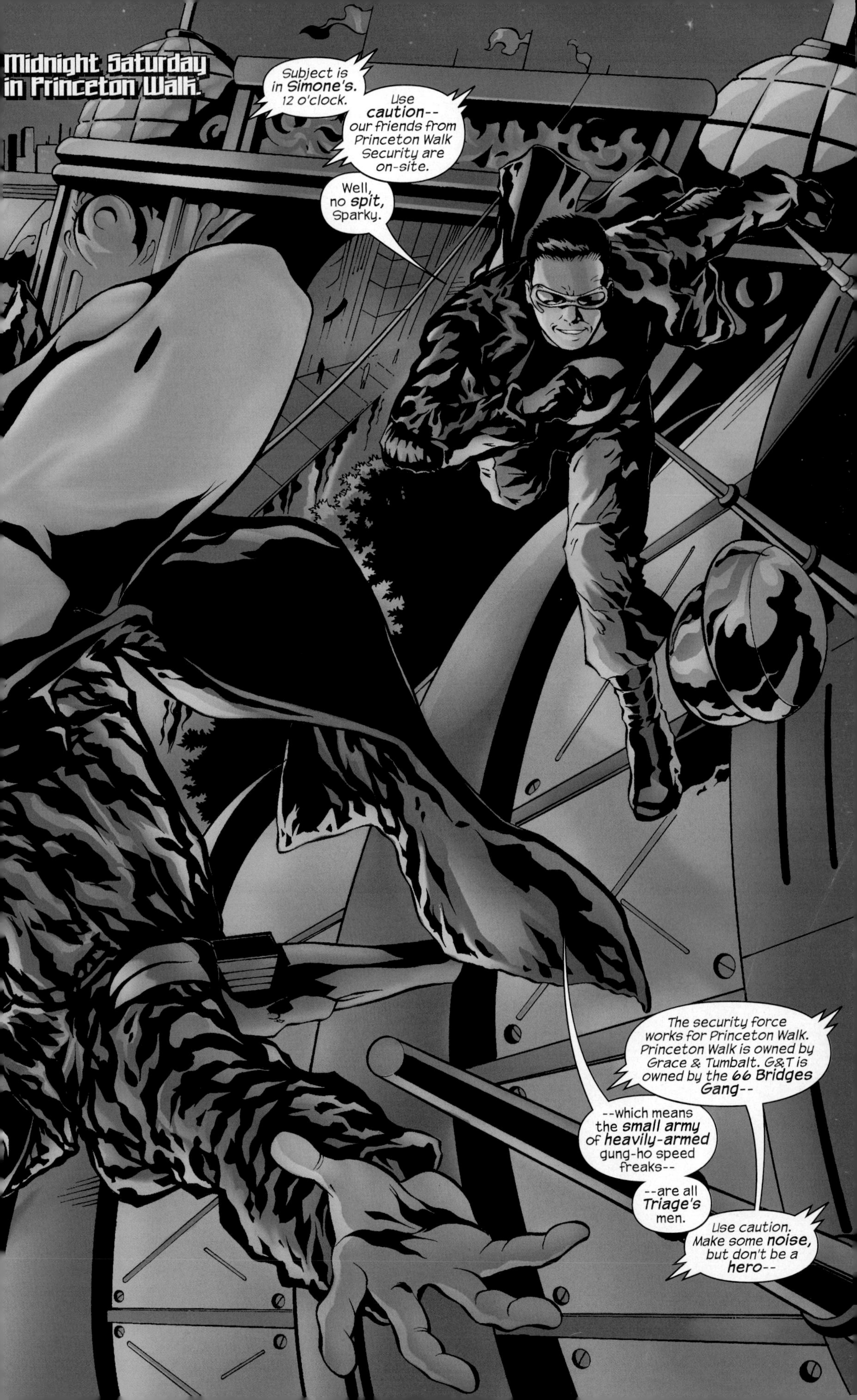
Midnight Saturday in Princeton Walk.
Subject is in Simone's. 12 o'clock.
Use caution--our friends from Princeton Walk Security are on-site.
Well, no spit, Sparky.
The security force works for Princeton Walk. Princeton Walk is owned by Grace & Tumbalt. G&T is owned by the 66 Bridges Gang--
--which means the small army of heavily-armed gung-ho speed freaks--
--are all Triage's men.
Use caution. Make some noise, but don't be a hero--

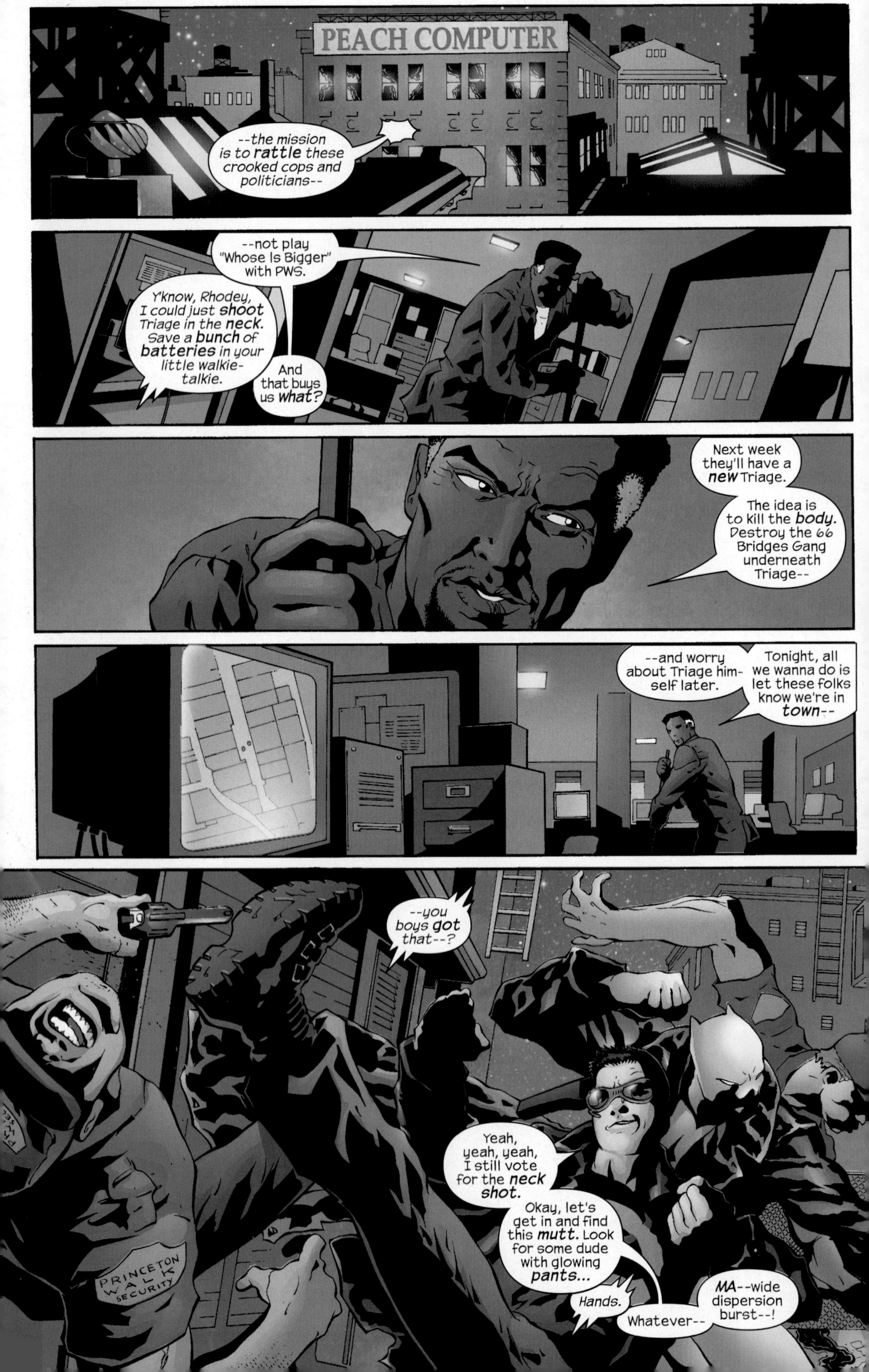
PEACH COMPUTER
--the mission is to rattle these crooked cops and politicians--
--not play "Whose Is Bigger" with PWS.
Y'know, Rhodey, I could just shoot Triage in the neck. Save a bunch of batteries in your little walkie-talkie.
And that buys us what?
Next week they'll have a new Triage.
The idea is to kill the body. Destroy the 66 Bridges Gang underneath Triage--
--and worry about Triage himself later.
Tonight, all we wanna do is let these folks know we're in town--
--you boys got that--?
Yeah, yeah, yeah, I still vote for the neck shot.
Okay, let's get in and find this mutt. Look for some dude with glowing pants...
Hands.
Whatever--
MA--wide dispersion burst--!
PRINCETON WALK SECURITY

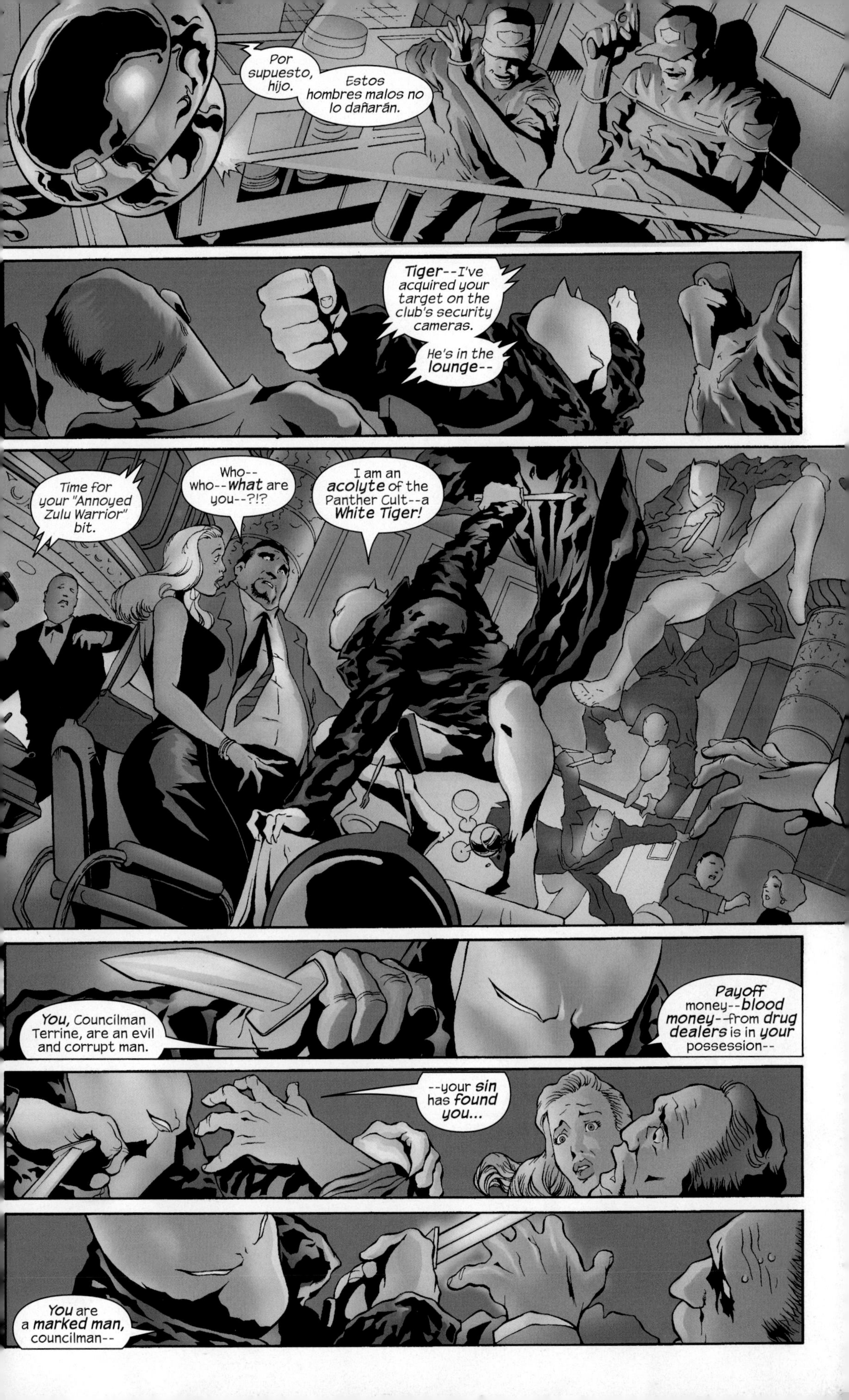
Por supuesto, hijo.
Estos hombres malos no lo dañarán.
Tiger--I've acquired your target on the club's security cameras.
He's in the lounge--
Time for your "Annoyed Zulu Warrior" bit.
Who-- who--what are you--?!?
I am an acolyte of the Panther Cult--a White Tiger!
You, Councilman Terrine, are an evil and corrupt man.
Payoff money--blood money--from drug dealers is in your possession--
--your sin has found you...
You are a marked man, councilman--

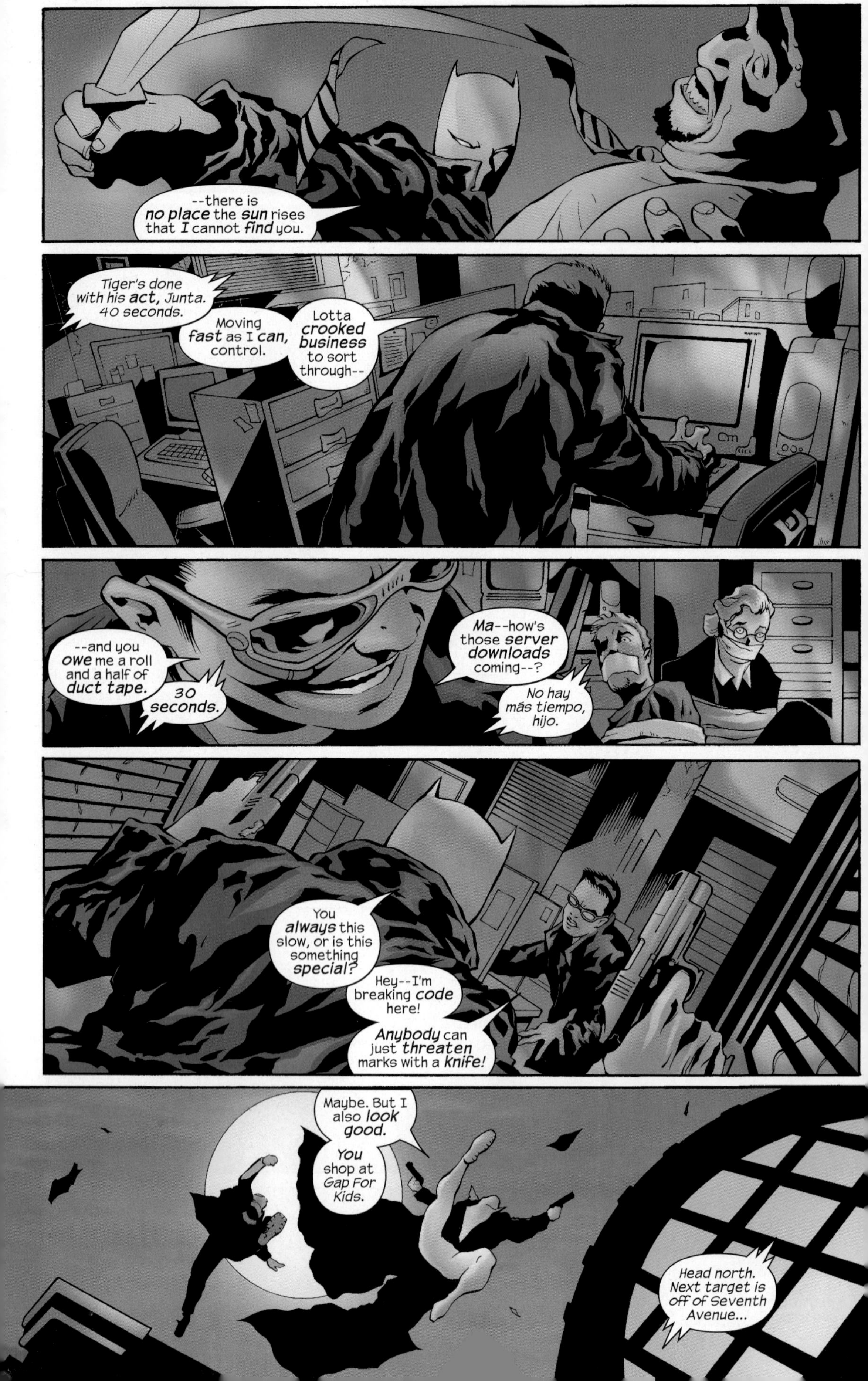
--there is no place the sun rises that I cannot find you.
Tiger's done with his act, Junta. 40 seconds.
Moving fast as I can, control.
Lotta crooked business to sort through--
--and you owe me a roll and a half of duct tape.
30 seconds.
Ma--how's those server downloads coming--?
No hay más tiempo, hijo.
You always this slow, or is this something special?
Hey--I'm breaking code here!
Anybody can just threaten marks with a knife!
Maybe. But I also look good.
You shop at Gap For Kids.
Head north. Next target is off of Seventh Avenue...

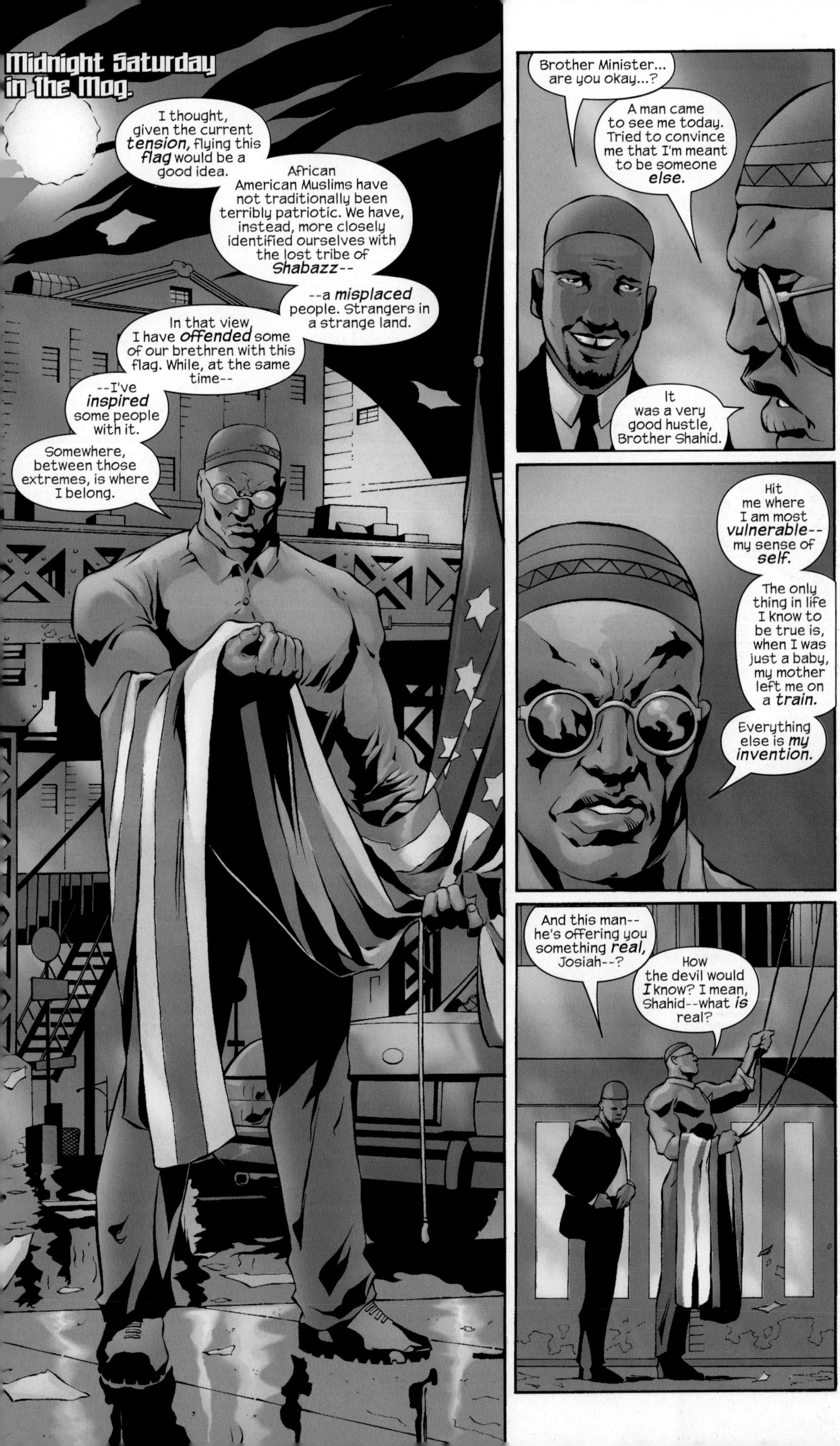
Midnight Saturday in the Mog.
I thought, given the current tension, flying this flag would be a good idea.
African American Muslims have not traditionally been terribly patriotic. We have, instead, more closely identified ourselves with the lost tribe of Shabazz--
--a misplaced people. Strangers in a strange land.
In that view, I have offended some of our brethren with this flag. While, at the same time--
--I've inspired some people with it.
Somewhere, between those extremes, is where I belong.
Brother Minister... are you okay...?
A man came to see me today. Tried to convince me that I'm meant to be someone else.
It was a very good hustle, Brother Shahid.
Hit me where I am most vulnerable--my sense of self.
The only thing in life I know to be true is, when I was just a baby, my mother left me on a train.
Everything else is my invention.
And this man--he's offering you something real, Josiah--?
How the devil would I know? I mean, Shahid--what is real?

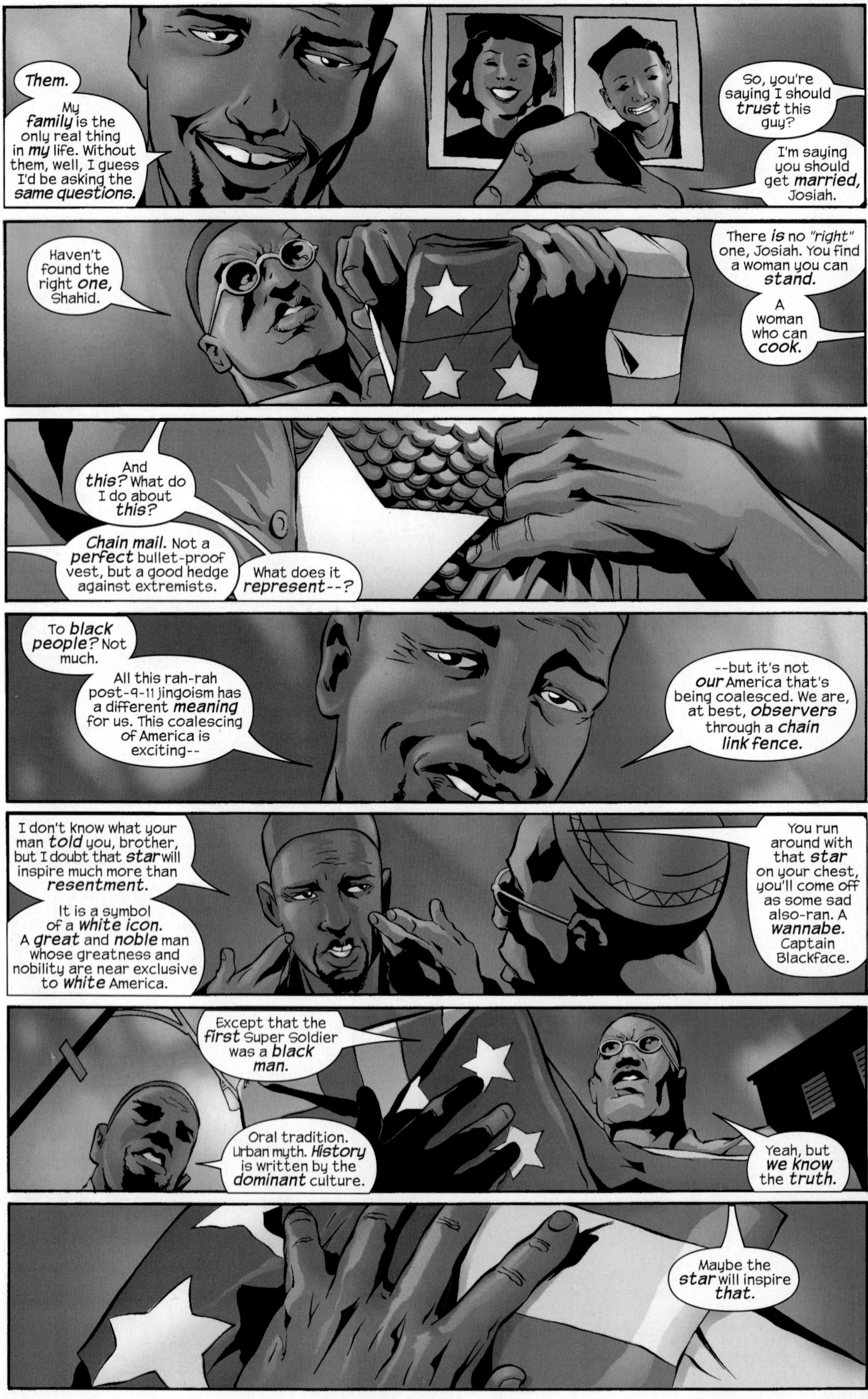
Them.
My family is the only real thing in my life. Without them, well, I guess I'd be asking the same questions.
So, you're saying I should trust this guy?
I'm saying you should get married, Josiah.
Haven't found the right one, Shahid.
There is no "right" one, Josiah. You find a woman you can stand.
A woman who can cook.
And this? What do I do about this?
Chain mail. Not a perfect bullet-proof vest, but a good hedge against extremists.
What does it represent--?
To black people? Not much.
All this rah-rah post-9-11 jingoism has a different meaning for us. This coalescing of America is exciting--
--but it's not our America that's being coalesced. We are, at best, observers through a chain link fence.
I don't know what your man told you, brother, but I doubt that star will inspire much more than resentment.
It is a symbol of a white icon. A great and noble man whose greatness and nobility are near exclusive to white America.
You run around with that star on your chest, you'll come off as some sad also-ran. A wannabe. Captain Blackface.
Except that the first Super Soldier was a black man.
Oral tradition. Urban myth. History is written by the dominant culture.
Yeah, but we know the truth.
Maybe the star will inspire that.

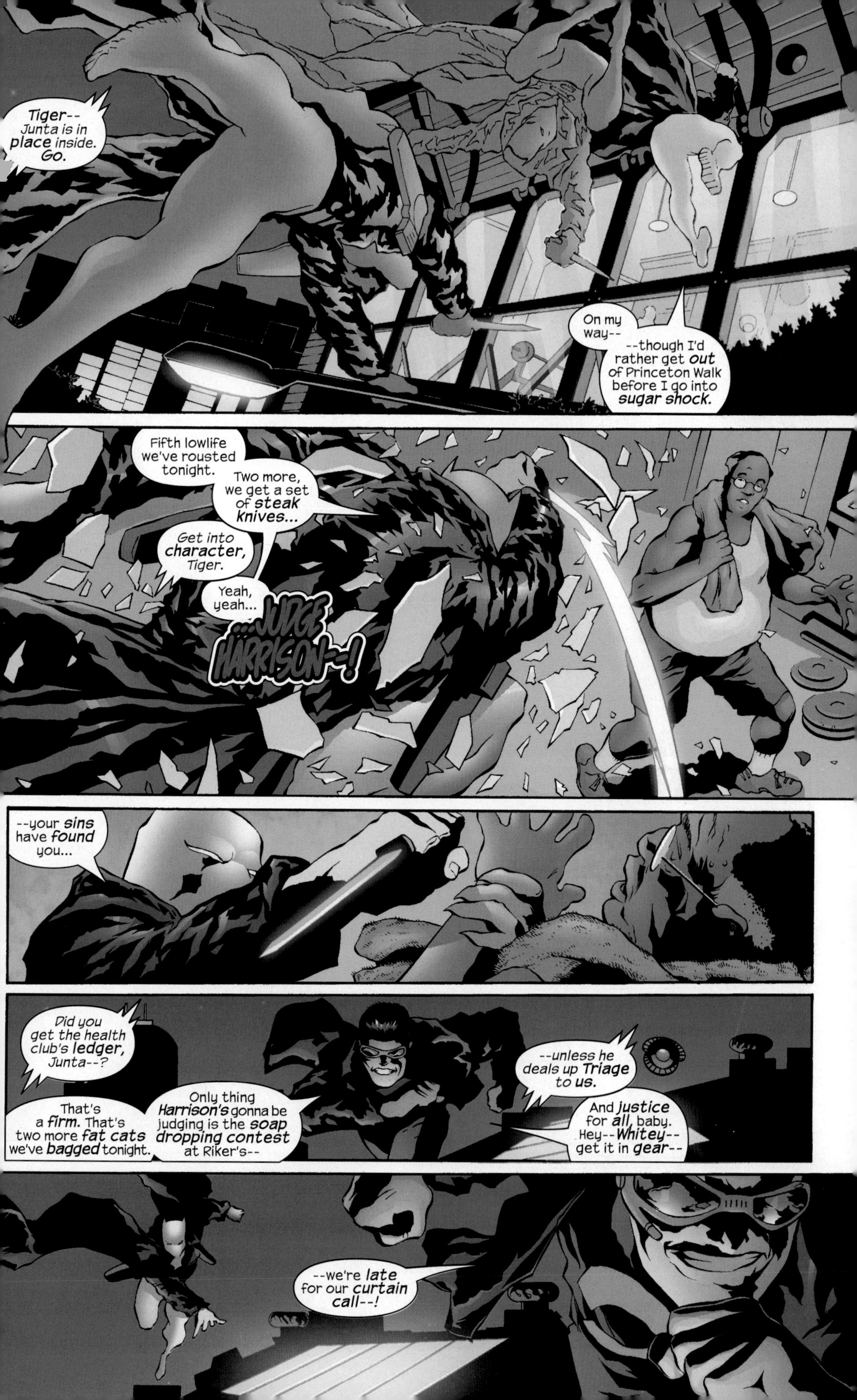
Tiger--
Junta is in place inside. Go.
On my way--
--though I'd rather get out of Princeton Walk before I go into sugar shock.
Fifth lowlife we've rousted tonight.
Two more, we get a set of steak knives...
Get into character, Tiger.
Yeah, yeah...
...JUDGE HARRISON--!
--your sins have found you...
Did you get the health club's ledger, Junta--?
That's a firm. That's two more fat cats we've bagged tonight.
Only thing Harrison's gonna be judging is the soap dropping contest at Riker's--
--unless he deals up Triage to us.
And justice for all, baby. Hey--Whitey--get it in gear--
--we're late for our curtain call--!

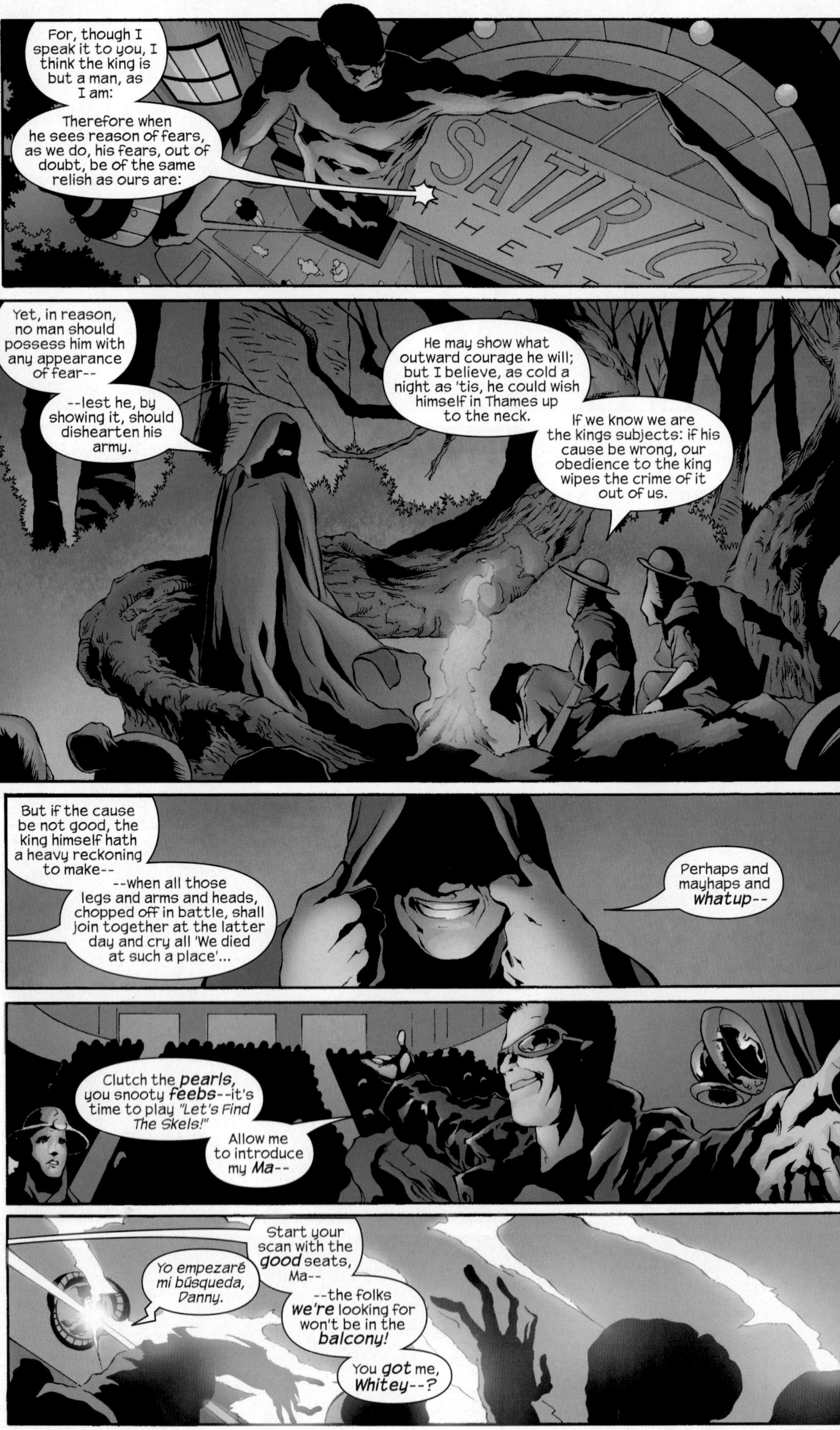
For, though I speak it to you, I think the king is but a man, as I am:
Therefore when he sees reason of fears, as we do, his fears, out of doubt, be of the same relish as ours are:
SATIRIC
HEAT
Yet, in reason, no man should possess him with any appearance of fear--
--lest he, by showing it, should dishearten his army.
He may show what outward courage he will; but I believe, as cold a night as 'tis, he could wish himself in Thames up to the neck.
If we know we are the kings subjects: if his cause be wrong, our obedience to the king wipes the crime of it out of us.
But if the cause be not good, the king himself hath a heavy reckoning to make--
--when all those legs and arms and heads, chopped off in battle, shall join together at the latter day and cry all 'We died at such a place'...
Perhaps and mayhaps and *whatup*--
Clutch the *pearls*, you snooty *feebs*--it's time to play *"Let's Find The Skels!"*
Allow me to introduce my *Ma*--
Start your scan with the *good* seats, Ma--
Yo empezaré mi búsqueda, Danny.
--the folks *we're* looking for won't be in the *balcony!*
You *got* me, *Whitey*--?

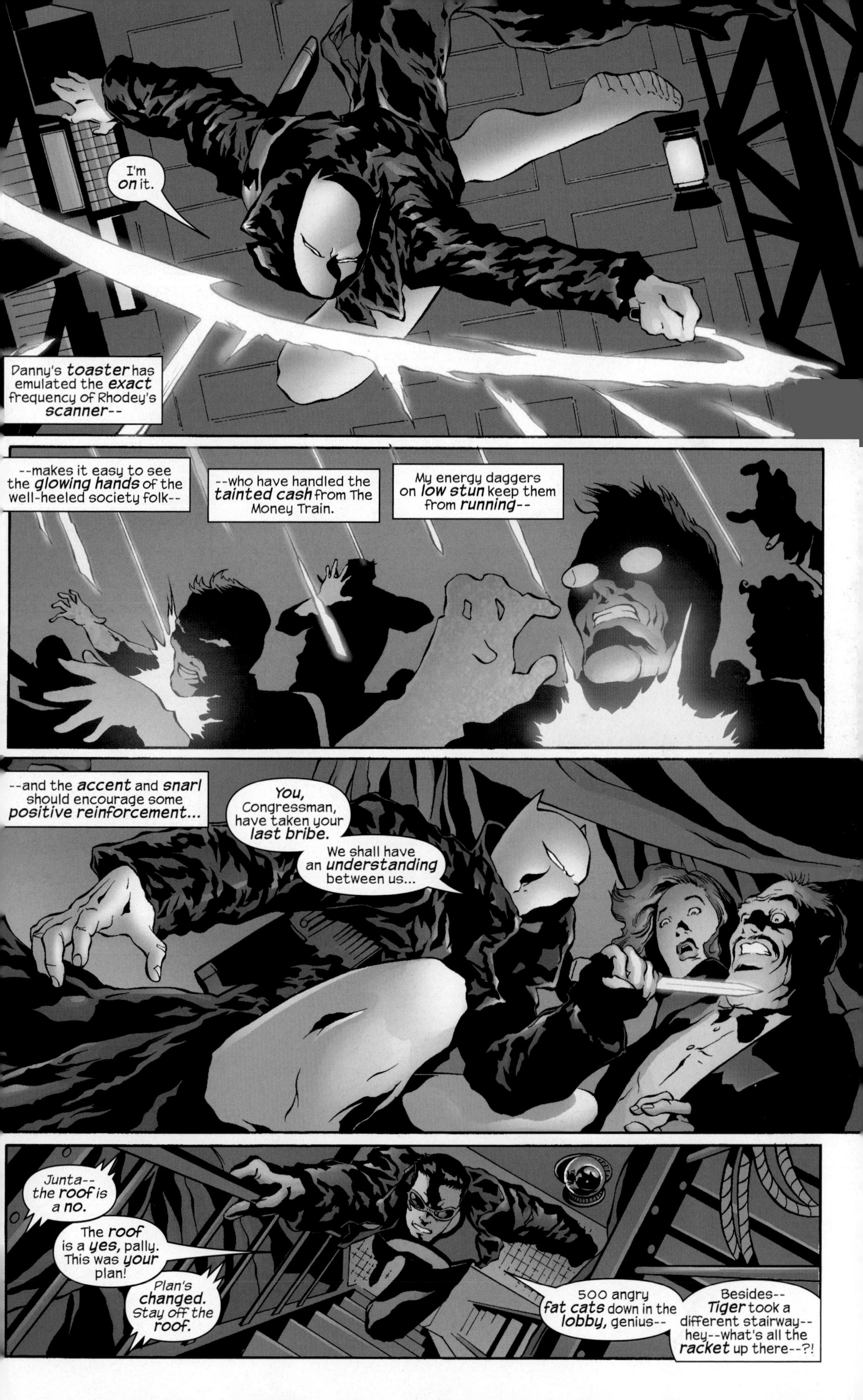
I'm on it.
Danny's toaster has emulated the exact frequency of Rhodey's scanner--
--makes it easy to see the glowing hands of the well-heeled society folk--
--who have handled the tainted cash from The Money Train.
My energy daggers on low stun keep them from running--
--and the accent and snarl should encourage some positive reinforcement...
You, Congressman, have taken your last bribe.
We shall have an understanding between us...
Junta-- the roof is a no.
The roof is a yes, pally. This was your plan!
Plan's changed. Stay off the roof.
500 angry fat cats down in the lobby, genius--
Besides-- Tiger took a different stairway-- hey--what's all the racket up there--?!

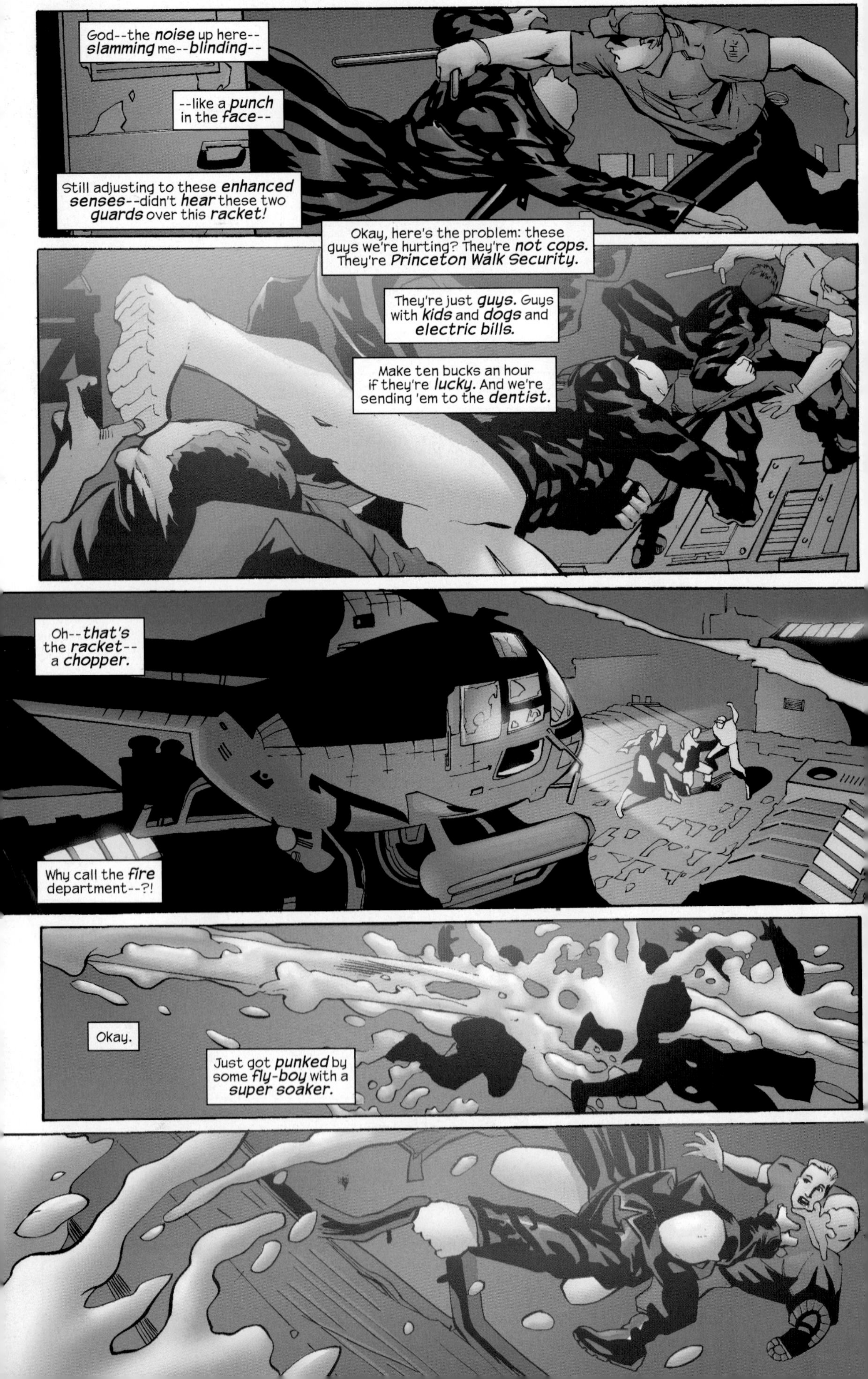
God--the noise up here--
slamming me--blinding--
--like a punch
in the face--
Still adjusting to these enhanced
senses--didn't hear these two
guards over this racket!
Okay, here's the problem: these
guys we're hurting? They're not cops.
They're Princeton Walk Security.
They're just guys. Guys
with kids and dogs and
electric bills.
Make ten bucks an hour
if they're lucky. And we're
sending 'em to the dentist.
Oh--that's
the racket--
a chopper.
Why call the fire
department--?!
Okay.
Just got punked by
some fly-boy with a
super soaker.

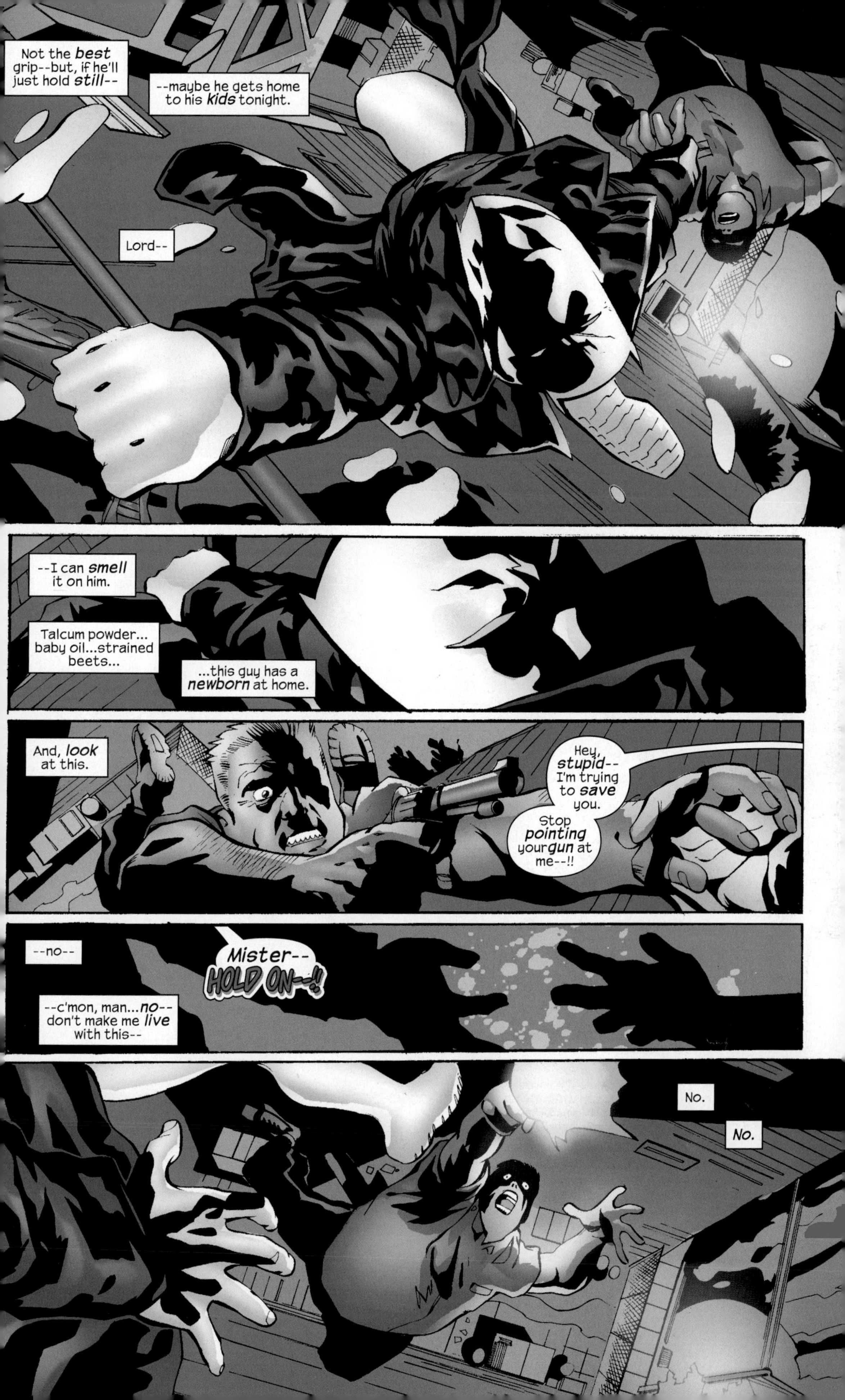

Not the best grip--but, if he'll just hold still--
--maybe he gets home to his kids tonight.
Lord--
--I can smell it on him.
Talcum powder... baby oil...strained beets...
...this guy has a newborn at home.
And, look at this.
Hey, stupid--I'm trying to save you.
Stop pointing your gun at me--!!
--no--
Mister--
HOLD ON--!!
--c'mon, man...no--don't make me live with this--
No.
No.

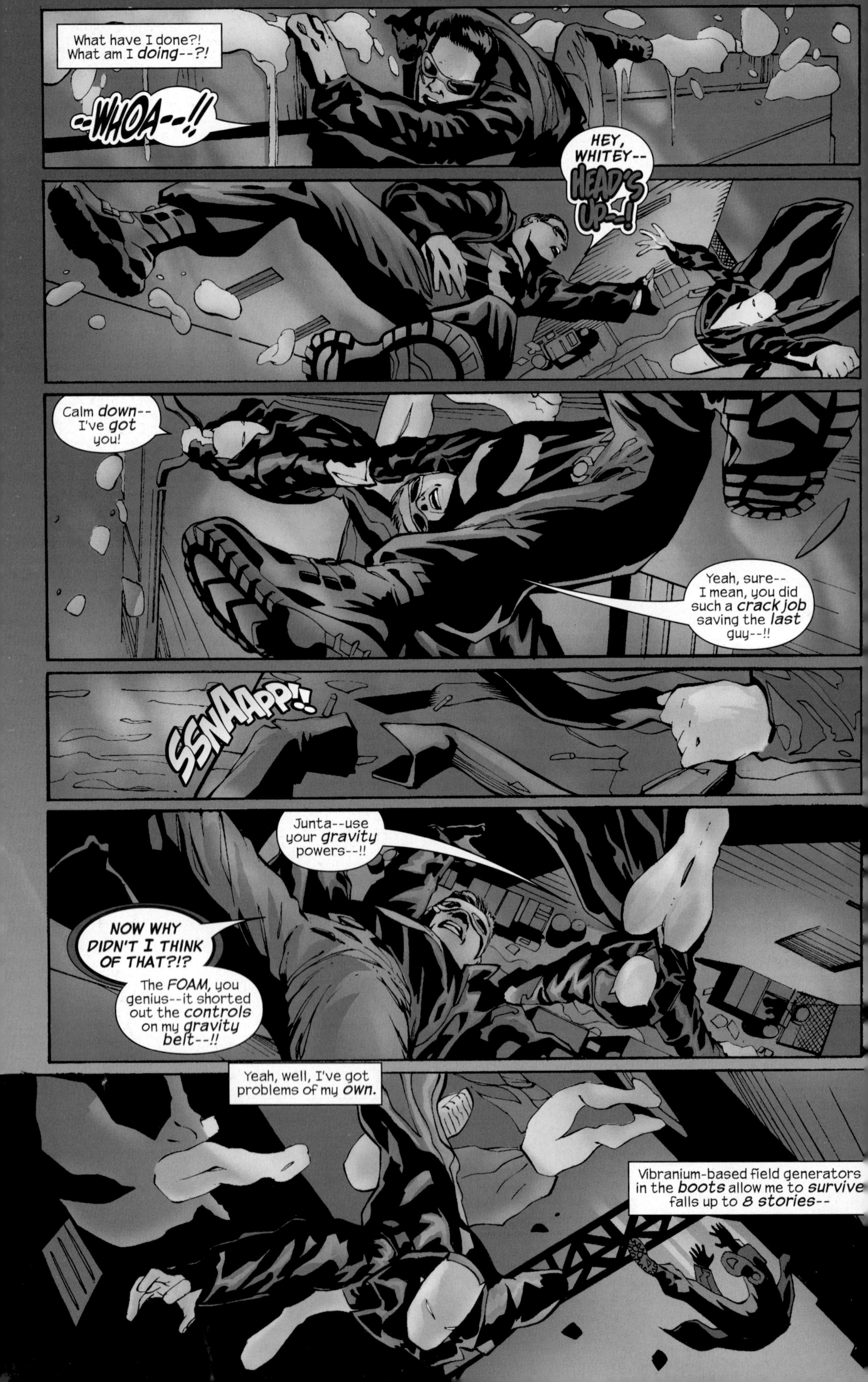

What have I done?! What am I doing--?!
--WHOA--!!
HEY, WHITEY-- HEAD'S UP--!
Calm down-- I've got you!
Yeah, sure-- I mean, you did such a crack job saving the last guy--!!
SSNAAPP!!
Junta--use your gravity powers--!!
NOW WHY DIDN'T I THINK OF THAT?!?
The FOAM, you genius--it shorted out the controls on my gravity belt--!!
Yeah, well, I've got problems of my own.
Vibranium-based field generators in the boots allow me to survive falls up to 8 stories--

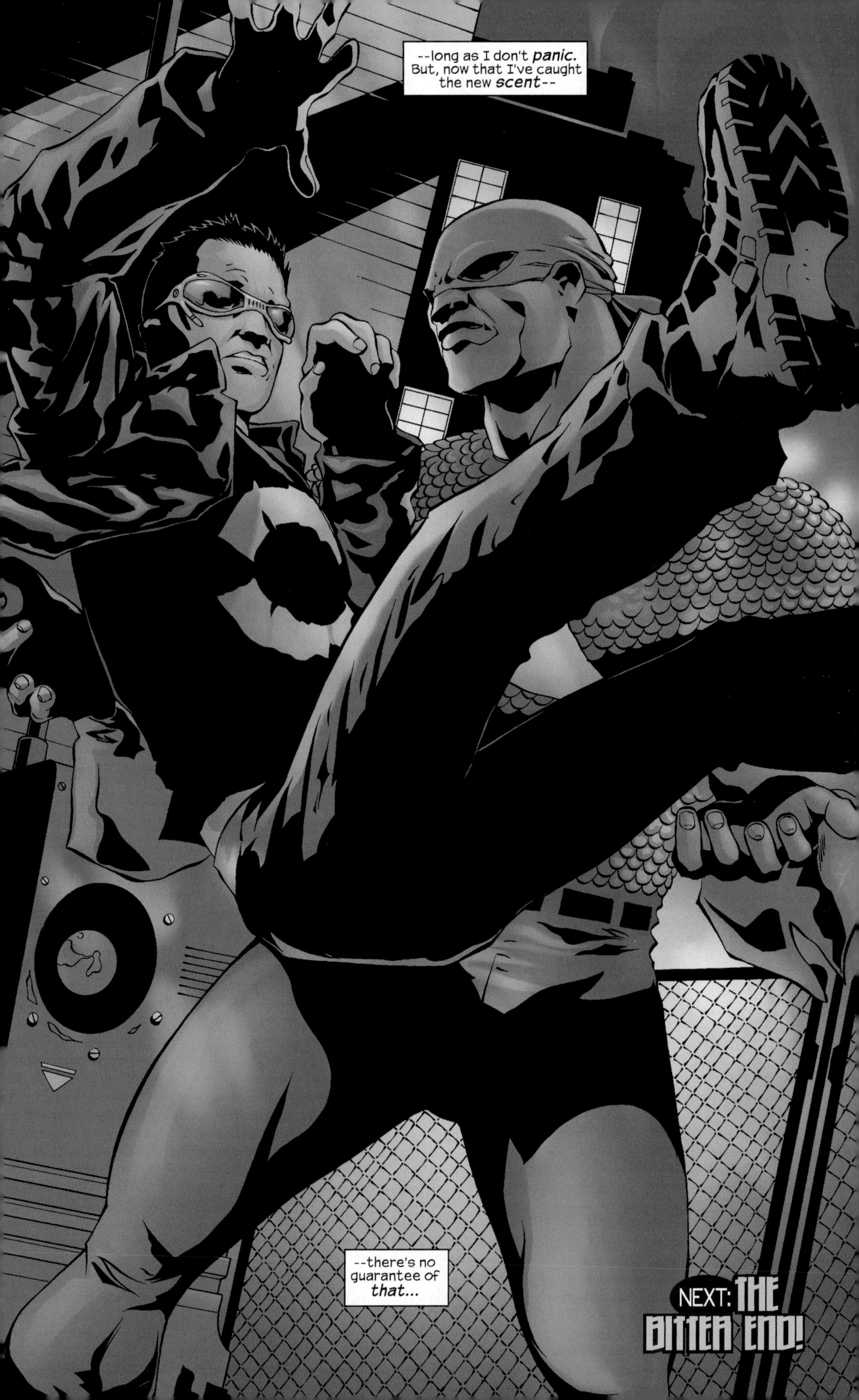
--long as I don't panic. But, now that I've caught the new scent--
--there's no guarantee of that...
NEXT: THE BITTER END!

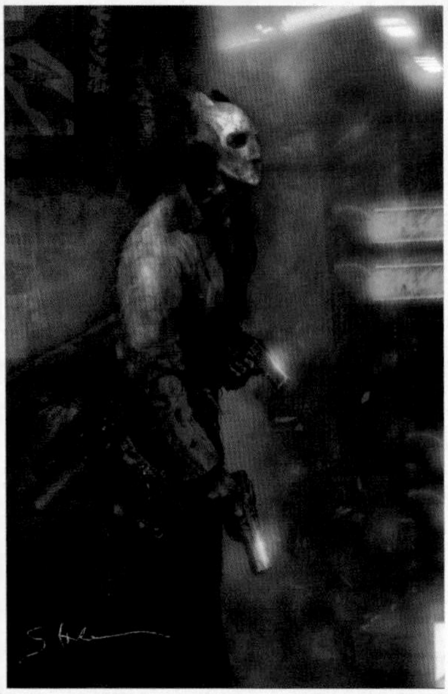
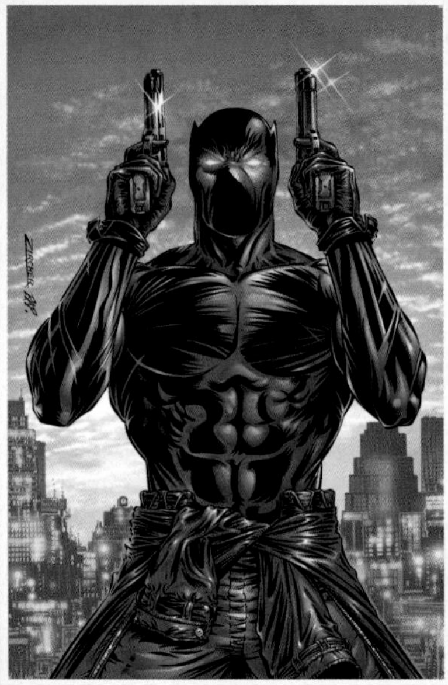
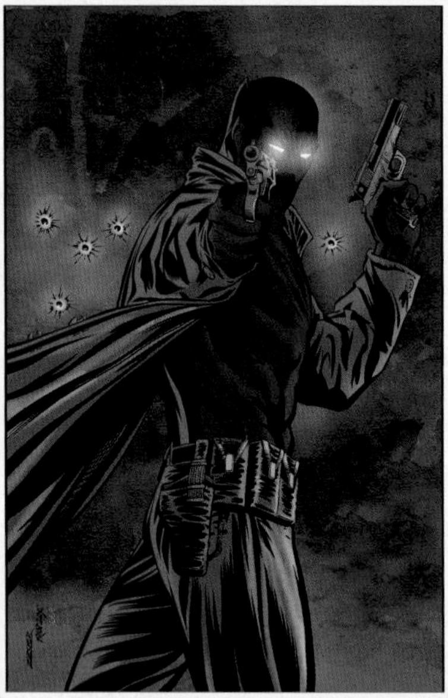
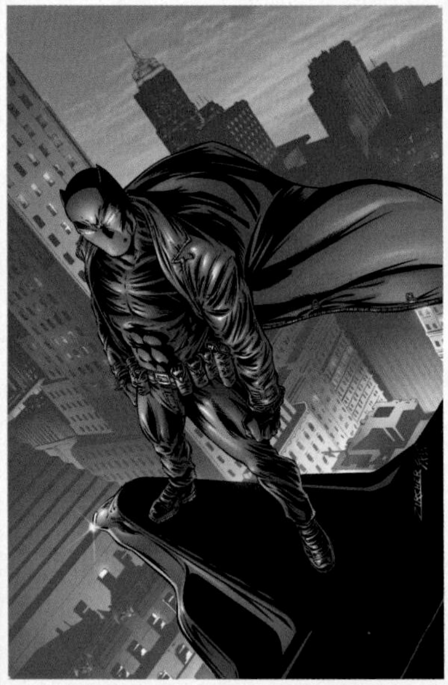
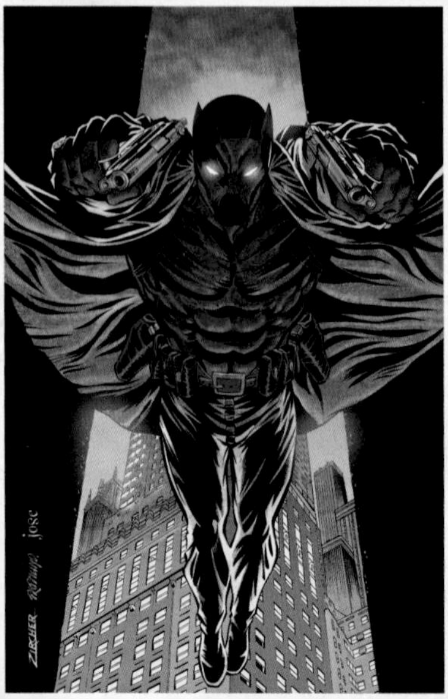
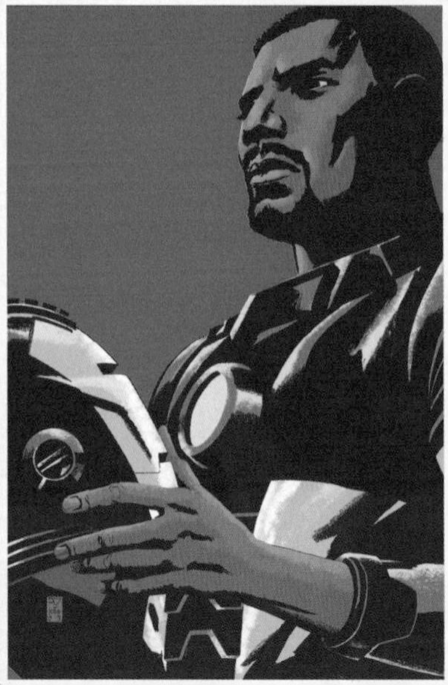

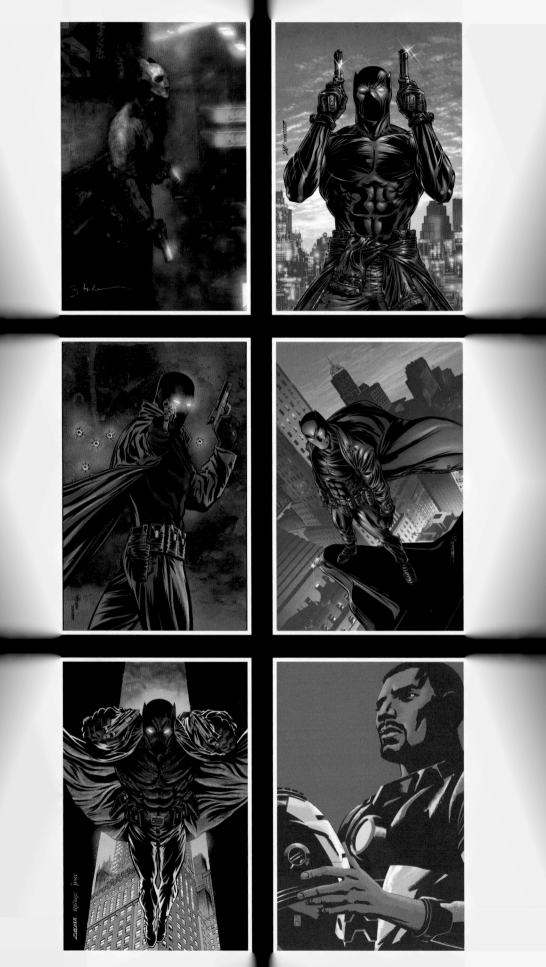

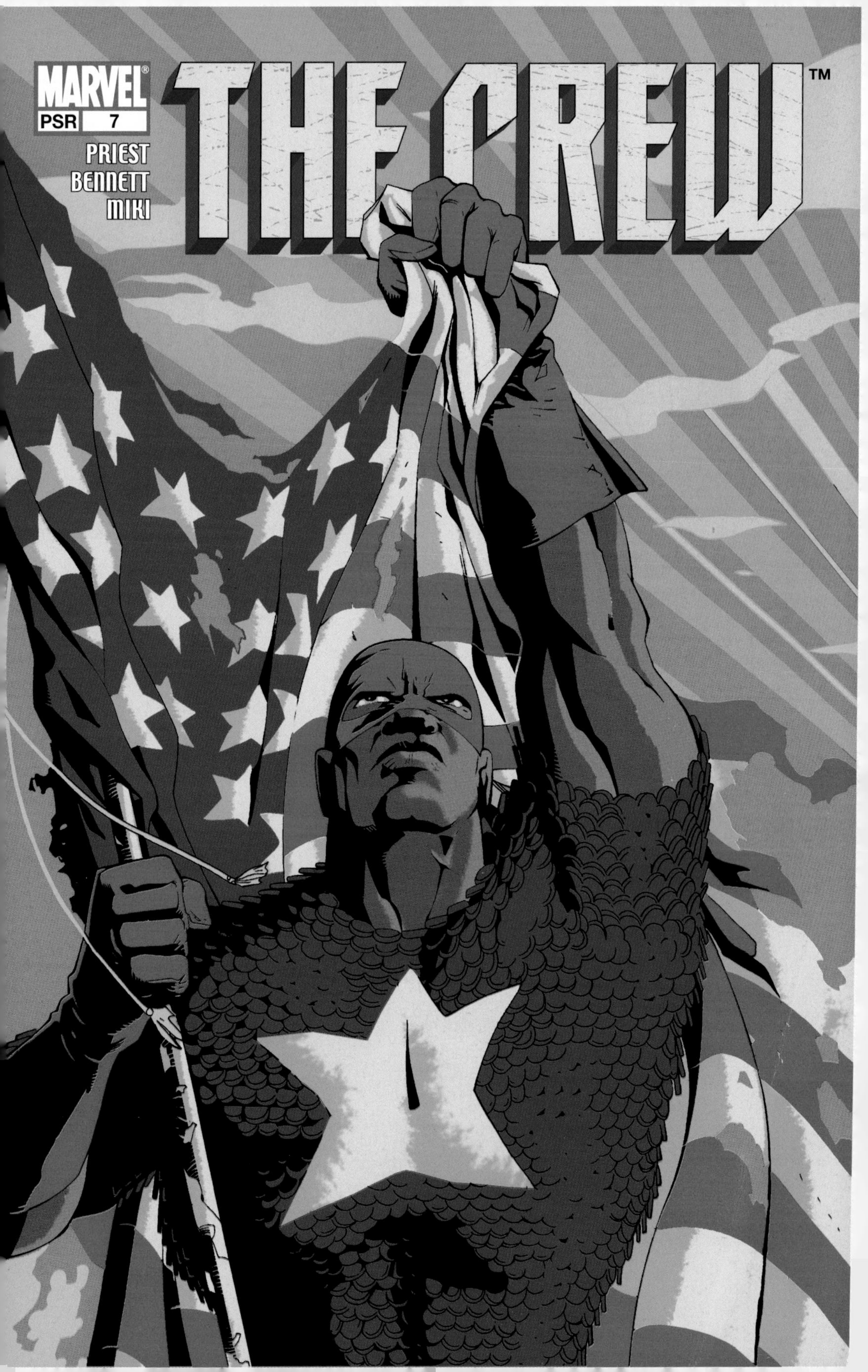
MARVEL
PSR 7
THE CREW™
PRIEST
BENNETT
MIKI

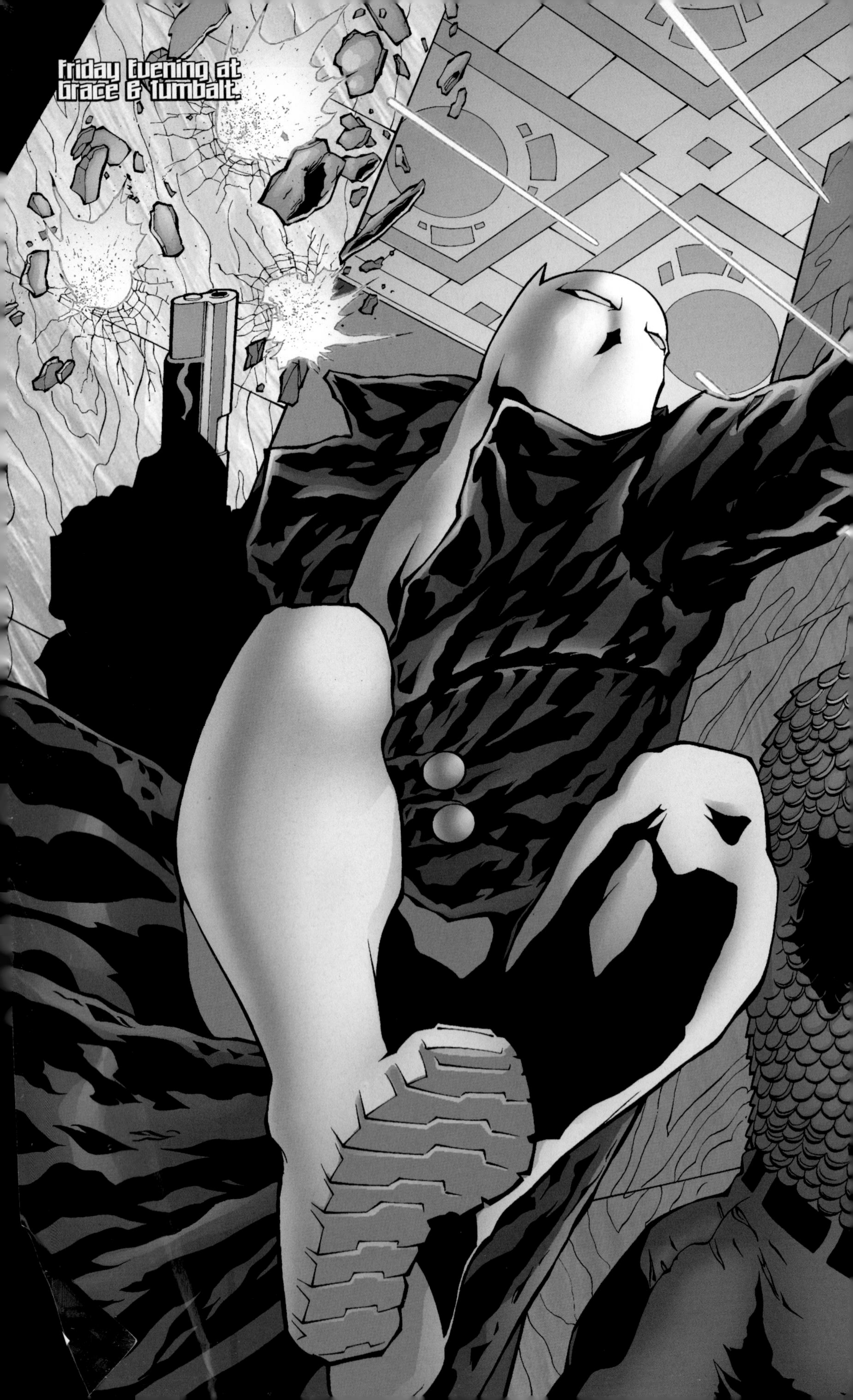
Friday Evening at
Grace & Tumbalt.

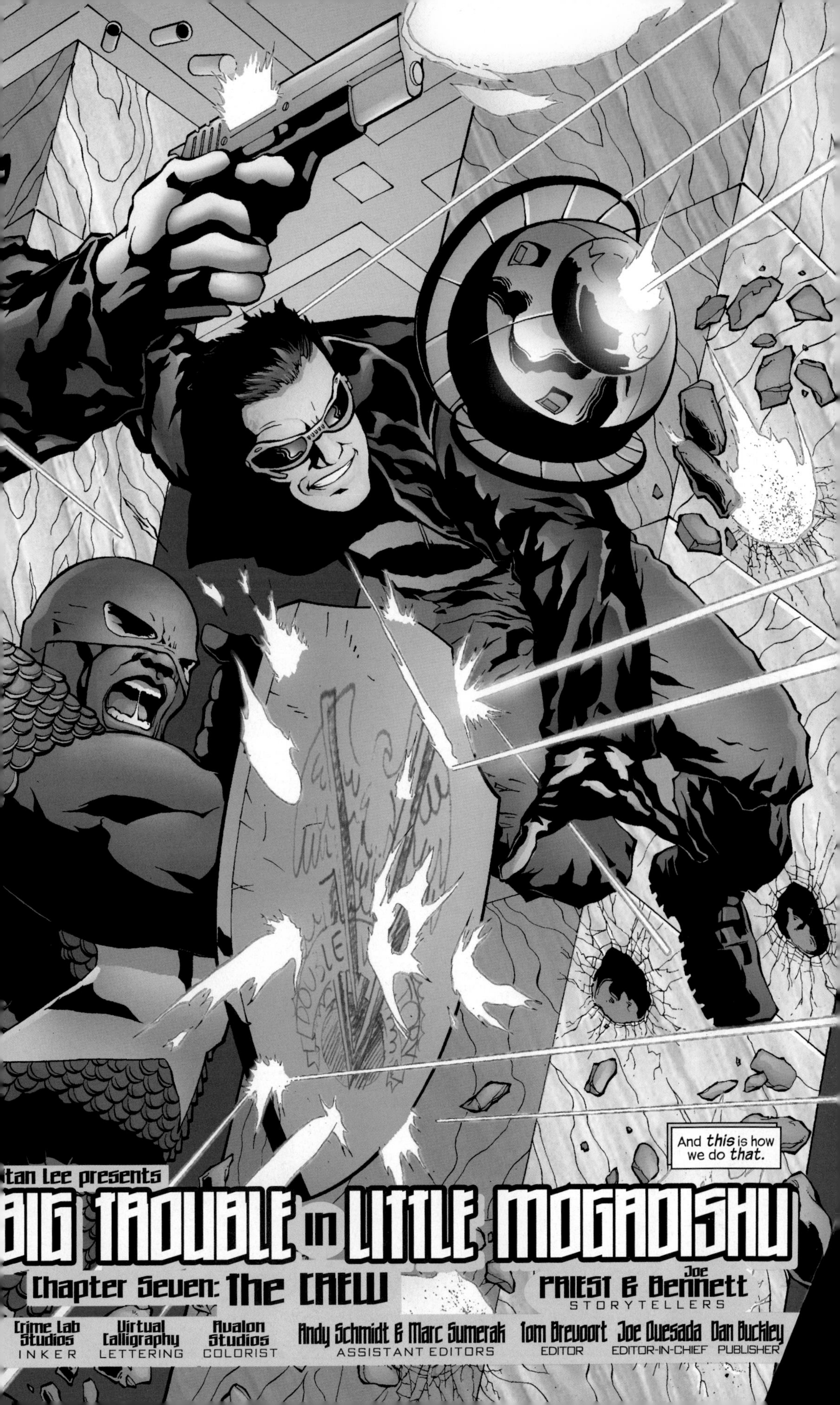
And this is how we do that.
Stan Lee presents
BIG TROUBLE in LITTLE MOGADISHU
Chapter Seven: The CREW
PRIEST & Joe Bennett
STORYTELLERS
Crime Lab Studios
INKER
Virtual Calligraphy
LETTERING
Avalon Studios
COLORIST
Andy Schmidt & Marc Sumerak
ASSISTANT EDITORS
Tom Brevoort
EDITOR
Joe Quesada
EDITOR-IN-CHIEF
Dan Buckley
PUBLISHER

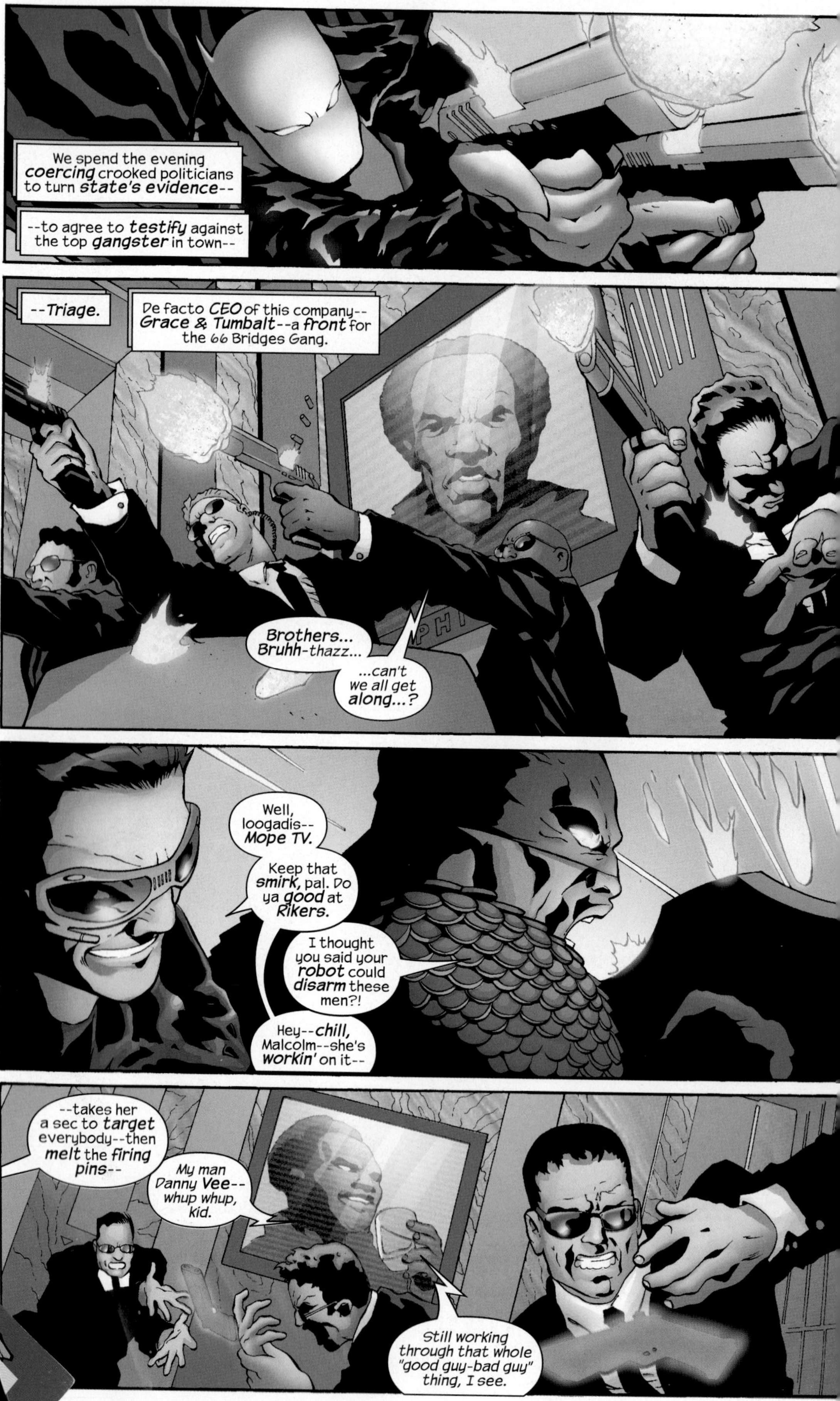

We spend the evening coercing crooked politicians to turn state's evidence--
--to agree to testify against the top gangster in town--
--Triage.
De facto CEO of this company--Grace & Tumbalt--a front for the 66 Bridges Gang.
Brothers... Bruhh-thazz...
...can't we all get along...?
Well, loogadis--Mope TV.
Keep that smirk, pal. Do ya good at Rikers.
I thought you said your robot could disarm these men?!
Hey--chill, Malcolm--she's workin' on it--
--takes her a sec to target everybody--then melt the firing pins--
My man Danny Vee--whup whup, kid.
Still working through that whole "good guy-bad guy" thing, I see.

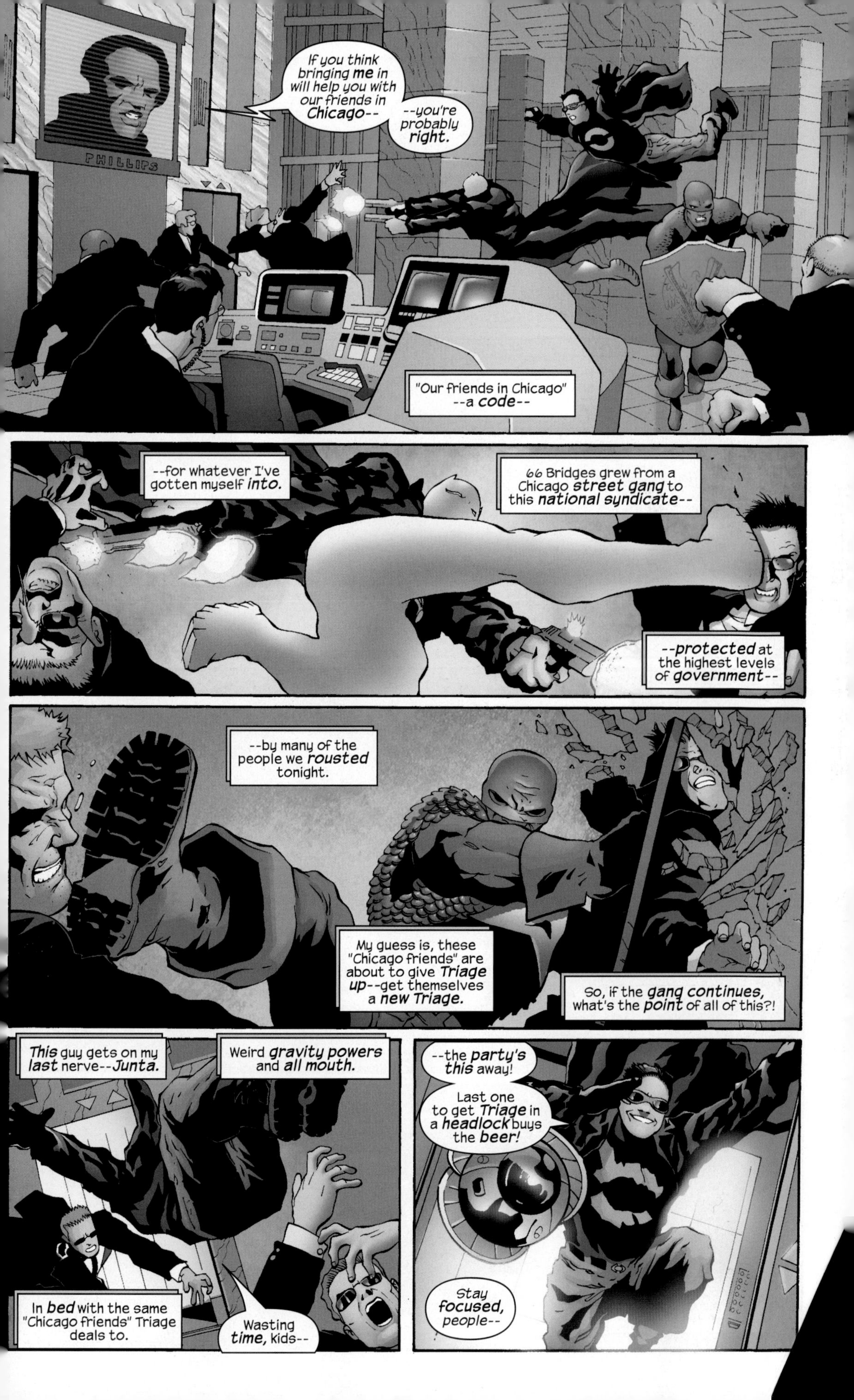
PHILLIPS
If you think bringing me in will help you with our friends in Chicago--
--you're probably right.
"Our friends in Chicago" --a code--
--for whatever I've gotten myself into.
66 Bridges grew from a Chicago street gang to this national syndicate--
--protected at the highest levels of government--
--by many of the people we rousted tonight.
My guess is, these "Chicago friends" are about to give Triage up--get themselves a new Triage.
So, if the gang continues, what's the point of all of this?!
This guy gets on my last nerve--Junta.
Weird gravity powers and all mouth.
In bed with the same "Chicago friends" Triage deals to.
Wasting time, kids--
--the party's this away!
Last one to get Triage in a headlock buys the beer!
Stay focused, people--

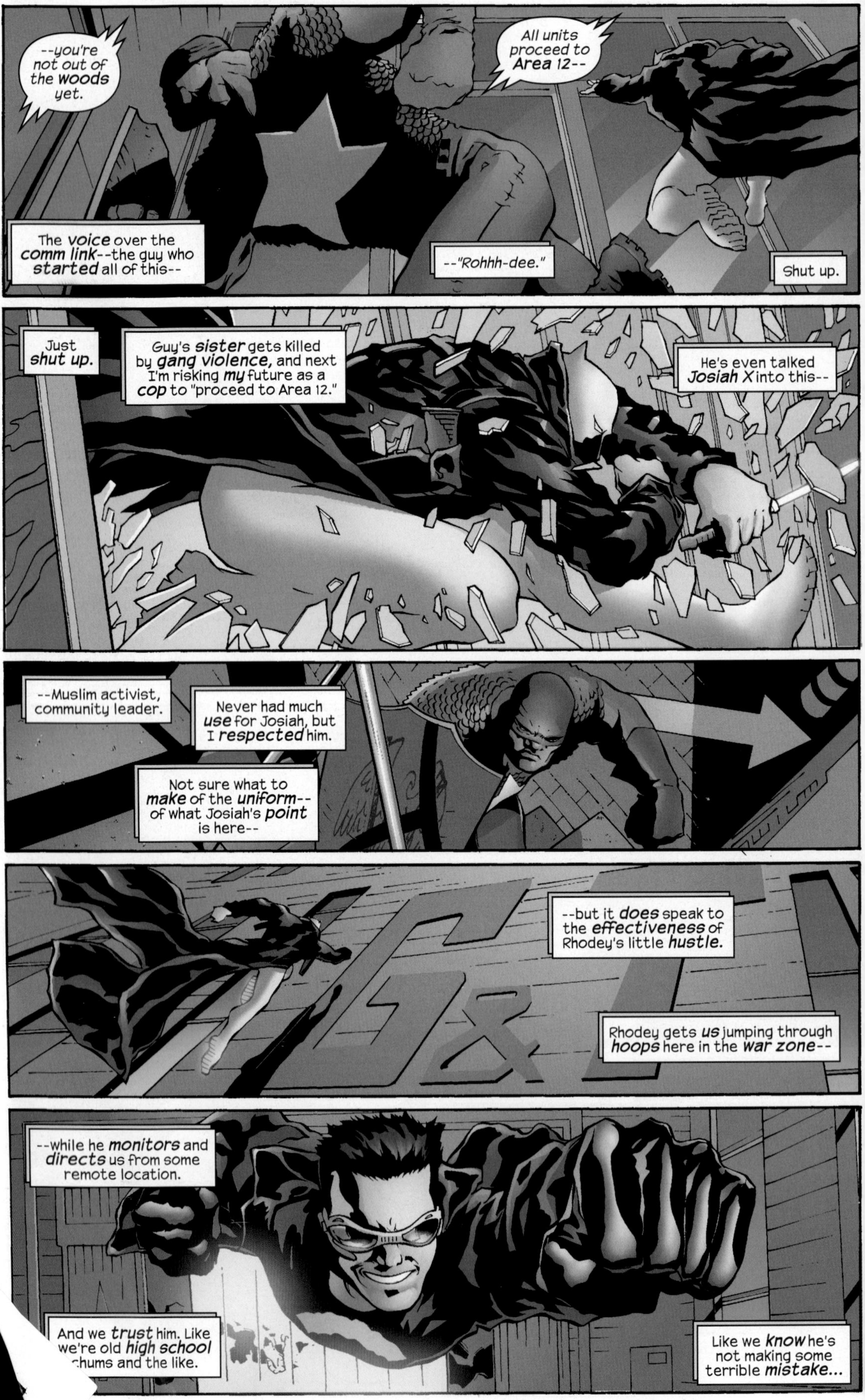
--you're not out of the woods yet.
All units proceed to Area 12--
The voice over the comm link--the guy who started all of this--
--"Rohhh-dee."
Shut up.
Just shut up.
Guy's sister gets killed by gang violence, and next I'm risking my future as a cop to "proceed to Area 12."
He's even talked Josiah X into this--
--Muslim activist, community leader.
Never had much use for Josiah, but I respected him.
Not sure what to make of the uniform--of what Josiah's point is here--
--but it does speak to the effectiveness of Rhodey's little hustle.
Rhodey gets us jumping through hoops here in the war zone--
--while he monitors and directs us from some remote location.
And we trust him. Like we're old high school chums and the like.
Like we know he's not making some terrible mistake...

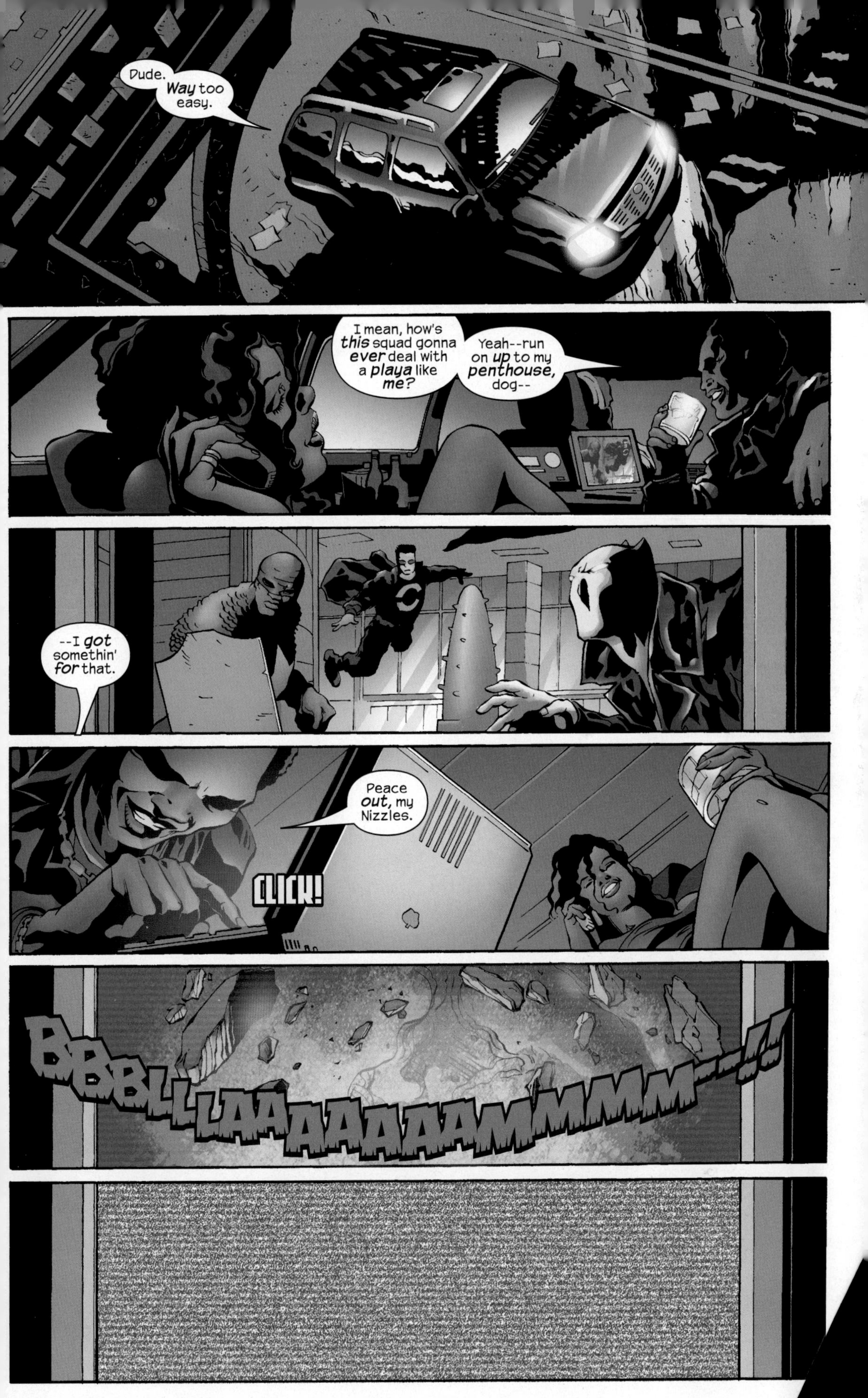
Dude. Way too easy.
I mean, how's this squad gonna ever deal with a playa like me?
Yeah--run on up to my penthouse, dog--
--I got somethin' for that.
Peace out, my Nizzles.
CLICK!
BBBLLLAAAAAAAMMMMM--!!

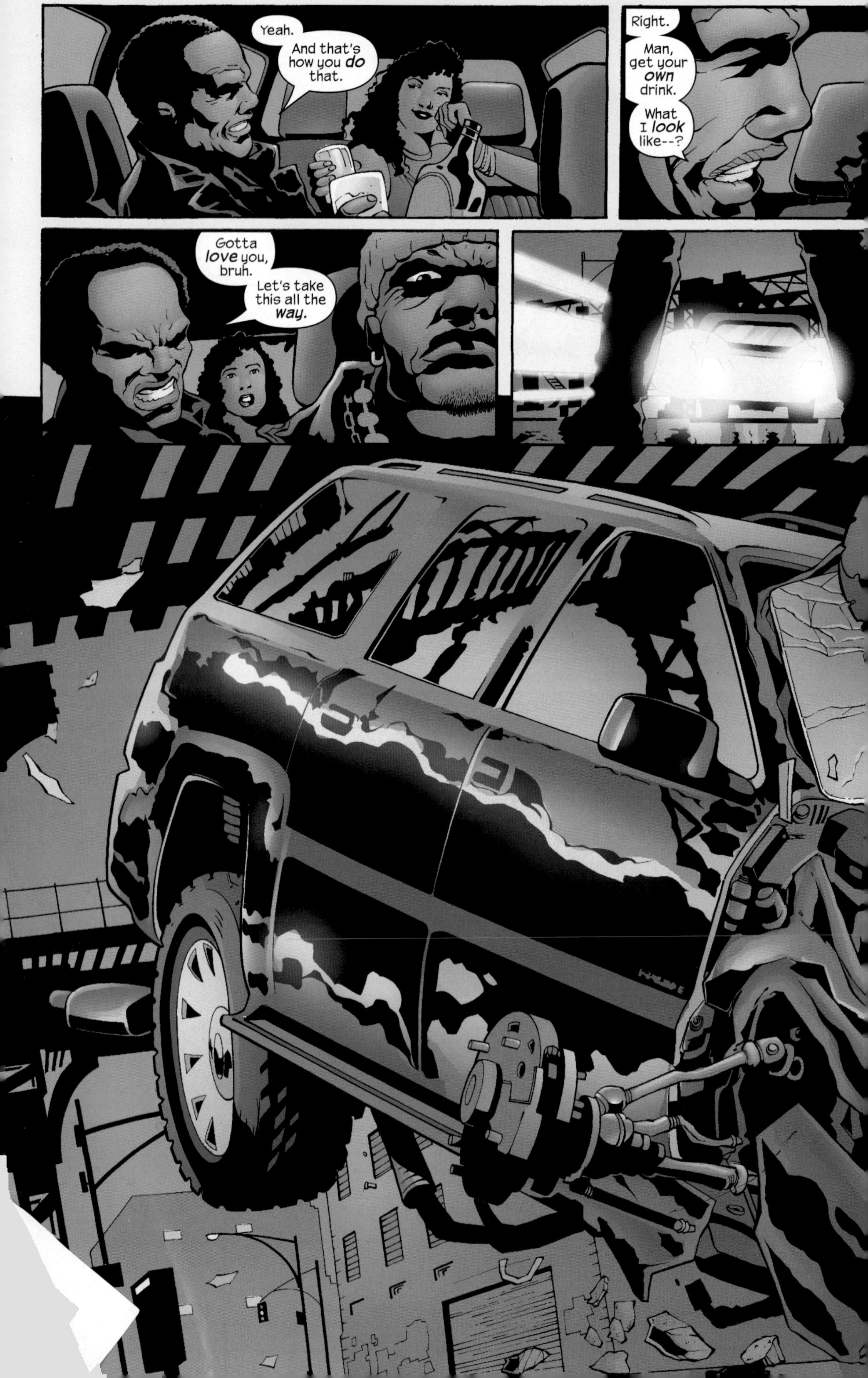
Yeah.
And that's how you do that.
Right.
Man, get your own drink.
What I look like--?
Gotta love you, bruh.
Let's take this all the way.

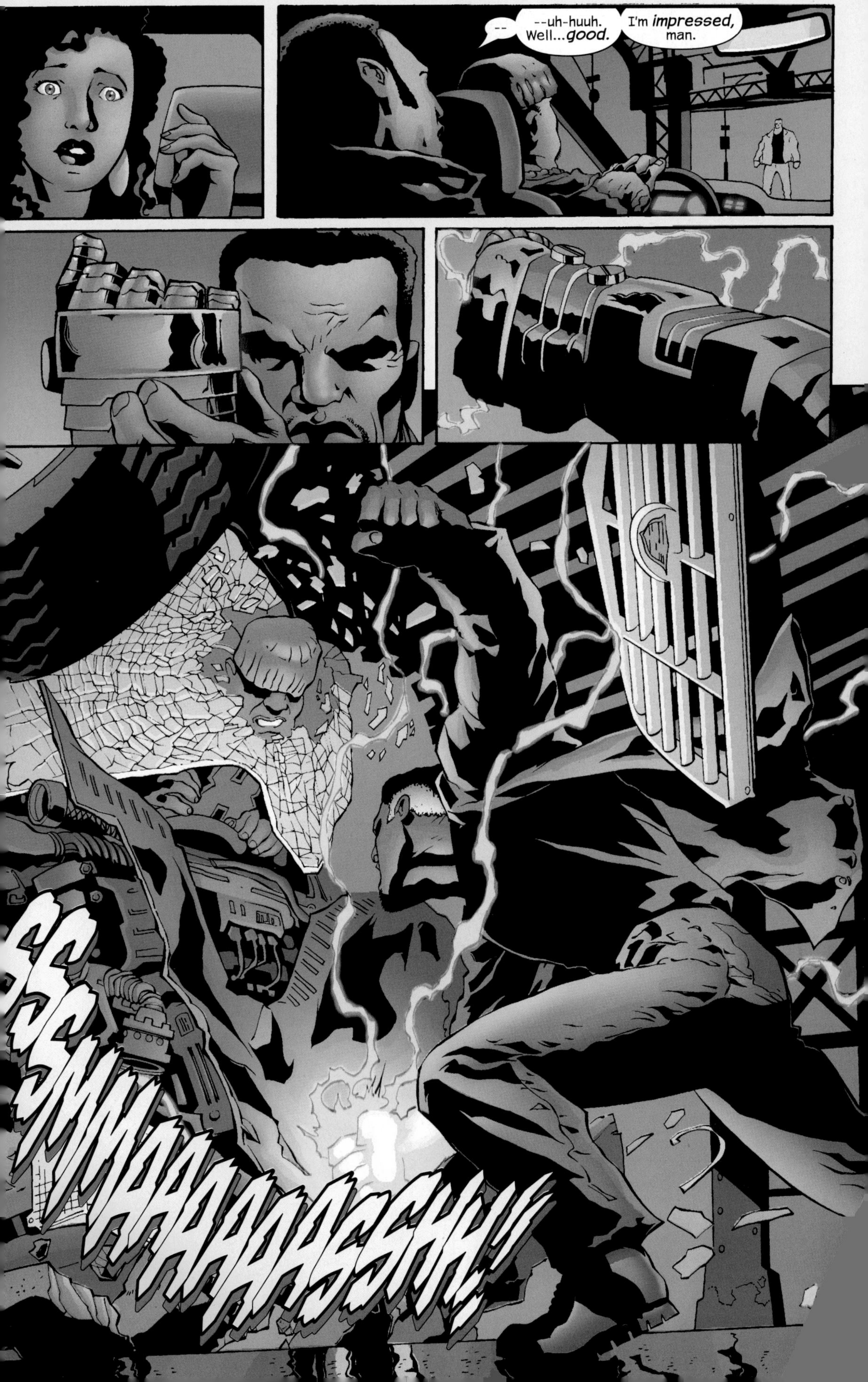
--
--uh-huuh. Well...*good.*
I'm *impressed,* man.
SSSMMAAAAAASSSHH!!

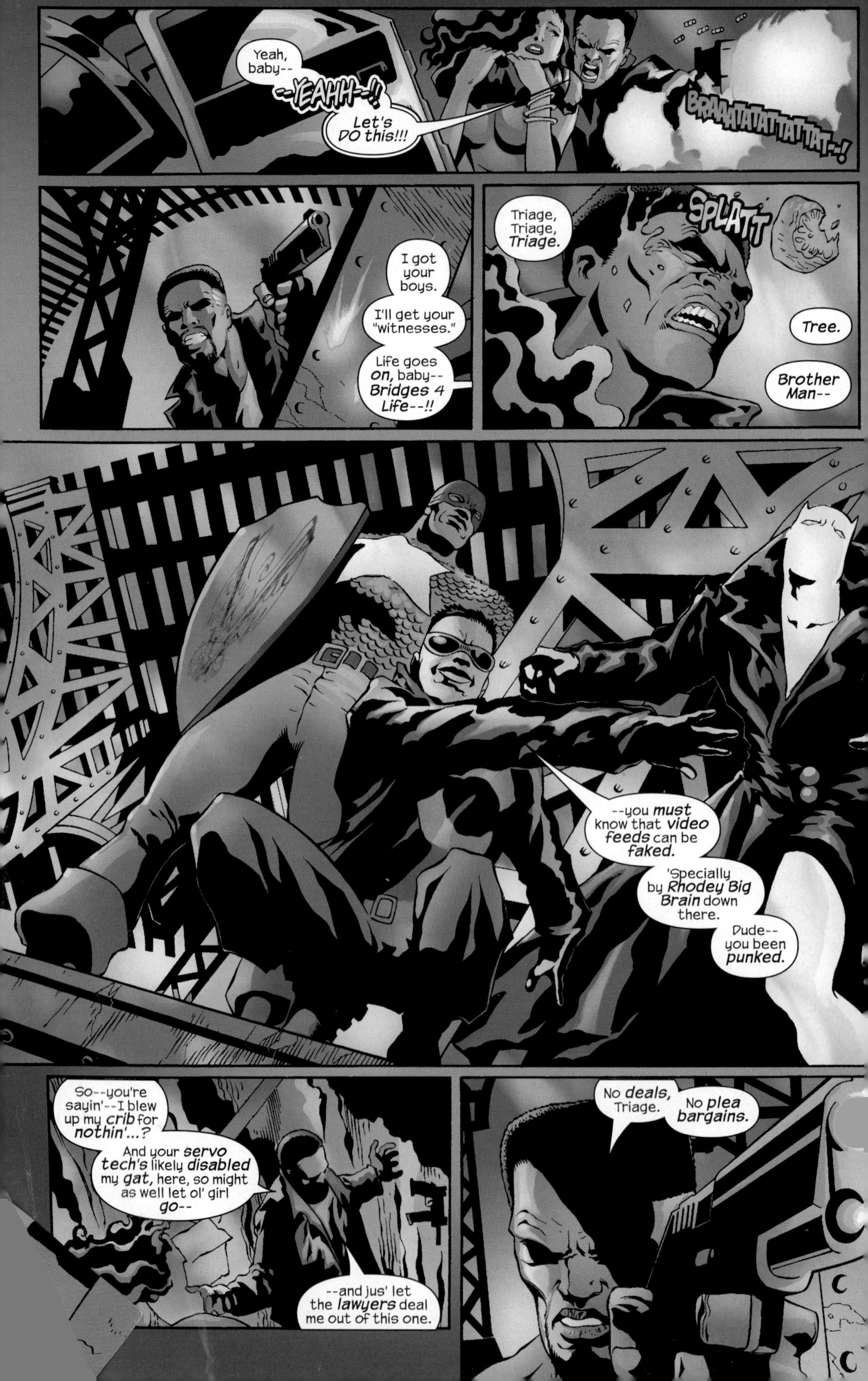
Yeah, baby--
--YEAHH--!!
Let's DO this!!!
BRAAATATATTATTAT--!
I got your boys.
I'll get your "witnesses."
Life goes on, baby-- Bridges 4 Life--!!
Triage, Triage, Triage.
SPLATT
Tree.
Brother Man--
--you must know that video feeds can be faked.
'Specially by Rhodey Big Brain down there.
Dude-- you been punked.
So--you're sayin'--I blew up my crib for nothin'...?
And your servo tech's likely disabled my gat, here, so might as well let ol' girl go--
--and jus' let the lawyers deal me out of this one.
No deals, Triage.
No plea bargains.

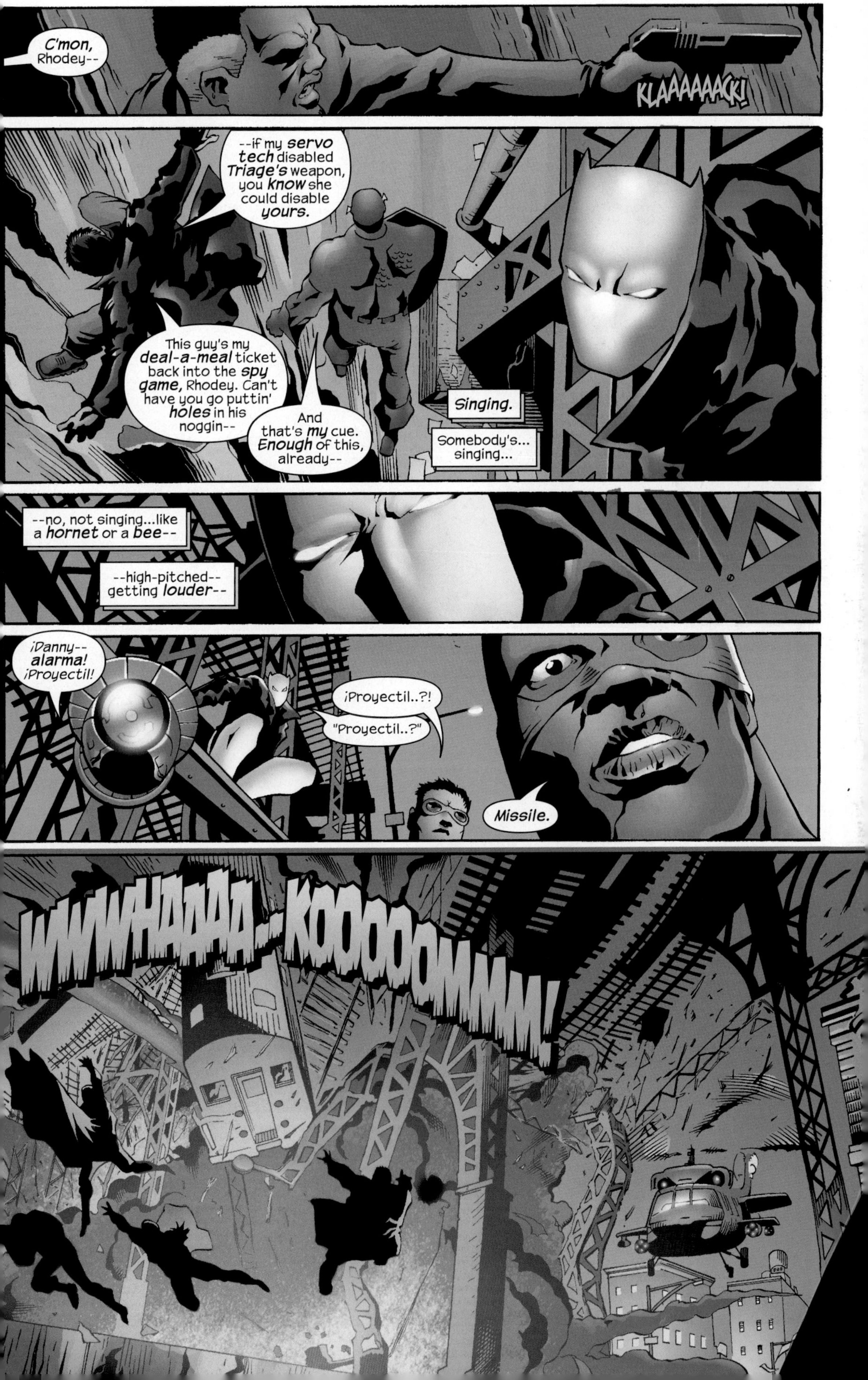
C'mon, Rhodey--
KLAAAAAACK!
--if my servo tech disabled Triage's weapon, you know she could disable yours.
This guy's my deal-a-meal ticket back into the spy game, Rhodey. Can't have you go puttin' holes in his noggin--
And that's my cue. Enough of this, already--
Singing.
Somebody's... singing...
--no, not singing...like a hornet or a bee--
--high-pitched-- getting louder--
¡Danny-- alarma! ¡Proyectil!
¡Proyectil..?!
"Proyectil..?"
Missile.
WWWHAAAA--KOOOOOMMMM!

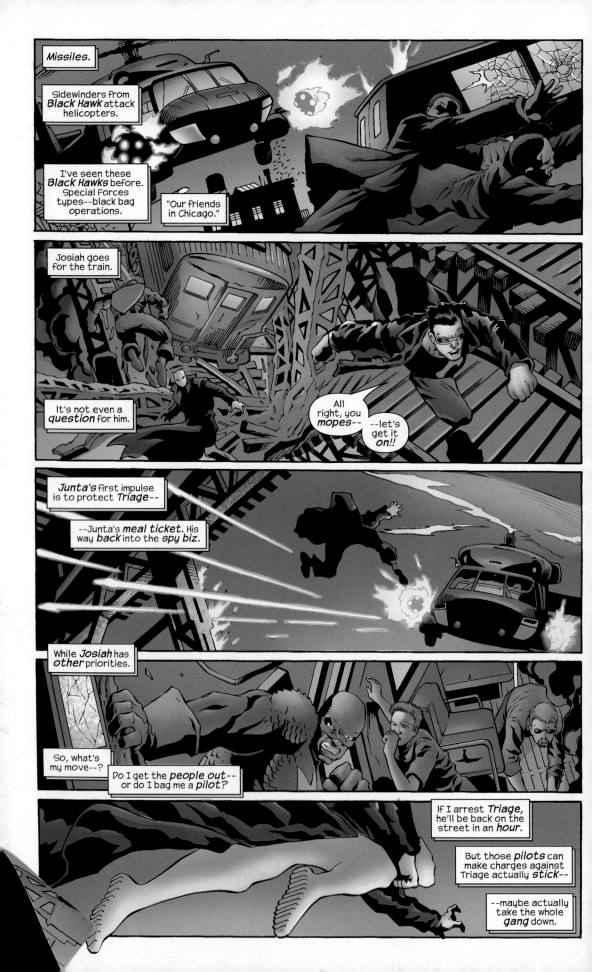

Missiles.

Sidewinders from *Black Hawk* attack helicopters.

I've seen these *Black Hawks* before. Special Forces types--black bag operations.

"Our friends in Chicago."

Josiah goes for the train.

It's not even a *question* for him.

All right, you *mopes*-- --let's get it *on!!*

Junta's first impulse is to protect *Triage*--

--Junta's *meal ticket.* His way *back* into the *spy biz.*

While *Josiah* has *other* priorities.

So, what's my move--?

Do I get the *people out*-- or do I bag me a *pilot?*

If I arrest *Triage,* he'll be back on the street in an *hour.*

But those *pilots* can make charges against Triage actually *stick*--

--maybe actually take the whole *gang* down.

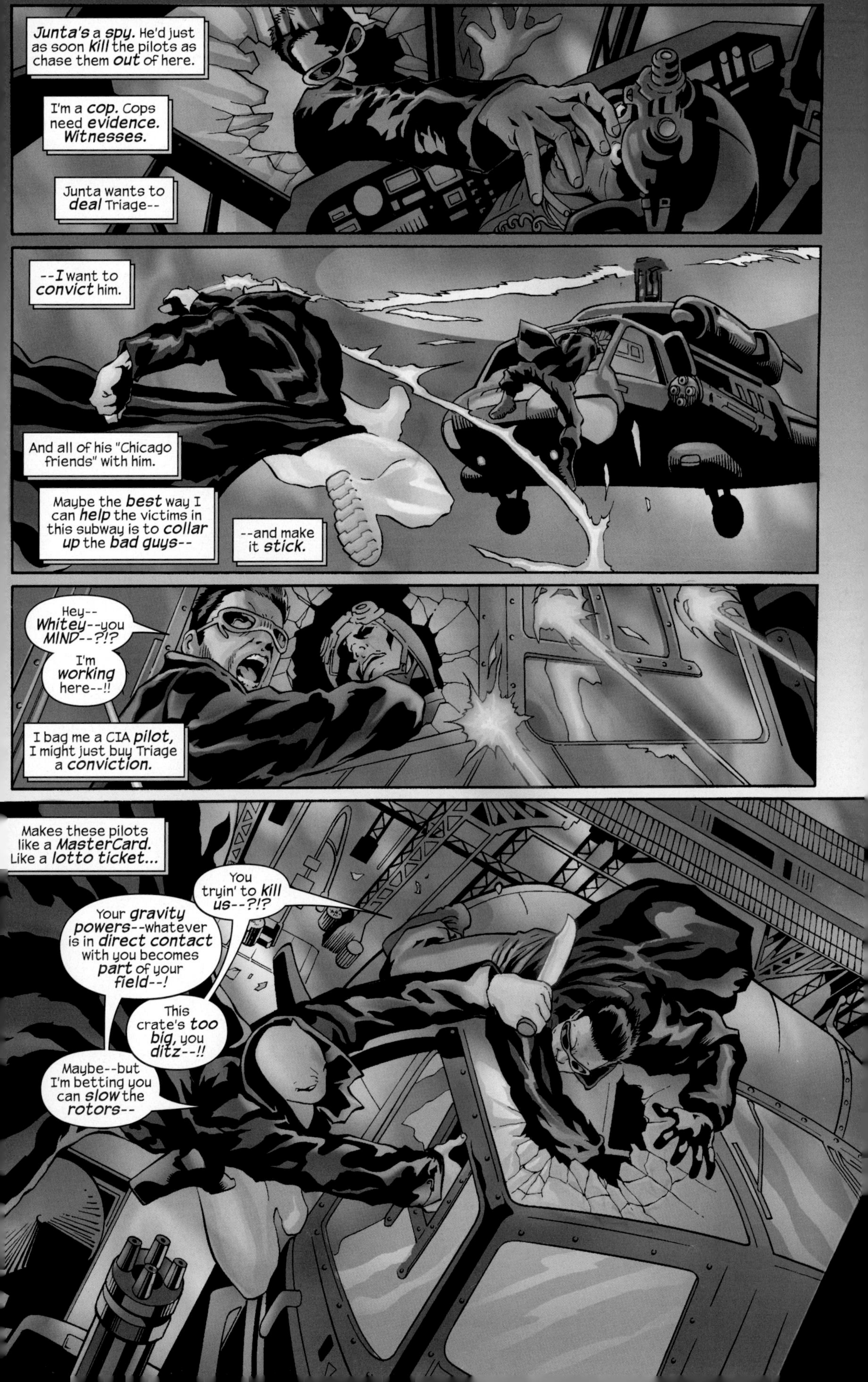
Junta's a spy. He'd just as soon kill the pilots as chase them out of here.
I'm a cop. Cops need evidence. Witnesses.
Junta wants to deal Triage--
--I want to convict him.
And all of his "Chicago friends" with him.
Maybe the best way I can help the victims in this subway is to collar up the bad guys--
--and make it stick.
Hey-- Whitey--you MIND--?!?
I'm working here--!!
I bag me a CIA pilot, I might just buy Triage a conviction.
Makes these pilots like a MasterCard. Like a lotto ticket...
You tryin' to kill us--?!?
Your gravity powers--whatever is in direct contact with you becomes part of your field--!
This crate's too big, you ditz--!!
Maybe--but I'm betting you can slow the rotors--

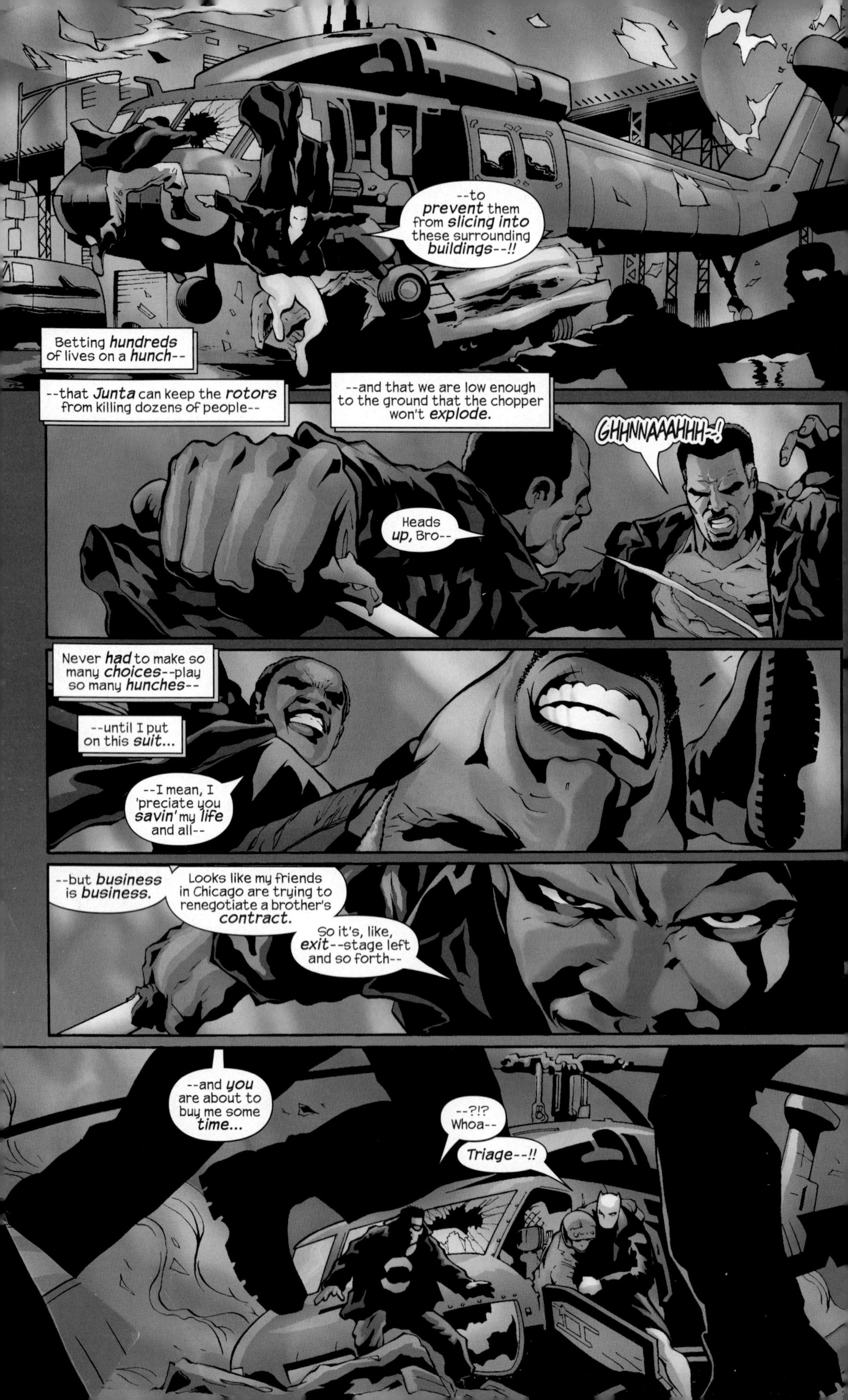
--to prevent them from slicing into these surrounding buildings--!!
Betting hundreds of lives on a hunch--
--that Junta can keep the rotors from killing dozens of people--
--and that we are low enough to the ground that the chopper won't explode.
GHHNNAAAHHH--!
Heads up, Bro--
Never had to make so many choices--play so many hunches--
--until I put on this suit...
--I mean, I 'preciate you savin' my life and all--
--but business is business.
Looks like my friends in Chicago are trying to renegotiate a brother's contract.
So it's, like, exit--stage left and so forth--
--and you are about to buy me some time...
--?!? Whoa--
Triage--!!

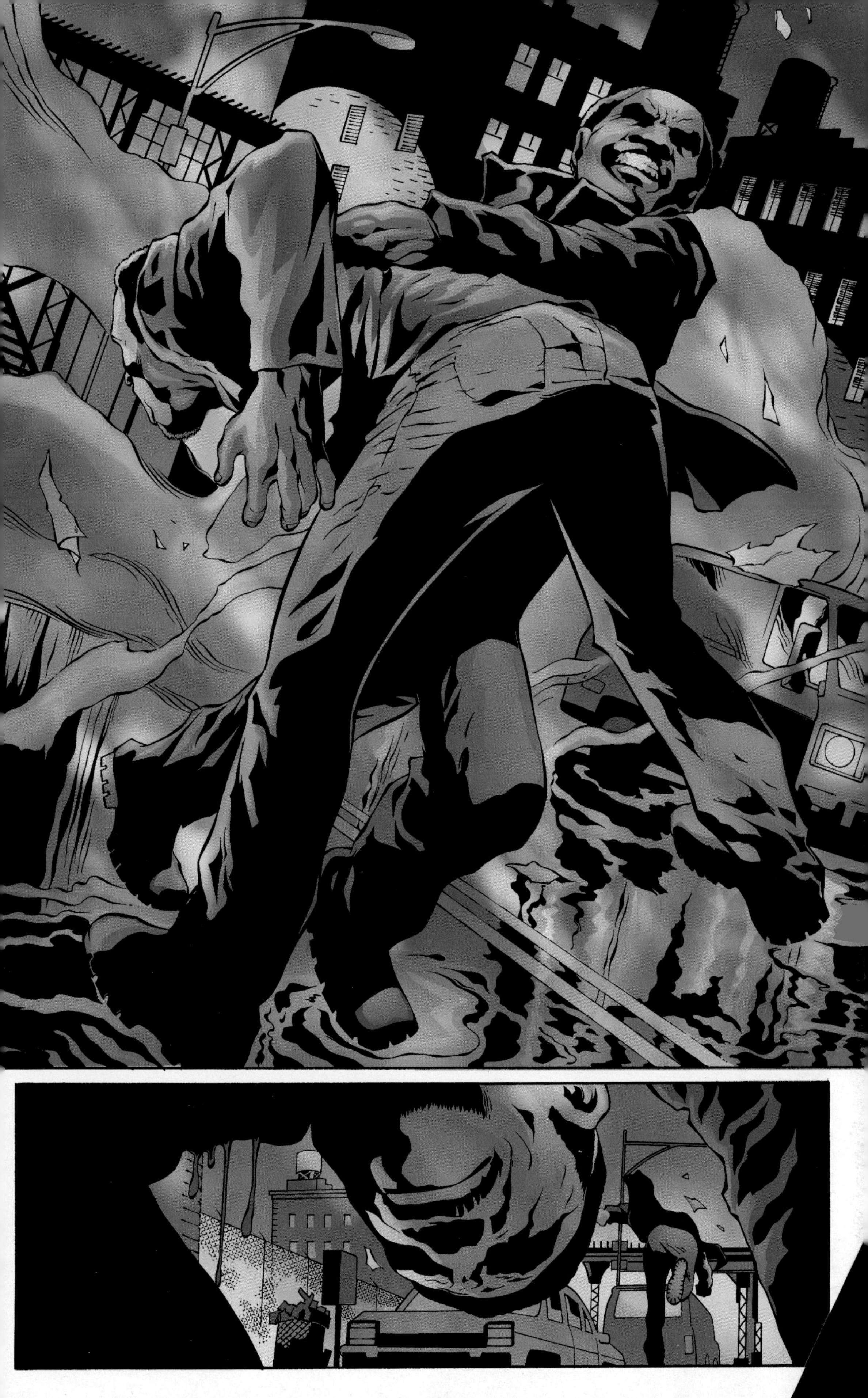

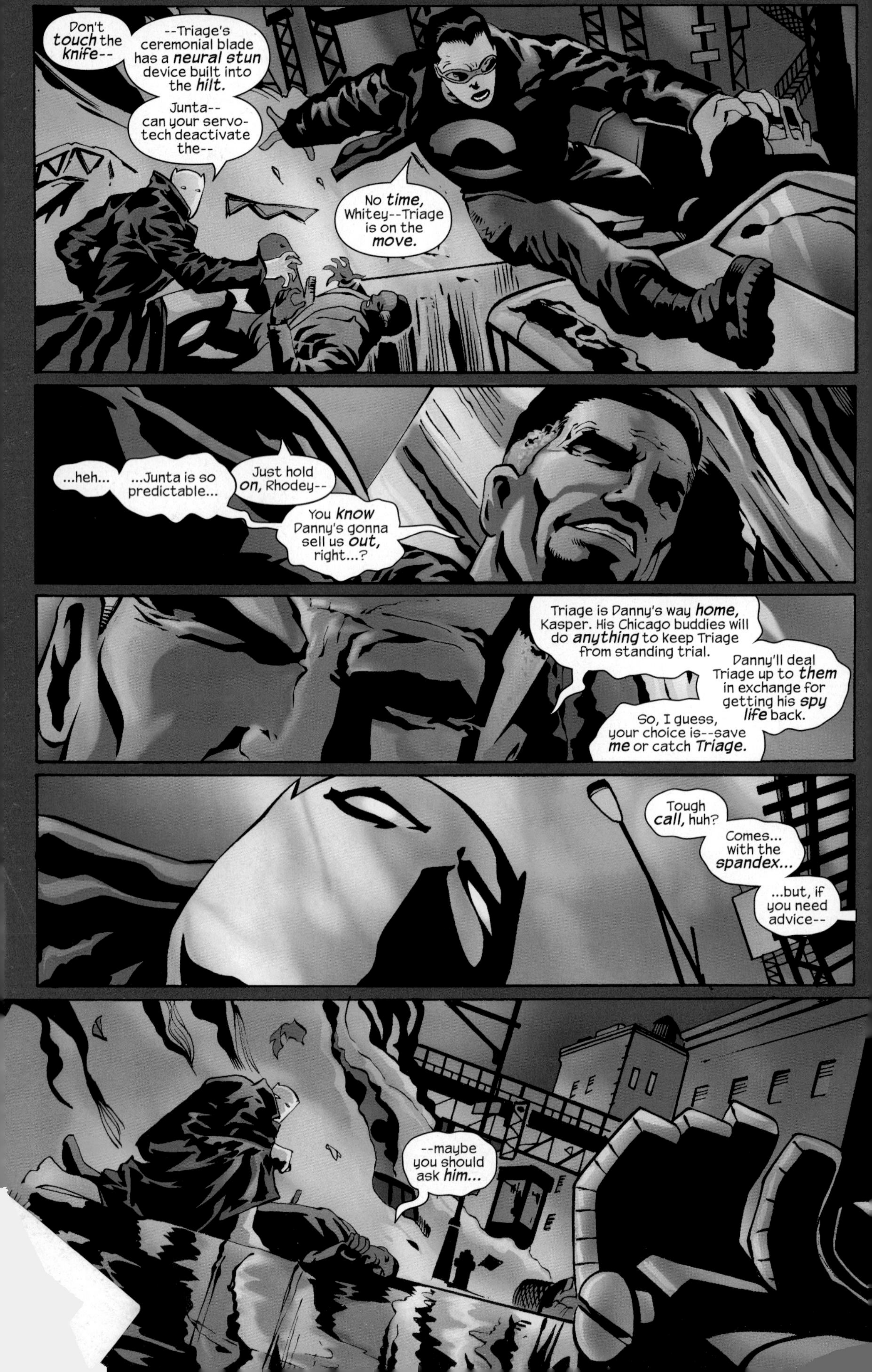

Don't touch the knife--
--Triage's ceremonial blade has a neural stun device built into the hilt.
Junta-- can your servo-tech deactivate the--
No time, Whitey--Triage is on the move.
...heh...
...Junta is so predictable...
Just hold on, Rhodey--
You know Danny's gonna sell us out, right...?
Triage is Danny's way home, Kasper. His Chicago buddies will do anything to keep Triage from standing trial.
Danny'll deal Triage up to them in exchange for getting his spy life back.
So, I guess, your choice is--save me or catch Triage.
Tough call, huh?
Comes... with the spandex...
...but, if you need advice--
--maybe you should ask him...

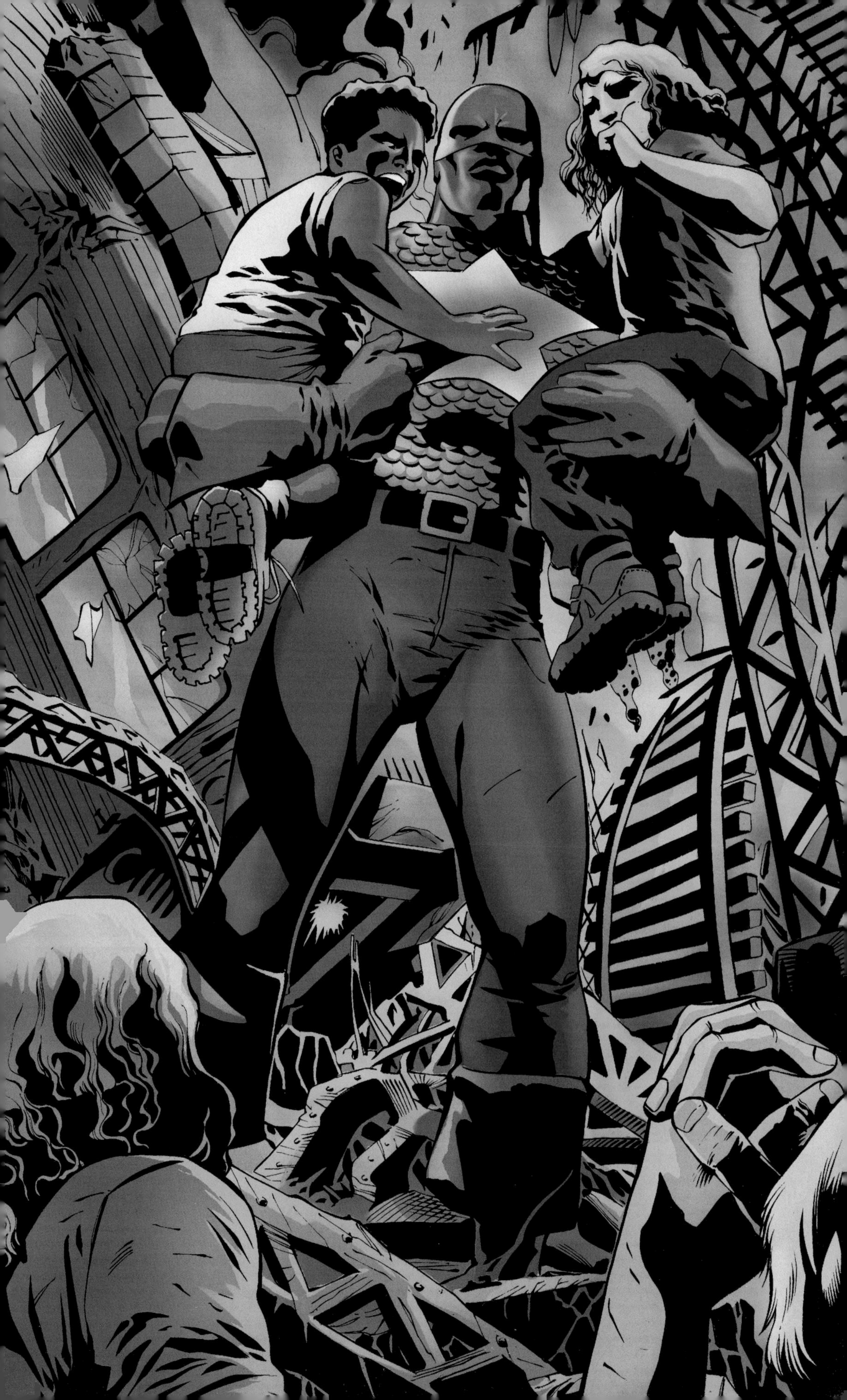

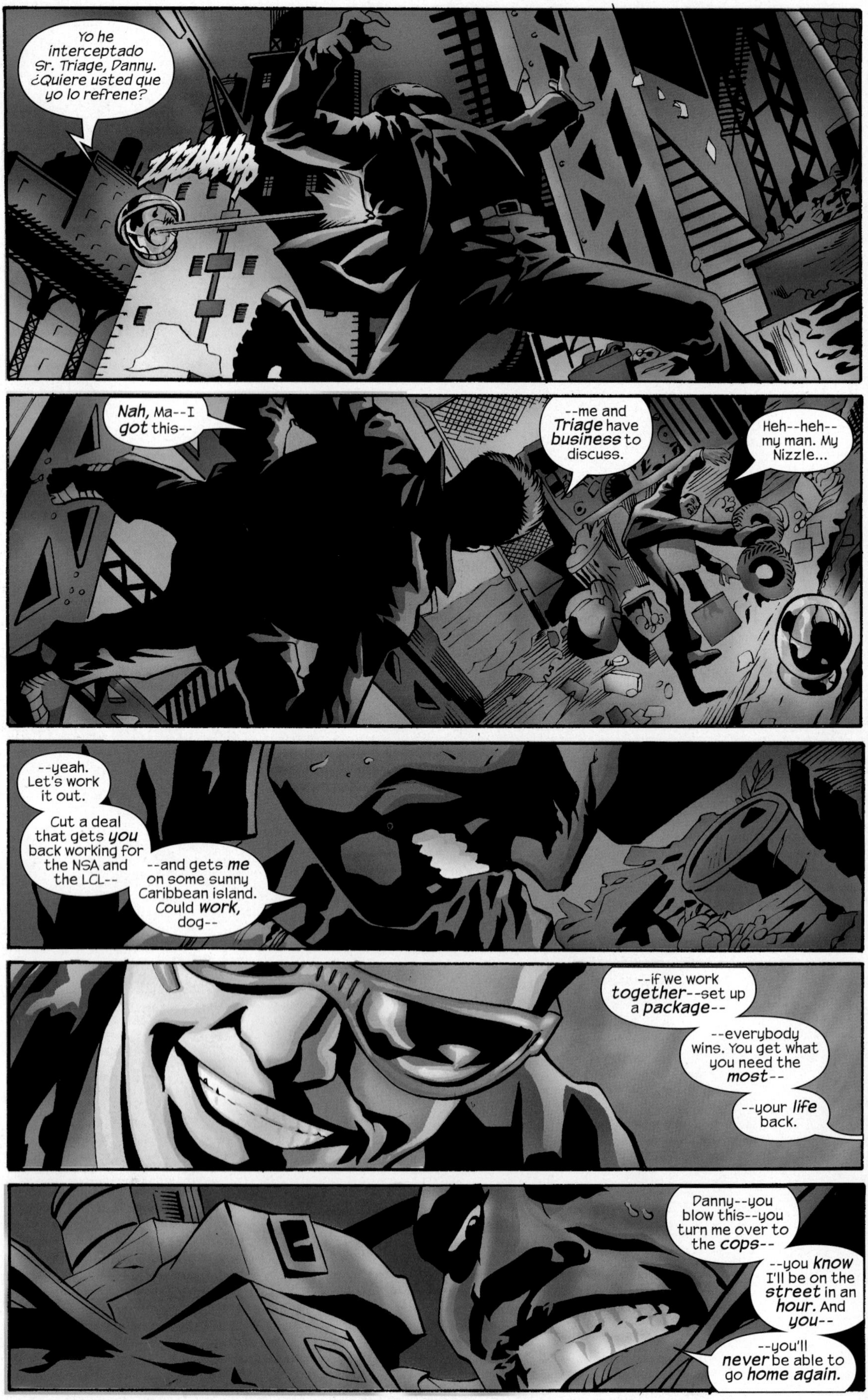

Yo he interceptado Sr. Triage, Danny. ¿Quiere usted que yo lo refrene?
ZZZZAAAAP
Nah, Ma--I got this--
--me and Triage have business to discuss.
Heh--heh--my man. My Nizzle...
--yeah. Let's work it out.
Cut a deal that gets you back working for the NSA and the LCL--
--and gets me on some sunny Caribbean island. Could work, dog--
--if we work together--set up a package--
--everybody wins. You get what you need the most--
--your life back.
Danny--you blow this--you turn me over to the cops--
--you know I'll be on the street in an hour. And you--
--you'll never be able to go home again.

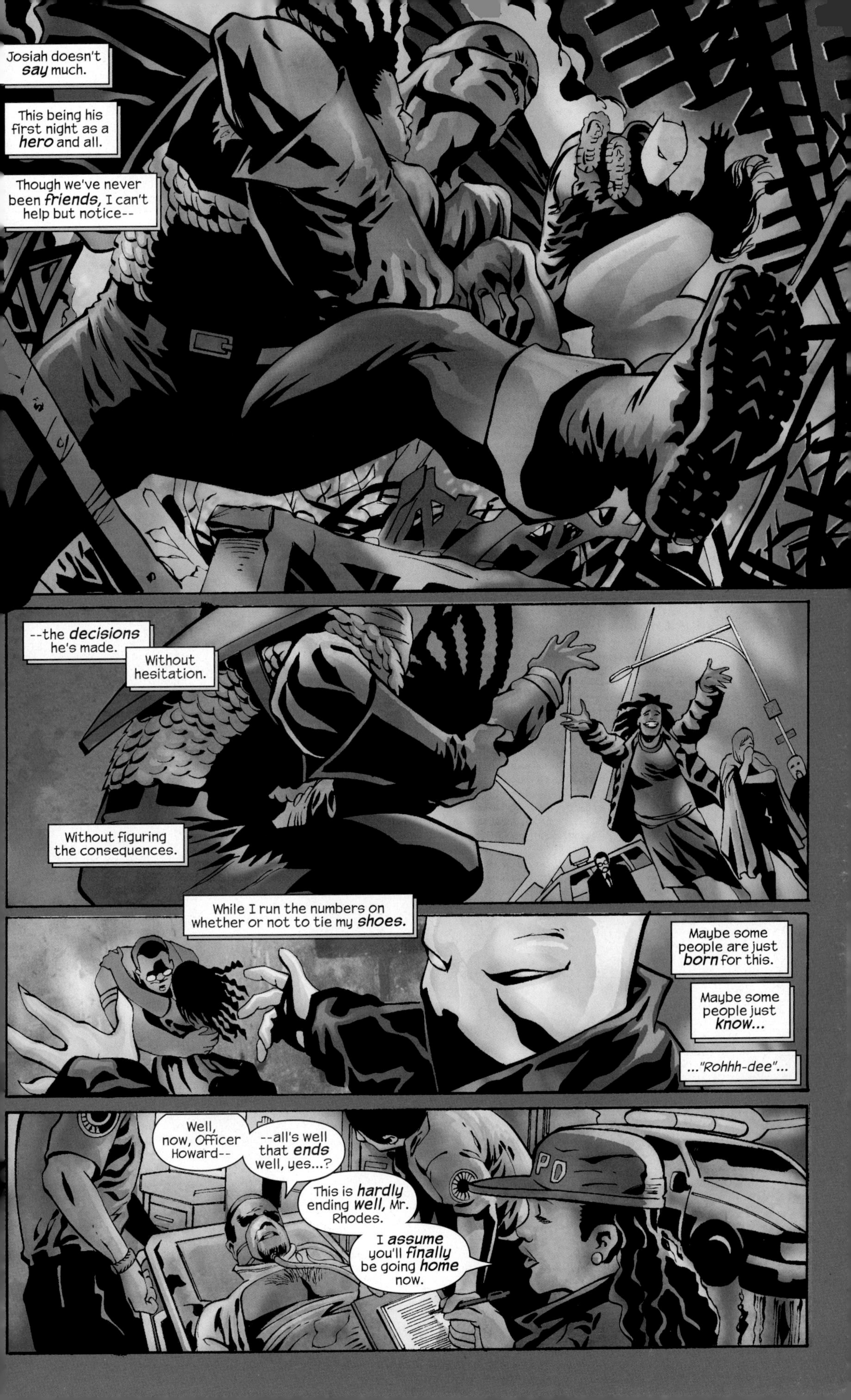

Josiah doesn't *say* much.
This being his first night as a *hero* and all.
Though we've never been *friends*, I can't help but notice--
--the *decisions* he's made.
Without hesitation.
Without figuring the consequences.
While I run the numbers on whether or not to tie my *shoes.*
Maybe some people are just *born* for this.
Maybe some people just *know...*
..."Rohhh-dee"...
Well, now, Officer Howard--
--all's well that *ends* well, yes...?
This is *hardly* ending *well,* Mr. Rhodes.
PD
I *assume* you'll *finally* be going *home* now.

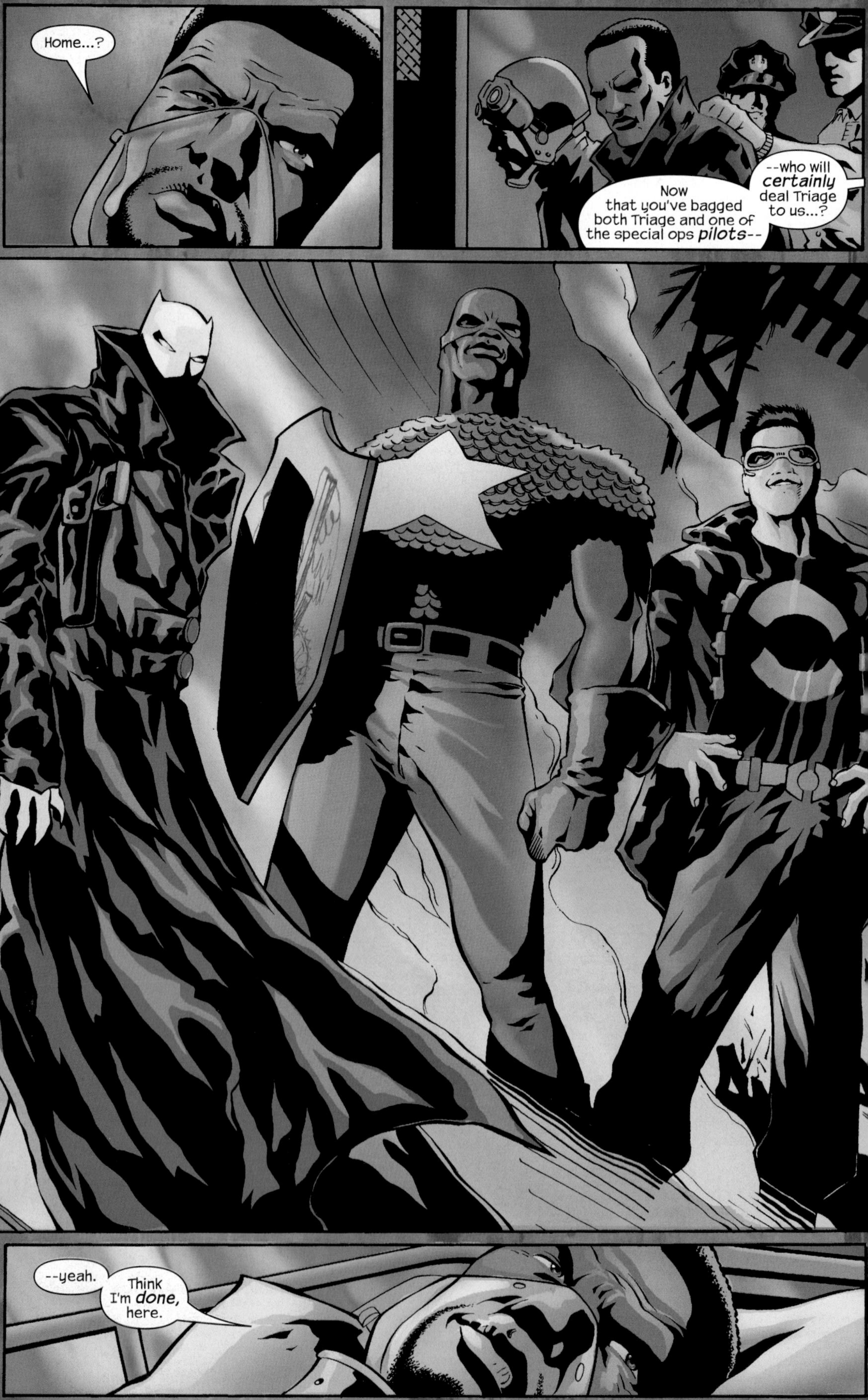
Home...?
Now that you've bagged both Triage and one of the special ops pilots--
--who will certainly deal Triage to us...?
--yeah.
Think I'm done, here.

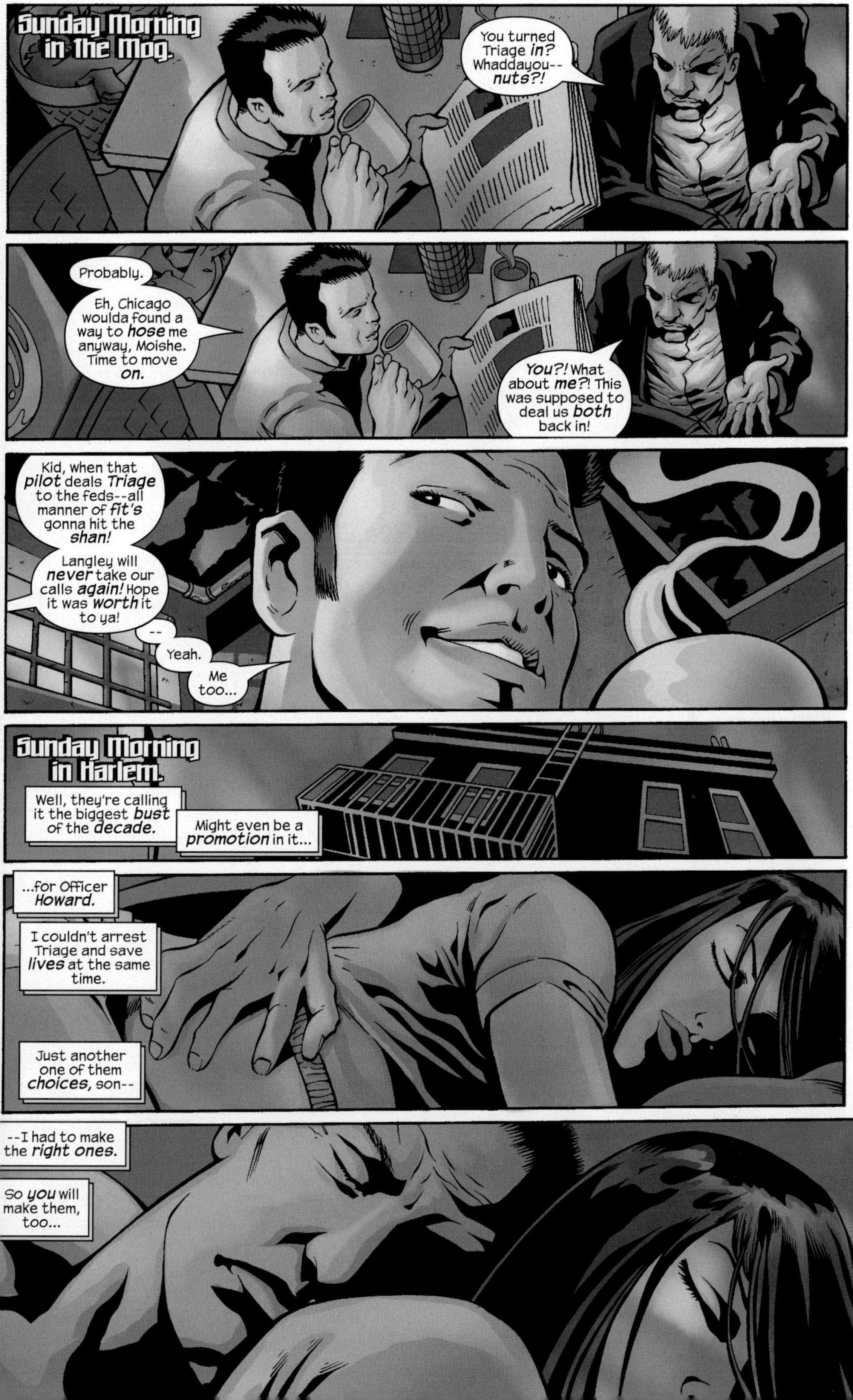
Sunday Morning in the Mog.
You turned Triage in? Whaddayou-- nuts?!
Probably.
Eh, Chicago woulda found a way to hose me anyway, Moishe. Time to move on.
You?! What about me?! This was supposed to deal us both back in!
Kid, when that pilot deals Triage to the feds--all manner of fit's gonna hit the shan!
Langley will never take our calls again! Hope it was worth it to ya!
--
Yeah.
Me too...
Sunday Morning in Harlem.
Well, they're calling it the biggest bust of the decade.
Might even be a promotion in it...
...for Officer Howard.
I couldn't arrest Triage and save lives at the same time.
Just another one of them choices, son--
--I had to make the right ones.
So you will make them, too...

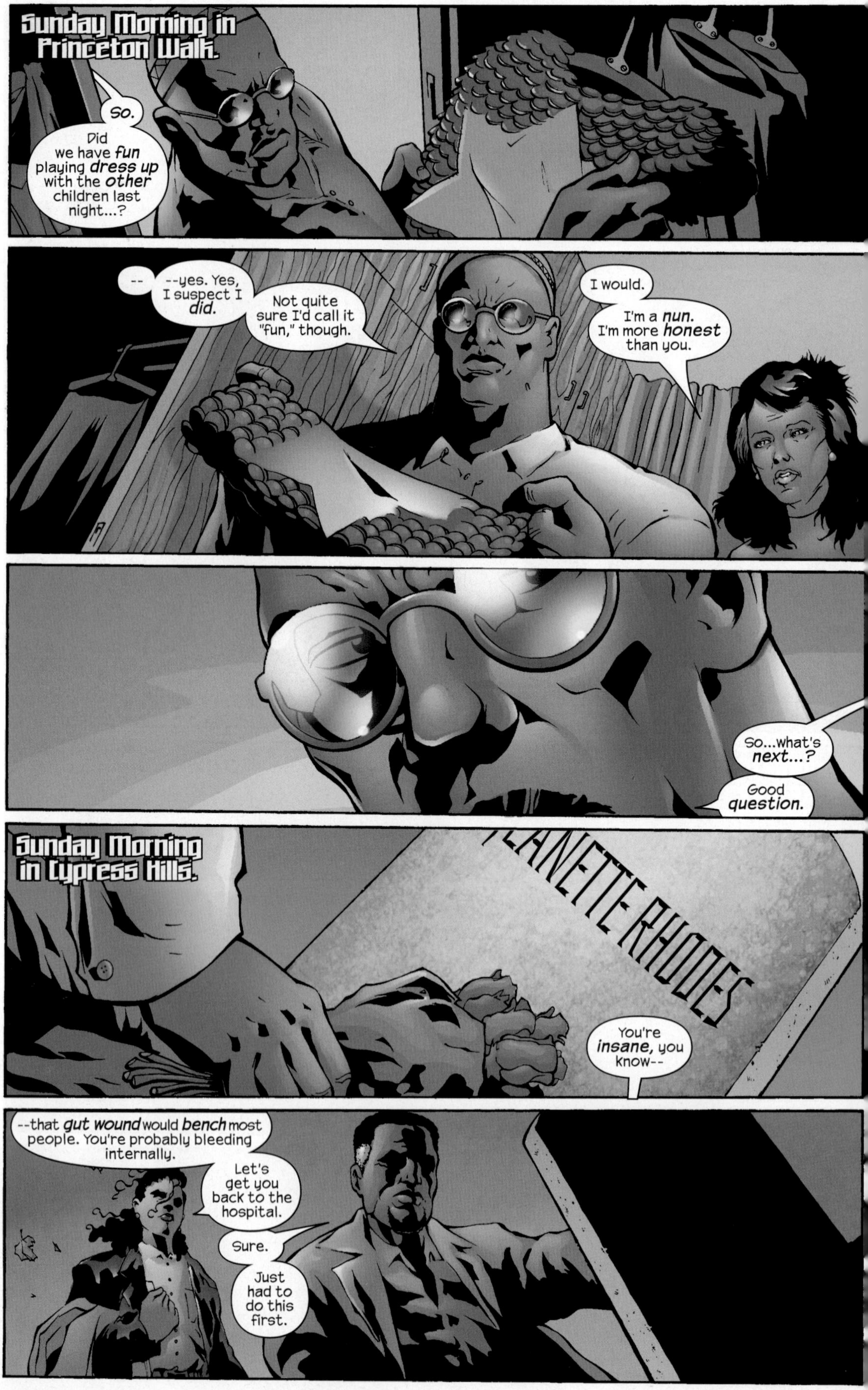
Sunday Morning in Princeton Walk.
So.
Did we have fun playing dress up with the other children last night...?
--
--yes. Yes, I suspect I did.
Not quite sure I'd call it "fun," though.
I would.
I'm a nun. I'm more honest than you.
So...what's next...?
Good question.
Sunday Morning in Cypress Hills.
JEANETTE RHODES
You're insane, you know--
--that gut wound would bench most people. You're probably bleeding internally.
Let's get you back to the hospital.
Sure.
Just had to do this first.

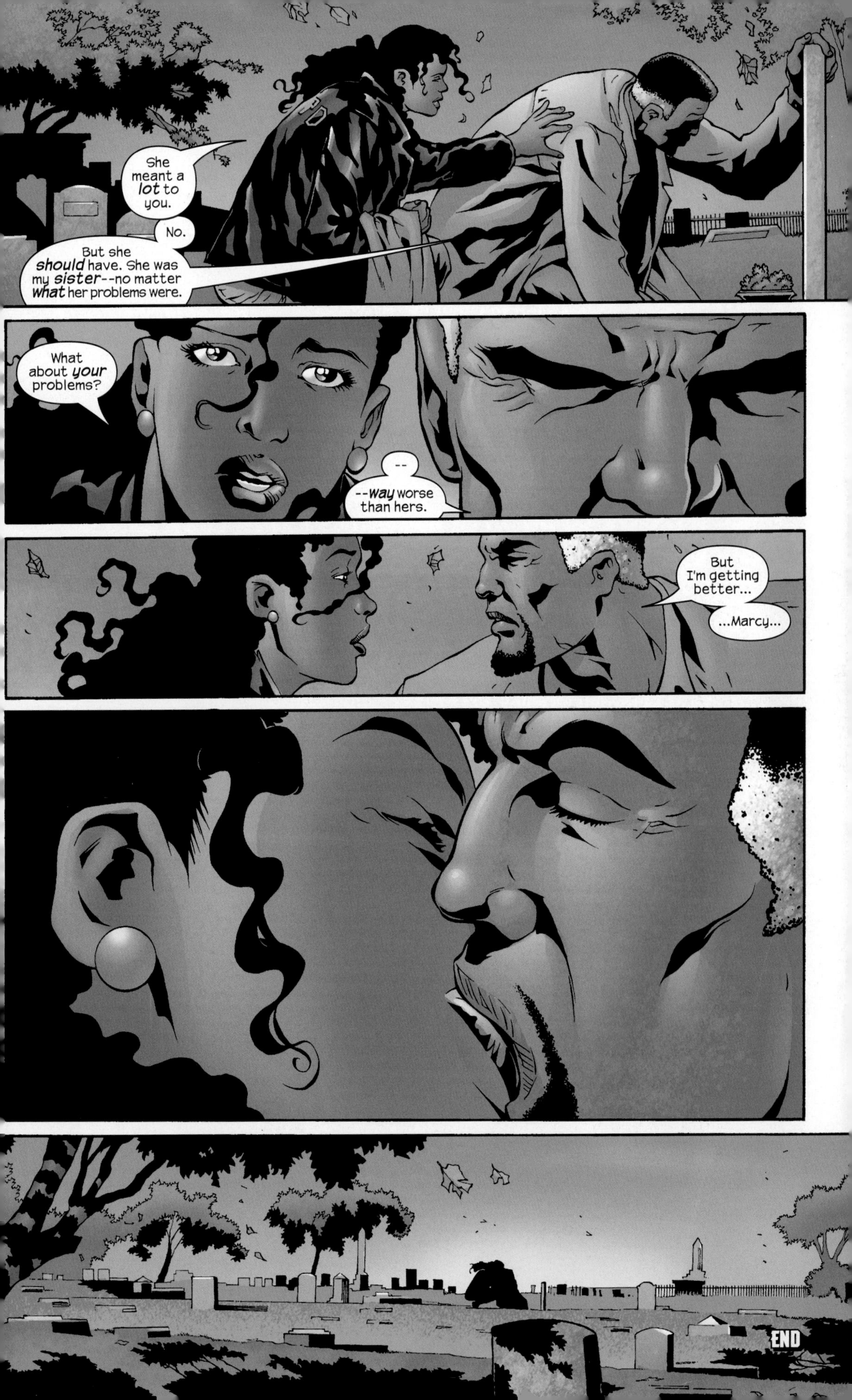
She meant a lot to you.
No.
But she should have. She was my sister--no matter what her problems were.
What about your problems?
--
--way worse than hers.
But I'm getting better...
...Marcy...
END

I know who she is.

How wack is that? The Daily Bugle can't figure it out, but me, an NYU sophomore — who can't even land a column on the student paper — knows who the new Black Panther is. But then again, they don't live in the same dorm that she does.

Believe me, I wasn't even trying to crack the case. Sure, I'd read the articles on her, seen the Method Man video ... but I didn't want to be like all the others, trying to figure out who it was that sparked a freakin' movement!

See, everyone's trying to claim her as their own. The Black Student Union, the gay/lesbian group ... whatever your cause, she fits. Maybe that's because so little is actually known about her. She just shows up and starts kicking butt ... which, in turn, inspires songs about hers.

Sal Velluto

BLACK PANTHER

New Girl in Town

And here's the kicker — she's not going after super-villains or freaks in tights. Nope. Instead, muggers, pushers, rapists ... those are her targets. It's like she's a one-woman crusade trying to take back the night.

And that's when I saw her — at night, about a week ago. I'm just sitting on my fire escape, having a smoke ... and who do I see on the roof across the quad, pulling on her mask? That's right, Ms. Panther herself ... who also happens to be in my African Culture class!

So here's my questions: Where'd she get the suit? She's not related to T'Challa, that's for sure ... so what's her connection? What would make someone dress up like that? Should I just ask her? Am I a reporter ... or a stalker? Am I invading her privacy? What's my duty as a journalist?

I don't know any of the answers. All I know is that there's a Panther on the hunt. Men who hurt women are her prey. She's hungry.

And I know who she is.

Inked by Bob Almond, Colored by Tom Chu and Text by Bill Rosemann

MARVEL KNIGHTS: MILLENNIAL VISIONS RE-IMAGINED THE MARVEL KNIGHTS CHARACTERS IN CREATIVE NEW WAYS.

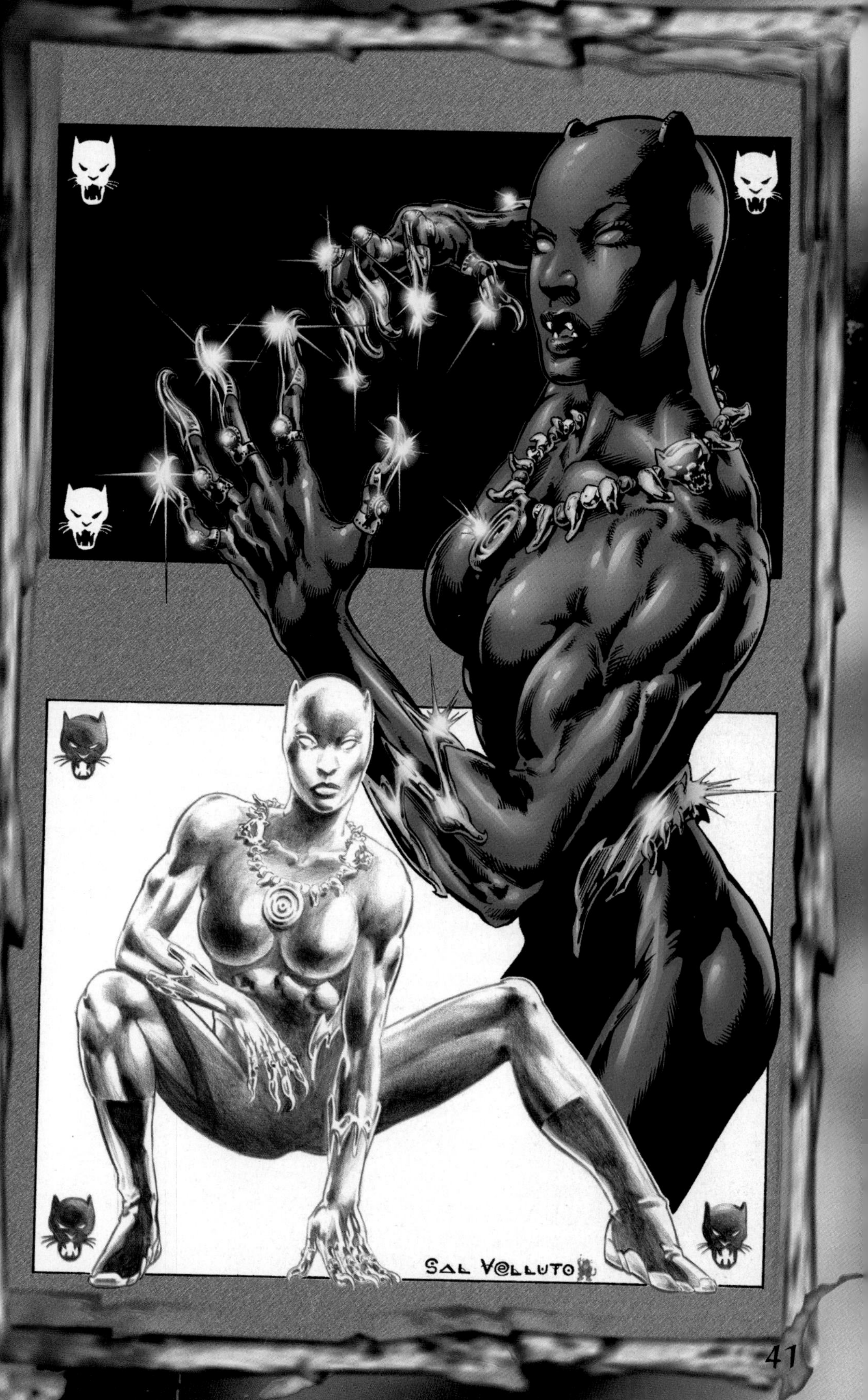
SAL VELLUTO

...beauty pageant contestant, unaware that she's developed the mutant power of probability, answers the question, "What is your greatest wish?" like every other contestant has in years past: "I wish for world peace." The only difference this time around is that her answer actually comes true and forever changes the Earth.

But in a world devoid of crime, what role will super heroes play? What role can they play?

DR. STRANGE now sits around watching Buffy, using his magic to levitate Cheeze Doodles® from the pantry.

CLOAK & DAGGER get married, but Cloak soon becomes what most American males become after marriage—fat and lazy. Dagger's having second thoughts.

Chris Eliopoulos
MARVEL KNIGHTS
America the Beautiful

ELEKTRA dies after getting hit by a bus, but soon after returns to life. She repeats the process three more times until finally getting hit by a train. She remains dead. Finally.

CAPTAIN AMERICA opens a car dealership where he sells Japanese imports.

GHOST RIDER sits around all day reading comic books.

NICK FURY pokes his one good eye out running through the house with a pair of scissors. His blindness, however, doesn't keep him from making fun of wife BLACK WIDOW's weight.

BLACK PANTHER continues to rule Wakanda, but wears his old costume only when his Spidey underoos are getting washed.

THE PUNISHER embraces his Italian heritage, devoting his life to the consumption of Cannolis.

DAREDEVIL runs for President and wins. Most of his term is spent hitting on female interns.

LUKE CAGE becomes a chiropractor. After four lawsuits for breaking people's spines, he moves to Las Vegas to become a host at Caesar's Palace.

The only person to prosper in these times is KINGPIN. No longer able to scheme or plot, he takes to long walks. He begins losing weight and soon opens a number of fitness clubs.

The beauty contestant ends up losing, but soon after wishes she could intern at the White House. Mr. and Mrs. Murdock are now happily married and living in D.C.

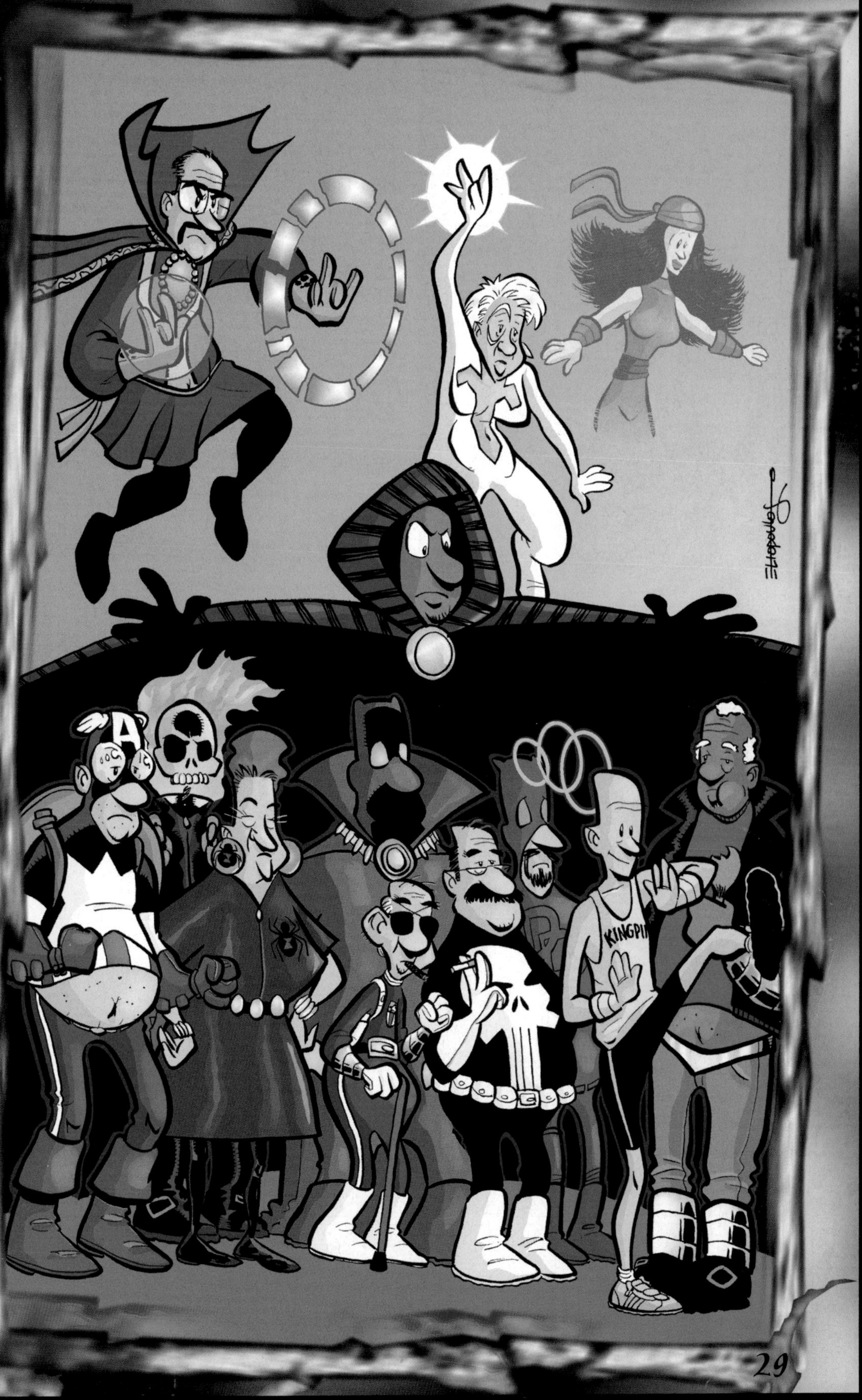
KINGPI

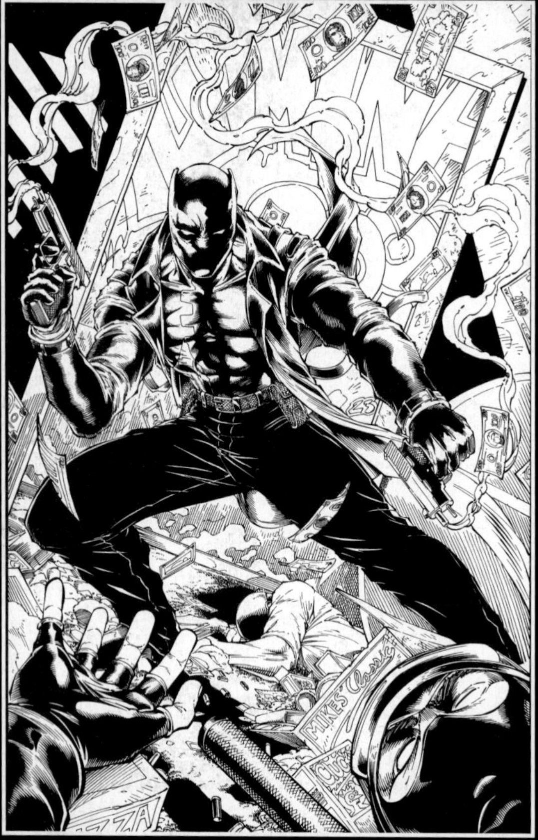

BLACK PANTHER #50, PAGE 4 ART BY **DAN FRAGA** & **LARY STUCKER**

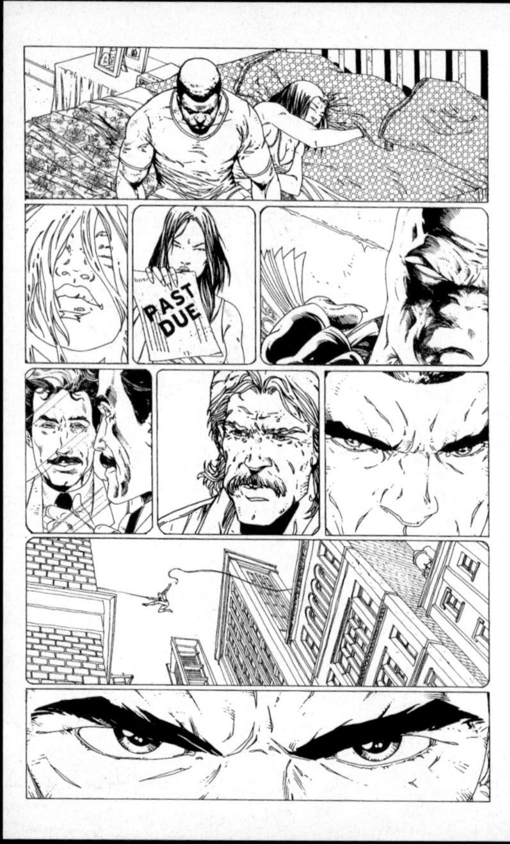
PAST DUE

BLACK PANTHER #52, PAGE 17 ART BY **JORGE LUCAS**

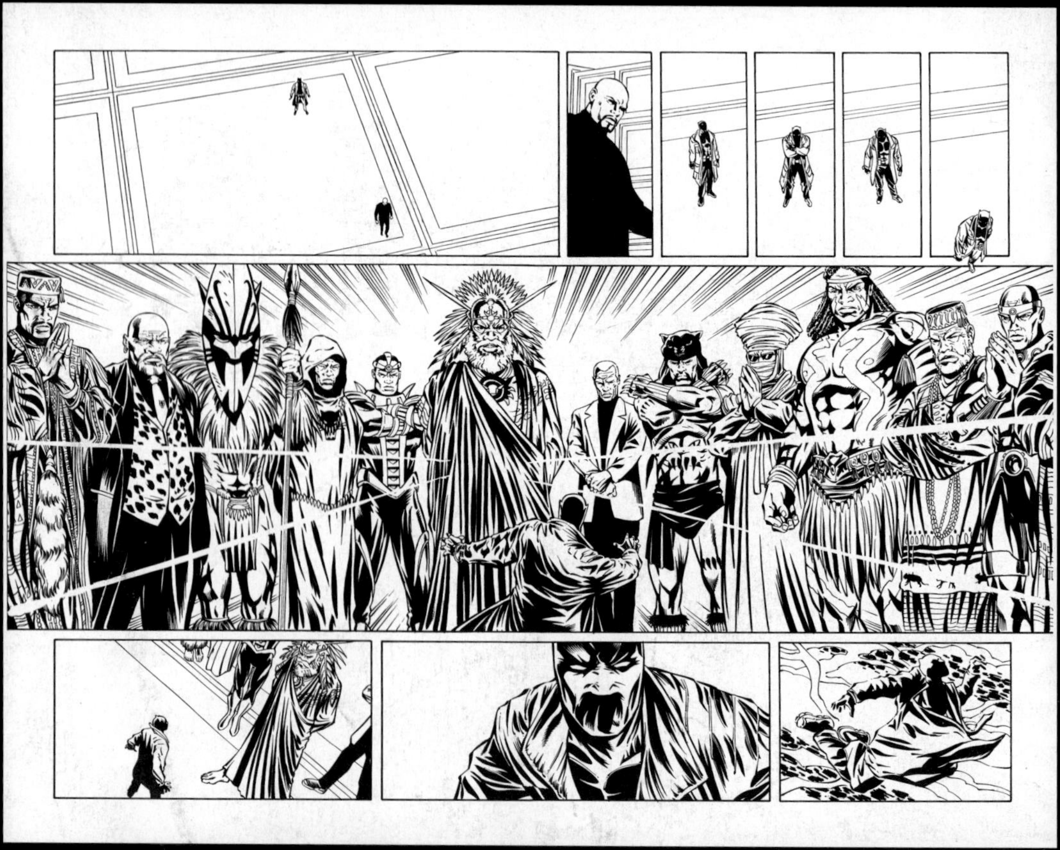

BLACK PANTHER #60, PAGES 14-15 ART BY **PATRICK ZIRCHER** & **NORM RAPMUND**

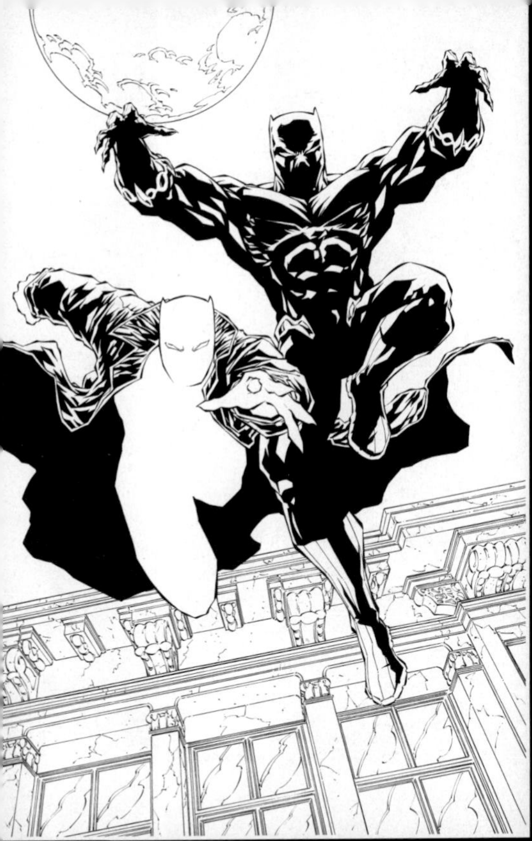

LACK PANTHER #62, PAGE 23 ART BY **JIM CALAFIORE** & **NORM RAPMUND**

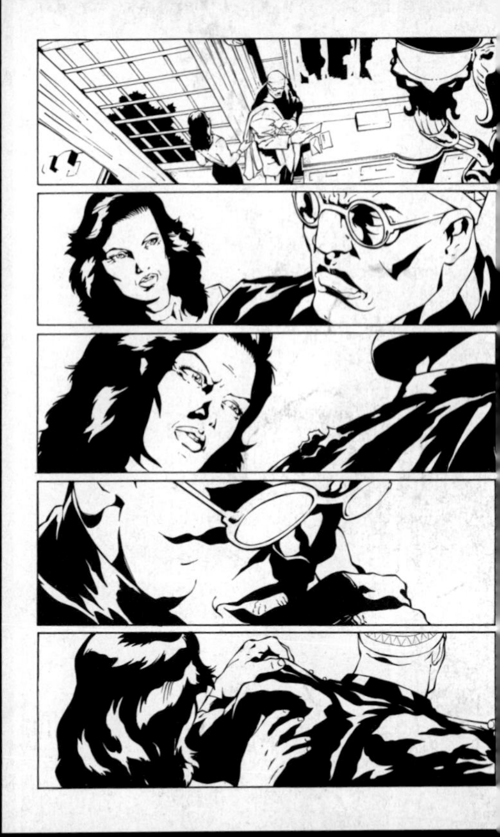

THE CREW #4, PAGE 21 ART BY **JOE BENNETT** & **CRIME LAB STUDIO**

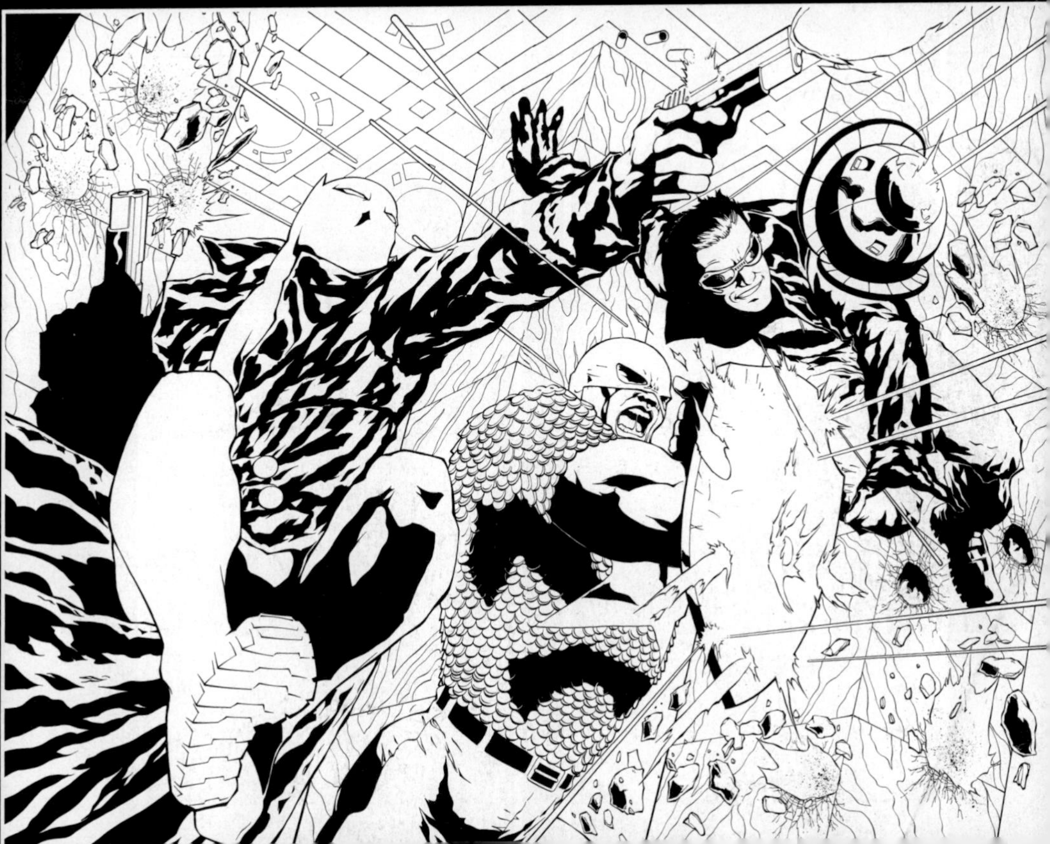

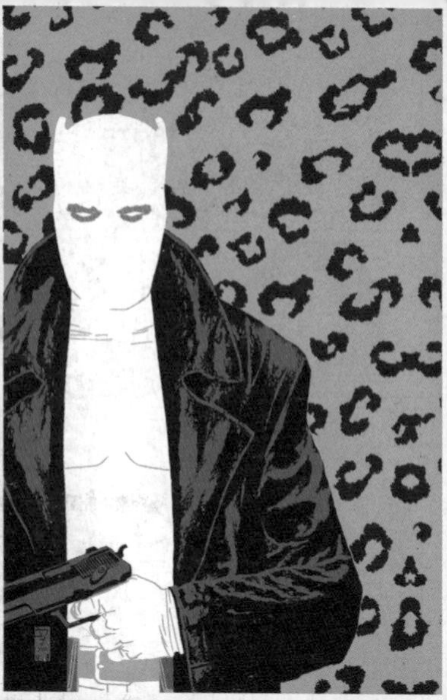

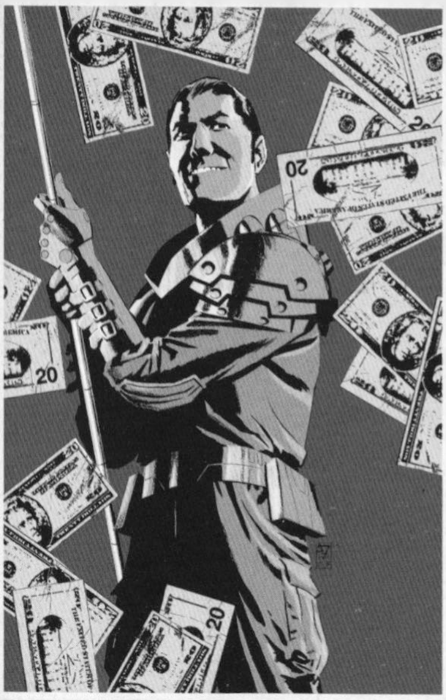

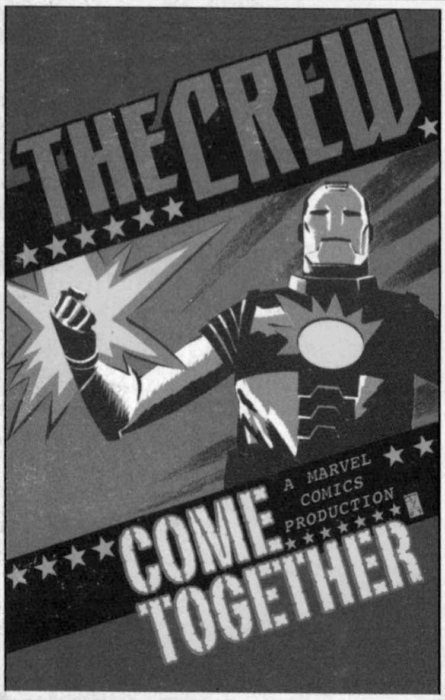
THE CREW
A MARVEL COMICS PRODUCTION
COME TOGETHER

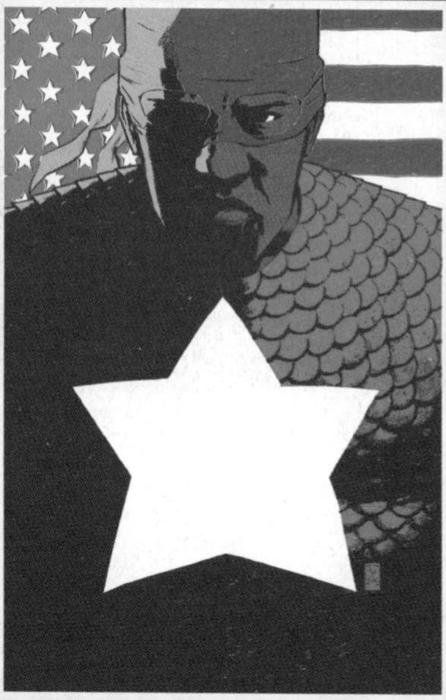

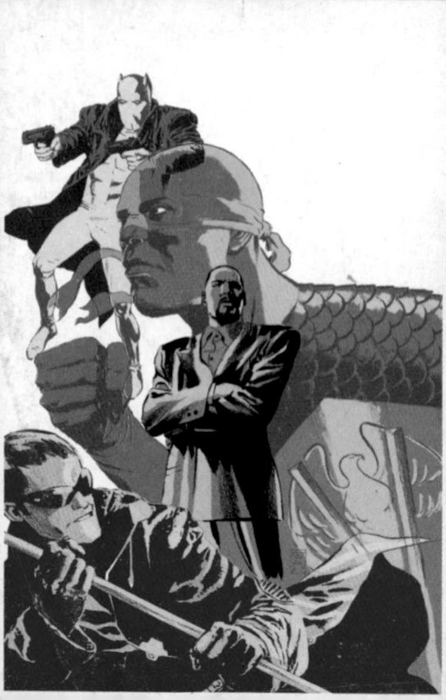

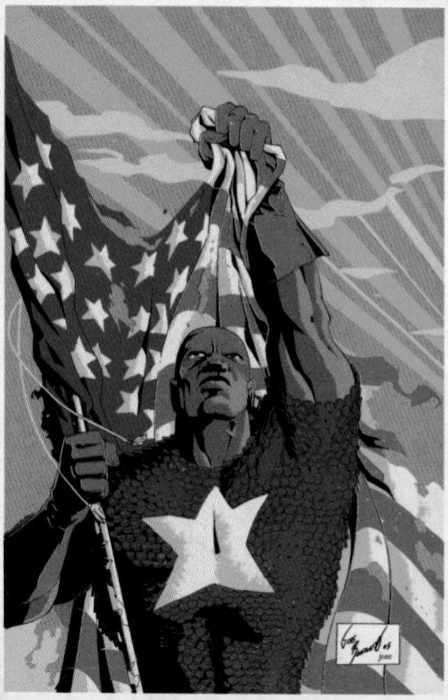

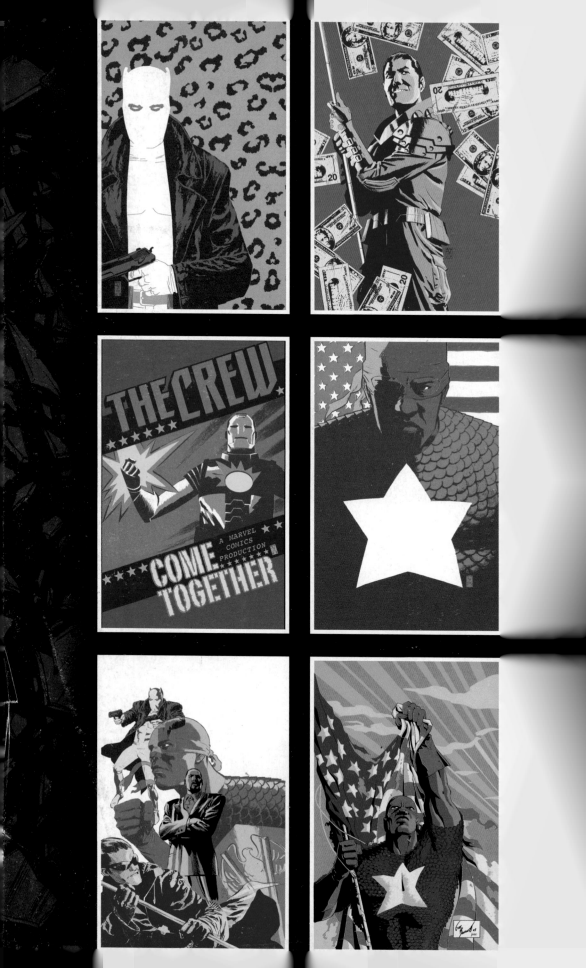